ROBERT BROWNING

AND

ELIZABETH BARRETT BARRETT

VOLUME II.

Elizabeth Barrett Browning

from a painting by Gordigiani

THE LETTERS OF

ROBERT BROWNING

AND

ELIZABETH BARRETT BARRETT

1845–1846

WITH PORTRAITS AND FACSIMILES

IN TWO VOLUMES

VOL. II.

HARPER & BROTHERS, PUBLISHERS
NEW YORK AND LONDON
1899

ILLUSTRATIONS

PORTRAIT OF ELIZABETH BARRETT BROWNING . . *Frontispiece*
After the picture by Gordigiani

FACSIMILE OF LETTER OF ELIZABETH BARRETT BARRETT . . . . *To face p.* 560

THE LETTERS OF ROBERT BROWNING AND ELIZABETH BARRETT

R. B. to E. B. B.

Wednesday.
[Post-mark, March 25, 1846.]

You were right to bid me never again wish my poor flowers were 'diamonds'—you could not, I think, speak so to my heart of any diamonds. God knows my life is for you to take just as you take flowers:—these last please you, serve you best when plucked—and 'my life's rose' . . if I dared profane *that* expression I would say, you have but to 'stoop' for it. Foolish, as all words are.

You *dwell* on that notion of your being peculiarly isolated,—of any kindness to you, in your present state, seeming doubled and quadrupled—what do I, what could anyone infer from *that* but, most obviously, that it was a very fortunate thing for such kindness, and that the presumable bestower of it got all his distinction from the fact that no better . . however, I hate this and cannot go on. Dearest, believe that under ordinary circumstances, with ordinary people, all operates differently—the *imaginary* kindness-bestower with his ideal methods of showing and proving his love,—*there* would be the rival to fear!

Do not let us talk of this—you always beat me, beside, turn my own illustrations into obscurations—as in the notable case of the *cards* and stakes and risks—I suppose, (to save my vanity!) that if I knew anything about cards,

I might go on, a step at least, with my argument. I once heard a dispute in the street between the proprietor of an oyster-stall and one of his customers—*who* was in the wrong . . that is, *who* used the clenching argument you shall hear presently, I don't remember; but *one* brought the other to this pass—'*Are* there three shells to an oyster?' —Just that! If there *were not*—he would clearly be found in the wrong, that as all!—'*Why,*' . . began the other; and I regret I did not catch the rest—there was such a clear possibility contained in that '*Why* . . an oyster *might* have three shells!'

Note the adroitness,—(calm heroic silence of the *act* rather than a merely attempted *word,*) the mastery with which, taking up Ba's implied challenge, I *do* furnish her with both 'amusement and instruction'—moreover I will at Ba's bidding amuse and instruct the world at large, and make them know all to be known—for my purposes—about 'Bells and Pomegranates'—yes, it will be better.

I said rather hastily that my head 'ached' yesterday: that meant, only that it was more observable because, after walking, it is usually well—and I had been walking. To-day it is much better; I sit reading 'Cromwell,' and the newspaper, and presently I shall go out—all will be better now, I hope—it shall not be my fault, at least, depend on that. All my work (work!)—well, such as it is, it is done—and I scarcely care *how*—I shall be prouder to begin one day—(may it be soon!—) with your hand in mine from the beginning—*that* is a very different thing in its effect from the same hand touching mine *after* I had begun, with no suspicion such a chance could befall! I repeat, both these things, 'Luria' and the other, are *manqué,* failures—the life-incidents ought to have been acted over again, experienced afresh; and I had no inclination nor ability. But one day, my siren!

Let me make haste and correct a stupid error. I spoke to my father last night about that tragedy of the *studs*—I was wholly *out* in the story—the sufferer was his *uncle,* and the scene should have been laid on the Guinea coast. Apropos of errors—the copyright matter is most likely a case of copy*wrong* by reporters—I never heard of it before—to be sure, I signed a petition of Miss Martineau's superintending once on a time—but long ago, 'I, I, I'—how, dear, all important 'I' takes care of himself, and issues bulletins, and corrects his wise mistakes, and all this to . . just 'one of his readers of the average intelligence.' Are you that, so much as that, Ba? I will tell you—if you do not write to me all about *your* dear, dearest self, I shall sink with shame at the recollection of what this letter and its like prove to be—*must* prove to be! Dear love, tell me—that you walk and are in good spirits, and I will try and write better. May God bless my own beloved!— Ever her own

R.

I think, am all but sure, there is a *Mrs.* Hornblower something!

Just a minute to say your second note has come, and that I *do* hate *hate* having to write, not kiss my answer on your dearest mouth—kindest, dearest—to-morrow I will try—and meantime—though Ba by the fire will not be cold at heart, cold *of* heart, at least, and I will talk to *her* and more than talk—My dearest, dearest one!

E. B. B. to R. B.

Wednesday Evening.
[Post-mark, March 26, 1846.]

But if people half say things,—intimate things, as when your disputant in the street (you are felicitous, I think, in your street-*experiences*) suggested the possible case of the 'three oyster shells to an oyster,'—why you must submit to be answered a little, and even confuted at need. Now just see—

. . 'Got all his distinction from the fact that no better'

. . That is precisely *the fact* . . *so* . . as you have stated it, and implied . . 'The fact that no better' . . *is to be found in the world—no better* . . *none.* There, is the peculiar combination. The isolation on one side, and the best in the whole world, coming in for company! And I 'dwell' upon it, never being tired . . and if *you* are tired already, you must be tired of *me*, because the 'dwelling' has grown to be a part of me and I cannot put it away. It is my especial miracle *à moi.* 'No better?' No, indeed! not in the seven worlds! and just *there*, lies the miraculous point.

But you mean it perhaps otherwise. You mean that it is a sort of *pis aller* on my part. A *pis aller* along the Via lactea . . is *that* what you mean?

Shall I let you off the rest, dearest, dearest? though you deserve ever so much more, for implying such monstrous things, and treading down all my violets, so and so. What did I say to set you writing so? I cannot remember at all? If I 'dwell' on anything, beloved, it is that I feel it strongly, be sure—and if I feel gratitude to you with the other feelings, you should not grudge what is a happy feeling in itself, and not dishonouring (I answer for *that*) to the object of it.

Now I shall tell you. I had a visitor to-day—Mrs. Jameson; and when she went away she left me ashamed of myself—I felt like a hypocrite—*I*, who was not born for one, I think. She began to talk of you . . talked like a wise woman, which she is . . led me on to say just what I might have said if I had not known you, (she, thoroughly impressed with the notion that we two are strangers!) and made me quite leap in my chair with a sudden consciousness, by exclaiming at last . . 'I am really glad to hear you speak so. Such appreciation' &c. &c. . . . imagine what she went on to say. Dearest—I believe she rather gives me a sort of credit for *appreciating you* without the jealousy '*de métier.*' Good Heavens . . how humiliating some conditions of praise are! She *approved* me with her eye—indeed she did. And this, while we were agreeing that you were the best . . 'none better' . . none so good . . of your country and age. Do you know, while we were talking, I felt inclined both to laugh and to cry, and if I had 'given way' the least, she would have been considerably astounded. As it was, my hands were so marble-cold when she took leave of me, that she observed it and began making apologies for exhausting me. Now here is a strip of the 'world,' . . see what colour it will turn to presently! We had better, I think, go farther than to your siren's island—into the desert . . shall we say? Such stories there will be! For certain, . . I shall have seen you just once out of the window! Shall you not be afraid? Well—and she talked of Italy too—it was before she talked of *you*—and she hoped I had not given up the thoughts of going there. To which I said that 'I had not . . but that it seemed like scheming to travel in the moon.' She talked of a difference, and set down the moon-travelling as simple lunacy. 'And simply lunatical,' . . I said, . . 'my thoughts, if chronicled, would be taken to be, perhaps'— 'No, no, no, ! . .' she insisted . . 'as long as I kept to the earth, everything was to be permitted to me.'

How people talk at cross-purposes in this world . . and act so too! It's the very spirit of worldly communion. Souls are gregarious in a sense, but no soul touches another, as a general rule. I like Mrs. Jameson nevertheless—I like her *more*. She appreciates you—and it is *my* turn to praise for that, now. I am to see her again to-morrow morning, when she has the goodness to promise to bring some etchings of her own, her illustrations of the new essays, for me to look at.

Ah—your '*failures* in "Luria" and the "Tragedy"'—Proud, we should all be, to fail exactly so.

Dearest, are you better indeed? Walk . . talk to the Ba in the chair . . go on to be better, ever dearest. May God bless you! Ah . . the 'I's.' You do not see that the 'I's'—as you make them, . . all turn to 'yous' by the time they get to me. The 'I's' indeed! How dare you talk against my eyes? For me, I was going downstairs to-day, but it was wet and windy and I was warned not to go. If I am in bad or good spirits, judge from this foolish letter—foolish and wise, both!—but not melancholy, *anywise*. When one drops into a pun, one might as well come to an end altogether—it cant be worse with one.

Nor can it be better than being

Your own

'No better' ! ! .

R. B. to E. B. B.

Thursday Morning.
[Post-mark, March 26, 1846.]

Sometimes I have a disposition to dispute with dearest Ba, to wrench her simile-weapons out of the dexterous hand (that is, try and do so) and have the truth of things my way and its own way, not hers, if she *be* Ba—(observe, I say nothing about ever meeting with remarkable success in such undertakings, only, that they *are* entered on sometimes). But at other times I seem as if I must lie down, like Flush, with all manner of coral necklaces about my neck, and two sweet mysterious hands on my head, and so be forced to hear verses on me, Ba's verses, in which I, that am but Flush of the lower nature, am called loving friend and praised for not preferring to go 'coursing hares' —with 'other dogs.' So I will lie now, as you will have it, and say in Flush-like tones (the looks that are dog's tones)—I don't *don't* know how it is, or why, or what it all will end in, but I am very happy and what I hear must mean right, by the music,—though the meaning is above me,—and here *are* the hands—which I may, and will, look up to, and kiss—determining not to insist any more this time that at Miss Mitford's were sundry dogs, brighter than 'brown'— See where, just where, Flush stops discreetly! 'Eternity' he would have added, 'but stern death' &c. &c.

I treat these things lightheartedly, as you see—instead of seriously, which would at first thought seem the wiser course—'for after all, she will find out one day' &c. *No*, dearest,—I do not fear that! Why make uneasy words of saying simply I shall continue to give you my best flowers, all I can find—if I bring violets, or grass, when you expected to get roses,—you will know there were none in my garden—that is all.

And for you—as I may have told you once,—as I tell myself always—you are *entirely* what I love—not just a rose plucked off with an inch of stalk, but presented as a rose should be, with a green world of boughs round: all about you is 'to my heart'—(to my mind, as they phrase it)—and were it not that, of course, I know *when* to have done with fancyings and merely flitting permissible 'inly-sayings with heart-playing,' and when it is time to look at the plain 'best' through the lock of 'good' and 'better' in circumstances and accident—I *do* say—were the best blessing of all, the blessing I trust and believe God intends, of your perfect restoration to health,—were *that* not so palpably best,—I should catch myself desirous that your present state of *unconfirmed* health might never pass away! Ba *understands*, I know!. After all, it will always stay, that luxury,—if but through the memory of what has been, and *may* recur, that deepest luxury that makes my very heart-strings tremble in the thought of—that I shall have a right, a duty—where in another case, they would be uncalled for, superfluous, impertinent. Tapers ordinarily burn best *let alone*, with all your light depending on the little flame, the darkest night but for it—why, stand off—what good can you do, so long as there is no extraordinary evil to avert, breaking down of the candlestick to prevent? But *here*—there will be reason as well as a delight beyond delights in always learning to close over, all but holding the flame in the hollow of one's hand! I shall have a right to think it is not mere pleasure, merely for myself, that I care and am close by—and that which thus is called 'not for myself' *is*, after all, in its essence, *most* for myself,—why it is a luxury, a last delight!—

In the procurement of which there will be this obstacle, or grave matter to be first taken into consideration,—that the world will 'change colour' about it, will have its own thoughts on the subject I have my own thoughts, on *its* subject, the affairs of the world and pieces of perfect good fortune it approves of, and stamps for enviable—and on the whole the world has quite a right to treat me unceremoniously,—I having begun it. As for the 'seeing out of the window once'—those who knew nothing about us but our names had better think *that* was the way, than most others; and the half-dozen who knew a little more, may hear the true account if they please, when they hear anything—those who know *all*, all necessary to know, will understand my 137 letters here and my 54 visits . . see, I write as if this were to be pleaded to-night—would it were! As if you had to write the *meeting* between Hector and Andromache, not the parting! By the way, dearest, what enchanted poetry all your translations for Miss Thomson are—as Carlyle says! 'Nobody can touch them, get at them!' How am I the better for Nonnus, and Apuleius? Now, do you serve me well *there?*

I shall hear to-morrow of Mrs. Jameson's etchings and discourses? and more good news of you, darling? I am *quite* well to-day—going out with my sister to dine next door—then, over to-morrow, and the letter, will come Saturday, my day.

Bless you, my own best, dearest—I am your own.

R.

E. B. B. to R. B.

Thursday.
[Post-mark, March 27, 1846.]

Not the 'dexterous hand'—say rather the good cause. For the rest, when you turn into a dog and lie down, are you not afraid that a sorcerer should go by and dash the water and speak the formula of the old tales. 'If thou wert born a dog, remain a dog, but if not' . . If not . . *what* is to happen? Aminè whipped her enchanted hounds ever so often in the day . . ah, what nonsense happens!

Dear, dearest, how you 'take me with guile,' or with stronger than guile, . . with that divine right you have, of talking absurdities! You make it clear at last that I am so much the better for being bad . . . and *I* . . . shall I laugh? *can* I? is it possible? The words go too deep . . . as deep as death which cannot laugh! And I am forbidden to 'dwell' on the meaning of them—I! There are '*I's*' to match yours!

I shall have the right of doing one thing, . . (passing to *my* rights). I shall hold to the right of remembering to my last hour, that *you*, who might well have passed by on the other side if we two had met on the road when I was riding at ease, . . *did not* when I was in the dust. I choose to remember *that* to the end of feeling. As for *men*, you are not to take me to be quite ignorant of what they are worth in the gross. The most blindfolded women may see a little under the folds . . and I have seen quite enough to be glad to shut my eyes. Did I not tell you that I never thought that any man whom *I* could love, would stoop to love *me*, even if I attained so far as the sight of such. Which I *never attained* . . until . . until! Then, that *you* should care for me. ! ! Oh—I hold to my rights, though you overcome me in most other things. And it is my right to love you better than I could do if I were more worthy to be loved by you.

Mrs. Jameson came late to-day, . . at five—and was hurried and could not stay ten minutes, . . but showed me her etchings and very kindly left a 'Dead St. Cecilia' which I admired most, for its beautiful lifelessness. She is not to be in town again, she said, till a month has gone —a month, at least. Oh—and 'quite uneasy' she was, about my 'cold hands'—yesterday—she thought she had put me to death with over-talking!—which made me smile a little . . 'sub-ridens.' But she is very kind and affectionate; and you were right to teach me to like her—and now, do you know, I look in vain for the 'steely eyes' I fancied I saw once, and see nothing but two good and true ones.

Well—here is an end till Saturday. It is too late . . or I could go on writing . . which I do not hate indeed. Talking of hating, . . . 'what you love entirely' means *that you love entirely* . . and no more and no less. If it did not mean so, I should be unhappy about the *mistake* . . but to 'love entirely' is not a mistake and cannot pass for one either on earth or in Heaven. May God bless you, ever dearest. Such haste I write in—as if the angels were running up Jacob's ladder!—or *down* it, rather, at this close!

Your own
Ba.

R. B. to E. B. B.

Friday.
[Post-mark, March 27, 1846.]

'Qui laborat, orat'; so they used to say, and in that case I have been devotional to a high degree this morning. Seven holes did I dig (to keep up inversions of style)—seven rose-trees did I plant—('Brennus'—and 'Madame Lafarge'! are two names I remember; very characteristic of old Gaul and young France—) and, for my pains, the first fruits, first blossoms some two or three months hence, will come, and will go to dearest Ba who first taught me what a rose really *was*, how sweet it might become with superadded memories of the room and the chair and the vase, and the cutting stalks and pouring fresh water . . ah, my own Ba!—And did you think to warn me out of the Flush-simile by the hint of Aminè's privilege which it would warrant? If the 'ever so much whipping' should please you! . . . And beside it was, if I recollect, for the creature's good, those poor imprisoned sisters, all the time. Moreover, I *was* 'born' all this and more, that you *will* know, at least—and only walked glorious and erect on two legs till dear Siren, an old friend of, and deep in the secrets of Circe, sprinkled the waters . . perhaps on those roses—No, before that!—

Well, to-morrow comes fast now—and I shall trust to be with you my beloved—and, first, you are to show me the portrait, remember.

I am glad you like Mrs. Jameson—do not *I* like her all the better, much the better! But it is fortunate I shall not see her by any chance just now—she would be sure to begin and tell me about *you*—and if my hands did not turn cold, my ear-tips would assuredly turn red. I daresay that St. Cecilia is the beautiful statue above her tomb at Rome; covered with a veil—affectingly beautiful; I well remember how she lies.

Now good-bye; and to-morrow! Bless you, ever dear, dearest Ba—

Your own
R.

R. B. to E. B. B.

Sunday Afternoon.

Now, I think, if I had been 'pricked at the heart' b. dear, dearest Ba's charge yesterday,—if I did not *certainly* know why it might sometimes seem better to be silent than to speak,—should I not be found taking out three or four sheets of paper, and beginning to write, and write! My own, dearest and best, it is *not* so,—not wrong, my heart's self tells me,—and tells you! But for the rest there shall never pass a day till my death wherein I will not write to you, so long as you let me, excepting those days I may spend with you, partly or . . altogether— Love, shall I have very, very long to be hating to write, yet writing?

You see sometimes how I *talk* to you,—even in mere talking what a strange work I make of it. I go on thinking quite another way; so, generally, I often have thought, the little I *have* written, has been an unconscious scrawling with the mind fixed somewhere else: the subject of the scrawl may have previously been the real object of the mind on some similar occasion,—the very thing which *then* to miss, (finding in its place *such another* result of a still prior fancy-fit)—which then to see escape, or find escaped, was the vexation of the time! One cannot, (or *I* cannot) *finish up* the work in one's mind, put away the old projects and take up new. Well, this which I feel on so many occasions, do you wonder if—if!

I should write on *this* for ever! It is all so strange, such a dream as you say!

Indeed, love, the picture is not like, nor 'flattered' by any means, yet I don't know how it is, I cannot be cross with it—there is a touch of truth in the eyes,—would one have believed *that?* I know my own way with portraits; how I let them master eventually my most decided sense of their *unlikeness*—and *this* finds me very prepared—still —it seems already more faithful than last night . . how do I determine where the miraculousness ends? (My Mother was greatly impressed by it—and my sister, coming (from my room) into the room where I was with a visitor, before whom she could not speak English, said '*È molto bella*' *!*)

Here is my 'proof'—I found it as I expected. I fear I must put you to that trouble of sending the other two acts—I hate to think of so troubling you! But do not, Ba, hurry yourself—nor take extraordinary pains—what is worth your pains in these poor things? I like Luria better now,—it may do, now,—probably because it *must;* but, as I said yesterday, I seriously hope and trust to shew my sense of gratitude for what is promised my future life, by doing some real work in it: work of yours, as through you. I have felt, not for the first time now, but from the beginning vexed, foolishly vexed perhaps, that I could not without attracting undesirable notice, 'dedicate,' in the true sense of the word, this or the last number to you.

But if any really worthy performance *should* follow, then my mouth will be unsealed. All is forewritten!

I wonder if you have ventured down this sunny afternoon—tell me how you are, and, once again, do not care about those papers; any time will do.

So, bless you, my own—my all-beloved Ba.

Your R. B.

E. B. B. to R. B.

Sunday Evening.
[Post-mark, March 30, 1846.]

Dearest, I have been trying your plan of thinking of you instead of writing, to-day, and the end is that I am driven to the last of the day and have scarcely room in it to write what I would. Observe if you please, how badly 'the system works,' as the practical people say. Then Mr. Kenyon came and talked,—asked when I had seen you, . . and desired, 'if ever I saw you again,' (ah, what an 'if ever'!) that I would enquire about the 'blue lilies' . . which I satisfied him were of the right colour, on your authority.

But, to go to the 'Tragedy'—I am not to admire it . . am I? And you really think that anyone who can think . . feel . . could help such an admiration, or ought to try to help it? Now just see. It is a new work with your mark on it. That is . . it would make some six or sixteen works for other people, if 'cut up into little stars'—rolled out . . diluted with rain-water. But it is your work as it is—and if you do not care for *that*, *I* care, and shall remember to care on. It is a work full of power and significance, and I am not at all sure (not that it is wise to make comparisons, but that I want you to understand how I am impressed!)—I am not at all sure that if I knew you now first and only by these two productions, . . 'Luria' and the 'Tragedy,' . . I should not involuntarily attribute more power and a higher faculty to the writer of the last—I *should*, I think—yet 'Luria' is the completer work . . I know it very well. Such thoughts, you have, in this second part of the Tragedy! a 'Soul's Tragedy' indeed! No one *thinks* like you—other poets talk like the merest women in comparison. Why it is full of hope for both of us, to look forward and consider what you may achieve with that com bination of authority over the reasons and the passions, and that wonderful variety of the plastic power! But I am going to tell you—Certainly I think you were right (though you know I doubted and cried out) I think now you were right in omitting the theological argument you told me of, from this second part. It would clog the action, and already I am half inclined to fancy it a little clogged in one or two places—but if this is true even, it would be easy to lighten it. Your Ogniben (here is my only criticism in the ways of objection) seems to me almost too wise for a crafty worldling—tell me if he is not! Such thoughts, for the rest, you are prodigal of! That about the child, . . . do you remember how you brought it to me in your first visit, nearly a year ago?

Nearly a year ago! how the time passes! If I had 'done my duty' like the enchanted fish leaping on the gridiron, and seen you never again after that first visit, you would have forgotten all about me by this day. Or at least, 'that prude' I should be! Somewhere under your feet, I should be put down by this day! Yes! and my enchanted dog would be coursing 'some small deer' . . some unicorn of a 'golden horn,' . . (*not* the Kilmansegg gold!) out of hearing if I should have a mind to whistle ever so, . . but out of harm's way perhaps besides.

Well, I do think of it sometimes as you see. Which proves that I love you better than myself by the whole width of the Heavens; the sevenfold Heavens. Yet I think again how He of the heavens and earth brought us together so wonderfully, holding two souls in His hand. If my fault was in it, my *will* at least was not. Believe it of me, dear dearest, that I who am as clear-sighted as other women, . . and not more humble (as to the approaches of common men), was quite resolutely blind when *you* came —I could not understand the possibility of *that*. It was too much . . too surpassing. And so it will seem to the end. The astonishment, I mean, will not cease to be. It is my own especial fairy-tale . . from the spells of which, may you be unharmed . . ! How one writes and writes over and over the same thing! But day by day the same sun rises, . . over, and over, and nobody is tired. May God bless you, dearest of all, and justify what has been by what shall be, . . and let me be free of spoiling any sun of yours! Shall you ever tell me in your thoughts, I wonder, to get out of your sun? No—no—Love keeps love too safe! and I have faith, you see, as a grain of mustard-seed!

Your own

Ba.

Say how you are . . mind!

R. B. to E. B. B.

Monday.
[Post-mark, March 30, 1846.]

'The system,' Ba?—Were *you* to stop writing, as if for my reasons? Could *I* do without your letters, on any pretence? You say well—it was a foolish fancy, and now—have done with it!

And do you think you *could* have refused to see me after that visit? I mean, do you think I did not resolve so to conduct myself; so to 'humble myself and go still and softly all my days'; that your suspicion should needs insensibly clear up . . (if it had been *so* pre-ordained, and that no more was in my destiny,) and at last I should have been written down your friend for ever, and let come and stay, on that footing. But you really think the confirmation of that sentence must have been attended with such an effect—that I should have forgotten you or *so* remembered you? You think that on the strength of such a love as *that*, I would have ventured a month of my future life . . much less, the whole of it? *Not you*, Ba,—my dearest, dearest!

How you surprise me (what ever may you think) by liking that 'Tragedy'! It seems as if, having got out of the present trouble, I shall never fall into its fellow—I will strike, for the future, on the glowing, malleable metal; afterward, *filing* is quite another process from hammering, and a more difficult one. Note, that 'filing' is the wrong word,—and the rest of it, the wrong simile,—and all of it, in its stupid wrongness very characteristic of what I try to illustrate—oh, the better, better days are before me *there* as in all else! But, do you notice how stupid I am to-day? My head begins again—that is the fact; it is better a good deal than in the morning—its œconomy passes my comprehension altogether, that is the other fact. With the deep joy in my heart below—this morning's letter here—what *does* the head mean by its perversity? I will go out presently and walk it back to its senses.

Dearest, did you receive my 'proof' this morning? Do not correct nor look at it, nor otherwise trouble yourself—there is plenty of time. But what day is ours to be? Of that you say nothing, and of my poems a great deal, 'O *you* inverter!' But *I* am, rather, a *re*verter—and *you* shall revert, and mind the natural order of things, and tell me first of all—(in to-night's letter, dearest?)—that it is to be on—?

Now let me kiss you here—my own Ba! Being stupid makes *some* difference in me—I am no poet, nor prose-writer, nor rational 'Christian, pagan nor man' this afternoon—but I *am* now—as yesterday—as the long 'year ago'—your own, utterly your own! May God bless you! (I wondered yesterday if you had gone downstairs—'*no*' I infer!)

E. B. B. to R. B.

Monday.

Dearest, I send you back the two parts of the 'Soul's Tragedy,' and the proof. On a strip of paper are two or three *inanities* in the form of doubts I had in reading the first part. I think upon the whole that you owe me all gratitude for the help of so much high critical wisdom—of which this paper is a fair proof and expression.

The proof, the printed 'Luria' I mean, has more than pleased me. It is noble and admirable; and grows greater, the closer seen. The most exceptionable part, it seems to me, is Domizia's retraction at the last, for which one looks round for the sufficient motive. But the impression of the whole work goes straight to the soul—it is heroic in the best sense.

I write in such haste. Oh—I should have liked to have read again the second part of the 'Tragedy,' but dare not keep it though you give me leave. I think of the printers—and you will let me have the proof, in this case also.

Your letter shall be answered presently. Your sister's word about the picture proves very conclusively how wonderfully like it must be as a portrait! *That* would settle the question to any 'Royal Commission' in the world—only we need not go so far.

Dearest I end here—to begin again in another half hour. Ah—and you promise, you promise—

No time—but ever your own.

Ba.

E. B. B. to R. B.

Monday Evening.
[Post-mark, March 31, 1846.]

Ah now, now, you *see!* Held up in *that* light, it *is* 'a foolish fancy,' and unlawful, besides! 'Not on any *pretence*' will you do without letters . . *you!* And you count it among the imaginations of your heart that *I* could do without them better perhaps . . *I* . . to whom they are sun, air, and human voices, at the very lowest calculation? Why seriously you dont imagine that your letters are not a thousand times more to *me*, than letters ever in the world were before, . . since 'Heaven first brought them to some wretch's aid.' If you *do*, that *is* the foolishest fancy of all.

So foolish as to be unspeakable. We will 'have done with it,' as you say. I only 'revert' and innocently,—I do not reproach, even ignorantly,—I am grateful rather. What you said in the letter this morning made me grateful, . . and oh, so glad! so glad! what you said, I mean, of writing to me on every day that we did not meet on otherwise. That promise seemed to bring us nearer (see how I think of letters!), nearer than another word *could*, though you went for it to the end of the universe, . . that other word. So I accept the promise as a promise of pure gold, and thank *you*, as pure gold too, which you are, or rather far above. Only my own dearest, you shall not write long letters . . long letters are out of the agreement . . I never feel the need of length *as long as* the writing is *there* . . just the little shred of the Koran, to be gathered up reverently . . (Inshallah!)—and then, you shall not write at all when you are not well . . no, you shall not. So remember from henceforth! Shall I whip my enchanted dog when he is so good and true?—not to say that the tags of the lashes (do you call them *tags?*) would swing round and strike me on the shoulders? Dearest, you are the best, kindest in the world—such a very, very, *very* 'little lower than the angels!' If ever I could take advantage of your goodness and tenderness, to teaze and vex you, . . what should *I* be, I have been seriously enquiring to-day, head on hand, when I had sent away 'Luria.' For I sent it away, and the 'Tragedy' with it, and I hope you will have all to-morrow morning at the furthest, . . before you get this letter. There was a note too in the parcel.

As to dedications . . . believe me that I would not

have them if I could . . that is, *even if there were no dangers.* I could not bear to have words from you which the world might listen to . . I mean, that to be commended of you in *that* way, on *that* ground, would make me feel cold to the heart. Oh no, no, no! It is better to have the proof-sheet as I had it this morning: it is the better glory . . as glory!

'Not worthy of my pains' . . you are right! But infinitely worthy of my *pleasures*—such pleasure as I could gather from nothing else, except from your letters and your very presence. Do you think that anything beside in the whole world could bring pleasure to me, as pleasure goes, . . . anything like reading your poetry? My 'pains' indeed! It is a felicitous word—'je vous en fais mon compliment.'

And all this time, while I write lightly, you are not well perhaps—you were unwell when you wrote to me; you were unwell a little yesterday even. Say how you are to-morrow—do not forget. For the cause of the unwellness, *I* see it, if *you* do not. It was *the proof-correcting*—I expected that you would be unwell—it is no worse than was threatened to my thoughts. The comfort is that all this wrong work is coming to an end, and that it is covenanted between us for you to *rest absolutely* from henceforth. Say how you are, dearest dearest. And walk, walk. For me, I have not been downstairs. It has been cold—too cold for *that*, I thought.

Oh—but I wanted to say one thing! That wonderful picture, which is not much like a unicorn or even 'a whale' . . but rather more perhaps than like *me*, you may keep for weeks or months, if you choose; if it continues 'not to make you cross.' Because *it* does not flatter, and because *you* do not flatter (in such equal proportions!): the sympathy accounts for the liking . . or absence of dislike; on your part.

Now I must end. *Thursday* is our day, I think:—and it is easier to say 'Thursday' on Monday than on Saturday . . a discovery of mine, *that*, as good as Faraday's last!

Say how you are. Do not forget. I had to say . . . . What I cannot, to-night.

But I am your own

Ba.

R. B. to E. B. B.

Tuesday.
[Post-mark, March 31, 1846.]

Dear, dear, Ba, what shall I say or not say? On a kind of principle, I have tried before this to *subdue* the expression of gratitude for the material, *worldly* good you do me —for my poor store of words would all pay themselves away here, at the beginning, and so leave the higher, peculiar, *Ba's own* gifts even without a *cry* of *acknowledgment*, not to say of thanks. But somehow you, you my dearest, my Ba, look out of all imaginable nooks and crevices in the materiality—I see you thro' your goodness, —I cannot distinguish between your acts now,—the greater, indeed, and the lesser! Which *is* the 'lesser'? *With you* all their heap of work seems no more than——. (I cannot even think of what may serve for some lesser act of kindness! *That* is just what I wanted to say—'the effect defective comes by cause' here—there *is* no 'lesser' blessing in your power, as I said!)

Now, darling,—it is late in the afternoon, as posts go —I have been out all the morning in town, and while I was happy with one letter (found waiting my return)—the parcel comes—so I will just say this much, (this *little*, this *least*)—this word now—and by to-night all shall be corrected, I hope, and got rid of fairly. And to-morrow, I will have you to myself, my best one, and will write till you cry out against me. I go now. God bless you and reward you—prays your very own R. B.

E. B. B. to R. B.

Tuesday Evening.
[Post-mark, March 31, 1846.]

If people were always as grateful to other people for being just kind to *themselves*, . . what a grateful world we should have of it! The actual *good* you get out of me, may be stated at about *two commas and a semi-colon*—do I overstate it, I wonder? *You*, on the other side, never overstate anything . . never enlarge . . never exaggerate! In fact, the immense 'worldly' advantages which fall to you from *me*, are plain to behold. Dearest, what nonsense you talk some times, for a man so wise! nonsense as wonderful in its way for 'Robert Browning' as the dancing of polkas! The worst is, that it sets me wishing impotently, to do some really good helpful thing for you—and I cannot,—cannot. The good comes to me from you, and will not go back again. Even the loving you, . . which is all I can, . . have I not had to question of it again and again . . . . "Is *that* good?" Now see.

I shall be anxious to hear your own thoughts of the 'Soul's Tragedy' when you have it in print. You liked 'Luria' better for seeing it printed—and I must have you like the 'Tragedy' in proportion. It *strikes* me. It is original, as they say. There is something in it awakening . . striking:—and when it has awakened, it won't let you go to sleep again immediately.

And of yourself, not a word. You might have said *one* word—but you have been in London which makes me hope that you are perhaps a little better . . or at least not worse. Oh, I do not hope *much* while you are about this printing. You are sure not to be well. That is to be accepted as a necessary consequence—it cannot be otherwise. The comfort is, that the whole will be put away in a week or ten days, and that then I may set myself to hope for you, as the roses to blow in June. Fit summer-business, *that* will be! And you will help me, and walk and take care.

What do you think I have been doing to-day to Mr. Kenyon? Sending him the 'enchanted poetry' which such as *you* are never to see . . the translation about Hector and Andromache!—yes, really. Yet after all it is not that I like him so much better than you . . I do not indeed . . it is just that Miss Thomson and her book are of consequence to him, and that he hears through Miss Bayley and herself of the attempt here and the failure there, . . and so, being interested altogether, he asked me to let him see what I did with Homer. And it is not much. Old Homer laughs his translators to very scorn . . and he does not spare *me*, for being a woman. Surpassingly and profoundly beautiful that scene is. I have tried it in blank verse. About a year ago, when I had a sudden fit of translating, I made an experiment on the first fifty lines of the Iliad in a rhymed measure which seemed to me rather nearer to the Greek cadence than our common heroic verse. Listen to what I remember—

> Thus he spake in his prayer: and Apollo gave ear to the whole;
> And came down from the steep of Olympus, with wrath in his soul;
> On his shoulder the bow, and the quiver fast woven by fate,
> And the darts hurtled on, as he trod, with the thrill of his hate
> And the step of his godhead. Like night did he travel below—
> And he sate down afar from the ships, and drew strong to the bow—

And so we get to the arrows you talked of . . ah, do you remember . . do you remember? . . which were to kill dogs and mules, you said! But they didn't. I have an enchanted dog ('which nobody *can* deny'!) and am not far to seek in my Apollo.

To-day I had a letter from Miss Mitford who says that, inasmuch as she does not go to Paris, she shall come for a fortnight to London and 'see me every day.'! ! No time is fixed—but I look a little aghast. *Am I not grateful and affectionate?* Is it right of you, not to let me love anyone as I used to do? Is it in *that* sense that you kill the dogs and mules? Perhaps. The truth is, I would rather she did not come—far rather. And she may not, after all—. . now I am ashamed of myself thoroughly.

I have not been downstairs to-day—the weather seemed so doubtful. To-morrow, if it is possible, I will . . must . . do it. So . . goodbye till the day after—Thursday. May God bless you everyday! and if only as I think of you . . you would not lose much!

Your Ba.

R. B. to E. B. B.

[Post-mark, April 1, 1846.]

Now—dear, dearest Ba—let me begin the only way!—And so you are kissed whether you feel it or not—through the distance, what matter? Dear love, I return from town—my writing has gone away—you remain, and we are together—as I said, it *would* be, so it is! And here is your letter, and here are recollections of all the letters for so long, all the perfect kindnesses which I did not answer, meaning to answer them one day—and, one day, look to receive (I may write you) a huge sheetful of answers to bygone interrogatories,—sins of omission remedied according to ability—and you will stare like a man, I read of somewhere, who asked his neighbour 'how he fed that mule of his, so as to keep it in such good case?'—and then, struck by some other fancy, went on to talk of other matters till the day's end—when, on alighting at their Inn (for these two were journeying, and the talk began with the stirrup-cup)—the other, who had been watching his opportunity, breaking silence for the first time, answered—'With oats and hay.' Observe that the only part of the story I parallel is the *surprise* at the end—for I am not going to get whipped before I deserve, Aminè (*Ba mine*). At all events I will answer this last dear note. The 'good' you do me, I see *you* cannot see nor understand *yet*—there is my answer! Here, in this instance, I corrected everything,—altered, improved. Did you notice the alterations (curtailments) in 'Luria'? Well, I put in a few phrases in the second part of the other,—where Ogniben speaks—and hope that they give a little more insight as to his character—which I meant for that of a man of wide speculation and narrow practice,—universal understanding of men and sympathy with them, yet professionally restricted claims for himself, for his own life. *There*, was the theology to have come in! He should have explained, 'the belief in a future state, with me, modifies every feeling derivable from this present life—I consider *that* as dependent on foregoing *this*—consequently, I may see that your principles are perfectly right and proper to be embraced so far as concerns this world, though I believe there is an eventual gain, to be obtained elsewhere, in either opposing or disregarding them,—in not availing myself of the advantages they procure.' Do you see?—as a man may not choose to drink wine, for his health's sake, or from a scruple of conscience, &c.—and yet may be a good judge of what wine should be, how it *ought* to taste—something like this was *meant*—and when it is forgotten almost, and only the written thing with a shadow of the meaning stays,—you wonder that the written thing gets to look better in time? Do you think if I could forget *you*, Ba, I should not reconcile myself to your picture—which already I love better than yesterday—and which, to revenge, I know I shall by this time to-morrow like less, so far less. Well, and then there is Domizia—I *could not* bring her to my purpose. I left the neck stiff that was to have bowed of its own accord—for nothing graceful could be accomplished by pressing with both hands on the head above! I meant to make her leave off her own projects through love of Luria. As it is, they in a manner fulfil themselves, so far as she has any power over them, and then, she being left unemployed, sees Luria, begins to see him, having hitherto seen only her own ends which he was to further. Oh, enough of it! I have told you, and tell you and will tell you, my Ba, because it is simple truth,—that you have been 'helping' me to cover a defeat, not gain a triumph. If I had not known you *so far* THESE works might have been the *better*:—as assuredly, the greater works, I trust will follow,—they would have suffered in proportion! If you take a man from prison and set him free . . do you not probably cause a signal interruption to his previously all ingrossing occupation, and sole labour of love, of carving bone-boxes, making chains of cherry-stones, and other such time-beguiling operations—does he ever take up that business with the old alacrity? No! But he begins ploughing, building—(castles he makes, no bone-boxes now). I may plough and build—but there,—leave them as they are!

Here an end till to-morrow—my best dearest. I am very well to-day—I forgot to say anything yesterday. You did not go down stairs, for all your good intentions, I hope—this morning I mean: observe how the days are made—the mornings are warm and sunny—after gets up such a wind as now howls—what a sound! The most melancholy in the whole world I think.

No—I can't do what I had set down—keep my remonstrance and upbraiding on the Homer-subject till to-morrow and then speak arrows. What do you mean, Ba, by 'remembering' those lines you give me—have you no more written down. *Quite* happy and original they are—but to-morrow this is waited for—dearest, bless you ever! your R.

E. B. B. to R. B.

Friday.
[Post-mark, April 3, 1846.]

Dearest, your flowers make the whole room look like April, they are so full of colours . . growing fuller and fuller as we get nearer to the sun. The wind was melancholy too, all last night—oh, *I* think the wind melancholy, just as *you* do,—or *more* than you do perhaps for having spent so many restless days and nights close on the sea-shore in Devonshire. I seem now always to hear the sea *in* the wind, voice within voice! But I like a sudden wind, not too loud,—a wind which you hear the rain in rather than the sea—and I like the half cloudy half sunny April weather, such as we have it here in England, with a west or south wind—I like and enjoy *that;* and remember vividly how I used to like to walk or wade nearly up to my waist in the wet grass or weeds, with the sun overhead, and the wind darkening or lightening the verdure all round.

But none of it was happiness, dearest dearest. Happiness does not come with the sun or the rain. Since my illness, when the door of the future seemed shut and locked before my face, and I did not tire myself with knocking any more, I thought I was happier, happy, I thought, just because I was tranquil *unto death.* Now I know life from death, . . and the unsorrowful life for the first time since I was a woman; though I sit here on the edge of a precipice in a position full of anxiety and danger. What matter, . . . if one shuts one's eyes, and listens to the birds singing? Do you know, I am glad—I could almost thank God—that Papa keeps so far from me . . that he has given up coming in the evening . . I could almost thank God. If he were affectionate, and made me, or *let* me, feel myself necessary to him, . . how should I bear (even with my reason on my side) to prepare to give him pain? So that the Pisa business last year, by sounding the waters, was good in its way . . and the pang that came with it to me, was also good. He feels!—he loves me . . but it is not (this, I mean to say) to the *trying* degrees of feeling and love . . trying to *me.* Ah, well! In any case, I should have ended probably, in giving up all for you—I do not profess otherwise. I used to think I should, if ever I loved anyone—and if the love of you is different from, it is greater than, anything preconceived . . divined.

Mrs. Jameson, the other day, brought out a theory of hers which I refuse to receive, and which I thought to myself she would apply to *me* some day, with the rest of what Miss Mitford calls 'those good-for-nothing poets and poetesses.' She maintained (Mrs. Jameson did) that 'artistical natures never learn wisdom from experience—that sorrow teaches them nothing—leaves no trace at all—that the mind is modified in no way by passion—suffering.' Which I disbelieved quite, and ventured to say on the other side, that although practically a man or woman might not be wiser, through perhaps the interception of a vivid apprehension of the present, which might put back the influence of the future over actions, . . yet that it was impossible for a selfconscious nature (which all these artistic natures are) and a sensitive nature, not to receive some sort of modification from things suffered— 'No'—she said, they did not! she had known and loved such—and they were like children, all of them,—essentially immature.' But she did not persuade me. What is *inequality* of nature, as Dugald Stewart observed it, (and did he not say that men of genius had lop-sided minds?) is different, I think, from immaturity in her sense of the word. We were talking of her friend Mrs. Butler, which brought us to the subject. Presently she will say of you and me . . 'Just see there! she meant no harm, poor thing, I dare say—but she acts like a child! And, for *him*, *his* is the imbecility of most regent genius . . such as I am to live to see confessed imperial, or I die a disappointed woman.'!

Do you hear? *I* do, distinctly. *You*, in the meantime, are looking at the 'locks' . . just as poor Louis Seize did when they were preparing his guillotine.

May God bless you, my own dearest—Think of me *a little*—as you say!

Your

Ba.

R. B. to E. B. B.

Friday.
[Post-mark, April 3, 1846.]

I want to tell you a thing before I forget it, my own Ba—a thing that pleased me to find out this morning. A few days ago there was a paragraph in the newspaper about Lord Compton and his ways at Rome. His address was to be read in the general list of working-artists kept for public inspection at Monaldini's news-room, and the Earl's self was to be found in fraternal association with 'young art,' at board and sporting-place, wearing the same distinctive *blouse* and Louis II. hat with great flaps; even his hair as picturesquely disordered as the best of them—(the artists, not flaps)—at all which the reporter seemed scarcely to know whether he ought to laugh or cry. This I read in the *Daily News* with other gossip about Rome, last Wednesday. But this morning a *Cambridge Advertiser* of the same day reaches me—and there, under the head of College news (after recording that Mr. A has been appointed to this vicarage, and Mr. B, licensed to the other curacy)—one finds this—'The Earl Compton, M.A. (Hon. 1837)—is of great fame in Rome as a Painter!'—which the other authority wholly forgot to mention; supposing, no doubt, all the love went to the blouse and flapped hat aforesaid! Now, is it not a good instance of that fascination which the *true* life at Rome (apart from the stupidities of the travelling English) exercises every now and then on susceptible people? The best thing for an English Earl to do,—(who will be a Marquis one day)—would be to stay here and vindicate his title by honest work with the opportunities it affords him—but if he *cannot* rise to the dignity of the best part, surely this, he chooses, is better than many others—being caught as some noblemen were yesterday, for instance, superintending a dog-fight in some horrible den of thieves in St. Giles'. I don't know, after all, why I tell you this,—but that amid all the dull doings of the notable dull ones there, and their 'honours'—(such a wonder of a man was Smith's prize-man,—another had got to be gloriously first in the Classical Tripos)—this bit of 'fame at Rome' seemed like a break of blue real sky with a star in it, shining through the canvass sham clouds and oil-paper moons of a theatre.

Now I get to you, my Ba! How strange! It does so happen that I took the pen and laid out the paper with, I really think, a completer, deeper yearning of love to *you* than usual even—I seemed to have a thousand things that I *could* say *now*—and on touching the paper . . see—I start off with a foolish story and still foolisher comment as if there were no Ba close at my head all the time, straight before my eyes too! So it is with me—I give the *expressing* part up at once! It must be understood, inferred,—(*proved*, never!) All nonsense, so I will stay—and try to be wise to-morrow—*now*, I have no note to guide me and half put into my mouth what I ought to say. So, dear, dear Ba, goodbye! I very well know what this letter is worth—yet because of the love and endeavour *un*seen, may I not have the hand to kiss—and without the glove? It *is* kissed, whether you give it or no,—for there are two long days more to wait—and then comes Monday! Bless you till then, and ever, my dearest: My own Ba—

Your R.

E. B. B. to R. B.

Friday Evening.
[Post-mark, April 4, 1846.]

Shall the heir to a Marquisate 'justify his title' in these days? Is not the best thing he can do for *himself*, to forget it in a studio at Rome?—and one of the best things he can do for his country, perhaps, to desecrate it at dog-fighting before the eyes of all men? I should not like to have to justify my Marquisate to reasonable men now-a-days, — should *you* . . seriously speaking? It would be a hard task, and rather dull in the performance. On the other hand, the noble dog-fighters (unconscious patriots!) find it easy and congenial occupation down in St. Giles's, rubbing out (as in the old game of fox and goose) figure by figure, prestige by prestige, the gross absurdity of hereditary legislators, lords, and the like. Yet of the three positions, I would rather be at Rome, certainly a man looks nobler there, is better, is happier . . a good deal nearer the angels than on his 'landed estates' playing at feudal proprietor, or even in St. Giles's dog-fighting. See what a republican you have for a . . *Ba*. Did you fancy me capable of writing such unlawful, disorderly things? And it is'nt out of bitterness, nor covetousness . . no, indeed. People in general would rather be Marquises than Roman artists, consulting their own wishes and inclination. I, for my part, ever since I could speak my mind and knew it, always openly and inwardly preferred the glory of those who live by their heads, to the opposite glory of those who carry other people's arms. So much for glory. Happiness goes the same way to my fancy. There is something fascinating to me, in that Bohemian way of living . . all the conventions of society cut so close and thin, that the soul can see through . . beyond . . above. It is 'real life' as you say . . whether at Rome or elsewhere. I am very glad that you like simplicity in habits of life—it has both reasonableness and sanctity. People are apt to suffocate their faculties by their manners—English people especially. I admire that you,—R B,—who have had temptation more than enough, I am certain, under every form, have lived in the midst of this London of ours, close to the great social vortex, yet have kept so safe, and free, and calm and pure from the besetting sins of our society. When you came to see me first, I did not expect so much of you in that one respect. How could I? You had lived in the world, I knew, and I thought . . . well!—what matter, *now*, what I thought?

I will tell you instead how to-day has gone by with me. Not like yesterday, indeed! In the first place, I went down stairs, walked up and down the drawing-room twice, and finding nobody there (they were all having luncheon in the dining-room) came up stairs again . . . half-way on the stairs met Flush, who having been asleep, had not missed me till just then, and was in the act of search. I was lost for ever, thought poor Flush. At least I think he thought so by his eyes. They were three times their usual largeness—he looked quite wild . . and leaped against me with such an ecstasy of astonished joy, that I nearly fell backward down the stairs (whereupon, you would have had to go to the Siren's island, dearest, all by yourself!) After which escape of mine and Flushie's, and when I had persuaded him to be good and quiet and to believe that I was not my own ghost, I came home with him and prepared to see . .

I will tell you. She is a Mrs. Paine who lives at Farnham, and learns Greek, and writes to me such overcoming letters, that at last, and in a moment of imprudent reaction from an ungrateful discourtesy on my part, I agreed to see her if she ever came to London. Upon which, she comes directly—I am taken in my trap. She comes and returns the same day, and all to see me. Well—she had been kind to me . . and she came at two to-day. Do you know, . . for the first five minutes, I *repented quite?* Dearest . . she came just with the sort of face which a child might take to see a real, alive lioness at the Zoological Gardens . . she just sate down on a chair, and stared. How can people do such things in this year of grace when they are abolishing the cornlaws, I wonder? For my part, it was so unlike anything civilized I had ever been used to, that I felt as if my voice and breath went together. It would have saved me to be able to *stare back again*, but *that* was out of my power. So I endured—and, after a pause, ran violently down a steep place into some sort of conversation (thinking of your immortal Simpson, and vowing never to be drawn into such a situation again) and in a little while, I was able to recognize that there was nothing worse than bad manners—*ignorant* manners—and that, for the rest, my antagonist was a young, pretty woman (*rather* pretty), enthusiastic and provincial, with a strong love for poetry and literature generally, loving Carlyle and *your*self, (could I hold out against *that?*) and telling me all her domestic happinesses with a frankness which quite appeased me and prevented my being too tired . . though she stayed two hours, and *wasn't you!*—

So there is my history of to-day for you! To-morrow you will have the proof—and perhaps, *I* shall! Monday will bring a better thing than a proof. May God bless you, beloved. Say how you are . . to-morrow! *Mind* to do it . . or I will not sit any more in your gondola-chair. How can you make me, unless I choose?

And you speak against my letter to-night? you shall not dare do such things. It is a good, dear letter, and it is mine to call so . . and I knew its fellows before I knew you and loved them before I loved you, and so you are not to be proud and scornful and try to put them down 'in *that* way.'

Your own

Ba.

R. B. to E. B. B.

Saturday.
[April 4, 1846.]

Oh, my two letters—and to turn from such letters to you, to my own Ba!—I very well know I am not grateful enough, if there is any grace in *that*, any power to avert punishment, as one hopes! But all my hope is in future endeavour—it *is*, my Ba,—this is earnest truth. And one thing that strikes me on hearing such prognostications of Mrs. Jameson's opinion on *our* subject—is that—as far as I am concerned . . or yourself, indeed—we must make up our mind to endure the stress of it, and of such opinions generally, with all resignation . . and by the time we *can* answer,—why, alas, they are gone and forgotten, so that there's no paying them for their impertinence. I mean, that I do not *expect*, as a foolish fanciful boy might, that on the sudden application of 'Hymen's torch' (to give the old simile one chance more) your happiness will blaze out apparent to the whole world lying in darkness, like a wondrous 'Catherine-wheel,' now all blue, now red, and so die at the bed amid an universal clapping of hands—I trust a long life of real work 'begun, carried on and ended,' as it never otherwise could have been (certainly by *me* . . and if I dare hope, *you*, dearest, it is because you teach me to aspire to the height)—that the attainment of all that happiness of daily, hourly life in entire affection, which seeing that men of genius need rather more—ah, these words, I cannot look back and take up the thread of the sentence,—but I wanted to say—we will live the real answer, will we not, dearest, all the stupidity against 'genius' 'poets,' and the like, is got past the stage of being treated with patient consideration and gentle pity—it is *too* vexatious, if it will not lie still, out of the way, by this time. What *is* the crime, to his fellow man or woman (not to God, I know that—these are peculiar sins to Him—whether greater in His eyes, who shall say?)—but to mankind, *what* is crime which would have been prevented but for the 'genius' involved in it? A man of genius ill-treats his wife—well, take away the 'genius'—does he so naturally improve? See the article in to-day's *Athenæum*, about the French Duel—far enough from 'men of genius' these Dujarriers &c.—but go to-night into half the *estaminets* of Paris, and see whether the quarrels over dice and some wine present any more pleasing matter of contemplation *au fond*. Sin is sin everywhere and the worse, I think, for the grossness. Being fired at by a duellist is a little better, I think also, than being struck on the face by some ruffian. These are extreme cases—but go higher and it is the same thing. Poor, cowardly miscreated natures abound—if you could throw 'genius' into their composition, they would become more degraded still, I suppose!

I know I want every faculty I can by any possibility dare—want all, and much more, to teach me what you are, my own Ba, and what I should do to prove that I am taught, and do know.

I will write at length to you to-morrow, my all beloved. I am, somehow, overflowing with things to say, and the time is *fearfully* short—my proofs have just arrived, here they are, not even *glanced* over by me—(To-morrow, love! not one thing answered in my letters, as when I read and read them to-night I shall say to myself). Bless you, dearest, dearest

R.

E. B. B. to R. B.

Sunday.
[April 5, 1846.]

It seems to me the safest way to send back the proofs by the early Monday post: you may choose perhaps to bring the sheet corrected into town when you come, and so I shall let you have what you sent me, before you come to take it . . though I thought first of waiting. To-morrow I shall force you to tell me how you like the 'Tragedy' *now!* For my part, it delights me—and must raise your reputation as a poet and thinker . . *must.* Chiappino is highly dramatic in that first part, and speaks so finely sometimes that it is a wrench to one's sympathies to find him overthrown. Do you know that, as far as the *temper* of the man goes, I am acquainted with a Chiappino . . just such a man, in the temper, the pride and the bitterness . . not in other things. When I read your manuscript I was reminded—but here in print, it seems to grow nearer and nearer. My Chiappino has tired me out at last—I have borne more from him than women ought to bear from men, because he was unfortunate and embittered in his nature and by circumstances, and because I regarded him as a friend of many years. Yet, as I have told him, anyone, who had not such confidence in me, would think really *ill of me* through reading the insolent letters which he has thought fit to address to me on what he called a pure principle of adoration. At last I made up my mind (and shall keep it so) to answer no letter of the kind. Men are ignoble in some things, past the conceiving of their fellows. Again and again I have said . . 'Specify your charge against me'—but there is no charge. With the most reckless and dauntless inconsistency I am lifted halfway to the skies, and made a mark there for mud pellets—so that I have been excited sometimes to say quite passionately . . 'If I am the filth of the earth, tread on me—if I am an angel of Heaven, respect me—but I can't be both, remember.' See where your Chiappino leads you . . and me! Though I shall not tell you the other name of mine. Whenever I see him now, I make Arabel stay in the room —otherwise I *am afraid*—he is such a violent man. A good man, though, in many respects, and quite an old friend. Some men grow incensed with the continual pricks of ill-fortune, like mad bulls: some grow tame and meek.

Well—*I* did not like the spirit of the *Athenæum* remarks either. I like what *you* say. These literary men are never so well pleased, as in having opportunities of barking against one another—and, for the *Athenæum* people, if they wanted to be didactic as to morals, they might have taken occasion to be so out of their own order, and in their own country. And then to bring in Balzac *so!* The worst of Balzac (who has not a fine moral sense at any time, great and gifted as he is), the very worst of him, is his bearing towards his literary brothers . . the manner in which he, who can so nobly present genius to the reverence of humanity in scientific men (as he describes them in his books), always dishonours and depreciates it in the man of letters and the poet. See his 'Grand Homme de Province à Paris,' one of the most powerful of his works, but the remark is true everywhere. I go on writing as if I were not to see you directly. It is past four oclock—and if Mr. Kenyon does not come to-day, he may come to-morrow, and find you, who were here last Thursday to his knowledge!—Half I fear.

Observe the proof. Since you have two, you say, I have not scrupled to write down on this ever so much improvidence, which you will glance at and decide upon finally.

'Grateful' . . 'grateful' . . what a word *that* is. I never would have such a word on any proof that came to me for correction. Do not use such inapplicable words—do not, dearest! for you know very well in your understanding (if not in your heart) that if such a word is to be used by either of us, it is *not by you*. My word, I shall keep mine,—*I* am 'grateful'—*you* cannot be 'grateful' . . for ineffable reasons . .

> 'Pour bonnes raisons
> Que l'on n'ose dire.
> Et que nous taisons.'

For the rest, it is certainly very likely that you may 'want all your faculties, *and more*' . . . to bear with me . . to support me with graceful resignation; and who can tell whether I may not be found intolerable after all?

By the way (talking of St. Catherine's wheels and the like torments) you wrote 'gag' . . did you not? . . where the proof says 'gadge'—I did not alter it. More and more I like 'Luria.'

Your Ba.

Mr. Kenyon has been here—so our Monday is safe,

R. B. to E. B. B.

Sunday.
[Post-mark, April 6, 1846.]

I sent you some even more than usual hasty foolish words,—not caring much, however—for dearest Ba shall have to forgive my shortcomings every hour in the day,—

it is her destiny, and I began unluckily with that stupidest of all notions,—that about the harm coming of genius &c., so I fell with my subject and we rolled in the mud together—*pas vrai?* But there was so many other matters alluded to in your *dearest* (because last) letter—there are many things in which I agree with you to such a tremblingly exquisite exactness, so to speak, that I hardly dare cry out lest the charm break, the imaginary oscillation prove incomplete and your soul, *now* directly over, pass beyond mine yet, and not *stay!* Do you understand, dear soul of my soul, dearest Ba? Oh, how different it all might be! In this House of life—where I go, you go—where I ascend you run before—when I descend it is after you. Now, one might have a piece of Ba, but a very little of her, and make it up into a lady and a mistress, and find her a room to her mind perhaps when she should sit and sing, 'warble eat and dwell' like Tennyson's blackbird, and to visit her there with due honour one might wear the finest of robes, use the courtliest of ceremonies—and then—after a time, leave her there and go, the door once shut, without much blame, to throw off the tunic and put on Lord Compton's blouse and go whither one liked—after, to me, the most melancholy fashion in the world. How different with us! If it were *not*, indeed—what a mad folly would marriage be! Do you know what quaint thought strikes me, out of old Bunyan, on this very subject? He says (with another meaning though) 'Who would keep a cow, that may buy milk at a penny the quart'—(elegant allusion). Just so,—whoever wants 'a quart' of this other comfort, as solace of whatever it may be (at breakfast or tea time too), why not go and 'buy' the same, and having discussed it, drink claret at dinner at his club? Why did not Mr. Butler *read* Fanny Kemble's verses, paying his penny of intellectual labour, and see her play 'Portia' at night, and make her a call or ride with her in the middle of the day—why 'keep the cow'? *But*—don't you know they prescribe to some constitutions the *per-*

petual living in a cow-house? the breath, the unremitting influence is everything,—not the milk—(now, Ba—Ba is suddenly Ἰω πλανωμένη and Mrs. Jameson is the Gadfly—and I am laughed at—not too cruelly, or the other lock of hair becomes mine—with which locks . . and not with Louis Seize iron knicknack ones, I rather think I was occupied last time, last farewell taking—)

From all which I infer—that I shall see you to-morrow! Yes, or I should not have the heart to be glad and absurd.

Well, to-morrow makes amends—dear, dear Ba! Why do you persist in trying to turn my head so? It does not turn, I look the more steadfastly at the feet and the ground, for all your crying and trying! But something shocking might happen—*would* happen, if it were not written that I am to get nothing but good from Ba,—and *who, who* began calling names—who used the word 'flatterer' first?

Bless you my own dearest flatterer—I love you with heart and soul. Are you downstairs to day? it is warm, the rain you like—yes you are down, I think. God keep you wherever you are!

Your own.

I went last night to Lord Compton's father's Soirée,—and for all our deep convictions, and philosophic rejoicing, I assure you that of the two or three words that we interchanged—congratulation on the bright fortune of his son formed no part,—any more than intelligence about ordering Regiments to India whenever I met the relatives of the ordered. And yesterday morning I planted a full dozen more rose-trees, all white—to take away the yellow-rose reproach!

R. B. to E. B. B.

Monday Morning.
[April 6, 1846.]

I shall receive a note from you presently, I trust—but this had better go now—for I expect a friend, and must attend to him as he wants to go walking—so, dearest—dearest, take my—last work I ever shall *send* you, if God please!

A word about a passage or two,—I had forgotten to say before—gadge is a real name (in Johnson, too) for a torturing iron—it is part of the horror of such things that they should be mysteriously named,—indefinitely,—'The Duke of Exeter's Daughter' for instance . . Ugh!—Besides, am I not a rhymester? Well, who knows but one may want to use such a word in a couplet with '*badge*'—which, if one reject the old and obsolete '*fadge*,' is rhymeless?

Then Chiappino remarks that men of genius usually do the *reverse* . . of beginning by dethroning &c. and so arriving with utmost reluctancy at the acknowledgment of a natural and unalterable *inequality* of Mankind—instead of *that*, they begin *at once*, he says, by recognizing it in their adulation &c. &c.—I have supplied the words '*at once*,' and taken out '*virtually*,' which was unnecessary; so that the parallel possibly reads clearlier. I know there are other things to say—but at this moment my memory is at fault.

Can you tell me Mrs. Jameson's address?

My sea-friend's opinion is altogether unfavourable to the notion of an invalid's trusting himself alone in a merchant vessel—he says—'it will certainly be the gentleman's death.' So very small a degree of comfort can be secured amid all the inevitable horrors of dirt, roughness, &c The expenses are trifling in any case, on that very account. Any number of the *Shipping Gazette* (I think) will give a list of all vessels about to sail, with choice of ports—or on the walls of the Exchange one may see their names placarded, with reference to the Agent—or he will, himself, (my friend Chas. Walton) do his utmost with a shipowner, we both know, and save some expense, perhaps. I made him remark the difference between my carelessness of accommodations and an invalid's proper attention beforehand—but he persisted in saying nothing can be done, nothing effectual. My time is out—but I must bless you my ever dearest Ba—and kiss you—

Ever your own.

E. B. B. to R. B.

Tuesday.
[Post-mark, April 7, 1846.]

Dearest, it is not I who am a 'flatterer'—and if I used the word first, it is because I had the right of it, I remember, long and long ago. There is the vainest of vanities in discussing the application of such a word . . and so, when you said the other day that you 'never flattered' forsooth . . . (oh no!) I would not contradict you for fear of the endless flattery it would lead to. Only that I do not choose (because such things are allowed to pass) to be called on my side 'a flatterer'—I! *That* is too much, and too out of place. What do I ever say that is like flattery? I am allowed, it may be hoped, to admire the 'Lurias' and the rest, quite like other people, and even to *say* that I admire them . . may I not lawfully? If *that* is flattery woe to me! I tell you the real truth, as I see the truth, even in respect to *them* . . the 'Lurias' . .

For instance, did I flatter you and say that you were right yesterday? Indeed I thought you as wrong as possible . . wonderfully wrong on such a subject, for *you* . . who, only a day or two before, seemed so free from conventional fallacies . . so free! You would abolish the punishment of death too . . and put away wars, I am sure! But honourable men are bound to keep their honours clean at the expense of so much gunpowder and so much risk of life . . *that* must be, ought to be, . . let judicial deaths and military glory be abolished ever so! For my part, I set all Christian principle aside, (although if it were carried out . . and principle is nothing unless carried out . . it would not mean cowardice but magnanimity) but I set it aside and go on the bare social rational ground . . . and I do advisedly declare to you that I cannot conceive of any *possible combination of circumstances* which could . . I will *not* say *justify*, but even *excuse*, an honourable man's having recourse to the duellist's pistol, either on his own account or another's. Not only it seems to me horribly wrong . . but absurdly wrong, it seems to me. Also . . as a matter of pure reason . . the Parisian method of taking aim and blowing off a man's head for the sins of his tongue, I do take to have a sort of judicial advantage over the Englishman's six paces . . throwing the dice for his life or another man's, because wounded by that man in his honour. His honour!—Who believes in such an honour . . liable to such amends, and capable of such recovery! *You* cannot, I think—in the secret of your mind. Or if *you can* . . *you*, who are a teacher of the world . . . poor world—it is more desperately wrong than I thought.

A man calls you 'a liar' in an assembly of other men. Because he is a calumniator, and, on that very account, a worse man than you, you ask him to go down with you on the only ground on which you two are equals . . the duelling-ground, . . and with pistols of the same length and friends numerically equal on each side, play at lives with him, both mortal men that you are. If it was proposed to you to play at real dice for the ratification or non-ratification of his calumny, the proposition would be laughed to scorn . . and yet the chance (as chance) seems much the same, . . and the death is an exterior circumstance which cannot be imagined to have much virtue. At best, what do you prove by your duel? . . that your calumniator, though a calumniator, is not a coward in the vulgar sense . . and that yourself, though you may still be a liar ten times over, are not a coward either! 'Here be proofs.'

And as to the custom of duelling preventing insults . . why you *say* that a man of honour should not go out with an unworthy adversary. Now supposing a man to be withheld from insult and calumny, just by the fear of being shot . . who is more unworthy than such a man? Therefore you conclude irrationally, illogically, that the system operates beyond the limit of its operations.—Oh! I shall write as quarrelsome letters as I choose. You are wrong, I know and feel, when you advocate the pitiful resources of this corrupt social life, . . and if you are wrong, how are we to get right, we all who look to you for teaching. Are *you* afraid too of being taken for a coward? or would you excuse that sort of fear . . that cowardice of cowardice, in other men? For me, I value your honour, just as you do . . more than your life . . of the two things: but the madness of this foolishness is so clear to my eyes, that instead of opening the door for you and keeping your secret, as that miserable woman did last year, for the man shot by her sister's husband, I would just *call in the police*, though you were to throw me out of the window afterwards. So, with that beautiful vision of domestic felicity, (which Mrs. Jameson would leap up to see!) I shall end my letter—is'nt it a letter worth thanking for?—

Ever dearest, do *you* promise me that you never will be provoked into such an act—never? Mr. O'Connell vowed it to himself, for a dead man . . and you may to me, for a living woman. Promises and vows may be foolish things for the most part . . but they cannot be more foolish than, in this case, the thing vowed against. So promise and vow. And I will 'flatter' you in return in the lawful way . . for you *will* 'make me happy' . . so far! May God bless you, beloved! It is so wet and dreary to-day that I

I do not go down stairs—I sit instead in the gondola chair . . do you not see? . . and think of you . . do you not feel? I even love you . . if *that* were worth mentioning . .

being your own

Ba.

How good of you to write so on Sunday! to compare with *my* bad!

R. B. to E. B. B.

Tuesday.
[Post-mark, April 7, 1846.]

They have just sent me *one* proof, only—so I have been correcting everything as fast as possible, that, returning it at once, a *revise* might arrive, fit to send, for *this* that comes is just as bad as if I had let it alone in the first instance. All your corrections are golden. In 'Luria,' I alter 'little circle' to 'circling faces'—which is more like what I meant. As for that point we spoke of yesterday—it seems 'past praying for'—if I make the speech an 'aside,' I *commit* Ogniben to that opinion:—did you notice, at the beginning of the second part, that on this Ogniben's very entry (as described by a bystander), he is made to say, for first speech, 'I have known so many leaders of revolts'—'*laughiny gently to himself*'? This, which was wrongly printed in italics, as if a comment of the bystander's own, was a characteristic circumstance, as I meant it. All these opinions should be delivered with a 'gentle laughter to himself'—but—as is said elsewhere,—we profess and we perform! Enough of it—Meliora sper*u*mus!

What am I to say next, my Ba? When I write my best and send 'grateful' to you—you send my proof back, '*grateful* (*h*)' Then I *must* do and say what you hate . . for I am one entire gratitude to you, God knows! May He reward you.

It is late; bless you once again, my dearest! You have nothing so much yours as

R.

My mother says that I paid only fifteen or sixteen pounds for the Venice voyage, and much less for the Naples one—*ten*, and no more, she thinks—and I think; but *that* represents *twenty*—as the other, twenty five or thirty pounds, to a person unconnected with the freighting party. (In the first ship, Rothschild sent a *locomotive* entire, with all its appurtenances, for one article, to Trieste). Can I make enquiries for you? Nay, I *will*, and at once.

E. B. B. to R. B.

Tuesday evening.
[Post-mark, April 8, 1846.]

In my *disagree* . . able letter this morning, I forgot to write how, after you went away, and I came to read again the dedication, I admired it more and more—it is most graceful and complete. Landor will be gratified and grateful . . he, allowably—and only *you* shall be 'hateful' . . and only to *me*, dearest, . . so that it does'nt matter much. As to Ogniben, you understand best of course—*I* understood the 'laughing gently to himself,' though I omitted to notice the italics. I perfectly understood that it was the bystander's observation.

Your letter came so late to-night that I despaired of it—the postman fell into a trance somewhere I fancy, and it was not till nine oclock that the knock (equal to the tapping of a fairy's wand) came to the door. Now I have two letters to thank you for together . . for the dear one on Monday, which lay in the shadow of your coming, and so was a little, little, less thought of than it could have been under any other possible circumstance . . and for this letter to-night. Well! and for Mr. Buckingham's voyage, if you will and can conveniently, (I use *that* word for my sake, not for your sake—because I think of *you* and not of *him!*) but if you can without inconvenience make enquiries about these vessels, why I shall be glad, and shall set it to your account as one goodness more. It would be easy for him (and *you* should have done it, in *your* voyage) to take with him those potted meats and portable soups and essences of game which would prevent his being reduced to common fare with the sailors. Then a mattress is as portable as the soups, nearly. Apart from the asafœtida he may endure, I should think. Do you know, I was amused at myself yesterday, after the first movement, for liking to hear you say that 'dry biscuits satisfied' you—because, after all, I should not be easy to see you living on dry biscuits . . Ceres and Bacchus forbid! Oh—I dont profess to apply, out of a pure poetical justice, Lord Byron's Pythagoreanism to the 'nobler half of creation'—do not be afraid'—but it *is* rather desecrating and disenchanting to mark how certain of those said Nobilities turn upon their dinners as on the pivot of the day, for their good pleasure and good temper besides. Did you ever observe a lord of creation knit his brows together because the cutlets were underdone, shooting enough fire from his eyes to overdo them to cinders . . . 'cinder-blast' them, as Æschylus would have it? Did you ever hear of the litany which some women say through the first course . . low to themselves? Perhaps not! it does not enter into your imagination to conceive of things, which nevertheless *are*.

Not that I ever thought of *you* with reference to *such*—oh no, no! But every variety of the 'Epicuri de grege porcus,' I have a sort of indisposition to . . even as the animal itself (pork of nature and the kitchen) I avoid like a Jewish woman. Do you smile? And did I half (or whole) make you angry this morning through being so didactic and detestable? Will you challenge me to six paces at Chalk Farm, and *will* you 'take aim' this time and put an end to every sort of pretence in me to other approaches between us two? Tell me if you are angry, dearest! I *ask* you to tell me if you felt (for the time even) vexed with me . . I want to know . . I *need* to know. Do *you* not know what my reflection must reasonably be? . . That is, *apart from provocation and excitement*, you believe in the necessity of such and such resources, . . provoked and excited you would apply to them—there could be no counteracting force . . no help nor hope.

So I spoke my mind—and you are vexed with me, which I feel in the air. May God bless you dearest, dearest! Forgive, as you can, best,

Your Ba.

R. B. to E. B. B.

Wednesday Morning.
[Post-mark, April 8, 1846.]

First of all, kiss me, dearest,—and again—and now, with the left arm round you, I will write what I think in as few words as possible. I think the fault of not carrying out principles is *yours*, here. Several principles would arrive at the result you desire—Christianity, Stoicism, Asceticism, Epicureanism (in the modern sense)—all these 'carried out' stop the procedure you deprecate—but I fancy, as you state your principle, that it is an *eclecticism* from these and others; and presently one branch crosses its fellow, and we *stop*, arrive at nothing. Do you accept 'life's warm-beating joy and dole,' for an object of that life? Is 'society' a thing to desire to participate in? not by the one exceptional case out of the million, but by men generally,—men who 'live' only for living's sake, in the first instance; next, men who, having ulterior objects and aims of happiness, yet derive various degrees of sustainment and comfort from the social life round them; and so on, higher up, till you come to the half-dozen, for whom we need not be pressingly urgent to legislate just yet, having to attend to the world first. Well, is social life, a good, generally to these? If so,—go back to another principle which I suppose you to admit,—that 'good' may be *lawfully* held, defended,—even to the death. Now see where the 'cross' takes place. Something occurs which forces a man to *hold* this, defend this—he *must* do this, or *renounce* it. You let him do neither. Do not say he *needs* not renounce it,—we go avowedly on the vulgar broad ground of fact—you very well know it is a *fact* that by his refusing to accept a challenge, or send one, on conventionally sufficient ground, he will be infallibly excluded from a certain class of society thenceforth and forever. What society *should* do rather, is wholly out of the question—what *will* be done? And now, candidly, can you well fancy a more terrible wrong than this to the ordinary multitude of men? Alter the principles of your reasoning—say, Christianity forbids this,—and *that* will do—rational Simon renounces on his pillar more than the pleasures of society if so he may save his soul: say, society is not worth living in,—it is no wrong to be forced to quit it—*that* will do, also,—a man with 'Paradise Lost' or 'Othello' to write; or with a Ba to live beside for his one companion,—or many other compensations,—*he* may retire to his own world easily. Say, on the lowest possible ground, 'out of society one eats, drinks &c. excellently well; what loss is there?'—all these principles *avail;* but *mix* them—and they surely neutralize each other. A man *may* live, enjoy life, oppose an attempt to prevent his enjoying life, —yet not—you see! 'The method is irrational, proves nothing &c.'—what is that to the question? Is the *effect* disputable or no? Wordsworth decides he had better go to court—then he must buy or borrow a court-dress. He goes because of the poetry in him. What irrationality in the bag and sword—in the grey duffil gown yonder, he wrote—half through the exceeding ease and roominess of it—'The Excursion'; how proper he should go in it, therefore . . beside it will wring his heartstrings to pay down the four pounds, ten and sixpence: good, Mr. Wordsworth! There's no compulsion; go back to the lakes and be entirely approved of by Miss Norwick! . . but, if you *do* choose to kiss hands (instead of cheeks 'smackingly') why, you must even resolve to 'grin and bear it' (a sea-phrase!)—and, Ba, your imaginary man, who is called 'liar' before a large assembly, must decide for one or the other course. 'He makes his antagonist double the wrong'? Nay—*here* the wrong begins—the poor author of the outrage should have known his *word* was *nothing*—the sense of it, he and his like express abundantly every hour of the day, if they please, in language only a shade removed from this that causes all the harm,—and who does other than utterly, ineffably despise them? but he chooses, as the very phrase is, to *oblige* his adversary to act thus. *He* is nothing (I am going on your own case of a supposed futile cause of quarrel)—he may *think* just what he pleases—but having *said* this and *so,—it is entirely society's affair*—and what *is* society's present decision? Directly it relaxes a regulation, allows another outlet to the natural contempt for, and indifference to such men and their opinions spoken or unspoken, everybody avails himself of it directly. If the Lord Chamberlain issues an order this morning, 'No swords need be worn at next levee'—who will appear with one? A politician is allowed to call his opponent a destructive &c. A critic may write that the author of such a book or such, is the poorest creature in the world—and who dreams of being angry? but society up to this time says, 'if a man calls another &c. &c., *then* he must'— Will you renounce society? *I for one, could, easily: so therefore shall Mr Kenyon!* Beside, I on purpose depreciate the value of an admission into society . . as if it were only for those who recognize no other value; and the wiser men might easily forego it. *Not so easily!* There are uses in it, great uses, for purposes quite beyond its limits—you pass through it, mix with it, to get something by it: you do *not* go in to the world to live on the breath of every fool there, but you reach something *out* of the world by being let go quietly, if not with a favourable welcome, among them. I leave *here* to go to Wimpole Street:—I want to have as little as possible to say to the people I find *between*—but, do you know, if I allow a foolish child to put the very smallest of fool's caps on my head instead of the hat I usually wear, though the comfort would be considerable in the change,—yet I shall be followed by an increasing crowd, say to Charing Cross, and thence pelted, perhaps, till I reach No 50—there, perhaps to find the servant hesitate about opening the door to such an apparition,—and when Papa comes to hear how illustriously your visitor was attended through the streets! why he will specially set apart Easter Monday to testify in person his sense of the sublime philosophy, will he not? My Ba—I tell the child on the first symptom of such a wish on his part 'Don't!' with all the eloquence in my power—if I can put it handsomely off my head, even, I will, and with pitying good nature—but if I *must* either wear the cap, and pay the penalty, or—slap his face, why—! 'Ah,' you say, 'but he has got a pistol that you don't see and will shoot you dead like a foolish child as he is.' That he may! Have I to be told that in this world men, foolish or wicked, do inflict tremendous injuries on their unoffending fellows? Let God look to it, I say with reverence, and do *you* look to this point, *where* the injury *is, begins.* The foolish man who throws some disfiguring liquid in your face, which to remove you must have recourse to some dangerous surgical operation,—perilling himself, too, by the consequent vengeance of the law, if you sink under knife or cauterizing iron,—shall I say 'the fault is *yours*—why submit to the operation?' The fault is *his* that institutes the very fault—which begin by teaching him from his cradle in every possible shape! But don't, don't say—'the operation in *unnecessary;* your blistered face will look, *does* look just as usual, not merely to me who know you, perhaps love you,— but to the whole world . . on whose opinion of its agreeableness, I confess that you are dependent for nearly every happy minute of your life.' In all this, I speak for the world, *not* for me—I have other, too many other sources of enjoyment—I could *easily*, I think, do what you require. I endeavour to care for others with none of these; as dear, dearest Ba, sitting in her room because of a dull day, would have *me* take a few miles' exercise. Has everybody a Ba? I had not last year—yet last year I had reasons, and still have, for, on occasion, renouncing society fifty times over: what I should do, therefore, is as improper to be held up for an example, as the exemplary behaviour of Walpole's old French officer of ninety, who 'hearing some youths diverting themselves with some girls in a tent close by, asked. 'Is this the example *I* set you, gentlemen?' . But I shall be dishonoured however—Ba will 'go and call the police'—why, so should I for your brother, in all but the extremest case!—because when I had told all the world, *with whom the concern solely* is, that, despite his uttermost endeavour, I had done this,—the world would be satisfied at once—and the whole procedure is *meant* to satisfy the world—even the foolishest know that the lion in a cage, through no fault of his, cannot snap at a fly outside the bars. The thing to know is, will Ba dictate to her husband 'a refusal to fight,' and then recommend him to go to a dinner-party? Say, 'give up the dinner for my sake,' if you like—one *or* the other it *must* be: you know, I hate and refuse dinner-parties. Does everybody?

But now in candour, hear me: I write all this to show the *not such irrationality* of the practice even on comparatively frivolous grounds . . and that those individuals to whom you once admit society may be a legitimate enjoyment, must take such a course to retain the privileges they value—and that the painful cconsequences should be as unhesitatingly attributed to the first offence and its author, —as the explosion and horror to the fool who *would* put the match, in play perhaps, to the powder-barrel. And I excepted myself from the operation of this necessity. But I must confess that I can conceive of 'combinations of circumstances' in which I see two things only . . or a Third: a miscreant to be put out the world, my own arm and best will to do it; and, perhaps, God to excuse; which is, approve. My Ba, what is Evil, in its unmistakable shape, but a thing to suppress at any price? I *do* approve of judicial punishment to death under some circumstances—I think we may, *must* say: 'when it comes to *that*, we will keep our pact of life, stand by God and put *that* out of us, our world—*it* shall not be endured, or *we* shall not be endured'! Dear Ba, is Life to become a child's game? A is wronged, B rights him, and is a hero as we say; B is wronged again, by C; but he must not right himself; *that* is D's proper part, who again is to let *E* do the same kind office for *him*—and so on. 'Defend the poor and fatherless'—and we all applaud—but if they could defend themselves, why not? I will not fancy cases—here's one that strikes me—a fact. Some soldiers were talking over a watch fire abroad—one said that once he was travelling in Scotland and knocked at a cottage-door—an old woman with one child let him in, gave him a supper and a bed—next morning he asked how they lived, and she said the cow, the milk of which he was then drinking, and the kale in the garden, such as he was eating—were all her '*mailien*' or sustenance—whereon, rising to go, he, for the fun, 'killed the cow and destroyed the kale'—'the old witch crying out she should certainly be starved'—then he went his way. 'And she *was* starved, of course,' said a young man; 'do you *rue* it?'— The other laughed 'Rue aught like that!' —The young man said, 'I was the boy, and that was my mother—now then!'—In a minute or two the preparer of this 'combination of circumstances' lay writhing with a sword through him up to the hilt—'If you had *rued* it'—the youth said—'you should have answered it only to God!'

More than enough of this—but I was anxious to stand clearer in your dear eyes. 'Vows and promises!'—I want to leave society for the Siren's isle,—and *now*, I *often seriously reproach* myself with conduct quite the reverse of what you would guard against: I have too much *indifferentism* to the opinions of Mr Smith and Mr Brown—by no means am anxious to have his notions agree with mine.

Smith thinks Cromwell a canting villain,—Brown believes no dissenter can be saved,—and I repeat Goethe's 'Be it your unerring rule, ne'er to contradict a fool, for if folly choose to brave you, all your wisdom cannot save you!' And sometimes I help out their arguments by a touch or two, after Ogniben's fashion—it all seems so wearisomely unprofitable; what comes of Smith's second thought if you change his first—out of *that* second will branch as great an error, you may be sure! (11 o'clock) Here comes your letter! My own Ba! My dearest best, best beloved! *I*, angry! oh, how you misinterpret, misunderstand the motions of my mind! In all that I said, or write here, I speak of others—others, if you please, of limited natures: I say why *they* may be excused . . that is all. '*You do not like pork*'? *But* those poor Irish Colliers whose only luxury is *bacon* once a month; you understand *them* liking it? I do not value society—others do: '*we are all His children*' says Euripides and quotes Paul.

Now, love, let this be a moot point to settle among the flowers one day—with Sir Thomas Browne's 'other hard questions yet not impossible to be solved' ('What song the sirens' sang to Ulysses,' is the first!) in which blessed hope let me leave off; for I confess to having written myself all-but-tired, headachy. But 'vexed with you'! Ba, Ba; you perplex me, bewilder me; let me get right again; kiss me, dearest, and all is right—God bless you ever—

Your R.

E. B. B. to R. B.

Wednesday Evening.
[Post-mark, April 9, 1846.]

After the question about the 'Siren's song to Ulysses,' dearest? Then directly *before*, I suppose, the other 'difficult question' talked of by your Sir Thomas Browne, as to 'what name Achilles bore when he lived among the women.' *That*, you think, will be an appropriate position for our 'moot point' which, once in England, was guilty of tiring you and making your head ache:—and as for Achilles's name when he lived among women, it was *Μῶρος* you will readily guess, and I shall not dare to deny. Only . . only . . I never shall be convinced on the 'previous question' by the arguments of your letter—it is not possible.

May I say just one thing, without touching that specific subject? There is a certain class of sacrifice which men who live in society, should pay willingly to society . . the sacrifice of little or indifferent things, . . in respect to mere manners and costume. There is another class of sacrifice which should be refused by every righteous man though ever so eminently a social man, and though to the loss of his social position. Now you would be the last, I am sure, to confound these two classes of sacrifice—and you will admit that our question is simply *between them* . . and to which of them, duelling belongs . . and not at all whether society is in itself a desirable thing and much rejoiced in by the Browns and Smiths. You refuse to wear a fool's cap in the street, because society forbids you—which is well: but if, in order to avoid wearing it, you shoot the 'foolish child' who forces it upon you . . why you do *not* well, by any means: it would not be well even for a Brown or a Smith—but for my poet of the 'Bells and Pomegranates,' it is very ill, wonderfully ill . . so ill, that I shut my eyes, and have the heartache (for the headache!) only to think of it. So I will not. Why should we see things so differently, ever dearest? If anyone had asked me, I could have answered for you that you saw it quite otherwise. And you would hang men even—you!

Well! Because I do 'not rue' (and am so much the more unfit to die) I am to be stabbed through the body by an act of 'private judgment' of my next neighbour. So I must take care and 'rue' when I do anything wrong—and I begin now, for being the means of tiring you, . . and for seeming to persist *so!* You may be right and I wrong, of course—I only speak as I *see*. And will not speak any more last words . . taking pardon for these. *I rue*.

To-day I was down stairs again—and if the sun shines on as brightly, I shall be out of doors before long perhaps.

Your headache! tell me how your headache is,—remember to tell me. When your letter came, I kissed it by a sort of instinct . . not that I do always at first sight (please to understand), but because the writing did not look angry . . not vexed writing. Then I read . . 'First of all, kiss' . .

So it seemed like magic.

Only I know that if I went on to write disagreeing disagreeable letters, you might not help to leave off loving me at the end. I seem to see through this crevice.

Good Heavens!—how dreadfully natural it would be to me, seem to me, if you *did* leave off loving me! How it would be like the sun's setting . . and no more wonder! Only, more darkness, more pain. May God bless you my only dearest! and me, by keeping me

Your

Ba.

R. B. to E. B. B.

Thursday. 8. a.m.
[Post-mark, April 9, 1846.]

Dearest, I have to go out presently and shall not be able to return before night . . so that the letter I expect will only be read *then*, and answered to-morrow—what will it be, the letter? Nothing but dear and kind, I know . . even deserve to know, in a sense,—because I am sure all in *my* letter was meant to be 'read by your light.' I submit, unfeignedly, to you, there as elsewhere—and,—as I said, I think,—I wrote *so*, precisely because it was never likely to be my own case. I should consider it the *most* unhappy thing that could possibly happen to me,—(putting aside the dreadful possibilities one refuses to consider at all,—the *most*)

Have you made any discoveries about the disposition of Saturday? May I come, dearest? (On Saturday evening I shall see a friend who will tell me all he knows about ships and voyage expenses—or refer me to higher authorities)

Bless you, now and ever, my own Ba. Do you know, next Saturday, in its position of successor to Good Friday, will be the anniversary of Mr. Kenyon's asking me, some four years ago, 'if *I would like to see* Miss B.' How I remember? I was staying with him for a couple of days. Now, I will ask myself 'would you like to kiss Ba?' '*Then comes the Selah.*' Goodbye, dearest-dearest!

Yours R,

E. B. B. to R. B.

Thursday Evening.
[Post-mark, April 10, 1846.]

I thought you had not written to me to-night, ever dearest! Nine o'clock came and went, and I heard no postman's knock; and I supposed that I did not deserve (in your mind) to hear it at all. At last I rang the bell and said to Wilson . . 'Look in the letter-box—there may be a letter perhaps. If there should be none, you need not come up stairs to tell me—I shall understand.' So she left me, and, *that* time, I listened for *footsteps* . . the footsteps of my letter. If I had not heard them directly, what should I have thought?

You are good and kind, . . *too* good and kind, . . always, always!—and I love you gratefully and shall to the end, and with an unspeakable apprehension of what you are in yourself, and towards me:—yet you cannot, you know,—you know you cannot, dearest . . 'submit' to me in an *opinion*, any more than I could to you, if I desired it ever so anxiously. We will talk no more however on this subject now. I have had some pain from it, of course . . but I am satisfied to have had the pain, for the knowledge . . which was as necessary as possible, under circumstances, for more reasons than one.

Dearest . . before I go to talk of something else . . will you be besought of me to consider within yourself, . . and not with me to tease you; *why* the 'case,' spoken of, should 'never in likelihood be your own?' Are you and yours charmed from the influence of offensive observations . . *personally* offensive? 'The most unhappy thing that could happen to you,' is it, on that account, the farthest thing?

Now—! Mrs. Jameson was here to-day, and in the room before, almost, I heard of her being on the stairs. It is goodnatured of her to remember me in her brief visits to London—and she brought me two or three St. Sebastians with the arrows through them, etched by herself, to look at—very goodnatured! Once she spoke of you—'Oh,' she said, 'you saw Mr. Browning's last number! yes, I remember how you spoke of it. I suppose Mr. Kenyon lent you his copy' . . . And before I could speak, she was on another subject. But I should not have had heart to say what I meant and predetermined to say, even if the opportunity to-day had been achieved. As if you could not be read except in Mr. Kenyon's copy! I might have confessed to my own copy, even if not to my own original . . do you not think?

Before she came, I went down to the drawing-room, I and Flush, and found no one there . . and walked drearily up and down the rooms, and, so, came back to mine. May you have spent your day better. There was sunshine for you, as I could see. God bless you and keep you. Saturday may be clear for us, or may not—and if it should not be clear, certainly Monday and Tuesday will not . . what shall be done? Will you wait till Wednesday? or will you (now let it be as you choose!) come on Saturday, running the risk of finding only a parcel . . a book and a letter . . and so going away, if there should be reasons against the visit. Because last Monday was *known* of, and I shall not ascertain until Saturday whether or not we shall be at liberty. Or . . shall we at once say *Wednesday?* It is for your decision. You go out on Saturday evening . . and perhaps altogether there may be a conspiracy against Saturday. Judge and decide.

I am writing as with the point of a pilgrim's staff rather than a pen. 'We are all strangers and pilgrims.' Can you read anywise?

I think of you, bless you, love you—but it would have been better for you never to have seen my face perhaps, though Mr. Kenyon gave the first leave. *Perhaps!!*—I 'flatter' *myself* to-night, in change for *you*.

Best beloved I am your

Ba.

E. B. B. to R. B.

Friday—2 o'clock p.m.
[Post-mark, April 10, 1846.]

Ever dearest I wrote last night what might make you doubtful and uncomfortable about Saturday; being doubtful myself and not knowing what word to say of it. But just now Papa has been here in the room with me,—and a beatific Jamaica packet has just come in, as the post declares . . (Benedetta sia l'ora &c!) and he will 'hear more,' he says, '*in the city to-morrow!*'— So we are safe. Come, if there should be no reason of your own for staying. For me, I seem to have more need than usual of seeing you. May God bless you. I am

Your
Ba.

R. B. to E. B. B.

Friday Morning.
[Post-mark, April 10, 1846.]

Dearest, sweetest best—how can you, seeing so much, yet see that 'possibility'—*I leave off loving* you! and be 'angry' and 'vexed' and the rest! Well—take care I don't answer fairly and plainly that I *can* do all this—as the poor women had to confess in their bewilderment when grave judges asked 'by which of the thirty-seven ways they were accustomed to signify their desire of his presence to Asmodeus'—&c &c— But I cannot jest, nor trifle here—I protest in the most solemn way I am capable of conceiving, that I am altogether unable to imagine how or whence or why any possible form of anger or vexation or any thing akin can or could or should or shall ever rise in me to you—it is a sense hitherto undreamed of, a new faculty—altogether an inexplicable, impossible feeling. I am not called on, surely, to suppose cases of pure impossibility? To say, 'if you did thus or thus,'—what I know you could no more do than go and kill cows with your own hand, and dig up kale grounds? But I *can* fancy your being angry with me, very angry—and speaking the truth of the anger—that is to be *fancied:* and God knows I should in that case kiss *my* letters, here, till you pleased to judge me not unworthy to kiss the hem of your garment again. My own Ba! My election is made or God made it for me,—and is irrevocable. I am wholly yours. I see you have yet to understand what that implies,—but you will one day. And in this, just said, I understand *serious* anger, for serious offences; to which, despite my earnest endeavour, who shall say I may not be liable? What are you given me for but to make me better—and, in that, happier? If you could save my soul, 'so as by fire,' would your dear love shrink from that? But in the matter we really refer to . . . Oh, Ba, did I not pray you at the beginning to *tell* me the instant you detected anything to be altered by *human* effort? to give me that chance of becoming more like you and worthier of you? and here where you think me gravely in the wrong, and I am growing conscious of being in the wrong,—one or two repetitions of such conduct as yours, such 'disagreeable letters,' and I *must* 'leave off' . . . When I do *that* on such ground . . I need imprecate no foolish sense on my head,—the very worst will be in full operation. I only wrote to justify an old feeling, exercised only in the case of others I have heard of—men called 'cool murderers,' 'deliberate imbruers of their hands in,' &c. &c.—and I meant just to say, —well,—I, and others, despise your society and only go into it now to be the surer that, when we leave it, we were not excluded as the children turn from the grapes because their teeth are set on edge, whatever may be the foxes' pretext—but, for your own devoted followers be a little more merciful, and while you encourage them to spend a dozen years in a law-suit, lest they lose a few pounds . . but I won't repeat the offence, dear—*you are right* and I am wrong and will lay it to heart, and now kiss, not your feet this time, because I am the prouder, far from the more humble, by this admission and retraction—

Your note arrives here—Ba;—it would have been 'better for me,' *that?* Oh, dearest, let us marry soon, very soon, and end all this! If I could begin taking exceptions again, I might charge you with such wild conventionalism, such wondrous perversity of sight or blindness rather! *Can* you, now, by this time tell me or yourself that you could believe me happy with any other woman that ever breathed? I tell *you*, without affectation, that I lay the whole blame to myself . . that I feel that if I had spoken my love out *sufficiently*, all this doubt could never have been possible. You quite believe I am in earnest, know my own mind and speak as I feel, on these points we disputed about—yet *I am* far from being sure of it, or so it seems now—but, as for loving you,—*there* I mistake, or may be wrong, or may, or might or or—

Now kiss me, my best-dearest beloved! It seems I am always understood *so*—the words are words, and faulty, and inexpressive, or wrongly expressive,—but when I live under your eyes, and die, you will never mistake,—you *do not now*, thank God, say to me 'you want to go elsewhere for all you say the visit seems too brief'—and, 'you would change me for another, for all you possess'—never do you *say* such things—but when I am away, all the mistaking begins—let it end soon, come, dearest life of my life, light of my soul, heart's joy of my heart!

You feel I *must* see you to-morrow if possible—at all events I will call for the parcel. (What made you suppose I was engaged to-morrow night? The saying that I should meet my sea-faring friend, perhaps? But that is to be *here*—he comes here—at all events, I recollect no other engagement—if I had one with Death himself, I almost think I would go,—folly! But let the parcel be ready (to put into my hand at once) and I will venture at 3 o'clock.

In truth, all yesterday I was very unwell,—going about sight-seeing with a friend and his lady-cousins, and afterward dining with them—I came home dead with intense boring—I rarely remember to have suffered so much. To-day I am rather better,—much better, indeed. If I can but see you for a few minutes to-morrow!

May God bless you, dearest—and show you the truth in me, the one truth which I dare hope compensates for much that is to be forgiven: when I told you at the beginning I was not worthy, was infinitely lower &c, you seemed incredulous! well now, you see! I, that you *would* persist in hoping better things of, held such opinions as those—and so you begin setting me right, and so I am set far on towards right—is not all well, love? And now go on, when I give next occasion, and tell me more, and let me alter more, and thank you, if I can, *more*,—but not, not love you more, you, Ba, whom I love wholly,—with all my faculties, all my being. May God bless you, again—it all ends there—!

Your own R.

E. B. B. to R. B.

Sunday.
[Post-mark, April 13, 1846.]

I will not speak much of the letter, as you desire that I should not. And because everything you write must be answered in some way and sense, . . must have some result, there is the less need of words in the present case. Let me say only then, ever dearest, dearest, that I never felt towards you as I felt when I had read that letter . . never loved you so entirely! . . that it went to my heart, and stayed there, and seemed to mix with the blood of it . . . believe this of me, dear dearest beloved! For the rest, there is no need for me to put aside carefully the assumption of being didactic to *you* . . of being better than *you*, so as to teach you! . . . ah, you are so fond of dressing me up in pontifical garments ('for fun,' as the children say!)—but because they are too large for me, they drop off always of themselves, . . they do not require my pulling them off: these extravagances get righted of their own accord. After all, too, you, . . with that præternatural submissiveness of yours, . . you know your power upon the whole, and understand, in the midst of the obeisances, that you can do very much what you please, with your High Priest. *Εἴ τις αἴσθησις* in the ghosts of the tribe of Levi, let them see and witness how it is!

And now, do *you* see. It was just natural that when we differed for the first time I should fall into low spirits. In the night, at dream-time, when instead of dreams 'deep thought falleth upon man,' suddenly I have been sad even to tears, do you know, to think of *that:* and whenever I am not *glad*, the old fears and misgivings come back—no, you *do not understand* . . you *cannot*, perhaps! But dear, dearest, never think of yourself that you have expressed 'insufficiently' your feelings for me. Insufficiently! No words but *just your own*, between heaven and earth, could have persuaded me that one such as you could love me! and the tongue of angels could not speak better words for that purpose, than just yours. Also, I know that you love me . . I do know it, my only dearest, and recognize it in the gratitude of my soul:—and it is through my want of familiarity with any happiness—through the want of use in carrying these weights of flowers, that I drop them again and again out of weak hands. Besides the *truth* is, that I am *not* worthy of you—and if you were to see it just as I see it, why there would be an end . . there, . . I sometimes think reasonably.

Well—now I shall be good for at least a fortnight. Do I not tease you and give you trouble? I feel ashamed of myself sometimes. Let me go away from myself to talk of Mr. Kenyon, therefore!

For he came to-day, and arrived in town on Friday evening—(what an escape on Saturday!) and said of you, . . with those detestable spectacles—like the Greek burning glasses, turned full on my face . . 'I suppose now that Mr. Browning's book is done and there are no more excuses for coming, he will come *without* excuses.' Then, after talk upon other subjects, he began a long wandering sentence, the end of which I could see a mile off, about how he 'ought to know better than I, but wished to enquire of me' . . . what, do you suppose? . . why, 'what Mr. Browning's objects in life were. Because Mrs. Procter had been saying that it was a pity he had not seven or eight hours a day of occupation,' &c. &c. It is a good thing to be angry, as a refuge from being confounded: I really *could say* something to *that*. And I did say that you 'did not *require* an occupation as a means of living . . having simple habits and desires—nor as an end of living, since you found one in the exercise of your genius! and that if Mr. Procter had looked as simply to his art as an end, he would have done better things.'

Which made Mr. Kenyon cry out . . 'Ah now! you are spiteful! and you need not be, for there was nothing unkind in what she said.' 'But *absurd*'! . . I insisted—'seeing that to put race horses into dray carts, was not usually done nor advised.'

You told me she was a worldly woman; and here is a proof, sent back to you. But what business have worldly women to talk their dusts and ashes over high altars in that way? I was angry and sinned not—angry for the moment. Then Mr. Kenyon agreed with me, I think, and illustrated the subject by telling me how Wordsworth had given himself to the service of the temple from the beginning—'though,' observed Mr. Kenyon, 'he did not escape *so* from worldliness.' But William Wordsworth is not Robert Browning. Mr. Kenyon spoke of your family and of yourself with the best and most reverent words.

And all this reminds me of what I have often and often mused about saying to you, and shrank back, and torn the paper now and then . . . You know the subject you wanted to discuss, on Saturday. Now whenever the time shall come for discussing that subject, let this be a point agreed upon by both of us. The peculiarity of our circumstances will enable us to be free of the world . . of our friends even . . of all observation and examination, in certain respects: now let us use the advantage which falls to us from our misfortune,—and, since we must act for ourselves at last, let us resist the curiosity of the whole race of third persons . . even the affectionate interest of such friends as dear Mr. Kenyon, . . and put it into the power of nobody to say to himself or to another, . . 'she had so much, and he, so much, in worldly possessions—or she had not so much and he had not so much.' Try to understand what I mean. As it is not the least importance to either of us, as long as we can live, whether the sixpence, we live by, came most from you or from me . . and as it will be as much mine as yours, and yours as mine, when we are together . . why let us join in throwing a little dust in all the winking eyes round—oh, it is nonsense and weakness, I know—but I would rather, rather, see winking eyes than staring eyes.

What has anybody to do with us? Even my own family . . why should they *ever* see the farthest figure of *our* affairs, as to mere money? There now—it is said, . . what I have had in my head so long to say. And one other word resumes my meditations on 'the subject' which will not be ripe for discussion for ever so many months . . and that other word is . . that if ever I am to wrong you so much as to be yours *so*, it is on the condition of leaving England within the fewest possible half hours afterwards. I told you *that*, long ago—so bear it in mind. I should not dare breathe in this England. Think!—There is my father—and there is yours! Do you imagine that I am *not afraid of your family?* and should be still more, if it were not for the great agony of fear on the side of my own house. Ah—I must love you unspeakably . . even to dare think of the possibility of such things. So we will not talk of them now. I write what I write, to throw it off my mind and have done. Bear it in yours, but do not refer to it—*I ask you not to refer to it.*

A long straggling letter, this is. I shall have mine to-morrow. And you will tell me if Wednesday or Thursday shall be our day; and above all, tell me how you are. Then the book will come. Remember to send one to Mrs. Jameson! I write in haste . . in haste—but one may think of you either in haste or at leisure, without blotting the air. Love me, beloved . . do not leave off to see if I deserve it. I am at least (which is at most)

Your very own.

R. B. to E. B. B.

Sunday.
[Post-mark, April 13, 1846.]

Dearest, unspeakably dear Ba,—would I were with you! But my heart stays with you: I write this, tired somewhat and out of spirits—for I have been writing notes this morning; getting rid of the arrears which turn out more considerable than I thought. And the moment I have done, I look to the chair and the picture and desire to be at rest with you; the perfect rest and happiness here on earth. But *do* think, my own Ba, in the direction I indicated yesterday—any obstacle now, would be more than I could bear—I feel I *must* live with you,—if but for a year, a month—to express the love which words cannot express, nor these letters, nor aught else.

See one thing! Through your adorable generosity, my beloved,—at the beginning you pleased to tell me my love was returned,—that I had gained your love; without your assurance, I should never have believed that possible, whatever you may think; but *you*, what you *say*, I *believe;* would in other matters believe, rather than my own senses; and *here* I believed—in humbleness, God knows; but so it was.—Then, is there not this one poor fruit of that generosity, one reassuring consideration, if you will accept it, that, nearly a year ago, I was in possession of all I aspired to?—so that if I had been too weak for my accorded happiness—likely to be in due time satiated with it, and less and less impressed by it, and so on, till at last '*I changed,*'—would not this have happened inevitably *before now?* I had gained your love; one could not go on gaining it—but some other love might be gained! Indeed, I don't see how, in certain instances (where there is what is called a 'pursuit,' and all the excitement of suspense, and alternating hope and fear, all ending in the marriage day, after the fashion of a Congreve comedy), how with the certainty of that kind of success, all the interest of the matter can avoid terminating. But it does seem to me, that the love I have gained is as nothing to the love I trust to gain. I want the love at our lives' end, the love after trial, the love of *my* love, when mine shall have had time and occasion to prove itself! I have already, from the beginning indeed, had quite enough magnanimity to avoid wishing for opportunitiés of doing so at your expense—I pray you may never be in dangers from which I rescue you, nor meet sorrow from which I divert you: but in the ordinary chances of life—I shall be there, and ready, and your own, heart and soul. Why do I say this to you?

All words are so weak,—*so* weak!

Here,—(no, I shall have to send it to-morrow, I believe—well, here in the course of the day)—comes 'Luria' and the other—and I lay it at my dear Lady's feet, wishing it were worthier of them, and only comforted, through all the conviction of the offering's unworthiness, by knowing that *she* will know,—the dear, peerless, all precious Ba I adore, will know—that I would give her my life gladlier at a word. See what I have written on the outside—'to Miss Barrett'!—because I thought even leaving out the name might look suspiciously! But where no eye can see; save your dear eye . . *there* is written a dedication.

Kiss me, dear Ba. May God bless you. Care for everything—if you should have taken cold last night, for instance! Talk of a sword suspended by a hair!—what is the feeling of one whose priceless jewel hangs over a gulf by a hair? Tell me all—I love you wholly and am wholly yours.

See the strangely dirty paper—it comes from my desk where, every now and then, a candle gets over-set; or the snuffers remain open, aghast at what I write!

E. B. B. to R. B.

Monday.
[Post-mark, April 14, 1846.]

Ever dearest I have your two letters; and because there are only two 'great lights' to rule the day and the night, I am not likely to hear from you again before to-morrow. Then you want Mrs. Jameson's direction . . (it is just *Mrs. Jameson, Ealing!*) and here is the last 'Bell and Pomegranate'—and, for all these reasons, I must write without waiting; I will not wait for the night. Thank you for the book, thank you! I turn over the leaves ever so proudly. Tell me how I can be proud of *you*, when I cannot be proud of your loving me:—I am certainly proud of *you*. One of my first searches was for the note explanatory of the title—and I looked, and looked, and looked, at the end, at the beginning, at the end again. At last I made up my mind that you had persisted in not explaining, or that the printer had dropped the manuscript. Why, what could make you thrust that note on all but the titlepage of the 'Soul's Tragedy'? Oh—I comprehend. Having submitted to explain, quite at the point of the bayonet, you determined at least to do it where nobody could see it done. Be frank and tell me that it was just *so*. Also the poor 'Soul's Tragedy,' you have repudiated *so* from the 'Bells and Pomegranates' . . pushing it gently aside. Well—you must allow it to be a curious dislocation—only it is not important—and I like the note, all except the sentence about 'Faith and Works,' which does not apply, I think, . . that instance. 'Bells and Pomegranates' is a symbolic phrase—which the other is not at all, however much difficult and doubtful theological argument may have arisen from it as a collective phrase. So I am the first critic, you see, notwithstanding that Mr. Forster waylaid the first copy. Ah no! I shall have my gladness out of the book presently, beyond the imagination of any possible critic. Who in the world shall measure gladnesses with me?

Tell me—I was going to write *that* 'Tell me' in my yesterday's letter, but at last I was hurried, and could not . . did you come into London on Sunday? did you walk past this house on the other side of the street, about two o'clock? Because just then I and Flush went down stairs. The drawing room had nobody in it, and the window being wide open, I walked straight to it to shut it. And there, across the street, walked somebody . . . I am so near sighted that I could only see a shadow in a dimness . . but the shadow had, or seemed to have, a sign of you, a trace of you . . . and instead of shutting the window I looked after it till it vanished. No, it was not *you*. I feel now that it was not you; and indeed yesterday I felt it was not you. But, for the moment, it made my heart stop beating, . . that insolent shadow, . . which pretended to be you and wasn't. Some one, I dare say, who 'has an occupation eight or nine hours a day' and never does anything! I may speak against him, for deceiving me—it's a pure justice.

To go back to the book . . you are perfectly right about 'gadge,' and in the view you take of the effect of such words. You misunderstood me if you fancied that I objected to the word—it was simply my ignorance which led me to doubt whether you had written 'gag.' Of course, the horror of those specialities is heightened by the very want of distinct understanding they meet with in us:—it is the rack in the shadow of the vault. Oh—I fully agree.

And now . . dearest dearest . . do not bring *reason* to me to prove . . . what, to prove? I never get anything by reason on this subject, be very sure!—and I like better to *feel* that unreasonably you love me—to *feel* that you love me as, last year, you did. Which I could not feel, last year, a whole day or even half a day together. *Now* the black intervals are rarer . . which is of your goodness, beloved, and not of mine. For me, you read me indeed a famous lesson about faith, . . and set me an example of how *you* 'believed'! . . . but it does not apply, this lesson, . . it does not resemble, this example!—inasmuch as what *you* had to believe . . viz that roses blow in June . . was not quite as difficult as what *I* am called to believe, . . viz that St. Cecilia's angel-visitant had a crown of roses on, which eternally were budding and blowing. But I believe . . believe . . and want no 'proof' of the love, but just itself to prove it,—for nothing else is worthy. On the other side, I have the audacity to believe, as I think I have told you, that no woman in the world *could* feel for you exactly what . . . but, here, too, I had better shun the reasons, . . the 'bonnes raisons' which 'le roy notre sire' cannot abide.—What foolishness I am writing really! And is it to be for a 'year,' or a 'month'—or a *week*,—better still? or we may end by a compromise for the two hours on Wednesdays, . . if it goes on so,—more sensibly.

I have heard to-day from Miss Martineau and from Mrs. Jameson, both—one talking Mesmer and the other Homer. I sent her (Mrs. J.) two versions of the daughters of Pandarus, the first in the metre you know, and the second in blank verse; . . and she does not decide which she likes best, she says graciously, whereas I could not guess which I liked worse, when I sent them on Saturday. Do let her have 'Luria' at once. She will take the right gladness in it, even as she appreciates you with the right words and thoughts. But surely you use too many stamps? Have you a pair of scales like Zeus and me? . . only mine are broken, or I would send you an authority on this important subject, as well as an opinion.

How did you *not* get my letter, pray, by the first post on Monday? You ought to have had it! it was not my fault. And thinking of 'causas rerum,' . . I was to 'catch cold,' I suppose, on Saturday, because you went away?—there was no stronger motive. I did not however catch cold—ah, how you make me giddy with such words, as if I did really 'hang over a gulph'!—not with *fear* though! Is it possible, I say to myself, that I can be so much to him? to *him!* May God bless him! There was no harm meant by the black seal, I think? Tell me too of the headache, and whether the dinner is for Wednesday, and whether, in that case, *it* is still to be preferred, with all its close clipping, to Thursday. Meantime the letter grows as if there was no such thing as shears!

Your own
Ba.

R. B. to E. B. B.

Tuesday Morning.
[Post-mark, April 14, 1846.]

I waited till this second letter should arrive—feeling that it would be easier to address the answer to *this*.

About the other,—that part which you bid me not refer to. You are obeyed now—my time will come in its turn, and I will try and speak. With respect to the immediate leaving England, you will let me say, I think, that *all* my own projects depend on that,—there will not be one least objection made to it by my father or mother, I know beforehand. You perhaps misconceived something I said last Saturday. I meant the obvious fact however—that while there would be a *best* way of finding myself with you, still, from the *worst* way (probably, of taking a house opposite Mrs. Procter's)—from that even, to the *best* way of any other life I can imagine,—what a descent! From the worst of roses to the most flourishing of—dandelions. But we breathe together, understand together, know, feel, live together . . I feel every day less and less need of trying to assure you *I* feel thus and thus—I seem to know that *you* must *know!*

Mrs. Procter is very exactly the Mrs. Procter I knew long ago. What she says is of course purely foolish. The world does seem incurably stupid on this, as other points. I understand Mr. Kenyon's implied kindness—that is,—understand he may think he sees my true good in this life with older and better instructed eyes than my own—so benevolent people beg me 'not to go out in the open air—without something about my neck,' and would gird on a triple worsted 'comforter' there, entirely for my good, if I would let them. 'Why, Mr. Procter wears one!' Ah, but without it, what a cold he would catch!

The explanatory note fills up an unseemly blank page—and does not come at the end of the 'Soul's Tragedy'—

prose after prose—still it does look awkwardly—but then I don't consider that it excludes this last from the 'Bells' —rather it says this *is* the last, (*no*, *nine* if you like,—as the title says eight *and* last'—from whence will be this advantage, that, in the case of another edition, all the lyrics &c. may go together under one common head of Lyrics and Romances—and the 'Soul's Tragedy,' profiting by the general move-up of the rest of the numbers, after the fashion of hackney coaches on a stand when one is called off, step into the place and take the style of No. 8—and the public not find themselves defrauded of the proper quantity!)

And shall I indeed see you to-morrow, Ba? I will tell you many things, it seems to me now, but when I am with you they always float out of mind. The feelings must remain unwritten—unsung too, I fear. I very often fancy that if I had never before resorted to *that* mode of expression, to singing,—poetry—*now* I should resort to it, discover it! Whereas now—my very use and experience of it deters me—if one phrase of mine should seem 'poetical' in Mrs. Procter's sense—a conscious exaggeration,—put in for effect! only *seem*, I say! So I dare not try yet —but one day!

Ba, I kept your letter yesterday, *about* me—it lay by my head at night—that its good might not go from me,—such perfect good! How strange to hear what you say of my letters,—of such and such a letter—some seem kind, and kinder and kindest—and how should I guess why? My life and love flow steadily under all those bubbles, or many or less—it is through the under current that, whatever you see, *does* appear, no doubt—but also where nothing appears,—all is one depth!

Bless you, all dearest beloved.

To-morrow, Wednesday!

Ever your very own,

E. B. B. to R. B.

Thursday.
[Post-mark, April 16, 1846.]

This morning, you would never guess what I have been doing.—Buying a bonnet! That looks like a serious purpose of going out, walking out, driving out . . now doesn't it? And having chosen one a little like a quaker's, as I thought to myself, I am immediately assured by the learned that 'nothing can be more fashionable' . . which is a most satisfactory proof of blind instinct, . . feeling towards the Bude lights of the world, and which Mrs. Procter would highly esteem me for, if she did but know it.

In the meanwhile assure yourself that I understand perfectly your feeling about the subject of yesterday. Flies are flies, and yet they are vexatious with their buzzing, *as* flies. Only Mrs. Jameson told me the other day that a remedy against the mosquitos . . *polvere di morchia* . . had been discovered lately in Italy, so that the world might sleep there in peace—as *you* may here . . let us talk no more of it. I think I should not have told you if I had not needed it for a talking-ladder to something else. For the rest, it is amusing to me, quite amusing, to observe how people cannot conceive of *work* except under certain familiar forms. Men who dig in ditches have an idea that the man who leads the plough rather rests than works: and all men of out-door labour distrust the industry of the manufacturers in-doors—while both manufacturers and out-door labourers consider the holders of offices and clerkships as idle men . . gentlemen at ease. Then between all these classes and the intellectual worker, the difference is wider, and the want of perception more complete. The work of creation, nobody will admit . . though everybody has by heart, without laying it to heart, that God rested on the seventh day. Looking up to the stars at nights, they might as well take all to be motionless—

though if there were no motion there would be no morning . . and they look for a morning after all. Why who could mind such obtuse stupidity? It is the stupidity of mankind, par excellence of foolishness! The hedger and ditcher they see working, but God they do not see working. If one built a palace without noise and confusion and the stroke of hammers, one would scarcely get credit for it in this world . . so full of virtue and admiration it is, to make a noise! Even I, you see, who said just now 'Talk no more of it,' talk more and more, and make more noise than is necessary. Here is an end though—we leave Mrs. Procter here. And do not think that the least word of disrespect was said of you—indeed it was not! neither disrespect nor reproach. So you and I will forgive everybody henceforward, for wishing you to be rich. And if Mrs. Procter would 'commit suicide' rather than live as you like to live, *I* will not, as long as you are not tired of me—and *that, just now* and as things are, is of a little more consequence perhaps. . .

Scarcely had you gone, dearest, yesterday, when I had two letters with the very prose of life in them, dropping its black blotchy oil upon all the bright colours of our poetry! I groaned in the spirit to read, and to have to answer them. First was a Miss Georgiana Bennet—did you ever hear of her?—*I* never did before, but that was my base ignorance; for she is a most voluminous writer it appears . . and sent me five or six '*works*' (observe), . . published under the 'high sanction' (and reiterated subscription) of ever so many Royal Highnesses and Right Reverends . . . written in prose and verse, upon female education and the portrait of Harrison Ainsworth ('I gaze upon that noble face, and bright expressive eyes!'), miscellaneous subjects of that sort!—also, there is a poem of some length, called 'The Poetess,' which sets forth in detail how Miss Georgiana Bennet has found the laurel on her brow a mere nightshade, and the glories of fame no comfort in the world. Well—all these books were sent to me, with a note hortative—giving indeed a very encouraging opinion of my poems generally, but desiring me to consider, that poets write both for the learned and the unlearned, and that in fact I am in the habit of using a great many hard words, much to the confusion of the latter large class of readers. She has heard (Georgiana has) that I am a classical scholar which of course (of course) accounts for this peculiarity . . but it is the duty of one's friends to tell one of one's faults, which is the principle she goes upon. In return for which benevolence, I am requested to send back a copy of my poems directly, and to 'think of her, as she thinks of me.' There an end. The next letter is from a Mrs. Milner, who used to edit the 'Christian Mother's Magazine'; the most idiotic tract-literature, that magazine was, but supported by the Queen dowager and a whole train of Duchesses proper—very proper indeed! She used to edit the 'Christian Mother,' but now she has 'generalised' it, she says, to the 'Englishwoman's Magazine' and wants me to write for it and says. . .

Oh—I cannot have patience to go on to tell you. Besides you will take me to be too bitter, when I ought to be grateful perhaps! But if you knew how hard it is for me to have to read and write sometimes, as if you were not in the world with me . . as if . . . Is it wrong to laugh a little, to put it off,—only to *you*, though? And do you know, I feel ill at ease in my conscience, on account of what I said (even to *you*) about Mrs. Paine, who came to see me, you remember; and because she has written me a letter which quite affected me, I shall send it for you to read, to undo any false impression. Then you will not dislike reading it on other grounds. She is very different from the Georgiana Bennets, and I am interested in her, and touched aright by what she says.

You will write. You think of me? I am better to-day, much—and it is strange to be so, when you are not here. Ever dearest, let your thoughts be with me—

I am your own . .

R. B. to E. B. B.

Thursday.
[Post-mark, April 16, 1846.]

How are you now, dearest? If the worse for my visit . . No, there is no affectation in what I would say—you might be worse, you know, through *excitement*, whether pleasurable or the reverse. One comfort is, the walking, going downstairs, &c. have not occasioned it. I expect everything from your going out of doors, that is to be—what a joy to write it, think of it, expect it! Oh, why are you not here—where I sit writing; whence, in a moment, I could get to know why the lambs are bleating so, in the field behind—I do not see it from either window in this room—but I see a beautiful sunshine (2½ p.m.) and a chestnut tree leafy all over, in a faint trembling chilly way, to be sure—and a holly hedge I see, and shrubs, and blossomed trees over the garden wall,—were you but here, dearest, dearest—how we would go out, with Flush on before, for with a key I have, I lock out the world, and then look down on it; for there is a vast view from our greatest hill—did I ever tell you that Wordsworth was shown that hill or its neighbour; someone saying 'R. B. lives over *there* by that HILL'—'Hill'? interposed Wordsworth—'*we* call that, such as that, a *rise*'! I must have told you, I think. (While I write, the sun gets ever brighter—you must be downstairs, I feel sure—)

I fully meant to go out this morning—but there is a pressing note from my old young friend, Frank Talfourd, to get me to witness—only another play and farce!—and what is to be done?

Here shall be my ending 'for reasons, for reasons.' To-morrow I will write more; my Monday—to have to wait so long! And when I *do* see you, I begin to pour out profusions of confusions of speech about Mrs. Procter and her vain notions—to what earthly good? . . as it is very easy to ask *now!* now that I am here again, alone again.

Dear, dearest Ba, I cannot serve you, nor even talk to you . . but love you,—oh, that I must dare say I *can* do, as none other could—as you have yet to know!

Bless you my very dearest, sweetest Ba—I am your own, heart and soul—

E. B. B. to R. B.

Thursday Evening.
[Post-mark, April 17, 1846.

Ah, the chestnut tree: do you think that I never saw the chestnut tree before? Long ago, I did . . a full year ago or more—more! A voice talked to me of the 'west wind' which 'set dancing the baby cones of my chestnut tree'—nearly I remember the words. Do *you*, the time? It was early in the morning—'before seven,' said the voice! —too early in the morning for my dream to be—because a dream, says Lord Brougham when he tries at philosophy, a dream, if ever so long a dream, is all contained in the last moment of sleep, at the turn towards waking—so, late and not early!

No—you did not tell me of Wordsworth—not at least, after *that* reading. Perhaps if Hatcham should not be swept away in the Railway 'scirocco,' I may see the 'hill' or the 'rise' at some distant day. Shall I, do you think? I would rather see it than Wordsworth's mountains—'for reasons, for reasons' as you say. And talking of reasons, and reasonable people in general, I thought, . . after you went away on Wednesday, and I began to remember how you had commended your own common sense and mine,—I thought that it might be very well for you to do it, inasmuch as nobody else would, for you——! ὑπέρ σου as the theological critics intensify ὑπέρ to the genitive, 'for reasons, for reasons.'

How 'Luria' takes possession of me more and more!

Such a noble work!—of a fulness, a moral grandeur!—and the language everywhere worthy. Tell me what you hear the people say—I shall be anxious, which you will not be—but, to *me*, you will forgive it. 'The Soul's Tragedy' is wonderful—it suggests the idea of more various power than was necessary to the completion of 'Luria' . . though in itself not a comparable work. But you never wrote more vivid dramatic dialogue than that first part—it is exquisite art, it appears to me. Tell me what the people say!—and tell me what the gods say . . Landor, for instance!

Mr. Kenyon has not been here—and I dare not, even in a letter, be the first to talk to anyone of you. If is foolish of me perhaps—but if I whisper your name I expect to be directly answered by all the thunders of Heaven and cannons of earth. When I was writing to Miss Martineau the other day, for full ten minutes I held the pen ready charged with ink over a little white place, just to say 'have you read,' . . or 'have you heard' . . . and at last I couldn't write one word of those words . . I believe I said something about landed proprietors and agrarian laws instead.

So you '*felt*' that I was down stairs to-day! See how wrong feeling may be, when it has to do with such as I. For, dearest, notwithstanding your bright sunshine I did not go down stairs . . only opened the window and let in the air. I have not been quite as well, as far as just sensation goes, as usual, these few days—but it is nothing, a passing common headache, as I told you, . . and your visit did good rather than harm, and to-morrow you may think of me as in the drawing-room. Oh, I *might* have been there to-day, or yesterday, or the day before! but it was pleasanter to sit in the chair and be idle, so I sate! But you did not see me in my gondola chair—not *you!* you were thinking of the lambs instead, and looking over the wall to the 'blossomed trees' . . (what trees? cherry-trees? appletrees? peartrees?) and so, altogether, you lost your second sight of me and made mistakes. Ever dearest, is your head better? You will not say. You are *afraid* to say, perhaps, that you were ill, through writing too many notes and not going out to take the right exercise. Ah, *do* remember me for *that* good! I heard yesterday that 'Mr. Browning looked very pale as he came upstairs.' Which comes of Mr. Browning's writing when he should be walking!—now doesn't it?

Do you go to Mr. Sergeant Talfourd's on *Monday?* and would it be better therefore if you came here on Tuesday? You could come on the next Saturday all the same—consider! Nobody shall leap into lions' dens for *me!* so let us measure the convenience of things, as Miss Mitford would in marriages. 'Convenance,' though, she would say—which is more foolish than 'convenience' as I write it. She asserts that *every marriage in her experience,* beginning by any sort of *love,* has ended miserably—thus run her statistics in matrimony. Add, that she thinks—she told me last autumn—that all men without exception are essentially tyrants,—and that poets are a worse species of men, seeing that, all human feelings, they put into their verses, and leave them there . . . add this, and this, and then calculate how, if I consulted her on our prospects (shall I?), she would see for me an infinite succession of indefinite thumbscrews and *gadges!!* Well—I am not afraid—except for *you* sometimes! for myself I accept my chances for life under the *peine forte et dure.* And I won't speak to Miss Mitford, if *you* don't to Mr. Kenyon . . and I beseech you to avoid by every legitimate means the doing *that* . . oh, DO NOT *ever speak* THAT *to him!*

May God bless you my beloved!— Walk for my sake, and be well, try to be well! For me, I am so without trying, . . just as I am

Your own
Ba.

R. B. to E. B. B.

Friday.
[Post-mark, April 17, 1846.]

No, my own dearest, I did not see you sit in your chair, nor in mine, yesterday—did I write nothing about your walking with me by the garden wall, and on the hill, and looking down on London? And afterwards you went with me, indeed, to Talfourd's (last night was that purgatorial business,—how could I make you think it related to Monday?) If I have to put the least thing into words, *so* I put it always! Being just like the family of somebody—'who were one and all so stupid' said he—'that if you bade them spell A B they answered *B A*—' Nay, I spell Happiness, and Blessing, and all other good words if ever so many letters by that same Ba! But I want to go on and say you kept me from such an undiluted evening of misery (because I saw you through it all)—oh, such an evening!—it shall be the last, I think—and the going out is so near,—*the bonnet* is bought! And you pretend not to know I would walk barefoot till I dropped, if so I might attain to the sight of you, *and it.* Do let me say, for gratitude's sake—it is like the sign of spring in Shelley's 'Prometheus'—

When 'mild winds shake the elder-brake,
And the wandering herdsmen know
That the white thorn soon *will blow*':

—that the flower of my life will blow! Now let me try and answer everything in Ba's darling letters and so not be 'vexed' afterward,—recollecting how she asked *this*, or bade me be sure to reply to *that*, and how I answered, spelling A B *for* B A! First, there is a famous contrivance against fly tormentors, a genuine *canopy*, gnat-repelling enclosure of muslin which covers your bed wholly, and into which once introduce yourself dexterously (because the plagues try to follow slily) and lo, you are in a syren's isle within the isle, a world cut off from the outer one by that fine hazy cloudish gauze—a delight it is! Only, if you let one persisting critic of a buzzer lie perdue, he will have you at a glorious advantage—(not that one *ever* bit ME, in England or elsewhere) And now—your letters,—Miss Bennets' letter *that* you received 'just after I had gone'—will you be edified if I tell you what *I* received the moment I got home? (once, beforehand—my experience or yours, which would you rather *not* have?) My sister pointed with immense solemnity to a packet,—*then* delivered a message, and *then*—but hear the message—a 'Mrs. George Sharp' (unless I mistake the name) lives next door to Dickens and awfully respects him—she asks one aunt of mine, to ask another, to ask my sister, to ask me . . who have never seen or heard of this Mrs. George, —*me*, who am, she has understood, a friend of Dickens,— to get inserted in the *Daily News* some paragraph of a reasonable length in recommendation of the accompanying packet of *cough-drops*, (lozenges, or pills—for I was not rightly instructed *which*)— *my fee*, I suppose, being the said packet of pills! All comment is beyond me.

Well, but your Mrs. Bennet—what a wretched, disgusting *sfacciataccia!* I would not be accessory to keeping those soapy bubbles of stupid vanity from bursting by sparing a rough finger, certainly not. *How* 'ought you to be grateful, perhaps?' For *what* on earth?

Dearest, dearest Ba,—a 'passing' headache of 'these few days,' what can I say, or do? May God bless you, and care for all. Still the comfort continues, it is not that you have made an effort, and so grown worse.

I am pretty well,—I half determine to go out and see Carlyle to-night,—so to forget a hasty resolution against all company ('other' company I had written . . as if to honour it— Ba's is one company, and those people's!— 'another'!)—I think I will go.

I spoke about Mr. Kenyon,—because I never would in my life take a step for *myself* (if that could be), apart from your good, without being guided by you where possible—much more, therefore, in a matter directly concerning you rather than me, did I want your opinion as to the course most proper, *in the event* of &c. I do not think it likely he will speak, or I shall have to answer . . but if that *did* happen, and you were not at hand, my own dearest,—how I should be grieved if, answering wrongly, I gave you annoyance! Here I seem to understand your wish.

My Ba, my only, utterly dear love, may God reward you for your blessing to me—my whole heart turns to you—and in your own. I kiss you, dearest—this morning a very ordinary motivetto in the overture to 'Rabuco' seemed to tell you more than *I* ever *shall*—I sit and speak to you by *that*, now!

R. B.

No letters yet from 'anybody'—the few received are laudatory however—I will send you one from the old sailor-friend I told you of—but, mark! you must not send it back, to show my eyes and grieve my heart, when the bulky letter proves to be only *this*—returned! Landor's in due time, I suppose! This I send is to make you laugh . . My Ba's dear laugh can hurt nobody, not even my friend here—who *has praised her poems* more to me, there's my consolation,—Consuelo—

E. B. B. to R. B.

Friday.
[Post-mark, April 18, 1846.]

But, dearest of all, you never said a word about Monday. So I did not misunderstand—I only *misguessed.* Because you did not mention any day, I took it into my head that you might perhaps be invited for Monday, and make an effort, which would make a fatigue, and go there and come here. I am glad you went to Carlyle's—and where is Tennyson, and the dinner at Forster's all this while? And how did the Talfourds torment you so? was it that you were *very unwell?* I fear you were unwell. For me, I have recovered from my dreadful illness of the last day or two . . I knew I should survive it after all . . and to-day, just that I might tell you, I went down stairs with Flush, he running before as when *we* walk together through the gate. I opened the drawing-room door; when instead of advancing he stopped short . . and I heard strange voices—and then he drew back and looked up in my face exactly as if to say, 'No! This will not do for us!—we had better go home again.' Surely enough, visitors were in the room . . and he and I returned upon our steps. But think of his sense! Flush beats us both in 'common sense,' dearest, we must acknowledge, let us praise each other for it ever so. Next to Flush we may be something, but Flush takes the *pas*, as when he runs down stairs.

To-day Mr. Kenyon came, spectacles and all. He sleeps in those spectacles now, I think. Well, and the first question was . . 'Have you seen Mr. Browning? And what did he come for again, pray?' 'Why I suppose,' I said, 'for the bad reason my visitors have in general, when they come to see me'— Then, very quickly I asked about 'Luria,' and if he had read it and what he thought of it—upon which, the whole pomegranate was pulled out of his pocket, and he began to talk like the agreeable man he can be when he doesn't ask questions and look discerningly through spectacles. 'Luria' was properly praised indeed. A very noble creation, he thought it, and heroically pathetic . . and much struck he seemed to be with the power you had thrown out on the secondary characters, lifting them all to the height of humanity, justifying them by their own lights. Oh—he saw the goodness, and the greatness, the art, and the moral glory; we had a great deal of talk. And when he tried to find out a few darknesses, I proved to him that they were clear noonday blazes instead, and that his eyes were just dazzled. Then the 'Soul's Tragedy' made the right impression—a wonderful work it is for suggestions, and the conception of it as good a test of the writer's genius, as any we can refer to. We talked and talked. And then he put the book into his pocket to carry it away to some friend of his, unnamed: and we had some conversation about poets in general and their way of living, of Wordsworth and Coleridge. I like to hear Mr. Kenyon talk of the gods and how he used to sit within the thunder-peal. Presently leaning up against the chimney-piece,—he said quietly . . 'Do you not think—oh, I am sure I need not ask you—in fact I know your thoughts of it . . but how strikingly upright and loyal in all his ways and acts, Mr. Browning is!—how impeccable as a gentleman' &c. &c. and so on and on . . I do not tell you any more, because I should be tired perhaps . . (do you understand?) and this is not the first time, nor second, nor third time that he has spoken of you personally, *so* . . and as no man could use more reverent language of another. And all this time, what has become of Walter Savage Landor? I shall be vexed in another day. He may be from home perhaps—there must be a reason.

Vive Pritchard! and thank you for letting me see what he wrote.

Oh—and you *shall* see what I did not send yesterday—I shall make you read this one sheet of Mrs. Paine's letter, because it really touched me, and because I am bound to undo the effects of my light speaking. As for the overpraise of *myself*, the overkindness in every respect, . . why we know how 'sermons are found in stones' . . . yet no praise to the stones on that account! But you shall read what I send, both for her sake and mine, . . because I like you to read it.

My own dearest, do you mind what I say, and take exercise? You are vexing yourself with those notes, as I see from here. Now take care—follow my example, and be well—if not, there will be no use in wellness to me! May God bless you! Do you remember when you wrote first to me '*May God bless you and me* in *that!*' It was before we met. Can you guess what I thought? I have the whole effect in my memory distinctly. I felt with a bitter feeling, that it was quite a pity to throw away such beautiful words out of the window into the dark. 'Bitterly' does not mean anything wrong or harsh, you know. But there was something painful . . as if the words were too near, for the speaker to be so far. Well—I am glad in looking back . . yes, glad . . glad to be certain at my heart, that I did not assume anything . . stretch out my hand for anything . . *dearest!* . .

It is always when one is asleep that the dream-angels come. Watchers see nothing but ghosts.

Yet I shall see you on Monday, and shall watch and wait as those who wait for the morning . . that is, the Monday-morning! Till when and ever after, I am

Your own

Ba.

R. B. to E. B. B.

Saturday.

[Post-mark, April 18, 1846.]

So my dear, own Ba *has* good sense, best sense—whatever Flush's may be! Do you think . . (to take the extreme horn of a certain dilemma I see) . . that—

Now, dearest, somehow I can't write the great proof down—I will tell you on Monday—as to *my* good sense. I was wrong to give such a praise to myself in the particular case you were alluding to at the time—the good sense of the bird which finds out its mate amid a forest-full of birds of another kind! Why the poorest brown butterfly will seek out a brown stone in a gravel walk, or brown leaf in a flower bed, to settle on and be happy——(And I suppose even dear Carlyle is no longer my brown leaf; at least, I could not go last night. I will, however, try again on Monday—after leaving you—with that elixir in my veins).

Mrs. Paine's note is charming. I thank you, dearest, for sending it—(How I like being reminded of thanks, due from me to you, which I may somehow come near the expression of! I am silent about an infinity of blessings —but I do say how grateful I am for this kindness!). Now, there is the legitimate process; the proper benefit received, in the first instance, and profited by, and thence grows in proper time the desire of being admitted to see you—so different from the vulgar 'Georgianas' who, possibly, hearing of the privilege extended to such a person as this we speak of, would say, with the triumphant chuckle of low cunning, 'ah,—I will get as far, by one stroke of the pen—by one bold desire "to be thought of as I think of her." She could but ask and be refused! Whereas Mrs. Paine was already in possession of much more dear, dear Ba, than could be taken away even by a refusal—besides, her reverence would have made her understand and acquiesce even in that. Therefore, I am glad, sympathisingly glad she is rewarded, that good, gentle Mrs. Paine! I will bring her note with me.

Because, here is Mr. Kenyon's, and Landor's (which had been sent to *Moxon's* some days ago, whence the delay)—and Mrs. Jameson's. All kind and indulgent and flattering in their various ways . . but, my Ba, my dear, dear Ba, other praises disregarding, I but harken those of yours—only saying—Ah, it is wrong to take the sacrificial vessel and say,—'See, it holds my draught of wine, too'!—I will not do so, not parody your verses again. And I like to be praised now, in a sense, much, much more than ever—but, darling, oh how easily, if need were, I could know the world was abusing at its loudest outside; if you were *inside* . . though but the thinnest of gauze canopies kept us from the buzzing! This is only said *on* this subject, struck out by it, not *of* it,—for the praise is good true praise and from the worthies of our time—*but—you*, I love, —and there is the world-wide difference. And what ought I to say to Mr. Kenyon's report of me? Stand quietly, assentingly? You will agree to *this* at least, that he cannot *know* what he says—only be disposed to hope and believe it is *so:* still, to speak so to *you*—what would I not do to repay him, if that could be! What a divinely merciful thought of God for our sake . . that we cannot *know* each other—infallibly know—as we know other things, in their qualities! For instance, I bid you know my love for you (which would be knowing *me*)—I complain that you do not, *cannot*—yet,—if you *could* . . my Ba, would you have been ever quite my Ba? If you said, calmly as when judging of material objects, 'there is affection, so much, and sincerity, and admiration &c, yes, *that* I see, of course, for it is *there*, plainly'—So I should lose the delight crowning the delight,—first of the fact, as *I* know it; and then of *this;* that you *desired* to know it, chose to lean forward, and take my poor testimony *for* a fact, believing through desire, or at least will to believe—so that I do, in the exercise of common sense, adore you, more and more, as I live to see more, and feel more. So let me kiss you, my pearl of woman. Do I 'remember' praying God to bless me *through* the blessing on you? Shall I ever forget to pray so, rather! My dear—dearest, I pray now, with all my heart; may He bless you—and what else can now bless your own R?—

R. B. to E. B. B.

Sunday Afternoon.
[Post-mark, April 20, 1846.]

Just now I read again your last note for a particular purpose of thinking about the end of it . . where you say, as you have said so many times, 'that your hand was not stretched out to the good—it came to you sleeping'—etc. I wanted to try and find out and be able to explain to myself, and perhaps to you, why the *wrongness* in you should be so exquisitely dear to me, dear as the rightness, or dearer, inasmuch as it is the topmost grace of all, seen latest on leaving the contemplation of the others, and first on returning to them——because, Ba, that adorable spirit in all these phrases, what I should adore without their embodiment in these phrases which fall into my heart and stay there, that strange unconsciousness of how the love-account really stands between us, *who* was giver altogether and *who* taker, and, by consequence, what is the befitting virtue for each of us, a generous disposition to forgetfulness on the giver's part, as of everlasting remembrance and gratitude on the other—this unconsciousness *is wrong*, my heart's darling, strangely wrong by the contrast with your marvellous apprehension on other points, every other point I am capable of following you to. I solemnly assure you I cannot imagine any point of view wherein I ought to appear to any rational creature the benefitting party and you the benefitted—nor any matter in which I can be supposed to be even magnanimous, (so that it might be said, '*there*, is a sacrifice'—'*that*, is to be borne with' &c)—none where such a supposition is not degrading to me, dishonouring and affronting. I know you, my Ba, not because you are *my* Ba, but through the best exercise of whatever power in me you too often praise, I *know*—that you are immeasurably my superior, while you talk most eloquently and affectingly to me, I *know* and could prove you are as much my Poet as my Mistress; if I suspected it before I knew you, personally, how is it with me *now?* I feel it every day, I tell myself every day it is so. Yet you do not feel nor know it—for you write thus to me. Well,—and this is what I meant to say from the beginning of the letter, I love your inability to feel it in spite of right and justice and rationality. I would,—I *will*, at a moment's notice, give you back your golden words, and lie under your mind supremacy as I take unutterable delight in doing under your eye, your hand. So Shakespeare chose to 'envy this man's art and that man's scope' in the Sonnets. But I did not mean to try and explain what is unexplainable after all—(though I wisely said I *would* try and explain!) You seem to me altogether . . (if you think my words sounded like flattery, *here* shall come at the end—anything but that!) you do seem, my precious Ba, *too* entirely *mine* this minute,—my heart's, my senses', my soul's precise τὸ καλόν to *last!* Too perfect for that! The true power with the ignorance of it, the real hold of my heart, as you can hold this letter,—yet the fear with it that you may 'vex me' by a word,—makes me angry. Well,—if one must see an end of all perfection—still, to know one *was* privileged to see it—Nay, it is safe now—for this present, all my future would not pay, whatever your own future turned to!

Yet if I had to say, 'I shall see her in a month or two —*perhaps*—as this time last year I was saying in a kind of contented feeling!

Thank God I shall see her to-morrow—my dearest, best, only Ba cannot change by to-morrow!—What nonsense! The words break down, yet I *will* be trying to use them!

God bless my dearest, ever bless her.

I shall be with you soon after this reaches you, I trust —now, I kiss you, however, and now, my Ba!

Letters! since you bid me send them,—do you not?—see what the longer says of the improved diction, freedom from difficulty &c. Who is to praise for that, my Ba? Oh, your R. B. wholly and solely to be sure!

E. B. B. to R. B.

Tuesday.
[April 21, 1846.]

I would not say to you yesterday, perhaps could not, that you wrote ever so much foolishness to me in the morning, dearest, and that I knew it ever so well. There is no use, no help, in discussing certain questions,—some sorts of extravagance grow by talking of,—shake this elixir, and you have more and more bubbles on the surface of it. So I would not speak—nor will I write much. Only I *protest*, from my understanding, from my heart—and besides I do assert the truth—clear of any 'affectation,' this time,—and it is that you always make me melancholy by using such words. It seems to me as if you were in the dark altogether, and held my hand for another's: let the shutter be opened suddenly; and the hand . . is dropped perhaps . . . must I not think such thoughts, when you speak such words? I ask you if it is not reasonable. No, I do not ask you. We will not argue whether eagles creep, or worms fly. And see if it is distrust on my part! *Love*, I have learnt to believe in. I see the new light which Reichenbach shows pouring forth visibly from these chrystals tossed out. But when you say that the blue, I see, is red, and that the little chrystals are the fixed stars of the Heavens, how am I to think of you but that you are deluded, mistaken?—and in *what?* in love itself? Ah,—if you could know—if you could but know for a full moment of conviction, how you depress and alarm me by saying such things, you never would say them afterwards, *I* know. So trust to me, even as I trust to you, and do not say them ever again, . . *you*, who 'never flatter'. Is it not enough that you love me? Is there anything greater? And will you run the risk of ruining that great wonder by bringing it to the test of an 'argumentum ad absurdum' such as I might draw from your letter? Have pity on me, my own dearest, and consider how I must feel to see myself idealized away, little by little, like Ossian's spirits into the mist . . till . . 'Gone is the daughter of Morven'! And what if it is mist or moon-glory, if I stretch out my hands to you in vain, and must still fade away farther? Now *you will not any more.* When the world comes to judge between us two, or rather over us both, the world will say (even the purblind world, as I myself with wide-open eyes!) that I have not been generous with my gifts—no; you are in a position to choose . . and you might have chosen better— . . that is my immoveable conviction. It has been only your love for me,—which I believe in perfectly as love—and which, being love, does not come by pure logic, as the world itself may guess . . it has been only, wholly and purely your love for me which has made a level for us two to meet and stand together. There is my fact against your fiction! Now let us talk no more. We cannot agree, because we stand in different positions . . . 'I hear a voice you cannot hear'! . . I am on the black side of the knight's shield. Presently you will hear perhaps, and see. Shall you love me *then?* When the ideal breaks off, when the light is gone, . . will you love me then for the love which I shall bear you then as now, . . the only real thing?

In the meantime I did but jest about the letters—I *know* you care for mine . . because I care for yours so infinitely: . it is a lesson learnt by heart. To-night I shall write again!—

Your own
Ba.

R. B. to E. B. B.

Tuesday.
[Post-mark, April 21, 1846.]

My dearest Ba, my sweetest, only love must sit, if she please, in the gondola chair and let me talk to-day, not write to her—for my head aches,—from pure perversity,—and a little from my morning spent over a novel of Balzac's—*that* is it, not any real illness, I know—however, the effect is the same. Beside I got tired with the long walk from Carlyle's last night—for I went and saw him to heart's content—and he talked characteristically and well, and *constringingly, bracingly.* He has been in the country a little,—that is, has gone down to see his wife occasionally who was on a visit at Croydon, whence she only returned on Saturday. He told me he had read my last number; and that he had 'been read to'—some good reader had recited 'The Duchess' to him. Altogether he said wonderfully kind things and was pleased to prophesy in the same spirit; God bless him! We talked for three or four hours—he asked me to come again soon, and I will.

Here are two letters—Chorley's, one—and the other from quite another kind of man, an old friend who 'docks' ships or something like it; a great lover of 'intelligibility in writing,' and heretofore a sufferer from my poetry.

My love, I lend you such things with exactly as much vanity as . . no comparison will serve! it is the French vulgarism—comme . . n'importe quoi! Celui me pousse à la vanité comme—n'importe quoi!

Will you have a significative 'comme' of another kind? 'je me trouve bête ce matin comme . . trente-six oies!'—(I assure you this is no flower culled from Balzac this morning—but a little '*souvenir*' of an old play.)

Now, if I were to say to myself something is dear as 'thirty-six Bas'—I should be scared, as when looking into a mirror cut into façettes one is met on every side by the same face, twenty times repeated. Nothing can add to my conception of the one Ba—my one, only—ever dear, dearest Ba—'what perfect nonsense' says Ba—and nonsensical I will be——all she pleases so long as let live and die her very own.

E. B. B. to R. B.

Tuesday Evening.
[Post-mark, April 22, 1846.]

'Vanity'! I never saw in you, my very dearest, even the short morning shadow of 'vanity.' 'Vanity' is not of you! You work as the cedars grow, upward, and without noise, and without turning to look on the darkness you cause upon the ground. It is only because you are best and dearest that you let me see the letters . . . yes, and besides, because I have a little a right to have them sent to me,—since they concern me more than you,—and are, after a fashion, *my* letters. *My* letters? what am I saying? *My* letters, *my true* letters, are different indeed—and one of them came to-night to prove so!

But Mr. Chorley's and the illegible man's whose name begins with a D (or doesn't) both gave me pleasure. If Mr. Chorley did not read 'Luria' at once, he speaks of you in the right words—and the naval illegible man, with his downright earnest way of being impressed, makes a better critic than need be sought for in the *Athenæum* synod. And what a triumph (after all!) and what a privilege, and what a good deed, is this carrying of the light down into the mines among the workmen, this bringing down of the angels of the Ideal into the very depth of the Real, where the hammer rings on the rough stone. The mission of Art, like that of Religion, is to the unlearned . . to the poor and to the blind—to make the rugged paths straight, and the wilderness to blossom as the rose—at least it seems so to me. And now, pray, why am I not to hear what Carlyle said? will you tell me? won't you tell me? how shall I persuade you? If I can or not, I will say God bless him too . . since he spoke the right word, to do you good. For the manifest advance in clearness and directness of expression . . I quite forgot to take notice of what you said to me—and you, who never flatter!—about being the cause of it—I! Now do observe that the 'Soul's Tragedy,' which is as light as day, I never touched with my finger, except in one place, I think . . to say . . 'Just here there is a little shade.' The fact is, that your obscurities, . . as far as they concern the *medium*, . . you have been throwing off gradually and surely this long while—you have a calmer mastery over imagery and language, and it was to be expected that you should. For me, I am the fly on the chariot, . . 'How we drive!' Shall I ever, ever, ever, be of any use or good to you? See what a thought you have thrown me into, from that height! Shall I ever, ever, be of any use, any good—and not, rather, the contrary to these? Love is something: and it is something to love you better than a better woman could: but . . but . .

There is no use nor good in writing so, and you with a

headache too! Why, how could you get that headache? First with not walking; then with walking—!! and reading Balzac. But you had been writing notes perhaps? or Carlyle had talked *too* 'bracingly?' or you fasted too long, being too late for his tea-kettle? The headache *came* at any rate. Did it *go?* tell me, dearest beloved! say how you are. And let me hear if your mother continues to be better. How happy that change must make you all! and shall I not thank God that it makes *you* happy?

Mr. Kenyon has not been here, and I have nothing, nothing, to tell you. The east wind has kept guard at the door, so that I should not go out, . . and nothing has happened. I seem not to have drawn breath scarcely, since we parted. 'Parted'—what a word! As if we could!—in the full sense!

I have written to Miss Bayley to ask her to come on any day except Saturday.

Shall the thirty-six Bas love you all together in that one Ba who is your own?

R. B. to E. B. B.

Wednesday.
[Post-mark, April 22, 1846.]

I never thought I should convince you, dearest—and I was foolish to write *so,* since it makes you reply so. At all events, I do not habitually offend in this kind—forty-nine days out of fifty I hear my own praises from your lips, and yet keep silence—on the fiftieth I protest gently—is that too much? Then I will be quiet altogether, my Ba, and get a comfort out of the consciousness of obedience there at least. But I should like some talking-bird to tell you the struggle there is and what I *could* say. Shall I idealize you into mere mist, Ba, and see the fine, fine, last of you? Well, I cannot even play with the fancy of *that*—so, one day, when so much is to be cleared up between us, look for a word or two on this matter also. Some savage speech about the 'hand I was to have dropped'—the whole ending with the Promethean—*Οὕτως ὑβρίζειν τοὺς ὑβρίζοντας χρέων.* Meantime my revenge on the hand must be to kiss it—I kiss it.

Yesterday's letters both arrived this morning by the 11½ post—was that right? I add my mite of savageness to the general treasury of wrath: every body is complaining. Still, so long as I *do* get my letters,—such letters!

The cold wind continues—you will have kept the room to-day no doubt—what colourless weather; not the moist fresh bright true April of old years! I shall go out presently—but with such an effort, such unwillingness! I am better however—and my mother still continues *well*—goes out every morning—so there is hope for everybody. I ought to tell you that I went to my doctor last evening—(remembering *to whom* I promised I would do so, if need were, or good seemed likely to follow)—and he speaks encouragingly and I have engaged to be obedient; perhaps, because he ordains no very intolerable laws. He says I am better than when he saw me last—and, as he wanted *then* to begin and prescribe, . . . there is clearly a gain of about two months comfort!

Here strikes fatal four-o'clock! To-morrow for more writing; and *now*, for the never-ending love, and thought of my dearest dearest. May God bless you, Ba.

Your own——

E. B. B. to R. B.

Wednesday Evening.
[Post-mark, April 23, 1846.]

Then seriously you are not well, since you went for the medical advice after all! *that* is the thought which is uppermost as the effect of your letter, though I ought to be grateful to you (and am!) for remembering to keep your promise, made two months ago. But how can I help thinking that you are ill . . help *knowing* that you felt very ill before you came to consider that promise? You *did* feel very ill . . now did you not? And I see in this letter that you *are not* well—I see plainly, plainly! Have you been using the shower-bath? tell me:—and tell me how you are—do not keep back anything. For the rest, you will submit to the advice, you say, and you *mean* to submit, I think, my own very dearest—remember that all my light comes, not only *through* you, but *from* you, let it be April light or November light. I say that for *you*. As for myself, when I am anxious about you, it is not, I hope, for such a reason as that my light comes from you. Before I had any light, . . before I knew you *so* . . do I not remember how Mr. Kenyon with that suggestive shake of the head and grave dropping of the voice, when he came and told me with other news, of your being *ill*, . . made me wonderfully unhappy and restless till I could not help writing for a directer account? Oh, those strange days to look back upon, . . which had no miraculous light, yet were strange days, with their 'darkness which might be felt' and was felt!

You will be careful, . . will you not? . . in these? I am not happy about you, to-night. I feel as if you are worse perhaps than you say. And it does you so much good to keep talking about this misgiving and that misgiving!—the 'trente-six oies' are nothing at all to me, really.

For those two letters, it was far from any intention of mine that you should have them both together,—and the first-written went to the post at two on the day before. Too bad it is! I observe that you never get a letter on the day it is posted, unless the posting is very early, . . say before eight, or, at latest, before nine. Which is abominable, when the distance is considered.

And you make a piteous case out for yourself against me, indeed, . . and it seems very hard to have to endure so much, 'forty-nine days out of fifty' . . . I did not think it was so bad with you! And when you protest gently on the fiftieth day . . so gently . . so gently!!

Well, the fact is that you forget perhaps what sort of a gentle protestation it was, you wrote to me on Sunday, you who protest so gently, and never flatter! And as for having your own 'praises blown in your eyes' for forty-nine days together, I cannot confess to the iniquity of it, . . you mistake, you mistake, as well as forget—only that I will not vex you and convict you too much now that you are not well. So we shall have peace, shall we not? on each side. *I* never write extravagances—ah, but we will not write *of* them, even. Any more letters about 'Luria'?

Yes—All day to-day in the gondola chair! There was no leaving this room for the cold wind, and it made me feel so tired without my taking a step scarcely, that after dinner . . guess what I did, and save me the shame of relating? after dinner, my dinner at one o'clock, I positively fell fast asleep with this pen in my hand, and went to see you in a dream I dare say, though, this time, I do not remember. Then I half expected Miss Bayley, and she did not come, and instead of talking to her I wrote letters to 'all the peoples' . . I hate writing letters, how I hate it now, except to you only. And to-day I thought only of you, let me write ever so away from you. Which is why you saw me in the gondola chair.

But you are not well—the 'refrain' comes round constantly—call it a *burden!* May God bless you, dearest beloved! Do you say harm of this April, when it is the best April I ever saw, let it be proved to want the vulgar sun and blue sky as much as you please! Yet you are not well! say how you are! I come clear out of the mist to call myself

Your very own
Ba.

R. B. to E. B. B.

Thursday.
[Post-mark, April 23, 1846.]

Dear, dear Ba, I was never very ill, and now am very much better, quite well, indeed. I mean to co-operate with your wishes, and my doctor's doings, which are luckily gentle enough,—and so, how should I fail of bringing into subjection this restive, ill-conditioned head of mine? .

This morning I have walked to town and back—leaving myself barely time to write—but just before going out, I got your letter, for which I was waiting; and the joy of it, the entire delight, carried me lightly out and in again. Ah, my own Ba,—of the two 'extravagances which you never write nor speak,'—after all, if I must, I concede the *praises*, and eagle-soaring and, and—because, if I please, I can say, if you do persist in making me, 'why, it *may* be so,—how should I know, or Ba *not* know?' And as a man may suppose himself poor and yet be rightful owner to a wonderful estate somewhere (in novels &c)—so, I, the intellectually poor &c &c— But, dearest, if you say 'My letters *tire* you'——say *that* again—and then *what* unknown *gadge* ought to stop the darling mouth? How does honey dew bind up the rose from opening? Moreover it is one peculiarity of my mind that it loses no pleasure,—must not forego the former for the latter pleasure. How shall I explain? I believe that, when I should have been your husband for years,—years—if I were separated from you for a day and a letter came—I think my heart would move to it *just as it now does*—because now, when I see you, know what that blessing is—still the very oldest first flutter of delight at 'Miss Barrett's' writing it is all here, *all!*

Shall my heart flutter, then, to-morrow, my dear dear heart's heart? And it shall be *not* April when I read it your letter—but June and May—if it tells me *you* are well, *as I am well*,—now, if I say *that*, can you doubt what I consider my present state? But be *better*, dear Ba, and make me better—I should like to breathe and move and live by your allowance and pleasure—being your very very own R. B.

I see this morning a characteristic piece of news in the paper. President Polk, with an eye to business, gets his brother, a tall gaunt hungry man, appointed Ambassador to Naples—why not? So he arrives a year ago,—finds the Neapolitans speak Italian, or else French, or else German —that is, the Diplomatic Body at Naples don't speak English—on which discovery, Polk secundus sees he may as well amuse himself, so goes to Paris for half a year,—then to Rome where he is now, seeing sights—who could tell the Italians were not able to talk English? Is not that American entirely? Carlyle told me of an American who was commissioned by some learned body of his countrymen to ask two questions . . 'What C's opinion was as to a future state?'—and next 'what relation Goethe was to Goethe's mother's husband?'—

E. B. B. to R. B.

Thursday Evening.
[Post-mark, April 24, 1846.]

Yes, you are better, I think. I thank God for *that*, first of all. And, do you know, your note only just comes, and it is past ten o'clock, and I had rung the bell to have the letter-box investigated . . and then came the knock and the letter! Such a sinning post, it is, more and more. But to come at last, is something—I am contented indeed. And for being well, I am well too, if that is all. The wind is a little hard on me; but I keep in the room and think of you and am thought of by you, and no wind, under such circumstances, can do much harm perhaps:—it does not to *me*, anywise. So keep well, and believe that I am so:— 'well as you are well' . . which sounds very well.

What nonsense one comes to write when one is glad! I observe *that* in myself constantly. All my wisdom seems to depend on being pricked with pins . . or rather with something sharper. And besides your being better, I am glad through what you say here about your 'peculiarity'! Ah—how you have words in your coffers, of all sorts, . . crowns to suit all heads . . and this, which I try on last, suits mine better than the other glittering ones. Those exaggerations, idealizations, with burning carbuncles in the front of them, which made me sigh under the weight, . . those are different—! But when you say now that you do not part with feelings,—that it is your peculiarity not to wear them out, and that you are likely to care for the sight of my handwriting as much after years as at first, why you make me happy when you say such things, and (see what faith I have!) *I believe them,* since you say them, speaking of yourself. They are not after the fashion of men, or women either—but, true of *you,* they may be, . . and I take upon trust that they are: I accept such words from you as means of gladness. The worst is—I mean, the worst reasonableness that goes out to oppose them, is, . . the fear lest, when your judgments have been corrected by experience, the feelings may correct themselves. But it is ungrateful to talk reason in the face of so much love. I take up the gladness rather, and thank you and bless you seven times over, to completion. You are the best, I know, of all in the world. Did I tell you once that my love was '*something*'? Yet it is nothing: because there is no woman, let her heart be ever so made of stone and steel, who could *help* loving you, . . I answer for all women!—so this is no merit of mine, though it is the best thing I ever did in my life.

Dearest beloved, when I used to tell you to give me up, and imagined to myself how I should feel if you did it, . . and thought it would not be much worse than it was before I knew you . . (a little better indeed, inasmuch as I had the memory for ever . .) the chief *pang* was the idea of another woman——! From *that*, I have turned back again and again, recoiling like a horse set against too high a wall. Therefore if I talk of what all women *would* do, I do not mean that they *should*. 'Thirty-six Bas,' we shall not have,—shall we? or I shall be like Flush, who, before he learnt to be a philosopher, used to shiver with rage at sight of the Flush in the looking-glass, and gnash his teeth impotently, and quite howl. Now,—we shall not, dearest, have the thirty-six Bas . . now, shall we? Besides, *one* will be more than enough, she fears to herself, for your comfort and patience.

No more letters about 'Luria'? Did you see Moxon when you were in town?

Miss Bayley has not been here yet. To-morrow, perhaps. When she comes, I shall not dare name you, but *she* will, I think . . I seem sure of hearing her mind about 'Luria' and the 'Tragedy.' George thinks the former 'very fine.' Mr. Kenyon does not come,—and to-morrow (Friday) he goes . . from London.

You will care for me always the same? But *that* is like promising a charmed life, or an impossible immortality to somebody—and nobody has either, except Louis Philippe. May God bless you,—say how you are when you write to-morrow.

Your own

Ba.

Oh—your learned Americans! was it literal of Carlyle, do you think, or a jest?

R. B. to E. B. B.

[Post-mark, April 24, 1846.]

How I sympathize with poor Cloten when he complains that 'he is in the habit of saying daily many things fully as witty as those of Posthumus, men praise so—*if men would but note them!*—I feel jealous of the success and 'praise' of my Ba,—falling as they do on the mere *asides* and interjectional fits and starts of the play,—when its earnest soliloquy, the very soul and substance of it all, never reaches her ear, nor calls down her dear, dear words.

Yet do I say that I feel jealous? Rather, I acquiesce gladly in the ignorance . . because when the words, the golden words, are brought in to me by the inferior agents, and honestly transferred by *them* to the real moving powers . . they, even, find the reward too much, too much, till they—till they resolve (on the other side of a sheet) to keep silence and be grateful till death help them to speak.

Well, my dear, own dearest . . the week has got to its weary end, and to-morrow I shall trust to be with you. I continue to feel better,—and this morning's rain, in the opinion of the learned, will be succeeded by warm weather. May is just here, beside.

Let me say how a word of praise from your brother gratifies me. I feel his kindness in other respects—feel it deeply—as I do that of the rest of your family. Because . . after these extravagant flatteries of mine you find such just fault with,—wherein I go the length of attributing to you the authorship of the 'Drama of Exile,' and 'Geraldine' and 'Bertha,' and many more poems which I used to suppose my Ba's,—after that undue glorification, you will bear to be told, by way of 'set-off'—that I cannot help thinking, you, of all your family, are the most ignorant of your own value—very ignorant you are, my sweet Ba,—but they cannot be, and their kindness to me becomes centupled 'for reasons, for reasons.'

Now let me kiss you—which kiss, as I am to really kiss you to-morrow, my sweetest, I shall dare tell the truth of to myself, and say 'The real will be better.' At other times, with a longer perspective of days, and days after them, until . . why, *then* I make the best of pity and say '*Can* the real be better—what can be better than the best'? Still—remember my 'peculiarity'—with the greater I keep the less, you let me say and praise me for saying—so, with all the dear hope of to-morrow,—*now*, my Ba—and now, I kiss you. May God bless you, best and dearest.

No letters that are letters—here is one however from Arnould[1] just arrived—an Oxford Prize Poet, and an admirable dear good fellow, for all his praise—which is better.

E. B. B. to R. B.

Sunday.
[Post-mark, April 27, 1846.]

Ever dearest you might have stayed ten minutes more. George did not come in till half past six after all—but there is the consciousness of being wise in one's generation, which consoles so many for their eternity as children of light, . . yet doesn't console *me* for my ten minutes, . . so it is as well to say no more on this head!

I have glanced over the paper in the *Athenæum* and am of an increased certainty that Mr. Chorley is the writer. It is his *way* from beginning to end—and that is the way, observe, in which little critics get to tread on the heels of great writers who are too great to kick backwards. Think of bringing George Sand to the level of the same sentence with such a woman as Mrs. Ellis! And then, the infinite trash about the three eras in the Frenchwoman's career, . . which never would have been dragged into application there, if the critic had heard of her last two volumes . . published since the 'Meunier d'Angibault,' 'Teverino' and 'Isidora.' One may be angry and sin not, over such inapplicable commonplace. The motive of it, the low expediency, is worse to me than the offence. Why mention her at all . . why name in any fashion any of these French writers, for the reception of whom the English mind is certainly not prepared, unless they are to be named worthily, recognised righteously? It is just the principle of the advice about the De Kocks; whom people are to go and see and deny their acquaintance afterwards. Why not say boldly 'These writers have high faculty, and imagina-

[1] [Afterwards Sir Joseph Arnould.]

tion such as none of our romance-writers can pretend to—but they have besides a devil—and we do not recommend them as fit reading for English families!' Now wouldn't it answer every purpose? Or silence would!—silence, at least. But this digging and nagging at great reputations, . . it is to me quite insufferable: and not compensated for by the motive, which is a truckling to conventions rather than to morals. As if earnestness of aim was not, from the beginning, from 'Rose et Blanche' and 'Indiana,' a characteristic of George Sand! Really it is pitiful.

The 'Mysteries of the Heaths,' I suppose to be a translation of 'Sept jours au château,' a very clever story from the monstrous Hydra-headed imagination of Frederic Soulié. Dumas is inferior to them all of course, yet a right good storyteller when he is in the mind for storytelling;—telling, telling, telling, and never having done. You know I like listening to stories—I agree with the great Sultan and would forego ever so much cutting off of heads for the sake of a story—it is a taste quite apart from a taste for literature: a storyteller, I like, apart from the sweet voice. Now that book of Dumas's on the League wars, which distressed me so the other day, by having the cruelty . . the 'villainie' . . of hanging its hero in the fourth volume . . (regularly hanging him on a pair of gallows—wasn't it too bad?) that book is amusing enough, more than amusing enough, to take with one's coffee . . which is my fashion, . . because you are not here and I have nobody to talk to me. The hero who was hanged, deserved it a little, I think, though the author meant it for a pure misfortune and though no good romance-reader in the world, such as I am, could bear to part with the hero of four volumes in *that* manner, without pain; but the hero did deserve it a little when one came to consider. In the first place, he was a traitor once or twice in war and politics, and was quite ready to be so a third or fourth time, . . *only* . . as he said to the lady he loved . . 'je perdrais votre estime.' 'Is that your only objection' she enquired.

'*The only one*' he answered! (*How* frightfully true, that those brilliant French writers have no moral sense at all! do not, for the most part, know right from wrong! here, an instance!) Then, from the beginning to the end of the four volumes, he loves two women together . . a 'phénomène' by no means uncommon, says the historian musingly, . . and, except for the hanging, there might have been a difficulty perhaps in the final arrangement. Yet oh . . to see one's hero, the hero of four volumes, and not a bad hero either in some respects, hung up before one's eyes! . . it wrongs the natural affections to think of it! it made me unhappy for a full hour! There should be a society for the prevention of cruelty to romance-readers, against the recurrence of such things!

Pure nonsense I write to you, it seems to me.

What beautiful flowers you brought me!—and the sweetbrier is unfolding its leaves to-day, as if you did them, so, no wrong. And I have been considering; and there are not, if you please, *five* but *four* days, between Saturday and Thursday. In the meanwhile say how you are, dearest dearest! My thoughts are with you constantly . . indeed. I could almost say, too much, . . because sometimes they grow weak and tired . . not of *you*, who are best and beloved, but of themselves, having been so long used to be sad. May God bless you, . . bless you! His best blessing for *me* (after *that!*) were to make me worthy of you—but it would take too many miracles.

Your

Ba.

Remember the letters, if they come.

R. B. to E. B. B.

Sunday.
[Post-mark, April 27, 1846.]

See what a brain I have,—which means, *you* have! The book I ought to put in my pocket,—and fancy I leave on the table,—is picked up in our lane and presented to me on my return; so my reason, which told you I had forgotten it, the book, was wrong, and my instinct which told me, all the time, that I could not forget even so poor a matter if it tended to you,—*that* was right, as usual? (Don't think that I forgot the said book on the former occasions . . I wanted to look through it first, so as to be able to correct any possible mistakings, in case you should ask, or should not ask, my siren! I read the book during the voyage.)

Will you tell me what number of the *League* contains the notice of you? I can get it directly. I did not ask you yesterday, being just as much master of myself as I commonly am when with you—but after-wisdom comes duly for a consolation, and mine was apparent in a remark I made last night—'Here is truly an illusion broken' I said —'for not very long ago I used to feel impatient at listening to other people's commendations of her, and as if they were usurping my especial office,—they *could* not see what I see, not utter what I could utter: and now, at the beginning of my utterance, the hand closes my mouth, while its dear fellow shuts my eyes,—I may not see what everybody sees, nor say what the whole world says,—I, that was to excel them all in either function! So now I will change my policy and bid them praise, praise, praise, praise, since I may not. Will you let me hear them, my Ba? You know Chesterfield forbids his son to play on the instrument himself—'for you can pay musicians' he says—'and hear them play.' Where may I hear this discourser of most excellent music?

In your last letter you spoke of 'other women,' and said they might 'love' me—just see! They might love me because of something in me, lovingness in me, which they never could have evoked . . so the effect produces the cause, my dear 'inverter'! If there had been a vague aimless feeling in me, turning hither and thither for some object to attach itself to and spend itself on, and you had chanced to be that object, I should understand you were very little flattered and how a poplar does as well for a vine-prop as a palm tree—but whatever love of mine clings to you was created by you, dearest,—they were not in me, I believed—those feelings,—till you came. So that, mournful and degrading as it sounds, still it would, I think, be more rational to confess the possibility of their living on, though you withdrew,—finding some other—oh no, it is,—that is as great an impossibility as the other,—they came from you, they go to you, what is the whole world to them!

May God bless you, repay you—He can—

Well Ba, do you see the *Examiner?* That is very kind, very generous of Forster. There are real difficulties in the way of this prompt, efficient, serviceable notice—for he has a tribe of friends, dramatists, actors 'conflicting interests' &c. &c. to keep the peace among,—and he quite understands his trade—how compensation is to be made, and an equilibrium kept in the praises so as to offend nobody,—yet see how he writes, and with a heap of other business on his shoulders! I thank him very sincerely, I am sure.

Tell me how you are, beloved—all-beloved! I am quite well to-day,—have been out.

Do you remember our friend Bennett of Blackheath? (Don't ejaculate 'le Benêt'!) He sent me letters lately—and I returned a copy of 'Luria' to save compliments and words—here is his answer . . (I will at once confess I could not read it, but Ba bids me send, and what am I but Ba's own, very very own?)

R. B. to E. B. B.

Monday.
[Post-mark, April 27, 1846.]

Oh yes; that paper is by Chorley, no doubt—I read it, and quite wonder at him. I suppose he follows somebody's 'lead'—writes as he is directed—because I well remember what he said on lending me 'Le Compagnon. There, there is that other silly expenditure of pen and ink on the English poets, or whatever they are. And in such work may a man spend his youth and not a few available energies—sad work altogether!

My love, *I* have done a fair day's work this Monday,—whoever may be idle—I thought I would call on Forster this morning—he was out, and I crossed over to Moxon's, not seeing him, neither, and thence walked home—so that to tell you I am *well* is superfluous enough, is it not? But while the sun shone brightest, (and it shines now) I said 'The cold wind is felt through it all,—*she keeps the room!*' The wind is unremitting,—savage. Do you bear it, dearest, or suffer, as I fear? (Speaking of Forster . . you see the *Examiner*, I believe? Or I will send it directly of course). I entirely agree with you in your estimate of the comparative value of French and English Romance-writers. I bade the completest adieu to the latter on my first introduction to Balzac, whom I greatly admire for his faculty, whatever he may choose to do with it. Do you know a little sketch 'La Messe de l'Athée,'—most affecting to me. And for *you*, with your love of a 'story,' what an unceasing delight must be that very ingenious way of his, by which he connects the new novel with its predecessors—keeps telling you more and more news yet of the people you have got interested in, but seemed to have done with. Rastignac, Mme. d'Espard, Desplein etc.—they keep alive, moving—is it not ingenious? Frédéric Soulié I know a little of (I let this reading drop some ten years ago) and only George Sand's early works: by the way, the worst thing of all in that blessed article we have been referring to, is the spiteful and quite uncalled for introduction of the names of A. de Musset and De Lamennais—what have the English families to do with *that?* Did you notice a stanza quoted from some lachrymose rhymester to be laughed at (in the Article on Poetry)—in which the writer complains of the illtreatment of false friends, for' says he,

'I have felt their *bangs.*' The notion of one's friend 'banging' one is exhilarating when one reflects that he might get a little pin, and prick, prick after this fashion. No, it is probably a manner of writing,—meant for the week's life and the dozen readers. Here is a note from his sister, by the way.

Now, dearest-dearest, good bye till to-morrow. I think of you all day, and, if I dream, dream of you—and the end of the thinking and of the dreaming is still new love, new love of you, my sweetest, only beloved! so I kiss you and bless you from my heart of heart.

Ever your R.

E. B. B. to R. B.

Monday Evening.
[Post-mark, April 28, 1846.]

Very good *Examiner!*—I am pleased with it and with Mr. Forster for the nonce, though he talks a little nonsense here and there, in order to be a true critic, and though he doesn't talk at all, scarcely, of the 'Soul's Tragedy' . . . how is one to bear it? That 'Tragedy' has wonderful things in it—thoughts, suggestions, . . and more and more I feel, that you never did better dialogue than in the first part. Every pulse of it is alive and individual—dramatic dialogue of the best. Nobody in the world could write such dialogue—now, you know, you must be patient and 'meke as maid,' being in the course of the forty-nine days of enduring praises. Praises, instead of 'bangs'!!—consider that it might be worse!—*dicit ipsissima Ba.*

Think of my not hearing a word about the article in the *Examiner*, until I had your note this morning. And the *Examiner* was in the house since Saturday night, and nobody to tell me! I was in high vexation, reproaching them all, to-day—till Stormie had the impertinence to turn round and tell me that only Papa had read the paper, and that 'he had of course put it away to keep me from the impropriety of thinking too much about . . about' . . yes, really Stormie *was* so impertinent. For the rest, when Papa came upstairs at one o'clock, he had it in his hand.

At two, Miss Bayley came, and sate here two hours, and thought me looking so well, with such improved looks from last autumn, that I don't mean to groan at all to you to-day about the wind—it is a savage wind, as you say, and I wish it were gone, and I am afraid of stirring from the room while it lasts, but there's an end . . and not of *me*, says Miss Bayley. She doffed her bonnet and talked and talked, and was agreeable and affectionate, and means to come constantly to see me . . . ('only not on Thursday,' I desired:) and do you know, you need not think any more of my going with you to Italy, for she has made up her mind to take me herself . . there is no escape for me that I can see—it's fixed . . certain! with a thousand generous benignities she stifled my 'no's' . . and all I had breath to say at last, was, that 'there was time enough for plans of that kind.' Seriously, I was quite embarrassed to know how to adjourn the debate. And she is capable of 'arranging everything'—of persisting, of insisting—who knows what? And so, . . when I am 'withdrawn' . . carried away . . then, shall all my 'feelings,' which are in you, be given to somebody else? is *that* the way — ?

Now I shall not make jests upon *that* . . I shall not: first, I shall not, because it is ungrateful—and next and principally, because my heart stands still only to think of it . . ! Why did you say *that* to me? I could be as jealous (did I not tell you once?) as any one of your melodramatic gitana heroines, who carries a poignard between the white-satin sash and the spangles? I perfectly understand, at this distance, what *jealousy* is, would be, ought to be, must be—though I never guessed at all what *love* was, at *that* distance, and startled I am often and confounded, to see the impotency of my imagination.

Forgive the blottings out—I have not blotted out lately . . *have* I now? and it is pardonable once in a hundred years or days.

The rest for to-morrow. Your correspondent of the first letter you sent me really does write like a Bennet, though he praises you. I could not help laughing very gently, though he praises you. Good-night my only beloved . . dearest! As *my* Bennet says (Georgiana) when she catches vehemently at the laurel . . '*I will not be forgot*' . . .

"I must die . . but I WILL NOT BE FORGOT' (in *large capitals!*) But what *she* applies to the Delphic groves, turns for *me* to something more ambitious. 'I will not be forgot' . . will I? shall I? not till Thursday at least . . being ever and ever

Your own
Ba.

R. B. to E. B. B.

Tuesday.
[Post-mark, April 28, 1846.]

Now bless you, my dearest, best Ba, for this letter that comes at the eleventh hour,—which means, at 3 o'clock. Was not I frightened! I made sure you would write. Why, our Post emulates the Italian glory . . nay, that is *too* savage a saying—for in Venice or Rome I should have to go for this to the office, and only get it at last through the forbearing honesty of every other applicant for letters during the day, or week—since to every man and woman who thrusts his or her head in at the window at Venice, the clerk hands coolly over the whole odd hundred, and turns to his rest again till as many are taken as may be thought necessary. But, Ba, dear dearest Ba, do you really mean to tell me I *said* '*that*' . . of 'transferring feelings' etc? I hope I did,—though I cannot imagine how I ever could—say so—for so the greater fault will be Ba's—who drives me from one Scylla (see my critic's account) into a worse Charybdis through pure fear and aversion,—and then cries 'see where you are *now!*' I was retreating as far as possible from that imaginary 'woman who called out those feelings,'—might have called them out,—just as this April sun of ours makes date-palms grow and bear—and because I said, of the two hypotheses, the one which taught you the palms *might* be transplanted and *live on* here,—*that* was the more rational . . you turn and ask 'So your garden will rear palms.' Now, I tell Ba,—no, I will kiss Ba and so tell her.

How happy Miss Bayley's testimony makes me! One never can be too sure of such a happiness. She has no motive for thus confirming it. You 'look so well'—and she not merely sees it, but *acts* upon it,—is for deriving a practical benefit from it, and forthwith. Then, Miss Bayley, let me try and 'transfer' . . ah, the palm is too firmly rooted in my very heart,—I can but sprinkle you over with yellow dust!

Oh, Ba; not to tell me of the *League;* the *number!*—will you please tell me? One letter more I get, do I not? Then comes Thursday—my Thursday.

What you style 'impertinence' in your Brother, is very kind and good natured to my thinking. Well, now—see the way a newspaper criticism affects one, nearly the only way! If this had been an attack—how it would affect you and me matters nothing—it might affect others disagreeably—and through them, us. So I feel very much obliged to Forster in this instance.

I kiss you with perfect love, my sweetest best Ba. May God bless you.

R

E. B. B. to R. B.

Tuesday.
[Post-mark, April 29, 1846.]

Dearest, you are not to blame the post, nor even me. The reason you did not get the letter was simply that

Henrietta slept over the hour, and let it lie on the table till past eight. Still, you should have had it before *three* perhaps. Only the wrong was less a wrong than you fancied.

For *my* wrongs, dearest beloved, they are mine I confess, and not yours . . ah, you are 'evilly persecuted, and entreated' of me, I must allow. Yet as, with all my calumnious imputations, I think softly to myself seven times seven times a day that no living man is worthy to stand in your footsteps, . . why you must try to forgive and (*not*) forget me. Do I teaze you past enduring, sometimes? Yes, yes. And wasn't it my fault about the 'imaginary woman;' that heiress, in an hypothesis, of the 'love' I 'made'? Yes, yes, yes—it was, of course. Unless indeed she came out of that famous mist, which you fined me away into, . . the day you slew and idealized me, remember!—and, now I begin to consider, I think she did! So we will share the fault between us, you and I. The odium of it, I was going to say—but *odium* is by no means the right word, perhaps.

The truth of all is, that you are too much in the excess of goodness, . . that you spoil me! There it is! Did I not tell you, warn you, that I never was used to the purple and fine linen of such an infinite tenderness? If you give me back my sackcloth, I shall know my right hand from my left again, perhaps, . . guess where I stand . . what I am . . recover my common sense. Will you? no—do not.

And for the *League* newspaper, you mistook me, and I forgot to say so in my letter yesterday. I told you only that the *League* paper had mentioned me—not noticed me. It was just . . I just shall *tell* you, that you may not spend another thought on such a deep subject . . it was a mere quotation from the 'cornships in the offing,' with a prefatory *as that exquisite poet Miss B . . says!* Now you are done with the winter of your discontent? You are with the snowdrops at any rate. But last year there was a regular criticism on my poems in that *League* paper, and I had every reason to thank the critic. I have heard too that Cobden is a very gracious reader of mine . . and that his Leeds (liege) subjects generally do me the honours of popularity, more than any other people in England. There's glory for you, talking of palm-trees.

Ah—talking of palm-trees, you do not know what a curious coincidence your thought is with a thought of mine, which I shall not tell you now . . but some day perhaps. There's a mystery! talking of Venice!

For Balzac, I have had my full or overfull pleasure from that habit of his you speak of, . . and which seems to prove his own good faith in the life and reality of his creations, in such a striking manner. He is a writer of most wonderful faculty—with an overflow of life everywhere—with the vision and the utterance of a great seer. His French is another language—he throws new metals into it . . malleable metals, which fuse with the heat of his genius. There is no writer in France, to my mind, at all comparable to Balzac—none—but where is the reader in England to make the admission?—*none*, again . . is almost to be said.

But, dearest, you do not say how you are; and *that* silence is not lawful, and *is* too significant. For me, when the wind changed for a few hours to-day, I went down stairs with Flush, and had my walk in the drawing-room. Mrs. Jameson has written to proclaim her coming to-morrow at four,—so I shall hear of 'Luria,' I think. Remember to bring my verses, if you please, on your Thursday. And if dreaming of me should be good for making you love me, let me be dreamt of . . go on to dream of me: and love me, my beloved, ever so much, without grudging,—because the love returns to you, all of it, . . as the wave to the sea; and with an addition of sundry grains of soiling sand, to make you properly grateful. Take care of yourself—may God take care of you for your own

Ba.

R. B. to E. B. B.

Wednesday.
[Post-mark, April 29, 1846.]

Oh, post, post, how I am plagued by what uses to delight me! No letter,—and I cannot but think you have written one, my Ba! It will come perhaps at 3 o'clock. Shame and again, shame!

Meantime I will tell you what a dear, merciful Ba you are, in only threatening me with daggers,—when you play at threatening,—instead of declaring you will *frown* at me. . . Oh, but here 'Fear recoils, he knows well why, even at the sound himself has made—'

The best of it is, that this was the second fright, and by no means the most formidable. When I read that paragraph beginning 'you need not think any more of going with me to Italy'—shall I only say I *was* alarmed? Without a particle of affectation, I tell Ba, I *am*, cannot help being, alarmed even now—we have been discussing possibilities—and it is rather more possible than probable that Miss Bayley may 'carry off' my Ba, and her Flush, and, say, an odd volume of the Cyclic Poets, all in her pocket . . she being, if I remember, of the race of the Anakim—than that I shall ever find in the wide world a flesh and blood woman able to bear the weight of the 'feelings,' I rest now upon the B and the A which spell Ba's name,—only her name!

Forster sent a note last evening urging me to go and dine with him and Leigh Hunt to-day,—there was no refusing. There is sunshine—you may have been downstairs—but the wind continues.

I shall know to-morrow—but surely a letter *is* to come presently—let me wait a little.

Nothing! Pray write if anything have happened, my own Ba!

No time—Ever your

R.

E. B. B. to R. B.

Friday.
[Post-mark, May 1, 1846.]

I am delighted with the verses and quite surprised by Mr. Arnould's, having expected to find nothing but love and law in them, and really there is a great deal besides. Hard to believe, it was, that a university prize poet (who was not Tennyson) could write such good verses: but he wrote them of *you*, and *that* was enough inspiration for *him*, I suppose, as it would be for others, my own dearest. How I delight in hearing you praised!—it is such a delightful assent to the word which is in me, in the deepest of me. You know that mysterious pleasure we have, in listening to echoes!—we hear nothing new, nothing we have not said ourselves—yet we stand on the side of the hill and listen . . listen . . as if to the oracles of Delphi. The very pleasure of it all is in the repetition . . the reverberation.

When you had gone yesterday and I had taken my coffee, holding my book . . 'La Gorgone' a sea-romance by *Landelle*, (those little duodecimo books are the only possible books to hold in one's hand at coffee-times . . and the people at Rolandi's library sent me this, which is not worth much, I think, but quite new and very marine) . . holding my book at one page, as if fixed . . transfixed, . . by a sudden eternity, . . . well, after all *that* was done with, coffee and all, . . in came George, and told me that the day before he had seen Tennyson at Mr. Vennables' house, or chambers rather. Mr. Vennables was unwell, and George went to see him, and while he was there, came the poet. He had left London for a few days, he said, and meant to stay here for a time . . 'háting it perfectly' like your Donne . . 'seeming to detest London,' said George . . 'abusing everything in unmeasured words.' Then he had been dining at Dickens's, and meeting various celebrities, and Dickens had asked him to go with him (Dickens) to Switzerland, where he [is] going, to write his new work: 'but,' laughed Tennyson, 'if I went, I should be entreating him to dismiss his sentimentality, and so we should quarrel and part, and never see one another any more. It was better to decline—and I have declined.' When George had told his story, I enquired if Tennyson was what was called an agreeable man—happy in conversation. And the reply was . . . 'yes—but quite inferior to Browning! He neither talks so well,' observed George with a grave consideration and balancing of the sentences, . . 'nor has so frank and open a manner. The advantages are all on Browning's side, *I should say.*' Now dear George is a little criticised you must know in this house for his official gravity and dignity—my sisters murmur at him very much sometimes . . poor dear George!— but he is good and kind, and high and right minded, as we all know, and I, for my part, never thought of criticising him yesterday when he said those words rather . . . perhaps . . barristerially, . . had they been other words.

My other words must go by my next letter—I am to write to you again presently, you are to be pleased to remember . . and that letter may reach you, for aught I can guess, at the same moment with this. In the meantime, ever beloved,

I am your

Ba.

R. B. to E. B. B.

Friday.
[Post-mark, May 1, 1846.]

I go to you, my Ba, with heart *full* of love, so it seems, —yet I come away always with a greater capacity of holding love,—for there is more and still more,—*that* seems too! At the beginning, I used to say (most truly) that words were all inadequate to express my feelings,—now, those very feelings seem, as I see them from this present moment, just as inadequate in their time to represent what I am conscious of now. I *do* feel more, widelier, strangelier . . how can I tell you? You must believe,—my only, only beloved! I daresay I have said this before, because it has struck me repeatedly,—and, judging by past experience, I shall need to say it again—and often again. Am I really destined to pass my life sitting by you? And you speak of *your* hesitation at trusting in miracles! Oh, my Ba, my heart's—well, Ba, I am so far guiltless of presumption, let come what will, that I never for the moment cease to be . . tremblingly anxious I will say,—and conscious that the good is too great for me in this world. You do not like one to write so, I know, but there is a safety in it —the presumptuous walk blindfold among pits, to a proverb —and no one shall record that of me. And if I have cares and scruples of this kind at times, or at all times, I have none where most other people would have very many. I never ask myself, as perhaps I should,—'Will *she* be happy too?'—All that seems removed from me, far above my concernment—she—you, my Ba . . will make *me* so entirely happy, that it seems enough to know . . my palm-trees grow well enough without knowing the cause of the sun's heat. Then I think again, that your nature is to make happy and to bless, and itself to be satisfied with that.—So instead of fruitless speculations how to give you back your own gift, I will rather resolve to lie quietly and let your dear will have its unrestricted way. All which I take up the paper determining *not* to write,—for it is foolish, poor endeavour at best, but,—just this time it is written. May God bless you—

R. B.

I called on Moxon, who is better, and reports cheeringly. Then I went to my friend's, and thence home, not much tired. I have to go out (to-day) with my sister but only next door. To-morrow I hear from you, love, and on Monday— (unless a pressing engagement &c.—ah!)

What do you say to this little familiar passage in the daily life of friend Howitt,—for which I am indebted to Moxon. Howitt is book-making about Poets, it seems—where they were born, how they live, 'what relation their mothers' sons are to their fathers'—etc. In the prosecution of this laudable object he finds his way to Ambleside, calls on Wordsworth 'quite promiscuously' as Mrs. Malaprop says, meaning nothing at all. And so after a little ordinary complimenting and *play*-talk, our man of business takes to good earnest, but dexterous questioning . . all for pure interest in poetry and Mr W. 'So, sir, after that school . . if I understand—you went to . . to . . ?—and so on. Mr. Wordsworth the younger having quicker eyes than his father detected a certain shuffling movement between the visitor's right hand and some mysterious region between the chair's back and his coat-pocket . . glimpses of a pocket case and paper note book were obtained. He thought it (the son) high time to go and tell Mrs. Wordsworth,—who came in and found the good old man in the full outpouring of all those delightful reminiscences hitherto supposed the exclusive property of Miss Fenner no doubt! Mrs. W—'desired to speak with William for a moment' (the old William)—and then came the amazement, horror &c. &c., and last of all came Mr. Howitt's bow and 'so no more at present from your loving &c.'— Seriously, in my instinct—instinct—instinct thrice I write it and thank my stars! Moxon said, Howitt is 'just gone to call on Tennyson for information—having left his card for that purpose.' 'And one day will call on *you*' quoth Moxon, who is but a sinister prophet, as you may have heard—Dii meliora piis! It is fair enough in Tennyson's case, for he is apprised by Howitt's self of the purpose of his visit, but to try and inveigle Wordsworth into doing what he would hate most . . to his credit be it said—why, it is abominable—abominable!

Then I heard another story—his wife, Mary, finds out,—at all events, translates Miss Bremer. Another publisher gets translated other works—or may be the same,—as who shall say him nay? Howitt writes him a letter (which is shown my informant), wherein 'rogue,' 'thief,' 'rascal' and similar elegancies dance pleasantly through period after period.

'Come out from among them my soul, neither be thou a partaker of their habitations!'

From all which I infer—I may kiss you, may I not, love Ba? It is done, may I or may I not— Ever your own

E. B. B. to R. B.

Friday.
[Post-mark, May 2, 1846.]

How you write to me! Is there any word to answer to these words . . which, when I have read, I shut my eyes as one bewildered, and think blindly . . or do not think—some feelings are deeper than the thoughts touch. My only beloved, it is thus with me . . . I stand by a miracle in your love, and because I stand in it and it covers me, just for *that*, you cannot see me! May God grant that you *never see me*—for then we two shall be 'happy' as you say, and I, in the only possible manner, be very sure. Meanwhile, you do quite well not to speculate about making me happy . . your instinct knows, if *you* do not know, that it is *implied* in your own happiness . . or rather (not to assume a magnanimity) in my sense of your being happy, not apart from me. As God sees me, and as I know at all the motions of my own soul, I may assert to you that from the first moment of our being to each other anything, I never conceived of happiness otherwise . . never thought of being happy through you or by you or in you, even—your good was all my idea of good, and *is*. I hear women say sometimes of men whom they love . . 'such a one will make me happy, I am sure,' or 'I shall be happy with *him*, I think'—or again . . 'He is so good and affectionate that nobody need be afraid for my happiness.' Now, whether you like or dislike it, I will tell you that I never had such thoughts of *you*, nor ever, for a moment, gave you that sort of praise. I do not know why . . or perhaps I do . . but I could not so think of you . . I have not time nor breath . . I could as soon play on the guitar when it is thundering. So be happy, my own dearest . . and if it should be worth a thought that you *cannot* be *alone, so,* you may think *that* too. You have so deep and intense a nature, that it were impossible for you to love after the fashion of other men, weakly and imperfectly, and your love, which comes out like your genius, may glorify enough to make you happy, perhaps. Which is my dream, my calculation rather, when I am happiest now. May God bless you. Suppose I should ever read in your eyes that you were not happy with me?—can I help, do you fancy, such thoughts? Could *you* help being not happy? The very word '*unhappiness*' implies that you cannot help it. Now forgive me my naughtiness, because I love you, and never loved but you, . . and because I promise not to go with Miss Bayley to Italy . . I promise. Ah—If you could pretend to be afraid of *that, indeed, I* have a right to be afraid, without pretence at all . . *I* who am a woman and frightened of lightning. And see the absurdity. If I did not go to Italy with *you*, the reason would be that you did not choose—and if *you* did not choose, I should not choose . . I would not see Italy without your eyes—*could* I, do you think? So if Miss Bayley takes me to Italy with a volume of the Cyclic poets, it will be as a dead Ba clasped up between the leaves of it. You talked of a 'Flora,' you remember, in the first letter I had from you.

How bad of William Howitt! How right you are, always! Yet not quite always, dear dearest beloved, happily for your own

Ba.

Say how you are I beseech you, and honestly! I was

down-stairs to-day, since the wind changed, and am the better for it. What writing for a postman!—or for *you* even!

R. B. to E. B. B.

Saturday.
[Post-mark, May 2, 1846.]

No, my Ba, your letter came as it ought last night,—and the promise it contained of another made me restless all the morning—to no purpose,—nothing more comes—*yet*—for there is a 'peradventure' yet unwithdrawn. When I do not hear from you, as now, I always fancy there was some signal reason why I ought to have heard . . that 'to-morrow,' I could better bear the not hearing . . though never, never do yesterday's letters slip by a hair's breadth from the place in my affection they once take,—*they* could not have been dispensed with,—but the imaginary letter of to-morrow *could*, by contrast with to-day's exigencies . . till to-morrow really comes and is found preferring such claims of its own—such claims.

This letter I have got, and will try and love enough for two . . I can do no harm by trying . . *this* I do not mean to say that I expected. May I say 'in heart-playing,' . . now, Ba, it will be a fancy, which you can pounce on and poke your humming-bird bill through, like a needle, in a very 'twinkling,' and so shall my flower's eye be ruined for ever, and when it turns black and shrivels up as dead flowers do, you can triumph and ask 'are these your best flowers, best feelings for me?'. But now, after this deprecation, you will be generous and only hover above, using the diamond eye rather than the needle-bill,—and I will go on and dare say that I should like, for one half second, *not to love you*, and then feel all the love lit up in a flame to the topmost height, at the falling of such a letter on my heart. Don't you know that foolish boys sometimes play at hanging themselves—suspend themselves by the neck actually for such a half second as this of my fancying—

that they may taste the luxury of catching back at existence, and being cut down again? There is a notable exemplification, a worthy simile! It all comes, I suppose, from the joy of being rid handsomely of my dinners and in a fair way for Monday . . nothing between but letters,—I shall continue to hope! At sea it always sounds pleasantly to hear . . after passing Cape This and Isle the other, 'now, *next* land we make is—Italy, or England, or Greece.'

Moxon told me Tennyson was still in Town. Switzerland? He is a fortnight going to wherever a Train takes him—'for,' says Moxon, 'he has to pack up, and is too late, and next day' . . I dare say he unaffectedly hates London where this poco-curanteism would entail all manner of disagreeabilities. If I caught rightly . . that is, now apply rightly, a word or two I heard . . one striking celebrity at Dickens' Dinner was—Lord Chesterfield—literary, inasmuch as a great 'maker *up* of books'—for the Derby. Macready may have been another personage—they, Tennyson and he, may 'fadge,' in Shakespearian phrase, if the writer of the 'Two Voices' &c. considers Home's 'Douglas' exquisite poetry,—otherwise,—it is a chance!

But with respect to your Brother . . first of all—nay, and last of all, for it all is attributable to *that*—I feel his kindness, in its way, as I feel yours; as truly, according to its degree and claim: but—'now think what I would speak!'—When he really *does* see me one day—no longer embarrassed as under the circumstances I could not but have been on these two or three occasions when we met—he will find something better than conversational powers to which I never pretended—and what he will accept in preference,—a true, faithful desire of repaying his goodness—he will find it, that is, because it must be *there,* and I have confidence in such feelings making sooner or later their way.

So now, at 2½ p.m., I must (*—here is the Post* . . from

you? *Yes*—the letter is here at last—I was waiting:—now to read; no, kissing it comes first.

And now . . I will not say a word, my love of loves, my dearest, dearest Ba,—not one word—but I will go out and walk where I can be alone, and think out all my thought of you, and bless you and love you with nothing to intercept the blessing and the love. I will look in the direction of London and send my heart there . . Dear, dear love, I kiss you and commend you to God. Your very own —

I am very well—quite well, dearest.

R. B. to E. B. B.

Sunday.
[Post-mark, May 4, 1846.]

When I said one more letter might come before to-morrow, I forgot. How used I to manage in the early 'day of small things'—comparatively—when letters came once a week at most, and yet I felt myself so rich, dearest!

I want you to remember, Ba, what I shall be nearly sure to forget when closer to you than now; tell me to-morrow. If I chance to see Mrs. Jameson in the course of the week what am I to say,—that is, what have you decided on saying? Does she know that you write to me? Because there is a point of simple good taste to be preserved . . I must not listen with indifference if I am told that 'her friend Miss B.' thought well of the last number. But she must know we write, I think,—never make any secret of that, when the subject is brought forward.

Here is warm May weather, my Ba; I do not shiver by sympathy as I fancy you going down stairs. I shall hope to see the sweet face look its . . now, what? 'Best' would be altogether an impertinence,—unless you help my meaning, which is 'best,' too.

I received two days ago a number of the *People's Jour-*

nal—from our illustrious contemporary, Bennett! Bennett figures where Barrett might have fronted the world. Fact! I will cut you out his very original lyric[1]—observe the felicitous emendation in the author's own blue ink . . that supplemental trochee makes a musical line of it! Mary Howitt follows with a pretty, washy, very meritorious Lyric of Life. There is 'a guilty one'—'Name her not!' 'Virtue turns aside for shame'

> She was born of guilty kin—
> Her life's course hath guilty been—
> Unto school she never went—
> And whate'er she learned was sin,—
> LET HER DIE!

And so on—what pure nonsense! Who cries 'let her die' in the whole world now? thank God, nobody. The sin of the world (of the lookers-on, not the causers of the wrong) consists, in these days, in looking-on and asking 'How can we help her dying—or factory children's dying —or evicted Irish peasantry's dying?' What ails these Howitts of a sudden, that they purvey this kind of cat-lap, —they that once did better? William Howitt grinds here an article on May day; past human power of reading of course, but I just noticed that not a venerablest commonplace was excused on account of its age—the quotation from Chaucer, Spenser, Herrick got once more into rank and file with the affecting alacrity shown the other day at a review of the Chelsea invalids! Oh, William, 'Let them die!'

So goodbye till to-morrow, my dearest. I love you and bless you ever, and am your

R. B.

R. B. to E. B. B.

Tuesday.
[Post-mark, May 5, 1846.]

Yes, you were right, my Ba—our meeting was on the 20th of last May: the next letter I received was the 14th and *that* ran in my head, no doubt, yesterday. You must

[1] ['Cry of the Spring Flower-seller,' by W. C. Bennett.]

have many such mistakes to forgive in me when I undertake to talk and 'stare' at the same time . . well for me if they are no more serious mistakes!

I referred to my letters—and found much beside the date to reflect on. I will tell you. Would it not be perilous in some cases,—many cases—to contrast the present with the very early Past: the first time, even when there is abundant fruit, with the dewy springing and blossoming? One would confess to a regret at the vanishing of that charm, at least, if it were felt to be somehow vanished out of the present. And, looking upon our experience as if it were another's,—undoubtedly the peril seems doubled—with that five months' previous correspondence . . only *then*,—after all the curiosity, and hope and fear,—the first visit to come! And after,—shortly after,—you know—the heightened excitement that followed . . I should not believe in the case of another,—or should not *have* believed, —that the strange delight could last . . no more than I should think it reasonable to wonder, or even grieve, that it did not last—so long as other delights came in due succession. Now, hear the truth! I never, God knows, felt the joy of being with you as I felt it YESTERDAY—the fruit of my happiness has grown under the blossom, lifting it and keeping it as a coronet—not one feeling is lost, and the new feelings are infinite. Ah, my Ba, can you wonder if I seem less inclined to see the adorable kindness in those provisions, and suppositions, and allowances for escape, change of mind &c., you furnish me with,—than to be struck at the strange fancy which, as I said, insists on my being free to leave off breathing vital air the moment it shall so please me?

And when I spoke of 'dishonouring suppositions' I had not the faintest approximation to an idea of standing in your eyes for a magnanimous keeper of promises, vow-observer, and the rest. All *that* is profoundly pitiable! But to change none of my views of the good of this life and the next, and yet to give up my love on the view (for instance) which sees that good in money, or worldly advancement,—what is that if not dishonouring?

All the while, I know your thought, your purpose in it all,—I believe and am sure—and I bless you from my heart—you will soon know, what *you* have to know—*I* believe, beforehand, I repeat.

I am rather out of spirits to-day—*thus* I feel toward you when at all melancholy . . you would undo me in withdrawing from me your help, *undo* me, I feel! When, as ordinarily, I am cheerful, I have precisely the same conviction. Does that prove nothing, my Ba?

Well, I give up proving, or trying to prove anything—from the beginning I abjured mere words—and now, much more!

Let me kiss you, ever best and dearest! My life is in the hand you call 'mine,'—if that hand would 'shake' less from letting it fall, I earnestly pray God may relieve you of it nor ever let you be even aware of what followed your relief! For what *should* one live or die in this world?

I am wholly yours—

Did I not meet two of your brothers yesterday in the Hall? Pray take care of this cold wind—be satisfied with the good deeds of the last few days.

E. B. B. to R. B.

Tuesday.
[Post-mark, May 6, 1846.]

Dearest, it has just come into my head that I should like to carry this letter to the post myself—but no, I shall not be able. Probably the post is far out of reach, and even if it were within reach, my grand scheme of walking in the street is scarcely a possible thing to-day, for I must keep watch in the house from two till five for Lady Margaret Cocks, an old friend of mine, who was kind to me when I was a child, in the country, and has not forgotten me since, when, two months in the year, she has been in the habit of going to London. A good, worthy person, with a certain cultivation as to languages and literature, but quite manquée on the side of the imagination . . talking of the poets, as a blind woman of colours, calling 'Pippa Passes' '*pretty and odd,*' and writing herself 'poems' in heaps of copy books which every now and then she brings to show me . . . 'odes' to Hope and Patience and all the cardinal virtues, with formulas of 'Begin my muse' in the fashion ended last century. She has helped to applaud and scold me since I could walk and write verses; and when I was so wicked as to go to dissenting chapels besides, she reproached me with tears in her eyes; but they were tears of earnest partizanship, and not of affection for me, . . she does not love me after all, nor guess at my heart, and *I* do not love her, I feel. Woe to us! for there are good and unlovable people in the world, and we cannot help it for our lives.

In the midst of writing which, comes the Leeds Miss Heaton, who used to send me those long confidential letters *à faire frémir*, and beg me to call her 'Ellen,' and as this is the second time that she has sent up her card, in an accidental visit to London, I thought I would be good-natured for once, and see her. An intelligent woman, with large black eyes and a pleasant voice, and young . . manners provincial enough, for the rest, and talking as if the world were equally divided between the 'Congregationalists' and the 'Churchpeople.' She assured me that 'Dr. Vaughan was very much annoyed' at the article on my poems which 'crept' into his review, and that it was fully intended to recant at length on the first convenient opportunity. 'And really,' she said, 'it seems to me that you have as many admirers among churchmen as among dissenters.'! There's glory!—and I kept my countenance. *Lost* it though, five minutes afterwards, when she observed pathetically, that a 'friend of hers who had known Mr. Browning *quite intimately*, had told her he was an infidel . . . more's the pity, when he has such a genius.' I desired the particular information of your intimate friend, a little more warmly perhaps than was necessary, . . but what could be expected of me, I wonder?

I shall write again to you to-night, you know, and this is enough for two o'clock. Now will you get my letter on this Tuesday? Do you think of me . . love me? And are you well to-day? The flowers look beautiful though you put their heads into the water instead of their feet.

Your Ba.

E. B. B. to R. B.

Tuesday Evening.
[Post-mark, May 6, 1846.]

But my own only beloved, I surely did not speak too 'insistingly' yesterday. I shrank from your question as you put it, because you put it wrong. If you had asked me instead, whether I meant to keep my promise to you, I would have answered 'yes' without hesitation: but the form you chose, referred to *you* more than to *me*, and was indeed and indeed a foolish form of a question, my own dearest! For the rest . . ah, you do not see my innermost nature, . . *you!*—you are happily too high, and cannot see into it . . cannot perceive how the once elastic spring is broken with the long weights! . . you wonder that it should drop, when you, who lifted it up, do not hold it up! you cannot understand! . you wonder! And *I* wonder too . . on the other side! *I* wonder how I can feel happy and alive . . as I can, *through you!* how I can turn my face toward life again . . as I can, *for you!* . . and chiefly of all, how I can ever imagine . . as I do, sometimes . . that such a one as you, may be happy perhaps with such a one as *I!* . . happy!

Do not judge me severely, you, to whom I have given *both* hands, for your own uses and ends!—you, who are more to me than I can be to you, even by your own statement—better to me than life . . or than death even, as death seemed to me before I knew you.

Certainly I love you enough, and trust you enough, if you knew what God knows. Yet, . . 'now hear me.' I shall not be able to please you, I think, by a firm continued belief of this engagement's being justifiable, until the event wholly *has* justified it . . I mean, . . until I shall see you not less happy for having lived near me for six months or a year—should God's mercy permit such justification. Do not blame me. I cannot help it . . I would, if I could, help it. Every time you say, as in this dearest letter, ever dearest, that you have been happy on such a day through being with me, I have a new astonishment—it runs through me from head to feet . . I open my eyes astonished, whenever my sun rises in the morning, as if I saw an angel in the sun. And I *do* see him, in a sense. Ah—if you make a crime to me of my *astonishments*, it is all over indeed! can I help it, indeed? So forgive me! let it not be too great a wrong to be covered by a pardon. Think that we are different, you and I—and do not think that I would send you to 'money and worldly advancement' . . do not think so meanly of my ambition for you.

Dearest dearest!—do you ever think that I could fail to you? Do you doubt for a moment, ever . . ever, . . that my hand might peradventure 'shake less' in being loosed from yours? Why, it might—and would! *Dead* hands do not shake at all,—and only *so*, could my hand be loosed from yours through a failing on my part. It is your hand, while you hold it: while you choose to hold it, and while it is a living hand.

Do you know what you are to me, . . *you?* We talk of the mild weather doing me good . . of the sun doing me good . . of going into the air as a means of good! Have you done me no good, do you fancy, in loving me and lifting me up? Has the unaccustomed divine love and tenderness been nothing to me? Think*!* Mrs. Jameson says earnestly . . said to *me* the other day . . that 'love was only magnetism.' And I say in my heart, that, magnet or no magnet, I have been drawn back into life by your means and for you . . that I see the dancing mystical lights which are seen through the eyelids . . and I think of you with an unspeakable gratitude always—always! No other could have done this for me—it was not possible, except by you.

But, no—do not, beloved, wish the first days here again. You saw your way better in them than I did. I had too bitter feelings sometimes: they looked to me like an epigram of destiny! as if 'He who sitteth on high should laugh her to scorn—should hold her in derision'—as why not? My best hope was that you should be my friend after all. We will not have them back again . . those days! And in these, you do not love me less but more? Would it be strange to thank you? I feel as if I *ought* to thank you!

I have written, written, and have more to write, yet must end here now. The letter I wrote this morning and gave to my sister to leave in the post, she was so naughty as to forget, and has been well scolded as a consequence; but the scolding did not avail, I fear, to take the letter to you to-night; there is no chance! Mrs. Jameson came to-day when I was engaged with Lady Margaret Cocks and I could not see her—and Mr. Kenyon came, when I could see him and was glad. I am tired with my multitude of visitors—oh, so tired!

Why are you melancholy, dear, dearest? Was it my fault! could *that* be? no—you were unwell, I think . . I fear. Say how you are; and believe that you may answer your own questions, for that I never can fail to you. If two persons have one will on a matter of that sort, they need not be thwarted here in London—so answer your own questions.

Wholly and ever yours I am.

R. B. to E. B. B.

Wednesday.
[Post-mark, May 6, 1846.]

Dearest Ba let me [be] silent, as on other occasions, over what you promise: one reads of 'a contest in generosity,' and how this party was as determined to give, as that party not to accept—far from anything so graceful, I am compelled to clutch at the offering, I take all, because, because—because I *must*, now! May God requite you, my best beloved!

I met Mrs. Jameson last evening and she began just as I prophesied . . 'but' said she 'I will tell you all when you come and breakfast with me on Thursday—which a note of mine now on its way to you, desires may happen!'

A large party at Chorley's, and admirable music—not without a pleasant person or two. I wish you could hear that marvellous Pischek, with his Rhine songs, and Bohemian melodies. Then a Herr Kellerman told a kind of crying story on the violoncello, full of quiet pathos, and Godefroi—if they so spell him—harped like a God harping, immortal victorious music indeed! Altogether a notable evening . . oh, the black ingratitude of man . . these few words are the poor 'set-off' to this morning's weary yawning, and stupefaction. To-night having to follow beside! So near you I shall be! Mrs. J. is to [be] at the Procters' to-night too. Oh, by the way, and in the straight way to make Ba laugh . . Mrs. J.'s *first* word was 'What? Are you *married?*' She having caught a bit of Miss Chorley's enquiry after 'Mrs. Browning's health' i.e. my mother's. Probably Miss Heaton's friend, who is my intimate, heard me profess complete infidelity as to—homœopathy . . *que sais-je?* But of all accusations in the world . . what do you say to my having been asked if I was not the Author of 'Romeo and Juliet,' and 'Othello'? A man actually asked me that, as I sate in Covent Garden Pit to see the second representation of 'Strafford'—I supposed he had been *set on* by somebody, but the simple face looked too quiet for that impertinence—I was muffled up in a cloak, too; so I said 'No—so far as I am aware.' (His question was, '*is not* THIS *Mr. Browning* the author of &c. &c.') After the play, all was made clear by somebody in Macready's dressing room—two burlesques on Shakspeare *were* in the course of performance at some minor theatre by a Mr. Brown, or Brownley, or something Brownlike—and to these my friend had alluded.

So is begot, so nourished '*il mondan rumore*'—*I*, author of 'Othello'!—when I can be, and am, and may tell Ba I am, her own, own R.

The news about the post—the walk there which might have been,—*that* is pure delight! But take care, my all-precious love—*festina lente*. All the same, what a vision I have of the *Bonnet!*

E. B. B. to R. B.

Wednesday Evening.
[Post-mark, May 7, 1846.]

Now, dearest, you are close by and I am writing to you as if you were ever so far off. People are not always the better, you see, for being near one another. There's a moral to put on with your gloves—and if you were not quite sufficiently frightened by Mrs. Jameson's salutation, it may be of some use to you perhaps—who knows?

She left word yesterday that she should come to-day or to-morrow, and as to-day she didn't, I shall hear of you from her to-morrow . . that is, if you go to her breakfast, which you will do I dare say, supposing that you are not perfectly ill and exhausted by what came before. Ah—you do not say how you are—and I know what *that* means. Even the music was half lost in the fatigue . . *that* is what you express by 'stupefaction.' And then to have to dine at Mr. Procter's without music . . say how you are . . do not omit it this time.

Nor think that I shall forget how to-morrow is the seventh of May . . your month as you call it somewhere . . in Sordello, I believe . . so that I knew before, you had a birthday there—and I shall remember it to-morrow and send you the thoughts which are yours, and pray for you that you may be saved from March-winds . . ever dearest!

I am glad you heard the music after all: it was something to hear, as you describe it.

To-day I had a book sent to me from America by the poetess Mrs. Osgood. Did you ever hear of a poetess Mrs. Osgood? . . and her note was of the very most affectionate, and her book is of the most gorgeous, all purple and gold—and she tells me . . oh, she tells me . . that I ought to go to New York, only 'to see Mr. Poe's wild eyes flash through tears' when he reads my verses. It is overcoming to think of, even . . isn't it? Talking of poetesses, such as Mrs. Osgood and me, Miss Heaton, . . the friend of your intimate friend, . . told me yesterday that the poetess proper of the city of Leeds was '*Mrs. A.*' . 'Mrs. A.?' said I with an enquiring innocence. 'Oh,' she went on, (divining sarcasms in every breath I drew) . . 'oh! I dare say, *you* wouldn't admit her to be a real poetess. But as she lives in Leeds and writes verses, we call her our poetess! and then, really, Mrs. A. is a charming woman. She was a Miss Roberts . . and her 'Spirit of the Woods,' and of the 'Flowers' has been admired, I assure you.' Well, in a moment I seemed to remember something,—because only a few months since, surely I had a letter from somebody who once was a spirit of the Woods or ghost of the Flowers. Still, I could not make out *Mrs. A.* . . ! 'Certainly' I confessed modestly, 'I never did hear of a Mrs. A. . . and yet, and yet' . . . A most glorious confusion I was in . . when suddenly my visitor thought of spelling the name . . '*Hey*' said she. Now conceive that! The Mrs. Hey who came by solution, had both written to me and sent me a book on the Lakes quite lately . . 'by the author of the Spirit of the Woods' . . *There* was the explanation! And my Leeds visitor will go back and say that I denied all knowledge of the charming Mrs. A. the Leeds poetess, and that it was with the greatest difficulty I could be brought to recognise her existence. Oh, the arrogance and ingratitude of me! And Mrs. A. . . being 'a churchwoman' . . . will expose me of course to the churchwardens! May you never fall into such ill luck! You could not expect me to walk to the post office afterwards—now could you?

What nonsense and foolishness I take it into my head to send you sometimes.

I was downstairs to-day but not out of the house. Now you are talking, now you are laughing—I think that almost I can hear you when I *listen hard* . . at Mr. Procter's!

Do *you*, on the other side, hear *me?* . . and how I am calling myself your very own

Ba

R. B. to E. B. B.

Thursday.
[Post-mark, May 7, 1846.]

No, dearest,—I get Mrs. Jameson's leave to put the breakfast off till to-morrow—and this morning, instead of resting as I had intended, I wisely went to town, to get a call on Forster off my mind—I have walked there and back again . . see the weakness you pity! I *cheat* you, my Ba, of all that pity . . yet when I have got it, however unjustly, I lay it to my heart.

And I was at Mrs. Procter's last night—Kinglake and Chorley, with a little of Milnes and Coventry Patmore—but no Howitts: because they have a sick child,—dying, I am afraid. On my return I found a note from Horne, who is in London of a sudden for a week.

Oh,—*The Daily News* passes into the redoubtable hands of Mr. Dilke,—and the price is to be reduced to 2½ᵈ, in emulation of the system recently adopted by the French Journals. Forster continues to write, on the new Editor's particular entreaty. I rather think the scheme will succeed, Dilke having the experience the present régime wants—he will buy his privileges cheaply too. So that Chorley may possibly be employed. Here ends my patronage of it, at all events—not another number do I groan over!

Patmore told me in his quiet way that his criticisms—his book on which he had been expending a world of pains, is altogether superseded by the appearance of 'Ulrici on Shakespeare'—'the very words of many of his more important paragraphs are the same.' *That* astounds one a little, does it not?

And what, *what* do you suppose Tennyson's business to have been at Dickens'—what caused all the dining and repining? He has been sponsor to Dickens' child *in company with Count D'Orsay*, and accordingly the *novus homo* glories in the prænomina, Alfred D'Orsay Tennyson Dickens! Ah, Charlie, if this don't prove to posterity that you might have been a Tennyson and were a D'Orsay—why excellent labour will have been lost! You observe, 'Alfred' is common to both the godfather and the—devilfather, as I take the Count to be: so Milnes has been goodnaturedly circulating the report that in good truth it is *the* Alfred of neither personage, but of—Mr Alfred Bunn. When you remember what the form of sponsorship is, to what it pledges you in the ritual of the Church of England——and *then* remember that Mr Dickens is an enlightened Unitarian,—you will get a curious notion of the man, I fancy.

Have you not forgotten that birthday? Do, my Ba, forget it—my day, as I told you, is the 20th—my true, happiest day! But I thank you all I can, dearest—All good to me comes through you, or for you—every wish and hope ends in you. May God bless you, ever dear Ba.—

Your own R.

E. B. B. to R. B.

May 7th, 1846.

Beloved, my thoughts go to you this morning, loving and blessing you! May God bless you for both His worlds—not for this alone. For me, if I can ever do or be anything to you, it will be my uttermost blessing of all I ever knew, or could know, as He knows. A year ago, I thought, with a sort of mournful exultation, that I was *pure of wishes*. Now, they recoil back on me in a spring-tide . . flow back, wave upon wave, . . till I should lose breath to speak them! and it is nothing, to say that they concern another . . . for they are so much the more intensely mine, and of me. May God bless you, very dear! dearest.

So I am to forget to-day, I am told in the letter. Ah! But I shall forget and remember what I please. In the meanwhile I was surprised while writing thus to you this morning . . as a good deed to begin with . . by Miss Bayley's coming. Remembering the seventh of May I forgot *Thursday*, which she had named for her visit, and altogether she took me by surprise. I thought it was Wednesday! She came—and then, Mr. Kenyon came, . . and as they both went down-stairs together, Mrs. Jameson came up. Miss Bayley is what is called *strong-minded*, and with all her feeling for art and Beauty, talks of utility like a Utilitarian of the highest, and professes to receive nothing without *proof*, like a reasoner of the lowest. She told me with a frankness for which I did not like her less, that she was a materialist of the strictest order, and believed in no soul and no future state. In the face of those conclusions, she said, she was calm and resigned. It is more than *I* could be, as I confessed. My whole nature would cry aloud against that most pitiful result of the struggle here—a wrestling only for the dust, and not for the crown. What a resistless melancholy would fall upon me if I had such thoughts!—and what a dreadful indifference. All grief, to have itself to end in!—all joy, to be based upon nothingness!—all love, to feel eternal separation under and over it! Dreary and ghastly, it would be! I should not have strength to love you, I think, if I had such a miserable creed. And for life itself, . . would it be worth holding on such terms,—with our blind Ideals making mocks and mows at us wherever we turned? A game to throw up, this life would be, as not worth playing to an end!

There's a fit letter for the seventh of May!—but why was *Thursday* the seventh, and not Wednesday rather, which would have let me escape visitors? I thank God that I can look over the grave with you, *past* the grave, . . and hope to be worthier of you *there* at least.

Mrs. Jameson did not say much, being hoarse and weak with a cold, but she told me of having met you at dinner, and found you 'very agreeable.' Also, beginning by a word about Professor Longfellow, who has married, it appears, and is a tolerably merciful husband for a poet . . ('solving the problem of the *possibility* of such a thing,' said she!) . . beginning so, she dropped into the subject of marriage generally, and was inclined to repropose Lady Mary Wortley Montagu's septennial act . . which might be a reform perhaps! . . . . what do you think? Have I not, altogether, been listening to improving and memorable discourse on this seventh of May? The *ninth's* will be more after my heart.

I like Mrs. Jameson, mind!—and I like her views on many subjects—*ex*clusive of the septennial marriage act, though.

How you amuse me by your account of the sponsorship! the illustrious D'Orsay with his *paletot* reputation, in a cleft stick of Alfred . . . Tennyson! Bunn in the distance! A curious combination it makes really . . and you read it like a vates that you are!—

So, good night—dearest!—I think of you behind all these passing clouds of subjects, my poet of the Lyre and Crown! Look down on your own Ba.

R. B. to E. B. B.

Friday.
[Post-mark, May 8, 1846.]

'*Look down on you*'—my Ba? I would die for you, with triumphant happiness, God knows, at a signal from your hand! But that,—look *down*,—never, though you bade me again and again, and in such words! I look *up*,—always up,—my Ba. When I indulge in my deepest luxury, I make you *stand* . . do you not know that? I sit, and my Ba chooses to let me sit, and stands by,—understanding all the same how the relation really *is* between us,—how I would, and do, kiss her feet,—my queen's feet!

Do you feel for me so, my love? I seldom dare to try and speak to you of *your love for me* . . my love I am allowed to profess . . I could not steadily (I have tried, whether you noticed it or no, and could not,) say aloud 'and you love *me*'! Because it is altogether a blessing of your gift,—irrespective of my love to you—however it may go to increase it. Here are the words however. Human conviction is weak enough, no doubt,—but, when I forget these words, and this answer of my heart to them,—I cannot say it—

May God bless you, dearest dearest,—my Ba! I was at Mrs. Jameson's this morning—she spoke of you so as to make my heart tremble with very delight—I never liked her so much . . I may say, never liked her before—by comparison. She read me your three translations,—clearly feeling their rare beauty; and now,—let me clap hands, my Ba, and ask you who knows best? She means to print BOTH versions—the blank verse and the *latter* rhymed one. Of course, of course! But she said so many things—I must tell you to-morrow,—if you *remind* me. She felt such gratifications, too, at your thinking her etching of St. Cecilia worthy to hang by your chair, in your sight. Do you know, Ba, at the end,—*à propos of her breakfast*, I fairly took her by both hands, and shook them with a cordiality which I just reflect, tardily, may subject the Literary Character to a possible misconstruction. 'He must have wanted a breakfast,' she will say!

I am going to the Museum on Monday with her, to see Italian prints. I like her very much. And after breakfast, Mr. Kenyon came in, and Mr. Bezzi—and Mr. K. means to make me go and see him next Monday also, I believe.

But my seeing, and hearing, and enjoying—Saturday is my day for all that? To-morrow—by this time!—too great happiness it is, I know.

And I, too, look long over the grave, to follow you, my own heart's love. Let Mrs. Jameson repeal those acts,—limit the seven years to seven days or less,—what matters? If the seven days have to be endured because of a law,—then I see the weariness of course—but in our case, if a benevolent Legislature should inform me, now, that if I choose, I may decline visiting you to-morrow—

. . Ah, nefandum,—kiss me, my own Ba, and let the world legislate and decree and relieve and be otherwise notable—so they let me be your own for ever

R.

E. B. B. to R. B.

Sunday.
[Post-mark, May 11, 1846.]

Dearest when you use such words as 'eligible . . .' (*investment* . . was it?) and I do not protest seriously and at length, it is through the very absurdity and unnaturalness . . as if you were to say that the last comet was made of macaroni, and Arago stood by, he would not think it worth while to confute you. Talking the worldly idiom, as you will tell me you just meant to do in those words, and considering the worldly considerations, why still the advantage is with you—I can do nothing that I can see, but stand in your sunshine. I solemnly assure you that only the apparent fact of your *loving me*, has overcome the scruple, which, on this ground, made me recoil from . . . Well! there is no use now in talking. But for *you* to talk of what is eligible and ineligible for *me*, is too absurd—indeed it is. You might be richer, to be sure—but *I* like it better as it is, a hundred times—I should *choose* it to be so, if it were left to my choice. In every other respect, using the world's measures, . . or the measure of the angel who measured the heavenly Jerusalem, . . you are beyond me . . above me—and nothing but your love for me could have brought us to a level. My love for you could not have *tried*, even! Now, if I teaze you with saying such things over and over, it is the right punishment for what *you* said yesterday about 'eligible marriages'—now, isn't it?

But your conclusion then was right. For if you were twice yourself, with a duchy of the moon to boot, it would avail nothing. We should have to carry all this underground work on precisely the same. Miserable it is, nevertheless—only, I keep my eyes from *that side*, as far as I can. I keep my eyes on your face. Yesterday Henrietta told me that Lady Carmichael, a cousin of ours, met her at the Royal Academy and took her aside to 'speak seriously to her' . . to observe that she looked thin and *worried*, and to urge her to act for herself . . to say too, that Mrs. Bayford, an old hereditary friend of ours, respected by us all for her serene, clear-headed views of most things,—and 'of the strictest sect,' too, for all domestic duties,—'did not like, as a mother, to give direct advice, but was of opinion that the case admitted certainly and plainly of the daughter's acting for herself.' In fact, it was a message, sent under cover of a supposed irresponsibility. Which is one of a hundred proofs to show how this case is considered exceptional among our family friends, and that no very hard judgment will be passed at the latest. Only, on other grounds, *I* shall be blamed . . and perhaps by another class of speakers. As for telling Mr. Kenyon, it is most unadvisable, both for his sake and ours. Did you never hear him talk of his organ of caution? We should involve him in ever so many fears for us, and force him to have his share of the odium at last. Papa would not speak to him again while he lived. And people might say, 'Mr Kenyon did it all.' No—if we are to be selfwilled, let us be selfwilled . . at least, let *me!* for you, of course, are free to follow your judgment in respect to your own friends. And then, it is rather a matter of feeling with me after all, that as I *cannot* give my confidence to my father, I should refuse it to others. I feel *that* a little.

Henrietta will do nothing, I think, this year—there are considerations of convenience to prevent it; and it is better for us that it should be so, and will not be worse for *her* in the end. I wish that man were a little nobler, higher . . more of a man! He is amiable, good-natured, easy-tempered, of good intentions in the main: but he eats and drinks and sleeps, and *shows* it all when he talks. Very popular in his regiment, very fond of his mother—there is good in him of course—and for the rest. . .

Dearest . . to compare others with you, would be too hard upon them. Besides, each is after his kind. Yet . . as far as love goes . . and although this man sincerely loves my sister, I do believe, . . I admit to myself, again and again, that if you were to adopt such a bearing towards *me*, as he does to her, I should break with you at once. And why? Not because I am spoilt, though you knit your brows and think so . . nor because I am exacting and offensible, though you may fancy that too. Nor because I hold loosely by you . . dearest beloved . . ready at a caprice to fall away. But because *then* I should know you did *not* love me enough to let you be happy hereafter with me . . you, who must love according to what you *are!* greatly, as you write 'Lurias'!

To-morrow, shall you be at Mr. Kenyon's? To-morrow I shall hear. Nothing has happened since I saw you. May God bless you.

Your own, I am.

R. B. to E. B. B.

Sunday.
[Post-mark, May 11, 1846.]

I am always telling you, because always feeling, that I can express nothing of what goes from my heart to you, my Ba; but there is a certain choice I have all along exercised, of subjects on which I would *try* and express somewhat—while others might be let alone with less disadvantage. When we first met, it was in your thought that I loved you only for your poetry . . I think you thought that. And because one *might* be imagined to love that and not you,—because everybody must love it, indeed, that is worthy, and yet needs not of necessity love you,—yet *might* mistake or determine to love you through loving *it* . . for all these reasons, there was not the immediate demand on me for a full expression of my admiration for your intellectuality,—do you see? Rather, it was proper to insist as little as possible on it, and speak to the woman, Ba, simply—and so I have tried to speak,—partly, in truth, because I love *her* best, and love her mind by the light and warmth of her heart—reading her verses, saying 'and these are Ba's,'—not kissing her less because they spoke the verses. But it does not follow that I have lost the sense of any delight that has its source in you, my dearest, dearest—however I may choose to live habitually with certain others in preference. I would shut myself up with you, and die to the world, and live out fifty long, long lives in bliss through your sole presence—but it is no less true that it will also be an ineffable pride,—something too sweet for the name of pride,—to avow myself, before anyone whose good opinion I am soliciting to retain, as *so* distinguished by you—it is *too* sweet, indeed,—so I guard against it,—for frequent allusion to it, might,—(as I stammer, and make plain things unintelligible) . . might cause you to misconceive me, which would be dreadful . . for after all, Ba's head has given the crown its worth,—though a wondrous crown it is, too! All this means . . the avowal we were speaking of, will be a heart's pride above every other pride whenever you decide on making such an avowal. You will understand as you do ever your own R.

On getting home I found letters and letters—the best being a summons to meet Tennyson at Moxon's on Tuesday,—and the frightfullest . . nay, I will send it. Now, Ba, hold my hand from the distant room, tighter than ever, at about 8 o'clock on Wednesday . . for I must go, I fear—'Unaccustomed as I am to public speaking' &c. &c. 'ἔα, ἔα, ἄπεχε, φεῦ.' Then Mr. Kenyon writes that his friend Commodore Jones is returned to England in bad health and that he must away to Portsmouth and see him —so I do not go on Monday. While I was away Chorley's brother (John Chorley) called,—having been put to the trouble of a journey hither for nothing.

I have been out this morning—to church with my sister —and the sun shone almost oppressively,—but now all is black and threatening. How I send my heart after your possible movements, my own all-beloved! Care for yourself, and for me. But a few months more,—if God shall please. May He bless you—

Ever your own

Hail and rain—at a quarter to four o'clock!

R. B. to E. B. B.

Monday 4 o'clock.
[Post-mark, May 11, 1846.]

Sweetest, I have this moment come from Town and Mrs. Jameson—the Marc-Antonio Prints kept us all the morning—and at last I said 'there is a letter for me at home which I *must* go and answer.' And now I cannot answer it—but I can love you and say so. God bless you, ever dearest. I have read your letter . . but only once. Now I shall begin my proper number of times—

Ever your very own

E. B. B. to R. B.

Monday.
[Post-mark, May 12, 1846.]

It is too bad, or too good, or something. Almost I could reproach you, and quite would thank you! . yet do not let it be so again. You are supernaturally kind . . kindestest, bestestest . . . and, so, dearestest by the merest justice; only, to think of your hastening home, as if you were under an obligation to write to me in the face of the seven worlds, . . *that* is too much, and shall not be again—now see that it shall not. I seem to hear the rattling of the chain all this distance. And do, for the future, let it be otherwise. When you are kept in London, or in any way hindered, or unwell, . . in any case of the sort, let the vow be kept by *one line*, which, too late for the day's post, may reach me the next day,—and I shall not be uneasy at eight o'clock, but wait 'as those who wait for the morning.' In the meanwhile how I thank you! The second dear letter comes close in the footsteps of the first, as your goodnesses are so apt to do.

Well!—and whatever you may think about Wednesday, *I* am pleased, and feel every inclination to 'return thanks' myself in reply to the bishop of Lincoln. I send the letter back lest you should want it. The worst is that you are likely to have a very bad headache with the noise and confusion—and the bishop's blessing on the dramatists of England, will not prevent it, I fear.

Look what is inside of this letter—look! I gathered it for you to-day when I was walking in the Regent's Park. Are you surprised? Arabel and Flush and I were in the carriage—and the sun was shining with that green light through the trees, as if he carried down with him the very essence of the leaves, to the ground, . . and I wished so much to walk through a half open gate along a shaded path, that we stopped the carriage and got out and walked, and I put both my feet on the grass, . . which was the strangest feeling! . . and gathered this laburnum for you. It hung quite high up on the tree, the little blossom did, and Arabel said that certainly I could not reach it—but you see! It is a too generous return for all your flowers: or, to speak seriously, a proof that I thought of you and wished for you—which it was natural to do, for I never enjoyed any of my excursions as I did to-day's—the standing under the trees and on the grass, was so delightful. It was like a bit of that Dreamland which is your especial dominion,—and I felt joyful enough for the moment, to look round for you, as for the cause. It seemed *illogical*, not to see you close by. And you were not far after all, if thoughts count as bringers near. Dearest, we shall walk together under the trees some day!

And all those strange people moving about like phantoms of life. How wonderful it looked to me!—and only you, . . the idea of you . . and myself seemed to be real there! And Flush a little, too!—

Ah—what . . *next* to nonsense, . . in the first letter, this morning! So you think that I meant to complain when we first met, of your '*loving me only for my poetry*'! Which I did not, simply because I did not believe that *you loved me!—for any reason.* For the rest, I am not over-particular, I fancy, about what I may be loved for. There is no good reason for loving me, certainly, and my earnest desire (as I have said again and again) is, that there should be by profession no reason at all. But if there is to be any sort of reason, why one is as welcome as another . . you may love me for my shoes, if you like it . . except that they wear out. I thought you did not love me at all—you loved out into the air, I thought—a love *a priori*, as the philosophers might say, and not *by induction*, any wise! Your only knowledge of me was by the poems (or most of it)—and what knowledge could *that* be, when I feel myself so far below my own aspirations, morally, spiritually? So I thought you did not love me at all—I did not believe in miracles *then*, nor in 'Divine Legations'—but *my* miracle is as good as Constantine's, you may tell your bishop on Wednesday when he has delivered his charge.

Is it *eight* o'clock, or *three?* You write a [figure] which looks like both, or at least either.

Love me, my only beloved; since you *can*. May God bless you!

I am ever and wholly your

Say how you are. Ba.

R. B. to E. B. B.

Tuesday.
[Post-mark, May 12, 1846.]

My Ba, your flower is the one flower I have seen, or see, or shall see—when it fades 'I will bless it till it shine,' and when I can bless you no longer it shall fade with me and my letters and . . perhaps . . my ring. Ba, if . . I was going to say, *if* you meant to make me most exquisitely happy . . and you *did* surely mean it . . well, you succeed, as you know! And I see you on the grass, and am with you as you properly acknowledge. And by this letter's presence and testimony, I may judge you to be not much the worse,—not fatigued . . is it so? Oh, it was a good inspiration that led you through the half-opened gate and under the laburnum, and, better still, that made you see us 'one day walking by the trees together' —when all I shall say is,—I hope, in spite of that felicity to remember and feel *this*, as vividly as now.

'For the chain you hear rattle' . . *there* comes the earthly mood again and the inspiration goes away altogether! So you being Miss Barrett and not my Ba for the moment, I will give you none of my, and Ba's, syren-island illustrations, but ask you, what a fine lady would say if you caught at her diamond necklace and cried— 'You shall wear no such chains,—indeed you shall not!' Why even Flush is proud of his corals and blue beads, you tell me! As for me,—being used to bear sundry heavier chains than this of writing to you—owning the degradation of being, for instance, forced to respire so many times a minute in order to live—to go out into the open air so as to continue well—with many similarly affronting impositions on a free spirit . . on the whole, I can very patiently submit to write a letter which is duly read, and forgiven for its imperfections, and interpreted into a rationality (sometimes) not its own, and then answered by the sweetest hand that ever ministered to the dearest, dearest Ba that ever was imagined, or can be! Ba,—there are three Syren's Isles, you know: I shall infallibly get into the farthest of them, a full thirty yards from you and the tower,—so as to need being written to —— for the *cicale* make such a noise that you will not be able to call to me—which is as well, for you may . . that is, *I* might—break my neck by a sudden leap on the needles of rocks . . as I remember the boatman told me.

As for what you wish yesterday . . the *mode* of my expressing my love . . I never think of it,—I *have* none—no system, nor attempt at such a thing—I begin and end by saying *I love you—whatever comes of it.* There is one obvious remark to make however . . that unless I *had* loved you and felt that every instant of my life depended on you for its support and comfort,—I should never have dreamed of what has been proposed and accepted . . Your own goodness at the very beginning would have rendered that superfluous; for I was put in possession of your friendship,—might write to you, and receive letters—might even hope to see you as often as anybody—would not this have sufficed a reasonable friendship? May not Mr. Kenyon be your satisfied friend? . But all was different—and so——

So I am blessed now—and can only bless you. But goodbye, dearest, till to-morrow—and next day, which is ours. At 8—eight I conjecture my martyrdom may take place . . oh, think of me and help me! I shall feel you, —as ever. You forgot the letter after all . . can you send it? It may be convenient to produce, as I know nobody of them all—terrible it is altogether! 'At six' the dinner begins——I shall get behind my brother Dramatists . . and say very little about them, even.

Kiss me, in any case, of failure, or success,—and the one will be forgotten, and the other doubled, centupled—to your own—

E. B. B. to R. B.

Tuesday.
[Post-mark, May 13, 1846.]

When you began to speak of the islands, the three islands, I thought you were going to propose that you should live in one, and Flush in one, and I in the third: and almost it was so, . . only that you took, besides, the '*farthest*' for yourself! Observe!—always I write nonsense, when you send me a letter which moves me like this, . . dearest, . . my own!

To-day Mrs. Jameson has been here, and having left with me a proof about Titian, she comes again to-morrow to take it. I think her quite a lovable person now—I like her more and more. How she talked of you to-day, and called you the most charming companion in the world, setting you too on your right throne as 'poet of the age.' Wouldn't it have been an '*effect*' in the midst of all, if I had burst out crying? And what with being flurried, frightened, and a little nervous from not sleeping well last night, I assure you it was quite possible—but happily, on every account, I escaped that 'dramatic situation.' I wish . . no, I can't wish that she wouldn't talk of you as she does whenever she comes here. And then, to make it better, she told me how you had recited 'in a voice and manner as good as singing,' my 'Catarina.' How are such things to be borne, do you think, when people are not made of marble? But I took a long breath, and held my mask on with both hands.

You will tell me of the Marc Antonio prints,—will you not? Remember them on Thursday. Raffael's—are they not? I shall expect ever so much teaching, and showing, and explaining . . I, who have seen and heard nothing of pictures and music, from you who know everything . . so the cicale must not be too loud for *that*. Did ever anyone say to you that you were like Raffael's portrait—not in the eyes, which are quite different, but in the lower part of the face, the mouth, and also the brow? It has struck me sometimes—and I had it on my lips to-day as a question to Mrs. Jameson. I think I was mad to-day altogether. But she did not see it—(I mean my madness . . not your likeness!) [and] went away unconsciously.

Here, at last, is the letter! Careless that I was yesterday!—

And you take me to be too generous if you fancy that I proposed giving up the daily letter which is my daily bread. I meant only that you should not, for the sake of a particular post, tire yourself, hurry yourself, . . do what you did yesterday. As for the daily letter, I am Ba—not Miss Barrett. Now, am I Miss Barrett? am I not Ba rather, and your Ba? I should like to hear what will be heard to-morrow. Oh—I should like to be under the table, or in a pasty, after the fashion of the queen's dwarf when Elizabeth was queen and Shakespeare poet. Shall you be nervous, as *I* was with Mrs. Jameson? Oh no,—why should you be nervous? You will do it all well and gracefully—I am not afraid for you. It is simply out of vain-glory that I wish to be there! Only . . the dramatists of England . . where in the world are they just now? Or will somebody prove *ten* of them,—because *nought* after *one*, makes exactly ten? Mr. Horne indeed. But I wish the toast had been 'the poets of England,' rather. May God bless you, any way! '*I love you whatever comes of it.*' Yes, unless sorrow of yours should come of it, *that* is what I like to hear. Better it is, than a thousand praises of this thing and that thing, which never were mine . . alas!

—Also, loving me *so*, you can be made happy with laburnum-leaves!—Dearest—most dear! Dare I speak, do you think?

Exactly at eight to-morrow, and exactly at three the next day, I shall be with you—being at any hour

Your very own.

The walk did me no harm. But you say nothing of yourself!

R. B. to E. B. B.

Wednesday.
[Post-mark, May 13, 1846.]

Dearest, dearest, I shall be with you to-morrow and be comforted—and will tell you all about everything. I am a little tired (but *very* well, altogether well, singularly so)—and I *do* feel a little about to-night's affair, though you may not. *You*, indeed, to judge me by yourself! But, after all I do not greatly care . . I can but get up and stammer and say 'thank you' and sit down again, like my betters,—and—as I say and say,—*you* are at the end of everything . . so long as I find *you!* I hoped that Tennyson was to have been Poet-respondent—but Moxon says 'no' . . and, moreover, that the Committee had meant (and he supposed had acted upon their meaning) to offer me the choice of taking either qualification, of Poetry or the Drama, as mine . . but they have altered their mind. As it *is* . . observe—(you will find a list of Stewards in last *Athenæum*)—observe that they are all Bishops or Deans or Doctors . . and that all will be grave and heavy enough, I dare say. So I shall try and speak for about five minutes on the advantages of the Press over the Stage as a medium of communication of the Drama . . and so get done, if Heaven please!

I saw Tennyson last night—and . . oh, let me tell you to-morrow. Also, Severn, I saw . . Keats' Severn, who bought his own posthumous picture of Keats, and talked pleasantly about him and Shelley (Tennyson asked me 'what I thought of Shelley'—in so many words). Moxon's care of him,—Tennyson, not Severn,—is the charmingest thing imaginable, and he seems to need it all—being in truth but a LONG, hazy kind of a man, at least just after dinner . . yet there is something 'naif' about him, too,—the genius you see, too.

May God bless you, my dearest dearest,—to-morrow repays for all—

Your own R.

E. B. B. to R. B.

Friday.
[Post-mark, May 15, 1846.]

The treader on your footsteps was Miss Bayley, who left a card and 'would come another day.' She must have seen you . . . One of these days, 'scirocco' will be 'loose'—we may as well be prepared for it. To keep it off as long as possible is all that can be. But when it comes it will not uproot my palm-trees, I think, though it should throw flat the olives.

Papa brought me some flowers yesterday when he came home . . and they went a little to my heart as I took them. I put them into glasses near yours, and they look faded this morning nevertheless, while your roses, for all your cruelty to them, are luxuriant in beauty as if they had just finished steeping themselves in garden-dew. I look gravely from one set of flowers to the other—I cannot draw a glad omen—I wish he had not given me these. Dearest, there seems little kindness in teazing you with such thoughts . . but they come and I write them: and let them come ever so sadly, I do not for a moment doubt . . hesitate. One may falter, where one does not fail. And for the rest, . . it is my fault, and not my sorrow rather, that we act so? It is by choice that we act so? If he had let me I should have loved him out of a heart altogether open to him. It is not my fault that he would not let me. Now it is too late—I am not his nor my own, any more.

This morning I have had American letters of the kindest . . from Massachusetts—and a review on my poems, quite extravagant indeed, in the *Methodist Quarterly*. One of these letters is so like another, that I need only tell you of them . . written too by people . . Lydias and Richards . . never heard of before by either of us. The review repeats the fabulous story in the 'Spirit of the Age,' about unknown tongues and a seven years eclipse in total darkness—but I say to myself . . . after all, the real myth is scarcely less wonderful. If I have not all this knowledge . . . I have *you* . . . which is greater, better! 'Not less wonderful' did I say? when it is the miracle . . . . .

Oh, these people!—I am seized and bound. More to-night! from

Your own
Ba.

Say how you are.

R. B. to E. B. B.

Friday.
[Post-mark, May 15, 1846.]

The sun is warm, and the day, I suppose, is fine,—but my Ba will have been kept at home by the vile wind—most vile—even I feel it! So the spring passes away without the true spring feeling—all the blossoms are fast going already—and one's spirits are affected, I dare say. Did you not think me intolerable yesterday with my yawning and other signs of fatigue you noticed? Well now—I *do* think a little is *said* by all that: might one not *like* or even *love* . . just short of *true* love, so long as the spirits were buoyant and the mind cheerful,—and when the contrary befell, some change might appear, surely!

The more I need you the more I love you, Ba—and I need you *always*—in joy, to make the joy seem what it is —and in any melancholy that I can imagine, *more* still, infinitely more, I need you—though *melancholy*, I certainly was not—only tired a little . . all I mean to say is, that at times when I could, I think, shut up Shelley, and turn aside from Beethoven, and look away from my noble Polidoro,—my Ba's ring—not to say the hand—ah, you know, Ba, what they are to me!

I have to go out to-day, to my sorrow—to the Garrick Club, and a friend there. (My sister tells me we have to go to the Flower-show next Wednesday unless the day be rainy. I shall hear from Mr. Kenyon, I expect.)

Let me end the chapter we began yesterday, about speech-making and adepts in it of various kinds, by telling you what my father made me laugh by an account of, the other day . . only it should be really *told*, and not written. He had a curiosity to know how would-be Parliamentary members *canvassed* . . and as the Chamberlain of the City, Sir James Shaw, came into the Bank for that purpose (there being Livery men there, or whatever they are called, with votes) my father followed to hear how he would address people. Sir James, a gigantic man, went about as his friends directed . . or rather pushed and shoved him . . and whenever they reached an Elector the whole cortège stopped, Sir James made his speech, the friends, book and pencil in hand, recorded the promise the moment it was made, and forthwith wheeled round their candidate to the next man . . no word of speechification being to be wasted once its object accomplished, since time pressed —so now fancy. *Friends* (to Sir J) 'Mr Snooks, Sir James!' Sir J. (*with his eyes shut, and head two feet above Snooks*) 'When Charles Fox came into Parliament, he came into Parliament with a profusion of promises, of which I'll defy Charles Fox's best friends to say that he ever kept a single one'—(Friends twitch him)—'Thankee Sir'— 'Mr Smith.' 'When Charles Fox came into Paliament . . thankee, Sir'—'Mr Thompson'—'When Charles Fox . . thankee!' &c &c And so on from man to man, never getting beyond this instructive piece of anecdotical history

—till at the very last a little Elector, reaching to the great man's elbow, let him go to the full length of the sentence's tether from admiration of such an orator . . did not say briefly 'yes' or 'no' as the others had done. So Sir James arrived duly at . . 'kept a single one. Thus—if . . as it were . . eh? oh!' Here he opened his eyes with a start, missing the pushing and driving from his friends in the rear—and finding it was only this little man; he abruptly stopped . . was not going to spend more eloquence on *him!* There, Ba; *you tell* me you write nonsense . . *I do* the thing, the precise thing! But no more nonsense because I am going to kiss you, which is wise, and love you with my whole heart and soul forever, which is wiser, and pray you to love me, dear, dear Ba, which is the wisest! Sweetest, may God bless you,—

Your very own.

E. B. B. to R. B.

Friday Evening.
[Post-mark, May 16, 1846.]

Not even do you yawn in vain then, O you! And this, then, is what Cicero called 'oscitans sapientia?' The *argument of the yawn* ought in fact, to be conclusive.!

But, dearest, if it was 'intolerable' to see you yawn yesterday, still less supportable was it to-day when I had all the yawning to myself, and proved nothing by it. Tired I am beyond your conceiving of . . tired! You saw how I broke off in my letter to you this morning. Well—that was Miss Heaton, who came yesterday and left the packet you saw, and came again to-day and sate here exactly three hours. Now imagine that! Three hours of incessant restless talking. At the end I was *blanched*, as everybody could see, and Mrs. Jameson who came afterwards for five minutes and was too unwell herself to stay, seriously exhorted me not to exert myself too much lest I should pay the penalty. And I had not been down-stairs even—only been ground down in the talking-mill. Arabel told her too, before she came up-stairs, that I was expecting a friend—'Oh' . . said she to me, 'I shall go away directly anyone comes.' And again presently . . 'Pray tell me when I ought to go away'! (As if I could say *Go.* She deserved it, but I *couldn't!*) And then . . 'How good of you to let me sit here and talk!' So good of me, when I was wishing her . . only at Leeds in the High Street, between a dissenter and a churchman—anywhere but opposite to my eyes! Yet *she* has very bright ones, and cheeks redder than your roses; and she is kind and cordial . . . as I thought in the anguish of my soul, when I tried to be grateful to her. Certainly I should have been more so, if she had stayed a little less, talked a little less—it is awful to think how some women can talk! Happily she leaves London to-morrow morning, and will not be here again till next year, if then. She talked biography too . . . ah, I did not mean to tell you—but it is better to tell you at once and have done . . only she desired me not to mention it . . only she little knew what she was doing! *You* will not mention it. She told me that 'her informant about Mr. Browning, . . was a lady *to whom he had been engaged* . . that there had been a very strong attachment on both sides, but that everything was broken off by *her* on the ground of religious differences—that it happened years ago and that the lady was married.' At first I exclaimed imprudently enough (but how could it be otherwise?) that it was not true—but I caught at the bridle in a minute or two and let her have it her own way. Do not answer this—it is nonsense, I know—but it helped to tire me with the rest. Wasn't it a delightful day for me? At the end of the three hours, she threw her arms round me and kissed me some half dozen times and wished me 'goodbye' till next year. Wilson found me standing in the middle of the room, looking as she said, 'like a ghost.' And no wonder! The 'vile wind' out of doors was nothing to it.

Dearest, you are well? Your letter says nothing. Only one more letter, and then Monday. Ah—it is the sweetest of flattery to say that you 'need' me—but isn't it difficult to understand? Yet while you even fancy that you have such a need, you may be sure (let Charles Fox break his promises ever so!) of your own

Ba.

R. B. to E. B. B.

Saturday.
[Post-mark, May 16, 1846.]

Then, dearest-dearest, *do* take Mrs. Jameson's advice —*do* take care of the results of this fatigue—why should you see any woman that pleases to ask to come? I am certain that some of the men you have refused to admit, would be more considerate—and Miss Heaton must be a kind of fool into the bargain with her inconsiderateness . . though *that* is the folly's very self. As for her 'Yorkshire Tragedy,' I hold myself rather aggrieved by it—they used to get up better stories of Lord Byron,—and even *I told* you, anticipatingly, that I caused that first wife of mine to drown and hang herself . . whereas, now, it turns out she did neither, but bade me do both . . nay, was not my wife after all! I hope she told Miss Heaton the story in the presence of the husband who had no irreligious scruples. But enough of this pure nonsense—I had, by this post that brings me your last letter, one from Horne —he leaves to-day for Ireland, and says kind things about my plays—and unkind things of Mr. Powell 'a dog he repudiates for ever.' So our 'clique' is deprived of yet another member!

For me, love,—I am pretty well—but *rather* out of spirits,—for no earthly cause. I shall take a walk and get better presently—your dear letters have their due effect, al that effect!

So, dear,—all my world, my life, all I look to or live

for, my own Ba—I will bless you and bid you goodbye for to-day—to-morrow I will write more—and on Monday—return, my Ba, this kiss . . my dearest above all dearness!

E. B. B. to R. B.

Saturday Morning.
[Post-mark, May 16, 1846.]

You shall hear from me on this Sunday, though it cannot be as an answer, dearest, to your letter of to-night. But I being so wretchedly tired last night, and 'yawning' being, to your mind, so 'intolerable,' it is as well to leave a better impression with you than *that* . . though there is nothing to say, and the east wind blows on virulently.

The *Athenæum* has put me out of humour for the day . . besides. Not a word of 'Luria'—not a word of the Literary Fund dinner, and a great, drawling carrying out of the 'Poetry for the Million' article . . as if all this trash could not die of itself!—as if it were not *dead* of itself!—That the critics of a country should set themselves to such work . . is as if the Premier of England took his official seat in the window to kill flies, . . talking, with his first finger out, of 'my administration.' Only flies are flies and have fly-life in them: they are nobler game than those.

Mrs. Jameson, while she was here the five minutes yesterday, talked, in an under-breath to my under-breath opposition, her opinion about the present age. 'That the present age did not, could not, ought not, to express itself by Art, . . though the next age would.' She is surprisingly wrong, it appears to me. There is no predominant character in the age, she says, to be so expressed! there is no unity, to bear expression.

But art surely, if art is anything, is the expression, not of the characteristics of an age except accidentally, . . essentially it is the expression of Humanity in the individual being—and unless we are men no longer, I cannot conceive how such an argument as hers can be upheld for a moment. Also it is exasperating to hear such things.

Then I do not believe, for one, that genius in the arts is a mere reflection of the character of the times. Genius precedes surely,—initiates. It is genius which gives an Age its character and imposes its own colour . . . . But I shall not write any more. Her paper on 'Titian's House at Venice,' which she let me read in proof, and which is one of the essays she is printing now, is full of beauty and truth, and I admired it heartily. Then there is a quotation about the 'calm, cold, beautiful regard,' of 'Virgin child and saint' . . . which you may remember perhaps. I know you will like the essay and feel it to be Venetian.

That you were feeling the east wind, beloved, meant that you were not well, though you have quite left off telling me a word of yourself lately. And why? It shall not be so next week,—now shall it? May God bless you. I am afraid of going down-stairs, because of the double-knocks. It will be great gain to have the loudest noises from the cicale. Except when somebody else is noisy,—which is a noise I am always forgetting, just as if it were impossible.

Your own

Ba.

R. B. to E. B. B.

Sunday.
(Day before to-morrow!)
[Post-mark, May 18, 1846.]

How kind to write to me and help me through the gloomy day with a light! I could certainly feel my way in the dark and reach to-morrow without very important stumbling, but now I go cheerfully on, spite of a little headache and weariness. Need you? I should hate life apart from you. Knowing what I say, I should hate it—the life of my soul as seen apart from that of the mere body . . to which, to the necessities of which, no human being ever ministered before, and which, now that I have known you, I myself cannot provide for,—or could not were you removed,—even after the imperfect fashion of former times. If you ask Mrs Jameson she will tell you, if she has thought it worth remembering, that I once, two or three years ago, *explained* to her that I could not believe in 'love' nor understand it,—nor be subject to it consequently. I said—'all you describe as characteristics of the passion—I should expect to find in *men* more easily and completely—' now I know better, and my year's life spent in this knowledge makes all before it look pale and all *after*, if an after could come, look black.

Why do I write so? I am rather dull, this horrible day, and cling to you the closelier.

All you write about Art is most true. Carlyle has turned and forged, reforged on his anvil that fact 'that no age ever appeared heroic to itself' . . and so, worthy of reproduction in Art by itself . . I thought after Carlyle's endeavours nobody could be ignorant of that,—nobody who was obliged to seek the proof of it out of his own experience. The cant is, that 'an age of transition' is the melancholy thing to contemplate and delineate—whereas the worst things of all to look back on are times of comparative standing still, rounded in their important completeness. So the young England imbeciles hold that 'belief' is the admirable point—*in what*, they judge comparatively immaterial! The other day I took up a book two centuries old in which 'glory', 'soldiering', 'rushing to conquer' and the rest, were most thoroughly 'believed in'—and if by some miracle the writer had conceived and described some unbeliever, unable to 'rush to conquer the Parthians' &c, it would have been as though you found a green bough inside a truss of straw.

But you know—

And I know one thing, one—but one—I love you, *shall* love you ever, living and dying your own—

E. B. B. to R. B.

Tuesday Morning.
[Post-mark, May 19, 1846.]

My own ever dearest, when I try to thank you for such a letter as yesterday's, . . for any proof, in fact, of your affection, . . I cannot speak: but you know, of this and all things, that I understand, feel—you must know it very well. There is only one thing I can do as I ought, and it is to love you; and the more I live, not '*the less*' but the *more* I am able to love you—believe it of me. And for *the less*, . . we never will return to that foolish subject, . . but for the 'less' you spoke of when you said 'you do not love me less?' . . . why I thought at the moment and feeel now, that it would be too late, as I am, ever, upon any possible ground, to love you less. If you loved *me* less . . even!—or (to leave that) if you were to come to me and say that you had murdered a man—why I may imagine such things, you know—but I cannot imagine the possibility of my loving you less, as a consequence of your failing so! I am yours in the deepest of my affections:—not unreasonably, certainly, as I see you and know you—but if it *were* to turn unreasonable . . I mean, if you took away the appearance of reasonableness . . still I should be yours in the deepest of my affections . . it is too late for a difference *there*.

Mrs. Jameson has just now sent me a proof with the 'Daughters of Pandarus,' which she is to call for presently, and therefore I must come to an end with this note. How I shall think of you to-morrow! And if it should be fine, I may perhaps drive in the park near the gardens . . take my sisters to the gate of the gardens, and feel that you are inside! That will be something, if it is feasible. And if it is fine or not, and if I go or not, I shall remember our first day, the only day of my life which God blessed visibly to me, the only day undimmed with a cloud . . my great compensation-day, which it was worth while being born for!

Your very own
Ba.

Oh—you will *not see me* to-morrow, remember! I tell you only out of cunning . . to win a thought!

R. B. to E. B. B.

Tuesday.
[Post-mark, May 19, 1846.]

With this day expires the first year since you have been yourself to me—putting aside the anticipations, and prognostications, and even assurances from all reasons short of absolute sight and hearing,—excluding the five or six months of these, there remains a year of this intimacy. You accuse me of talking extravagantly sometimes. I will be quiet here,—is the tone *too* subdued if I say, such a life—made-up of such years—I would deliberately take rather than any other imaginable one in which fame and worldly prosperity and the love of the whole human race should combine, excluding 'that of yours—to which I hearken'—only wishing the rest were there for a moment that you might see and know that I did turn from them to you. My dearest, inexpressibly dearest. How can I thank you? I feel sure you *need* not have been so kind to me, so perfectly kind and good,—I should have remained your own, gratefully, entirely your own, through the bare permission to love you, or even without it—seeing that I never dreamed of stipulating at the beginning for 'a return,' and 'reward,'—but I also believe, joyfully, that no course but the course you have taken would have raised me above my very self, as I feel on looking back. I began by loving you in comparison with all the world,—now, I love you, my Ba, in the face of your past self, as I remember it.

All words are foolish—but I kiss your feet and offer you my heart and soul, dearest, dearest Ba.

I left you last evening without the usual privilege—you did not rise, Ba! But,—I don't know why,—I got nervous of a sudden, it seemed late and I remembered the Drawing-room and its occupants.

E. B. B. to R. B.

Tuesday Evening.
[Post-mark, May 20, 1846.]

Do you remember how, when poor Abou Hassan, in the Arabian story, awakens from sleep in the Sultan's chamber, to the sound of instruments of music, he is presently complimented by the grand vizier on the royal wisdom displayed throughout his reign . . do you remember? Because just as he listened, do *I* listen, when you talk to me about 'the course I have taken' . . . *I*, who have just had the wit to sit still in my chair with my eyes half shut, and dream . . dream!—Ah, whether I am asleep or awake, what do I know . . even now? As to the 'course I have taken,' it has been somewhere among the stars . . or under the trees of the Hesperides, at lowest. . .

Why how can I write to you such foolishness? Rather I should be serious, grave, and keep away from myths and images, and speak the truth plainly. And speaking the truth plainly, I, when I look back, dearest beloved, see that you have done for me everything, instead of my doing anything for you—that you have lifted me . . . Can I speak? Heavens!—how I had different thoughts of you and of myself and of the world and of life, last year at this hour! The spirits who look backward over the grave, cannot feel much otherwise from my feeling as I look back. As to *your* thanking *me*, *that* is monstrous, it seems to me. It is the action of your own heart alone, which has appeared to do you any good. For myself, if I do not spoil your life, it is the nearest to deserving thanks that I can come. Think what I was when you saw me first . . laid there on the sofa as an object of the merest compassion!

and of a sadder spirit than even the face showed! and then think of all your generosity and persistence in goodness. Think of it!—shall I ever cease? Not while the heart beats, which beats for you.

And now as the year has rounded itself to 'the perfect round,' I will speak of that first letter, about which so many words were, . . just to say, this time, that I am glad now, yes, glad, . . as we were to have a miracle, . . to have it *so*, a born-miracle from the beginning. I feel glad, now, that nothing was *between* the knowing and the loving . . and that the beloved eyes were never cold discerners and analyzers of me at any time. I am glad and grateful to you, my own altogether dearest! Yet the letter was read in pain and agitation, and you have scarcely guessed how much. I could not sleep night after night,—could not,—and my fear was at nights, lest the feverishness should make me talk deliriously and tell the secret aloud. Judge if the deeps of my heart were not shaken. From the first you had that power over me, notwithstanding those convictions which I also had and which you know.

For it was not the character of the letter apart from you, which shook me,—I could prove that to you—I received and answered very calmly, with most absolute calmness, a letter of the kind last summer . . knowing in respect to the writer of it, (just as I thought of *you*), that a moment's enthusiasm had carried him a good way past his discretion. I am sure that he was perfectly satisfied with my way of answering his letter . . as I was myself. But *you* . . *you* . . I could not escape so from *you*. You were stronger than I, from the beginning, and I felt the mastery in you by the first word and first look.

Dearest and most generous. No man was ever like you, I know! May God keep me from laying a blot on one day of yours!—on one hour! and rather blot out mine!

For my life, it is yours, as this year has been yours. But how can it make you happy, such a thing as my life?

There, I wonder still. It never made *me* happy, without you!—

Your very own
Ba.

Mrs. Jameson was here to-day and brought a message from Mr. Kenyon, who comes to-morrow *at one*. The sun does not promise to come besides—does he?

Mrs. Jameson goes to Brighton on Thursday, and returns in a day or two to spend another month or six weeks in town, changing her lodgings.

R. B. to E. B. B.

Wednesday.
[Post-mark, May 20, 1846.]

My Ba, I can just kneel down to you and be kissed,—I cannot do more, nor speak, nor thank you—and I seem to have no more chance of getting new love to give you,—all is given,—so I have said before, and must keep saying now—all of me is your very own.

My sister (whose engagement, and not mine, this was) decides to act according to the letter of Mr. Kenyon's kind instructions, and keeps at home on account of the rain. She is very subject to colds and sore-throat which the least dampness underfoot is sure to produce in her. So I am not near you! You would not go, however,—I think, would not go,—to the Park gate as you conditionally promised—I do not, therefore, miss *my* flower-show, my 'rose tree that bareth seven times seven.' But the other chance which your last letter apprises me of,—the visit of Mr. Kenyon,—which, by going in time to him, I might perhaps make my own too—*that*, on a second thought, I determine to forego . . because it jeopardizes my Saturday, which will be worth so many, many such visits,—does it not? There is no precedent in our golden year for three visits taking place in a single week—not even in that end of October when all the doubt was about the voyage—how I remember!

I shall be more with you than if in the presence of people before whom I may not say 'Miss Barrett' with impunity while professing to talk of Miss—I forget who! But '*more* with you' I who am always with you!

Always with you in the spirit, always yearning to be with you in the body,—always, when with you, praying, as for the happiest of fortunes, that I may remain with you for ever. So may it be, prays your

own, own R.

E. B. B. to R. B.

Wednesday, May 20.

Was it very wrong of me that never did I once think of the possibility of your coming here with Mr. Kenyon? Never once had I the thought of it. If I had, I should have put it away by saying aloud 'Don't come;' because as you say, it would have prevented Saturday's coming, the coming to-day would, . . and also, as you do not say, it would have been infinitely hard for me to meet you and Mr. Kenyon in one battalion. Oh no, no! The gods forefend that you should come in that way! It was bad enough as it was, to-day, when, while he sate here his ten minutes, (first showing me a sonnet from America, which began 'Daughter of Græcian Genius!') he turned those horrible spectacles full on me and asked, 'Does Mrs. Jameson know that Mr. Browning comes here?' 'No,' said I,—suddenly abashed, though I had borne the sonnet like a hero. 'Well, then! I advise you to give directions to the servants that when she or anyone else asks for you, they should not say *Mr. Browning is with you,*—as they said the other day to Miss Bayley who told me of it.' Now, wasn't *that* pleasant to hear? I thanked him for his advice, and felt as uncomfortable as was well possible—and am, at this moment, a little in doubt how he was thinking while he spoke.

Perhaps after the fashion of my sisters, when they cry out 'Such a state of things never was heard of before!' Not that they have uttered one word of opposition . . not, from the first they knew, . . understand!—but that they are frightened at what may be said by people who take for granted that we are strangers, you and I, to one another. Ah!—a little more, a little less . . of what consequence is it?

Such a day, to-day!—it was finer last year I remember! and Tuesday, instead of Wednesday! Your sister was right, very right—though mine went—but the distance was less, with us. A party of *twelve* went from this house—'among us but not of us.' For my part, I have not stirred from my room of course—the carriage was out of the question. And, if you please, I never '*promised*' to be at the park gate—oh indeed, I never meditated seeing you even from afar—I thought only that I should hear a little distant music and remember that, where it sounded, you were, *that* was all, . . and too much, the stars made out, and so drove down the clouds.

Poor Mr. Kenyon was grave—depressed about his friend, who is in a desperate state—dying in fact. He returns to Portsmouth to-morrow to be with him till the change comes.

Dearest, how are you? Never now will you condescend to say how you are. Which is not to be allowed in this second year of our reign. I am very well. Yesterday I heard some delightful matrimonial details of an 'establishment' in Regent's Park, quite like an old pastoral in the quickness of the repartee. 'I hate you'— 'I abhor you'—'I never liked you'—'I always detested you.' A cup and saucer thrown bodily, here, by the lady! On which the gentleman upsets her, . . chair and all, . . flat on the floor. The witness, who is a friend of mine, gets frightened and begins to cry. She was invited to the house to be godmother to their child, and now she is pressed to stay longer to witness the articles of separation.

Oh, I suppose such things are common enough!—But what is remarkable *here*, is the fact that neither party is a *poet*, by the remotest courtesy.

Goodnight, dear dearest—

I am your
Ba.

R. B. to E. B. B.

Thursday.
[Post-mark, May 21, 1846.]

Just as I write, the weather is a little more proper for this 'the blest ascension-day of the cheerful month of May': may you not go out therefore, my Ba? Or downstairs, at all events. We were sorry, Sarianna and I, to see the bright afternoon yesterday . . we ought to have gone, perhaps—but Mr. Kenyon is good and will understand; spite of the spectacles. But what sonnet is that, you perverse Ba, of which you give me the two or three words,—in print,—how, where? And if I do not request and request I shall be sure to hear nothing of that American review again,—so, I do request, Ba!

Last night brought Dickens' 'Pictures from Italy'—which I read this morning. He seems to have expended his power on the least interesting places,—and then gone on hurriedly, seeing or describing less and less, till at last the mere names of places do duty for pictures of them, and at Naples he fairly gives it up . . the Vesuvius' journey excepted. But the book is readable and clever—shall I bring it?—(or next week when everybody here has done with it.)

I know, dearest, you did not *promise* me that beatific vision by the gate—but was not enough said to justify me in waiting for you there? Indeed, yes—only the rain and wind seemed to forbid you; as they did. Were your sisters pleased? I am not sure I should have been glad to meet them *so*—I could not have left my sister (whom nobody would have known)—and then, with that unspoken secret between us. Also I please myself by hoping that Mr. Kenyon was only relieved of a great trouble and annoyance in the present state of his anxieties by our keeping away. Poor Captain Jones—really a fine, manly, noble fellow—I am heartily sorry. As for me, since Ba asks, I am pretty well,—much better in some points, and no worse in the rest—all is right but the little sound in the head which *will* be intrusive—but I must walk it away presently, or *think* it away at worst.

For, dearest, dearest Ba, I *can* cure all pains at once with you to think of, and to love, and to bless. So, bless you!

Your R.

E. B. B. to R. B.

Thursday.
[Post-mark, May 22, 1846.]

Dearest, when your letter came I was cutting open the leaves of Dickens' 'Letters from Italy' which Papa had brought in—so I am glad to have your thoughts of the book to begin with. Before your letter came I had sent you the review, as you will find. What changes, what changes! And the sonnet was purely manuscript, and for the good of the world should remain so. Oh—you cannot care for all this trash—such trash! Why I had a manuscript sonnet sent to me last autumn by 'person or persons unknown,' . . . 'To EBB on her departure from England *to Pisa.*' Can you fancy that melodious piece of gossipping? Then a lady of the city, famous, I believe, for haberdashery, used to address *all* her poems to me—which really was original . . for she would write five or six 'poems' on an evening, and sweep them up and send them to me once a fortnight, upon faith, hope and charity, seaweed and moonshine, cornlaws and the immortality of the soul, and take me for her standing muse, properly *thou*'d and *thee*'d all through. What a good vengeance it would be upon your unjust charges, if I set you to read a volume or two of those 'poems' . . . which all went into the fire—so you need not be frightened.

And to-day I had a rose-tree sent to me by somebody who has laid close siege to me this long while, and whom I have escaped hitherto . . but who has encamped, she says, 'till July' in *16* Wimpole Street. She writes too on her card . . 'When are you going to Italy?'

Ah! you, who blame me (half blame me) for 'seeing women,' do not know how difficult it is to help it sometimes, without being in appeaance ungrateful and almost brutal. Just because I am unwell, they teaze me more, I believe. Now that Miss Heaton . . oh, I need not go back, but it was not of my choice, be sure. You being a man are different,—and perhaps you make people afraid and keep them off. They do not thrust their hands through the bars where the lion is, as they do with the giraffe. Once I had this proposition—'If we mayn't come in, *will you stand up at the window that we may see?*' Now!—And there's the essence of at least ten MS. sonnets!——so don't complain any more.

As for Mr. Kenyon, he had his 'collation,' I understand—and he said that he was expecting Mrs. Jameson and *sundries*—but he referred to some 'friends from the country who would not be so mad as to come,' and whom I knew to be yourselves. You were quite, quite right not to come. To-day you are right too . . in thinking that I—was out. I was in the park nearly an hour, Arabel and Flush and I: and perhaps if to-morrow should be fine, I may walk in the street; so think of me and help me. This is my last letter before I see you again, dear dearest. Oh—but I heard yesterday . . and it was not a tradition of the elders this time . . it was 'vivid in the pages of contemporary history' . . . in fact one of my brothers heard it at the Flower Show and brought it home as the newest news, . . that 'Mr. Browning is to be married immediately to Miss Campbell.' The tellers of the news were 'intimate friends' of yours, they said, and knew it from the highest authority—

Laugh!—Why should not they talk, being women? My brother did not tell *me*, but he told it down-stairs—and Arabel was amused, she said, at some of the faces round. At that turn of the road they lost the track of the hare. Not an observation was made by anybody.

May God bless you—Think of me. I am ever and ever

Your own

Ba.

E. B. B. to R. B.

Thursday.

This is not to be called a letter, please to understand, because to write a letter to you once a day is enough in all reason. But I want to send you the review you asked for at the same time with the drawings which I kept too long I thought months ago,—but I have looked over them again and again. Then there is the book on Junius—and lastly, the song which I want you to have . . the 'Toll Slowly'—*that* is my gift to you, for as much as it is worth, and not to be sent back to me if you please. As for the Notes on Naples, I shall keep them for the present, having need to study about Amalfi.

Now I am going out in the carriage, and shall drive round the park perhaps. You will not think much of the music—but it being the first music I had heard for years and years, and in itself so overwhelmingly melancholy, it affected me so that I should scarcely hear it to the end. I went down-stairs on purpose to hear it and be able to thank the composer rightly. But she has done better things, I am sure.

Your own

Ba.

Observe—I disobey in nothing by sending this parcel. There is too much for you to carry. Don't forget to bring me my *Statesmen* which is a lawful burden.

R. B. to E. B. B.

Friday.
[Post-mark, May 22, 1846.]

I have a great mind to retract . . I *do* retract altogether whatever I said the other day in explanation of Miss Heaton's story. I make no doubt, now, it was a pure dream to which my over-scrupulousness of conscience gave a local habitation and name both, through the favourable dimness and illusion of 'a good many years ago'—because this last charge about 'Miss Campbell'—briefly—I never in my life saw, to my knowledge, a woman of that name—nor can there be any woman of any other name from my acquaintance with whom the merest misunderstanding in the world could possibly arise to a third person . . I mean, that it must be a simple falsehood and not gossip or distortion of fact, as I supposed in the other case. I told you of the one instance where such distortion *might* take place,—(Miss Haworth, to avoid mistake). This charge after the other . . I will tell you of what it reminds me—in my early boyhood I had a habit of calling people 'fools,' with as little reverence as could be, . . and it used to be solemnly represented to me after such offences that 'whoso calleth his brother "fool," is in danger &c. for he hath committed murder in his heart already' &c. in short,—there was no help for it,—I stood there a convicted *murderer* . . to which I was forced penitently to agree . . Here is Miss Heaton's charge and my confession. Now, let a policeman come here presently to ask what I know about the 'Deptford Murder' or the 'Marshalsea Massacre'—and you will have my 'intimate friend's' charge. By the way, did your brother overhear this, or was it spoken to someone in his company, or is my friend his acquaintance also? Because in either of the latter cases I can interfere easily. (There is a *Mr. Browning*—Henry I think—living in, or near the Regent's Park.) At all events, please say that I know no such person, nor ever knew,—that the whole is a pure falsehood—(and I only use so mild a word because I write to *you*, and because on reading the letter again I see the speakers were women).

It is a *fact* that I have made myself almost ridiculous by a kind of male prudery with respect to 'young ladies' . . that I have seemed to imply—'If I gave you the least encouragement something would be sure to follow.' In fact never seeing any attractiveness in the class, I was very little inclined to get involved in troubles and troubles for nothing at all. And as for marrying . . that is a point on which I have certainly not chosen to dilate before *you*, nor shall I now dilate on it.

Well, I shall see you to-morrow, that remedies everything. And that is your way of letting me see the Review,—you send it! Not that it has arrived yet. Dear Ba, how ever good you are!

All about the lady enthusiasts makes me laugh—don't think I fail of the proper respect to them, however—it is only once in a week that one sees a real painted Emperor settle on a flower, and then perhaps for a few minutes—while at all times, if you look, you will find a good half dozen of earnest yet sleepy drones *living* there, working away at the sweet,—after all, these get the most out of the flower.

Did you really go out yesterday? I was not sure, for the wind was Easterly—but it appears to have done you no harm,—you may 'go into the street' to-day—I am most happy,—most happy—and always entirely happy in you,—in thinking of you, and hoping,—my life is in you now—

Bless you, dearest—I am your own.

2 o'clock, the parcel arrives . . thank you, best of Ba's! I will read and tell you—(only what on earth do you mean by sending back those sketches?)

R. B. to E. B. B.

Sunday Morning.
[Post-mark, May 25, 1846.]

My own Ba is entreated to observe, that when she sends me reviews about herself, and songs by herself, and a make-weight book about 'Junius' happens to be sent also . . I do not ordinarily plunge into the Junius-discussion at once—perhaps from having made up my mind that the Author is Miss Campbell:—at all events, while the review was read and re-read and the music done justice and injustice to, the Junius was opened for the first time this morning, at eight of the clock, and Ba's letter which lay between pages 16 and 17, 'came to hand'—was brought to me by my mother, from my father! but for whose lucky inspiration of curiosity the said note had perhaps lain shut in till the book's secret was found out . . certainly *I* should never have touched the book before then! And from this note, duly studied, I learn that yesterday I must have appeared to Ba touched by a general mental paralysis—inasmuch as I was surprised, over and above the joyfulness, to hear that she was in the Park on Thursday, as well as Friday . . (oh, I know the letter I *did* receive mentioned it, but it seems as if *one* of the two excursions were unrecorded)—and seeing that I enquired whether Ba had heard with her own ears the song . . and altogether omitted thanking her for the gift of it: and lastly, brought no *Statesmen*, even on Ba's request! Of all which matters I *ought* to have been made acquainted by the note: what must you think of me, you Ba; dearest-dearest, that expect me to know the face through the bonnet, and the letter through the book covers—(Ba sitting in the Bookseller's shop was a type, I see!). What did you think of me yesterday, I want to know?

Well, and now my letter does come I thank you—(for all the trouble this precedent will give me—next time a parcel comes—of poking into all impossible places to see and to see!) You are the dearest, dearest, impossibly dear Ba that heart ever adored,

> 'And the roses which thou strowest,
> All the cheerful way thou goest,
> Would direct to follow thee,'

as Shirley sings—and every now and then the full sense of the sweetness *collects* itself and overcomes me entirely, as now, on the occasion of this note that I find; I am blessed by you in the hundred unspeakable ways—but were it only for *this* and similar pure kindness, I find it in my heart to give you my life could it profit you! Here ought I, by every law and right and propriety . . ask Miss Campbell! . . to be ministering to you, caring for you; and . . oh, Ba, do please, please, throw a coffee cup at me!—(giving some *grounds* for complaint!)—and after it the *soucoupe* (' glaring with *saucer* eyes ')—and see what you shall see, and hear what you shall hear! You 'strongest woman that has written yet'! Have *they* found that out? *I* know it, I think, by this! So I will go and think over it in the garden, and tell you more in the afternoon.

12 o'clock!—What strange weather!—but pleasant, I think—you have been out, or will go out, perhaps. Tell me all, dearest, and how you feel after it. To-morrow I will send you the Review and some of the other books you have spoken of from time to time—but, I almost dare to keep the *Statesmen*, spite of your positive request. Why, dear, want to see what I desire to forget altogether? So my other poems, 'Sordello' &c.—I most unaffectedly shudder at the notion of your reading them, as I said yesterday. *My* poetry is far from the 'completest expression of my being'—I hate to refer to it, or I could tell you why, wherefore, . . *prove* how imperfect (for a mild word), how unsatisfactory it must of necessity be. Still, I should not so much object, if, such as it is, it were the best, the flower of my life . . but that is all to come, and through you, mainly, or more certainly. So will it not be better to let me write one last poem this summer,—quite easily, stringing every day's thoughts instead of letting them fall,—and laying them at the dear feet at the summer's end for a memorial? I have been almost determining to do this, or try to do it, as I walked in the garden just now. A poem to publish or not to publish; but a proper introduction to the afterwork. What do you think, my Ba, my dearest siren, and muse, and Mistress, and . . something beyond all, above all and better . . shall I do this? And what are you studying about Amalfi, my Ba? Will you please keep that Naples' Note-book till I ask for it—at Amalfi. Till holy church incorporate two in one; and I take the degree of my aspiration. Rt. Bg. *B.A.*—in earnest of which, kiss me dear, 'earnest, most earnest of poets,' and let me kiss you as I do . . loving you as I love you. Bless you, best and dearest.

E. B. B. to R. B.

Sunday.
[Post-mark, May 25, 1846.]

When you came yesterday I had scarcely done my grumbling over the *Athenæum*, which really seems to me to select its subjects from the things least likely to interest and elevate. It goes on its own level perhaps—but to call itself a Journal of Art and Literature afterwards, is too much to bear patiently when one turns it over and considers. Lady Hester Stanhope's physician, antiquities of the mayors of London, stories re-collected from the magazines by Signor Marcotti—and this is literature . . art! Without thinking of 'Luria,' it is natural and righteous to be angry even after the sun has gone down. These are your teachers, O Israel! Mr. Dilke may well fly to the *Daily News* for congenial occupation and leave literature behind him, and nobody hang on the wheels of his chariot, crying, 'Come back, Mr. Dilke.'

Talking of chariots, George met you, he said, yesterday, wheeling down Oxford Street, . . (this he told me when he came in . .) going as fast as an express train, and far too fast, of course, either to recognize or be recognized.

Oh—I forgot to tell you one thing about the review in the *Methodist Quarterly*. You observe there some very absurd remarks about Tennyson—but, just *there*, is an extract from the 'Spirit of the Age,' about his 'coming out of himself as the nightingale from under the leaves,' . . you see *that?* Well . . it is curious that precisely what is quoted *there*, is some of my writing, when I contributed to Mr. Horne's book. It amused me to recognize it, (as you did not George) . . but I was vexed too at the foolish deduction, because . . .

In the midst I had to hold my Sunday-levee, when for the only day in the week and for one half hour I have to see all my brothers and sisters at once: on the week days, one being in one place and one in another, and the visits to me only coming by twos and threes. Well, and Alfred, who never had said a word to me before, gave me the opportunity of saying '*no, no, it is not true*'—followed hard by a remark from somebody else, that 'of course Ba must know, as she and Mr. Browning are such *very* intimate friends,' and a good deal of laughter on all sides: on which, without any transition and with an exceeding impertinence, Alfred threw himself down on the sofa and declared that he felt inclined to be very ill, . . for that then perhaps (such things being heard of) some young lady might come to visit *him*, to talk sympathetically on the broad and narrow gauge! Altogether, I shall leave you for the future to . . . contradict yourself! I did not mean to do it this time, only that Alfred forced me into it. But he said . . . 'How the Miss Cokers praised him! . . . "It was delightful," they cried, "to see a man of such a great genius condescend to little people like them."' So they are better than the *Athenæum*, and I shall not have them spoken of ungently, mind, even if they do romance a little wildly, and marry *me*, next time, to the man in the moon.

In the meantime, dearest, it is no moonshine that I was out walking to-day again, and that I walked up all these stairs with my own feet on returning. I sate down on the stairs two or three times, but I could not rest in the drawing-room because somebody was there, and I was not carried, as usual—see how vain-glorious I am. And what a summer-sense in the air—and how lovely the strips of sky between the houses! And yet I may tell you truly, that, constantly, through these vivid impressions, I am thinking and feeling that mournful and bitter would be to me this return into life, apart from you, apart from the consideration of you. How could ever I have borne it, I keep feeling constantly. But you are *there*, in the place of memory. Ah—you said yesterday that you were not ungrateful! *I* cannot say so. I blame myself often. And yet again I think that the wrong may be pardoned to me, for that those affections had worked out on me their uttermost pang—nearly unto death I had felt them—and now if I am to live, it must be by other means—or I should die still, and not live. Also I owe *you* gratitude——do I not owe *you* gratitude? Then, *I cannot help it* . . right or wrong, I cannot help it . . you are all to me, and, beloved —whichever way I look, I only can see *you*. If wrong, it is not for *you* to be severe on me—

Your own
Ba.

R. B. to E. B. B.

Monday. 12 o'clock.

I get nothing by the post this morning:—perhaps at next delivery! Well, I had the unexpected largess yesterday, you know. At this time last year the letters came once a week! Now the manna falls as manna should, omitting only the seventh day. Do you know, my Ba,—the Campbell mystery is all but solved, to my thinking, by supposing, as one may, that, those foolish ladies confound their cousin's friend *Brown*, an indubitable Scot and Lord Jeffrey's nephew,—(and their intimate for aught I know)—with *me*. He is in town now; *did* dine with them just before I saw him a fortnight ago; and *may* meditate happiness with Miss Campbell, and be provided with a paragon of a 'sister' besides. Those ladies have been to Scotland—may easily know him there and see 'sights' with him here. Is not all this likely? It is not worth writing about to White, nor a visit to him at Doctor's Commons, but when I next chance on his company, I will enquire.

Here is the review,—which I like very much—the introductory, abstract remarks might be better, but so it always is when a man, having really something to say about one precise thing (your poems), thinks he had better preface it by a little graceful *generality*. All he *wanted* to write, I agree in, thoroughly agree,—though I cannot but fancy my own selection,—that *might* be,—of passages and single poems!

And, dearest, I venture to keep back the *Statesmen*, as I asked leave to do yesterday, for the reasons then given—may I keep it back?

Also I return those sketches,—now they have been in your hand, they cannot lie about here—(I keep brown paper with your writing on it, and string, and the wrappage of this pen of mine—to be sure) so I shall get you to bear with them again, two or three being added, just as I find them. There is, too, the ode which was presented to me on my departure from Rome by an enthusiastic Roman; red ribbon and all! And last of all you have my play as altered by Macready: greater excisions had been determined on, but on the appearance of the printed copy had the effect it intended . . it would have been too ludicrous to leave out the whole of the first scene, for instance (as was in contemplation), and then to tell the public 'my play' had been acted. I refer to this silly business only to show you what sucess or non-success on the stage means and is worth. It is all behind me now—so far behind!

Now I will wait and see what next post may bring me from dearest Ba—Ba, the dear, and the beloved, e sopra tutto, the tall! Does she not 'stand high in the affection' —of her very own

R. B.?

R. B. to E. B. B.

Monday.
[Post-mark, May 25, 1846.]

Dear, dear love, your letter comes at half past *three* by a new Postman,—(very bewildered). You will perhaps have received my parcel and note—if not, such things are on the road. All in *your* note delights me entirely. As for my walking fast, *that* is exactly my use and wont . . I am famous for it,—as my father is for driving old lady-friends into illnesses, and then saying innocently, 'I took care to walk *very* slowly.' When I have anything to occupy my mind, I all but run—but the pen can't run, for this letter must go, and nothing said.

So, Ba, my Ba, Goodbye till tomorrow from

Your own, own.

E. B. B. to R. B.

Monday Morning.
[Post-mark, May 26, 1846.]

My beloved I scarcely know what to say about the poem. It is almost profane and a sin to keep you from writing it when your mind goes that way,—yet I am afraid that you cannot begin without doing too much and without suffering as a consequence in your head. Now if you make yourself ill, what will be the end? So you see my fears! Let it be however as it must be! Only you will promise to keep from all excesses, and to write very very gently. Ah—can you keep such a promise, if it is made ever so? There are the fears again.

You are very strange in what you say about my reading your poetry—as if it were not my peculiar gladness and glory!—my own, which no man can take from me. And not *you*, indeed! Yet I am not likely to mistake your poetry for the flower of your nature, knowing what that flower is, knowing something of what that flower is without a name, and feeling something of the mystical perfume of it. When I said, or when others said for me, that my poetry was the flower of me, was it praise, did you think, or blame? might it not stand for a sarcasm? It might,—if it were not true, miserably true after a fashion.

Yet something of the sort is true, of course, with all poets who write directly from their personal experience and emotions—their ideal rises to the surface and floats like the bell of the waterlily. The roots and the muddy water are *subaudita*, you know—as surely there, as the flower.

But *you* . . you have the superabundant mental life and individuality which admits of shifting a personality and speaking the truth still. *That* is the highest faculty, the strongest and rarest, which exercises itself in Art,—we are all agreed there is none so great faculty as the dramatic. Several times you have hinted to me that I made you careless for the drama, and it has puzzled me to fancy how it could be, when I understand myself so clearly both the difficulty and the glory of dramatic art. Yet I am conscious of wishing you to take the other crown besides—and after having made your own creatures speak in clear human voices, to speak yourself out of that personality which God made, and with the voice which He tuned into such power and sweetness of speech. I do not think that, with all that music in you, only your own personality should be dumb, nor that having thought so much and deeply on life and its ends, you should not teach what you have learnt, in the directest and most impressive way, the mask thrown off however moist with the breath. And it is not, I believe, by the dramatic medium, that poets teach most impressively—I have seemed to observe *that!* . . it is too difficult for the common reader to analyse, and to discern between the vivid and the earnest. Also he is apt to understand better always, when he sees the lips move. Now, here is yourself, with your wonderful faculty!—it is wondered at and recognised on all sides where there are eyes to see—it is called wonderful and admirable! Yet, with an inferior power, you might have taken yourself closer to the hearts and lives of men, and made yourself dearer, though being less great. Therefore I do want you to do this with your surpassing power—it will be so easy to you to speak, and so noble, when spoken.

Not that I usen't to fancy I could see you and know you, in a reflex image, in your creations! I used, you remember. How these broken lights and forms look strange and unlike now to me, when I stand by the complete idea. Yes, *now* I feel that no one can know you worthily by those poems. Only . . I guessed a little. *Now* let us have your own voice speaking of yourself—if the voice may not hurt the speaker—which is my fear.

Evening.—Thank you, dearest dearest! I have your parcel—I have your letters . . . three letters to-day, it is certainly feast day with me. Thank you my own dearest. The drawings I had just fixed in my mind, courageously to ask for, because as you *meant* me to keep them I did not see why I should throw away a fortune—and they return to me with interest . . I observe these new vivid sketches! Some day I shall put them into a book, as *you* should have done. Then for the Roman ode, and all the rest, thank you, thank you. *I* looked here and looked there, though, for a letter—I could not find it at first, and was just saying to myself quite articulately 'What wickedness'! . . . meaning that it was wickedness in you to send me a parcel without a word, . . when I came upon the folded paper. For *I* looked inside the books, be sure. *I* did not toss them away . . .

There's the gratitude of the world, you see! and of womankind in particular! there's the malign spirit of the *genus coffee-cup-throw-arum!* Talking of which coffee cups, you dare me to it. Which is imprudent, to say the least of it. I heard once of her most gracious Majesty's throwing a tea cup,—whereupon Albertus Magnus, who is no conjurer, could find nothing better to do than to walk out of the room in solemn silence. If I had been he, I should have tied the royal hands, I think; for when women get to be warlike after that demonstrative fashion, it seems to me to be allowable to teach that they are not the strongest. I say it, never thinking of my 'licence to' throw coffee-cups—which you granted, knowing very well what I know intimately, . . that . . that . .

I have a theory about you. Was ever anybody in the world, . . a woman at least, . . *angry with you?* If anyone ever tried, did she not fail in the first breath of the trying?—go out to curse like the prophet, and bless instead? Tell me if anyone was ever angry with you? It is impossible, I know perfectly. Therefore, as to the coffee-cup license, . . the divine Achilles, invulnerable all but the heel, might as well have said to his dearest foe 'Draw out your sword, O Diomede, and strike me across the head, prick me in the forehead, slash me over the ears, . . ' and *that* stand for a proof of courage!

What stuff I do write, to be sure. I was out to-day walking, with Arabel and Flush, and rested at the bookseller's; but as I went farther than the other day, I let Stormie carry me upstairs, . . it is such a long way! Say how you are, dearest—you do not! Shall you walk so fast when you walk with me under the trees? I shall not let you—I shall hang back, as Flush does, when he won't go with a string. Ah—little (altogether) you know perhaps what a hard Degree that B: A: is, to take——the BA which is not a Bachelor's.

No, no, for the rest. It was not any Brown on earth, but the only Browning of the great genius, who was shown up as intimate friend to the Miss Cokers and elect husband of that cloud, Miss Campbell the 'great heiress'—all in proportion, observe! But I do entreat you not to say a word to Dr. White or another. Why should you? It is mere nonsense,—so do let it evaporate quietly. Why, with all my doubts for which you have blamed me, . . at the thickest and saddest of the doubting, it never was what people could *say of you* that could move me. And this is so foolish, and unbelieved even by the very persons who say it, perhaps! Let it pass away with other dust, in the wind. It is not worth the watering.

May God bless you! This is my last letter . . already! I had another criticism to-day from America, in a book called 'Thoughts on the Poets,' which is written by a Mr. Tuckermann, and selects its poets on the most singular principle . . or rather on none at all . . beginning with Petrarch, ending with Bryant, receiving Tennyson, Procter, Hunt, and your Ba . . and not a word of you! Stupid book—Petrarch and Alfieri are the only foreign poets admitted—criticisms, swept back to the desk from the magazines, I dare say. Very kind to me—you shall see if you like.

And now . . good-night at last! it must come. Have I not written you one letter as long as the three? Only not worth a third as much—*that* I know.

Wholly and ever your

Ba.

Oh I must speak, though I meant to be silent! though first, I meant to keep the great subject of the *Statesmen* for an explosion on Wednesday. I gave up the early poems because I felt contented to read them afterwards—but listen . . my *Statesmen*, I *will not give up*. Now listen—I expect nothing at all from them—they were written for another person, and under peculiar circumstances . . they are probably as bad as anything written by you, can be. Will *that* do, to say? And *may* I see them? Now I ask ever so humbly . . *Dearest!*

R. B. to E. B. B.

3½ P.M. Tuesday.
[Post-mark, May 26, 1846.]

Dearest, your dearest of notes only arrived at 2 o'clock—and Carlyle has just been with me,—come on horseback for the express purpose of strolling about—so that I was forced, forced . . you see! He is gone again—and there is only time to tell you why no more is told—but to-morrow will supply all deficiency. Bless you, my dearest best Ba. How I love you!

Your own—

Poor Capt. Jones is dead,—you may see in the papers.

E. B. B. to R. B.

Thursday Morning.
[Post-mark, May 28, 1846.]

Dearest it is my fancy to write quickly this morning and take my letter to the post myself. Oh, I shall do it this time—there will be no obstacle. The office is just below Hodgson's, the bookseller's. And so with this letter, please to understand that I go to you twice and wholly, once in the spirit, and again in the body.

But there is nothing to tell you, except that I think of you with the thought which never can change essentially, while it deepens always. What I meant to say yesterday was simply, that I, *knowing that,* should be 'bad' if I could fail practically to myself and you. I have known from the beginning the whole painful side of what is before me, also . . I should have no excuse therefore for any weakness in any fear. Should I not be 'bad' then, and more unworthy of you than even according to my own account, if the obstacle came from *me? It never can.* Remember to be sure of it.

A change of feeling indeed would be a different thing,

and we think exactly alike on the fit consequences of it. Which change is however absolutely impossible in my position and to *me*, 'for reasons . . for reasons' . . . . you guess at some of them, some are spoken, and others cannot be.

In one word for all, life seems to come to me only through you.

I am your very own.

Ba.

R. B. to E. B. B.

Thursday.
[Post-mark, May 28, 1846.]

There is a long four days more of waiting—I feel more and more and ever more how, wanting you, my life wants all it can have. Dear Ba, never wonder that I fancy at times such an event's occurrence as you tell me I need not fear. I shall always fear,—never *can* I hold you sufficiently fast, I shall think. So, if my jewel must be taken from me, let some eagle stoop down for it suddenly, baffling all human precaution, as I look on my treasure on a tower's top miles and miles inland,—don't let me have to remember, though but in a minute of life afterwards, that I let it drop into the sea through foolishly balancing it in my open hand over the water. There is one of Ba's 'myths,' excepting all Ba's felicitousness of application and glory of invention,—but then it has all my own love and worship of Ba's self, all I care to be distinguished by.

I hope you go out this fine morning—the wind is cold, to be sure, but London is much warmer than this place, and the wind kept off by the houses. I have got two of Mr. Kenyon's kind notes, to confirm the appointment for Wednesday (when Mrs. Jameson is to be of the party), and to invite me to meet Landor on Tuesday—so that for three days running I shall be in Ba's very neighbourhood . . for if the wind can't get through houses and walls, Ba can and does, as my heart knows. Might I not see you for a moment on the Wednesday? Ah, there will be time to contrive, to concert—but the worst is that when I see you I contrive nothing, nor do you help me, you Ba! Else, out of these walks,—who is to object to my going to see the Thames Tunnel or the Tower, by way of Wimpole Street,—wanting the organ of locality as I am said to? Whereas I am all one consciousness of the influence of one locality, turning as my whole heart and soul turn to Ba,—my dearest, dearest, whom may God bless and requite. I can only kiss you, as I do, and be your very own, my Ba, as I am and shall be ever.

E. B. B. to R. B.

Thursday.
[Post-mark, May 29, 1846.]

Dearest dearest, I thought I had lost my letter to-night, for not a sound came like a postman's knock . . I thought I had lost my letter, talking of losing jewels. I waited and waited, and at last broke silence to Arabel with, 'when *will* the post come?' 'Not to-night,' said she—'it is nearly ten.' On which I exclaimed so pitifully and with such a desperate sense of loss, 'You mean to say that I shall have no letter tonight,'? . . that after she had laughed a very little, she went down-stairs to search the letterbox and brought me what I wanted.

And you think it possible that I should give up my letters and their golden fountain?—*I!* . . while I live and have understanding! I can't fancy what manner of eagles you believe in. If in real live eagles, . . why it is as probable as any other thing of the sort, that I (or you) should be snatched away by an eagle . . . the eagle who used to live, for instance, at the Coliseum of Regent's Park. And when I ride away upon an eagle, I may take a wrong counsel perhaps that hour from other birds of the air: . . . but *till then*, I am yours to have and to hold, . . unless, as you say, you open your hand wide and cry with a distinct voice, 'Go.' It shall be your doing and not mine, if we two are to part—or God's own doing, through illness and death. And the way to avert danger is to avoid observation and discussion, as much as we can—and we have not been frightened much yet, . . now have we? As for Wednesday, there is time to think. But how can you leave your sister? you cannot. So unless you derange your 'myth' altogether, and find a trysting place for us, . . . each mounted on an eagle, . . in Nephelococcygia, we had better be satisfied, it seems to me, with Monday and Saturday.

I was out to-day as you saw by my letter, which with my own hand I dropped into the post. I liked to do it beyond what you discern. And how the sun shone,—and the little breath of wind could do nobody harm, I felt. Also there was the 'Autography' in the shop-window to see, before I sate down in the shop. So you were thought of by necessity, besides the freewill.

Do you not see that I am bound to you hand and foot? Why do you not see what God sees?

But it is late, and the rest must be for to-morrow. The sender of the rose-tree sent to-day a great heliotrope—so, presently, you will have to seek me in a wood.

Everywhere your own

Ba.

R. B. to E. B. B.

Friday.
[Post-mark, May 29, 1846.]

My own darling, your little note was a great delight to me last night, when I expected nothing; and though I do not hear to-day, I will believe you are well after the walk—the walk, what a 'divine fancy'; not mentioned by Quarles!

And then the words that follow the good news of the walk . . those assurances . . oh, my best, dearest Ba,—it is all right that I cannot speak here,—if I *could,* by some miracle, speak, it would be foolish:—but my life lies before you to take and direct, and keep or give away,—I am altogether your own.

I come in rather tired from Town—having spent the morning at the Exhibition, and made calls beside. (Etty's picture of the *sirens* is abominable; though it looks admirable beside another picture of his: did I not tell you he had chosen the sirens for a subject?)

Oh, dearest beyond all dearness, *now*, at this moment only, your last and *pro tempore best* letter comes to me! One can't scold and kiss at the same time . . so let the wretched Post arrangements be unmentioned for the moment; there is enough to get up a revolution about, I do think! But you, you spoil me and undo me almost,—*ought* to do so, at least,—they were *too* delicious to bear, the things you say to me! Why will you not say rather what I feel,—for you can, perhaps, being what you are,—and let me subscribe it! It is a real pain to me to feel as I feel, and speak no more than I speak.

And again the time urges . . just when I want most to go on writing—but to-morrow I will do nothing else. Take this now, sweet, sweet Ba, with my whole heart that loves, loves you! your R.

E. B. B. to R. B.

Friday.
[Post-mark, May 30, 1846.]

I have your letter . . you who cannot write! The contrariety is a part of the 'miracle.' After all it seems to me that you can write for yourself pretty well—rather too well I used to think from the beginning. But if you persist in the proposition about my doing it for you, leaving room for your signature . . . shall it be this way?

Show me how to get rid of you.

(signed) *R. B.*

Now isn't it *I* who am . . not 'balancing my jewel' over the gulph . . but actually tossing it up in the air out of sheer levity of joyousness? Only it is not perhaps such dangerous play as it looks: there may be a little string perhaps, tying it to my finger. Which, if it is not imprudence in act, is imprudence in fact, you see!

Dearest, I committed a felony for your sake to-day—so never doubt that I love you. We went to the Botanical Gardens, where it is unlawful to gather flowers, and I was determined to gather this for you, and the gardeners were here and there . . they seemed everywhere . . but I stooped down and gathered it. Is it felony, or burglary on green leaves—or what is the name of the crime? would the people give me up to the police, I wonder? *Transie de peur*, I was, . . listening to Arabel's declaration that all gathering of flowers in these gardens is highly improper,—and I made her finish her discourse, standing between me and the gardeners—to prove that I was the better for it.

How pretty those gardens are, by the way! We went to the summer-house and sate there, and then on, to the empty seats where the band sit on your high days. What I enjoy most to see, is the green under the green . . where the grass stretches under trees. *That* is something unspeakable to me, in the beauty of it. And to stand under a tree and feel the green shadow of the tree! I never knew before the difference of the *sensation* of a green shadow and a brown one. I seemed to feel that green shadow through and through me, till it went out at the soles of my feet and mixed with the other green below. Is it nonsense, or not? Remember that by too much use we lose the knowledge and apprehension of things, and that I may feel therefore what you do not feel.

But in everything I felt *you*—and always, dearest beloved, you were nearer to me than the best.

Well; to go on with my story. Coming home and submitting to be carried up-stairs because I was tired, the news was that Miss Bayley had waited to see me three quarters of an hour. Then she sate with me an hour—

and oh, such kind, insisting, persisting plans about Italy! I did not know what to say, so I was *niaise* and grateful, and said 'thank you, thank you' as I could. Did Mrs. Jameson tell you of her scheme of going to Florence for two years and to Venice for one, taking her niece with her in order to an 'artistical education'? And Mr. Bezzi, who is the 'most accurate of men,' furnishes the details of necessary expenses, and assures her in his programme that she may 'walk in silk attire' and drive her carriage like an English aristocrat, for three hundred a year, at Florence—but the place is English-ridden . . filled and polluted. Sorrento is better or even Pisa. We will keep our Siren-isles to ourselves . . will we not?

And now tell me. Was there not a picture of Sirens by Etty, exhibited years ago . . which was also 'abominable,' as I thought when I saw it? Is it the same picture returning like a disquieted ghoule . . much more *that*, than like a Siren at all, if it is the same, . . I remember it was scarcely to be looked at for hideousness . . though I heard some carnivorous connoisseurs praising the 'colouring'!! Foreigners might refer such artistical successes to our national 'beef' . . . 'le bifteak' ideal. The materialism of Art.

Can you love me *so? do* you? . . will you always? And is any of that love 'lost,' do you think, . . as the saying is? Indeed it is not. I put golden basins all round (the reverse shape of lachrymatories) to catch every drop as it falls, . . so that when we two shall meet together in the new world, I may look in your face (as I cannot at this moment) and say 'None of the love was lost, though all of it was undeserved.' May God bless you, dearest, best! My heart is *in* you, I think. You would laugh to see the books I take up . . first, 'Strafford' . . then Suetonius to see about your Cæsar . . then the Naples book. Oh, but I find you out in the *Statesmen* . . for all the dim light.

Your very own

Ba.

R. B. to E. B. B.

Saturday.
[Post-mark, May 30, 1846.]

Oh, yes, do 'show me how to get rid of you,' my best Ba,—for so I shall have the virtuous delight of deciding to keep you, instead of being wholly kept by you,—it is all out of my head, now, how I used to live when I was my own: and if you can, by one more witchery, give me back that feeling for once . . Ba, I have no heart to write more nonsense, when I can take your dearest self into my arms; yet I shall never quite lie quiet and happy, I do think . . I shall be always wishing you would be angry and cruel and unjust, for a moment, — for my love overflows the bounds, needs to prove itself—all which is foolish, I know. To-day, for some unknown reason, is a day of hope with me . . all bright things seem possible; I was feeling them so, when your note came—as I sate in the garden—and when I saw the flower (Paracelsus' *own* . . they usually ornament his pictures with it,—I said something on the subject in the poem, too, and gave a note about 'Flammula citrinula — herba Paracelso multum familiaris'—) when I saw that, and read on and on,—every now and then laying the letter down to feel the entire joy,—and when the end came,—Ba, dearest Ba, it was with me then as now, as always after steady thinking of *what* you are to me . . I cannot tell you—but for the past, utterly irrespective of the future,—for what you *have* been, this love cannot cease though you were transformed into all you are not nor could ever be. I mean, that after the blow struck, the natural vibration must follow and continue its proper period—and that my love for what I have received from you already *must* last to my life's end—cannot end sooner! 'Shall I continue to love you!'

You said in Thursday's letter—'We have not been frightened much yet,' our meetings have been uninterrupted hitherto, and these letters: yes, *that* I am most thankful for—whatever should happen, our real relation one to the other is wholly known—that fact has been established beyond possibility of doubt at least. I don't make myself understood here, I know,—but, think,—if at the very beginning any accident had separated us . .

But I will believe in the end now and henceforth—I will believe you *are* my very own Ba,—my best dream's realization, my life's fulfilment and consummation—and having discovered you, I shall live and die with you. So may God dispose.

I will write the rest,—(nothing is here) a longer letter to-morrow—but now my mind is too full of you—the poor hand gets despised for lagging after! All my thoughts are with you, dearest. May God bless you and make me less unworthy— being your own, own R.

One more day—one, and Monday!

(See what kindness of Mr. Kenyon! I do not accept, having no need to trouble him as he desires—but see how kind.)

E. B. B. to R. B.

Saturday.
[Post-mark, May 30, 1846.]

You shall have a visit from me on the seventh day as on the others, I think, because I remember you every day equally, and because, without waiting for your Saturday's letter, I have always with me enough of you, to thank you. This morning, Henrietta and I went as usual to Hodgson's and took possession of the chair in waiting, as Flush did of the whole territory, setting himself, with all the airs of a landed proprietor, to snap at the shop boy. Nota bene—Flush is likely to injure my popularity if I take him about with me much. He has been used, you see, to be '*Cæsar* in his own house,' and the transition to being Cæsar everywhere is the easiest thing in the world. Yet as to leaving him at home, it is impossible, . . not to mention other objections! His delight in going out in the carriage is scarcely a natural thing—but I have told you of it. Yesterday I was in the back drawing-room waiting to go out, and just said to him, 'Flush! go and see if the carriage is come'—instantly he ran to the front windows, standing on his hind legs and looking up the street and down. Now Mr. Kenyon would declare that *that* was my invention. Yet it is the literal truth of history.

Coming back from Hodgson's, we passed our door and walked to 57 and home, which is an improvement in the distance. Then I walked upstairs to the drawing-room, and was carried the rest of the way. May I be tired a little, after it all? Just a little, perhaps.

Henrietta dined at Mr. Lough's yesterday, and met Miss Camilla Toulmin who was gracious . . and Professor Forbes, who can do nothing without the polka, . . and sundries. There was a splendid dinner, and wine of all vintages—one is in a strait in such cases to know how to praise at once the hospitable intentions and to blame the bad taste—surely it *is* bad taste in a man like Mr. Lough who lives by his genius, to give ambitious dinners like a man who lives by his dinners. The true dignity of simplicity in these things were worth such a man's holding, one might think. But he is kind and liberal, and a good artist, . . and sent me a very gracious invitation to go and see his works.

The Hedleys are likely to be in England this summer again——more's the pity. I am fond of them, but would rather, rather, not see them just now, and not be seen by them—for eyes have they, and can see. My uncle Hedley comes next week, . . comes to London for several weeks . . that is certain—and my aunt after settling the younger part of her family at Barégos for the summer, *ponders* coming, . . as I behold from afar off, . . with her daughter Arabella, who is to be married immediately to the younger brother of the great Brewery partner, Barclay and Bevan, a Mr. Bevan. But they will not be in this house, and we must manage as we can, dearest! One leap over Sunday, and Monday comes bringing you! Then, I shall have you near on Tuesday besides, and Wednesday, afterwards! how the cup overflows! May God bless you my beloved! It is not exaggeration to say that I feel you in the air and the sun.

Ever and ever your own I am!

Ba.

R. B. to E. B. B.

Sunday.
[Post-mark, June 1, 1846.]

My own Ba, do you want to turn my head with good fortune and get at my secrets, that you give me two letters in one day? For there was too much life and warmth, I do think, in these last, to be kept in the Postman's pouch as before—he delivered them punctually as he was obliged, not before his cold newspapers and railway-prospectuses felt astonished, you may be sure; so, as I say, do you want to try my temper and bring out infirmities of mind that may be latent, as kings used to put robes and crowns on their favourites to see what they would do then?

I will try and say as soberly as I can,—if you did not write to me for a week, I would remember and love you the same—you are not bound to any kindness, much less to this extravagance—which yet so blesses me that—

Let me leave what I can never say, and make the few remarks I ought to have made before. Mrs. Jameson did tell me something about her intended journey to Italy—but not in detail as to you. Miss Bayley seems worthy to be your friend, dearest,—and it is satisfactory, very satisfactory to find her opinion thus confirming yours, of the good you will derive from travelling. You know I look on you with absolute awe, in a sense,—I don't understand how such a creature lives and breathes and moves and does *not* move into fine air altogether and leave us of the Etty-manufacture! I have solemnly set down in the tablets of my brain that Ba prefers morphine to pork, but can eat so much of a chicken as Flush refuses—a chapter in my natural history quite as important as one in Pliny's (and Ælian's too)— 'When the Lion is sick, nothing can cure him but to eat an Ape!'—though not so important as my great, greatest record of all—'A cup of coffee will generally cure Ba's headaches—'

As for Pisa or Florence, or Sorrento, or New Orleans, —*ubi* Ba, *ibi* R B! Florence, however, you describe exactly . . the English there are intolerable,—even from a distance you see *that.* Indeed, I have heard here in England of a regular system of tactics by which *parvenus* manage to get among the privileged classes which at home would keep them off inexorably. Such go to Florence, make acquaintance as 'travellers,' keeping the native connexions in the farthest of back grounds, and after a year or two's expatriation, come back and go boldly to rejoice the friends they 'passed those amusing days with' &c.

What you say of Lough is right and true in one point of view—but I excuse him, knowing the way of life in London—what alternative has he? Even when you ask people by ones and twos, and think to be rational, what do you get for your pains? Not long ago somebody invited himself to dine with me—and got of course the plainest fare, and just hock and claret, because I like them better than heavier wines myself, and suppose others may. I had to dine in the same manner with my friend a week after, and he judiciously began by iced champagne, forced vegetables &c. What was that but telling me *such* was his notion of the duty of the giver of 'just a chop' according to stipulation? It is all detestable—a mere pretext! there is simply a '*fait accompli*' in every such dinner,—it is an eternal record (to the seasons' end) that you witnessed (because you may let it alone for aught anybody cares, so long as you have eyes and can see)—*such* a succession of turbot, and spring-soup and—*basta!* I shall go and take tea with Carlyle before very long. Lough has asked me more than once, but I never went. I like him when he is not on the subject of himself or other artists. Of one particular in his liberality I can bear testimony, he promises at a great rate. Some three years ago he most preposterously signified his intention of giving me a cast of one of his busts—me who had neither claim on him, the slightest, nor much desire for the bust; but on this intimation I was bound to express as many thanks as if the bust had arrived in very plaster,—which it has not done to this day; so that I was too prodigal, you see, and instead of thanks ought to have contented myself with making over to him the whole profits of 'Luria'—value received. But, jokes apart, he is a good, kind man I believe, so don't mention this absurdity to your sister—which I am sorry for having mentioned now that mentioned it is! So sorrow shall be turned into joy, for I will only think that the evening is come, and night will follow, and morning end . . 3 o'clock with all of dearest, dearest Ba,—with the walkings and drivings to evidence in her face? *My* face, thank God, I am let say to my unutterable joy and pride and love above all other feelings.

Ever your own.

E. B. B. to R. B.

Tuesday.
[Post-mark, June 2, 1846.]

You understand, dearest beloved, all I *could* mean about your sister's coming here. Both I was afraid of not being liked enough . . which was one reason, and none the less reasonable because of your being 'infatuated' . . (oh, *that* is precisely the word to use, and indeed I never falter to myself in the applying of it!) and I felt it to be impossible for me to receive so near a relative of yours, your own only sister, as I should another and a stranger. There would be the need in me of being affectionate to your sister! how could I not? and yet, *how could I?* Everything is at once too near and too far—it is enough to make me tremble to think of it—it *did*, when Mr. Kenyon made his proposition. I would rather, ten times over, receive Queen Victoria and all her court——do you understand? can you misunderstand? can you pretend to fancy, as you talked yesterday, that the reluctance came from my having 'too many visitors,' or from any of those common causes. Why, she is your sister—and *that* was the cause of the reluctance. You will not *dare* to turn it into a wrong against yourself.

Now I am going to ask you a question, dearest of mine, and you will consider it carefully and examine your own wishes in respect to it, before I have any answer. In fact it is not necessary to treat of the subject of it at all at this moment—we have a great deal of time before us. Still, I want to know whether, upon reflection, you see it to be wise and better for me to go to Italy with Miss Bayley, or with any other person who may be willing to take me, (supposing I should find such a plan possible) and that you should follow with Mr. Chorley or alone, . . leaving other thoughts for another year. Or if I find this scheme, as far as I am concerned, impossible, shall we gain anything, do you think, on any side of the question that you can see, by remaining quietly as we are, you at New Cross, and I here, until next year's summer or autumn? Shall we be wiser, more prudent, for any reason, or in any degree, by such a delay?

It is the question I ask you—it is no proposal of mine, understand—nor shall I tell you my own impression about it. I have told you that I would do as you should decide, and I will do that and no other. Only on that very account it is the more necessary that you should decide well, and according to the best lights of your own judgment and reason.

I forgot to talk to you yesterday of your *Statesmen*

which I read with a peculiar sort of pleasure, coming and going as I see you and miss you. There is no mistaking your footsteps along the sands.

May God bless you, dear dearest! Say how your head is, and love me *so* much more than Machiavelli, as to spare it from farther injury. It is not hard to think of you to-day in this chair, where you were sitting yesterday—do you think it *is?*

Your own

Ba.

R. B. to E. B. B.

Tuesday.
[Post-mark, June 2, 1846.]

You are the most entirely lovable creature I ever dreamed perhaps might be in a better world—altogether made up of affectionateness and generosity. I do not much fear, now, I shall ever offend you—in the miserable way of giving you direct offence which mortal will and endeavour could avert (although I speak—by design, on profession—doubtfully about the happiness of the future in some respects, yet I dare be quite bold here, and feel sure, as of my life at this moment, that I shall never do *that*, . .)—but at present I almost love even the apprehension that I may be found out too useless, too unworthy in the end; let it be said so, since I feel it so, my own Ba! I love this, because your dear love seems fit to cover any imperfection of mine: I dare say you do *not* see them, as you say—but you will perhaps, and then I trust to the love wholly. I want forms, ways, of expressing my devotion to you—but such as I am, all is yours.

I will write more to-morrow—the stupid head will not be quiet to-day—my mother's is sadly affected too—it is partly my fault for reading . . . a state to be proud of! Don't let my frankness do me wrong, however,—the inconvenience is very little, but I was desired to tell you, was I not? I shall go out presently and get well.

Are *you* out to-day, beloved? It is very warm; be careful like the dearest Ba you are! And kiss me as I kiss you . . all except the adoration which is mine indefeasibly.

May God bless you ever for your very own.

E. B. B. to R. B.

Tuesday Night.
[Post-mark, June 3, 1846.]

My own dearest who are never to offend me!—And, true, *that* is—because I have *tried*, before now, to be offended, and could not, . . being under a charm. So it is not my fault but yours, that never you see me angry.

But your head, *my* head . . is it better, dearest, by this time, or is it ringing and aching even, under the crashing throat-peals of Mr. Landor's laughter? he laughs, I remember like an ogre—he laughs as if laughter could kill, and he knew it, thinking of an enemy. May it do his friends no harm to-night! How I think of you, and, in every thought, love you! Yes, surely I can love you as if I were worthier! and better perhaps than if *I* were better, . . though that may sound like a riddle. And dear dearest, why do you talk of your faults *so?* It is not at all gracious of you indeed. You are on a high hill above me where I cannot reach your hand—(in the myths, be it understood) and you sigh and say querulously . . . 'By and bye I may have to take a step down lower.' Now is that gracious of you, or worthy of your usual chivalry? You ought to be *glad*, on the contrary, to be so much nearer *me*—! in the myths, be it understood! For *out* of the myths we are near enough, as near as two hearts can be, . . I believe . . I trust!

You will not mistake what I said to you this morning my own beloved—you will not? My promise to you was to place the decision in your hands—and my desire is simply that you should decide according to your judgment and understanding . . I do not say, your affections, this time. Now it has struck me that you have a sort of *instinct* . .

But no—I shall not write on that subject to-night. Rather I will tell you what I have been doing to-day to be so very, very tired. To-day I paid my first visit—not to Mr. Kenyon but to an older friend than even he—to Miss *Trepsack* . . learn that name by heart . . whom we all of us have called 'Treppy' ever since we could speak. Moreover she has nursed . . tossed up . . held on her knee—Papa when he was an infant; the dearest friend of his mother and her equal, I believe, in age—so you may suppose that she is old now. Yet she can outwalk my sisters, and except for deafness, which, dear thing, she carefully explains as 'a mere nervous affection,'—is as young as ever. But she calls us all 'her children' . . and I, you are to understand, am 'her child,' *par excellence* . . her acknowledged darling and favourite,—perhaps because tenderly she thinks it right to carry on the love of her beloved friend, whom she lived with to the last. Once she saw you in the drawing-room—and you perhaps saw her. She dines here every Sunday, and on the other days of course often, and has the privilege of scolding everybody in the house when she is out of humour, and of being 'coaxed' by slow degrees back into graciousness. So, she had full right to have me on my first visit—had she not? and the goodness and kindness and funniness of the reception were enough to laugh and cry over. First . . half way up-stairs, I found a chair, to sit and rest on. Then the windows were all shut up, because I liked it so in my room. And then, for occulter reasons, a feast was spread for Arabel and Flush and me, which made me groan in the spirit, and Flush wag his tail, to look upon . . ice cream and cakes, which I was to taste and taste in despite of all memories of dinner an hour before . . and *cherrybrandy!!!* which I had to taste too, . . just then saved alive by an oath, on Arabel's part, that I was 'better without it.' Think of dear Treppy!—of all the kindness, and fondness! Almost she kissed me to pieces as the 'darlingest of children.' So I am glad I went—and so is Flush, who highly approves of that class of hospitable attentions, and wishes it were the way of the world every day. But I am tired! so tired! The visiting is a new thing.

It is an old one that I should write such long letters. If I am tired, you might retort with the *Ed io anche!*—Yet you will not, because you are supernaturally good; and as it was in the beginning, ever shall be, you say!

But will you explain to me some day why you are sorry for Italy having been mentioned between us, and why you would rather prefer Nova Zembla? *So as to kill me the faster, is it?*

Your Ælian says that the oldest painters used to write under a tree, when they painted one, 'This is a tree.' So *I* must do, I suddenly remember, under my jests . . I being, it would appear, as bad an artist in jesting, as they were in painting. Therefore . . see the last line of the last paragraph . . '*This is a jest.*'

And *this* is the earnest thing of all . . that I love you as I can love—and am for ever . . living and dying . .

Your own—

Take care of the head, *I entreat!* and say how you are! and how your mother is! I am grieved to hear of that relapse!

R. B. to E. B. B.

Wednesday Morning.
[Post-mark, June 3, 1846.]

I will tell you, dearest: your good is my good, and your will mine; if you were convinced *that* good would be promoted by our remaining as we are for twenty years instead of one, I should endeavour to submit in the end . . after the natural attempts to find out and remove the imagined obstacle. If, as you seem to do here, you turn and ask about *my* good—yours being supposed to be uninfluenced by what I answer . . then, here is my TRUTH on that subject, in that view,—my good for myself. Every day that passes before *that day* is one the more of hardly endurable anxiety and irritation, to say the least; and the thought of another year's intervention of hope deferred—altogether intolerable! Is there anything I can do in that year—or that you can do—to forward our object? Anything impossible to be done sooner? If not—

You may misunderstand me now at first, dear, dearest Ba: at first I sate quietly, you thought; do I live quietly now, do you think? Ought I to show the evidence of the unselfishness I *strive*, at least, to associate with my love, by coolly informing you 'what would please me.'

But I will not say more, you must know . . and *I* seem to know that this question was one of Ba's old questions . . a branch-licence, perhaps, of the original inestimable one, that charter of my liberties, by which I am empowered to 'hold myself unengaged, unbound' &c. &c.

Good Heaven; I would not,—even to save the being asked such questions,—have played the horseleech that cries 'give, give,' in Solomon's phrase—'Do you let me see you once a week? Give me a sight once a day!—May I dare kiss you? Let me marry you to-morrow!'

But to the end, the very end, I am yours: God knows I would not do you harm for worlds—worlds! I may easily mistake what *is* harm or not. I will ask your leave to speak—at your foot, my Ba: I would not have dared to take the blessing of kissing your hand, much less your lip, but that it seemed as if I was leading you into a mistake—as did happen—and that you might fancy I only felt a dreamy, abstract passion for a phantom of my own creating out of your books and letters, and which only took your name. . . *That* once understood, the rest you shall give me.. In every event, I am your own.

12 *o'clock.*—I thought another letter might arrive. This must go as we shall set off presently to Mr. Kenyon's.

I *did* understand the question about my sister. I mean, that you felt somewhat so, incredible as it seems—only I believe *all* you say, all—to the letter, the iota. Think of *that*, whenever I *might* ask and do not—or speak, and am silent . . but I am getting back to the question discussed above, which I ought not to do—understand me, dearest dearest! See me, open the eyes, the dear eyes, and see the love of your R.

E. B. B. to R. B.

Wednesday—5. p.m.
[Post-mark, June 4, 1846.]

Then let it be as we meant it should be. And do you forgive me, my own, if I have teazed you . . vexed you. Do I not always tell you that you are too good for me?

Yet the last of my intentions was, this time, to doubt of your attachment for me. Believe *that*. I will write to-night more fully—but never can be more than at this moment

Your

Ba.

E. B. B. to R. B.

Wednesday Evening.
[Post-mark, June 4, 1846.]

Nothing at all had it to do with your Magna Charta, beloved, that question of mine. After you were gone, the other day and I began turning your words over and over, . . (*so* I make hay of them to feed the horses of the sun!) it struck me that you had perhaps an instinct of common sense, which, with a hand I did not see and a voice I could not hear, drew you perhaps. So I thought I would ask. For after all, this is rather a serious matter we are upon, and if you think that you are not to have your share of responsibility . . that you are not to consider and arrange and decide, and perform your own part, . . you are as much mistaken as ever *I* was. 'Judge what I say.' For my part, I have done, it seems to me, nearly as much as I can do. I do not, at least, seem to myself to have any power to *doubt* even, of the path to choose for the future. If for any reason you had seen wisdom in delay, it would have been a different thing—and the seeing was a *possible* thing, you will admit. I did not ask you if you *desired* a delay, but if you saw a reason for it. In the meantime I was absolutely yours, I remembered thoroughly, . . and the question went simply to enquire what you thought it best to do with your own.

For me I agree with your view—I never once thought of proposing a delay on my own account. We are standing on hot scythes, and because we do not burn in the feet, by a miracle, we have no right to count on the miracle's prolongation. Then nothing is to be gained—and everything may be lost—and the sense of mask-wearing for another year would be suffocating. This for *me*. And for yourself, I shall not be much younger or better otherwise, I suppose, next year. I make no motion, then, for a delay, further than we have talked of, . . to the summer's end.

My good . . happiness! Have I any that did not come from you, that is not *in* you, that you should talk of my good apart from yours? I shudder to look back to the days when you were not for me. Was ever life so like death before? My face was so close against the tombstones, that there seemed no room even for the tears. And it is unexampled generosity of yours, that, having done all for me, you should write as you always do, about *my giving* . . giving! Among the sons of men there is none like you as I believe and know, . . and every now and then declare to my sisters.

Dearest, if I vexed you, teazed you, by that question which proved unnecessary . . forgive me! Had you uncomfortable thoughts in the gardens to-day? Perhaps!

And I could not smooth them away, though I drew as near as I dared . . though I was in a carriage at seven o'clock, running a mystical circle round your tents and music. Did you feel me, any more than if I were a 'quick spider,' I wonder.

Henrietta and Arabel were going to spend the evening with cousins of ours, and as the carriage waited for the plaiting of Henrietta's hair, or the twisting of the ringlets, Arabel said to me 'Will you go for a quarter of an hour?' And in a minute, we were off . . she and Flush and Lizzie and I. Never did I expect again to see so many people—but I thought of *one* so much that my head was kept from turning round—and we drove once round the 'inner circle,' so called, and looked up to Mr. Kenyon's windows—and *there,* or *there,* you were, certainly!—and either *there,* or *there,* you were being disquieted in your thoughts by me, as certainly! Ah forgive me. After all, . . listen . . I love you with the fulness of my nature. Nothing of all this unspeakable goodness and tenderness is lost on me . . I catch on my face and hands every drop of all this dew.

So now . . you are not teazed? we are at one again, and may talk of outside things again?

But first, I must hear how the head is. *How* is it, best and dearest? And you had my letter at last, had you not? Because I wrote it as usual, of course. May God bless you—and *me* as I am altogether your own.

Twice (observe) I have been out to-day—the first time, walking. Also, twice have I written to you.

Say how your mother is—and *yourself!*—

George and Henrietta were asked to meet you at Mr. Kenyon's—but only to-day, and too late to forestall other engagements. Did you enjoy any of it? Tell me.

R. B. to E. B. B.

Thursday.
[Post-mark, June 4, 1846.]

'Vex me,' or 'teaze me,' my own Ba, you cannot. I look on it indeed, after a moment, as the only natural effect of your strange disbelief in yourself, and ignorance of our true relation one to the other by every right and reason. Only, Ba, you *are* wrong—doubly,—that is, you would be wrong if your own estimate of your power over me were the true one—for,—though it is difficult for me to fancy these abstractions and fantastic metamorphoses (as how one could feel without one's head,—or how I could live without the love of you now I have once got it)—yet, since you make me, I will fancy I love my head and love you no longer . . and then (which is *now*) *now*, do you think I am so poor a creature as to go on adding to my faults, and letting you gently down, as the phrase is, with cowardly excuses, 'postponing' this, and 'consenting to delay' the other,—and perhaps managing to get you to do the whole business for me in the end? I hope and think I should say at once—Oh, no more of this! But see how right I was—'*an instinct*, you seem to see.' So, I have been thinking,—there are but few topics of our conversation from which any such impressions could arise—was it that I have asked more than once, if you could really bear another winter in London, (in all probability a severe one)—and again, if you could get to Italy by any ordinary means without the same opposition you will have to encounter for my sake? . . My Ba, as God knows, *all that* was so much pure trembling attempting to justify myself for the over-greatness of the fortune, the excess of the joy,—if I could but feel that there was a little of your own good in it too—that you would gain that much advantage at least by my own inestimable advantage! If you knew how,—spite of all endeavours,—how happy I have been—

which is a shame to confess—but how very happy to hear that you could not without a degree of danger stay here—could no more easily leave England with Miss Bayley than with me! It seemed to justify me, as I say. And so of 'the wishing I had not mentioned Italy'—I wish your will to be mine, to originate mine, your pleasure to be only mine. Expressed first—it *will be* my pleasure . . but all is wrong if you take the effect, seek to know it, before the cause. What does it matter that I should prefer Italy to Nova Zembla? So, you *ought to have begun by saying* 'we will go there,' and then my pleasure in obedience had been naturally expressed. Did I not ask you whether you had not, after all, thought of going to Italy first—to Pisa, or Malta,—from the very beginning? *Always to justify myself!* Always!

But—this too is misunderstood. Let me say humbly, I *should* prefer to go with you to Italy or any place where we can live alone for some little time, till you can *know* me, be as sure of me as of yourself. Nor am I so selfish, I hope, as that (because my uttermost pride and privilege and glory above all glories would be to live in your sick-room and serve you,)—as that, on that account, I would not rather see you in a condition to need none of my service . . the next thing to serving you, is to be—what shall I say?—served by you . . loved by you, made happy by you—it is the being an angel, though there might be *arch*-angels—

And if *now* you do not understand,—well, I kneel to you, my Ba, and pray you to give yourself to me in deed as in word, the body as the heart and mind,—and *now!*—at any time,—you know what I cannot say, I cannot, I think,—if I know myself—love you more than I do . . but I shall always love you *thus*—and *thus*, in any case, happen what God may ordain—

Your R.

I know this is taking the simple experimental question

too seriously to heart . . but such experiments touch at the very quick and core of the heart . . I cannot treat them otherwise—*ought* I?

You will see Miss Bayley to-day—Mr. Kenyon asked if I were going to call to-day . . 'if not, Miss B. would.'

I have your letter . . the short note, not the promised one . . for all this writing about the question . . but I could not merely say—'Oh no, you mistake . . I had rather, upon the whole, not wait.'

Even now the feeling, in its subsiding, hinders me from speaking of the delightful account of 'Treppy' . . whom I remember now, perfectly—and what comfort is in *thy* dear note!

Bless you, *my* 'darlingest creature,'—my Ba!

E. B. B. to R. B.

Thursday.
[Post-mark, June 5, 1846.]

You are too perfect, too overcomingly good and tender—dearest you are, and I have no words with which to answer you. There is little wonder indeed that *I*, being used so long to the dark, should stumble and mistake, and see men like trees walking—and yet I must tell you that I did *not* mistake to the extent you have set down for me . . and that never was I so dull, so idiotic and ungrateful, as to fancy you into one 'wishing to let me down gently with cowardly excuses.' Since I first looked you in the face, and before that day, I have been incapable of defiling the idea of you with such an unworthy imputation. And surely what I *did* fancy, was consistent with the fullest faith in you and in the completest verity of your affection for myself. You might have had reasons, surely, which I did not see, without aggrieving me in any fashion. So do not make me out *too* stupid—it is bad enough actually. Yes—those questions you refer to, turned me down that path—and do tell me how I could be expected to guess at the real drift of them, after having been accustomed to walk rather with men than with angels! Ah—and now even, that I *see*, it makes me smile and sigh together. To say that I am not worthy, all at once grows too little to say. *No one* could be worthy of such words from *you*. You are best, best!! How much more do you want me to owe to you, when I *begin* by owing to you all things, . . the only happiness of my life?

As to Italy, I thought of it first, so I am in no danger of thinking that you engage me as female courier and companion . . the feminine of what Mr. Bezzi wants to be, Miss Bayley told me to-day. So if it is the same thing to you, we will put off Nova Zembla a little. But how is it possible to jest, with this letter close by? Dearest of all, believe that I am grateful to you as I ought to be . . penetrated . . touched to the bottom of my heart with the sense of what you have been to me and are; dearest beloved!

So do not reproach me with my dull questions, on Saturday. I won't ask them any more, . . and I did not mean by them the wickedness you thought . . so now let us be tranquil and happy till the fine weather ends. Brightly it begins, does it not? So hot it is to-day—so very hot in this room! Miss Bayley came just as I had been out walking and was tired; but she talked and interested me, and I found out from her that you were not in the gardens when we drove round them, but in the house when I looked up at the windows. Very happy and agreeable you all were, she said, at Mr. Kenyon's—though Mrs. Jameson missed the flower-show.

I forgot to tell you that Treppy is a Creole—she would say so as if she said she was a Roman. She lived, as an adopted favourite, in the house of my great grandfather in Jamaica for years, and talks to the delight of my brothers, of that 'dear man' who, with fifty thousand a year, wore patches at his knees and elbows, upon principle. Then there are infinite traditions of the great great grandfather, who flogged his slaves like a divinity: and upon the beatitude of the slaves as slaves, let no one presume to doubt, before Treppy. If ever she sighs over the slaves, it is to think of their emancipation. Poor creatures, to be emancipated!

May God bless you, dear dearest! Shall I ever be better, I wonder, than the torment of your life? It is *I* who wanted to be '*justified*,' and not *you* my beloved,—except as to your good sense for having made such a choice.

Such as I am however, I am

Your very own

Ba.

R. B. to E. B. B.

Friday.
[Post-mark, June 5, 1846.]

Nor did *I* mean so bad, dearest dearest, as that you *were* suspecting me of *that* . . Oh no, since 'Scorn of me (*that* "me") would recoil on you' . . you would have no right to bear with such a person for a moment: but I put the broadest case possible to declare upon broadly. As I would do *so* if I felt *so* . . felt no love longer . . so, in due degree, I would tell you frankly a fear or a doubt if I felt either. I thought you suspected me, perhaps, of being deficient in this last point of courage: but it was not altogether so,—or if it was, you shall doubt no more, but believe the more strongly for the future . . let us kiss on that convention, dearest! You see, I knew it *could not but be that* . . for if anything had struck *you* as really to be gained by delay, you must feel whether I should listen to that or no—last year, for instance, when you said 'let us wait.'

Ah, Ba, my own, many things *are* that ought not to be . . and I hide nothing . . cannot hide from you some feelings . . as that—after all, after all—talk, and indeed think, as one may—it is, let us say, a *pleasant* thing, at least, to be able to prove one's words,—even one's lighter words. The proof may justify *some* words, I mean, and the rest, that admit of no proof, get believed on the score of *them*,—the first words and proofs. I should like to prove a very, very little . . if I could but do so in turning fifty-thousand a year, or less, to some account and building Flush a house 'fair to see'—after which I could go on talking about the longings never to be satisfied here . .

Now this is foolish,—so the causeless blame, if you please, shall be transferred here . . as naughty children punished by mistake are promised a remission of next offence.

Oh to-morrow kisses all right . . all so right again, dearest! I have so much to say. Make me remember, love, to tell you something I have just learned about Mr. Kenyon which makes one—no, all is proper,—he *should* have the money, and I the admiration and love of his divine use of it: something to love him for, and he happy that God will reward it. Remember—for even *that* I should forget by you!

And all has been charming at Mr. Kenyon's—Landor's dinner, and our flower-show feast,—I will tell you to-morrow—and last night I went to Mrs. Procter's in downright spirits '*pour cause*' (with my first letter . . not my second, which only arrived this morning)—and I danced, to put it on record there that I was altogether happy, and saw Mrs. Jameson, and the Countess Hahn-Hahn, and Milnes and the Howitts and others in a multitude,—and I got to this house door at 4-o'clock, with the birds singing loud and the day bright and broad—and my head is *quite well*,—as my mother's is better, I hope—quite well, I am at this minute. For the rest, the news of your two exits and entrances in one day . . oh, thank you, thank the golden heart of my own, own Ba! whom I shall see to-morrow, but can . . *how* I can kiss her now—being her own

R. B.

E. B. B. to R. B.

Sunday.
[Post-mark, June 6, 1846.]

This is the first word I have written out of my room, these five years, I think . . if I dare count anything beyond two . . for I do know that one comes after two . . (now just see what I have written!) that two comes after one, I meant to say, . . as well as a mathematician. I am writing now in the back drawing-room, half out of the window for air, driven out of my own territory by the angel of the sun this morning. Oh—it is so hot—and the darkness does not help when the lack is just of *air*. There is a thick mist lacquered over with light—it is cauldron-heat, rather than fire-heat. So different in the country it must be! Well, everybody being at church or chapel, I knew I could have this room to myself, without fear even of the dreadful knocker . . more awful to me than the famous knocks which used to visit the Wesley family—so here I curl up my feet '*more meo*' on the settee, and help to keep the sabbath by *resting* upon you. Would Miss Goldsmid call it as 'profane' as anything in your poems? But it will not be more profane for *that*—as I could prove if we wanted proofs—only we do not.

Such flowers as you brought me yesterday—such roses! The roses are best, as coming from your garden! When I began to arrange them, I thought I never saw such splendid roses anywhere—they are more beautiful than what you brought last year surely! It seems so to me. Dearest, how did you get home, and how are you? and how is your mother? Remember to answer my questions, if you please.

After you were gone I received from Mr. Lough a very gracious intimation that if I would go to see his studio, his statue of the Queen and other works, he would take care that no creature should be present, he would uncover all the works and provide a clear solitude for me—he 'would not do it for a Duchess,' he said, but he 'would for *me*'! Now what am I to say. My sisters tell me that I can go quite easily. The place is very near, and there are no stairs. Well, I think I must go. It is very kind and considerate, and there would be a pleasure, of course. Do you know that statues have more power over me than all the pictures and all the colours thereof which the world can show? Mr. Kenyon told me once that it was a pure affectation of mine to say so—and for my own part I could not see for a long while what was the *reason* of a most unaffected preference. I think I see it now. Painting flatters the senses and makes the Ideal credible in a vulgar way. But with sculpture it is different—and there is a grand audacity in the power of an Ideal which, appealing directly to the Senses, and to the coarsest of them, the Touch, as well as the Sight, yet forces them to receive Beauty through the door of an Abstraction which is a means abhorrent to them. Have I written what I mean, I wonder, or do you understand it, without? Then there is a great deal, of course, in that grand white repose! Like the Ideas of the Platonic system, these great sculptures seem—when looked at from a distance.

When you were gone yesterday, and I had had my coffee and put on my bonnet, I went, with the intention of walking out, as far as the drawing-room, and there, failed: not even with your recommendation in my ears, beloved, could I get any further. Notwithstanding all my flatteries (meaning the flatteries of me!) I was not at best and strongest, yesterday, nor am even to-day, though it is nothing to mind or to mention—only I think I shall not try to walk out in this heat even to-day, and yesterday it seemed impossible. So I came back and lay on my own sofa, and presently began to read 'Le Comte de Monte Cristo,' the new book by Dumas, (observe how I waste my time—while you learn how *not* to fortify cities, out of Machiavelli!) and really he amuses me with his 'Monte Cristo' . . six volumes I am glad to see—he is the male Scheherazade certainly. Now that the hero is safe in a dungeon (of the Château d'If) it will be delightful to see how he will get out—somebody knocks at the wall already. Only the narrative is not always very clear to me, inasmuch as, when I read, I unconsciously interleave it with such thoughts of you as make very curious cross readings . . j'avais cru remarquer quelques infidelités . . he really seems to love me—l'homme n'est jamais qu'un homme . . never was any man like him—ses traits étaient bouleversés . . the calmest eyes I ever saw . . So, Dumas or Machiavelli, it is of the less consequence what I read, I suppose, while I apply so undestractedly.

May God bless you, ever beloved! I think of you, I love you—I forgot again your 'Strafford'—Mr. Forster's 'Strafford,' I beg his pardon for not attributing to him other men's works. Not that I mean to be cross—not to him even.

I am your own.

R. B. to E. B. B.

Sunday.
[Post-mark, June 8, 1846.]

One thing you said yesterday which I want to notice and protest against, my Ba—you charged me with speaking depreciatingly of myself because you had set the example—'I should not have thought of it but that you began.' Now I am tired, just at this moment, and submissive altogether, and *hopeful* besides, on the whole,—so I will let you off with a simple but firmest of protests,—I did NOT think of imitating you, but spoke as I felt and knew,—and feel and know still. The world, generally, will inform you of this in its own good time and way, so . . *taceo!* (The last opinion of the world's on the respective value of people and people, is unhappily too decisive. 'And, after all, Mr. Langton is quite as good as the Duke's daughter . . for he will have full twenty thousand a year!') I suspect I was going to turn a pretty phrase and tell you I have only a heart, as the play-books prescribe,—when the said heart pricks me as if I reserved something—so I will confess to owning a 'forehead and an eye'—one advantage over Pope, to whom folks used to remark 'Sir, you have an eye'—and no more—whereas yesterday evening after leaving Ba, while I settled myself in the corner of our omnibus to think of her, a spruce gentleman stretched over, and amid the rumbling begged my pardon for being forced to remark that my forehead and eye interested him deeply, phrenologist as he was; and he was sure I must needs be *somebody* . . besides a passenger to Greenwich! So if Ba will trust in phrenology!—I will at least not be unkind to her as to the learned man—who left the vehicle in due time, lamenting that in return for his own confidence and pink bill ('Mr. Hamilton, phrenologist and lecturer' &c. &c.) I would not break my obstinate reserve and augustly pronounce 'Am I a Beefeater now?'

Assez de sottises: Ba, my Ba, I am happy in you beyond hope of expression—you know how happy . . And have not I some shade of a right,—I who loved the dear, dear pale cheek and the thin hand,—a right to be blessed in the wonders I see . . so long as I continue to be thankful to God whose direct doing I know it to be: how can I ever doubt the rest . . the so easy matters remaining—I will not doubt more, I think.

Tell me, write of yourself, love: remember the fierce heat . . and *never* go up the long stairs—or, at least, *rest* at proper intervals. I think of the Homeric stone heaved nearly to the hill-top and *then!* . . An accident now would be horrible,—think, and take every precaution—because it is *my* life, (if that will influence you) my whole happiness you are carrying safely or letting slip. May God overwatch all and care for us!

Good bye, best beloved,—I fear I ought to go to Mrs.

Jameson's to-night: there is a breakfast engagement for Wednesday, to meet this and the other notable; and a simple 'at home' promised to anybody calling this evening—and my pride won't let me accept *one*, nor my liking to Mrs. J. suffer me to refuse both . . Yet the fatigue! I have been at church to-day, seeing people faint.

Your own, your own R.

R. B. to E. B. B.

Monday.
[Post-mark, June 8, 1846.]

My 'recommendation' to dearest Ba was properly interpreted by her when she regarded the spirit and not the letter of it.

The day was hot—even *I* thought who thrive in heat—and yesterday you did well to keep the house—but last night's rain, and this comfort of cloudiness may allow you to resume the exercise,—only with *all* ease, darling! Mrs. Jameson told me she called the other day on Miss Barrett, and was informed that lady was 'walking before her door'—for I went last night, and deserved to be amused, perhaps, for the effort, . . and so I was, I never liked our friend as I now like her, I more than like the good nature and good feeling and versatility of ready intelligence and quick general sympathy. She is to see you to-day. She told this to a Miss Kindersley who had been reading the 'Drama of Exile' to her complete delight—but in listening silently,—and after, when Mrs. J. obligingly turned and said 'How I should like to introduce *you* to Miss Barrett . . did you ever see her?' . . to which I answered in the old way, 'that nobody, as she knew, saw you.' At all these times did not I feel the 'mask' you speak of! I am, fortunately, out of the way of enquiries . . but if the thing were of constant occurrence, it would be intolerable. Shall it indeed end soon? May I count by months, by weeks? It is not safe—beginning to write on this subject—I can do nothing moreover.

Well, Lough has some good works, and you will be pleased I daresay: but of all things, hold him to his bond of maintaining the strictest privacy—for Mr. Powell or his kith and kin go there, and *his* impudence and brazen insensibility are dreadful to encounter beyond all belief. He would book-make about 'the meeting,' and in his ordinary talk, be supplied with a subject to tell lies about for the next year or two,—unless he got a lesson earlier. But Lough will understand and keep his promise, no doubt, if you exact it strictly.

My mother is decidedly better, . . I am quite well—considering Thursday is so far off!—considering the end of summer is so far off. Would it be profane to think of that lament . . 'the Summer is ended and we are not saved'?

I am obliged to leave off here—I love you ever my best dearest, own Ba!

E. B. B. to R. B.

Monday *Morning.*
[Post-mark, June 9, 1846.]

The stars threaten you with a long letter to-day, it seems, for I stretch out my hand and take blindly the largest sheet. Dearest, I have been driving out before your letter came . . and to *Hampstead!* think of *that*. And see the proof of it—this grew in the hedges when the sun rose to-day. We had a great branch gathered, and 'this was of it,' starred over with dog-roses. I did in the morning long for air, through the suffocation yesterday, and the walking being better for another day, my sisters persuaded me into the carriage. Only I wanted to wait for your letter, my letter, and could not—it did not come by the usual early post, and the carriage was here before it . . so I had to go, thinking of it all the way, and having it on my return ready to gladden me. How you make me laugh with your phrenologist! 'For the interests of science' you should have given your name. Then, would have come the whole history in the next lecture, . . how 'Once in an omnibus he met an individual with a forehead and eyes of mark, and knew him at a glance for the first poet of the age.' It would have made a feature in the lecture, and highly developed, I dare say, . . to suit the features in the omnibus. Just at the moment of this observation *I* too was thinking of eyes—'calm eyes' did I say? Yes, calm, serene . . which was what struck me first of all, in the look of them—was it ever observed before, I wonder? The most serene spiritual eyes, I ever saw—I thought *that* the first day I saw *you*. They may be called by other names beside, but they shall not lose the name I then gave them. Now to bear with the horrible portrait in the matter of the eyes, is a hard thing—Mr. Howitt must have *his* shut nearly, I think. The hair is like—and nothing else. The mouth, the form of the cheek, one is as unlike as the other. And the character of the whole is *most* unlike of the whole—it is a vulgarized caricature—and I only wonder how I could have fastened it inside of my 'Paracelsus' frontispiece-fashion. When it was hung up and framed, I did not know you face to face, remember. Mr. Kenyon told me it was 'rather like.' But always and uninstructed I seemed to know that it was not like you in some things . .

Monday Evening.—Observe how the sentence breaks off! While I was writing it, came a 'tapping, tapping at the chamber door,' as sings my dedicator Edgar Poe. Flush barked vociferously; I threw down the pen and shut up the writing case, . . and lo, Mrs. Jameson! I suppose she did not guess that I was writing to you. She brought me the engravings of Xanthian marbles, and also her new essays . . and was very kind as usual, and proposed to come some day next week with a carriage to take me out, —and all this time, how we treat her! Will she not have a right to complain of being denied the degree of confidence we gave (. . Mr. Kenyon gave for me . .) to Miss

Bayley? Will she not think hereafter 'There was no need of their deceiving *me?*' And yet I doubt how to retreat now. Could I possibly say to her the next time she speaks of you . . or could I not? it would set her on suspecting perhaps. She talked a little to-day of Italy, and plainly asked me what thoughts I had of it,—to which I could answer truthfully 'No thoughts, but dreams.' Then she insisted, 'But whenever you have thoughts, you will let me know them? You will not be in Italy when I am there, without my knowing it? And where will you go—? to Pisa? . . to Sienna? to Naples?' And she advised . . 'Don't go where the English are, in any case.' And encouraged like an oracle, . . 'Remember that where there's a will there's a way'—knowing no more what she spoke, than a Pythian on the serpent's skin.

Beloved, you are right in your fear about Mr. Lough. I have decided not to go there. Oh, it is best certainly; and, quietly considered, I shall be happier as well as safer in not going. We must walk softly on the snowdrifts of the world, now that we have got to them.

For the rest, . . that is for the chief thing . . you wrote foolishly in your first letter to-day, my beloved,—you *can* write foolishly on occasion, let me grant to the critics. I have just so much logic as to be able to see (though I am a woman) that for *me* to be too good for *you*, and for *you* to be too good for *me*, cannot be true at once, both ways. Now I could discern and prove, from the beginning of the beginning, that *you* were too good for *me*—it is too late therefore to take up the other argument—the handle of it was broken last year.

Also, I do not go to the world to ask it to appraise you—I would fain leave to Robins the things of Robins. I hope you have repented all day to-day having written so foolishly yesterday. Even Robins would not justify you.

Dearest, the avalanches are on us! Uncle and aunts coming down in a great crash! My uncle Hedley comes next week!—on the second or third of July, the eldest of my aunts, . . from Paris, . . who proposes to reside in this house for a week—it may be longer! and, still in July, the rest of the Hedleys, I think!—everybody coming, coming! Their welcome will be somewhat of a ghastly smile from *me*—for indeed I cannot be quite delighted, after the fashion of a thoroughly dutiful niece.

Ah, never mind them! Nobody can change anything, if you do not change yourself. You have 'a right' . . not the 'shadow' of one, but the very right . . to all I am, and to all the life I live. Did you not see before, what I have felt so long, that indeed you have a right to me and over me?

I am your own

Ba.

R. B. to E. B. B.

Tuesday.
[Post-mark, June 9, 1846.]

Is your letter 'long,' my own Ba? I seem to get to the end, each time I read it, just as sorrowfully soon as usual —so much for thankfulness! But if Ba is not to be 'tall,' depend on it, her letter shall not describe itself as 'long' —though in a sense nothing ever written, ever read by me, drew such a trail of light after it as her letters—your letters, my own, own love! While I write this, my lips rest on the eglantine . . well, it shall be '*dog*-rose' for Flushie's sake! You say truly about the folly—it is very foolish,—when I fancy you proposing to give *me* a golden Papal rose and gift for a King, instead of this! And if *I* feel this, why should not you, and more vividly even? A rose from Hampstead! And you bore the journey well? You should tell me, precisely, detailedly.

As for Lough's statues . . now, I have said more than I meant if it deters you from going to see them! If he will abide strictly by his promise, there is much to reward the trouble of going.

Always remember, my Ba, that the secret is *your* secret

and not mine . . that I keep it while you bid me, but that you may communicate it to whom you please, *when* you please, without waiting to apprize me. I should, I think, have preferred telling Mrs. Jameson from the beginning about the mere visits . . or, I don't know . . by one such piece of frankness you only expose yourself to fifty new—whatever they are! For there would be so much the more talk about you,—and either the quick woman's wit and discernment are to be eluded, or they are not,—foiled or not—and how manage without . . without those *particular* evasions which seem to degrade most of all? Miss Mitford's promises began the embarrassment. In short I think the best way in such a case is to tell *all* or none. I believe you might tell all to Mrs. Jameson with perfect safety, but, for *her* sake, I doubt the propriety . . for it would be to introduce her forthwith to exactly our own annoyances with respect to Mr. Kenyon, Chorley &c. Once knowing, she cannot *un*-know. In any case, I promise my conscience to give her,—and anybody else that may have a right to it,—a full explanation at the earliest safe moment . . may *that* be at no great distance! My own feeling is for telling Mr. Kenyon . . though you would considerably startle me if you answered 'well, *do!*' But, of the whole world, I seem only to care for *his* not feeling aggrieved: oh, he will understand!—and *can*, because he knows the circumstances at your house. Come what will, I am sure of you; 'if you live, and are well'—even this last clause I might exclude; it has often been in my thought to tell you . . only, dearest, there is always, when I plan never so dreamily and vaguely, always an understood submission the most absolute to your own desire . . but I fancied, that, in the case of any *real* obstacle arising so as to necessitate the 'postponement,' &c., I should have *stipulated* . . in the right yourself have given me . . I should have said—'we will postpone it, if you will marry me *now* . . merely as to the form . . but so as to enable me, if difficulties should thicken, to be by your bed*side* at least.' You see, what you want 'to relieve' me of, is just what my life should be thrice paid down for and cheaply. How could you ever be so truly mine as *so?* Even the poor service does not 'part us' before 'death' ——'till *sickness* do us part!'

But there will be no sickness and all happiness, I trust in God! Dear, dear Ba, I love you wholly and for ever— true as I kiss your rose, and will keep it for ever. Bless you.

My first letter 'did not reach you by the first post on Monday morning'—No! How should it . . when I carried it to town on Sunday night and went half a mile out of my way to put it in the general post office at the corner of Oxford Street!

You know I am to breakfast with Mrs. Jameson to-morrow—and perhaps I may make some calls after: if anything keeps me in Town so as to hinder the letter by the 8 o'clock post, you will know the reason . and expect the letter the next morning; but I will endeavour to get back in time.

E. B. B. to R. B.

Tuesday Evening.
[Post-mark, June 10, 1846.]

Best, dearest beloved, . . would it not be strange if you were not so to me? How do you think I feel, hearing you say such things . . finding such thoughts in your mind? If it is not worthy of you to have a burden set on your shoulders and to be forced into the shadow of disquietudes not your own, yet this divine tenderness is worthy of you . . worthy of your nature; as I know and recognise! May God help me to thank you, for I have not a word.

Practically however, see how your proposal would work. It could not work *at all*, unless circumstances were known—and if they were known, at the very moment of their being known you would be saved, dearest, all the trouble of coming upstairs to me, by my being thrown out of the window to you . . upon which, you might certainly pick up the pieces of me and put them into a bag and set off for Nova Zembla. *That* would be the event of the working of your proposition. Yet remember that I will accede to whatever you shall choose—so *think for us both.* You know more of the world and have more practical sense than I—and if you did not, had not, you may *do what you like with your own,* as surely as the Duke of Newcastle might.

For Mrs. Jameson, I should never think of telling her '*all*'—I should not, could not, would not! and the gods forefend that you should think of telling Mr. Kenyon any more. Now, listen. Perfectly I understand your reasons, your scruples . . what are they to be called? But I promise to take the blame of it. I will tell dear Mr. Kenyon hereafter that you would have spoken, but that I *would not let you*—won't *that* do? won't it stop the pricking of the conscience? Because, you see, I know Mr. Kenyon, . . and I know perfectly that either he would be unhappy himself, or he would make us so. He never could bear the sense of responsibility. Then, as he told me to-day, and as long ago I knew, . . he is 'irresolute,' timid in deciding. Then he shrinks before the dæmon of the world—and 'what may be said' is louder to him than thunder. And then again, and worst of all, he sees afar off casualty within casualty, and a marriage without lawyers would be an abomination in his sight. Moreover, to discover ourselves to him, and *not submit to his counsels,* would be a real offence . . would it not? As it is, it may seem natural and excusable that we two of ourselves should poetically rush into a foolishness—but if we heard counsel, and rejected it! ! Do you see? . . .

He came here to-day, dear Mr. Kenyon, and is to come with Miss Bayley on Friday, and take me in the carriage to drive, and to see his house. I must go, but dread it . . shrink from it—yes, indeed. As for Mr. Lough, how could I have 'bound him with Styx nine times round him?' It is easier to bind Mrs. Jameson. Oh no! You were right, and I was wrong in my first inclination about Mr. Lough.

And yesterday I was not tired to signify. I shall not be ill, my beloved,—I think I shall not. I am as perfectly well now in all respects (except that I have not strength for much exercise and noise and confusion, . .) as it is possible to be. So do not be anxious about me—rather spend your dear thoughts of me in loving me, . . dear, dearest!

You breakfast with Mrs. Jameson, and I shall remember not to long too much for the eight o'clock letter at night. Remember *you*, not to be hurried as to the writing of it.

Oh! I had a letter from my particular Bennet this morning, . . and my Georgiana desires me instantly to say why I presumed not to write to her before. I am commanded out of all further delays. '*Did* I receive her letter,' she wonders!!!! Georgiana is imperative.

May God bless you, you who bless me!

I am wholly your own.

E. B. B. to R. B.

Friday Morning.
[Post-mark, June 12, 1846.]

I must write very little to-day, dearest, because Mr. Kenyon, as a note from him just tells me, comes at half past two for me, and in the meantime I am expecting a visit from my uncle Hedley, who arrived yesterday while we were together. Scarcely could Henrietta keep him, she says, from coming upstairs 'to see Ba!' We just escaped, therefore. I have been thinking that having the barbarians down on us may be at least a means of preserving us from going into the wilderness ourselves . . *my*self . . if I were taken away, as I told you, to Tunbridge, Dover, or other provinces of Siberia. How should I bear, do you think, to be taken away from you? Very badly!—though you will not hear of my being able to love you as I ought——when *that* is precisely the only thing I can do, it seems to me, at all worthily of you.

Ora pro me in Mr. Kenyon's carriage to-day—I am getting so nervous and frightened! I shall feel all the while as if set on a vane on the top of St. Paul's . . can you fancy the feeling? I do wish I were safe at home again, reading your letter . . which *will* come to-night—*will* . . *shall* . . *must* . . according to the letter and spirit of the Law.

You made the proposal to me about New Cross, yesterday, out of consideration and kindness to *me!* I understand it so, thanking you. For the rest, I need not, I am certain, assure you that it would be the greatest pain to me at any time, to be wanting in even the forms of respect and affection towards your family—and that I would not, from a mere motive of shyness, hazard a fault against *them*—you will believe this of me. But the usual worldly form (if the world is to give the measure) would be *against* my paying such a visit—and under ordinary circumstances it never is paid—not *so*. Therefore the not paying it is not an omission of an ordinary form of attention—*that* is what I mean to say. And to keep all dear to you quite safe and away from all splashing of the mud which we cannot ourselves hope to escape, is the great object,—it does seem to me. Your father and mother would be blamed (in this house, I know, if not in others) for not apprizing my father of what they knew. As it is, there is evil enough—though there is a way of escaping *that* evil.

As it is.— Now I do beseech you to consider well whether you will not have too much pain in finding that they suffer it (after every precaution taken) . . to render all this which we are about, wise and advisable. They will suffer, to hear you spoken of as we both shall be spoken of . . be perfectly sure! They will suffer, to have to part with you *so*——and the circumstances, perhaps, will not help to give them confidence in the stranger, who presumes *so* to enter their family. I *ask you* not to answer this!—only, to think of it in time, lest you should come to think of it too late. Put it between the leaves of Machiavel,—that at need you may confute yourself as well as M. Thiers.

Beloved, say how you are—and how your mother is. Here I must end—to be ready for dear Mr. Kenyon, and casualties of uncles &c. Think of me, love me—my heart is full of you.

I am your Ba.

R. B. to E. B. B.

Friday.
[Post-mark, June 12, 1846.]

When I am close to you in your very room, I see through your eyes and feel what you feel—but after, the sight widens with the circle of outside things—I cannot fear for a moment what seemed redoubtable enough yesterday—nor do I believe that there will be two opinions anywhere in the world as to your perfect right to do as you please under the present circumstances. People are not quite so tolerant to other people's preposterousness, and that which yourself tell me exceeds anything I ever heard of or imagined—but, dearest, on twice thinking, one surely ought not to countenance it as you propose—why should not my father and mother know? What possible harm can follow from their knowing? Why should I wound them to the very soul and for ever, by as gratuitous a piece of unkindness as if,—no,—there is no comparison will do! Because, since I was a child I never looked for the least or greatest thing within the compass of their means to give, but given it was,—nor for liberty but it was conceded, nor confidence but it was bestowed. I dare say they would break their hearts at such an end of all. For in any case they will take my feeling for their own with implicit trust

—and if I brought them a beggar, or a famous actress even, they would believe in her because of me,—if a Duchess or Miss Hudson, or Lady Selina Huntingdon rediviva . . they would do just the same, sorrow to say! As to any harm or blame that can attach itself to *them*,—it is too absurd to think of! What earthly control can they have over me? They live here,—I go my own way, being of age and capability. How can they interfere?

And then, blame for *what*, in either God's or the devil's name? I believe you to be the one woman in the world I am able to marry because able to love. I wish, on some accounts, I had foreseen the contingency of such an one's crossing my path in this life—but I did not, and on all ordinary grounds preferred being free and poor, accordingly. All is altered now. Does anybody doubt that I can by application in proper quarters obtain quite enough to support us both in return for no extraordinary expenditure of such faculties as I have? If it *is* to be doubted, I have been greatly misinformed, that is all. Or, setting all friends and their proposals and the rest of the hatefulness aside—I should say that so simple a procedure as writing to anybody . . Lord Monteagle, for instance, who reads and likes my works, as he said at Moxon's two days ago on calling there for a copy to give away . . surely to write to him, 'When you are minister next month, as is expected, will you give me for my utmost services about as much as you give Tennyson for nothing?'—*this* would be rational and as easy as all rationality. *Let me do so, and at once, my own* Ba! And do you, like the unutterably noble creature I know you, transfer your own advantages to your brothers or sisters . . making if you please a proper reservation in the case of my own exertions failing, as failure comes everywhere. So shall the one possible occasion of calumny be removed and all other charges go for the simple absurdities they will be. I am entirely in earnest about this, and indeed had thought for a moment of putting my own share of the project into immediate execution—but on consideration,—no! *So* I will live and so die with you. I will not be poorly endeavouring to startle you with unforeseen generosities, catch you in pretty pitfalls of magnanimities, be always surprising you, or trying to do it. No, I resolve to do my best, *through* you—by your counsel, with your help, under your eye . . the most strenuous endeavour will only approximate to an achievement of *that*,—and to suppose a superfluousness of devotion to you (as all these surprises do) would be miserably foolish. So, dear, dear Ba, understand and advise me. I took up the paper with ordinary feelings . . but the absurdity and tyranny suddenly flashed upon me . . it must not be borne—indeed its only safety in this instance is in its impotency. I am not without fear of some things in this world—but the 'wrath of men,' all the men living put together, I fear as I fear the fly I have just put out of the window; but I fear *God*—and am ready, he knows, to die this moment in taking his part against any piece of injustice and oppression, *so* I aspire to die!

See this long letter, and all about a tiny one, a plain palpable commonplace matter about which you agree with me, you the dear quiet Ba of my heart, with me that make all this unnecessary fuss! See what is behind all the 'bated breath and whispered humbleness?'—but it is *right*, after all, to revolt against such monstrous tyranny. And I ought not, I feel, to have forgotten the feelings of my father and mother as I did—because I know as certainly as I know anything that if I could bring myself to ask them to give up everything in the world; they would do it and cheerfully.

So see, and forgive your own R.

E. B. B. to R. B.

Friday.
[Post-mark, June 13, 1846.]

But dearest, dearest, . . *when* did I try to dissuade you from telling all to your father and mother? Surely I did not and could not. That you should 'wound them to the very soul and for ever' . . I am so far from counselling it, that I would rather, I think, as was intimated in my letter of this morning, have all at an end at once—*rather!* Certainly *rather*, . . when the alternative would be your certain unhappiness and remorse. *A right*, they have, to your entire confidence;—for *me* to say a word against your giving it—may God forbid! Even that you should submit your wishes to theirs in this matter, would be no excess of duty—I said so, I think, in my letter of this morning.

At the same time, I *am* of opinion, . . which was what I meant to put into words, . . that, *in the case* of their approving in the sufficient degree . . and of your resolving finally on carrying out our engagement . . you should avoid committing them further than is necessary, and so exposing them to unpleasant remarks and reproaches from *my family* . . to go no farther. You think that nothing can be said—I wish *I* could think so. You are not to be restrained perhaps . . but you are to be *advised* . . and it would be a natural step for your father, to go straight to his friend Mr. Kenyon. Do you see what might be done though you are 'of age'—and for not doing which, your father might be reproached? And more there would be to do, besides. Therefore I thought that you should avoid, as far as possible, committing him openly . . making him a party in the eyes of the world (as would be done by my visit to New Cross for instance)—yet I may be wrong here, . . and you, in any case, are the master, to act as you see best.

And, looking steadily at the subject, do you not see, . . now that we look closely besides, . . how mortifying to the just pride of your family, as well as to your own self-respect, is every possible egress from these unhappy circumstances? Ah—I told you—I told you long ago! I saw that at the beginning. Giving the largest confidence to your family, you still must pain them—still.

For the rest . you are generous and noble as always —but, no, . . I shall refuse steadily for reasons which are plain, to put away from me God's gifts . . given perhaps in order to this very end . . and apart from which, I should not have seen myself justified, . . even as far as now I vaguely, dimly seem . . to cast the burden of me upon you. *No.* I care as little for money as you do—but this thing I will not agree to, because I ought not. At the same time, you shall be at liberty to arrange that after the deaths of us two, the money should return to my family . . this, if you choose—for it shall be by your own act hereafter, that they may know you for what you are. In the meanwhile, I should laugh to scorn all *that* sort of calumny . . even if I could believe it to be possible. Supposing that you sought *money*, you would not be quite so stupid, the world may judge for itself, as to take hundreds instead of thousands, and pence instead of guineas. To do the world justice, it is not likely to make a blunder on such a point as this.

I wish, if you can wish so, that you were the richer. I could be content to have just nothing, if we could live easily so. But as I have a little without seeking it, you must, on the other hand, try to be content, and not be too proud.

As to Lord Monteagle, . . dearest . . . you will do what you like of course, though I do not understand exactly what your object is. A pension on literary grounds is the more difficult to obtain, that the fund set apart for that end is insufficient, I believe. Then if you are to do diplomacy for it, . . how do you know that you may not be sent to Russia, or somewhere impossible for me to winter in? If you were fixed even in London, . . what then? You know best what your own views are, and wishes are—I would not cross them, if you should be happier so, or so.

And do you think that because this may be done, or not done . . and because *that* ought *not* to be borne . . we can make any change . . act any more openly . . face to face, perhaps—voice to voice? Alas, no!—You said once that women were as strong as men, . . unless in the concurrence of physical force. Which is a mistake. I would rather be kicked with a foot, . . (I, for one woman! . .) than be overcome by a loud voice speaking cruel words. I would not yield before such words—I would not give you up if they were said . . but, being a woman and a very weak one (in more senses than the bodily), they would act on me as a dagger would, . . I could not help *dropping*, dying before them. I say it that you may understand. Tyranny? Perhaps. Yet in that strange, stern nature, there is a capacity to love—and I love him—and I shall suffer, in causing him to suffer. May God bless you. You will scarcely make out these hurried straggling words—and scarcely do they carry out my meaning. I am for ever your

Ba.

R. B. to E. B. B.

Saturday.
[Post-mark, June 13, 1846.]

Dearest, all dearest beyond my heart's uttering, will you forgive me for that foolish letter, and the warmth, and—FOR ALL,—more than ever I thought to have needed to ask forgiveness for! I love you in every imaginable way. All was wrong, absurd, in that letter—do you forgive—now, while I kiss your feet, my own, own Ba?

For see why it was wrong . . my father and mother will NOT BE PAINED IN ANY DEGREE: they will believe what I say, exactly what I say. I wrote on and on in a heat at the sudden ridiculous fancy of the matter's taking place some fine morning, without a word of previous intimation,—'I am going away, never mind where,—with somebody, never concern yourselves whom,—to stay, if for ever, is it any business of yours to enquire?' All which was . . *what* was it? a method of confirming you in your complimentary belief in my 'calmness'—or that other in my good practical sense'—oh, Ba, Ba, how I deserve you!

I will only say, I agree in all you write—it will be clearly best, and I can obviate every untowardness here . . show that all is pure kindness and provident caution . . so easy all will be! And for the other matters, I will fear nothing.

But you do—you DO understand what caused the sudden fancy . . how I thought 'not show them my pride of prides, my miraculous, altogether peerless and incomparable Ba!' It was not flying from your counsel,—oh, no!

So, is your hand in mine, or rather mine in yours again, sweetest, best love? All will be well. Follow out your intention, as you spoke of it to me, in every point. *Do not for God's sake* run the risk, or rather, encounter the certainty of hearing words which most likely have not anything like the significance to the speaker that they would convey to the hearer—and so let us go quietly away. I will care nothing about diplomatism or money-getting extraordinary—why, my own works sell and sell and are likely to sell, Moxon says. And I mean to write wondrous works, you may be sure, and sell them too,—and out of it all may easily come some fifty or sixty horrible pounds a year,—on which one lives famously in Ravenna, I dare say: think of Ravenna, Ba!—it seems the place of places, with the pines and the sea, and Dante, and *no* English, and all Ba.

My Ba, I see you on Monday, do I not? You let me come then, do you not? I am on fire to see you and know you love me . . *not as* I love you . . that can never be! I am your own

R.

I resolve, after a long pause and much irresolution, to write down as much as I shall be able, of an obvious fact . . If the saddest fate I can imagine should be reserved for me . . I should wish, *you* would wish to live the days out worthily,—not end them—nor go mad in them—to prevent which, I should need distraction, the more violent the better,—and it would have to be *forced* on me in the only way possible—therefore, *after my death*, I return nothing to your family, be assured. You will not recur to *this!*

E. B. B. to R. B.

Saturday Morning.
[Post-mark, June 15, 1846.]

I wrote last night when my head was still struggling and swimming between two tides of impressions received from the excitement and fatigue of the day. Mr. Kenyon (dear Mr. Kenyon in his exquisite kindness!) took me to see the strange new sight (to *me!*) of the Great Western . . the train coming in: and we left the carriage and had chairs—and the rush of the people and the earth-thunder of the engine almost overcame me . . not being used to such sights and sounds in this room, remember!! and afterwards I read and answered your letter with a whirling head. I cannot be sure *how* I answered it, my head whirled so. I only hope . . hope . . hope . . that it did not seem unworthy of your goodness and generosity—for *that* would be unworthy of my perception of them and reverence for them, besides. You do not, in particular, I do hope, misunderstand my reasons for refusing to improve what you call my 'advantages,' by turning them into disadvantages for *you*. Really it struck me at the moment and strikes me new every time I think of it, that it would be monstrous in me to stop at such an idea long enough to examine it. To do such a thing would complete the 'advantages' of my alliance—if *that* is a desire of yours. And if I were to be ill afterwards, there would be the crown of the crown. Now ask yourself if *I ought*——

I cannot conceive of the possibility of a 'calumny' on such a pretext—there seems no room for it. You will however have it in your power hereafter, without injury to either of us, to do yourself full justice in this particular ——only neither now nor hereafter shall I consent to let in sordid withering cares with your life. God has not made it so, and it shall not be so by an act of mine.

And after all, shall we be so much . . so much tòo rich? do you fancy that Miss Kilmansegg is made of brass compared to me? It is not so bad, be very sure. If Arabel should not offend Papa, she will be richer hereafter than we are . . yet not rich even so. Why are you fanciful in *that* way? People are more likely to say that *I have taken you in.* The sign of the Red Dragon! as you suggested once yourself!

I could make you laugh, if it were not too hot to laugh, with telling you how I really do not know what my 'advantages' are—specifically—so many, and so many. I am not 'allowed' to spend what I might—but the motive is of course a kind one——there is no mistaking *that.* Poor Papa! He attends just to those pecuniary interests which no one cares for, with a scrupulous attention. Nearly two hundred a year of ship shares I never touch. Then there is the interest of six thousand pounds (not *less* at any rate) in the funds—and I referred to the principal of *that,* when I said yesterday, that when we had ceased to need it, it might return to my family, since it came from them, if you chose. But this is all air—and *nothing shall be said of it now*—and whatever may be said hereafter, shall come from *you,* and be your word rather than mine. So I beseech you, by your affection for me, to speak no more of this hateful subject, which I have entered for a *moment* lest you should exaggerate to yourself and mistake me for the least in the world of an heiress. As to Lord Monteagle, we can do without him, *I* think—and unless he would give us a house to keep, or something of that sort, at Sorrento or Ravenna, I do not exactly see what he can do for us. To make an agreement with a periodical, would be more a possibility perhaps—but it is not a necessity—there is no sort of need, in fact—and why should you be tormented 'in the multitude of the thoughts within you,' utterly in vain?

As to your family . . I understand your natural desire of giving your confidence at the fullest to your father and mother, who deserve and claim it . . I understand that you should speak and listen to them, and cross no wish of theirs, and in nothing displease and pain them. But I do not understand the argument by which you involve the question with other questions . . when you say, for instance, that I 'ought not to countenance the preposterousness and tyranny.' How do I seem to countenance what I revolt from? Do you mean that we ought to do what we are about, *openly?* It is the only meaning I can attach to your words. Well—If you choose it to be so, knowing what I have told you, *let* it be so. I can however, as I said yesterday, answer only for my will and mind, and not for my strength and body—and if the end should be different from the end you looked for, you will not blame me, being just, . . any more than I shall blame myself. May God bless you, ever dearest!—

I am your own as ever.

R. B. to E. B. B.

Sunday.
[Post-mark, June 15, 1846.]

May I venture to speak to dearest Ba as if I had seen her or heard from her since I wrote yesterday,—and that seeing or that hearing had brought the usual comfort and assurance,—and forgiveness when needed, but delight at all times? Do you forgive me indeed, Ba?

I shall know to-morrow—which 'to-morrow' is your *to*-day. I am soon to be with you *to-day*. I trust there is [no] occasion to exercise fancy and say—'When we meet on your return from Tunbridge a month hence,' or two, or three . . to go on fancying! What should I do,—be able to do? and if I understood you rightly the letter-communication would be hindered, if not stopped altogether. Thus is one the sport of one's own wishes. Fine weather is desired . . fine enough to drive people out of town into the country!

As it is, I have been sufficiently punished for that foolish letter, which has lost me the last two or three days of your life and deeds, my Ba. You went to Mr. Kenyon's—may have gone elsewhere (and gathered roses I did not deserve to receive)—but I do not know, and shall not recover my loss—not ever . . because if you tell me *now*, you exclude something new you would say otherwise . . if you write it on Tuesday, what becomes of Tuesday's own stock of matter for chronicling?

Well, the proper word in my mouth is—I am sorry to the heart, and will try never to offend so again. How you wrote to me, also! How you rise above yourself while I get no nearer where you were first of all, no nearer than ever! But so it should be! so may it ever be!

I believe the fault comes from a too-sweet sense of the freedom of being *true* with you, telling you all, hiding nothing. Carlyle was saying in his fine way, he understood why the Romans confined acting to their slaves . . it was no employment for a free man to amuse people . . be bound to do that, and if other faculties interposed, tending to other results on an audience than amusement, be bidden suppress them accordingly . . and so, he thought, it would be one day with our *amusers*, writers of fun, concocters of comic pieces. *I* feel it delicious to be free when most bound to you, Ba,—to be able to love on in all the liberty of the implied subjection . . so I am angry *to* you, desponding sometimes *to* you, as well as joyous and hopeful—well, well, I *love*, at any rate,—do love you with heart and soul, my Ba,—ever shall love you, dearest above all dearness: God bless you!

E. B. B. to R. B.

Tuesday.
[Post-mark, June 16, 1846.]

As to 'practical sense' I never saw, I confess, much to praise you for—but you began by making a great profession of it, please to remember—and, otherwise, you certainly ought to know more of the world and the wisdom thereof than I, or you are *dull*, dearest mine, and one might as well call the sun so on this burning dazzling morning, when everything is at a white heat. Then for the 'calmness' . . . . I did not call your eyes 'green' after all . . nor did I mean what you would force on me for a meaning in the other way:—you pretend to misunderstand? Eyes, at least, that had the mastery with me from the beginning! and it was so long, so long (as you observed yourself), that I could not lift up mine against them—they were the mystic crystal walls, so long!

After you were gone yesterday and I had done with the roses (exquisite roses!) and had my coffee, I saw my uncle Hedley who had been inquiring about me, said my sisters, all the afternoon, . . for it was he who came when we heard the greetings on the stairs—and he told me that his wife and daughter were to be in London early in July . . so that we shall have the whole squadron sooner than we thought—drawn up like a very squadron . . my other aunt, Miss Clarke, coming at the same time, and my cousin with her, Arlette Butler. But only those two will be in the house here, and they will not be for very long, nor will they be much in the way, I hope.

Shall I tell you? I repented yesterday . . I repented last night . . I repent to-day, having made the promise you asked of me. I could scarcely sleep at all last night, through thinking that I ought not to have made it. Be generous, and free me from that promise. To be true to you in the real right sense, I need no promises at all—and if an argument were addressed to me *in order* to *separate us*, I should see through the piteous ingenuity of it, I think, whatever ground it took, and admit no judgment and authority over your life to be higher than your own. But I have misgivings about that promise, because I can conceive of circumstances . . Loose me from my promise, and let me be grateful to you, my beloved, in all things and ways, and hold you to be generous in the least as in the greatest. What *I* asked of *you*, was as different as our positions are—different beyond what you see or can see. No third person can see,—no second person can see . . what my position is and has been . . I do not enter on it here. But there is just and only *one* way in which I may be injured by you, . . and *that* is, in being allowed to *injure you*—so remember, remember, . . to the last available moment.

Then . . I have lived so in a dream for very long!—and everything, all undertakings, all movements, seem easy in dream-life. The sense of this has lately startled me. To waken up suddenly and find that I have wronged you—what more misery?—and I feel already that I am bringing you into a position which will by some or many be accounted unworthy of you. Well—we will not talk of it—not now! there is time for the grave consideration which *must be*. Let us both think.

And may God bless you, ever dearest! You are the best and most generous of all in the world! Whatever my mistake may be, it is not concerning *that*. Also I love you, love you. Premature things I say sometimes, which are foolish always. Tell me how you are . . tell me how your mother is——but speak of your own head . . tam chari . . particularly. Overcoming, the heat is—and I do hope that Mrs. Jameson won't come after all.

Your
Ba.

R. B. to E. B. B.

Tuesday.
[Post-mark, June 16, 1846.]

I have just returned from Town—some twelve miles at least I must have walked in this extreme heat . . so what has become of the headache? And now I sit down to write what Ba will read . . what has become of the heat and fatigue? In this sense Ba 'looks cool at me!'

I shall just write that I love, and love you, and love you again—my own Ba—just this, lest you learn the comfort of a respite from hearing what you are doomed to hear, with variations, all the days of your life. But not much more than this shall I write, because the love lies still in me, and deep, as water does,—cannot run forth in rivulets and sparkle, this hot weather; but then how I love her when I can only say so,—how I feel her . . as in an old opera's one line that stays in my recollection the tropical sun is described on the ocean—'fervid on the glittering flood'—so she lies on me.

See the pure nonsense, my own Ba, and laugh at it, but not at what lies at bottom of it, because that is true as truth, true as Ba's self in its way.

I called on Forster this morning: he says Landor is in high delight at the congratulatory letters he has received—so you must write, dearest, and add the queen-rose to his garland. F— talks about some 500 copies—or did he say 300?—being sold already . . so there is hope for Landor's lovers.

So I should have written once . . but like Virgil's shepherd . . 'know I now what love is!'—Do you remember that the first word I ever wrote to you was 'I love you, dear Miss Barrett?' It was so,—could not but be so—and I always loved you, as I shall always.

Tell me all you can about your dearest self, my own love. I am so happy in you, in your perfect goodness and truth,—in all of you.

Be careful this fatiguing weather . . the evenings and mornings are the only working time of the day, as in the beginning of things. But all day long is rest-time to love you, dear, and kiss you, as now—kisses

Your own.

E. B. B. to R. B.

Tuesday, 6 o'clock.
[Post-mark, June 17, 1846.]

Beloved, this weather, which makes Flush cross, perhaps helped to make me depressed this morning. I had not slept well, and ought not to have written to you till the effect of it had gone off. Now I feel more as if I had been with you yesterday. Ah well! I don't, can't remember what I wrote . . and some of it was *wise* . . for I ought not to have promised *that*, . . and you must loose me, that I may be loosed in Heaven, from the bands of it. Only you are not to go to Greenwich (you go to Greenwich to-morrow, do you not?) thinking that I wanted to teaze you. There is just one meaning to all my words, let them be sad or gay . . and it is, that *your happiness is precious*. For myself, if we were to part now and for ever, I should still owe you the only happiness of my life. But nobody is talking of parting, you know—I am yours, and cannot be put away from you except by your own hand. Which is decided! What I ask of you, is to spare me the pang of causing you to suffer on my account, . . and you may suffer sometimes, I fear, through all your affection for me, . . and indirectly, if not directly.

Two visitors I have had to-day—dear Mr. Kenyon, and Lady Margaret Cocks. She is going to Italy—(oh, of course!) to Rome. He came to tell me that the books came to me from Landor himself, and that I must write to him to thank him properly. Mrs. Jameson I do not see, nor Miss Bayley.

How hot it will be for you to-morrow! Try to be

amused and not too tired, dearest beloved, and tell me in your letters how the head is.

While the heart beats (mine!) I am your own.

I am going in the carriage presently and shall write again to-night. Won't that be *three times in a day* according to order?

E. B. B. to R. B.

Tuesday Evening.
[Post-mark, June 17, 1846.]

Best, . . best, you are, to write to me when you were tired, and *so!* When *I* am tired and write to *you*, it is too apt to be what may trouble you. With *you*, how different! In nothing do you show your strength more than in your divine patience and tenderness towards me, till . . not being used to it, I grow overwhelmed by it all, and would give you my life at a word. Why did you love *me*, my beloved, when you might have chosen from the most perfect of all women and each would have loved you with the perfectest of her nature? That is my riddle in this world. I can understand everything else . . I was never stopped for the meaning of sorrow upon sorrow . . but that you should love me I do not understand, and I think that I never shall.

Do I remember? Yes indeed, I remember. How I recurred and wondered afterwards, though at the moment it seemed very simple and what was to be met with in our philosophy every day. But there, you see, there's the danger of using *mala verba!* The Fates catch them up and knit them into the web! Then I remember all the more (though I should at any rate) through an imprudence of my own (or a piece of ill-luck rather . . it shall not be called an imprudence) of which I will tell you. I was writing to Miss Mitford and of you—we differed about you often, . . because she did not appreciate you properly, and was fond of dwelling on the 'obscurity' when I talked of the light,—and I just then writing of you, added in my headlong unreflecting way that I had had a real letter from you which said that you loved me—'Oh—but,' I wrote on, 'you are not to mistake this, not to repeat it—for of course, it is simply the purest of philanthropies' . . . some words to that effect—and if yours was the purest of philanthropies, mine was the purest of innocences, as you may well believe, . . for if I had had the shadow of a foresight, I should not have fallen into the snare. So vexed I was afterwards! Not that she thought anything at the time, or has referred to it since, or remembers a word now. Only I was vexed in my innermost heart . . and *am* . . do you know? . . that I should have spoken lightly of such an expression of yours—though you meant it lightly too. Dearest! It was a disguised angel and I should have known it by its wings though they did not fly.

But I foresaw nothing, . . looked to you for nothing, . . nothing can prove better to myself, than my having mentioned the quaint word at all. For I know, and I hope *you* know, how impossible it always has been to me to choose for a subject of conversation and jest, things which never should be spoken to friend or sister. But how was I to foresee? So the quaintness passed as quaintness with me. And never from that time (you grew sacred too soon!), never again from that moment, did I mention you to Miss Mitford—oh yes, I did, when she talked of introducing Mr. Chorley, and when I replied that, being a woman, I would have my wilful way, and that my wilful way was to see *you* instead. But except *then* . . and when I sent her Mr. Landor's verses on you . . not a word have I spoken . . except in bare response. She thinks perhaps that my old fervour about you has sunk into the socket—she suspects nothing—in fact she does not understand what *love* is . . and I never should think of asking her for sympathy. She is one of the Black Stones, which, when I climb up towards my Singing Tree and Golden Water, will howl behind me and call names.

You had my second letter to-day, speaking of Landor, and of Mr. Kenyon's visit. At half-past six came Miss Bayley, talking exceeding kindnesses of Italy, and entreating me to use her . . to let her go with me and take care of me and do me all manner of good. What kindness, really, in a woman whom I have not seen six times in all! I am very grateful to her. She held my hands, and told me to write to her if ever I had need of her—she would come at a moment, go for a year!—she would do anything for me I desired! And this woman to believe of herself that she has no soul! Help me to thank her in your thoughts of her! She said, by the way, that Mrs. Jameson had talked to her of wishing to take me, . . but she thought (Miss Bayley thought) that she (Mrs. Jameson) had too many objects and too much vivacity . . it would not do so well, she thought. In reply—I could just thank her, and scarcely could do *that*, . . only I am sure she saw and felt that I was grateful to her aright, let the words come ever so wrong. To-morrow she leaves London for an indefinite time.

She told me too that a friend of hers, calling on Mrs. Jameson, had found her on the point of coming to me to-day, to drive out . . but she suffered from toothache and was going to Cartwright's first . . . and last, I suppose. I dare say he put her to torture, to be classified with 'the thumbscrew and the gadge' . . some disabling torture, for I have not seen her at all. So as at half-past seven Henrietta was going out to dinner, Lizzie and I and Flush took our places by her in the carriage, and went to Hyde Park . . drove close by the Serpentine, and saw by the ruffling of the water that there was a breath of wind more than we felt. The shadows were gathering in quite fast, shade upon shade; and at last the silvery water seemed to hold all the light left, as on the flat of a hand. Very much I liked and enjoyed it. And, as we came home, the gas was in the shops . . another strange sight for me—and we all liked everything. Flush had his head out of the window the whole way . . except when he saw a long whip, . . or had a frightful vision at the water of somebody washing a little dog . . which made him draw back into the carriage with dilated eyes and quivering ears, and set about licking my hands, for an 'Ora pro nobis.' And Lizzie confided to me, that, when she is 'grown up,' she never will go out to dinners like Henrietta, but drive in the park like Ba, instead . . unless she can improve upon both, and live in a cottage covered with roses, in the country. I, in the meantime, between my companions, thought of neither of them more than was necessary, but of somebody whom I had been teazing perhaps . . dearest, was it so, indeed? . . but I avenge you by teazing myself back again! A long rambling letter, with nothing in it! 'Passages, that lead to nothing'—and staircases, too! May I be loved nevertheless, as usual? and forgiven for my 'secret faults?' You are the whole world to me—and the stars besides!

And I am your very own

Ba.

R. B. to E. B. B.

Wednesday Morning.
[Post-mark, June 17, 1846.]

My own Ba, I release you from just as much as you would easily dispense me from observing in that mutual promise. Indeed, it has become one unnecessary for our present relation and knowledge: it was right at the beginning for either to say to the other, using calm words, 'It is your good I seek, not mine,' and as if it were demonstrated that I should secure yours at the expense of mine by leaving you I would endeavour to do it—so, you assure me, you would act by me. The one point to ascertain therefore, is—what will amount to a demonstration; and I for my part apprize you that no other person in the world can by any possibility know so much of me as to be entitled to pronounce in the matter—to say 'it is for good or for evil'—therefore, you will no more be justified in giving up to *that* kind of demonstration what I consent you shall give up to one clearly furnished by *myself*, the only authentic one—than you would be justified in paying my money, entrusted to you, on the presentation of a cheque signed by somebody else . . somebody who loves me better than himself, my best of friends, truest of advisers &c. &c. It skills not, boots not—'John Smith' is not R.B., nor B.A. and because R.B. or B.A. shall be instantly attended to,—the counterfeit must be refused.' Just this, so rational and right, I understood you to bid me promise—and so much you have promised me, a proper precaution for the earlier time when the friend might seem to argue with some plausibility 'really I understand my friend's interests better than you can.' But now, who dares assure me that? I disbelieve it—one only knows better, can ever know better—yourself; and I will obey yourself. So with me—I know better my own good than you do yet, I think. When I tell you that good requires such a step as you speak of, you shall acquiesce; I will tell you on the instant, as you, in your own case, should tell me on the instant. I needed not ask you to promise, as I foolishly did, that you would not act in the saddest of ways—professing to see what could never be, and believe what must be untrue. At the beginning, at the first day, suppose Mr. Kenyon had said—you prevent his getting such a place, which brings in so much honour and wealth—or marrying such a person who would effect the same—you might have assented then, in your comparative ignorance, just as you could not have objected had he said, 'If you hold Mr. B. to his engagement to come here on the Derby Day you will ruin him assuredly, for his heart and soul are on "the turf" and his betting-book will go to wreck.' To this you could never bring yourself to pretend an assent—it would be no argument if he went on saying—'Why, A and B and C go to races and bet on them'—*you know* I *do not*—so you know my estimate of honour and wealth and the rest, apart . . I will not say from the love of you,—but from my own life as I had traced it years ago, and as it is still traced for me to its end,—your love coming to help it in every smallest particular, to supply the undreamed-of omissions in the plan of it, and remove the obstructions best seen now that they are removed or removable. There is a calmest 'of calm' statements of the good of you to me.

My dearest Ba, you say 'let us both think'—think of this, you! Do not for God's sake introduce an element of uncertainty and restlessness and dissatisfaction into the feeling whereon *my* life lies. To speak for myself, this matter is concluded, done with,—I am yours, you are mine, and not to give use to refinements upon refinements as to what is the being most of all each others, which might end in your loving me best while I was turned a Turk in the East, or my—you know the inquisition does all for the pure love of the victim's soul. Let us have common sense—and think, in its most ordinary exercise, what would my life be worth now without you—as I,—putting on your own crown, accepting your own dearest assurance,—dare believe your life would be incomplete now without mine—*so* you have allowed me to believe. Then our course is plain. If you dare make the effort, we will do as we propose,—if not, not: I have nothing to do but take your hand . . there is not one difficulty in my path,—nor in yours on my account,—that is for me. If I change my views, and desire hereafter what I altogether turn from now,—in what conceivable respect will your being my wife hinder me? If I accept the Embassy which Young England in the person of Milnes has promised me—you shall offer no impediment. If I rather aspire to 'dine out' here in London, you shall stay at home and be good-natured. I shall attain to all these delights just as easily with you as without you, I suppose; 'No, I cannot marry some other woman and by her means and connections and connexions'—No—because—first and least of all, I begin by drawing on myself the entire cataract of shame and disgrace in the mouth of the world,—direct accusation or rather condemnation, against which not a word can be urged in mitigation, because all would be the pure simple truth—*I* do this, who have been fretfully wincing under the mere apprehension of catching a mere spatter or two of gossiping scandal—which a very few words would get rid of, seeing that, in fact, the falseness of the imputation will be apparent to everybody with eyes to see—for after all, here I am, living to my own pleasure and my father and mother's, and at liberty to do so for ever, as mortals say. Well, and *so* having gone under the whole real cataract instead of the sprinkling impertinence of the half a dozen sprinklings from the mop at the nursery-window which an upward look and cry will stop at once,—*so* having mended the matter, I commit a sin which I turn and ask you, should you be ever at peace with God and yourself if you sate still and suffered me to commit,—not on account of me and my harm to follow in both worlds,—but in mere justice to your 'neighbour,'—on whom you would see inflicted this infamous wrong?

Dear, dear, dear Ba, I kiss you, kiss my heart out unto you,—best love, one love! *I* see above what I will not think over again, look over again—but what then? Can I be quiet when I hear the least, least motion about my treasure, and my heart that is there, with it? Then *no more*, I beseech you, love, never one word more of all that! Whenever I can hear such words calmly, I shall be fit for agreeing to them,—let all be now. These two kindest of letters both come in together to my blessing—my entire blessing! I was writing the last line when they came—I will just say now, that the Greenwich affair is put off till Friday. Do not I understand Miss Bayley? And do I understand you, my Ba, when I venture this time—because of the *words* and the pain I shall not hide that they *did* give me,—to feel that, even beyond my kissing you, you kiss this one time your own R.B.

My mother is much better, and out—she is walking

with my sister. I am very well—in the joy perhaps . . but really much better—and have been so.

My two hundredth letter from her! I, *poor?*

E. B. B. to R. B.

Wednesday.
[Post-mark, June 18, 1846.]

Dearest and ever dearest, try to forgive me when I fall so manifestly short of you in all things! It is the very sense of this which throws me on despairs sometimes of being other than a bane to your life—and then . . by way of a remedy . . I begin to be a torment to it directly. *Forgive me.* Whatever I may say I am as wholly yours as if you held me in your hand, and I would do for you any extravagance, as if it were a common thing, at a word —and what is before us is *only* a common thing, since I have looked to it from the beginning. Oh—I may talk when I am out of spirits—but you know, and *I* know best of all, that I could not withdraw myself from you, unless you said 'Go'—could not—I have no power. Fine talking, it is of me, to talk of withdrawing myself from you! You know I could not at all do it, let ever so many special pleaders come to prove to me that you would be more prosperous and happy without me. 'Then' I would say . . 'let him put me away. I can't put myself away, because I am not mine but his.' Assuredly I would say just that, and no more. So do you forget that I have teazed you and pained you . . . *pained* you! . . I will try not to pain you, my own, own dearest, any more. I have grown to love you instead of the whole world; and only one thing . . (you understand what *that* is . .) is dreadful and intolerable to me to imagine. But now it is done with; and you shall teach me hereafter to make you happy instead of the contrary. So . . yes—you are kissed this time! upon both eyes, . . that they may not see my faults. And afterwards I will tell you a paradox . . that if I loved you a hundred times less, I should run into such offences less in exact proportion. And finally I will give you a promise . . not to teaze you for a week—which were a wonderful feat for *me!* the teazer *par excellence.*

To-day I deserved to hear of your head being worse—but it is better, I thank God—and your mother is better—all such comforting news! But it was no news that you did not go to Greenwich to-day,—for Mrs. Jameson came for me to drive at about six, and she and I were in Regent's Park until nearly eight. Then she went somewhere to dinner, and I, who had had tea, came home to supper! I like her very much—more and more, certainly—and we need not be mysterious up to the usual mark of mystery, because I told her . . told her . . what might be told—and she was gracious to the uttermost—not angry at all,—and said that 'Truth was truth, and one could breathe in the atmosphere of it, and she was glad I had told her.' Of you, she said, that she admired you more than ever—yes, more than ever—for the 'manner in which as a man of honour you had kept the secret'—so you were praised, and I, not blamed . . and we shall not complain, if our end is as good as our beginning. Also we talked of your poetry and of you personally, and I was *pleased,* . . which proves a little what was said—and I heard how you were invited as a 'celebrity' for the Countess Hahn-Hahn to see you, and how you effaced yourself with ever so much gracefulness; yet not too much, to omit charming the whole room. Mrs. Jameson praises you always, as nobody does better. And to-morrow . . will you be surprised to hear that to-morrow at half-past four, I am to go again with her, . . to see Rogers's pictures? Is it wrong? shall I get into a scrape? She promised laughingly that I should be *incognita* to the only companion she thought of taking . . a Mrs. Bracebridge, I think . . and Mr. Rogers himself is not to be visible—and she herself will mention it to nobody. It was hard to say '*no*'—yes perhaps 'no' would have been better. Do you think so? Mrs. Bracebridge is an artist and lives or lived on *Mount Hymettus!*—and she is not to hear my name even.

Now—good night, very dear!—most dear of all! I will not teaze you for a fortnight, I think. Ah—if ever I can do that again, you shall not be *pained*, . . you shall think that my heart and life are in you, and that, if they seem to flatter, it is that they go deeper. All I *am* is yours—which is different from . . all I *have*. 'All I *have*,' is when I may lean my head down on the shoulder—

So let me be your own

Ba.

Of those two letters, one was in the post before seven the evening before. Now, is it not too bad?

R. B. to E. B. B.

Thursday.
[Post-mark, June 18, 1846.]

Did you really kiss me on the two eyes, my Ba? I cannot say 'perhaps at the very time I was thinking of you,'—more than 'when I was breathing'—I breathe always, think of you always,—kiss you almost always. You dear, dearest Ba! Do *pain* me so again and again,—if you will *so* cure me every time! But you should not imagine that I can mistake the motive,—as if you loved me less and therefore wrote—oh, no—but there is no getting rid of these mistakings before the time: they bear their fruit and die away naturally . . the hoe never cuts up all their roots. I shall trust to hear you say one day I am past such mistaking—but—at Amalfi?

I am very glad, *love*, you go to Mr. Rogers' to-day—what harm *can* follow? The evil in the other case was a very precise and especial one. They say his pictures are well worth seeing. Tell me, make me see *you* seeing! I am glad, too, Mrs. Jameson knows . . but her graciousness I expected, because the causes you were able to give her would really operate just in that manner: indeed they *are* the sole causes of the secresy we have observed. I cannot help liking Mrs. Jameson more, much more since her acquaintance with you. Hazlitt says somewhere that the misery of consorting with country-people is felt when you try for their sympathy as to favourite actors—'Liston?' says the provincial, 'never heard of him'—but—whoever knows Miss Barrett . . 'Ba,' they are not going to be let known . . of such a person *I* know something more than of any other.

Talking of Hahn-Hahn, read this note of Mrs. Carlyle's—although to my mortification I find that the wise man is not so peremptory on the virtue of one of Ba's qualities as I, the ignorant man, must continue to be. Never mind,—perhaps 'in the long run' I may love you as if you were exactly to Mrs. Carlyle's mind!

I want to tell you a thing not to be forgotten about Florence as a residence for any time. You spoke of the *bad water* at Ravenna . . which if a serious inconvenience anywhere is a very plague in Italy; well, the medical people, according to Valléry, attribute the black hollow cheeks and sunk eyes and general ill health of the Florentines to their vile water; impregnated with lead, I think. There is only one good fountain in the city—that opposite Santa Croce; I religiously abstained from drinking water there—and felt the privation the more from having just left Rome, where the water is the most perfectly delicious and abundant and, they say, wholesome—in the world. That one objection is decisive against Ravenna—but then, why do the English all live at Florence?

It makes me happy to hear of your achievements and *not* of any ill result—*happy!* Is it quite so warm to-day? If it were to rain to-morrow (!), IF—our party would be postponed till the next day, Saturday, I believe . . there was a kind of understanding to that effect—now, in that case, might I go to you to-morrow? In the case of real heavy rain only——the letter to-morrow will tell me perhaps . .

Goodbye, dearest dearest; I love you wholly—

E. B. B. to R. B.

Thursday Evening.
[Post-mark, June 19, 1846.]

But I have not been to Mr. Rogers's to-day, after all. I had a note from Mrs. Jameson, to put off our excursion to Saturday . . if I consented to Saturday! but of course I would not consent to Saturday—and as she intimated that another day would do as well, we shall have another day fixed, I suppose. What a good fruit it would be of the confession I made in the park, if she were to ask *you* to go! ! ! Oh, I should like *that*—I should like it notwithstanding the drawbacks. It would be a fair gain upon the usual times of meeting—only that I could not care quite as much for the pictures—yet, those too, I should like to see with you, rather than apart from you. And *you* never saw them . . *you!* Is there a hope of her asking you when you are at Greenwich together? Now I have got this into my head, it will not go out again—oh, you must try and enchant her properly at Greenwich and lead her into asking you. Yet, with you or without you in the body, the spirit of you and the influence of you are always close to my spirit when it discerns any beauty or feels any joy; if I am happy on any day it is through you wholly, whether you are absent or present, dearest, and ever dearest!

And so, instead of Mr. Rogers's pictures, I have been seeing you in my thoughts, as I sate here all alone to-day. When everybody was at dinner I remembered that I had not been out—it was nearly eight . . there was no companion for me unless I called one from the dinner-table; and Wilson, whom I thought of, had taken holiday. Therefore I put on my bonnet, as a knight of old took his sword,—aspiring to the pure heroic,—and called Flush, and walked downstairs and into the street, all alone—*that* was something great! And, with just Flush, I walked there, up and down in glorious independence. Belgium might have felt so in casting off the yoke. As to Flush, he frightened me a little and spoilt my vain-glory—for Flush has a very good, stout vain-glory of his own, and, although perfectly fond of me, has no idea whatever of being ruled over by me!—(he looks beautiful scorn out of his golden eyes, when I order him to do this or this) . . and *Flush* chose to walk on the opposite side of the street, —he *would*,—he insisted on it! and every moment I expected him to disappear into some bag of the dogstealers, as an end to *his* glory, *à lui*. Happily, however, I have no moral with which to point my tale—it's a very immoral story, and shows neither Flush nor myself punished for our sins. Often, I am not punished for my sins, . . am I? *You* know *that* . . dearest, dearest! But then, even *you* are not punished for your sins . . . when you flatter so! Ah, it is happy for you, and for your reputation in good taste and sense, that you cannot very well say such things except to me, who cannot believe them. For the rest, the eyes were certainly blinded, . . being kissed too hard.

How I like Mrs. Carlyle's note! You will go of course. But it will *not* rain to-morrow, and you shall *not* have the advantage of coming through it to me, . . for this reason (among others far better), that I have engaged to see, at three or four perhaps, a friend of ours from the country. She is in London for only two days and wrote to beg me to see her, and to-day I escaped by half a rudeness, and, if I do to-morrow, it will be by a whole rudeness. So, not to-morrow! And, if Saturday should be taken from us, we must find three days somehow next week—it will be easily done.

As to Florence, the flood of English is the worst water of all in the argument. And then Dr. Chambers 'warned me off' Florence, as being too cold for the winter. It would be as well not to begin by being ill; and half I am afraid of Ravenna—though Ravenna may *not* be cold, and though Shelley may belie it altogether. 'A miserable place' he calls it in the 'Letters.' Still I observe that his first impressions are apt to be darker than remain. For instance, he began by hating Pisa, and preferred it to most places, afterwards. There is Pisa by the way! Or your Sorrento . . Salerno . . Amalfi . . you shall consider if you please—find a new place if you like.

It is my last letter perhaps till I see you. May God bless you, I lift up my heart to say. How happy I ought to be, . . and am, . . with your thoughts all round me, *so*, as you describe! Let them call me your very own

Ba.

R. B. to E. B. B.

Friday Morning.
[Post-mark, June 19, 1846.]

I shall hardly be able, I am afraid, to get your letter . . if one should come through your dear goodness, my own Ba . . . before I go out . . having to meet the Procters' party in Town: so I will just write my joy at its being little more now than twenty-four hours before I shall see you, I trust. The day is cool and nearer rain than I fancied probable—but, oh the task-work, Egyptian bondage, that *much* going-out would be to me, who am tired (*unreasonably*) beforehand on this first and most likely last occasion during the year. It is a pity that I am so ignorant about Hahn-Hahn's books—one, 'Faustina,' I got last night, but have neither heart nor time to 'get it up' in a couple of hours.

Something you said on Mrs. Jameson's authority amused me—the encomium on my grace in sitting still to see the play and not jumping on the stage to act too—as if it were not the best privilege one finds in being 'known' never so little, that it dispenses one from having to make oneself known. When you are shipwrecked among Caribbee Indians you are forced to begin professing 'I can make baskets, and tell fortunes, and foresee eclipses—so don't eat me!' And even there if they threatened nothing of the kind, I should be content to live and die as unhonoured as one of their own cabbage-trees.

I must go now—the day gets hotter, but then *our* day draws nearer—All my heart is yours, best of dearest loves, my own Ba, as I am your own—

R. B. to E. B. B.

Sunday.
[Post-mark, June 22, 1846.]

What I told you yesterday is very often in my thoughts, my own Ba—that with respect to the love for you 'I see what I know and testify what I have seen.' I know what *is*, and *why* it is—so far as my faculties of perception allow, of course—I rest on you just as I sate on the grass in the garden this morning with the very earth's immensity beneath: that is very different from trusting to this chair which is firm enough now, but might break down from a thousand causes. How entirely I believe in you, Ba! When you praise me, I believe that you are in error, yet believe it none——I know I am not so truthful to you—not so invariably, in the least as in the greatest matters—in the *greatest*, in the ordinary even, I speak pure truth,—but the old conventional habits cling, as I find out on reflection sometimes—but I aspire no less to become altogether open to your sight as you are to me,—I in my degree,—like a smallest of lake's face under the sky's: and for this also I shall have to bless you, my only Ba,—my only Ba!

I ought never . . I think I will not again . . attempt to write down why I love you . . (not, NOT that it is done here, but alluded-to, touched upon . .) The elements of the love . . (I say 'the' love, *mine,* because I *will* not know, nor hear, nor be taught anything by anybody else about 'love,' the one love everybody knows, it seems, and lives and dies by)—my love's elements are so many that the attempt to describe them is to bring about this failure . . the first that comes is taken up and treated of at length . . as that element of '*trust*' just now . . and then, in the feeling of incompetence which makes the pen sink away and turns the mind off, the others are let pass by unnamed, much less described, or at least acknowledged for the undeniable elements they are. What were all the *trust* without—and thus I could begin again! Let me say no more now—and forgive all the foolishness . . it is not for my wisdom you are to love me, Ba! Except that if you agreed too heartily with me on that point, I should very likely be found turning round on you with 'not wise, when I adore you *so?*' Wise or unwise, I *do* adore you, my Ba! And more and evermore! But see how I need your letters to *train* mine, to lead them into something more like the true way . . and to-morrow the letter will come—will it not? And mine shall be less about myself and more about you—whom may God bless, prays your own

R.

E. B. B. to R. B.

Sunday.
[Post-mark, June 22, 1846.]

I write to you in the drawing-room, and have brought down with me, I find, no smaller paper—but it can't be filled, can it? though I have to tell you the great news about the lilies . . that all, except *two,* are in full blow . . and that the two are unfolding . . I can almost see the leaves move. I told you how it would be. They will live, . . and last longer than the roses, . . which I shall have to tell you by history as well as prediction, presently. The next news is not so good,—for I have had a note from

Mrs. Jameson to the effect that she will come to take me to the pictures to-morrow, Monday—so that there will be no time to be diplomatic. My hope was of your meeting her at Mr. Carlyle's, before she could arrange anything finally, —and really I do feel as disappointed as if I had had a reason for the hope. Now, unless we have another miracle, there's an end, I suppose.

Think of my having left Flush behind me fast asleep. He dashes at the door in the most peremptory way, and nearly throws me backward when I open it, with his leaping-up-joy . . if it is not rather his reproach.

Now I am here all alone, except Flush—sitting, leaning against the open window with my feet curled up, and, at them, Flush curled up too; and I writing on my knee *more meo*. Rather cooler it seems, but rather too hot still it is, I think. How did you get home? how are you, dearest? And your mother? tell me of her, and of you! You always, you know (*do* you know?), leave your presence with me in the flowers; and, as the lilies unfold, of course I see more and more of you in each apocalypse. Still, the Saturday's visit is the worst of all to come to an end, as always I feel. In the first place stands Sunday, like a wall without a door in it! no letter! Monday is a good day and makes up a little, but it does not prevent Tuesday and Wednesday following . . more intervening days than between the other meetings—or so it seems. I forgot to tell you that yesterday I went to Mr. Boyd's house . . not to see him, but as a preliminary step to seeing him. Arabel went to his room to tell him of my being there—we are both perhaps rather afraid of meeting after all these years of separation. Quite blind he is—and though scarcely older than Mr. Kenyon (perhaps a year or two or three), so nervous, that he has really made himself infirm, and now he refuses to walk out or even to go downstairs. A very peculiar life he has led ever since he lost his sight, which he did when he was quite a young man—and a very peculiar person he is in all possible ways. His great faculty is . . *memory* . . and his great passion . . Greek—to which of late he has added *Ossian*. Otherwise, he talks like a man of slow mind, which he is, . . and with a child's way of looking at things, such as would make you smile—oh, he talks in the most wonderfully childish way! Poor Mr. Boyd. He cares for me perhaps more than he cares for any one else . . far more than for his own only daughter; but he is not a man of deep sensibility, and, if he heard of my death, would merely sleep a little sounder the next night. Once he said to me that whenever he felt sorry about anything, he was inclined to go to sleep. An affectionate and grateful regard . . grateful for many kindnesses . . I bear him, for my part. He says that I should wear the crown in poetry, if I would but follow Pope—but that the dreadful system of running lines one into another ruins everything. When I talk of *memory*, I mean merely the mechanical faculty. The *associative*, which makes the other a high power, he wants. So I went to his house in St. John's Wood yesterday, and saw the little garden. Poor Mr. Boyd. There, he lives, all alone—and never leaving his chair! yet cheerful still, I hear, in all that desolation. As for you and Tennyson, he never heard of you . . he never guesses at the way of modern literature . . and it is the intense compliment to me when he reads verses of mine, 'notwithstanding my corrupt taste,' . . to quote his own words.

Dearest, do you love me to-day? I think of you, which is quite the same thing. Think of *me* to-morrow at half-past four when Mrs. Jameson comes, and I shall have all that exertion to go through without the hope of you. Only that you are always *there* . . *here!*—and I, your very own

Ba.

R. B. to E. B. B.

Monday.
[Post-mark, June 22, 1846.]

If I only thought for myself in this instance, I should at once go and mount guard before your house so as to see you, at least, for a moment as you leave it.

To hope for a word would never do . . you might be startled, or simply not like such a measure, and *in simili incontri* I will not run risks, but I should be able to *see* you, my Ba . . why do I not go then? People at doors and windows are also able, alas, to see *me* too—so I stay . . if this *is* staying away when I can see the curled-up feet and kiss them beside,—ever-dear feet!

Do *you* know the days and the times and the long interval,—you, as *I* know? How strange that you should complain, and I become the happier! If I could alter it, and make you feel no subject for complaint any longer, I *would*,—surely I would, and be happy in that too, I hope . . yet the other happiness needs must be given up in that case . . I cannot reason it out. I excuse my present selfish happiness by feeling I would not exchange the sadness of being away from you for any imaginable delight in which you had no part. But I will have this delight, too, my Ba, of imagining that you are gratified by what you will see to-day. Tell me all, and what is said, and how you are at the end.

Thank you meanwhile for the picture of poor Mr. Boyd . . then he never *has* seen you, since he was blind so long ago! How strange and melancholy—you say he is 'cheerful,' however. In that case—think of unhappy Countess Faustina with her 'irresistible longings,' and give her as much of your commiseration as she ought to get. What a horrible book . . how have I brought in what I prescribed to myself 'silence about.' Such characters as Faustina produce the very worst possible effect on me—I don't know how they strike other people—but I am at once incited 'debellare superbos'—to try at least and pull down the arrogant—*contempt* would be the most Christian of all the feelings possible to be called forth by such a woman. Let me get back to you, my own dearest-dearest,—I *do* 'love you to-day,' if you must ask,—and bidding me think of you is all very well—never bid me not think of you!—and so never find out that there could be a bidding I am unable to obey. But what is mere '*thinking*'? I kiss your hand, and your eyes, and now your lips,—and ask for my heart back again, to give it and be ever giving it. No words can tell how I am your own.

My mother is much better,—observably so, to-day. Oh, dearest,—I want you to read Landor's Dialogue between Tasso and his Sister, in the second volume,—with the exquisite Sorrentine scenery—do read it. I see your Tasso with his prominent eyes as if they were ever just brightening out of a sorrow that has broken over them.

How I like ('love' is not my word now) but like Landor, more and more!

E. B. B. to R. B.

Monday Evening.
[Post-mark, June 23, 1846.]

Well—I did look everywhere for you to-day,—but not more than I always do—always I do, when I go out, look for you in the streets . . round the corners! And Mrs. Jameson came *alone* and she and I were alone at Mr. Rogers's, and you must help me to thank her some day for her unspeakable kindness to me, though she did not leap to the height of the inspiration of managing to let us see those pictures together. Ah—if she had, it would have been too much. As it is, she gave me a great deal of pleasure in the kindest of ways . . and I let it *be* pleasure, by mixing it with enough thoughts of you—(otherwise how could it be pleasure?)—and she showed the pictures, and instructed me, really taking pains and instructing me . . and telling me how Rubens painted landscapes . . as how should my ignorance guess? . . . and various other unknown things. The first word as we reached the door, frightened me—for she said that perhaps we might see Mr. Rogers . . which was a little beyond our covenant—but we did not see him, and I suppose the Antinous on the staircase is not at all like him. Grand it is, in its serene beauty. On a colossal scale, in white marble. For the pictures, they are full of wonder and divinity—each giving the measure of a man's soul. And think . . sketches from the hand of Michael Angelo and Raphael! And a statuette in clay, alive with the life of Michael Angelo's finger—the blind eyes looking . . seeing . . as if in scorn of all clay! And the union of energy and meditation in the whole attitude! You have seen the marble of that figure in Florence. Then, a divine Virgin and child, worn and faded to a shadow of Raphael's genius, as Mrs. Jameson explained to me—and the famous 'Ecce Homo' of Guido . . and Rubens' magnificent '*version*,' as she called it, of Andrea Mantegna's 'Triumph of Julius Cæsar.' So triumphing to this day! And Titian, and Tintoretto . . . and what did not strike me the least, . . a portrait of Rembrandt by himself, which if his landscapes, as they say, were 'dug out of nature,' looks as if it were dug out of humanity. Such a rugged, dark, deep subterraneous face, . . yet inspired—! seeming to realize that God took clay and breathed into the nostrils of it. There are both the clay, and the divinity! And think! I saw the agreement between the bookseller and Milton for the sale of Paradise Lost! with Milton's signature and seal! and '*Witnessed by William Greene, Mr. Milton's servant.*' How was it possible not to feel giddy with such sights! Almost I could have run my head against the wall, I felt, with bewilderment—and Mrs. Jameson must have been edified, I have thought since, through my intense stupidity. I saw too the first edition of 'Paradise Lost.' The rooms are elegant, with no pretension to splendour . . which is good taste, a *part* of the good taste everywhere. Only, on the chimney-piece of the dining-room, were two small busts, beautiful busts, white with marble, . . and representing——now, whom, of gods and men, would you select for your Lares . . to help your digestion and social merriment? . . . Caligula and Nero in *childhood!* The '*childhood*' is horribly suggestive to me! On the side-board is Pope's bust, by Roubillac—a too expressive, miserable face—drawn with disease and bitter thoughts, and very painful, I felt, to look at. These things I liked least, in the selection and arrangement. Everything beside was admirable: and I write and write of it all as if I were not tired—but I am . . and most with the excitement and newness. Mrs. Jameson breakfasted with Mr. Rogers yesterday, she said, and met the Countess Hahn-Hahn, who was talking of modern literature when her host suddenly stopped her with a question . . 'Did you ever read Addison?'

How late it is. Must I have done, before I have half done?

What I did *not* tell you yesterday is very much in my thoughts . . do you know? *I*, too, 'see what I know and testify what I have felt . . and, as far as my faculties of perception go!' I am confident that you had better not look for a single reason for loving me. Which is worst? A bad reason, or no reason at all? A bad reason, *I* think —and accept the alternative. Ah . . my own only beloved. And how you write to me to-night! I will read what you tell me in Landor . . but no words of inspired lips or pen . . no poet's word, of the divinest, . . ever went to my heart as yours in these letters! Do I not love you? am I not your own? And while deserving nothing of all of it, I *feel* it at least—respond to it—my heart is in your hand. May God bless you . . '*and me in that,*'—

because even He could not bless me without *that*. Which He knows.

Your own.

But there is much beauty in Faustina—oh, surely! The lilies, all in blow except one . . which is blowing. Are we going to have a storm to-night? It lightens lightens!

R. B. to E. B. B.

Tuesday Morning.
[Post-mark, June 23, 1846.]

I was just on the point of answering your dear letter, in all the good spirits it might be expected to wake in me, when the sad news of poor Haydon's death stopped all; much I feel it, for the light words of my own about his extravagance, as I had been told of it, but very much more on your account, who were so lately in communication with him. I earnestly hope,—I will trust—you have not been rudely apprised of this—I am happy to remember that you do not see the newspaper in the morning,—others will see it first; perhaps there may be no notice in the *Chronicle* at all, or on the other hand, a more circumstantial one than this in the *Times* which barely says—'that B.R.H. died suddenly at his residence—yesterday morning. He was in his usual health on the previous evening, and it is believed that his decease was hastened by pecuniary embarrassment'—and he is called 'the unfortunate gentleman'—which with the rest implies the very worst, I fear. If by any chance *this* should be the first intimation you receive of it . . do not think me stupid nor brutal,—for I thought again and again as to the right course to take . . whether it would not be best to be silent alogether and wait and see . . but in that case I should have surprised you more by my cold letter,—such an one as I could bring myself to write,—for how were it possible to speak of pictures and indifferent matters when you perhaps have been shocked, made ill by this news? If I have done wrong, forgive me, my own best, dearest Ba—I would give the world to know how you are. The storm, too, and lightning may have made you even more than ordinarily unfit to be startled and grieved. God knows and must help you! I am but your devoted—

How glad I am you told me you had never seen him. And perhaps he may be after all a mere acquaintance . . anything I will fancy that is likely to relieve you of pain! Dearest dearest!

E. B. B. to R. B.

Tuesday.
[Post-mark, June 24, 1846.]

Ever tenderest, kindest and most beloved, I thank you from the quick of my heart, where the thought of you lives constantly! In this world full of sadness, of which I have had my part . . full of sadness and bitterness and wrong . . full of most ghastly contrasts of life and death, strength and weakness side by side . . it is too much, to have *you* to hold by, as the river rushes on . . too much good, too much grace for such as I, . . as I feel always, and cannot cease to feel!

Oh yes—it has shocked me, this dreadful news of poor Mr. Haydon—it chilled the blood in my veins when I heard it from Alfred, who, seeing the *Times* at the Great Western Terminus, wrote out the bare extract and sent it to me by the post. He just thought that the *Chronicle* did not mention it, . . and that I had not seen Mr. Haydon . . he did not perhaps think how it would shock me

For, *this I* cannot help thinking. Could anyone—*could my own hand even . . have averted what has happened?* My head and heart have ached to-day over the inactive hand! But, for the moment, it was out of my power, without an application where it would have been useless—and then, I never fancied this case to be more than a piece of a continuous case . . of a habit fixed. Two years ago he sent me boxes and pictures precisely so, and took them back again—poor, poor Haydon!—as he will not this time. And he said last week that Peel had sent him fifty pounds . . . adding . . 'I do not however want *charity*, but employment.' Also, I have been told again and again (oh, never by *you* my beloved!) that to give money *there*, was to drop it into a hole of the ground.

But if to have dropped it so, dust to dust, would have saved a living man—what then?

Yet of the three notes I had from him last week, the first was written so lightly, that the second came to desire me not to attribute to him a 'want of feeling.' And who could think . . contemplate . . this calamity? May God have mercy on the strongest of us, for we are weak. Oh, that a man so high hearted and highly endowed . . a bold man, who has thrown down gauntlet after gauntlet in the face of the world—that such a man should go mad for a few paltry pounds! For he was *mad* if he killed himself! of that I am as sure as if I knew it. If he killed himself, he was mad first.

Some day, when I have the heart to look for it, you shall see his last note. I understand now that there are touches in it of a desperate pathos—but never could he have meditated self-destruction while writing that note. He said he should write six sets of lectures more . . six more volumes. He said he was painting a new background to a picture, which made him 'feel as if his soul had wings.' And then he hoped his brain would not turn. And he 'gloried' in the naval dangers of his son at sea. And he repeated an old phrase of his, which I had heard from him often before, and which now rings hollowly to the ears of my memory . . that he *couldn't and wouldn't die*. Strange and dreadful!

It is nearly two years since we had a correspondence of some few months—from which at last I receded, notwithstanding the individuality and spirit of his letters, and my admiration for a certain fervour and magnanimity of genius, no one could deny to him. His very faults partook of that nobleness. But for a year and a half or more perhaps, I scarcely have written or heard from him—until last week when he wrote to ask for a shelter for his boxes and pictures. If you had enquired of me the week before, I might have answered that I did not *wish to renew the intercourse*—yet who could help being shocked and saddened? *Would* it have availed, to have dropped something into that 'hole in the ground?' Oh, to imagine *that!* Yet a little would have been but as nothing!—and he did not ask even for a little—and I should have been ashamed to have offered but a little. Yet I cannot turn the thought away—*that I did not offer.*

Henry went to the house as I begged him. His son came to the door, and to a general enquiry 'after the family,' said that 'Mr. Haydon was dead and that his family were quite as well as could be expected.' That horrible banality is all I know more than you know.

Yesterday at Rogers's, Mrs. Jameson led me to his picture of Napoleon at St. Helena. At the moment we looked at it, his hand was scarcely cold, perhaps. Surely it was not made of the commonest clay of men—that hand!

I pour out my thoughts to you, dearest dearest, as if it were right rather to think of doing myself that good and relief, than of *you* who have to read all. But you spoil me into an excess of liberty, by your tenderness. Best in the world! Oh—you help me to live—I am better and lighter since I have drawn near to you even on this paper—already I am better and lighter. And now I am going to dream of you . . to meet you on some mystical landing place . . in order to be quite well to-morrow. Oh—we are so selfish on this earth, that nothing grieves us very long, let it be ever so grievous, unless we are touched in *ourselves* . . in the apple of our eye . . in the quick of our heart . . in *what* you are, and *where* you are . . my own dearest beloved! So you need not be afraid for *me!* We all look to our own, as I to *you;* the thunderbolts may strike the tops of the cedars, and, except in the first start, none of us be moved. True it is of *me*—not of *you* perhaps—certainly you are better than I, in all things. Best in the world, you are!—no one is like you. Can you read what I have written? Do not love me less! Do you think that I cannot *feel* you love me, through all this distance? If you loved me less, I should know, without a word or a sign. Because I live by your loving me! I am your

Ba.

R. B. to E. B. B.

Wednesday.
[Post-mark, June 24, 1846.]

But, dearest love—I have just come in later than I expected, I am happy to say . . for your note only just arrives too, they say . . and I should have been frightened more than I need say. All blessing on you, Ba. I have seen no paper,—but Countess Hahn-Hahn said across Carlyle's table that poor H. had attempted to shoot himself and then chosen another method—too successful. Horrible indeed— All to say now is, I shall be with you to-morrow,—my very own, dearest of all dear created things—my life and pride and joy—(Bless you). R.

There is nothing in to-day's *Times* I find—

R. B. to E. B. B.

Friday Morning.
[Post-mark, June 26, 1846.]

I drew the table to the fire before I wrote this. Here is cool weather, grateful to those overcome by last week's heat, I suppose!—much as one conceives of a day's starvation being grateful to people who were overfeasted some time back. But the coolness (that is, piercing cold as the north wind can make) sets me to ponder on what you said yesterday,—of considering summer as beginning next Wednesday, or there about, and ending by consequence with September. Our time is 'at the Summer's end': and it does strike me that there may be but too many interpositions beside that of 'my own will' . . far too many. If those equinoctial winds disturb the sea, the cold weather adds to the difficulties of the land-journey . . then the will may interpose or stand aloof . . I cannot take you and kill you . . really, inevitably kill you! As it is . . or rather, as it might be, I should feel during a transit under the most favourable circumstances possible, somewhat as the performer of that trick by which a full glass of water resting in the open hand is made to describe a circle from above to below and back without spilling a drop—through some good-natured suspension, in the operator's interest, of just a fundamental law of the universe, no more! Therefore if any September weather shall happen in September . . let us understand and wait . . another year! and another, and another.

Now, have I ever, with all those askings, asked you once too often, that is, unnecessarily—'if this should be,'—or 'when this should be?' What is my 'will' to do with it? Can I keep the winds away, alas? My own will has all along been annihilated before you,—with respect to you—I should never be able to say 'she shall dine on fish, or fruit,' 'She shall wear silk gloves or thread gloves'—even to exercise in fancy that much 'will *over you*' is revolting —I *will this*, never to be 'over you' if I could!

So, you decide here as elsewhere—but *do* decide, Ba, my own only Ba—do *think*, to decide. I *can* know nothing here as to what is gained or lost by delay or anticipation—I only refer to the few obvious points of the advantage of our 'flight not being in the winter'—and the consideration that the difficulty in another quarter will never be less nor more,—therefore is out of the question.

I will tell you something I meant to speak of yesterday.

Mrs. Jameson said Mr. Kenyon had assured her, with the kindest intentions, that it was quite vain to make those offers of company to Pisa or elsewhere, for your Father would never give his consent, and the very rationality of the plan, and probability of the utmost benefit following the adoption of it, would be the harder to forego the more they were entertained—whereupon, 'having the passions of his kind he spoke some certain things'—bitter and unavoidable. Then Mrs. J. spoke too, as you may imagine; apparently from better knowledge than even I possess. Now I repeat this to your *common-sense*, my Ba—it is not hard to see that *you* must be silent and suffering, where no other can or will be either—so that if a verdict needs must be pronounced on our conduct, it will be 'the world's' and not an individual's—and for once a fair one. Mrs. Jameson's very words were . . (writing from what *has been*, observe—what is irrevocably past, and not what *may* be)—'I feel unhappy when in her presence . . impelled to do her some service, and impeded. *Can* nothing be done to rescue her from this? *ought* it to continue?' So speaks—not your lover!—who, as he told you, *did* long to answer 'someone with attempt, at least!' But it was best, for Mrs. Jameson would be blamed afterward, as Mr. K. might be abused, as ourselves will be vituperated, as my family must be calumniated . . by *whom?*

Do you feel me kiss your feet while I write this? I think you must, Ba! There is surely,—I trust, surely no impatience here, in this as in the other letter—if there is, I will endeavour to repress it . . but it will be difficult—for I love you, and am not a stock nor a stone.

And as we are now,—another year!

Well, kissing the feet answers everything, declares everything—and I kiss yours, my own Ba.

E. B. B. to R. B.

Friday Morning.
[Post-mark, June 26, 1846.]

Arabel insists on my going out in the carriage, but I will not, I say, before I have written my letter—and while we talk, the rain comes down like a guardian angel, and I *cannot* go out before I have written my letter, as is apparent to all. Dearest, you did me such good yesterday with seeing you and hearing you, that I slept better and am better altogether, and after a little change into the air, shall be well—and how is your head? Now do not forget to tell me particularly. Say too whether you found your friend and had the right quantity of talk and got home without being the worse for him . . or *me!*

I have not had the heart to look at the newspapers, but hear that Sir Robert Peel has provided liberally for the present necessities of the poor Haydons. And do you know, the more I think the more I am inclined to conclude that the money-distress was merely an additional irritation, and that the despair leading to the revolt against life, had its root in disappointed ambition. The world did not recognize his genius, and he punished the world by withdrawing the light. If he had not that thought in him, I am wrong. The cartoon business, and his being refused employment in the Houses of Parliament . . *that* was bitter: and then came his opposition with Tom Thumb and the dwarf's triumph . . he talked bitterly of *that* in a letter to me of last week. He was a man, you see, who carried his whole being and sensibility on the outside of him; nay, worse than *so*, since in the thoughts and opinions of the world. All the audacity and bravery and self-exultation which drew on him so much ridicule were an agony in disguise—he could not live without reputation, and he wrestled for it, struggled for it, *kicked* for it, forgetting grace of attitude in the pang. When all was vain, he went mad and died. Poor Haydon! He measures things differently now! and let *us* now be right and just in our admeasurement of what he was—for, with all his weaknesses, he was not certainly *far* from being a great man.

It is hope and help, to be able to look away from all such thoughts, to *you*, dearest beloved, who do not partake of the faults and feeblenesses of these lower geniuses. There is hope and help for the world in you—and if for the world, why for me indeed much more. You do not know . . ah, you do not know—how I look up to you and trust perfectly in you. You are above all these clouds—your element is otherwise—men are not your taskmasters that you should turn to them for recompense. 'Shall I always think the same of you,' you asked yesterday. But I *never* think the same of you; because day by day you look greater and feel dearer. Only there is a deep gulph of another question, close beside *that*, which suggests itself, and makes me shudder to look down.

And now, the rain is over, and I shall dine briefly, and go out in the carriage.

May God bless you . . très bon!—très cher, pour cause.

Toute à toi—pour toujours.

E. B. B. to R. B.

Friday Evening.
[Post-mark, June 27, 1846.]

Ever dearest, I send you a bare line to-night, for it is late and I am very tired; having . . while you were sitting by the fire . . been, for my part, driving to Highgate . . now think of *that!* Also it has done me good, I think, and I shall sleep for it to-night perhaps, though I am tired certainly.

Your letter shall be answered to-morrow—and here is a green answer to your leaves![1]—what leaves? whence and

[1] [A sprig from rose-tree enclosed. R. B.'s previous letter contained some leaves.]

how? My green little branch, I gathered myself out of the hedge, snatching at it from the carriage-window. The roses were gone, or nearly gone, and the few left, quite out of reach; and the leaves keep behind to assure you that they do not look for snow-storms in *September*. No! it was not *that*, they said. I am belying what they said.

I gathered them in the hedge of the pretty close green lane which you go through to Hampstead. Were you ever there, I wonder?

Dearest, I will write to-morrow. Never are you 'impatient,' inconsiderate—and as for selfishness, I have been uneasy sometimes, precisely because you are so *little* selfish. I am not likely to mistake . . to wrench the wrong way . . any word of yours. As for mine, it was not a *mere* word, when I said that you should decide everything. Could I hold out for November, or October, or for September even, if *you* choose against? Indeed I could not. We—you will think—I am yours, and if *you* never repent *that*, *I* shall not:—I am too entirely yours.

And so good-night—dearest beloved! Because you have a fire in June, is the snow to fall in September, and earth and ocean to become impassable? Ah well! we shall see! But you shall not see that I deceive you—

I am your very own

Ba.

Dear brown leaves! where did they come from, besides from *you?*

Not a north wind. Only a north-west wind, as I could have proved to you if you had been with me! Yet it is a detestable climate, this English climate, let us all confess. Say how your head is.

R. B. to E. B. B.

Saturday.
[Post-mark, June 27, 1846.]

Your dear gentle laugh, as I seem to hear it, makes all well again for the moment undoubtedly. I cannot help trusting you implicitly . . so whenever I seem able to reason a little, and set you reasoning for me, ought I not to try,—and then give up, and sink my head over you . . dearest! In fact, I was a little frightened by what I heard and saw . . for *you*, if you please, began by saying 'it was too cold to go out'—and you were paler, I thought. The news of Highgate and the green leaves are re-assuring indeed—but my brown leaves might be sent to you by myriads for all that, for all the light laugh,—all roses fast going, lilies going . . autumnal hollyhocks in full blow . . and now to count three months over before summer is to end! These rains may do something, or hinder somewhat—and certainly our fire was left alone early yesterday morning. Well, I have not been presumptuous except . . . ah, the exception!

How could I presume, for one thing, to hope for last evening's letter . . a pure piece of kindness in you, Ba! And all your kindness is pure, entire, pearl-like for roundness and completeness . . there is no one rough side as when a crystal is broken off and given: do you think it no good augury of our after life in what must be called, I suppose, another relation,—that *this* has been so perfect . . to me . . this last year, let me only say? In this relation there are as many 'écueils' as in the other,—as many, though of a different nature,—lovers quarrel on as various grounds as the wedded—and though with the hue and softness of love the most energetic words and deeds may change their character; yet one might write savage sentences in Chinese celestial-blue ink, which after a powdering with gold-dust should look prettier than the truest blessing in ordinary black. But you have been PERFECT to me hitherto—perfect! And of course only to *you* is the praise . . for I have to be entirely confided in by you, seeing that you cannot keep an eye on me after I leave your room . . whereas,—not I, but a gross, stupid fool who conceived of no liberty but that of the body, nor that the soul may be far more unfaithful—such an one might exult in the notion of the closed door and the excluded world of rivals.

Bless you, darling—Monday is not very far off now! And I am to hear again. I am much better,—my mother much better too. I saw my French friend and talked and heard him talk. Yesterday, the whole day, (after the fire went out) was given to a cousin of mine, a girl, just married, and here from Paris with her husband—these two had to be amused somehow. Ever your very own— R.

E. B. B. to R. B.

Saturday.
[Post-mark, June 27, 1846.]

I said I would answer your letter to-day, my beloved, but how shall I say more than I have said and you know? *Do* you not know, you who will not will 'over' me, that I *cannot* will against you, and that if you set yourself seriously to take September for October, and August for September, it is all at an end with me and the calendar? Still, seriously . . there is time for deciding, is there not? . . . even if I grant to you, which I do at once, that the road does not grow smoother for us by prolonged delays. The single advantage perhaps of delay is, that in the summer I get stronger every week and fitter to travel—and then, it never was thought of before (that I have heard) to precede September *so*. Last year, was I not ordered to leave England in October, and *permitted* to leave it in November? Yet I agree, November and perhaps October might be late —might be running a risk through lingering . . in our case; and you will believe me when I say I should be loth to run the risk of being forced to the further delay of a year—the position being scarcely tenable. Now for September, it generally passes for a hot month—it ripens the peaches—it is the figtime in Italy. Well—nobody decides for September nevertheless. The end of August is nearer—and at any rate we can consider, and observe the signs of the heavens and earth in the meanwhile—there is so much to think of first; and the end, remember, is only too frightfully easy. Also you shall not have it on your conscience to have killed me, let ever so much snow fall in September. If the sea should be frozen over, almost we might go by the land—might we not? and apart from fabulous ports, there are the rivers—the Seine, the Soane, the Rhone—which might be cheaper than the sea and the steamers; and *would*, I almost should fancy. These are things among the multitude, to think of, and you shall think of them, dearest, in your wisdom. Oh—there is time—full time.

No—there is not, in a sense. I wanted to write so much more, so much—and I went out to walk first, and, on returning, met Mr. Kenyon, who came up-stairs with me.

Now it is too late to add a word.

May God bless you. I shall see you on Monday. I am better for Highgate—I walked longer to-day than usual. How strong you make me, you who make me happy!

I am your own.

R. B. to E. B. B.

Sunday.
[Post-mark, June 29, 1846.]

My last letter will have answered this of yours, my dearest,—I agree in all you say; and sooner or later comes to the same thing, if to any possible increase of difficulty is brought a proportionate increase of strength to undergo it—as let us hope will be the case! So you see you have to 'understand' and understand me,—I keep your faculty in constant exercise, now with seeming to wish for postponement, and now, for anticipation! And all the time do I really 'grow greater' in your eyes? I might grow less woefully,—'for reasons—for reasons'—

The sea will not be frozen, beside . . which makes me think to tell you that Carlyle is wanting to visit only one foreign country—*Iceland.* The true cradle of the Northmen and their virtues . . all that is worth a Northman's caring to see is there, he thinks, and nowise in Italy. Perhaps! Indeed, so I *reason* and say—Did I not once turn on myself and speak against the Southern spirit, and even Dante, just because of that conviction?—(or *imperfect* conviction, whence the uneasy exaggeration). Carlyle thinks modern Italy's abasement a direct judgment from God. 'Here is a nation in whose breast arise men who *could* doubt, examine the new problems of the reformation &c—trim the balance at intervals, and throw overboard the accumulation of falsehood—all other nations around, less favoured, are doing it laboriously for themselves . . now is the time for the acumen of the Bembos, the Bentivoglios and so forth . . and these and their like, one and all, turn round, decline the trouble, say 'these things *may* be true, or they may not, meantime let us go on verse-making, painting, music-scoring'—to which all the nation accedes as if relieved of a trouble—upon which God bids the Germans go in and possess them; pluck their fruits and feel their sun after their own hard work.' Carlyle said the *sense* of this, between two huge pipe-whiffs, the other afternoon.

'Pluck their fruits'—some four years ago I planted . . or held straight while my mother planted, a fig-tree,—for love of Italy! This year it bears its first fruit . . a single one! what does that bode?

Since I wrote the last paragraph, the wind took my thoughts away, as it always does, and I saw you again as I used to see, *before* I knew you, so very substanceless, faint, unreal—when I was struck by the reality again,—by this paper,—by to-morrow's visit I shall pay . . it was as if someone had said ' but that star is your own.'

I fancied you just what I find you—I knew you from the beginning.

Let me kiss you dearest dearest—

E. B. B. to R. B.

Tuesday Morning.
[Post-mark, June 30, 1846.]

The gods and men call you by your name, but I never do—never dare. In case of invocation, tell me how you should be called by such as I? not to be always the 'inexpressive *He*' which I make of you. In case of courage for invocation!—

Dearest . . (which is a name too) read on the paper inside what I have been studying about Salerno since we parted yesterday. Forsyth is too severe in his deductions, perhaps, from the apothecaries, but your Naples book will not help me to contradict him, saying neither the one thing nor the other. The word we could not read in the letter yesterday, was *La Cava*—and La Cava is a town on the way between Naples and Salerno, which Mrs. Stark describes as 'a large town with porticoes on each side of the High Street, like those at Bologna.' To which the letter adds, remember, 'enchantingly beautiful, very good air and no English.' Then there is Vietri, mentioned by Forsyth, between La Cava and Salerno, and *on the bay*. It is as well to think of all three. Were you ever at either? Amalfi itself appears to be very habitable. Oh—and your Naples book says of Salerno, that it is illuminated by fireflies, and that the chanting of frogs cover the noises of the city. You will like the frogs, if you don't the apothecaries, and I shall like the fireflies if I don't the frogs—but I *do* like frogs, you know, and it was quite a mistake of yours when you once thought otherwise.

Now I am going out in the carriage, to call on Mr. Kenyon, and perhaps to see Mr. Boyd. Your flowers are more beautiful than they were yesterday, if possible: and the fresh coolness helps them to live, so, that I hope you may see some of them on Saturday when you come. On Saturday! What a time to wait! if not for *them*, yet for *me*. Of the two, it is easier for them, certainly. *They* only miss a little dew and air.

I shall write again to-night,—but I cannot be more then than now, nor less *ever* than now

Your own

Ba.

Here is a coincidence. Hardly had you left me, when, passing near the table at the end of the room, I saw a parcel there. Remember your question about the '*Year of the World.*' Precisely that! With a note, the counterpart of yours—desiring an opinion!

May God bless you, dear, *dear!*— Did I ever think I should live to thank God that I did not die five years ago?—Not that I quite, quite dare to do it yet. I must be sure first of something.

Which is not your *love*, my beloved—it is a something still dearer and of more consequence.

SALERNO.

'Though placed between the beauties of sea and land, of cultivated and rude nature, the city is *so unhealthy* that its richer inhabitants remove to Vietri during the hot months. In proof of its bad air, I remark here a number of apothecaries!' FORSYTH.

'Its white houses curving round the haven at the water's brink, the mountains crowding close behind the city, the ruins of its Gothic castle on the olive-covered hill above, together mirrored on the waveless water, itself alternate shine and shadow—'tis a noble sight.

'The view from Salerno is one of the loveliest pictures in Italy. A clear-complexioned, open-eyed, and bright-faced city is modern Salerno,—and its streets and piazza were all astir.' *Letters from Naples.*

'This town, the approach to which is enchanting, boasts a tolerably good *inn!!*' MRS. STARKE.

R. B. to E. B. B.

Tuesday.
[Post-mark, June 30, 1846.]

I have looked in the map for 'L——,' the place praised in the letter, and conclude it must be either Ceva, (La Ceva, between Nocera and Salerno, about four miles from the latter, and on the mountain-side, I suppose . . see a map, my Ba!)—or else *Lucera,* (which looks very like the word . . and which lies at about sixty miles to the N.E. of Naples, in a straight line over the mountains and roadless country, but perhaps twice as far by the main way through *Avellino, Ariano, Bovino,* and Savia—(exactly 120 Italian miles now that I count the posts). So that there would be somewhat of a formidable journey to undertake after the sea voyage. I daresay at Ceva there is abundance of quietness, as the few who visit Salerno do not go four miles inland,—can you enquire into this?

How inexpressibly charming it is to me to have a pretext for writing thus . . about such approaches to the real event—these business-like words, and names of places! If at the end you should bring yourself to say 'But you never seriously believed this would take place'—what should I answer, I wonder?

Let me think on what is real, indisputable, however . . the improvement in the health as I read it on the dear, dear cheeks yesterday. This morning is favourable again . . you will go out, will you not?

Mr. Kenyon sends me one of his kindest letters to ask

me to dine with him next week—on Wednesday. I feel *his* kindness, just as you feel in the other case, and in its lesser degree, I feel it,—and then I know,—dare think I know whether he will be so sorry in the end,—loving you as he does. I will send his letter that you may understand here as elsewhere.

I think my head is dizzy with reading the debates this morning—Peel's speech and farewell. How exquisitely absurd, it just strikes me, would be any measure after Miss Martineau's own heart, which should introduce women to Parliament as we understand its functions at present—how essentially retrograde a measure! Parliament seems no place for originating, creative minds—but for second-rate minds influenced by and bent on working out the results of these—and the most efficient qualities for such a purpose are confessedly found oftener with men than with women—physical power having a great deal to do with it beside. So why shuffle the heaps together which, however arbitrarily divided at first, happen luckily to lie pretty much as one would desire,—here the great flint stones, here the pebbles—and diamonds too. The men of genius knew all this, said more than all this, in their way and proper place on the outside, where Miss M. is still saying something of the kind—to be taken up in its time by some other Mr. Cobden and talked about, and beleaguered. But such people cannot or will not see where their office begins and advantageously ends; and that there is such a thing as influencing the influencers, playing the Bentham to the Cobden, the Barry to a Commission for Public Works, the Lough to the three or four industrious men with square paper caps who get rules and plummets and dot the blocks of marble all over as his drawings indicate. So you and I will go to Salerno or L—— (not to the L—akes, Heaven forefend!) and if we 'let sail winged words, freighted with truth from the throne of God'—we may be sure——

Ah, presumption all of it! Then, you shall fill the words with their freight, and I will look on and love you,

—is that too much? *Yes*—for any other—*No*—for one you [know] is *yours*—

Your very own.

For the quick departing yesterday our day was not spoken of . . it is Saturday, is it not?

E. B. B. to R. B.

Tuesday Evening.
[Post-mark, July 1, 1846.]

Thank you for letting me see dear Mr. Kenyon's letter. He loves you, admires you, trusts you. When what is done cannot be undone, then he will forgive you besides—that is, he will forgive both of us, and set himself to see all manner of good where now he would see evil if we asked him to look. So we will not, if you please, ask him to look on the encouragement of ever so many more kind notes, pleasant as they are to read, and worthy to trust to, under certain conditions. Dear Mr. Kenyon—but how good he is! And I love him more (shall it be *under-love?*) because of his right perception and understanding of *you*—no one among men sets you higher than he does as a man and as a poet—even if he misses the subtle sense, sometimes.

So you dine with him—don't you? And I shall have you on Wednesday instead of Thursday! yes, certainly. And on Saturday, of course, next time.

In the carriage, to-day, I went first to Mr. Kenyon's, and as he was not at home, left a card for a footstep. Then Arabel and Flush and I proceeded on our way to Mr. Boyd's in St. John's Wood, and I was so nervous . . so anxious for an excuse for turning back . . that . . can you guess what Arabel said to me? 'Oh Ba'; she said, 'such a coward as *you* are, never will be . . married, while the world lasts.' Which made me laugh if it did not make me persevere—for you see by it what her notion is of an heroic deed! So, there, I stood at last, at the door of poor Mr. Boyd's dark little room, and saw him sitting . . as if he had not moved these seven years—these seven heavy, changeful years. Seeing him, my heart was too full to speak at first, but I stooped and kissed his poor bent-down forehead, which he never lifts up, his chin being quite buried in his breast. Presently we began to talk of Ossian and Cyprus wine, and I was forced, as I would not have Ossian for a god, to take a little of the Cyprus,—there was no help for me, nor alternative: so I took as little as I could, while he went on proving to me that the Adamic fall and corruption of human nature (Mr. Boyd is a great theologian) were never in any single instance so disgustingly exemplified as in the *literary controversy about Ossian;* every man of the Highland Society having a lost soul in him; and Walter Scott . . . oh, the woman who poisoned all her children the other day, is a saint to Walter Scott, . . so we need not talk of him any more. 'Arabel!—how much has she taken of that wine? not half a glass.' 'But, Mr. Boyd, you would not have me obliged to carry her home.'

That visit being over, we went into the Park, Hyde Park, and drove close to the Serpentine, and then returned. Flush would not keep his head out of the window (his favourite pleasure) all the way, because several drops of rain trickled down his ears. Flush has no idea of wetting his ears:—his nose so near, too!

Right you are, I think, in opposition to Miss Martineau, though your reasons are too gracious to be right . . except indeed as to the physical inaptitude, which is an obvious truth. Another truth (to my mind) is, that women, as they *are* (whatever they *may be*) have not mental strength any more than they have bodily; have not instruction, capacity, wholeness of intellect enough. To deny that women, as a class, have defects, is as false I think, as to deny that women have wrongs.

Then you are right again in affirming that the creators

have no business *there*, with the practical men—*you* should not be *there* for instance. And *I* (if I am to be thought of) would be prouder to eat cresses and maccaroni (Dearest—there is a manufactory of maccaroni and writing-paper at Amalfi close by—observe that combination! maccaroni and writing-paper!) *I* would be prouder to eat cresses and maccaroni with *you* as *you*, than to sit with diamonds in my ears, under the shelter of the woolsack, *you* being a law-lord and parliamentary maker of speeches! By the way, I *couldn't* have diamonds in my ears: they never were *bored* for it . . as I never was *born* for it. A physical inaptitude, here too!

Shall I say what you tell me . . 'You never seriously believed' . . . shall I? I will, if you like. But it is not *C*eva, if you like—it is Cava . . La Cava . . in my map, and according to my authorities. Otherwise, the place is the same—four miles from Salerno, I think, and 'enchantingly beautiful.' It is worth an enquiry certainly, this enchanting place which has no English in it, with porticoes like Bologna, and too little known to be spelt correctly by the most accomplished geographers.

Ah—your head is '*dizzy*,' my beloved! Tell me how it is now. And tell me how your mother is. I think of you—love you. I, who am discontented with myself, . . self-condemned as unworthy of you, in all else . . am yet satisfied with the *love* I have for you—it seems worthy of you, as far as an abstract affection can go, without taking note of the personality loving.

Do you see the meaning through the mist? Do you accept

Your very own
Ba?

R. B. to E. B. B.

Wednesday.
[Post-mark, July 1, 1846.]

Dearest—dearest, you *did* once, one time only, call me by my name—Robert; and though it was to bid 'R. not talk extravagances' (your very words) still the name so spoken became what it never had been before to me. I never am called by any pet-name, nor abbreviation, here at home or elsewhere . . Oh, best let it alone . . it is one of my incommunicable advantages to have a Ba of my own, and call her so—indeed, yes, my Ba! I write 'dearest,' and 'most dearest,' but it all ends in—'Ba,' and the 'my' is its framework,—its surrounding arm—Ba—my own Ba! 'Robert' is in Saxon, (*ni fallor*), 'famous in counsel,' so let him give a proof of his quality in counselling you to hold your good, happy inspiration about La Cava (my French map-maker must have had *Ceva in Piedmont* in his head) for at such a place, so situate, we renounce not one sight at Salerno, nor Amalfi, nor Sorrento . . four miles . . the distance between your house and Highgate, perhaps! Cava,—the hollow of a hill; and such hills and such hollows are in that land! Oh, let it be La Cava—or Seven Dials, *with you!*

I passed through Seven Dials this morning—and afterward, by your house,—with a heart full of thoughts,—not fuller than usual, but they were more stirring and alive, near their source. I called at Mrs. Procter's door (proceeding from Forster's) and then on Mrs. Jameson whom I found and talked with pleasantly till a visitor came. I do extremely appreciate her, delight in her . . to avoid saying 'love'—I was never just to her before, far from it. I saw her niece, a quiet earnest-looking little girl. But did it not please me to call in at Moxon's and hear that (amongst other literary news dexterously enquired after) Miss Barrett's poems were selling very well and would ere long be out of print? And, after that pleasure, came the other of finding dear, generous noble Carlyle had sent his new edition of 'Cromwell,' three great volumes, with his brave energetic assurance of 'regards' and 'many' of them, in black manly writing on the first page. So may he continue to like me till he knows you; when it will be 'mine' instead of me, that he shall love—'love'? I let the whole world love you—if they can overtake my love. As I read on, about the visit to Mr. Boyd, I thought, 'I trust she will kiss his forehead,'—and I kiss yours—thus—for *that*, too—is gratitude for that. You dear, good, blessing of a Ba, how I kiss you!— R. B.

I am quite well to-day, and my mother is quite well—The good account of the visit is enough to make me happy on a Wednesday—leading to a Saturday! Then my two letters!

I did not see Moxon—only the brother—who tells odd stories drily; one made me laugh to-day. Poor Mr. Reade, Landor's love, sent a book to Campbell the Poet, and then called on him . . . to discover him in the very act of wiping a razor on a leaf torn out of the book, laid commodiously by his toilet-table for the express purpose.

E. B. B. to R. B.

Wednesday.
[Post-mark, July 2, 1846.]

No, No! indeed I never did. If you heard me say 'Robert,' it was on a stair-landing in the House of Dreams —never anywhere else! Why how could you fancy such a thing? Wasn't it rather your own disquieted Conscience which spoke instead of me, saying 'Robert, don't be extravagant.' Yes—just the speech *that* is, for a 'good *un*-easy,' discerning Conscience—and you took it for my speech! 'Don't be extravagant' I may certainly have said. Both I and the Conscience might have said so obvious a thing.

Ah—and now I have got the name, shall I have courage to say it? tell me, best councillor! I like it better than any other name, though I never spoke it with my own lips —I never called any one by such a name . . except once when I was in the lane with Bertha. One uncle I have, called Robert—but to me he is an 'uncle Hedley' and no more. So it is a white name to take into life. Isn't this an Hebraic expression of a preferring affection . . '*I have called thee by thy name.*'? And therefore, because you are the best, only dearest!——*Robert.*

You passed by and I never knew! How foolish—but really it quite strikes me as something wonderful, that I should not have known. I knew however of your being in London, because . . . (don't expect supernatural evidence) Mrs. Jameson told me. She was here with me about five, and brought her niece whom I liked just for the reasons you give; and herself was feeling and affectionate as ever: —it is well that you should give me leave to love her a little. Once she touched upon Italy . . and I admitted that I thought of it, and thought it probable as an event . . on which she pressed gently to know 'on what I counted.' 'Perhaps on my own courage,' I said. 'Oh,' she exclaimed 'now I see clearly.'

Which made me smile . . the idea of her seeing clearly, but earnestly and cordially she desired me to remember that to be useful to me in any manner, would give her pleasure. Such kindness! The sense of it has sunk into my heart. You cannot praise her too much for *me.* She was so kind, and when she asked me to go to see her in Mortimer Street on Friday, I could not help agreeing at once: and I am to have the sofa and no company—that's a promise. She asked me to go at twelve o'clock, and to bring Mr. Kenyon for an escort—but I would not answer for Mr. Kenyon's going, only half promising for myself. Now I must try to fix a later hour, because . .

Listen to the *because.* My aunt, Miss Clarke, and my cousin, her adopted daughter and niece, come to-morrow evening, and stay in this house . . oh, I cannot tell you how long: for a whole week as a beginning, certainly. I have been sighing and moaning so about it that Arabel calls it quite a scandal—but when one can't be glad, why should it be so undutiful to appear sad? If she had but stayed in Paris six months longer! Well!—and to-morrow morning Miss Mitford comes to spend the day like the kind dear friend she is; and I, not the least in the world glad to see her! Why have you turned my heart into such hard porphyry? Once, when it was plain clay, every finger (of these womanly fingers) left a mark on it—and now, . . you see! Even Mrs. Jameson makes me grateful to her chiefly (as I know in myself) because she sees you as you are in part, and will forgive me for loving you as soon as she hears of it . . however she may, and must consistently, expect us to torment one another, according to the way of the 'artistic temperament,' evermore, and ever more and more. But for the rest, the others who do not know you and value you . . *I hate to see them* . . and there's the truth! There is something too in the concealment, the reserve, the doubleness enforced on occasion! . which is painful and hateful. Detestable it all is.

And *I* like La Cava too! Think of a hollow in the mountain . . something like a cave, do you think? At least it must be a hollow in the mountains. I wrote to my friend this morning to ask if the place is considered warm, and if she knew any more of it. The '*porticoes as at Bologna*' look attractive too by the dreamlight we look at them by; and *Baba* may escape the forty thieves of English in the *Cave*, with a good watchword like Sesame—now that's half *my* nonsense and half yours, I beg you to observe. I won't be at the charge of it all.

I was out to-day—walked up, walked down, in my old fashion—only I do improve in walking, I think, and gain strength.

May God bless you dear dearest! I am your own.

R. B. to E. B. B.

Thursday.
[Post-mark, July 2, 1846.]

Dear, you might as well imagine you had never given me any other of the gifts, as that you did not call me, as I tell you. You spoke quickly, interrupting me, and, for the name, 'I can hear it, 'twixt my spirit and the earth-noise intervene'; do you think I forget one gift in another, even a greater? I should still taste the first freshness of the vinegar, (or whatever was the charm of it)—though Cleopatra had gone on dissolving pearl after pearl in it. I love you for these gifts to me now—hereafter, it seems almost as if I must love you even better, should you choose to continue them to me in spite of complete knowledge: I feel this as often as I think of it, which is not seldom.

Do you know, Mrs. Jameson asked *me* to go and see her on Friday morning—would you like me to go? What *I* like . . do not fancy,—because your own pleasure is to be consulted. Should you fear the eyes, which *can*, on occasion, wear spectacles? If not . . and if our Saturday will not be interfered with . . and if you can tell me the hour 'later than twelve' you mean to appoint, . . so that my call may be neither too early nor too late . . why, then, Ba, dearest, dearest—

La Cava—is surely our cave, Ba—early in October will be vintage-time,—no fire flies. There will be the advantage in the vicinity of Naples, that through the Rothschilds' House there we can, I believe, receive and dispatch letters without any charge, which otherwise would be an expensive business in Italy. The economy of the Post Office there is astounding. A stranger goes to a window and asks for 'A's' or 'Z's' letters . . not even professing himself to be 'A,' or 'Z'—whereupon the official hands over sundry dozens of letters, without a word of enquiry, out of which the said stranger picks what pleases him, and paying for his selections, goes away and there an end. At Venice, I remember, they offered me, with other letters, about ten or fifteen for the Marquis of Hastings who was not arrived yet—I had only to say 'I am sent for them' . . At Rome a lady lamented to me the sad state of things 'A letter might contain Heaven only knew what and lie at the office and'—'*I* might go and get it,' I said—'You? Nay, my husband might!' she answered as one mightily wronged.

But of your dear self now—the going out will soon and effectually cure the nervousness, we may be sure. I am most happy, love, to hear of the walking and increased strength. So you used to like riding on a donkey? Then you shall have a mule, un bel mulo, and I will be your muleteer, walk by your side—and you will think the moment you see him of the wicked shoeing of cats with walnut-shells, for they make a mule's shoes turn up, for all the world like large shells—those on his forefeet at least. Will the time really come then? Meanwhile, your visitors . . let us hope they will go sight-seeing or call-making, do anything but keep the house on our days . . The three hours seem as a minute . . if they are to be curtailed,—oh, no, no, I hope. Tell me all you can, dearest . . and let me tell you all I can, little as it is, in kissing you, my best and dearest Ba, as now kisses your very own.

E. B. B. to R. B.

Thursday Evening.
[Post-mark, July 3, 1846.]

But, ever dearest, I do so fear that I shall not be able to get to Mrs. Jameson's to-morrow at all! not at twelve, I fear, I fear. Our visitors are to arrive late to-night, too late for me to see them: and for me to go away at twelve in the morning, just about the hour when they might reasonably expect to have and to hold me, . . seems altogether unlawful, according to my sisters. Yet the temptation is strong. Would half-past twelve be too early for you, if I could manage to go at twelve? Ah—but I shall not be able, I do fear. Just see how it becomes possible and impossible at once for us to touch hands! I could almost wring mine, to see! For I *could* dare the spectacles, the hypothetical spectacles, and the eyes discerning without them: she has no idea to begin with—and you would not say 'Ba, let us order the mules,' I suppose. If I went, it would be *alone*—but probably I shall not be able—so you had better not think of me, and pay your visit at your own hour 'after the devices of your heart.'

In the meanwhile, quite you make me laugh by your positiveness about the name-calling. Well—if ever I did such a thing, it was in a moment of unconsciousness all the more surprising, that, even to my own soul, in the lowest spirit-whisper, I have not been in the *habit* of saying 'Robert,' speaking of you. You have only been The One. No word ever stood for you. The Idea admitted of no representative—the words fell down before it and were silent. Still such very positive people must be right of course—they always are. At any rate it is only one illusion more—and some day I expect to hear you say and swear that you saw me fly out of one window and fly in at another. So much for your Cleopatra's Roman pearls, oh my famous in council!—and appreciation of sour vinegar!

Dear Miss Mitford came at two to-day and stayed until seven, and all those hours you were not once mentioned—*I* had not courage—and she perhaps avoided an old subject of controversy . . I do not know. It is singular that for this year past you are not mentioned between us, while other names come up like grass in the rain. No single person will be more utterly confounded than she, when she comes to be aware of what you are to me now—and *that* I was thinking to-day, while she talked to never a listener. She will be confounded, and angry perhaps—it will be beyond her sympathies—or if they reach so far, the effort to make them do so will prove a more lively affection for me, than, with all my trust in her goodness, I dare count on. Yet very good and kind and tender, she was to me to-day. And very variously intelligent and agreeable. Do you know, I should say that her *natural* faculties were stronger than Mrs. Jameson's—though the latter has a higher aspiration and, in some ways, a finer sensibility of intellect. You would certainly call her superior to her own books—certainly you would. She walks strongly on her two feet in this world—but nobody shall see her (not even *you*) fly out of a window. Too closely she keeps to the ground, I always feel. Now Mrs. Jameson can 'aspire' like Paracelsus; and believes enough in her own soul, to know a poet when she sees one. Ah—but all cannot be all.

Miss Mitford wrung a promise from me—that 'if I were well enough and in England next summer, I would go to see *her*.' So remember. Isn't it a promise for two?

Only we shall be mule-riding in those days—unless I shall have tired you. *Shall* you be tired of me in one winter, I wonder? My programme is, to let you try me for one winter, and if you are tired (as I shall know without any confession on your side) why then I shall set the mule on a canter and leave you in La Cava, and go and live in Greece somewhere all alone, taking enough with me for bread and salt. Is it a jest, do you think? Indeed it is not. It is very grave earnest, be sure. I believe that I never could quarrel with you; but the same cause would absolutely hinder my living with you if you did not love me. We could not lead the abominable lives of 'married people' all round—you *know* we could not—*I* at least know that *I* could not, and just because I love you so entirely. Then, you know, you could come to England by yourself—and . . 'Where's Ba?'—'Oh, she's somewhere in the world, I suppose. How can *I* tell?' And then Mrs. Jameson would shake her head, and observe that the problem was solved exactly as she expected, and that artistical natures smelt of sulphur and brimstone, without any exceptions.

Am I laughing? am I crying? who can tell. But I am not *teasing*, . . Robert! . because, my Robert, if gravely I distrusted your affection, I could not use such light-sounding words on the whole—now could I? It is only the supposition of a *possible* future . . just possible . . (as the end of human affections passes for a possible thing)—which made me say what I would do in such a case.

But I am yours—your own: and it is impossible, in my *belief*, that I can ever fail to you so as to be less yours, on this side the grave or across it. *So*, I think of *im*possibilities—whatever I may, of possibilities!

Will it be possible to see you to-morrow, I wonder! I ask myself and not you.

And if you love me only nearly as much (instead of the prodigal 'more') *afterward*, I shall be satisfied, and shall not run from you further than to the bottom of the page.

Where you see me as your own

Ba.

E. B. B. to R. B.

Friday Morning.
[Post-mark, July 3, 1846.]

I am forced to say something now which you will not like and which I, for my part, hate to say—but you shall judge how impossible it is for me to see you to-morrow.

The visitors did not come last night; and as this morning we expected them hourly, the post brought a letter instead, to the effect that they were to arrive just *on Saturday* . . leaving us to calculate the time of arrival between one p.m. to five or six. If at one, . . Papa will be in the house and likely to stay in it all day after . . which would be a complication of disadvantages for us, and if at three . . why even so, my aunt would 'admire' a little the reason of my not seeing her at once, and there would be questions and answers a faire frémir. So dearest dearest, I must try to live these two days more without seeing you—and indeed it will be hard work—the very light of the sun to-morrow, let it be ever so bright a sun, will only reproach the day with what it *ought* to have been . . *our* day, instead of everybody's day or nobody's day, a poor, blank, dreary day. What, when the clock is at three . . oh *what* will keep me, I wonder, from being sullen to my aunt and sulky to my cousin? They will think me (if my ministering angel should not throw me some hallowing thought of *you*, best beloved!) considerably fallen off in the *morale*, however the improvement may be of the bodily health—I shall be as cross, as cross . . well, if I am less than cross, you must be right after all, and I, 'une femme miraculeuse' without illusion! It is too bad, too bad. The whole week—from Monday to Monday! And I do not positively fix even Monday, though I hope for Monday:—but Monday may be taken from us just as Saturday is, and the Hedleys are to come on *Tuesday* . . only not to this house. I wish they were all at Seringapatam.

Do not mind it however. Yes, mind it a little, . . Robert! but not overmuch—because the day shall not be lost utterly—I shall take care. I will be on the watch for half-days when people go out to shop . . that solemn business of life, . . and we will have our lost day back again . . you will see. But I could not get to Mrs. Jameson's this morning, not being quite well enough. It is *nothing* as illness,—I tell you the truth, dear—and even now I feel better than I did in the early morning. It was only just enough to prevent my going. And if I had gone I should not have seen you—you would not go in time—you would not perhaps even have my letter in time. The stars are against us for the moment, it seems.

Write to me, think of me, love me. You shall hear on Saturday and on Sunday, and we will settle about Monday.

After all, it would have been difficult to have met you

at Mrs. Jameson's, observing the 'fitness of things':—and as I am subject to the madness of saying 'Robert' without knowing it . . . !

May God bless you. Say how you are! Don't let me slide out of your mind through this rift in the rock. I catch at the jutting stones.

I am your own Ba.

R. B. to E. B. B.

Friday.
[Post-mark, July 3, 1846.]

No, dear, dear Ba, I shall not see you to-day in spite of all the hoping and fancying . . for I could not, as I calculate, reach Mrs. Jameson's before 1 o'clock or a little later . . and there would be the worst of vexations, to know you had been and gone again! I persuade myself you may not pay tho visit to-day, . . ('it is impossible' you say), and that it may be paid next week, the week in which there is only one day for us . . how do you say, dearest? all complaining is vain—let to-morrow make haste and arrive!

Ba, there is nothing in your letter that shocks me,—nothing: if you choose to imagine *that* 'possibility,' you are consistent in imagining the proper step to take . . it is all imagining. But I feel altogether as you feel about the horribleness of married friends, mutual esteemers &c.—when your name sounds in my ear like any other name, your voice like other voices,—when we wisely cease to interfere with each other's pursuits,—respect differences of taste &c. &c., all will be over *then!*

I cannot myself conceive of one respect in which I shall ever fall from this feeling for you . . there never has been one word, one gesture unprompted by the living, immediate love beneath—but there have been many, many, *so* many that the same love has suppressed, refused to be represented by! I say this, because I can suppose a man taking up a service of looks and words, which service is only to last for a time, and so may be endured,—after which the 'real affection,' 'honest attachment' &c. &c. means to go to its ends by a shorter road, saving useless ceremony and phrases . . do you know what I mean? I hardly do . . except that it is, whatever it is, opposed, as heaven to earth, to what I feel is. I count confidently on being more and more able to find the true words and ways (which may not be *spoken* words perhaps), the true rites by which you should be worshipped, you dear, dear Ba, my entire blessing now and ever—and *ever;* if God shall save me also.

Let me kiss you now, and long for to-morrow—I shall bring you the poorest flowers——all is brown, dry, autumnal. The sun shines and reproves me . . After all, there would have been some rocks in the pleasant water of to-day's meeting . . 'Oh, hardness to dissemble'!

Here is no dissembling . . I kiss you, my very own!

E. B. B. to R. B.

Friday Night.
[Post-mark, July 4, 1846.]

Ah! 'to-morrow, make haste and arrive.' And what good will to-morrow do when it comes?

Dearest, with your letter to-night, I have a note from Mrs. Jameson, who proposes that I should go to her just on this to-morrow, between twelve and one: she will wait for me till one and then go out. Moreover she leaves town on Tuesday. Now I think I ought to try to be with her this time, therefore, on the hour she mentions, and I will try . . I mean to try. But as for seeing you even *so*, and for a moment, . . I understand that it scarcely is possible—no, *not* possible—you cannot have time, I think. Thinking which, understanding which, I shall yet, in spite of reason, listen for the footstep and the voice: certainly I shall not help doing *that.*

Our to-morrow!—How they have spoilt it for us! In revenge, I shall love you to-morrow twice as much, looking at my dead flowers. Twice as much!! '*Ba, never talk extravagances.*' *Twice as much* is a giant fifty feet high. It is foolish to be fabulous.

Being better this evening (almost as if I were sure to see you in the morning) I went out to drive with Arabel and Flush, about six o'clock,—and we were not at home until eight, after having seen a mirage (as it appeared) of green fields and trees. Beyond Harrow cemetery we went, through silent lanes and hedgerows—so silent, so full of repose! Quite far away over the tops of the trees, was '*London,*' Arabel said . . but I could see only a cloud:—it seemed no more, nor otherwise. Once she got out and went into a field to give Flush a run—and I, left to myself and you, read your last letter in the carriage, under the branches which were dropping separate shadows of every leaf they had. The setting sun forced them to it. Oh—but I send you no leaves, because I could not reach any, and did not get out to walk to-day where I might have gathered them. Arabel tried hard to persuade me to go into the cemetery—but let me deserve all she said to me about weakness and foolishness, . . really that sort of thing does sadden me—my spirits fall flat with it: it is the dark side of death. So I begged her to go by herself and to leave me . . I would wait for her—and she should have as long a pleasure in that pleasure-ground of the Dead, as she liked. 'Very pretty,' it is said to be—the dissenters and the churchpeople planted in separate beds; and the Roman Catholics conspicuous for their roses! Oh that ghastly mixture of horror and frivolity! The *niaiserie* of their divisions and subdivisions taken down so carefully into the dust! But Arabel did not go at last, and we were at home quite late enough.

May God bless you, dear, dear! Give me all my thoughts (those that belong to me) to-morrow. Poor disinherited to-morrow.

I will *write* to-morrow, at any rate—and *hear*—let me hear.

And you are the best, best! When I speak lead, you answer gold. Because I 'do not shock' you, you melt my heart away with joy.

Yet I can love you enough, even I!

Your Ba.

R. B. to E. B. B.

Saturday.
[Post-mark, July 4, 1846.]

Dearest Ba, I am at Mrs. Jameson's . . to hear you cannot come; most properly. She wants me to go and see an Exhibition, and I cannot refuse . . so this is my poor long letter (with kisses in the words), that was to have been! But on Monday, dearest, dearest, I shall see you? All thanks for your letter . . I dare write no more, as there *must* be some difference in my way of writing to you from other ways.

Bless you, ever, as I am ever yours—

R.

E. B. B. to R. B.

Saturday.
[Post-mark, July 4, 1846.]

Ah, this Saturday! how heavily the wheels of it turn round! as if 'with all the weights of sleep and death hung at them.' After all it was not possible for me to get to Mrs. Jameson's this morning . . not that I was unwell to *signify*, mind—but unfit for the exertion—and it would not have been agreeable to anybody if I had gone there and fainted. So here I am, the picture of helpless indolence, stretched out at full length between the chair and the high stool, thinking how you will not to-day sit on the low one, nor in your old own place by me——oh how I think, think, think of you, to make imperfect amends! Are you disappointed . . *you?* I hope you are, and I fear you are. My generosity does not carry me through the hope of it to the end. I love your love too much. And *that* is the worst fault, my beloved, I ever can find in my love of *you.*

Look, what Miss Mitford has sent me from the *Daily News*—Mr. Horne's lament for poor Haydon. Tell me if you do not like it. It has moved me much, and as a composition it is fine, I think,—worthy of 'Orion.' I shall write to Mr. Horne to thank him, as one reader of many, for touching that solemn string into such a right melody. To my mind, it is worth, and more than worth, twenty such books as his ballad-book—tell me if it isn't. It has much affected me.

Papa went out early—so we should have escaped the 'complication'—but every half-hour we are expecting our visitors. And for Monday . . I scarcely dare say yet 'Come on Monday.' Only we will find our lost Pleiads . . of that, be very sure—*I* am very sure. Still to miss one for a moment draws me into darkness—or . . do you not know that you are *all* my stars? yes, and the sun, besides! The thing which people call a sun seems to shine quite coldly to-day, because you are not on this side of my window. 'All complaining is vain,' do you say?

Let me pass the time a little, then, by confessing to you that what you said, some letters ago, about the character of our intercourse, in our present relation, being a sort of security for the future, . . that *that* did strike me as a true and reasonable observation as far as it goes. I think, at least, that if I were inclined to fear for my own happiness apart from yours (which, as God knows, is a fear that never comes into my head), I should have sense to reason myself clear of it all by seeing in you none of the common rampant man-vices which tread down a woman's peace—and which begin the work often long before marriage. Oh, I understand perfectly, how as soon as ever a common man is sure of a woman's affections, he takes up the tone of right and might . . and he *will* have it so

. . and he *won't* have it so! I have heard of the bitterest tears being shed by the victim as soon as ever, by one word of hers, she had placed herself in his power. Of such are 'Lovers' quarrels' for the most part. The growth of power on one side . . and the struggle against it, by means legal and illegal, on the other. There are other causes, of course—but for none of them could it be possible for *me* to quarrel with *you* now or ever. Neither now nor ever do I look forward to the ordinary dangers. What I have feared has been so different! May God bless you my own . . own! For my part, you have my leave to make me unhappy if you please. It only would be just that the happiness you have given, you should take away —it is yours, as I am yours.

Say how your head is—say how your mother is. Think of me with the thoughts that do good.

Your own

Ba.

TO THE MEMORY OF B. R. HAYDON.

By the Author of 'Orion.'

Mourn, fatal Voice, whom ancients called the Muse!
Thy fiery whispers rule this mortal hour,
Wherein the toiling Artist's constant soul
Revels in glories of a visioned world,—
Power, like a god, exalting the full heart;
Beauty with subtlest ravishment of grace
Refining all the senses; while afar
Through vistas of the stars where strange friends dwell,
A temple smiles for him to take his seat
Among the happy Dead whose work is done.

Mourn, fatal Voice, whom ancients called the Muse!
Thou lead'st the devotee through fruitful bowers
Wherein Imagination multiplies
Divinely, and, with noblest ecstasy,
To nature ever renders truth for truth.

Mourn, fatal Voice, whom ancients called the Muse!
Thou teachest to be strong and virtuous;

In labour, patient; clear-eyed as a star,
Self-truthful; vigilant within; and full
Of faith to be, and do, and send it forth;—
But teachest no man how to know himself,
His over-measures or his fallings short,
Nor how to know when he should step aside
Into the quiet shade, to wait his hour
And foil the common dragon of the earth.

O fatal Voice! so syren-sweet, yet rife
With years of sorrow, deathbeds terrible!
Mourn for a worthy son whose aims were high,
Whose faith was strong amidst a scoffing age.
No warning giv'st thou, on the perilous path,
To those who need the gold thy teaching scorns,
Heedless if other knowledge hold due watch.
Thou fill'st with heavenly bliss the enraptured eyes,
While the feet move to ruin and the grave.
Therefore, O voice, inscrutably divine,
Uplifting sunward, casting in the dust,
Forgetting man as man, and mindful only
Of the man-angel even while on earth,—
Mourn now with all thine ancient tenderness,
Mingled with tears that fall in heavy drops,
For One who lost himself, remembering thee!

R. B. to E. B. B.

Sunday.
[Post-mark, July 6, 1846.]

You will have known by my two or three words that I received your letter in time to set out for Mrs. J.'s—she said to me, directly and naturally, 'you have missed a great pleasure'—and then accounted for your absence. Do not be sorry, Ba, at my gladness . . for I was, I hope, glad . . yes, I am sure, glad that you ran no risk, if you will not think of *that*, think of *my* risk if you had '*fainted*' . . should I have kept the secret, do you suppose? Oh, dearest of all dreamt-of dearness,—incur no unnecessary danger now, at . . shall I dare trust,— the end of the adventure! I cannot fear for any mischance that may follow, once let my arms be round you . . I mean, the blow seems then to fall on both alike—now, what dismal, obscure months might be prolonged between us, before we meet next, by a caprice where the power is! When have I been so long without the blessing of your sight! Yet how considerately you have written, what amends you make, all that the case admits of! If I were less sure of my own mind, and what it knows for *best*, I might understand the French lover's fancy of being separated from his mistress that he might be written to and write . . but the *very best* I know, and have ever in sight, and constantly shall strive after . . to see you face to face, to live so and to die so—which I say, because it ends all, all that can be ended . . and yet seems in itself *so* encountered—no death, no end.

After all, I *may* see you to-morrow, may I not? There is no more than a danger, an apprehension, that we may lose to-morrow also, is there? You cannot tell me after this is read . . I shall know before. If I receive *no* letter, mind, I go to you . . so that if the Post is in fault after its custom, and your note arrives at 3 o'clock, you will know why I seem to disobey it and call . . and I shall understand why you are not to be seen—but I will hope.

When you say these exquisitely dear and tender things, you know Ba, it is as if the sweet hand were on my mouth —I cannot speak . . I try to seem as if I heard not, for all the joy of hearing . . you give me a jewel and I cannot repeat 'you, you *do* give me a jewel.' I am not worthy of any gift, you *must* know, Ba,—never say you do not—but what you press on me, let me feel, and half-see, and in the end, carry away, but do not think I can, in set words, *take* them. At most, they are, and shall be, half-gift half-loan for adornment's sake,—mine to wear, yours to take back again. Even this, all this ungracefulness, is proper, appropriate in its way—I am penetrated with shame thinking on what you say, and what my utmost devotion will deserve . . so infinitely less will it deserve! You are my very, very angel.

Mrs. Jameson showed me the lines you had sent her, Horne's very beautiful poem,—very earnest, very solemn and pathetic,—worthy of Horne and the subject—and you will do well to reward him as you propose. I think I will also write two or three lines,—telling him that you called my attention to the poem,—so that he may understand the new friend does not drive out the old, as the old proverb says. I will wait a day or two and write. And you are herein, too, a dear good Ba,—to write me out the verses in the characters I love best of all! I may keep them, I hope.

The weather is hot as ever: Ba, remember how I believe in you—is the indisposition 'nothing to signify'? And remember the confidence I make you of every slightest headache or what looks like it—tell me frankly as Ba should, and will if she loves me! I am very well . . and my mother much better. I observe while I write, the clouds gather propitiously for coolness if not rain—may all be as is best for you—'and for me?' Then kiss me, really, through the distance, and love me, my sweetest Ba!

I am your own—

E. B. B. to R. B.

Sunday.
[Post-mark, July 6, 1846.]

Will it do if you come on Wednesday, dearest? It will be safer I think—and, with people staying in the house, it is necessary, you see, to consider a little. My aunt is so tired with her journey that she is not likely to go out at all to-morrow—and when I remember that you dine with Mr. Kenyon on that Wednesday, it seems marked out for our day. Still I leave it to you. Never have we been so long parted, and perhaps by Wednesday you may forget me—ah no! Now I will not make the time longer by being unkind . . or even unjust.

I meant to write you a long letter to-day,—but first my

aunt and cousin were here telling me all the statistics of Arabella Hedley's marriage,—and then Mr. Kenyon came, . . and on such a very different subject, *his* talk was, that he has left me quite depressed. It appears that poor Mr. Haydon, in a paper entering into his reasons for self-destruction, says that he has left his manuscripts to *me*, with a desire for me to arrange the terms of their publication with Longman. Of course it has affected me naturally . . such a proof of trust when he had so many friends wiser and stronger to look to—but I believe the reference to be simply to the *fact* of his having committed to my care all his private papers in a great trunk . . one of three which he sent here. Two years ago when we corresponded, he made me read a good part of his memoirs, which he thought of publishing at that time; and then he asked me (no, it was a year and a half ago) to speak about them to some bookseller . . to Longman, he said, I remember, then. I explained, in reply, how I had not any influence with any bookseller in the world; advising him besides not to think of printing, without considerable modification, what I had read. In fact it was—with much that was individual and interesting,—as unfit as possible for the general reader—fervid and coarse at once, with personal references blood-dyed at every page. At the last, I suppose, the idea came back to him of my name in conjunction with Longman's—I cannot think that he meant me to do any *editor's* work, for which (with whatever earnestness of will) I must be comparatively unfit, both as a woman and as personally and historically ignorant of the persons and times he writes of. I should not know how one reference would fall innocently, and another like a thunderbolt, on surviving persons. I only know that without great modification, the Memoirs should not appear at all . . that the scandal would be great if they did. At the same time you will feel with me, I am sure, you who always feel with me, that whatever is clearly set for me to do, I should not shrink from under these circumstances, whatever the unpleasantness may be, more or less, involved in the doing. But if Mr. Serjeant Talfourd is the executor . . is he not the obviously fit person? Well! there is no need to talk any more. Mr. Kenyon is to try to see the paper. It was Mr. Forster who came to tell him of this matter and to get him to communicate it to me. Poor Haydon!

Dearest, I long for you to come and bring me a little light. Tell me how you are—now tell me. Tell me too how your mother is.

My aunt's presence here has seemed to throw me back suddenly and painfully into real life out of my dream-life with you——into the old dreary flats of real life. She does not know your name even—she sees in me just *Ba* who is not your Ba—and when she talks to me . . seeing me so . . I catch the reflection of the old abstraction as *she* apprehends it, and feel myself for a moment a Ba who is not your Ba . . sliding back into the melancholy of it! Do you understand the curious process, I talk of so mistily? Do you understand that she makes me sorrowful with not talking of *you* while she talks to *me?* Everything, in fact, that divides us, I must suffer from—so I need not treat metaphysically of causes and causes . . splitting the thinner straws.

Once she looked to the table where the remains of your flowers are, . . and said, 'I suppose Miss Mitford brought you those flowers.' 'No,' I answered, 'she did not.' 'Oh no,' began Arabel with a more suggestive voice, 'not Miss Mitford's flowers.' But I turned the subject quickly.

Robert!—how did you manage to write me the dear note from Mrs. Jameson's? how could you dare write and direct it before her eyes? What an audacity that was of yours. Oh—and how I regretted the missing you, as you proved it was a missing, by the letter! Twice to miss you on one day, seemed too much ill-luck . . . even for *me*, I was going to write . . but *that* would have been a word of my old life, before I knew that I was born to the best fortune and happiest, which any woman could have, . . in being loved by *you*.

Dearest, do not leave off loving me. Do not forget me by Wednesday. Shall it be Wednesday? or must it be Thursday? answer *you*.

I am your own

Ba.

R. B. to E. B. B.

Monday.
[Post-mark, July 6, 1846.]

When I read, after the reasons for not seeing you to-day, this—'still I leave it to you,'—believe, dearest, that I at once made the sacrifice and determined to wait till Wednesday,—as seemed best for you, and therefore for me: but at the letter's very end, amid the sweetest, comes 'Wednesday . . or must it be Thursday?' What is *that?* What '*must*' is mine? Shall you fear, or otherwise suffer, if we appoint Wednesday?

Oh, another year of this! Yet I am not, I feel, ungrateful to the Past . . all the obstacles in the world can do nothing now, nothing: earlier they might have proved formidable annoyances. I have seen enough of you, Ba, for an eternity of belief in you . . and you, as you confess, you cannot think 'I shall forget.'

All you can, you compensate me for the absence—that such letters, instead of being themselves the supremest reward and last of gains, should be—compensation, at the best! Am I really to have you, all of you and altogether, and always? If you go out of your dream-life, can I lie quietly in mine? But I hold your hand and hear your voice through it all.

How do these abrupt changes in the temperature affect you? Yesterday at noon, so oppressively hot—this morning, a wind and a cold. Do you feel no worse than usual? If you do not tell me,—you know, I cannot keep away. Then, this disinspiriting bequest of poor Haydon's journal

. . his 'writings'—from which all the harm came, and, it should seem, is still to come to himself and everybody beside—let us all forget what came of those descriptions and vindications and explanations interminable; but as for beginning another sorrowful issue of them,—it is part and parcel of the insanity—and to lay the business of editing the 'twenty-six' (I think) volumes, with the responsibility, on *you*—most insane! Unless, which one would avoid supposing, the author trusted precisely to your ignorance of facts and isolation from the people able to instruct you. Take one little instance of how 'facts' may be set down—in the *Athenæum* was an account of Haydon's quoting Waller's verse about the eagle reached by his own feather on the arrow,—which he applied to Maclise and some others, who had profited by their intimacy with him to turn his precepts to account and so surpass him in public estimation: now, Maclise was in Haydon's company for the first time at Talfourd's on that evening when I met your brother there,—so said Talfourd in an after-supper speech,—and Forster, to whom I mentioned the circumstance, assured me that Maclise 'called on Haydon for the first time only a few months ago' . . I suppose, shortly after. Now, what right has Maclise, a fine generous fellow, to be subjected to such an imputation as that? With an impartial prudent man, acquainted with the artists of the last thirty years, the editing might turn to profit: I do hope for an exercise of Mr. Kenyon's caution here, at all events. And then how horrible are all these posthumous revelations,—these passions of the now passionless, errors of the at length better-instructed! All falls unfitly, ungraciously—the triumphs or the despondencies, the hopes or fears, of—whom? He is so far above it all now! Even in this life—imagine a proficient in an art or science, who, after thirty or sixty years of progressive discovery, finds that some bookseller has disinterred and is about publishing the raw first attempt at a work which he was guilty of in the outset!

All of which you know better than I—what do you not know better? Nor as well?—that I love you with my whole heart, Ba, dearest Ba, and look up into your eyes for all light and life. Bless you.

Your very own—

I am going to Talfourd's to-morrow (to dine)—and perhaps to Chorley's in the evening. If I can do any bidding of yours at Talfourd's . . but that seems improbable,—with Mr. Kenyon, too! But (*this between our very selves*) the Talfourds, or at least Mrs. T., please to take one of their unimaginably stupid groundless dislikes to him.

E. B. B. to R. B.

Monday.
[Post-mark, July 7, 1846.]

But I meant to 'leave it to you,' not to come before Wednesday but after Wednesday, in case of some Wednesday's engagement coming to cross mine. 'Ba's old way' . . do you cry out! Perhaps—only that an engagement is a possible thing always. Not meaning an engagement with Miss Campbell. I hope, hope, then, to be able to see you, dearest Robert, on Wednesday. On Wednesday, at last!

Here is a letter which I had this morning from Mr. Landor, than which can anything be more gracious? It appears . . I forgot to tell you yesterday after I heard it from Mr. Kenyon . . it appears that my note of thanks had my signature affixed to it in such a state of bad writing, that Mr. Landor, being sorely puzzled, sent the letter up to Mr. Forster to be read. Mr. Forster read it (so it *could* be read!) and then took it to Mr. Kenyon, who read it too, and afterwards came to scold me for being perfectly illegible. It was signed at full length too, Elizabeth Barrett Barrett . . and really I couldn't believe that I was very guilty till Mr. Landor's own letter persuaded me this morning of its being so much pleasanter to be guilty than innocent, for the nonce.

Ah—you use the right word for the other subject. *If* a bequest, it is indeed a '*dispiriting* bequest,' this of poor Haydon's. But I hope to the last that he meant simply to point to *me* as the actual holder of the papers—and certainly when he sent the great trunk here, it was with no intention of dying; Mr. Kenyon agreed with me to that effect—I showed him the notes which I had found and laid aside for you, and which you shall take with you on Wednesday. Still, there must be an editor found somewhere—because the papers cannot go as they are to a publisher's hands from mine, if I *only hold* them. Does any one say that I am a fit editor? Have I *the power?* the knowledge of art and artists? of the world? of the times? of the persons? All these things are against me—and others besides.

Now I will tell you one thing which he told me in confidence, but which is at length perhaps in those papers—I tell you because you are myself, and will understand the need and obligation to silence—and I want you to understand besides how the twenty-six volumes hang heavily on my thoughts. He told me in so many words that Mrs. Norton had made advances towards him—and that his children, in sympathy towards their mother, had dashed into atoms the bust of the poetess as it stood in his painting room.

If you can say anything *safely* for me at Mr. Talfourd's, of course I shall be glad . . and Mr. Kenyon will speak to Mr. Forster, he said. I want to get back my letters too as soon as I can do it without disturbing anyone's peace. What is in those letters, I cannot tell, so impulsively and foolishly, sometimes, I am apt to write; and at that time, through caring for nobody and feeling so loose to life, I threw away my thoughts without looking where they fell. Often my sisters have blamed me for writing in that wild way to strangers—and I should like to have the letters back before they shall have served to amuse two or three executors—but of this too, I spoke to Mr. Kenyon.

Still it is not of *me* that we are called to think—and I would not for the world refuse any last desire, if clearly signified, and if the power should be with me. He was not a common man—he had in him the stuff of greatness, this poor Haydon had; and we must consider reverently whatever rent garment he shall have left behind. Quite, in some respects, I think with you—but your argument does appear to me to sweep out too far on one side, so that if you do not draw it back, Robert, you will efface all autobiography and confession—tear out a page bent over by many learners—I mean when you say because he is above (now) the passions and frailties he has recorded, we should put from us the record. True, he is above it all—true, he has done with the old Haydon; like a man outgrowing his own childhood he will not spin this top any more. Oh, it is true—I feel it all just as you do. But, after all, a man outgrowing his childhood, may leave his top to children, and no one smile! This record is not for the angels, but for *us*, who are a little lower at highest. Three volumes perhaps may be taken from the twenty-six full of character and interest, and not without melancholy teaching. Only some competent and sturdy hand should manage the selection; as surely as mine is unfit for it. But where to seek *discretion? delicacy?*

Dearest, I speak the truth to you—I am not ill indeed. When I was at best in health I used sometimes to be a little weak and faint, and it has only been *so* for this last day or two. By Wednesday the cloud will have passed. And, do you know, I have found out something from our long parting, . . I have found out that I love you better than even I thought. There's a piece of finding out! My own dearest—what would become of me indeed, *if* I could not see you on Wednesday nor on Thursday nor on Friday?—no breath I have, for going on. No breath I should have, for living on. I do kiss you through the distance ——since you tell me. I love you with my soul.

Your own I am.

Three of the flowers and nearly all the little blue ones stay with me all this while to comfort me! ! isn't it kind of them?

Two letters to-day—and such letters! Ah—if you love me always but half as much—I will agree with you now for half! Yet, O Hesiod, half is not better than the whole, by any means! Yet . . if the whole went away, and did not leave me half!—

When I was a child I heard two married women talking. One said to the other . . 'The most painful part of marriage is the first year, when the lover changes into the husband by slow degrees.' The other woman agreed, as a matter of fact is agreed to. I listened with my eyes and ears, and never forgot it . . as you observe. It seemed to me, child as I was, a dreadful thing to have a husband by such a process. Now, it seems to me more dreadful.

Si l'âme est immortelle
L'amour ne l'est-il pas?

Beautiful verses—just to prove to you that I do not remember *only* the disagreeable things . . only to teaze you with, like so many undeserved reproaches. And you so good, so best— Ah—but it is *that* which frightens me! so far *best!*

You were foolish to begin to love me, you know, as always I told you, my beloved!—but since you *would* begin, . . go on to do it as long as you can . . do not leave me in the wilderness. God bless you for me!—

I am your Ba.

Think if people were to get hold of that imputation on poor Mrs. Norton—think!

E. B. B. to R. B.

Tuesday Morning
in haste.
[Post-mark, July 7, 1846.]

Dearest, I am uncertain whether I can see you to-morrow. To-night I will write again—you shall hear. You tell me to *risk nothing* . . which is what I feel. But I long, long to see you. You shall hear in the morning.

Read the note which Mr. Kenyon sends me from Mr. Forster. Very averse I feel, from applying, in the way prescribed, to Mr. Serjeant Talfourd. Tell me what to do, Robert . . my 'famous in council!' Sick at heart, it all makes me. Am I to write to Mr. Talfourd, do you think?

Oh, *you* would manage it for me—but to mix *you* up in it, will make a danger of a worse evil. May God bless you, my own. I may see you to-morrow perhaps after all—it is a '*perhaps*' though . . and I am surely

Your Ba.

R. B. to E. B. B.

Tuesday.
[Post-mark, July 7, 1846.]

Dearest, the first thing to say is the deep joyfulness of expecting to see you, really, to-morrow—mind, the engagement with Mr. Kenyon is nothing in the way. If you cannot let me stay the usual time—I can call, pass away the interval easily . . this is a superfluous word to your goodness which is superfluous in these 'old ways of Ba's'—dear Ba, whom I kiss with perfect love—and shall soon kiss in no dream! Landor is all well enough in one sentence . . happily turned *that* is,—but I am vexed at his strange opinion of Goethe's poem,—and the more, that a few years ago he wrote down as boldly that nothing had been written *so* 'Hellenic' these two thousand years—(in a note to the 'Satire on the Satirists')—and of these opinions I think the earlier much nearer the truth. *Then* he wrote so, because Wordsworth had depreciated Goethe—now, very likely, some maladroit applauder has said Landor's own 'Iphigenia' is worthy of Goethe,—or similar platitudes.

Yes, dearest, you are quite right—and my words have a wrong sense, and one I did not mean they should bear, if they object to confessions and autobiographies in general. Only the littleness and temporary troubles, the petty battle with foes, which is but a moment's work however the success may be, all *that* might go when the occasion, real or fancied, is gone. I would have the customary 'habits,' as we say, of the man preserved, and if they were quilted and stiffened with steel and bristling all over with the offensive and defensive weapons the man judged necessary for his safety,—they should be composed and hung up decently—telling the true story of his life. But I should not preserve the fretful gesture,—lift the arm, as it was angrily lifted to keep off a wolf—which now turns out to have been only Flush in a fever of vigilance—half-drew the sword which—Ah, let me have done with this! You understand, if I do not. For the bad story,—the telling *that*, if it were true, is nearly as bad as inventing it. That poor woman is the hack-block of a certain class of redoubtable braggarts—there are such stories by the *dozen* in circulation. All may have been misconception . . 'advances'—to induce one more painter to introduce her face in his works.

My time is out . . I had much to say, but this letter of mine arrived by the afternoon post,—shame on the office! To-morrow!

Bless you, ever dearest dearest—

Your own.

E. B. B. to R. B.

Tuesday Evening.
[Post-mark, July 8, 1846.]

Yes—I understand you perfectly—and it should be exactly as you say—and it is just *that*, which requires so much adroitness,—and such decision and strength of hand, to manage these responsibilities. Somebody is wanted to cut and burn, and be silent afterwards. I remember that bitter things are said of Shelley and Leigh Hunt beyond all the bitterness of alcohol. Olives do not taste so, though steeped in salt. There are some curious letters by poor Keats about Hunt, and *they* too are bitter. It would be dreadful to suffer these miseries to sow themselves about the world, like so much thistle-down . . the world, where there are thistles enough already, to make fodder for its wild asses!

As to Landor . . oh, I did not remember the note you speak of in the satire you speak of—but you remember everything . . . even *me*. Is it not true that Landor, too, is one of the men who carry their passions about with them into everything, as a boy would, pebbles . . muddying every clear water, with a stone here and a stone there. The end is, that we lose the image of himself in the serene depth, as we might have had it—and the little stone comes to stand for him. How unworthy of such a man as Landor, such weakness is! To *think* with one's temper! ! One might as well be at once Don Quixote, and fight with a warming-pan.

But I did not remember the *former* opinion. I took it for a constitutional fancy of Landor's, and did not smile much more at it than at my own 'profundity in German,' which was a matter of course . . of course . . of course. For have I not the gift of tongues? Don't I talk Syriac . . as well as Flush talks English—and Hebrew, like a prophetess . . and various other languages and dialects less familiarly known to persons in general than these aforesaid? So, profound indeed, must be the German and the Dutch! And perhaps it may not be worth while to answer Mr. Landor's note for the mere purpose of telling him anything about it.

Dearest!—I have written all this before I would say a word of your coming, just to think a little more—and down all these pages I have been thinking, thinking, of *you* . . of your possible coming . . what nonsense they must be! Well! and the end is that, let it be wise or unwise, I *must and will see you to-morrow*—I cannot do otherwise. It is just as if Flush had been shut up in a box for so many days. My spirits flag . . and I could find it in my heart to grow cross like Landor and deny Goethe. So come, dearest dearest—and let the world bark at our heels if it pleases. I will just turn round and set Flush at it.

For two or three days I have not been out—not for two days . . not out of this room. This evening at seven, when they were all going to dinner, I took Wilson with me and drove into the park for air. It will do me good perhaps—but your coming will, certainly. So come, my dearest beloved!—At three, remember.

Your own

Ba.

R. B. to E. B. B.

PRIVATE

Wednesday 7. A.M.
[Post-mark, July 8, 1846.]

My own Ba, I received your note on my return from Talfourd's last night. I am anxious to get the first post for this, so can only use the bare words,—if those. After dinner, Forster put a question to our host about the amount of the subscription; and in a minute the paper-bequest was introduced. Talfourd had received a letter from Miss Mitford, enclosing one from you (or a copy of one . . I did not hear)—whereat he pronounced so emphatically upon H.'s conduct in making you,—' who could never have known the nature of the transaction nor the very serious consequences it involved'—the depositary of his pictures &c. on such occasions,—the words, 'H. it seems, has been in the habit of using Miss B's house &c.' (or to that effect) had so offensive an implication,—that I felt obliged to say simply, you had never seen Haydon and were altogether amazed and distressed at his desire,—and that, for the other matter, what he chose to send, you could not, I supposed, bring yourself to refuse admittance to the house. I gave no particular account of my own means of knowledge, nor spoke further than to remove the impression from the minds of the people present that you must have 'known' Haydon, as they call 'knowing'—and Forster, for one, expressed surprise at it. I ventured to repeat what I mentioned to you—'that it seemed likely you were selected for the Editorship precisely on account of your isolation from the world.'

Soon after, Forster went away—and, upstairs, I got Talfourd alone, and just told him that I was in the habit of corresponding with you, that you had made me acquainted with a few of the circumstances, and that you had at once thought of *him*, Talfourd, as the proper source of instruction on the subject. Talfourd's reply amounted to this,—(in the fewest words possible). The *will* &c is of course an absurdity. The papers are the undoubted property of the creditors . . any attempt to publish them would subject you to an action at law. They were given prospectively to you *exactly for the reason I suggested:* they having been in the first instance offered to Talfourd. Haydon knew that T. would never print them in their offensive integrity, and hoped that *you would*—being quite of the average astuteness in worldly matters when his own vanity and selfishness were not concerned. They might, these papers, be published with advantage to Mrs. Haydon at some future time if the creditors permit—or without their permitting, if woven into a substantially new framework; as some 'Haydon and his Times,' or the like . . but there is nothing to call for such a step at present, even in that view of advantage to the family . . the subscription and other assistances being sufficient for their necessities. Therefore the course T. would recommend you to adopt is to let the deposit (*if* you have one . . for he did not *know*, and I said nothing)—lie untouched—not giving them up to anybody, any creditor, to Mrs. H's prejudice.

Now, can you do better than as Forster advises? Talfourd goes on circuit *to-morrow*—he said, 'I can hear, or arrange anything with Miss B's brother'—so that, if there should be no time, you can write by him, and entrust explanations &c. But would it not be best to get done with this matter directly—to write a BRIEF note in the course of to-day, mentioning the facts, and requesting advice? In order to leave you the time to do this,—should the post presently bring me a letter allowing me to see you at three . . unless the allowance is *very* free, *very* irresistible . . I will rather take to-morrow . . a piece of self-denial I fear I should not so readily bring myself to exhibit, were I not really obliged to pass your house to-day; so that even Ba will understand!

Miss Mitford's note appears to have been none of the wisest—indeed a phrase or two I heard, were purely foolish: H. was said to have practised 'Ion's principle'!

T. had known Haydon most intimately and for a long time: he does not believe H. was mad—of a mad vanity, of course. His *last* paper . . 'Haydon's Thoughts' . . was a dissertation on the respective merits of Napoleon and Wellington—how wrong Haydon felt he had been to prefer the former . . and the why and the wherefore. All this wretched stuff, in a room theatrically arranged,—here his pictures, there . . God forgive us all, fools or wise by comparison! The debts are said to be £3,000 . . he having been an insolvent debtor . . how long before? His landlord, a poor man, is creditor for £1,200.

Here I will end, and wait: this is written in *all* haste . . and is so altogether no proper letter of *mine* that I shall put the necessary 'Private' at the top of it. *My* letter shall go presently, if *I* do not go, to my own Ba—

R. B.

Should you write to your brother . . will he need reminding that Talfourd is only to know we correspond,—not that we are personally acquainted? Had you not better mention this in any case?

God bless you, dearest,—what a letter from me to you—to Ba! *Time*, Time!

R. B. to E. B. B.

Thursday.
[Post-mark, July 9, 1846.]

My own darling, my Ba, do you know when I read those letters (as soon as I remembered I had got them,—for you hold me long after both doors, up and down stairs, shut) when I looked through them, under a gateway . . I was pricked at the heart to have thought so, and spoken so, of the poor writer. I will believe that he was good and even great when in communication with you—indeed all men are made, or make themselves, different in their approaches to different men—and the secret of goodness and greatness is in choosing *whom* you will approach, and live with, in memory or imagination, through the crowding obvious people who seem to live with you. That letter about the glory of being a painter 'if only for the neglect' is most touching and admirable . . there is the serene spot attained, the solid siren's isle amid the sea; and while *there*, he was safe and well . . but he would put out to sea again, after a breathing time, I suppose? though even a smaller strip of land was enough to maintain Blake, for one instance, in power and glory through the poor, fleeting 'sixty years'—then comes the rest from cartooning and exhibiting. But there is no standing, one foot on land and one on the waves, now with the high aim in view, now with the low aim,—and all the strange mistaken talk about 'prestiges,' 'Youth and its luck,' Napoleon and the world's surprise and interest. There comes the low aim between the other,—an organ grinds Mr. Jullien's newest dance-tune, and Camoens is vexed that the 'choral singing which brought angels down,' can't also draw street-passengers round.

I take your view of H.'s freedom, at that time, from the thoughts of what followed.

He was weak—a strong man would have borne what so many bear—what were his griefs, as grief *goes?* Do you remember I told you, when the news of Aliwal and the other battles came to England, of our gardener, and his son, a sergeant in one of the regiments engaged . . how the father could learn nothing at first, of course . . how they told him at the Horse Guards he should be duly informed in time, after his betters, whether this son was dead, or wounded. Since then, no news came . . 'which is *good* news' the father persuaded himself to think . . so the apprehensions subside, and the hope confirms itself, more and more, while the old fellow digs and mows and rakes away, like a man painting historical pictures . . only without the love of it. Well, this morning we had his daughter here to say 'the letter' had arrived at last . . her brother was killed in the first battle, so there's an end of the three months' sickness of heart,—and the poor fellow must bear his loss 'like a man'—or like a woman . . for I recollect another case, of an old woman whom my mother was in the habit of relieving,—who brought a letter one day which she could hardly understand—it was from her son, a sailor, and went on for a couple of pages about his good health and expectations,—then, in a different handwriting, somebody, 'your son's shipmate' 'took up his pen to inform you that he fell from the masthead into the sea and was drowned yesterday,—which he therefore thought it right to put in the unfinished letter.' All which the old woman bore somehow,—seeing she lives yet.

Well,—ought not I to say Mr. Kenyon was as kind as usual, and his party as pleasant? No, for you know—what you cannot by possibility know, it seems, is, that I am not particularly engaged next Saturday! Ba, shall I really see you so soon? Bless you ever, my very, very own! I shall not hear to-day . . but to-morrow,—do but not keep me waiting for *that* letter, and the mules shall be ready hours and hours, for any sign I will have, at La Cava!

Ever your R.

E. B. B. to R. B.

Thursday.
[Post-mark, July 9, 1846.]

See what an account we have this morning of La Cava . . 'quite impossible for the winter.' What does 'quite impossible' quite mean, I wonder? I feel disappointed. As to Palermo, you would rather be in Italy, and so would I, perhaps. Salerno seems questionable too; and Vietri . . what of Vietri? I don't at all see why we should receive the responses of this friend of my friend who is not so very much my friend, as if they were oracular and final. There must be the right of appeal for us to other authorities. Will you investigate and think a little? For my part I shall not care to what place we go, except for the climate's sake—the cheapness too should be considered a little: and, for the rest, every place which you should like, I should like, and which you liked most, I should like most—everything is novelty to *me*, remember.

My uncle Hedley has just come now, and I must quicken my writing. Oh—to be so troubled just now . . just now!— But I wrote to Mr. Serjeant Talfourd last night, and told him as fully and as briefly as I could the whole position . . and *that* vexation I shall try now to throw behind me, after the fashion of dear Mr. Kenyon's philosophy. I put the thought of you, beloved, between me and all other thoughts—surely I *can*, when you were here only yesterday. So much to think of, there is! One thing made me laugh in the recollection. Do you mean to tell Mrs. Jameson that you are going to marry me, 'because it is intolerable to hear me talked of?' That would be an original motive. 'So speaks the great poet.'—

Ah Flush, Flush!—he did not hurt you really? You will forgive him for me? The truth is that he hates all unpetticoated people, and that though he does not hate *you*, he has a certain distrust of you, which any outward sign, such as the umbrella, reawakens. But if you had seen how sorry and ashamed he was yesterday! I slapped his ears and told him that he never should be loved again: and he sate on the sofa (sitting, not lying) with his eyes fixed on me all the time I did the flowers, with an expression of quite despair in his face. At last I said, 'If you are good, Flush, you may come and say that you are sorry' . . on which he dashed across the room and, trembling all over, kissed first one of my hands and then another, and put up his paws to be shaken, and looked into my face with such great beseeching eyes that you would certainly have forgiven him just as I did. It is not savageness. If he once loved you, you might pull his ears and his tail, and take a bone out of his mouth even, and he would not bite you. He has no savage caprices like other dogs and men I have known.

Writing of Flush, in my uncle comes, and then my cousin, and then my aunt . . . *by relays!* and now it is nearly four and this letter may be too late for the post which reaches you irregularly. So provoked I am!—but I shall write again, to-night, you know.

Dearest, you did me so much good yesterday! Say how your head is—and remember Saturday. Saturday will be clear through Chiswick—may the sun shine on it!—

Your own Ba.

Think of the dreadful alternative as set forth in this MS.!— The English . . or a bad climate!—*Can* it be true?

ENCLOSURE.

[La Cava is *impossible* for the winter owing to the damp and cold. At no season should any person remain out at the hour of sunset. An hour *afterwards* the air is dry and healthy—[Is this at La Cava? Ba] This applies to all Italy, and is a precaution too often neglected. Salerno has bad air too near it, to be safe as a residence. Besides, it is totally without the resources of books, good food, or medical advice. Palermo would be agreeable in the winter, and not *very* much frequented by English. *However, where good climate exists, English are to be found.* Murray's 'Southern Italy' would give every particular as to the distance of La Cava from the sea.]

E. B. B. to R. B.

Thursday Evening.
[Post-mark, July 10, 1846.]

How I have waited for your letter to-night,—and it comes nearly at ten!—It comes at last—thank you for it, ever dearest.

And I knew—quite understood yesterday, that you were sorry for *me*, which made you angry with another . . but, as to poor Haydon, you are too generous and too pitiful to refuse him any justice. I was sure that the letters would touch you. The particular letter about the 'back-ground' and the 'neglect' and Napoleon, . . *that*, you will observe, was the last I had from him. Every word you say of it, I think and feel. Yes, it was just *so!* His conscience was not a sufficient witness, . . nor was God. He must also have the Royal Academy and the appreciators of Tom Thumb. A 'weak man,' of course he was,—for all vain men are weak men. They cannot stand alone. But that he had in him the elements of greatness—that he looked to noble aims in art and life, however distractedly, . . that his thoughts and feelings were not those of a common man, . . it is true, it is undeniable,—and you would think so more and more if you read through the packets of letters which I have of his—so fervid, so full of earnestness and individuality . . so alive with egotism which yet seemed to redeem itself. Mr. Kenyon said of the letter we have spoken of, that it was scarcely the production of a sane mind. But I, who was used to his letters, saw nothing in it in the least unusual—he has written to me far wilder letters! That he 'never should die,' he had said once or twice before. Then Napoleon was a favourite subject of his . . constantly recurred to. He was not mad *then!*

Poor Haydon! Think what an agony, life was to him, so constituted!—his own genius a clinging curse! the fire and the clay in him seething and quenching one another!—the man seeing maniacally in all men the assassins of his fame! and, with the whole world against him, struggling for the thing which was his life, through night and day, in thoughts and in dreams . . struggling, stifling, breaking the hearts of the creatures dearest to him, in the conflict for which there was no victory, though he could not choose but fight it. Tell me if Laocoon's anguish was not as an infant's sleep, compared to this? And could a man, suffering *so,* stop to calculate very nicely the consideration due to A, and the delicacy which should be observed toward B? Was he scrupulously to ask himself whether this or that cry of his might not give C a headache? Indeed no, no. It is for *us* rather to look back and consider! Poor Haydon.

As to grief as grief—of course he had no killing grief. But he *suffered.*

Often it has struck me as a curious thing (yet it is not perhaps curious) that suicides are occasioned nearly always by a mortified self-love . . by losses in money, which force a man into painful positions . . and scarcely ever by bereavement through death . . scarcely ever. The wound on the vanity is more irritating than the wound on the affections—and the word *Death*, if it does not make us recoil (which it does I think sometimes, . . even from the graves of beloved beings!), yet keeps us humble . . casts us down from our heights. We may despond, but we do not rebel—we feel God over us.

Ah—your poor gardener! All that hope is vain—and the many, many hopes which in a father's heart must have preceded it! How sorry I am for him.[1]

You never can have a grief, dearest dearest, of which I shall not have half for my share. That is my right from henceforth . . and if I could have it *all* . . *would* I not, do you think, . . and give my love to you to keep instead? Yes, . . indeed yes! May God bless you always. I have walked out to-day, you did me so much good yesterday. As for Saturday, it certainly is our day, since you are not 'particularly engaged' to Miss Campbell. Saturday, the day after to-morrow! But the mules may wait long at La Cava for us, if the tradition, which I sent you, is trustworthy—may they not? I feel as disappointed . . as disappointed— Your own, very own Ba.

R. B. to E. B. B.

Friday.
[Post-mark, July 10, 1846.]

And *I* am disappointed, dearest, in this news of La Cava—after which it would be madness to think of going there: the one reason we have to go at all is simply *for your health*—I mean, that if the seclusion were the main object, we might easily compass *that* here. All places are utterly indifferent to me if I can inhabit them with you—why should Palermo please me less than Italy proper? The distance is considerable, however, and the journey expensive—I wonder whether the steamer will sail for Leghorn as last year. As for the travelling English, they

[1] [Some months later the discovery was made that there had been a mistake in the War Office in the name, and that the son was unharmed. R. B. B.]

are horrible, and at Florence, unbearable . . their voices in your ear at every turn . . and such voices!—I got to very nearly hate the Tribune for their sakes. Vietri is close to Salerno and must be obvious to the same condemnation. Your friend speaks from personal experience, I presume—she may well say that the baneful effects of the hour of sunset (*i.e.* the Ave-maria) are too much overlooked 'in all Italy'—I never heard of them before—but an infinity of 'crotchets' go from Italian brain to brain about what, in eating or drinking or walking or sleeping, will be the death of you: still, they may know best. The most dreadful event that could happen to me would be your getting worse instead of better . . God knows what I should do! So whatever precaution we *can* take, let us take.

Oh, poor Flush,—do you think I do not love and respect him for his jealous supervision,—his slowness to know another, having once known you? All my apprehension is that, in the imaginations down-stairs, he may very unconsciously play the part of the dog that is heard to 'bark violently' while something dreadful takes place: yet I do not sorrow over his slapped ears, as if they ever pained him very much—you dear Ba!

And to-morrow I shall see you. Are you, can you be, really 'better' after I have seen you? If it is not truth . . which I will not say . . such an assurance is the most consummate flattery I can imagine . . it may be recorded on my tombstone 'R. B.—to whom this flattery was addressed, that, after the sight of him, Ba was better, she said.' If it is truth . . may you say *that*, neither more nor less, day by day, year by year through our lives—and I shall have lived indeed!

How it rains—how it varies from hot to cold! a pretty vantage-ground whence we English can look and call other climates bad or indifferent! Now if to-morrow resembles to-day, will the Chiswick expedition hold good? I shall consider that I may go unless a letter comes to-morrow

. . which would have to be written to-day. How pleasant it would be to make our days *always* Wednesday and Saturday . . could not that be contrived? So much for considerateness and contentedness!

I want, now, to refer as little as possible to the sad subject . . but I am glad you have written,—glad too that you are not severe on me for some hasty speeches—which did, indeed, mean as you say . . vexation at your having been vexed. And, I will just add, you remark excellently on the wound to self-love making itself that remedy, rather than the wound to the affections . . yet there are instances . . Romilly loses his wife . . so does poor Laman Blanchard.

So I go on writing, writing about all but what my heart is full of! Let me kiss you, ever dearest—to-morrow will soon arrive—meanwhile, and forever I am your own.

R. B. to E. B. B.

Sunday.
[Post-mark, July 12, 1846.]

When I made you promise to refer no more to that subject in your letter (which I must wait a day and a night for, alas!), I did not engage myself to the like silence . . perhaps because I was not bidden—or, no! there is a better reason; I want to beg your pardon, dearest, for all that petulancy,—for the manner of what I said rather than the matter,—there is a rationality in it all, if I could express trulier what I feel—but the manner was foolish and wrong and unneessary to *you*—so do forgive and forget it. You would understand and sympathize if you knew—not me, whom you do know in some degree,—but so much of my early life as would account for the actual horror and hatred I have of those particular doctrines of the world—and the especially foolish word about the 'travelling' meant something like the not unnatural thought that if in this main, sole event for all good and all evil in my life,—if *here* the world plucked you from me by any of the innumerable lines it casts, with that indirectness, too,—*then*, I should simply go and live the rest of my days as far out of it as I could.

The simple thing to say is, that I who know you to be above me in all great or good feelings and therefore worship you, must be without excuse to talk inconsiderately as if I, sitting by you and speaking of the same subject, must needs feel more acutely, more strongly in one respect where, indeed, it wants very little pre-eminence in heart or brain to feel entirely the truth—a simplest of truths. It would have been laughable if I had broken out on Mrs. Proctor's bitterness of speech, for instance . . just as though you were the slower of us two to see the nature of it! So I do again ask your pardon, dearest Ba! You said you loved me no less yesterday than ever—how must I love you and press closer to you more and more, and desire to see nothing of the world behind you, when I hear how the world thinks, and how you think! You only, only adorable woman, only imaginable love for me! And all the hastiness and petulancy comes from that . . someone seems to come close (in every such maxim of the world's) and say 'What is *she*—to so much a year? Could you be happy with her except in Mayfair—and there whom could you not be happy with!'

It is as I expected—Rachel plays on Wednesday in 'Phèdre,' and our friend writes to say he has secured places. May nothing overcast the perfect three hours on Tuesday,—those dear, dear spaces of dear brightness—why cannot a life be made up of these . . with the proper interposition of work, to justify God's goodness so far as poor mortality and its endeavours can,—a week of Tuesdays—then a month—a year—a life! I must long to see you again,—always by far the most I long, the *next day*—the very day after I have seen you—when it is freshest in my mind what I did *not* say while I might have said it,—nor ask while I might have been answered—nor learn while you would have taught me—no, it is indescribable. Did I call yesterday 'unsatisfactory'? Would I had it back now! Or better, I will wish you here when I write, with the trees to see and the birds to hear through the open window—I see you on this old chair against the purple back . . or shall you lie on the sofa? Ba, how I love you, my own perfect unapproachable mistress.

Let me kiss your feet—and now your hands and your eyes—and your lips now, for the full pardon's sake, my sweetest love—

Ever your own—

E. B. B. to R. B.

Sunday. 6 P.M.
[Post-mark, July 13, 1846.]

Ever, ever dearest, I have to *feel* for you all through Sunday, and I hear no sound and see no light. How are you? how did you get home yesterday? I thought of you more than usual after you went, if I did not love you as much as usual . . . What could *that* doubt have been made of?

Dearest, I had a letter last night from Mrs. Jameson, who says that on *Tuesday or Wednesday* at about four o'clock (though she is as little sure of the hour apparently as of the day), she means to come to see me. Now you are to consider whether this *grand peutêtre* will shake our Tuesday, . . whether you would rather take Thursday instead, or will run the risk as it appears. I am ready to agree, either way. She is the most uncertain of uncertain people, and may not come at all . . it's a case for what Hume used to call sceptical scepticism. Judge! Then I have heard (I forgot to tell you) from Mr. Horne—and . . did *you* have two letters last week from your Bennet? . . because *I* had,—flying leaves of 'Mignonette,' and other lyrical flowers.

When you had gone Arabel came to persuade me to go

to the park in a cab, notwithstanding my too lively recollections of the last we chanced upon,—and I was persuaded, and so we tumbled one over another (yet not all those cabs are so rough!) to the nearest gate opening on the grass, and got out and walked a little. A lovely evening it was, but I wished somehow rather to be at home, and Flush had his foot pinched in shutting the cab-door, . . and altogether there was not much gain:—only, as for Flush's foot, though he cried piteously and held it up, looking straight to me for sympathy, no sooner had he touched the grass than he began to run without a thought of it. Flush always makes the most of his misfortunes—he is of the Byronic school—*il se pose en victime.*

Now I will not write any more—I long to have my letter of to-morrow morning—I *long* to have it . . Shall I not have it to-morrow morning? This is posted by my hand.

I loved you yesterday . . I love you to-day . . I shall love you to-morrow.

Every day I am yours.

Ba.

R. B. to E. B. B.

Monday.
[Post-mark, July 13, 1846.]

My own Ba, your letter kisses me in its entire kindness—and I kiss it and you.—Mrs. Jameson may come or keep away . . (since you let me speak and decide, which is like you) . . she may appoint and reappoint, but Tuesday was given me and I will have it if her visit is the only obstacle—for what was all the confessing worth if not to account for such a phenomenon as my presence in your room when by any chance she might discover it? Beside, as you say, she is the most uncertain of engagement-holders . . no, indeed,—no Tuesday ought to be given up for *her!* Therefore, unless fresh orders arrive,—at three on

Tuesday . . which is happily, happily to-morrow! You are my own sweetest to reach a letter to me with your own hand, as you tell me,—and the drive, and the walk to the Post Office—thank you, Ba! Perhaps . . dare I say . . you will answer that letter I sent yesterday . . because now I remember there is no prayer at the end to prevent you . . that is, from answering the main part of it—the reverting &c.

I wrote to Mr. Horne, but shall not hear from him—on Saturday I wrote. And Mr. Bennett's two letters are considerately written,—directed, I mean,—in a hand and with a blue ink that I recognise,—consequently the contents give me no trouble. I wrote two or three lines to the 'year of the world' poet,—did you take the pains? Once on a time some unknown author sent me a Tragedy, 'not published,' called 'Alessandro de' Medici,' with some striking scenes . . I wonder who could be the writer—did it ever fall in your way?

. . As if I care!—can I care about anything that is not Ba? All else seems as idle as . . as,—now you shall have a real instance in point—as my dream last night. This morning at breakfast my mother asked me, the first thing, what could so amuse me as to make me call loudly 'Bravo' again and again, with abundance of laughter? (My room is next to hers and the door is left ajar). Whereupon I tried to recall my dream—and all that I can seize is a passage through a gallery of *Haydon's* pictures, one of which was a portrait of his wife; nor did a suspicion once cross my mind that the artist was not well and working somewhere in the vicinity all the time—How strange! I never dream if *quite* well—and I suppose the present state of my head just amounts to *not* being quite well. (It is better at any rate, and to-morrow—ought to be worse, that—Ba may prove her potency as of old).

Now I will kiss you and wait as well as I can till the full blessing. Dearest—dearest I am your own—

E. B. B. to R. B.

Monday, Morning.
[Post-mark, July 14, 1846.]

I must write . . even if you come to-morrow. Dearest, if I told you all that nonsense on Saturday, it was for the sake of telling you all and of hearing you say 'What nonsense' afterwards. I never began by disguising anything from you . . did I? I always wished you to see how the arrows would strike out at us from that bush and this bush. At *us*. For, granting that you seriously thought it possible for such motives to divide me from you, . . . ah, *granting* it, . . and *you may well ask my pardon!*

The world! the world could as soon catch me with a 'line' so baited, as you could catch a trout with a silver sixpence at the end of a string. Not only do I think with you entirely on that subject, but I always thought like you. Always I have hated all their worldly systems, and not merely *now,* and since I *have loved you.* With a hundred a year between us, I would have married you, if *you* had not been afraid. And so, think whether directly or 'indirectly' I am likely to be frightened into the breach of an engagement by what I repeated to you or by what is like unto it. No—my weaknesses are of a different class altogether.

The talk I talked over again to you, seemed to burn in my ears the longer on that Saturday, because, while it was being originally talked between Papa and my aunt (touching Arabella Hedley's marriage), he had brought a paper for me to sign about some money placed on a railway, (not speculatively) . . and my aunt, by way of saying a lively thing, exclaimed, 'Is that your marriage-settlement, my dear?' . . which made me so nervous that I wrote my name wrong and vexed Papa into being almost cross with me. So one word got entwined with another, and all seemed to hang around me—Do you understand?

But you *do not*, how you pained me when you said *that*. Ah—I thought I saw you gone . . 'so far, so far,' as you said . . and myself left.

Yet I should deserve it of course, if I were to give you up for the sake of *that!* . . or for any other motive, . . except your advantage . . your own. I should deserve everything in such a case, but should feel nothing . . not even my punishment. *Could* I? . . *being without a heart?*

Ah—after all my mistrust, did I ever mistrust you *so?* I have doubted your power to love me as you believed you loved me, perhaps—but your will to be true to one you loved, without reference to worldly influences, I never doubted, nor *could*. I think I will let you beg my pardon; you unjust, dearest . .

To so much over-praise, there should be a little wronging, too . . and therefore you are not, after all, 'unjust' . . only 'dearest'! . . . .

Such a letter, besides, you have written, . . and there are two of them to-day! You will not go from me, I think, 'so far, so far.' You will not leave me behind, with the harpoon in me, to make red the salt wilderness of waters.

Altogether, then, I forgive you, Robert—and it is glorious for me to have something to forgive you for, who are the *best* so out of measure!— I seize the opportunity.

And you come to-morrow! Which is right . . right! I was afraid that you would not come— And Mrs. Jameson is perfectly uncertain as you may read in this new note which reached me with yours to-night.

All the Hedleys have dined here. To-morrow will be clear of them . . *pure* of them, I was going to write . . but I thought of Mrs. Hedley's beaming affectionate face . . (so still lovely, she looked this evening, when she came upstairs to kiss me!) . . and could not say such a wronging word. You would like her—you could not help it.

I was in the carriage to-day in Oxford Street . . and a sealed letter was thrown exactly at my head, my aunt and cousin and Henrietta being with me—a sealed letter sealed with arms (not of Agincourt!) and directed 'For your perusal.' Guess the meaning of that!—why just a tract by the Rev. Villiers of that parish, upon the enormous wickedness of frequenting plays and balls! Perhaps I looked as if my soul had entered into the secret of the Polka-dancers!—who can say?

So, good-night, dearest dearest!—

I cannot give myself again to you,

being your own.

Of course this was written with the poker, as you will see by the calligraphy.

E. B. B. to R. B.

Wednesday Morning.
[Post-mark, July 15, 1846.]

And is it true of to-day as you said it would be, ever dearest, that you wish to be with me? Let me have the comfort, or luxury rather, of the thought of it, before to-morrow takes you a step farther off.

At dinner my aunt said to Papa . . 'I have not seen Ba all day—and when I went to her room, to my astonishment a gentleman was sitting there.' 'Who was *that?*' said Papa's eyes to Arabel— 'Mr. Browning called here to-day,' she answered— 'And Ba bowed her head,' continued my aunt, 'as if she meant to signify to me that I was not to come in'— 'Oh,' cried Henrietta, '*that* must have been a mistake of yours. Perhaps she meant just the contrary.' 'You should have gone in,' Papa said, 'and seen the *poet.*' Now if she really were to do that the next time!— Yet I did not, you know, make the expelling gesture she thought she saw. Simply I was startled. As to Saturday we must try whether we cannot defend the position . . set the guns against the approaches to right and left . . we must try.

In speaking too of your visit this morning, Stormy said

to her . . 'Oh Mr. Browning is a *great* friend of Ba's! He comes here twice a week—is it twice a week or once, Arabel?'

While I write, the Hedleys come—and Mrs. Hedley is beseeching me into seeing Mr. Bevan, whom perhaps I must see, notwithstanding Flush's wrongs.

By the way, I made quite clear to Flush that you left the cakes, and they were very graciously received indeed.

Dearest, since the last word was written, Mrs. Hedley came back leading Mr. Bevan, and Papa who had just entered the room found the door shut upon him . . I was nervous . . oh, so nervous! and the six feet, and something more, of Mr. Bevan seemed to me as if they never would end, so tall the man is. Well—and he sate down by me according to my aunt's arrangement; and I, who began to talk a thousand miles from any such subject, with a good reason for the precaution, found myself thrown head-foremost into ecclesiastical architecture at the close of about three minutes—how he got there all his saints know best! It's his subject . . par excellence. He talks to Arabella about arches and mullions—he can't talk of anything else, I suspect. And because the Trinity is expressed in *such* a form of church-building, the altar at the east, and the baptistery at the door, . . there's no other lawful form of a church, none at all! Not that he has an opinion! he 'adopts opinions,' but would not think for himself for the world at the risk of ultimate damnation! Which was the amount of his talk to-day . . and really it does not strike me as wisdom, now that I set it down so. Yet the man expressed himself well and has a sensible face—he is a clever third-class man, I think—better than the mass for sense, but commonplace essentially. Only, inasmuch as ecclesiastical architecture is not *my* subject, I may think otherwise of him when I know him otherwise. I do not dislike him now. And then I am conscious how you spoil me for common men, dearest! It is scarcely fair on them.

My aunt (Mrs. Hedley) said when she introduced him: 'You are to understand this to be a great honour—for she never lets anybody come here except Mr. Kenyon, . . and a few other gentlemen' . . . (laughing). Said Papa—'Only *one* other gentleman, indeed. Only Mr. Browning, the poet—the man of the pomegranates.' Was *that* likely to calm me, do you think? How late it is—I must break off. To-night I shall write again. Dearest beloved,

I am your own always.

R. B. to E. B. B.

Wednesday.
[Post-mark, July 15, 1846.]

Dearest Ba, I am anxious to know what cannot yet be told me, how that unforseen visit has worked—tell me the moment you can,—and fully, whatever happens.

'Suspicious'—anything in the world rather than *that*, you are! When you have mistrusted your own power over me, I believed always in the mistrust . . which, indeed, matters little except to yourself. For if I would, certainly, have the truth seen as the truth, and our true position understood,—yet . . there is,—ought I not to be ashamed at saying?—an exquisite, *final* grace and *endearingness* in the ignorance, strange as I must account it. You doubly trust me,—with the treasure, and then, with the knowledge that it is a treasure, or *such* a treasure.

Ba, when I think of it all, my whole heart becomes one gratitude to you,—I am only yours, grateful for ever. It is the only kind of thoughts in which you *shall* not share (there are many in which you *cannot*) the thoughts to my inmost self as I go over what you say and do and try to clear up to myself the precise fascination in each : you shall not know what you do . . but shall continue to do and to let *me know*. I love you entirely. Where can you change so that I shall not love you more and more as I grow more able and worthier? I cannot sit for twenty-four hours by you as I sit for three—as it is, I take myself to task for not doing something here at home to justify in some measure my privilege and blessing—and the only thing that keeps conscience quiet comparatively is . . the old expedient that the Future engages to do for me what the Present cannot. Under your eyes, I will hope to work and attain your approval. *I know* that when you were only the great Poet and not my Ba, I would have preferred *your* praise, as competent to praise, to that of the whole world—I remember distinctly, and *know* I should have done so. And now if I put aside the Poet and only (what an 'only') see my dearest, dearest lady of that hair and eyes, and hands, and voice, and all the completeness that was trusted to my arms yesterday—why I feel that if she, never having written a line, said 'What Miss Barrett may think I do not know, but *I* am content with what you show me'—then, dearest, should not *I* be content—?

I called on Moxon—and called at Carlyle's to no purpose. He was out, and will leave town (said the servant) next Saturday. Mrs. Carlyle has already left it. So, no Rag Fair for the present, or probably ever! This was my fault,—I having let several Sundays go by—I must write to Mr. Kenyon and try if he will come on his own account. Moxon tells me that he has sold fifteen hundred of Tennyson's Poems in a year—and is about to print another edition in consequence. If that is the case, and Tennyson gets, say, only half a crown by the sale of each copy, expenses deducted, he will have received 178*l.*,—little enough, as payments are made to *Punch*-literature, but enough to live upon, whatever the awful fiat decides! Tennyson 'is going' to Switzerland presently with Moxon—but is liable to fits of indecision. He did talk of going to Italy (of course), but the other day, time being up, his brother was forced to proceed alone. Moxon is coming here first.

Now I will kiss you, dearest, and hope that Wimpole

Street stands where it did, unhurt by explosions of any-kind. I have got a letter from Procter asking me to go to-day, which I cannot do. Ever your own, very own R.

E. B. B. to R. B.

Wednesday Evening.
[Post-mark, July 16, 1846.]

Well! I anticipated your asking, I think, and told you *fully* this morning. It was a chronicle I sent you, rather than a letter. And nothing is left to tell you—for I did not go out all day . . nor yesterday. Which was wrong. But I had visitor on visitor to-day, . . my old maid coming to bring me her baby to look at, to Flush's infinite delight. Whenever she comes he devotes himself to her, stays with her downstairs, lies on the corner of her gown, and, for the most part, forbears going to sleep. To-morrow I mean to go out . . to-morrow,—when you are beginning to think rather less of me.

Isn't it ungrateful of me? *I think so.*

I am glad, at least, that I do not appear to you 'suspicious.' Because I dislike suspicious people myself, and it has struck me often in the midst of the dislike . . '*That* is how I must appear to *him*.' Ah—but you are too indulgent to me, my own dearest . . too dearest! . . . and you draw crooked inferences for me, shutting *both* the eyes . . the near-sighted eye and far-sighted eye. Or is it, in that strange sight of yours, that I walk between the far and the near objects, in an invisible security? Or is it (which were best) that I am too near to be seen even by the near-sighted eye, . . like a hand brought close to the eyelashes, which, for over-closeness, nobody can see? *Let* me be too near to be seen—always too near!—dearest, dearest! Never will I complain that you do not see me! Be sure of that, now.

Once I used to be more uneasy, and to think that I ought to *make* you see me. But Love is better than Sight, and Love will do without Sight. Which I did not understand at first. I knew it was enough for *me*, that you should love me. That it was enough for *you*, I had to learn afterwards.

And '*Grateful*' is my word and not yours. I am grateful to you, if to owe you all the sense of life, all the renewal of hope, all the possibility of happiness . . if to owe these things to another, consciously, feelingly, shall pass for gratitude, . . then *I* am grateful to *you*, Robert. Do you not know it, that I should say it again? For me, it seems to me that I can do nothing in return. To love you! Why no woman in the world could do less.

I am glad, both for the public and Tennyson, that his poems sell so well—and presently you will do as well or better—and I, half as well perhaps; so that we shall be too rich, which will spoil it all . . won't it?

Mr. Horne sent me the *Daily News* to-day, . . the number containing his verses on Haydon . . and I cut from it an advertisement, for the purpose of bidding you observe that the land journey, or river-voyage, is very much cheaper than the sea-voyage by the steamers—unless the direct vessel to Leghorn should go as last year, and I fear it will not. The steamer-charges of the Oriental company are immense. Nineteen guineas to Gibraltar even! Twenty-eight, I think, to Naples. As for the advertisement, I send it only for what it suggests. And there is time enough for calculations, all ways suggestible.

May God bless you, dear, *dear!* How is the head? shall it be better, without me, until Saturday? Say how it is.

Among all my visitors, the only one I expected, never came! No Mrs. Jameson again to-day!—

Dearest, I am your very own

Ba.

R. B. to E. B. B.

Thursday
[Post-mark, July 16, 1846.]

I should be doing your own dear face (which I see so perfectly through the distance)—too great a wrong if I so much as answered the charge of 'not remembering.' I see the face smile above the hand that writes! As if one may not say that a division, a wound, smarts more on the first day, and aches more on the next! As if I do not prefer the fresh sharp regret to the settling of . . what I trust in God and you I never shall feel! However, if it will please you to know, I *do* feel to-day as earnest a longing to be with you again as if your two letters were not here, —as if Tuesday lay only an hour behind instead of the two long days!

I think your Father's words on these two occasions, very kind,—very! They confuse,—perhaps humble me . . that is not the expression, but it may stay. I dare say he is infinitely kind at bottom—I think so, that is, on my own account,—because, come what will or may, I shall never see otherwise than with your sight. If he could know me, I think he would soon reconcile himself to all of it,—know my heart's purposes toward you. But that is impossible—and with the sincere will to please him by any exertion or sacrifice in my power, I shall very likely never have the opportunity of picking up a glove he might drop. In old novels, the implacable father is not seldom set upon by a round dozen of ruffians with blacked faces from behind a hedge,—and just as the odds prove too many, suddenly a stranger (to all save the reader) leaps over an adjacent ditch, &c 'Sir, under Providence, I owe you my life!' &c &c How does Dumas improve on this in 'Monte Cristo'—are there 'new effects?' Absurdity! Yet I would fain . . fain! you understand.

To talk about my 'spoiling you for other conversers'

is . . oh, leap over hedge and ditch, somebody, to the rescue! If I praise myself for anything in our intimacy it is that I never . . but I won't go into it. And putting my own experience aside and in its place, it strikes me that what Ba ranks as a 'third-rate man' may pass justly for a paragon and marvel among men as the world has a right to class them. I am quite sure if I had been present and much had uttered itself about mullions . . *somebody* would have looked a very babe in knowledge, and perhaps made Ba blush for him and her own waste of love and praise— So he retreats where he may keep it all in virtue of being what he *is*, ever is, and shall be, her own R.

The river-voyage is not only the cheaper but by far the more interesting . . *all* to consider is the fatigue to you; what else?

I am very well to-day. Rachel's 'Phèdre' was admirable last night; quite *through* Racine up to Euripides—the declaration-scene with Hippolytus exquisite . . I must tell you—

E. B. B. to R. B.

Thursday.
[Post-mark, July 17, 1846.]

Dearest, if *you* feel *that*, must I not feel it more deeply? Twice or three times lately he has said to me 'my love' and even 'my puss,' his old words before he was angry last year, . . and I quite quailed before them as if they were so many knife-strokes. Anything but his *kindness*, I can bear now.

Yet I am glad that you feel *that* . . The difficulty, (almost the despair!) has been with me, to make you understand the two ends of truth . . both that he is *not* stone . . and that he *is* immovable *as* stone. Perhaps only a very peculiar nature could have held so long the position he holds in his family. His hand would not lie so heavily, without a pulse in it. Then he is upright—faithful to his conscience. You would respect him, . . and love him perhaps in the end. For me, he might have been king and father over me *to* the end, if he had thought it worth while to love me openly enough—yet, even *so*, he should not have let you come too near. And you could not (so) have come too near—for he would have had my confidence from the beginning, and no opportunity would have been permitted to you of proving your affection for me, and I should have thought always what I thought at first. So the nightshade and the eglantine are twisted, twined, one in the other, . . and the little pink roses lean up against the pale poison of the berries—we cannot tear this from that, let us think of it ever so much!

We must be humble and beseeching *afterwards* at least, and try to get forgiven— Poor Papa! I have turned it over and over in my mind, whether it would be less offensive, less *shocking* to him, if an application were made first. If I were strong, I think I should incline to it at all risks —but as it is, . . it might . . would, probably, . . take away the power of action from me altogether. We should be separated, you see, from *that moment*, . . hindered from writing . . hindered from meeting . . and I could evade nothing, as I am—not to say that I should have fainting fits at every lifting of his voice, through that inconvenient nervous temperament of mine which has so often made me ashamed of myself. Then . . the positive disobedience might be a greater offence than the unauthorised act. I shut my eyes in terror sometimes. May God direct us to the best.

Oh—do not write about this, dearest, dearest?— I throw myself out of it into the pure, sweet, deep thought of you . . which is the love of you always. I am yours . . your own. I never doubt of being yours. I feel too much yours. It is might and right together. You are more to me, beside, than the whole world.

Write nothing of this, dearest of all!—it is of no use. To-day . . this morning . . I went out in the carriage, and we drove round the Park; and Mrs. Jameson did not come afterward. Will she put it off till Saturday? I have heard nothing against Saturday, by the way, worse than that conjecture of mine.

And I have written you, perhaps, a teazing, painful letter . . I, who love you to-day 'as much as ever.' It is my destiny, I sometimes think, to torment you. And let me say what I will, remember how nothing that I say can mean *a doubt*—you never shall have reason to reproach me for the falseness of cowardice—that double falseness . . both to me and to you. Only I wish this were Christmas-Day, and we . . . even at Salerno . . in the 'bad air'! There's no harm in such a wish—now *is* there?

Ever and ever I am your own

Ba.

R. B. to E. B. B.

Friday.
[Post-mark, July 17, 1846.]

Did you ever see a more uncongenial, colourless day than this—that brings me no letter! I do not despair yet, however—there will be a post presently. When I am without the sight of you, and the voice of you, which a letter seems . . I feel very accurately the justice of that figure by which I am represented as 'able to leave you alone—leaving you and following my pleasure elsewhere' —so you have written and spoken! Well, to-day, I may follow my pleasures.

I will follow you, Ba,—the thoughts of you, and long for to-morrow.

No letter for me,—the time is past. If you are well, my own Ba, I will not mind . . more than I can. You had not been out for two days—the wind is high, too. May God keep you at all times, ever dearest!

The sun shines again—now I will hope to hear at six o'clock.

I can tell you nothing better, I think, than this I heard

from Moxon the other day . . it really ought to be remembered. Moxon was speaking of critics, the badness of their pay, how many pounds a column the *Times* allowed, and shillings the *Athenæum*,—and of the inevitable effects on the performances of the poor fellows. 'How should they be at the trouble of reading any *difficult* book so as to review it,—Landor, for instance?' and indeed a friend of my own has promised to write a notice in the *Times*—but he complains bitterly,—he shall have to *read* the book,—he can do no less,—and all for five or ten pounds'! All which Moxon quite seemed to understand—'it will really take him some three or four mornings to read *enough* of Landor to be able to do anything effectually.' I asked if there had been any notices of the Book already—'Just so many,' he said, 'as Forster had the power of *getting done*'— Mr. White, a clergyman, has written a play for Macready, which everybody describes as the poorest stuff imaginable,—it is immediately reviewed in *Blackwood* and the *Edinburgh* 'Because' continues M, 'he is a *Blackwood* reviewer, and may do the like good turn to any of the confraternity.'

So—here I will end,—wanting to come to the kissing dearest Ba, and bidding her remember to-morrow how my heart sinks to-day in the silence.

Ever, dearest dearest, your very own.

E. B. B. to R. B.

Friday.
[Post-mark, July 18, 1846.]

It is out of time to-night to write to you, since to-morrow we are to meet—but the letter which did not reach you, has been recoiling on me all day. Perhaps you have it by this time . . an uncomfortable letter, better away from you, notwithstanding all the kindness you speak, about my silence and the effect of *that*. So I write just a few words— The post office was in fault as usual. May it do perfecter duty to-morrow.

Saturday!—our day! At least if anything should be against it, you shall hear at the door by a note, when you come at three o'clock. I have put away my Thursday night's melancholy . . except the repentance of troubling you with it——understand that I have!

Mrs. Jameson was here to-day, and her niece, . . and *you*, never named,—but she is coming another day, she says, to pay me a longer visit. I like her . . I like her. Then, there came another visitor, . . my uncle Hedley, who began, as usual, to talk of Italy—he advises me to go this year.— 'If you don't go this year, *you never will go* . . and you ought at once to make an effort, and go.' We talked of places and of ways, and after he had said many words in favour of Pisa, desired, if I went through Paris, that I would pay him a visit. 'Ah,' said I, 'uncle Hedley, you are very good to me always, but when that day arrives, you may be inclined, perhaps, to cast me off.' 'Cast you off, Ba,' he cried in the most puzzled astonishment—'why what *can* you mean? what words to use! Cast you off! now do explain what you mean.' 'Ah, no one can tell,' said I musingly. 'Do you mean,' he insisted, 'because you will be a rebel and a runaway?' . . (laughing!) 'no, no—*I* won't cast you off, I promise you! Only I hope that you may be able to manage it quietly' &c. &c.

He is a most amiable man, so gentle and tender; and fond of me; *exclusively* of the poetry. I am certain that he never can make out how anyone in the world can consent to read my verses. But Ba, as Ba, is a decided favourite of his, beyond all in the house—not that he is a real uncle . . only the husband of my aunt, and caring more for me than both my real uncles, who, each of them, much prefer a glass of claret,—thank you! The very comparison does me too much honour for either of them. Claret is a holy thing. If I had said half a glass, and mixed it with water, I should have been more accurate by so much.

Now, dearest, dearest, I say good-night and have done.

I am wholly yours and always.

R. B. to E. B. B.

Sunday.
[Post-mark, July 20, 1846.]

Dearest Ba's face of yesterday, with the smiles and perfect sweetness,—oh, the comfort it is to me through this day of my especial heaviness! I don't know when I have felt more stupid, and I seem to keep the closelier to you, Ba. Is that one of my felicities of compliment? I think if you were here I should lay my head on your bosom, my own beloved, and never raise it again. In your last letter, you speak of those who care less for you than for a 'glass of claret'—there is something sublime, —at all events, astounding, in the position we occupy each of us,—I, and those less-carers,—standing in respect to each other so like England and Owhyhee, at which, they told me when I was a boy, I should be pretty sure to arrive if I dug a hole just through the earth, dropped to the centre and then, turning round, climbed straight up!

I left here, yesterday, without taking the prints of Dumas and Hugo—*there* is a head 'for remembering!' and justifying your commodations! Chorley says, you see, my acquisitions are rather accumulated than digested —or words to that effect—I am sure at this moment the stupid, heavy head *knows* not one thing,—as a clear point of knowledge, taken in and laid by, orderly and separately. So let me say here, while I *do* remember, that a letter from Forster puts off his visit and Moxon's till Monday—should any reason, therefore, prevent your confirming to me the gift of Tuesday, this other day will lie open—but *only* in that case, I trust—because Tuesday objects not to Saturday, does it? while Wednesday looks grave, and Thursday frowns downright on the same! *Friday*, remember, is Mr. Kenyon's day.

I wish, dearest, you would tell me precisely what you have written—all my affectionate pride in you rises at once when I think of your poetry, that is and that is to be—you dear, dear Ba, can you not write on my shoulder while my head lies as you permit?

I found at home on my return yesterday my friend Pritchard, who brought me an old notice of Rachel by Jules Janin—of course there is no believing a word—but he *does* say that she was,—at the time he wrote,—perfectly ignorant of the most ordinary rules of grammar,—that, for instance, on meeting him she remarked (alluding to her having played previously at another theatre than the T. Français) —'C'était moi que j'était au Gymnase!'—to which he ought to have answered, he thinks, 'Je le savions!'—I will bring her portrait, too, if you please—and this memoir, untrustworthy as it is.

I will go now and walk about, I think—did you go out, as you promised, love? Ah, dearest,—*you* to wonder I could look up to you for ever as you stand,—you who once wrote to me that, in order to verify a date about Shelley in a book I lent you, 'You had accomplished a journey to the other end of the room, even'! And *now!* I thankfully *know* this to be miraculous—nor have I to ask my spiritual director's opinion thereon—to whom, how on earth can one surrender one's private right of judgment when it is only by the exercise of that very right that I select him from the multitude of would-be directors of me and the whole world? What but a deliberate act of judgment takes up Dr. Pusey of Oxford rather than Mrs. Fox of Finsbury—and is it for *that* pernicious first step that I determine on never risking a second?

Bless you, ever dearest—and do you bless your

very own R.

E. B. B. to R. B.

Sunday.
[Post-mark, July 20, 1846.]

Dearest, the leaf of yesterday was folded down quite smoothly and softly. A dinner party swept the thought of you out of people's minds. Otherwise I was prepared to be a little afraid,—for my aunt said to Arabel, upon being dispensed with so cavalierly from this room, . . (said in the passage, Arabel told me, with a half-laugh,) 'Pray which of Ba's lovers may *this* be?' So Arabel had to tell the name of the visitor. But the dinner-party set all right, and this morning I was asked simply whether it had been an agreeable visit, and what you had written, and banalities after such a fashion.

Oh, and I went out . . remembering your desire . . was it not a desire, dearest, dearest? I went out, any way —but the wind blew, and I had to hold my veil against my mouth, doubled, and trebled . . with as many folds, indeed, as Ajax's shield . . to keep myself in breathing order. The wind always gives me a sort of strangling sensation, which is the effect, I suppose, of having weak lungs. So it was not a long walk, but I liked it because you seemed to be with me still,—and Arabel, who walked with me, was 'sure, without being told, that I had had a happy visit, just from my manner.' The wisest of interpreters, I called her, and *pour cause.*

If ever I mistake you, Robert, doing you an injustice, . . you ought to be angry, I think, *rather* and *more* with me than with another—I should have far less excuse it appears to me, for making such a mistake, than any other person in the world. I thought so yesterday when you were speaking, and now upon consideration I think so with an increasing certainty. Is it your opinion that the members of our family, . . those who live with us always, . . know us best? They know us on the side we offer to them . . a bare profile . . or the head turned round to the ear—yes!—they do not, except by the merest chance, look into our eyes. They know us in a conventional way . . as far from God's way of knowing us, as from the world's—mid-way, it is—and the truest and most cordial and tender affection will not hinder this from being so partial a knowledge. Love! I love those who at the present moment, . . who love me (and tenderly on both sides) . . but who are so far from *understanding* me, that I never think of speaking myself into their ears . . of trying to speak myself. It is wonderful, it is among the great mysteries of life, to observe how people can love one another in the dark, blindly . . loving without knowing. And, as a matter of general observation, if I sought to have a man or woman revealed to me in his or her innermost nature, I would not go to the *family* of the person in question—though I should learn there best, of course, about personal habits, and the social bearing of him or her. George Sand delights me in one of her late works, where she says that the souls of blood relations seldom *touch* except at one or two points. Perfectly true, *that* is, I think—perfectly.

Remember how you used to say that I did not know you . . which was true in a measure . . yet I felt I knew you, and I did actually know you, in another larger measure. And if *now* you are not known to me altogether, it is my dulness which makes me unknowing.

But I know you—and I should be without excuse if ever I wronged you with a moment's injustice. I do not think I ever could depreciate you for a moment,—*that* would not be possible. There are other sins against you (*are* they against you?) which bring their own punishment! You shall never be angry with me for those.

While I was writing, came Mr. Kenyon. As usual he said that there was no use in his coming—that you had taken his place, and so on. He was in a high good humour, though, and spirits, and I did not mind much what he was pleased to say. More I minded, that he means 'to stay in London all the summer' . . which I can't be glad of, . . though I was glad at his not persisting in going to Scotland against his own wishes. But he might like to go somewhere else—it would be a pleasure, *that*, in which I should sympathize! The more shame for me!

Mr. Chorley pleases me more *than he ever pleased me before!* Only, as an analysis, he has done curiously with 'Pippa.' But it is good appreciation, good and righteous, and he has given me, altogether, a great, great deal of pleasure. As to the letter, I liked that too in its degree—and the advice is wise for the head, if foolish for the work. How *can* wise people be so foolish?

I am going out to walk now with Henrietta, and shall put this letter into the post with my own hand. It is seven p.m. May God bless you. Do say how you are, dear, dearest!

I am your very own Ba.

R. B. to E. B. B.

Monday Evening.
[Post-mark, July 20, 1846.]

Certainly you *do* know me, my own Ba, beyond all other knowledge possible to relatives,—*that* I know—in fact, I found myself speaking unwarily on a subject where speech is obliged to stop abruptly—the fault was mine for bringing up terms, remarks &c. quite inapplicable out of this house,—where all, as you understand, have seen me so long that they do not see differences in me,—increases or diminutions; I am twice as blind, most likely, to *them*, after the same fashion. Still, one is slow to concede an excuse to such blindness—hence the 'hasty words' I told you they charge me with uttering.

I apprehend no danger from *that*, to your feeling for me—it is your own speech my Ba, which I will take from you, and use—my own general short-comings, you will inevitably see and be sorry for—but there will be the more need of your love, which I shall go on asking for daily and nightly as if I never could have enough—which is the exact fact; and also, I shall grow fitter through the love to be what you would have me, so the end may be better than the beginning, let us hope.

Will you not do what you can with me who am your very own? as you are my own too, but for a different end—I am yours to operate on, as you are my only lady to dispose of what belongs to you. Dear, dearest Ba, it *is* so; will ever be so!

Yes, that notice by Chorley is very kind and gratifying. I wanted—(*quite* apart from the poor good to me or my books—but for Chorley's own sake, I rather wanted)—some decided streak of red, or spot, or spark,—some life in the increasing grey of the ashes—this is true, *live* lovingness of him—I will tell him so.

For Domett's letter,—he means, by all that nonsense, that my health is more in his estimation than any works producible at its expense. All the calculation about so many lines a day, so many a month &c., *he* knows to be absurd . . you *can't* write 'so many lines to-day,' and add next day's complement, and so 'grow to an end'—any more than you can paint a picture by thumb-breadths. The other paragraph about intelligibility laughs at itself all the time . . is not to be taken for serious.

Indeed I *did* desire with a great desiring that you should go out, and now I thank you for all the good account of the walk, and victory over the wind: and how kind that sister is!—I shall never forget it.

My own head, since you *will* be teazed with intelligence about it, was not very well yesterday, but is better decidedly this morning—*I*, too, will go and put this letter in the post and think of to-morrow . . for do not I keep to-morrow? I shall be with you unless another order comes . . may it be averted! And may you be happy always *with* me, as I shall be through you . . nay, but half as happy, dearest Ba, my very own! Your R.

R. B. to E. B. B.

Tuesday.
[Post-mark, July 22, 1846.]

How I long, my sweetest Ba, to know whether any heavy price is to be paid for our three hours yesterday,—if your Aunt knew or has discovered since? I shall not murmur in any case, I hope . . they are too delicious, these three-hour visits—and if *I* could pay for them by myself, Ba,—what would I not pay?

Will you let me write something, and forgive me? Because it is, I know, quite unnecessary to be written, and, beside, may almost seem an interference with your own delicacy,—teaching it its duty! However, I will venture to go on, with your hand before my two eyes. Then,—you remember what we were speaking of yesterday,—house-rents and styles of living? You will never overlook, through its very obviousness, that to consult my feelings on the only point in which they are sensitive to the world you must endeavour to live as simply and cheaply as possible, down to my own habitual simplicity and cheapness,—so that you shall come and live with me, in a sense, rather than I with Miss Campbell! You see, Ba, if you have more money than you want, you shall save it or spend it in pictures or parrots or what you please . . you avoid all offence to *me* who never either saved money nor spent it—but the large house, I should be forced to stay in,—the carriage, to enter, I suppose. And you see too, Ba, that the one point on which I desire the world to be informed concerning our future life, will be that it is ordered *so*—I wish they could hear we lived in one room like George Sand in 'that happy year—'

No, there I have put down an absurdity—because, I shall have to confess a weakness, at some time or other, which is hardly reconcilable to that method of being happy—why may I not tell you now, my adored Ba, to whom

I tell everything as it rises to me? Now put the hand on my eyes again—now that I have kissed it. I shall begin by begging a separate room from yours—I could never brush my hair and wash my face, I do think, before my own father—I could not, I am sure, take off my coat before you *now*—why should I ever? The kitchen is an unknown horror to me,—I come to the dining-room for whatever repast there may be,—nor willingly stay too long there,—and on the day on which poor Countess Peppa taught me how maccaroni is made,—*then* began a quiet revolution, (indeed a rapid one) against 'tagliolini,' 'fettucce,' 'lasagne,' etc., etc., etc.—typical, typical!

What foolishness . . spare me, my own Ba, and don't answer one word,—do not even laugh,—for I *know* the exceeding unnecessary foolishness of it!

Chorley has just sent me a note which I will send you because it is most graceful in its modesty—but you must not, if you please, return it to me in an envelope that ought only to hold your own writing,—and so make my heart beat at first, and my brows knit at last! (Toss it into 'my room,' at Pisa! !)

Thus it is to be made happy and unwise! Never mind —make me happier still by telling me you are well and have been out, and where, and when, and how—the footsteps of you, Ba, should be kissed if I could follow them.

Bless you, ever dearest, dearest, as yesterday, and always you bless me—I love you with all my heart and soul —*yes* Ba!

Your own, very own.

E. B. B. to R. B.

Wednesday Morning.
[Post-mark, July 22, 1846.]

I did not go out yesterday, and was very glad not to have a command laid on me to go out, the wind blew so full of damp and dreariness. Then it was pleasanter to lie on the sofa and think of you, which I did, till at last I actually dreamed of you, falling asleep for that purpose. As to Flush, he came upstairs with a good deal of shame in the bearing of his ears, and straight to me—no indeed! I would not speak to him—then he went up to Arabel . . 'naughty Flush, go away' . . and Wilson, . . who had whipped him before, 'because it was right,' she said . . in a fit of poetical justice, . . did not give him any consolation. So he lay down on the floor at my feet looking from under his eyebrows at me. I did not forgive him till nearly eight o'clock however. And I have not yet given him your cakes. Almost I am inclined to think now that he has not *a soul*. To behave so to you! It is nearly as bad as if I had thrown the coffee cup! Wicked Flush!—Do you imagine that I scolded Wilson when she confessed to having whipped him? I did not. It was done with her hand, and not very hardly perhaps, though 'he cried,' she averred to me—and if people, like Flush, choose to behave like dogs savagely, they must take the consequences indeed, as dogs usually do! And *you*, so good and gentle to him! Anyone but *you*, would have said 'hasty words' at least. I think I shall have a muzzle for him, to make him harmless while he learns to know you. Would it not be a good plan?

But nobody heard yesterday of either your visit or of Flush's misdoings . . so Wilson was discreet, I suppose, as she usually is, by the instinct of her vocation. Of all the persons who are *not* in our confidence, she has the most certain knowledge of the truth. Dearest, we shall be able to have Saturday. There will be no danger in it.

Perhaps in the days to come we shall look back on these days as covetable things. Will *you* do so, because you were loved in them as a beginning, or because you were *free?* (Am *I* not as bad as Flush, to ask such questions?) *I* shall look back on these days gratefully and gladly, because the good in them has overcome the evil, for the first time in days of mine. Yet my position is worse than yours on some accounts—*now*. Henrietta has had a letter from Capt. Surtees Cook who says in it, she says, . . 'I hope that poor Ba will have courage to the end.' There's a generous sympathy! Tell me that there is none in the world!

Will you let me know how you are? Such a letter you wrote to me on Sunday! Ah!—to *be anything to you* . . . what is the colour of *ambition* afterwards? When I look forwards I can see no work and no rest, but what is for you and in you. Even Duty seems to concentrate itself into one Debt— Dearest!

Yet it will be a little otherwise perhaps!—not that ever I shall love you otherwise or less— No.

You shall see some day at Pisa what I will not show you now. Does not Solomon say that 'there is a time to read what is written.' If he doesn't, he *ought*.

Your very own Ba.

E. B. B. to R. B.

Wednesday.
[Post-mark, July 23, 1846.]

Dearest, what you say is unnecessary for you to say—it is in everything *so* of course and obvious! You must have an eccentric idea of *me* if you can suppose for a moment such things to be necessary to say. If they had been *unsaid*, it would have been precisely the same, believe me, in the event.

As to the way of living—now you shall arrange *that* for yourself. You shall choose your own lodging, order your own dinner . . and if you choose to live on locusts and wild honey, I promise not to complain . . I shall not indeed be *inclined* to complain . . having no manner of ambition about carriages and large houses, even if they were within our possibilities,—which they may not be, according to Mr. Surtees's calculation or experience. The more simply we live, the better for *me!* So you shall arrange it for yourself, lest I should make a mistake! . . which, in *that* question, is a just possible thing.

One extravagance I had intended to propose to you . . but it shall be exactly as you like, and I hesitate a little as I begin to speak of it. I have thought of taking Wilson with me, . . for a year, say, if we returned then—if not, we might send her home alone . . and by that time, I should be stronger perhaps and wiser . . rather less sublimely helpless and impotent than I am now. My sisters have urged me a good deal in this matter—but if you would rather it were otherwise, be honest and say so, and let me alter my thoughts at once. There is one consideration which I submit to yours, . . that I cannot leave this house with the necessary number of shoes and pocket handkerchiefs, without help from somebody. Now whoever helps me, will suffer through me. If I left her behind she would be turned into the street before sunset. Would it be right and just of me, to permit it? Consider! I must manage a sheltering ignorance for my poor sisters, at the last, . . and for all our sakes. And in order to *that*, again, I must have some one else in my confidence. Whom, again, I would unwillingly single out for an absolute *victim*.

Wilson is attached to me, I believe—and, in all the discussions about Italy, she has professed herself willing to 'go anywhere in the world with me.' Indeed I rather fancy that she was disappointed bitterly last year, and that it would not be a pure devotion. She is an expensive servant—she has sixteen pounds a year, . . but she has her utilities besides, and is very amiable and easily satisfied, and would not add to the expenses, or diminish from the economies, even in the matter of room—*I* would manage *that* for her. Then she would lighten your responsibilities . . as the Archbishop of Canterbury and company do Mr. Bevan's. Well—you have only to consider your own wishes. I shall not care many straws, if you decide this way or that way. Let it be as may seem to you wisest.

I like Mr. Chorley's note. I began to write so late that

I, too, must send you a bare note to-night. May God bless you, ever dearest. I am tired . . so tired—yet I have not a long story to tell you of myself for the day's chronicle. I was just out for the few minutes my walking occupies, and came home and had coffee at half-past four; and scarcely was the cup empty, when Mrs. Jameson arrived—she stayed while you might count to a hundred—and your name was not once mentioned. And now, good-night. I hope the 'testimonials' may be 'satisfactory,' in this note which will not wait to be a letter! Dearest, say how your head is—do.

I am your Ba, always!

R. B. to E. B. B.

Wednesday.
[Post-mark, July 23, 1846.]

I have just returned from Town and Mr. Kenyon's, my own Ba. I called, according to compact, to point out the precise way he must go to reach us. He seemed to make sure I was going to Wimpole Street—'Oh, no!'

So, losing Wimpole Street, I made haste home, and gain my letter,—my dear letter: yesterday night, too, the first letter arrived duly—you perfect in kindness!

My dearest—dearest,—you might go to Pisa without shoes,—or feet to wear them, for aught I know, since you may have wings, only folded away from me—but without your Wilson, or some one in her capacity, you . . no, I will not undertake to speak of *you;* then, *I*, should be simply, exactly, INSANE to move a step; I would rather propose, let us live on bread and water, and sail in the hold of a merchant-ship; THIS CANNOT be dispensed with! It is most fortunate, most providential, that Wilson is inclined to go—I am *very* happy; for a new servant, with even the best dispositions, would never be able to anticipate your wants and wishes during the voyage, at the very beginning. Yet you write of this to me *so*, my Ba! I think I will, in policy, begin the anger at a good place. Yes, all the anger I am capable of descends on the head—(not in kisses, whatever you may fancy).

And so poor Flush suffered after all! Dogs that are dog-like would be at no such pains to tell you they would not see you with comfort approached by a stranger who might be—! A 'muzzle'? oh, no,—but suppose you have him removed next time, and perhaps the next, till the whole occurrence is out of his mind as the fly bite of last week—because, if he sees me and begins his barking and valiant snapping, and gets more and heavier vengeance downstairs, perhaps,—his transient suspicion of me will confirm itself into absolute dislike, hatred, whereas, after an interval, we can renew acquaintance on a better footing. Dogs have such memories! My sister told me last week she saw in a provincial newspaper an anecdote of one,—a miller's dog, that was a good fellow in the main, but chose to take an especial dislike to one of his master's customers, whom he invariably flew at and annoyed—so much so that the man declared he must carry his custom elsewhere unless the dog was parted with: this the miller was unwilling to do; so he hit on an expedient—by some contrivance, the dog was suffered to fall into a deep well, and bark himself hoarse there in vain—no help came—till the obnoxious individual arrived, let himself down and brought up the prisoner. From which time nothing could exceed the devotion of the dog to his rescuer; whom he always insisted henceforth on accompanying as far as his home, for one instance of it.

I wonder whether I have anywhere one of the sketches my father made of my bulldog's face.

What 'tired' you, dearest? You are not *less* well, I trust? Pray tell me,—and remember there are three days before our Saturday. I am very much better—the walking and riding of this morning did me good, too—and what profits it, if you are not better also? Love me in caring for yourself, which is *my* truest self! And I will go on and try to love you more than I do—for what may happen?

Ever your own R.

E. B. B. to R. B.

Thursday Evening.
[Post-mark, July 24, 1846.]

No letter for me to-night! not a word!—Perhaps the post is sinning again. If so, I shall hear to-morrow morning, if not . . may it be anything rather than that you are more unwell than usual! anything!

There is not much to say on my part. I had a letter from Miss Mitford this morning, and she encloses to me . . . you will not guess what—a lyric of the ubiquitous Bennett—the 'Mignonette.' Are you not amused? That's the way to 'agitate' for readers and praisers. She sees something in Bennett. He is to be 'heard of in our literature.' She shed tears over the 'Mignonette,' herself—

Your portrait of Victor Hugo, I like less and less—there is something ignoble in the face—and even the forehead is rather big than large. *He* does not 'look like a poet' in any case—now does he?

Dearest, did I annoy you . . frighten you, . . about Wilson yesterday? Did *that* prevent you from writing to me to-day—if really you did not write to me to-day? It yet was the merest *question*, . . I wished you to understand—the merest question for a yes or a no—and I shall not mind, *however* you may answer, be certain. I have been thinking to-day that it would be possible enough to leave a direction which might supply everything, and so escape inflicting the injury apprehended—yes, and as for myself, I shall manage perfectly. Observe how I pinned your coat, miraculously pricking you at the same moment. I shall do for myself and by myself, as well as possible. And therefore, judge, speak your thoughts out to the purpose and without drawback. I shall always feel to thank you for speaking the *truth*, even where it goes against me. But *this* will not go against me, *however* you speak it, . . understand.

And as for what my sisters think, it is nothing to the purpose. Say your 'no,' and they never shall hear it. I will avoid the subject from henceforth, with them . . *that* is all.

And take care of Mr. Kenyon to-morrow. I feel afraid of Mr. Kenyon. But take care of yourself most—look well that you never let me do, in the least or greatest matter, what would seem better undone hereafter. Not in the least, not in the greatest. For me, if I am to be thought of, remember that you *kill* me, if you suffer me to injure you. That is for *me*.

See how I exhort people who do not write to me! . . Ah no! It must be the post's fault. You could not be very much vexed with me, I think, for a mere proposal about Wilson. And the rest of my letter was all made up of assent and agreement. You could not be vexed about Wilson. And you *shall* not be ill, because I cannot bear to think of it—which, dearest, is a good reason and irrefragable.

The Hedleys dine here, and others. I hear the voices and the laughing. I wish I could, your voice, as near. May God bless you . . bless you—

Your own Ba.

R. B. to E. B. B.

Friday.
[Post-mark, July 24, 1846.]

Sweet, sweet, sweet Ba, look to be kissed to-morrow till it hurts you,—punished you ought to be for such a letter! When the ancients were in doubt about a man's identity (the ancient fathers) they called him 'aut Erasmus (or whoever it might be) aut—diabolus!'—no gradation, no mean between best and worst! Or do you think Flush bit me and inoculated me with super-cynical snappishness? Well, I *do* think I should not have conducted myself as you consider highly possible,—even if you *had* made, let me say at once, the *most* preposterous of proposals, even that of going *without* Wilson, or her substitute. I think and am sure I should, like a rational being, write all the faster to try and get you to reconsider the matter—convinced as I should be that your perfect good sense would, after a few minutes' examination, see that I could no more take you away without such assistance than desire you to perform the passage of the Mont Cenis on foot. Do I not remember that you intended to be thus accompanied even when your sister was to be of the party? But the absolute necessity of what you fancy I may object to . . it is not *that*, I complain about—but of the strange notion, that whenever Fate shall decree that you say, or do, or think anything, from which I shall be forced to differ,—my proceedings will needs take this fashion and colour—I shall 'sulk' and *say* nothing,—or perhaps turn aside grandly offended and meditative of noble vengeance! Oh, Ba, dearest, dearest beyond all words, come for *once* and always *into* the heart which is your own, and see how full it is of you, and if you say, *that* does not prevent the head being weak and acting accordingly, I will begin exemplifying the very point I want to convince you of by at once writing and speaking and by every imaginable means making you know, that the heart *does* teach the head better than such foolishness—ought to do it, and *does* do it!

Do you believe me, Ba, my own? Or, what nonsense! Did you *wonder* at my letter when it did come? Or *did* it come? It was duly posted at Deptford—moreover the 'Thursday' at the top was written 'Wednesday'—because all day long I was in that error—having been used to see you on Mondays, and to calculate my time by the number of days since I saw you—whence, knowing to my cost that two days had gone by since such an event, I thought what I wrote.

Now kiss me, my very own, for an end to every thing —your doubt and my impudent making the most of it,— for I do not doubt *you*, sweetest, truest, best love!

To-morrow brings me to you, Ba, I trust—I will be careful to-day, never fear your

own devoted R.

E. B. B. to R. B.

Sunday.
[Post-mark, July 27, 1846.]

Why should you ask such a question of me yesterday, as to whether I loved you as much then as ever? Love you as much? Why should I not love you *more?* . . to give question for question. And it does seem to me, too, that *my* question is more reasonable than yours. 'Is it afternoon at six o'clock,' you might have asked in the same breath with yours, and touched, *so*, as questionable a matter.

Tell me how the evening passed at Mr. Kenyon's. I have seen nobody yet—not him, not Mrs. Jameson.

Seen nobody? Except all the Hedleys, who have just left my room. Do you know, the pomp and circumstance, the noise and fuss and publicity of this marriage of theirs happen just in time to make me satisfied with 'quite the other principle' as you said. The system they are carrying out is detestable to its own extreme. Fifty or sixty people are to breakfast at Fenton's Hotel, . . with processions to and fro! . . which altogether, though the bride will bear it very well, (for she has been used to be a Belle *ex-officio*, and this business has been arranged by her and for her—otherwise they would have all been in Paris) is likely, I think, to half kill the bride's mother. My poor aunt wonders how she will get through it. To have to part with her daughter in that crowd! So barbarous a system it is, this system of public marriages, under whatever light considered. Both my sisters are invited; and so was *I!* (in vain) and Henrietta officiates as a bridesmaid. Did I tell you that Arabella Hedley is a glorious convert to Puseyism, as might have been expected, and talked here like a theologian a few days since, and 'considered the dissenters in a most dangerous position,' much to the amusement of my brothers.

What am I writing of all this time? Dearest, how did you get home yesterday through the ambush at Mr. Kenyon's? Tell me everything. And *know* that I love you 'as much,' my own beloved!—you may know it.

When Flush came into the room and had spoken to me (in the Flush-language) and had examined your chair, he suddenly fell into a rapture and reminded me that the cakes you left, were on the table. So I explained thoroughly to him that *you* had brought them for him, and that he ought to be properly ashamed therefore for his past wickedness, and make up his mind to love you and not bite you for the future—and then he was allowed to profit from your goodness to him. How *over*-good of you! It is an encouragement to throw coffee-cups, . . such over-goodness!

Nobody knew of your being here yesterday—at least, not that *I* know! So Tuesday looks brightly, at a distance. At a distance! The day after to-morrow! Ah, it seems too near! Too near, in the sense of saying '*Too good* . . to be true.'

I will write the paper as you bid me. Only, in the face of all that is to come, I solemnly tell you that neither I nor mine . . certainly not I . . will consent to an act of injustice, disinheriting my last hours (whenever they shall come) of a natural satisfaction. You are noble in all things—but this will not be in your power—I will not discuss it so as to teaze you. Your reputation is dear to me of course . . the thoughts which men shall have of you in the least matter, I would choose to keep clean . . . free from every possible taint. But it will be obvious to all, that if you pleased, you might throw out of the windows everything called mine, the moment after our marriage—interest and principal—why not? And if you abstain from this, and after your own death allow the sum which originally came from my family, to relapse there . . why it is all of pure generosity on your part—and they will understand it as I do, . . as generosity . . as more than justice. Well—let *that* be! It is your act, and not mine, letting it be—and I have no objection to show you what my wishes are, (mere wishes), so helping you to carry out such an act in the best way. I send you the paper therefore—to that end—and only that end. There, you must stop—I never will consent to the extravagance you propose about yourself. You shall not, *if you love me*, think of carrying it out. If I thought you *could be so hard on me*, . . do you know, I would rather throw it all up now into the hands of my sisters, and be poor with you at once—I could bear *that* so much better than the thoughts of *leaving* you to be poor. Or, would you be easier, dearest—if a *part* were relinquished *now?* would it make you easier . . and would you promise me, *so*, that what is mine should be accepted as yours to the end? The worst is that if I were ill, I should be a burden to you, and thus we might have reasons for regret. Still it shall be as pleases you best. But *I* must be pleased a little too. It is *fair* that I should.

Certainly you exaggerate to yourself the position. What would have become of you if you had loved a real heiress instead? That *would* have been a misfortune. As it is, while you are plotting how to get rid of these penny-pieces, everybody will be pitying you for having fixed yourself in such conditions of starvation. *You*, who *might —have married Miss Burdett Coutts!*

See how I tease you!—first promising not to tease you! But always I am worse than I meant to be. Wasn't it your fault a little for bringing up this horrible subject? —but here is the paper, the only sort of 'settlement' we shall have! Always I have said and sworn that I never, if I married, would have a settlement—and now I thank God to be able to keep my word *so*. *This* only is a settlement of the question.

Beloved, how is your head? I love you out of the deepest of my heart, and shall not cease.

Your very own
Ba.

Is this what is called a *document?* It seems to me that I have a sort of legal genius—and that I should be on the Woolsack in the Martineau Parliament. But it seems, too, rather *bold* to attach such a specification to your name. Laugh and pardon it all!

In compliance with the request of Robert Browning, who may possibly become my husband, that I would express in writing my wishes respecting the ultimate disposal of whatever property I possess at this time, whether in the funds or elsewhere, . . I here declare my wishes to be . . that he, Robert Browning, . . having, of course, as it is his right to do, first held and used the property in question for the term of his natural life, . . should bequeath the same, by an equal division, to my two sisters, or, in the case of the previous death of either or both of them, to such of my surviving brothers as most shall need it by the judgment of my eldest surviving brother.

ELIZABETH BARRETT BARRETT.

Wimpole Street: July, 1846.

R. B. to E. B. B.

Sunday.
[Post-mark, July 27, 1846.]

Mr. Kenyon said nothing,—except a few words at dinner about the mistake of Talfourd, to Forster,—nothing whatever, though we sat together and talked for some time before the arrival of the company. And all that I heard about Mrs. Jameson, was her return to Ealing and some wish she meant to express in a letter, of seeing me there.

So you will have to tell me and tell me, dearest, when you know anything—to-day perhaps.

My own Ba, *do not refer to what we spoke of*—the next vile thing to the vilest is, being too conscious of avoiding *that*,—painfully, ostentatiously, protesting and debating—only it seemed absolutely necessary to say thus much at some time, and early:—now it is done with,—you understanding what I expect at your hands.

Mr. Longman was of the party yesterday—speaking of Haydon, he remarked on his omitting to mention in the list of his creditors, 'the House'—to which he owed about 100*l*. being the loss consequent on publishing his 'Book'—the Lectures, I suppose—then, in a break, he said, in answer to a question from Forster, that the Book in question had gone into a second edition, but 'Oh, no—the Author had received nothing for it!' And he lost the money, poor fellow, besides! Is not that inexplicable to all save booksellers? Also, what could be his need for another person's intermediation with the Longmans since he knew them so well and so long!

I hope there is nothing to prevent our meeting on Tuesday. Do you think I am any longer able to appreciate properly the additional gift of the day in the week? I only know that I do not see you *now*, my Ba—and I feel as if I were—the words must not be written! I need *all* of you,—utterly dearest dearest that you are! My next day, *my* 'Sunday' is the forlornest imaginable. I never wasted time (in the worldly sense of not working in it) as at present,—I read books and at the turning of every page go back again for shame . . the words only before the eyes, the thoughts of you before the mind.

I found a new litter of poetry in a letter of our indefatigable Bennett,—the happy man! By the way (a very roundabout one), someone mentioned yesterday as an agreeable, or at least characteristic trait in Sydney Smith, that after dinner, or during dinner, he would occasionally pour water down, or *up*, as we say, his coat-sleeves, for coolness' sake. Nobody made a remark—nor spoke of such a feat's disqualifying its performer from going into good society. Now do you remember poor Horne and the censorship of his manners?—were not his more rational libations found abominable? See the association—Bennett—Miss Mitford—Horne? But I cannot write sensibly to-day, nor *in*sensibly, which would be more amusing perhaps—I can only know I am—*here*, on Sunday!—and whatever the pen may force itself to put down, my one thought is, that you are not here. To-morrow I shall hear, and get fresh strength in the anticipation of Tuesday,—if the letter tells me you are well—the 'headache for two days,'—tell me, my own Ba!

Bless you, ever best and dearest.

R. B. to E. B. B.

Monday Morning.
[Post-mark, July 27, 1846.]

That is sufficient, ever dearest: now dismiss the matter from your thoughts, as I shall—having forced myself once to admit that most dreadful of possibilities and to provide for it, I need not have compunction at dwelling on the brighter, better chances which God's previous dispensations encourage me to expect. There may be even a *claimant*, instead of a recipient, of whatever either of us can bequeath—who knows? For which reason, but most of all for the stronger yourself adduce—the contingency of your illness—I do not ask you to 'relinquish a part'—not as our arrangements now are ordered: for I have never been so foolish as to think we could live without money, if not of my obtaining, then of your possessing, and though, in certain respects I should have preferred to try the first course,—at the beginning at least, when my faculties seemed more my own and that 'end of the summer' had a less absorbing interest (as I perceive now)—yet, as that is not to be, I have only to be thankful that you are not dependent on my exertions,—which I could not be *sure* of,—particularly with this uncertain head of mine. I hope when we once are together, the world will not hear of us again until the very end—it would be horrible to have to come back to it and ask its help.

I wish Mr. Kenyon had paid his visit—our Tuesday would be safer—I shall be with you *unless* a letter forbids. I can only say this now, because I expect my visitors nearly directly,—Moxon and Forster, do you remember? And the post is always late in arriving on Mondays. But I should fill sheets of paper to no purpose if I thought to tell you how I love you—'more than ever'—I am wholly your own, dearest dearest.

Pat Flush for me—after having let me kiss you, Ba!

E. B. B. to R. B.

Monday Morning.
[Post-mark, July 28, 1846.]

Ever dearest, your 'Hush' came too late. I had spoken. Do not blame me however,—for I do not blame myself. It was not very possible that I should allow your fine schemes to lie unmolested by a breath. Nevertheless we will not carry on this discussion any farther: my simple protest is enough for the present,—and we shall have time, I hope, in the future, for your nobleness to unteach itself from being too proud. At any rate, let the subject *be*, now! I mentioned my 'eldest surviving brother' in that way in the paper, because he is put out of the question by the estates being entailed . . the Jamaica estates, I mean. And now, to have done! Unless I could *make you easier—!*

Dearest, you may come to-morrow, Tuesday . . for my aunt goes out and we shall have a clear ground. Ah—can it be true that you wish me to be with you *so*—dearest, dearest? That you miss me as you say, the day after? Yet I am with you in my thoughts, in my affections, always. Let them count for something, that it may not be entirely an absence.

Bennett to Bennett. When Wilson brought up my coffee on the little tray on Saturday, there was a Bennett ready on one corner. Then I must not forget to tell you how Mrs. Paine (you remember Mrs. Paine?) writes of you to *me*, . . speaking what she little knows the effects of . . 'I hope,' she says, 'that you admire 'Luria' greatly. I don't know whether you will call it a sweeping conclusion, but I feel inclined to call Browning the greatest dramatic genius we have had for hundreds of years.' Can anybody be more than the 'greatest' to anybody? Half inclined I might be to be jealous of my prerogative of knowing you—yet no. Dearest is greater than Greatest . . even if one Greatest were not greater than another.

As to my headache, you might as well enquire about Troy—*Fait*. It was the air, perhaps—the heat or the cold . . the causes are forgotten with the effects. And, since I began this letter, I have been out with my aunt and Henrietta, the former having visits to pay in all the noisiest streets of the town, as appeared to me. The stone pavements seemed to accumulate on all sides to run to meet us, and I was stunned and giddy, and *am* so tired that I shall finish my letter in a hurry, looking to to-morrow. We were out nearly three hours. Think of travelling three hours in a 'Diligence,' with a Clap of Thunder! It may be something like *that!* And as we were coming homeward . . there was Mr. Kenyon! He shook hands through the window and declared that he was on the point of paying a visit to me, holding up as witness, his lump of sugar for Flush . . which Flush leapt from the other side of the carriage to accept, *ore rotundo*. Then the next word was . . 'Did you see our friend B' . . (pronounced Bee) . . 'on Saturday.?' 'No,' said I . . saying no for yes in the confusion . . . 'but I shall to-morrow.' 'He dined with me,' continued Mr. Kenyon. The sound of which struck me into a fit of clairvoyance and I had to unsay myself with an 'Oh yes—I *did* see him on Saturday.' Mr. Kenyon must have thought me purely stupid or foolish or something of the sort—and really I agree with him. To imagine my telling in that unsolicited way, too, both to my aunt and himself, that you were coming here to-morrow! So provoking! Well—it can't be helped. He won't come to-morrow in any case.

And *you* will! Dearest, how glad I am that you are coming!

Being your own
Ba.

E. B. B. to R. B.

Tuesday Evening.
[Post-mark, July 29, 1846.]

Dearest, as I lost nearly an hour of you to-day, I make amends to myself by beginning to write to you as if I had not seen you at all. A large sheet of paper, too, has flown into my hands—the Fates giving ample room and verge enough, my characters . . not 'of *Hell*' . . to trace, *as* I am not going to swear at Mr. Kenyon, whatever the provocation! Dear Mr. Kenyon!

It appears that he talked to my sisters some time before he let himself be announced to me—he said to them 'I want to talk to you . . sit down by me and listen.' Then he began to tell them of Mrs. Jameson, repeating what *you* told me, of her desire to take me to Italy, . . and of her earnestness about it. To which, he added, he had replied by every representation likely to defeat those thoughts—that only a relative would be a fit companion for me, and that no person out of my family could be justified in accepting such a responsibility, on other grounds, entering on the occurrences of last year, and reasoning on from them to the possibility that if I offended by an act of disobedience, I might be 'cast off' as for a crime. Oh—poor Papa was not spared at all—not to Mrs. Jameson, not to my sisters. Mr. Kenyon said . . 'It is painful to you perhaps to hear me talk so, but it is a sore subject with me, and I cannot restrain the expression of my opinions.' He 'had told Mrs. Jameson everything—it was due to her to have a full knowledge, he thought . . and he had tried to set before her the impossibility she was under, of doing any good.' Then he asked my sisters . . if I ever spoke of Italy . . if they thought I dwelt on the idea of it. 'Yes,' they answered 'in *their* opinion, I had made up my mind to go.' 'But *how?* what is the practical side of the question? She can't go alone—and which of you will go with her? You know, last year, she properly rejected the means which involved you in danger.' Henrietta advised that nothing should be said or done. 'Ba must do everything for herself. Her friends cannot help her. She must help herself.' 'But she must not go to Italy by herself. Then, *how?*' 'She has determination of character,' continued Henrietta—'She will surprise everybody some day.'

'*But how?*'—Mr. Kenyon repeated . . looking uneasy. (And how imprudent of Henrietta to say *that!* I have been scolding her a little.)

The discussion ended by his instructing them to tell *me* of Mrs. Jameson's proposal; 'because it was only right that I should have the knowledge of her generous kindness, though for his part, he did not like to agitate me by conversing on the subject.'

Yes, one thing more was said. He mentioned having had some conversation with my uncle Hedley, who was 'very angry'—and he asked if my aunt Hedley had no influence with the highest authority. My sisters answered in the negative. And this is all. He appears to have no 'plan' of his particular own.

What do you say, Robert, to all this? Since I am officially *informed* of Mrs. Jameson's goodness, I must thank her certainly—and in what words? '*How*'!—— as Mr. Kenyon asks. Half I have felt inclined to write and thank her gratefully, and confide to her, not the secret itself, but the secret of *there being a secret* with the weight of which I am unwilling to oppress her at this time. Could it be done, I wonder? Perhaps not. Yet how hard, how very difficult, it seems to me, to thank her worthily, and be silent wholly on my motives in rejecting her companionship! And a *whole confidence* NOW is dangerous . . would torment her with a sense of responsibility. Think which way it should be.

Once you asked me about joining travelling-company with Mrs. Jameson. Should you like it? prefer it for any cause? . if it could be done without involving her in trouble, of course.

Ah, dearest . . what a loss the three quarters of an hour were to me! like the loss of four quarters of a moon on a dark night! When dear Mr. Kenyon came to me, he found me with my thoughts astray—following you up the street! He asked how long you had been here . . 'Some time,' I said—by an answer made to fit anything. The rest of my answers were not so apt!—were more like 'cross-questions,' perhaps, than answers of the common. But he roused me a little by telling me that he wanted you to 'make an excursion' with Landor and himself, and that you did not 'encourage the idea'—and by proceeding to tell me further, that at a dinner the other day at his house, your poetry being taken up and praised to the right measure, before that wretched Mr. Reade, he wrote a letter by the morning's post to Mr. Kenyon, to express a regret that he (Mr. Reade) should have found it impossible to join in the plaudits 'of a brother-bard,' but that Edmund Reade *could not* recognize Robert Browning as a master-mind of the period, 'for reasons, which were given at length.' '*He*, (Robert Browning) had never rushed, with a passionate genius, into the production of long poems' . . (like 'Italy') 'and long dramas . . (like . . like . . . what's the name of Mr. Reade's last?) Poor, wretched man! Mr. Kenyon tore up the letter in compassion too tender toward humanity! Also he told me your excellent story on the stairs.

On the stairs! I heard the talking and the laughing, and felt ready to cry out the burden. Well—, Saturday will come, as surely as *you* could go. May God bless you, my own!—are you my own? and not rather, yes, rather, far rather, *I* am your own, your very own

Ba.

I doubt your being able to read what is written. Only don't send the 'manuscript' to Mr. Forster, to be interpreted . . after the fashion of others!

R. B. to E. B. B.

Wednesday Morning.
[Post-mark, July 29, 1846.]

This is just the way, the only way, my ever, ever dearest, you make cares for me—it *is* hard to dare to settle whether the pain of the lost quarters of the hour yesterday be not balanced by the gladness and gain of this letter; as it is hard saying whether to kiss your hand (mind, only the hand!) with shut eyes, be better than seeing you and only seeing: you cause me abundance of *such* troubles, dearest, best, divinest that you are! Oh, how *can* you, blessing me so, speak as you spoke yesterday—for the *first* time! I thought you would only write such suppositions, such desires—(for it was a desire) . . and that along with you I was safe from them,—yet you are adorable amid it all—only I *do* feel such speaking, Ba, lightly as it fell—no, not *now* I feel it,—this letter is before my heart like the hand on my eyes. I feel this letter, only how good, good, good of you to write it! Yes, I *did* meet Mr. Kenyon on the stairs—with a half opened door that discovered sundry presences, and *then* had I to speak of a sudden—put it to my credit on one side that I *did* speak and laugh; and on the other side, that I did neither *too à propos*. He most kindly (SEEING IT

ALL) began asking about Forster and Moxon—and I remember some kind of stammering remark of the latter which I retailed . . to the effect that 'now would be a favourable time to print a volume of poems' this I did, to *seem* to have something on my mind calling for a consultation with you! Then he made that proposal about Landor and Mr. Eagles . . whether I 'encouraged the idea,' or no, it encouraged me, and helped me a good deal this morning,—for Eliot Warburton sent two days ago a pressing letter to invite me to go to Ireland,—I should have yachting and other delights,—and I was glad to return for an answer, that I had an engagement, 'conditional on my accepting any.' As for my 'excellent story on the stairs'—you *alarm* me! Upon my honour, I have not the least recollection of having told one, or said another word than the above mentioned. So people are congratulated on displaying this or the other bravery in battle or fire, when their own memory is left a blank of all save the confusion! Let me say here, that he amused me also with the characteristic anecdote of poor Mr. Reade, on Saturday.

And—now! now, Ba, to the subject-matter: whatever you decide on writing to Mrs. Jameson will be rightly written—it seems to me *nearly* immaterial; (putting out of the question the confiding the whole secret, which, from its responsibility, as you feel, must not be done) whether you decline her kindness for untold reasons which two months (Ba?) will make abundantly plain,—or whether you farther inform her that there *is* a special secret—of which she must bear the burthen, even in that mitigated form, for the same two months,—as I say, it seems immaterial—but it is most material that you should see how the ground is crumbling from beneath our feet, with its chances and opportunities —do not talk about 'four months,'—till December, that is —unless you mean what *must* follow as a consequence. The next thing will be Mr. Kenyon's application to me— *he certainly knows everything* . . how else, after such a speech from your sister? But his wisdom as well as his habits incline him to use the force that is in kindness, patience, gentleness: your father might have entered the room suddenly yesterday and given vent to all the passionate indignation in the world. I dare say we should have been married to-day: but I shall have the quietest, most considerate of expositions made me (with one arm on my shoulder), of how I am sure to be about to kill you, to ruin you, your social reputation, your public estimation, destroy the peace of this member of your family, the prospects of that other,—and the end will be?

Because I *can* not only die for you but live without you *for you*—once sure it IS for you: I know what you once bade me promise—but I do not know what assurances on assurance, all on the ground of a presumed knowledge of your good above your own possible knowledge,—might not effect! *I do not know!*

This is *through you!* You *ought* to know now that 'it would *not* be better for me to leave you'! That after this devotion of myself to you I cannot undo it all, and devote myself to objects so utterly insignificant that yourself do not venture to specify them—'it would be better—people will say such things' . . I will never *force* you to know this, however—if your admirable senses do not instruct you, I shall never seem to, as it were, threaten you, by prophecies of what my life would probably be, disengaged from you—it should certainly not be passed where the 'people' are, nor where their 'sayings' influenced me any more—but I ask you to look into my heart, and into your own belief in what is worthy and durable and *the better*—and then *decide*:—for instance, to speak of waiting for four months will be a decision.

See, dearest—I began lightly,—I cannot end so. I know, after all, the words were divine, self-forgetting words—after all, that you *are* mine, by the one tenure, of your own free gift,—that all the *other* words have not been mere breath, nor the love, a playful show, an acting, an error you will correct. I believe in you, or what shall I believe in? I wish I could take my life, my affections, my ambitions, all my very self, and fold over them your little hand, and leave them there—then you would see what belief is mine! But if you had *not* seen it, would you have uttered one word, written one line, given one kiss to me? May God bless you, Ba—

R. B.

E. B. B. to R. B.

Wednesday Evening.
[Post-mark, July 30, 1846.]

'Such desires—(for it was a desire—')

Well put into a parenthesis *that* is!—ashamed and hiding itself between the brackets!

Because—my own dearest—it was *not* a 'desire'—it was the farthest possible from being a 'desire' . . the word I spoke to you on Tuesday . . yesterday!

And if I spoke it for the first time instead of writing it ——what did *that* prove, but I *was able* to speak it, and that just it was so much less earnest and painfully felt? Why it was not a proposition even—. I said only 'You had better give me up!' It was only the reflection, in the still water, of what *had been* a proposition. 'Better' perhaps!—'Better' for you, that you should desire to give me up and do it—my 'Idée fixe' you know. But *said* with such different feelings from those which have again and again made the tears run down my cheeks while I wrote to you the vexatious letter . . . that I smile at you seeing no difference. You, blind!— Which is wrong of me again. I will not smile for having vexed you . . teased you. Which is wrong of *you*, though . . the being vexed for so little! because 'you *ought* to know by this time' . . (now I will use your reproachful words)—you ought certainly to know that I am your own, and ready to go through with the matter we are upon, and willing to leave the times and the seasons in your hand! Four months! meant nothing at all. Take September, if you please. All I thought of answering to you, was, that there was no need yet of specifying the exact time. And yet—

Ah—yes!— I feel as *you* feel, the risks and the difficulties which close around us. And *you* feel *that* about Mr. Kenyon? Is it by an instinct that I tremble to think of *him*, more than to think of others? The hazel-rod turns round in my hand when I stand *here*. And as you show him speaking and reasoning . . his arm laid on your shoulder . . oh, what a vision, *that* is! before *that*, I cannot stand any longer!—it takes away my breath—the likelihood of it is so awful that it seems to *promise* to realise itself, one day!

But *you promised*. I have your solemn promise, Robert! If ever you should be moved by a single one of those vain reasons, it will be an unfaithful cruelty in you. You will have trusted *another*, against *me*. You would not do it, my beloved.

For I have none in the world who will hold me to make me live in it, except only you. I have come back for you alone . . at your voice and because you have use for me! I have come back to live a little for you— I see *you*. My fault is . . not that I think too much of what people will say. I see you and hear you. 'People' did not make me live for *them*. I am not theirs, but yours. I deserve that you should believe in me, beloved, because my love for you is '*Me*.'

Now tell me again to 'decide'—and I will tell you that the words are not 'breath,' nor the affection 'a show.' Dearest beyond words, did I deserve you telling me to 'decide'?

Let it be September then, if *you* do not decide otherwise—I would not lean to dangerous delays which are unnecessary—I wish we were at Pisa, rather!

So try to find out if and how (certainly) we can get from Nevers to Chalons . . *I* could not to-day, with my French travelling-book, find a way, either by the *chemin de fer* or *coche d'eau.*— All the rest is easy and direct . . and very cheap. We must not hesitate between the French route and the sea voyage.

Now I will tell you your good story. You said that you had only heard six words from Mr. Reade—but that they were characteristic. Someone was talking before him and you of the illness of Anacreon Moore—'He is very ill' said the someone. '*But he is no poet*' said Mr. Reade.

Isn't it a good story? Mr. Kenyon called it 'exquisite.' It is what your man of science would have called 'A beautiful specimen'—now isn't it?

May God bless you, dearest, dearest!— I owe all to you, and love you wholly—I am your very own—

R. B. to E. B. B.

Thursday.
[Post-mark, July 30, 1846.]

Now you are my very own best, sweetest, dearest Ba— Do you think after such a letter as mine any amount of confidence in my own intentions, or of the reasonableness of being earnest on such a subject, can avail to save me from mortal misgivings? I should not have said those words, certainly I should not—but you forgive them and me, do you not?

It was through seeing the peril about Mr. Kenyon just as you see it; but do not suppose I could break my promise,—to every point urged after that sad irresistible fashion, my answer would be,—would in the end amount to,—'provided she consents.' And then he would return to you, put away altogether the arguments just used to me, take up in their stead the corresponding ones founded on *my* interests as he would profess to understand them, and the result would be that a similar answer would be obtained from you,—which he would call your 'consent.' This is not what I fear *now*,—oh, no!—but the fancy that I was frightened by, yesterday, while I wrote. Now, I seem to have my powers about me, and could get to the truth and hold by it through every difficulty,—and if I, how much more you!

Then, this is expecting the *worst* of Mr. Kenyon,—and the best is at least as likely. In any case, one may be sure of cautions and warnings and a wise, good, shaking of the head—he is none of the ardent anticipators of exuberant happiness from any scheme begun and ended here below. But after that,—why, ours is the only thoroughly rational match that ever came under my notice, and he is too clever not to see some justification in it. At all events, he will say 'we shall see!'—whether he sigh or smile in the saying—and if he waits, he *will* see.

And we will 'decide' on nothing, being sure of the *one* decision—I mean, that, if the summer *be* long, and likely to lead in as fine an Autumn, and if no new obstacles arise, —September shall go as it comes, and October too, if your convenience is attained thereby in the least degree,—afterward, you will be all my own, all your days and hours and minutes. I forgot, by the way, to reply to your question concerning Mrs. J.—*if there is good to you*, decided or even not impossible good—of course, let her be with us if she will, otherwise, oh let us be alone, Ba! I find by the first map, that from Nevers the Loire proceeds S.E. till the *Arroux* joins it, and that just below it communicates with the Canal du Centre, which runs N.E. from *Paray* to *Chagny* and thence to Châlons sur Saône. It is a roundabout way, but not more so than the post-road by Autun—the Canal must be there for something, and in that case, you travel from Orleans to Leghorn by water and with the least fatigue possible. I observe that steam-boats leave St. Katherine's Wharf every Thursday and Sunday morning at 8 o'clock for Havre, Rouen and Paris—would that way be advisable? I will ascertain the facts about Nevers and Châlons by the time we meet.

Dearest Ba, my very own, I love you with a love—not

to die before any sorrow! perhaps that is the one remaining circumstance of power to heighten it! May God bless you for me—

E. B. B. to R. B.

Thursday Evening.
[Post-mark, July 31, 1846.]

Well, then,—it wasn't, after all, so extravagant of me to make the proposition about 'four months?' How innocent people may be treated like guilty ones, through no *mistake* even, of theirs!

But I hold to my first impression about Mr. Kenyon, whatever your second ones may be. I know him entirely, and his views of life, and his terrors of responsibility . . his irresolution, his apprehensiveness. He never would 'shake his head' good-naturedly, . . until he could do nothing else. Just in proportion to the affection he bears each of us, would he labour to drive us apart. And by the means you describe! And we who can foresee and analyze those means from this distance, would not, either of us, resist the actual process! There . . do not suffer yourself, ever dearest, to be drawn into any degree of confidence *there!* It would end miserably, I know . . see . . am confidently sure. Let him, on the contrary, see the thing done, before he sees it at all, and *then* he will see the best of it . . the good in it . . *then* we shall stand on the sunshiny side of his philosophy and have all the benefit of *that*, instead of having to endure, as we should now, the darkness of his irresolution and the weight of his over-caution. Observe of dear Mr. Kenyon, that, generous and noble as he is, *he fears like a mere man of the world.* Moreover he might find very rational cause for fearing, in a distant view of this . . 'most rational' of marriages!—oh, but I am wrong in my quotation!—this only rational marriage that ever was heard of!—! !—it is *so*, I think.

Where did you guess that I was to-day? In Westminster Abbey! But we were there at the wrong hour, as the service was near to begin . . and I was so frightened of the organ, that I hurried and besought my companions out of the door after a moment or two. Frightened of the organ!—yes, just exactly *that*—and you may laugh a little as they did. Through being so disused to music, it affects me quite absurdly. Again the other day, in the drawing room, because my cousin sang a song from the 'Puritani,' of no such great melancholy, I had to go away to finish my sobbing by myself. Which is all foolish and absurd, I know—but people cannot help their nerves—and I was ready to cry to-day, only to *think* of the organ, without hearing it— I, who do not cry easily, either! and all Arabel's jests about how I was sure of my life even if I *should* hear one note, . . did not reassure me in the least. We walked within the chapel . . merely within . . and looked up and looked down! How grand—how solemn! Time itself seemed turned to stone there! Then we stood where the poets were laid—oh, it is very fine—it is better than Laureateships and pensions. Do you remember what is written on Spenser's monument—'Here lyeth, in expectation of the second coming of Jesus Christ, . . Edmond Spenser, having given proof of his divine spirit in his poems'—something to that effect; and it struck me as being earnest and beautiful, and as if the writer believed in him. We should not dare, nowadays, to put such words on a poet's monument. We should say . . the author of such a book . . at most! Michael Drayton's inscription has crept back into the brown heart of the stone . . all but the name and a date, which somebody has renewed with black lines . . black as ink.

Dearest, it will not do at all . . the going at eight o'clock in the morning. I could not leave this house—it would not be possible. And then, why should we *wish* even, for that long passage to no end; Southampton or Brighton being, each of them, accessible and unobjectionable. As for the expense, it is nearly equal, by railway or sea.

For Mrs. Jameson, I mentioned her because you did once, and because her being so kind reminded me of it. I thought perhaps you might like her being with us (how should *I* know?), in which case . . Well—but you do not wish it, . . and indeed *I* do not. Therefore she shall go by herself . . dear Mrs. Jameson . . I will however write to her, which I have not done yet. It is not so easy as you think, perhaps, to write at once so much and so little.

Why not tell me how you are, Robert? When you do not, I fancy that you are not well! Say how you are, and love me till Saturday—and even afterwards.

Your very own Ba.

As to forgiveness—*ought* I to have been angry when I was not? All I felt in that letter, was, that you loved me—and as to your pretending to think that it was 'show and acting' on my part, I knew you did not really, and could not:—but at any rate I was the farthest possible from being angry—and the *very* farthest possible, peradventure!

R. B. to E. B. B.

Friday.
[Post-mark, July 31, 1846.]

Dearest Ba, the love *was* as you admit, beneath all the foolish words—I will lay your pardon to my heart with the other blessings. All this missing of instant understanding—(for it does not amount to *mis*understanding)—comes of letters, and our being divided. In my anxiety about a point, I go too much on the other side from mere earnestness,—as if the written words had need to make up in force what they want in sound and promptness—and assuredly if I *had* received such an impression *directly* from your suggestion (since not a 'desire,'—you dear, dear Ba!) I should have begun at once to ask and argue . . whereas, it *was* only to the memory of what you said, an after impression, that I wrote in answer. Well, I will certainly 'love you till Saturday,—and even after.'

Did you indeed go to the Abbey? How right to go! Every such expedition is the removal of a world of apprehension. And why not accept Mrs. Jameson's offer now, stipulating for privacy, and go and see the Museum,—the Marbles? And the National Gallery, and whatever you would wish to see. At Pisa, Ba, the Cathedral will be ours, wholly—divinely beautiful it is—more impressive in itself than the Florence Duomo—and then the green grass round, over the pavement it hides.

And considerably more impressive than the party at Mrs. Milner Gibson's last night—whereof I made one through a sudden goodnatured invitation which only came yesterday—so I went 'for reasons.' Chorley was there, looking very tired as he said he was. I left very early, having accomplished my purpose.

You know you are right, and that I knew you to be right about Mr. Kenyon—no *confidence* shall I make to him, be assured—but in the case of a direct application, with all those kind apologies in case his suspicion should be wrongly excited, what should I say?—to Mr. Kenyon, with his kindness and its right, mind—not to any other inquirer—think of the facilities during the week among the Quantock Hills! But no matter,—nothing but your own real, unmistakable consent, divides us—I believe *nothing* till that comes. The Havre voyage was of course merely a fact noted—all courses, ways, routes are entirely the same to me.

Thank you, dearest—I am very much better, well, indeed—so said my doctor who came last evening to see my father, whose eye is a little inflamed—so shall Ba see, but not take the trouble to say, when I rejoice in her presence to-morrow. Dearest, I love you with my whole heart and soul—may God bless you—

E. B. B. to R. B.

Sunday Morning and Evening.
[Post-mark, August 3, 1846.]

Ever dearest, you were wet surely? The rain came before you reached the front door; and for a moment (before I heard it shut) I hoped you might return. Dearest, how I blame myself for letting you go—for not sending you a cab in despite of you! I was frightened out of all wisdom by the idea of who was down-stairs and listening perhaps, and watching—as if the cab would have made you appear more emphatically *you*! And then you said 'the rain was over'—and I believed you as usual. If this isn't a precedent of the evils of too much belief . . . ! !

Altogether, yesterday may pass among the 'unsatisfactory days,' I think—for if I was not frightened of the storm, and *indeed* I was not, much—of the state of affairs down in the provinces, I was most sorely frightened—uneasy the whole time. I seem to be with you, Robert, at this moment, more than yesterday I was . . though if I look up now, I do not see you sitting there!—but when you sate there yesterday, I was looking at Papa's face as I saw it through the floor, and now I see only yours.

Dearest, he came into the room at about seven, before he went to dinner—I was lying on the sofa and had on a white dressing gown, to get rid of the strings . . so oppressive the air was, for all the purifications of lightning. He looked a little as if the thunder had passed into him, and said, 'Has this been your costume since the morning, pray?'

'Oh no'—I answered— 'Only just now, because of the heat.'

'Well,' he resumed, with a still graver aspect . . (so displeased he looked, dearest!) 'it appears, Ba, that *that man* has spent the whole day with you.' To which I replied as quietly as I could, that you had several times meant to go away, but that the rain would not let you,—and there the colloquy ended. Brief enough—but it took my breath away . . or what was left by the previous fear. And think how it must have been a terrible day, when the lightning of it made the least terror.

I was right too about the message—he took up the fancy that I might be ill perhaps with fear . . 'and only Mr. Browning in the room'! ! which was not to be permitted. He was *peremptory* with Arabel, she told me.

Well—we need not talk any more of it—it has made one of us uncomfortable long enough. Shall you dare come on Tuesday after all? He will be out. If he is not—if my aunt should not be . . if a new obstacle should occur . . why you shall hear on Tuesday. At any rate I shall write, I think. He did not see you go yesterday—he had himself preceded you by an hour . . at five o'clock . . which if it had been known, would have relieved me infinitely. Yet it did not prevent . . you see . . the appalling commentary at seven— No.

With all the rest I am afraid besides of Mr. Chorley and his idea about your 'mysteriousness.' Let Mr. Kenyon hold that thread in one hand, and in the other the thread Henrietta gave him so carelessly, why he need not ask you for information—which reminds me of the case you put to me, Robert—and certainly you could not help a confession, in such possible circumstances. Only, even granting the circumstances, you need not confess more than is wrung from you—need you? Because Mr. Kenyon would undo us.

Before yesterday's triple storms, I had a presentiment which oppressed me during two days . . a presentiment that it would all end *ill*, through some sudden accident or misery of some kind. What is the use of telling you this? I do not know. I will tell you besides, that it cannot . . shall not . . be, by my fault or failing. I may be broken indeed, but never bent.

If things should go smoothly, however, I want to say one word, once for all, in relation to them. Once or twice you have talked as if a change were to take place in your life through marrying—whereas I do beg you to keep in mind that not a pebble in the path changes, nor is pushed aside because of me. If you should make me feel myself in the way, should I like it, do you think? And how could I disturb a single habit or manner of yours . . as an unmarried man . . though being within call—I? Tho best of me is, that I am really very quiet and not difficult to content—having not been spoilt by an excess of prosperity even in little things. It will be prosperity in the greatest, if you seem to be happy—believe that, and leave all the rest. You will go out just as you do now . . when you choose, and as a matter of course, and without need of a word—you will be precisely as you are now in everything, —lord of the house-door-key, and of your own ways—so that when I shall go to Greece, you shall not feel yourself much better off than before I went. That shall be a reserved vengeance, Robert.

While I write, comes Mr. Kenyon,—and through a special interposition of guardian-angels, he has broken his spectacles and carries them in his hand. On which I caught at the opportunity and told him that they were the most unbecoming things in the world, and that fervently (and sincerely) I hoped never to see them mended. The next word was . . 'Did you see Browning yesterday?' 'Yes.' 'I thought so, I intended to come myself, but I thought it probable that he would be here, and so I stayed away—'

Now——I confess to you that that thought carries me a good way over to your impression. It is at least 'suspicious,' that he who knew you were with me on Saturday and Tuesday should expect to find you again on the next Saturday. 'Oh—how uncomfortable'—the miracle of the broken spectacles not saving one from the discomfort of the position open to the bare eyes!—

He talked of you a little—asked what you were doing—praised you as usual . . for inexhaustible knowledge and general reasonableness, this time. Did I not think so? Yes—of course I thought so.

Presently he made me look aghast by just this question —'Is there an attachment between your sister Henrietta and Capt. Cook?'—(put as abruptly as I put it here).

My heart leapt up—as Wordsworth's to the rainbow in the sky—but there was a recoil in my leap. 'Why, Mr. Kenyon?'—I said . . 'what extraordinary questions, opening into unspeakable secrets, you do ask.'

'But I did not know that it was a secret. How was I to know? I have seen him here very often, and it is a natural enquiry which I might have put to anybody in the house touching a matter open to general observation. I thought the affair might be an arranged one by anybody's consent.'

'But you ought to know,' I answered, 'that such things are never permitted in this house. So much for the consent. As for the matter itself you are right in your supposition—but it is a great secret,—and I entreat you not to put questions about it to anybody in or out of the house.' Something to that effect I believe I said—I was frightened . . frightened . . and not exactly for Henrietta. What did he mean?— Had *he* too in his mind . . .

He touched on Mrs. Jameson . . just *touched* . . He had desired my sisters to tell me. He thought I had better write a note to thank her for her kindness. He had told her that if I had any thoughts of Italy they could be accomplished only by a sea-voyage, which was impossible to her.

I briefly expressed a sense of the kindness and said that I meant to write. On which the subject was changed in mutual haste, as seemed to me.

Is not this the book of the chronicles? . . And you shall hear again on Tuesday, if the post should be faithful to me that morning. I might be inclined to put off our Tuesday's meeting, but Mrs. Hedley remains in London for a few days after her daughter's marriage, and 'means to see a great deal' of me—therefore Wednesday, Thursday, Friday, . . where should we look, from Tuesday? but I must consider and will write. May God bless you! Do say how you are after that rain. The storm is calm,

and ever and ever I am your own Ba

R. B. to E. B. B.

Sunday.
[Post-mark, August 3, 1846.]

What can I tell you, ever dearest, while I am expecting all you are to tell *me?* I will not conjecture, nor be afraid (for you) before the time—I felt your dear hand press mine closer while the thunder sounded—so it will always be, I know, in life, in death—and when a thunder shall break, of a kind that I can fear, I will hold *your* hand, my Ba. Perhaps there is nothing formidable here . . indeed there can hardly be—tell me *all.* I got to your Hodgson's, waited a few minutes till a cab passed, and then was properly depcsited at the Haymarket. The streets, at least the roads out of Town, were flooded—very canals. Here, at home our skylight was broken,—and our chimneys behaved just as yours.

And now—shall I see you really on Tuesday after this Saturday of perils? And how will your head be,—your health in general be, you sweetest Ba? Is it the worse for the storm and the apprehension,—to say nothing of what may have followed? Oh, if but a 'sign' might be vouchsafed me—if I might go to Wimpole Street presently, and merely know by the disposition of a blind or of a shutter, that you were better, or no worse! I ought to have contrived something of the kind yesterday—but 'presence of mind'!

Ba, I have been reading those poems—now to speak soberly—I had no conception, Mrs. Butler could have written anything so mournfully mediocre . . to go as near flattery as I can. With the exception of three or four pieces respectable from their apparent earnestness, all that album writing about 'sprites,' and the lily-bell, and 'wishes'—now to be dead and now alive,—descriptions without colour, songs without tune,—why, Bennett towers above it! *Either* Bennett—for the one touch you recorded, 'I will not be forgot'—seems grandly succinct contrasted with

> Yet not in tears remembered be my name—
> Weep over those ye loved—for me, for me,
> Give me the wreath of glory and let fame
> Over my tomb spread immortality.

How many of these unfortunate Sundays are in store for me, I wonder—eight or nine, then the two months . . 'when constant faith and holy hope shall die,' one lost in certainty and one in the deep deep joy of the ever present ever dearest Ba! Oh, Ba, how I love you!

Your own R.

R. B. to E. B. B.

Monday Morning.
[Post-mark, August 3, 1846.]

Oh, the comfort you are to me, Ba—the perpetual blessing and sustainment! And what a piece of you, how instinct with you, this letter is! I will not try to thank you, but my whole life shall.

See! *Now* talk of 'three or four months'! And is not the wonder, that this should wait for the eighty-second visit to happen? Or could anything be more fortunate, more *mitigating* than the circumstances under which it *did* happen at last? The rain and thunder,—the two hours (see the accounts—nothing like it has been known, for years), at most, *proved* against us,—the ignorance of the visits last week—in spite of all which, see what comes and is likely to come!

Let me say at once that, at the worst, it *may* come! You have had time to know enough of me, my Ba,—and

I, who from the first knew you, have taken one by one your promises from your lips,—I *believe* what you write here; I accept it as the foundation of all my future happiness—'you will never fail me'—I will never fail you, dearest dearest.

How you have mistaken my words, whatever they may have been, about the 'change' to be expected in my life! I have, most sincerely I tell you, no one habit nor manner to change or persevere in,—if you once accept the general constitution of me as accordant to yours in a sufficient degree,—my incompleteness with your completeness, dearest,—there is no further difficulty. I want to be a Poet—to read books which make wise in their various ways, to see just so much of nature and the ways of men as seems necessary—and having done this already in some degree, I can easily and cheerfully afford to go without any or all of it for the future, if called upon,—and so live on, and 'use up,' my past acquisitions such as they are. I will go to Pisa and learn,—or stay here and learn in another way—putting, as I always have done, my whole pride, if that is the proper name, in the being able to work with the least possible materials. There is my scheme of life *without* you, *before* you existed for me; prosecuted hitherto with every sort of weakness, but always kept in view and believed in. Now then, please to introduce Ba, and say what is the habit she changes? But do not try to say what divinest confirmation she brings to 'whatever is good and holy and true' in this scheme, because even She cannot say that! All the liberty and forbearance . . most graceful, most characteristic of you, sweet! But why should I play with you, at taking what I mean to give again?—or rather, what it would be a horror to have to keep—why make fantastic stipulations only to have the glory of not abiding by them? If I may speak of my own desires for a moment unconnected with your happiness,—of what I want *for myself*, purely—what I mean by marrying you,—it is, that I may be with you forever—I cannot have enough of you in any other relation: why then should I pretend to make reservations and say 'Yes, you shall deprive me of yourself' (of your sympathy, of your knowledge, and good wishes, and counsel) on such and such occasions? But I feel your entire goodness, dear angel of my life,—ever more I feel it, though all seems felt and recorded.

And now of your 'chronicling'—of course Mr. Kenyon *knows*—and this is the beginning of his considerate, cautious kindness—he has determined to hurry nothing, interfere abruptly in no case, to make you *infer* rather than pretend to instruct you—as you must,—for 'if the visits of Captain Cook *have* that appearance &c., must not those of R.B. &c., &c.,' So, this is not from Chorley's information, mind, but from his own spectacled *acumen*.

After this, it seems very natural to remark that the Havre packets leave now at nine instead of eight o'clock on Thursdays and Sundays—while the departures from Southampton are on Tuesdays and Fridays. My presentiment is that suddenly you will be removed to Devonshire or Sussex or—. In which case, our difficulties will multiply considerably—be prepared for such events!

And for to-morrow—only think of yourself, *lest* you should forget my interests: *pray write to-night*, if but two or three words. If I am allowed to call, I will bring Mrs. Butler's book in a cover, and, if I find a note from you, leave *that*, as an excuse for the knock. Will you contrive that a note shall be ready—in case of your Aunt's presence &c. If it saves you from a danger, let me stay away—until the letters stop, I can bear absence *till* the *two months end*—any such journey as I apprehend would be most annoying, deplorable indeed.

Would you not, if the worst came,—*what* would you do?

May God bless you, infinitely bless you, ever dearest dearest, prays ever your very own—

R.

Mrs. Procter wants me to go to her on Thursday—is there anything to get out of *that* arrangement?—probably not—but write!

Do *re*consider, Ba,—had I better stay away to-morrow? You cannot misunderstand me,—I *only* think of you—any man's anger to me is Flushie's barking, without the respectability of motive,—but, once the door shut on me, if he took to biting you! Think for us both! Is there any possibility of a suspicious sudden return *because* of the facilities of the day? Or of the servant being desired to mention my visits—or to 'deny you,' as unwell &c.? Ah my soul revolts at the notion of a scene in your presence—my own tied tongue, and a system of patience I can well *resolve* upon, but not be *sure* of, as experience makes sure.

E. B. B. to R. B.

Monday.
[Post-mark, August 4, 1846.]

Two precious letters to make amends for yesterday! and in return only just two or three words to say . . 'yes, come.' And I meant to have proposed to you something like what you suggest when you talk of the book and the note. If the ground is not clear at three, and Papa (above all) still in the house, you shall have a note, instead of admittance, . . and you will understand by the sign that it is wise for us not to meet. My hope and expectation are, however, that no obstacle will occur—that *he* will be in the city, and *she* at Fenton's Hotel, engaged in some office of consolation beside her sister. I seriously exhorted her to remain there the rest of the day to wipe away the tears of the bride's mother . . as an appendix to the breakfast:—ah, and seriously I thought she ought to stay, as well as seriously wishing it. And thus, altogether, we shall probably have open ground when it is desirable. If not, the note!—

For the rest, dearest, do not exaggerate to yourself my

report of what passed on Saturday. It was an unpleasant impression, and that is all, . . and nothing, I believe, has been thought of it since. Once before, remember, your apparition made an unpleasant impression, which was perfectly transitory then as now. Now as then, do not suffer such things to vex you beyond their due import. There will be no coming back, no directions to servants, nothing of the sort. Only it would not do to deepen Saturday's impression with to-morrow's—we must be prudent a little.

And you see me, my prophet, sent to Sussex or Devonshire, in a flash of lightning? That is your presentiment, do you say? Well! Sussex is possible, Kent is not impossible. This house, . . *vox populi clamat,*—wants cleaning, painting, papering—the inhabitants thereof, too, cry aloud for fresh air. Nevertheless, summer after summer, there have been the same reasons for going, and nobody goes. We shall see.

So till to-morrow! Dear, dearest! you are always best—to justify the *dearest,* I suppose! I remember your having said before some of this . . which, never could I forget, having once heard. But think how Alfred the king divided his days—and how Solomon the king would tell you of 'a time' for sitting with *me.* 'Bid me . . not . . discourse' however—we shall both know what is right presently—and I in the meanwhile perfectly do know that I could not consent to your shutting yourself up for my sake—no, indeed!

Shall I fail to you? Could I? Could it be needful for me to say '*I will not fail.*'

Your own, I am.

E. B. B. to R. B.

Tuesday Evening.
[Post-mark, August 5, 1846.]

One word or two to-night and no more, let the paper spread itself as it may. Dearest, it was wise of you, perhaps, to go to-day. Wisdom was the first to wear sackcloth. My aunt, who had just had time to hear of your being in the house, found my door open, and you were noticed by a passing jest . . too passing to meet ears in authority—and I was made to put on my bonnet and go out in the carriage with *our* deparment of the bridal party, who had come home first, in order to change their costume into something wearable for comfort . . into gowns which had not a devil, torturing the wearers with a morbid sense of flounces. So they came home for *that*, and we were vexed and frightened for *that* reason—and I was taken to Kensington Gardens to leave some walkers there, and then to Fenton's Hotel, to leave my aunt as comforter for the evening. Altogether, oh, how provoked I was! But it was wise perhaps. I will not say that it was not very wise indeed. Papa knows nothing of your having been here, and Saturday is not far off. Still, to think of two hours being cut off; and of the long journey from New Cross, just for the one hour! Shall I hear to-morrow *fully*, to make up for it, Robert? And tell me if you accept Mrs. Jameson's invitation. And *your head?*

Flush thanks you! I asked him if he loved you even, and he wagged his tail. Generally when I ask him that question he won't answer at all,—but you have overcome him with generosity . . as you do me!

I forgot to tell you— There is a letter from Mr. Horne which makes me vexed a little. He is coming to England, and says, that, if still I will not see him, he shall bring his guitar to play and sing for my sisters, leaving the door open that I may hear upstairs. What a vexation! How shall I escape a checkmate now? He castles his king, and the next move undoes me. There's a bishop though to be played first, for he wants an introduction to Whately, which I am to write for to Miss Mitford, if I *don't know him myself*.

My consolation for to-day, is, that to-morrow is not Sunday. In the meanwhile, nothing is talked except of the glories of Fenton's Hotel. The bride behaved with the most indisputable grace, and had words and smiles for everybody. The bridegroom appears to have been rather petrified (he was saying orisons to St. James, I dare say) and was condemned by the severer critics, for being able to produce no better speech at the breakfast, when his health was drunk with ever so much elaboration of eloquence, than 'I thank you—I propose yours.' For my part I sympathize more with him in that point of specific stupidity, than on any other I have yet heard of. If he had said as little about ecclesiastical architecture, he would have been unobjectionable, wholly. They went away with four horses, in disdain of the railroads.

But poor Mrs. Hedley was dreadfully affected—I knew she would be. This is the only grown-up daughter, you see,—the others being all children, the youngest three years old—and she loses a constant companion, besides the hourly sight of a very lovely girl, the delight of her eyes and heart.

Dearest, you understood why I told you to-day of Mr. Kenyon's professed opinions? It was to make you know *him*. The rest, we know alike. And for *him* even, when he looks back on a thing instead of looking forward to it (where the Bude Light of the world is in his eyes and blinds them) he will see aright and as we do. Only you frightened me by your idea about his application to you. May God forbid!

May God bless you, rather, in the best way! Why should I choose how? I '*ought*' *not*, I think, to fancy that I know the best for you, enough to use such words.

But I am your own. That, we both know! *May* I be yours, not to do you harm, my beloved! Good-night, now!

R. B. to E. B. B.

Wednesday Morning.
[Post-mark, August 5, 1846.]

If I had felt, as you pleased to feel yesterday, that it had been 'only one hour' which my coming gained—I should richly deserve to find out to-day, as I do fully, what the precise value of such an hour is. But I never act so ungratefully and foolishly—you are more than ever you have been to me,—yet at any time I would have gone for the moment's sight of you,—one moment's—and returned happy. You never doubt this because I do not waylay you in your walks and rides? I consider your sisters, and your apprehension for them, and other reasons that make such a step objectionable. Do you remember what I said yesterday—what I have told myself so often? It is one proof how I love you that I am jealous of any conversation with you which should be too interesting *for itself*, apart from the joy of your presence—it is better to sit and see you, or hear you, or only say something which, in its insignificance, shall be obviously of no account beside the main and proper delight—as at wine-feasts you get the wine and a plate of thin dry tasteless biscuits—(observe, for instance, that this noble simile was not set before you yesterday—no, my Ba!)

And you *did* understand also why I left, on that mere chance of danger to you,—for it was not, do you think it was only the irksomeness to myself I sought to escape—though that would have been considerable. There is no unstable footing for me in the whole world except just in your house—which is *not* yours. I ought not to be in that one place—all I could do in any circumstances (were a meeting to happen) would be *wrong*, unfortunate. The certainty of misconception would spoil everything—so much of gentleness as is included in *gentle*manliness would pass for a very different quality—and the *manliness* which one observes there too, would look like whatever it is farthest from. This is a real avowal of weakness—because, being in the right, as I dare trust I am, so far as I can see through the involvement, I ought to be able to take my stand upon it,—and so I shall be able, and easily—but not *here*, just here. With Mr. Kenyon, in spite of a few misgivings, I shall know what to say—I can justify myself, if not convince him. Never fancy, dearest, that he has any 'clay' in his composition—he may show a drop of water at the heart of the else entire chrystal he is—did you ever see that pretty phenomenon—of which Claudian wrote so prettily? 'Non potuit toto mentiri corpore gemmam, sed medio latuit proditor orbe latex.' Our Druids used to make balls for divining out of such *all-but-solid* gems with the central weakness—I have had them in my hand. Such doubts and fears are infinitely more becoming in him, situated as he is, than their absence would be —if he said for instance, 'Oh yes,—I am used to a certain style of living, which of course I do not change for *no* reason at all,—but who doubts that I *could* do so, without difficulty or regret? I shall hardly bestow any sympathy on what I am sure must be the easiest life in the world!' One would rather hear an epicure say frankly he cannot conceive how people can end a dinner without Tokay, than ask over his Tokay (as Sheridan's Abbot in the 'Duenna') of the poor starved wistful attendant monk, 'Haven't you the chrystal spring?'

In this case, he is directly looking to your possible undertakings, not merely expressing his general 'remembrance that we are dust' and need gilding—and certainly if in some respects you have, as I believe, less use, fewer uses for money than ordinary women,—you also have an absolute *necessity* for whatever portion you *do* require,—such a necessity as *they* have not, neither. I shall never grieve over the lace handkerchiefs you cannot get—but whatever you possess already in this room of yours, or might possess on the contingency of such illness, you must *keep*,—to your life's end. I would not take you away on any other condition. Now listen Ba—not think for a moment that it puts me to the least, least pain imaginable to talk on this subject, while I know you wholly, as *there* I am sure I do, and while you too know me, as I also am sure,—we may discuss this, as we do the better or worse routes to Italy, in the fullest confidence of our aims and desires being absolutely identical,—so that it is but a prize for the ingenuity of either,—a prize from the common stock of our advantage,—whenever a facility is discovered or a difficulty avoided. So listen,—will you, at once, or as soon as practicable, ascertain what you certainly possess—what is quite yours, and in your sole power, to take or to let remain—what will be just as available to you in Italy as in England? I want to know, being your possible husband. My notion of the perfection of money arrangements is that of a fairy purse which every day should hold *so* much, and there an end of trouble. Houses and land always seem like a vineyard to a man who wants a draught of wine for present thirst: so tell me how much will be found in the purse—because when we are in Italy or halfway there telling will be superfluous or beyond remedy,—easy remedy at least.

Since writing the above I have been down-stairs—and now return to tell you, a miracle has just happened, which my father, mother and sister are at this moment engaged in admiring—I hear their voices in the garden. We have a fig-tree which I planted four years ago—this year it produces its first fruit, a small fig, '*seule et unique*,' which is still on the tree—not another fig, ripe or unripe, living or dead, has ever been carried into the garden—yet this morning is discovered in the exact centre of the garden, and parallel with the fig-tree aforesaid, another indubitable seedling fig-tree,—'how begot, how nourished?' *Ipse vidi*—does that prognosticate, my own Siren, my soothsayer and wise lady?

And now, have you been incommoded by the storm,—and thunder, which was loud and lasting here? I thought of you with such thoughts.

And what came of my visit? Was it really your Aunt—did my precipitation improve matters? Will Saturday have to fear?

Yesterday I was not in a mood to go quietly home—'for my soul kept up too much light under my eyelids for the night, and thus I *went* disquieted' till at Charing Cross it struck me that going home by water (to Greenwich, at least) would be a calmative—so I went on board a steamer. Close by me sate three elderly respectable men,—I could not help hearing them talk rationally about the prospects of the planters, the 'compensation there is to be in the article of Rum,'—how we 'get labour,' which is the main thing, and may defy, with that, Cuba, the Brazils &c. One who talked thus was a fat genial fellow, ending every sentence in a laugh from pure good-nature his companions somehow got to 'the Church,' then Puseyism, then Dissent—on all which this personage had his little opinion,—when one friend happened to ask 'you think so?'—'I do,' said the the other, 'and indeed I *know* it.' 'How so?'—'Because it was revealed to me in a vision.' 'A . . . vision?'—'Yes, a vision'—and so he began to describe it, quite in earnest, but with the selfsame precision and assurance, with which he had been a little before describing the effect of the lightning on an iron steam boat at Woolwich as he witnessed it. In this vision he had seen the devil cast out of himself—which he took for an earnest of God's purposes for good to the world at large—I thought, 'we mad poets,—and this very unpoetical person!' who had also previously been entering on the momentous question 'why I grow fatter than of old, seeing that I eat no more—'

Come, Ba, say, is not this too bad, too far from the line?—I may *talk* this *by* you,—but *write* this *away* from you,—oh, no! Be with me then, dearest, for one moment, for many moments, in spite of the miles, while I kiss your sweetest lips, as now—Beloved!

I am ever your very own

Oh,—I determine not to go *yet* to Mrs. J's 'for reasons'—a phrase which ought to be ready stereotyped.

E. B. B. to R. B.

Wednesday Night.
[Post-mark, August 6, 1846.]

Dearest, you did not have my letter, I think—the letter I wrote on Tuesday, yesterday. These iniquitous post-people—who are not likely to see in a vision (like your fat prophet) the devil cast out of them for the good of the world! Indeed it is too bad.

To answer first the question—(You are wise beyond me in all things . . let me say *that* in a parenthesis!) I will tell you what I know. Stormie told me the other day that I had eight thousand pounds in the funds; of which the interest comes to me quarterly, the money being in two different per cents . . (do you understand better than I do?) and from forty to forty-five pounds Papa gives me every three months, the income tax being first deducted. It may be eight thousand pounds, or more or less, . . it is difficult to ask about it . . but what comes to me every three months, I know certainly. Then there is the ship money . . a little under two hundred a year on an average . . which I have not used at all (but must for the future use), and the annual amount of which therefore, has been added to the Fund-money until this year, when I was directed to sign a paper which invested it (*i.e.* the annual return) in the Eastern Railroad. That investment is to yield a large percentage, I heard, and Stormie tried to persuade me to ask Papa to place everything I had, on the same railroad. Papa had said down-stairs the other day that it would be best so—and I ought to remind him to do it, repeated Stormie, as it would very much increase . . increase by doubling almost . . the available income; and without the slightest risk of any kind. But I could not take the advice under the circumstances—I could not mention such a word as money to him, giving the appearance even of trouble about my affairs, now. And he would wonder how I should take a fancy suddenly to touch such matters with the end of my finger. Then there are the ten shares in Drury Lane Theatre—out of which comes nothing.

You wonder how I can spend, perhaps, the quarterly forty pounds and upward that come to me? I *do spend* them. Yet let me hold you from being frightened, and teach you to consider how easy it is to spend money, and not upon oneself. Never in any one year of my life, even when I was well, have my expenses in dress (as I told Mr. Kenyon the other day) exceeded twenty pounds. My greatest personal expense lately has been *the morphine*. Still the money flows out of window and door—you will understand how it flows like a stream. I have not the gift (if it is a gift) of making dresses . . in my situation, here. Elsewhere, all changes, you know. You shall not call me extravagant—you will see. If I was 'surprised' at what you told me of Mrs. Norton, it was only because I had had other ideas of her—for my own gown cost five shillings . . the one I had on when you spoke. So she was better than I by a mere sixpence. Ah—it came into my head afterwards that my being 'surprised' about Mrs. Norton, might argue my own extravagance. See!—

But the Goddess Dulness inspires me to write about it and about it, to no end. I say briefly at last, that whatever I have, is mine . . and for use in Italy, as in England. Papa has managed . . has taken a power of attorney, to manage for me kindly . . but everything is in my name—and if it were not, he could not for a moment think of interfering with an incontestable right of property. Still, I do see a difficulty at the beginning—I mean that, *as I am here*, I could not put my hand out for a large sum, such as would be necessary perhaps. I have had a great deal to pay and do lately,—and the next quarter will not be until the middle of October. Still there would be something, but less than is necessary. We might either wait on the road till the required sum were called for and sent—or get a hundred pounds advanced by someone for a few weeks until everything was settled . . which would be pleasanter, if possible. Poor Papa's first act will be to abandon his management. Ah, may God grant him to do it rather angrily than painfully.

A letter, I have written to you, like the chiming of two penny pieces—a miserable letter! And there is much to tell you . . but nothing painful . . do not fear. The Hedleys dined here, and Mrs. Hedley has been sitting with me . . keeping me from writing. Good-night now it must be! When you write so of caring to be with me, my heart seems to *rock* with pleasure. Shouldn't this letter have been written on 'Change, and isn't it unworthy of all you are to me . . and even of all I am to *you?* But such things must be, after a fashion. Have I told you right, dearest? does it make any sense, altogether? You are wise in little subjects as in great ones, and I will let you make me wiser if you can. And there *is* no clay in dear Mr. Kenyon . . but just the drop in the chrystal you tell me of—only you shall not divine by him, my Druid, or you will sit by yourself under the oak tree to the end of the day!

Wholly yours and ever—in the greatest haste—

R. B. to E. B. B.

Thursday Morning.
[Post-mark, August 6, 1846.]

No, dearest,—the post brought me no letter till early this morning, a few hours before the second arrival: so, in case of any unexpected stoppage in our visit-affairs, if the post *can* have been to blame, always be sure it *is;* if I do not arrive at any time when I ought to arrive, having been sent for—there is the great instance and possibility, which you are to remember! However at present, *post naufragia tutus sum* with my two treasures.

Thank you, dearest, for all that kind care of answering—will you now let me lay it all quietly up in my head to mature, before I . . really *think* upon it, much more, speak of it? If one can do both *once for all*, what a blessing! But a little leaven of uncertainty and apprehension, just enough to be tasted bitterly in the whole lump of our life,—that cannot be too diligently guarded against while there is time.

Well, love, your excursion to Kensington was a real good, well purchased by my early going—and I am glad the great event stood before all eyes and mouths. I seem to notice that you do not leave the house quite so often as, say, a month ago; and that you are not the better for it. Of course you cannot go out in storm and rain. Will you do what is best for *my* Ba, you who say you love me,—that is, love her?

Don't I sympathize with Horne, and see with his eyes, and want with his senses! But why can he not want after the two months, I ask selfishly—seeing, or fancying I see, this inconvenience . . that, as his *report* will probably be the *latest* to the world, it would be advisable for you to look as well as possible,—would it not? It would not do for him to tell people 'All I can say is, that a few weeks only *before it happened*, she appeared to me thus and thus'—while, on the other hand, if you receive him in the drawing room,—*there* are difficulties too.

You never told me how yesterday's thunder affected you—nor how your general health is—yet I will answer you that I am very well to-day—about to go to Mrs. Procter's, alas—it is good that this letter cannot reach you before night or nine o'clock—I should fail to deny myself the moment's glance at the window—if you could be prayed to stand there! But it is past praying for now. I told you that I have excused myself to Mrs. Jameson on the ground of some kind of uncertainty that rules the next fortnight's engagements—who shall say what a fortnight may not bring forth? I shall not mind Mr. Kenyon being of the party to-night, should it be so ordered . . for, if he asks me, I can say with dignity—'No,—I did not call to-day,—meaning to call on Saturday, perhaps'—'Well, there is *some* forbearance,' he will think! However, he will not be present, I prophesy, and Chorley *will* . . or no, perhaps, Rachel's Jeanne D'Arc may tempt him. Important to Ba, very! almost as much as to me—so at once to the really, truly, exclusively important thing, by comparison—Love me ever, dearest dearest, as I must ever love you,—and take my heart, as if it were a better offering. Also write to me and tell me that Saturday is safe . . will it be safe? Your aunt may perhaps leave you soon—and one observation of hers would be enough to ruin us—consider and decide!

Since these words were written, my mother, who was out, entered the room to confirm a horrible paragraph in the paper. You know our light momentary annoyance at the storm on Saturday; it is over for *us*. The next day, Mr. Chandler, the cultivator of camellias at Wandsworth, died of grief at the loss from the damage to his conservatories and flowers—which new calamity added to the other, deprived his eldest son, and partner—of his senses . . 'he was found to be raving mad on Monday' are the words of the *Times*. My mother's informant called theirs 'the most amicable of families.'

How strange—and a few weeks ago I read, in the same paper, a letter from Constantinople—wherein the writer mentioned that he had seen (I think, that morning) Pacha somebody, whose malpractices had just drawn down on him the Sultan's vengeance, and who had been left with barely his life,—having lost his immense treasures, palaces and gardens &c., along with his dignity,—the writer saw this old man selling slices of melon on a bridge in the city; and on stopping in wonderment to praise such constancy, the Turk asked him with at least equal astonishment, whether it was not fitter to praise Allah who had lent him such wealth for forty years, than to repine that he had judged right to recall it now?

Could we but practise it, as we reason on it!—May God continue me that blessing I have all unworthily received . . but not, I trust, insensibly received!

May he keep you, dearest dearest

R.

E. B. B. to R. B.

Thursday.
[Post-mark, August 7, 1846.]

I told you nothing yesterday; but the interruption left me no time, and the house was half asleep before I had done writing what I was able to write. Otherwise I wanted to tell you that Mrs. Jameson had been here . . that she came yesterday, and without having received my note. So I was thrown from my resources. I was obliged to thank her with my voice . . so much weaker than my hand. If you knew how frightened I was! The thunder, the morning before, (which I did not hear holding *your* hand!) shook me less, upon the whole. I thanked her at least . . I could do *that*. And then I said it was in vain . . impossible.

'Mr. Kenyon threw cold water on the whole scheme. But *you!* Have *you* given up going to Italy?'

I said 'no, that I have not certainly.' I said 'I felt deeply how her great kindness demanded every sort of frankness and openness from me towards her,——and yet, that at that moment I could not be frank—there were reasons which prevented it. Would she promise not to renew the subject to Mr. Kenyon? not to repeat to him what I said? and to wait until the whole should be explained to herself?'

She promised. She was kind beyond imagination—at least, far beyond expectation. She looked at me a little curiously, but asked no more questions until she rose to go way. And then——

'But you will go?' 'Perhaps—if something unforeseen does not happen.' 'And you will let me know, and when you can,—when everything is settled?' 'Yes.' 'And you think you shall go?' 'Yes.' 'And with efficient companionship?' 'Yes.' 'And happily and quietly?' . 'Ye . .' I could not say the full 'Yes,' to *that*—If it had been utterable, the idea of 'quiet' would have been something peculiar. She loosened her grasp of her catechumen, therefore——nothing was to be done with me.

I forgot, however, to tell you that in the earlier part of the discussion she spoke of having half given up her plan of going herself. In her infinite goodness she said, 'she seemed to want an object, and it was in the merest selfishness, she had proposed taking *me* as an object'— 'And if you go even without me, would it not be possible to meet you on the road? I shall go to Paris in any case. *If* you go, *how* do you go?'

'Perhaps across France—by the rivers.'

'Precisely. That is as it should be. Mr. Kenyon talked of a long sea-voyage.'

Now I have recited the whole dialogue to you, I think, except where my gratitude grew rhetorical, as well it might. She is the kindest, most affectionate woman in the world! and you shall let me love her for you and for me.

As for me, my own dearest, you are fanciful when you say that I do not go out so much, nor look so well. Now I will just tell you—Henrietta cried out in loud astonishment at me to-day, desiring Treppy to look at my face, when we were all standing together in this room—'Look at Ba, Treppy!— Did you ever see anyone looking so much better; it really is wonderful, the difference within these few weeks.' That's Henrietta's opinion! She quite startled me with crying out . . as if suddenly she had missed my head!— And *you!*

Then I have been out in the carriage to-day, just to Charing Cross, and then to Mr. Boyd's in St. John's Wood. I am as well at this moment as anyone in the world. I have not had one symptom of illness throughout the summer—perfectly well, I am. At the same time, being *strong* is different; and sometimes for a day or two together, when I do not feel the strongest, it is *right* to be quiet and not to walk up and down stairs. So as I 'love *Ba*,' (quite enough, I assure you!) I am quiet. There's the only meaning of not going out every day! But the health is perfectly unaffected, I do assure you,—so keep yourself from every vexing thought of me, *so* far at least. Are you getting frightened for me, my beloved? Do not be frightened, I would not deceive you by an exaggeration, for the sake even of your temporary satisfaction—you may trust what I say.

For the thunder . . if you thought of me during it, as *you* say, . . why it did me just so much good. Think of me, dearest, in the thunder and out of the thunder; the longest peal's worth of your thought would not content me now, because you have made me too covetous.

As to Mr. Horne, you write *Sordelloisms* of him—and you shall tell me your real meaning in a new edition on Saturday. Might your meaning be that I *look worse* in this room than in the drawing-room? Have you an objection to this room as a room? I rub my eyes and look for a little more light—(but can't be more impertinent!—can I?)

So, till Saturday—yes, Saturday! To-morrow there is a clearance of aunts—one going at nine in the morning, and one at five in the afternoon: and uncles and cousins do not stay behind. You are glad, I think—and I, not sorry.

How striking your two stories are! Wonderful it is to me, when mere worldly reverses affect men *so*—I cannot comprehend it—I stand musing *there*. But the sublime sentiment of the Melon-seller applies to the griefs I *can* understand—and we may most of us (called Christians) go to him for his teaching.

May God bless you for *me!* Your Ba.

(I want to say one word more and so leave the subject Stormie told me this morning, in answer to an enquiry of mine, that certainly I did not receive the whole interest of the fund-money, . . could not . . making ever so much allowance for the income-tax. And now, upon consideration, I seem to see that I cannot have done so. The ship-shares are in the 'David Lyon,' a vessel in the West Indian trade, in which Papa also has shares. Stormie said 'There must be three hundred a year of interest from the fund-money—even at the low rate of interest paid there.' Now it would be the easiest thing in the world (as I saw even in to-day's newspaper) to have money advanced upon this—only there is a risk of its being known perhaps, which neither of us would at all like.) *Burn this.*

R. B. to E. B. B.

Friday Morning.
[Post-mark, August 7, 1846.]

(First of all, let me tell you that the whole story about that death through grief, madness &c, turns out to be a vile fabrication,—false from beginning to end. My mother's informant, I now find, had derived the knowledge from newspaper also—I hope the *other* tale, of the Turk, is true at least.)

And now, love, I can go on to say that no letter comes—is it the post's fault? Yes—I think,—so does your goodness spoil me—you have to tell me about to-morrow, beside. I shall wait hopefully till 2 or 3 o'clock.

Mr. Kenyon was there last evening, for all my prognostications—he had already twice passed this place in the course of the day on his way to Lewisham. He soon asked me as I expected—or something that sounded like it—for, in the half whisper of his tone, I can only hope he did not put the question thus 'Have you seen Miss Barrett *since Saturday*,—or have you called to-day?' My mind misgives a little—at all events I only answered the last part of the sentence—and now, mark you!—after dinner he proposed that I should go to him on Wednesday, and make one of a party he is organising. I tried some faint excuse or other—'You know,' interposed he, 'you can pay a visit to Wimpole Street and I shall know and keep away from troubling you'—or words to that effect. I thought it really better to simply (in every sense of the word) smile, and attempt to say nothing. Now, I feel sure that if I were to remark, 'I will call on Mrs. Jameson'—for instance—he would say, 'So will I, then, if I can'—on that day, rather than any other—unless some special business had been mentioned as the object of my visit. And here is another inconvenience he will perhaps consider 'As he means to call on Wednesday,—there is no reason I should keep away to-morrow—Saturday—'

It will be, however, a justification in his eyes at the end—'he knew her so well, saw so much of her,—who could wonder?'

I sate by a pleasant chatting Jewess, Goldsmid, or whatever the name is,—also by Thackeray—and Milnes came in the evening,—yet the dulness was mortal, and I am far from my ordinary self to-day. I am convinced that general society depresses my spirits more than any other cause. I could keep by myself for a month till I recovered my mind's health. But you are part or all of that self now,—and would be, were you only present in memory, in fancy. As it is, oh, to be with you, Ba?

Three o'clock, no letter! I will put my own philosophy in practice and be consoled that you are not in any circumstances to justify and require anxiety—not unwell—

nor have any fresh obstacles arisen *necessarily* . . Any alleviations so long as I am allowed to keep a good substantial misfortune at the end!

Once you said in your very own way . . when I sent you some roses in a box, and no letter with them, 'Now I shall write no more to-day, not having been written to!' I cannot write more—I see! Ah, Ba, here the letter comes!! and I will wait from reading it to kiss my gratitude to you, you utterly best and dearest! And I repeat my kisses while I write the few words there is time for—what a giver you are of all good things all together. Let me take the best first, not minding ingratitude to the rest, and say *yes*, to-morrow I will see you—even if Mr. Kenyon comes, it will be easy saying—'I cannot go on Wednesday.' Did you manage so well with Mrs. Jameson? As for Horne,—why, there may have been Sordelloisms, I daresay—I only meant, 'if you look an invalid to him,—he will say so, just when your improved health is my one excuse for the journey and its fatigues—and if you look plainly no longer an invalid'—Oh, I don't know . . I thought he might talk of that too, and bring in a host! There is the secret, rendered more obscurely perhaps! As for the room, the dearest four walls that I ever have been enclosed by—I only thought of the possible phrase—'Still confined to her room'—or the like—and as—that is the fact,—I rather understood the whole tone in which you spoke of the circumstance, as of slight dissatisfaction at the notion of the intended visit . . *in tuam sententiam discedens*, I sordelloized!

The words about your health reassure me, beloved! I had no positive fears *quite* as you suppose . . but I coupled one circumstance with another, do you see, and *did* get to apprehend what you now show me to be groundless, thank God!

Oh, my time! Bless you, ever, ever, beloved!

Your own R.

R. B. to E. B. B.

Sunday.
[Post-mark, August 10, 1846.]

Just now I tore the few words I had begun of the letter to you, Ba—they all went away, strangely afar from the meaning begun in them, through my mind taking up the thought that you were 'waiting' for what I should write—'waiting all day'—and ready to call the poor joyful service of love, 'goodness' in me! When such thoughts arise, I am not fit to pay even that imperfect service—I have only arms to receive you, kisses to give you—the words seem too cold, indeed! I sincerely believe this I am to write now, will be the shorter because of the intervention of you,—and that, like Flush, I shall behave best when not looked at too much!

Then, in our life,—what I do earnestly in intention and from love of you, *that* you will always accept and make the best of! How happy you make me, *now* and *ever*—in the present happiness, in the assurance of the future's even greater happiness, I am obliged to believe! It seemed like a dream as I walked home last night and thought of all over again, after a few hours' talk with my old friends on subjects from which you were excluded, and of a kind that brought my former feelings back again; so as to be understood, at least, and recognised as mine. 'All which is changed now,' I thought going home in the moonlight. Chorley was apprised of my being there and came good-naturedly—and we discussed delinquencies political and literary: he says, times were never so bad as now—people come without a notion of offending a critic, and offer him money—'will you do this for so much'—praise this or blame this! He was in a bad humour, he said; at least teazed and tired—and really looked both, so that I asked 'had you not better throw away a day on our green dulness at Hatcham, strolling through it with me?'—'Yes

—this day next week, if you like'—he answered at once . . so that our Saturday will be gone . . so that our Tuesday *must* be secured, my own Ba, and after it the Friday, at an equal interval of time—do you let it be so? Saturday would seem to be his only available day, poor Chorley—he walked through the park with me and over the Bridge, at one in the morning—in return for my proving, (I don't quite think *that*, however!)—proving, to *Arnould's* great satisfaction at least, that Mr. Horne *was a poet*, and moreover a dramatic one,—Chorley sees no good in him beyond talent with an abundance of 'crotchets,' and 'could not read "Orion" for his life.' I proved another thing too—that Foster was not a whit behind his brethren of the faculty, in literary morals—that the *Examiner*, named, was quite as just and good as another paper, unnamed. Whereat Chorley grew warm and lost his guard, and at last; declaring I forced him into corners and that speak he *must; instanced the 'Examiner's' treatment of myself as not generous* . . 'Luria' having been noticed as you remember a week after the publication, and *yet*, or never, to be reviewed in the Unnamed:—*Ces Misères!*

A fortnight ago when Rachel played in 'Andromaque' 'for the last time'—Sarianna and I agreed that if she did ever play again in it, we would go and see . . and lo, contrary to all expectation she *does* repeat Hermione to-morrow night, and we are to go. And you, Ba, you cannot go—ought I to go? One day, one not distant day, and 'cannot' will apply to us both—*now*, it seems to do me good, with the crowd of its suggestions, this seeing Rachel; beside, Sarianna has just this only opportunity of going.

I am anxious to let the folly of that person spend itself unaggravated by any notice of mine—I mean *to you;* any notice which should make you think it—(the folly)—affected *me* as well as you; but I do trust you will not carry toleration too far in this case, nor furnish an ungenerous, selfish man with weapons for your own annoyance. '*Insolent* letters' you ought to put up with from *no one*—and as there is no need of concealment of my position now, I think you will see a point when I may interfere. Always rely on my being *quietly* firm, and never violent nor exasperating: you alluded to some things which I cannot let my fancy stop upon. Remember you are mine, now,—my own, my very own. I know very well what a wretched drunkenness there is in that sort of self-indulgence—what it permits itself to do, all on the strength of its 'strong feeling' 'earnestness'—stupid in execrable sophistry as it is! I have too a strong belief that the man who would *bully* you, would drop into a fit at the sight of a man's uplifted little finger. Can this person be the 'old friend in an ill humour' who followed me up-stairs one day? I *trust* to you—that is the end of all.

Now I will kiss you, my own Ba, and wait for my letter, and then, Tuesday. Dearest, I am your own, your very own.

E. B. B. to R. B.

Sunday.
[Post-mark, August 10, 1846.]

Ever dearest, I shall write to you a little this morning and try to manage to post myself what shall be written, too early to permit the possibility (almost) of your being without a letter to-morrow. Dearest, how you were with me yesterday, after you went away!—I thought, thought, thought of you,—and the books I took up one by one . . (I tried a romance too 'Les Femmes' by a writer called Desnoyers . . quite new, and weak and foolish enough as a story, but full of clever things about shoe tyes . . philosophy in small:) the books were all so many *lorgnons* through which I looked at you again and again. Did you ever hear a story of the late Lord Grey, that he was haunted by a head, a head without a body? If he turned to the right or left there it was—if he looked up in the air, there it hung . . or down to the floor, there it lay—or walked up or down stairs, there it bounded before him—

flop . . flop . . just on its chin, 'Alas, poor ghost?' And just such another, as far as the haunting goes, were you to me, dearest, yesterday—only that *you* were of the celestial rather than ghastly apparitionery, and bore plainly with you airs from Heaven full against my forehead. How did I ever deserve you—how ever? Never indeed! And how can it seem right to submit to so much happiness undeservedly as the knowledge of your affection gives, you who are 'great in everything,' as Mr. Kenyon said the other day! Shall I tell you how I reconcile myself to the good? Thus it is. First I think that no woman in the world, let her be ever so much better than I, could quite be said to deserve you—and that therefore there may not be such harm in your taking the one who will owe you most with the fullest consciousness! If it may not be merit, it shall be gratitude—*that* is how I look at it when I would keep myself from falling back into the old fears. Ah! you may prevent my rising up to receive you . . though I did not know that I did . . it was a pure instinct!—but you cannot prevent my sinking down to the feet of your spirit when I think of the love it has given me from the beginning and *not* taken away. Dearest, dearest—I am content to owe all to you—it is not too much humiliation!

While I was writing, came Mr. Kenyon . . the spectacles mended, and looking whole catechisms from behind them. The first word was, 'Have you seen Browning lately?' I, taken by surprise, answered *en niaise*, 'Yes, yesterday.' 'And did he tell you that he was coming on Wednesday, next Wednesday?' 'He said something of it.'

A simpleton would have done better—to call me one were too much honour!—yet it seemed impossible to be adroit under the fire of the full face, spectacles included. The words came without the will. And now, what had we better do? Take Tuesday, that you may be able to say on Wednesday, 'I was not there to-day' . . ? or be frank for the hour and let it all pass? Think for us, Robert—I am quite frightened at what I have done. It seemed to me too, afterwards, that Mr. Kenyon looked grave. Still he talked of Miss Mitford and Mr. Buckingham, and Landor, and of going to the Lakes himself for a few days, and laughed and jested in great good humour, the subject being turned—he asked me too if I had ever discussed your poetry with Miss Mitford, on which I said that she did not much believe in you—'Not even in "Saul"?' said he. I don't know what to think. I am in a fog off the Nore. And he proposed coming to-morrow with a carriage, to drive me up the Harrow road to see the train coming in, and then to take me to his house, and, so, home,—all in his infinite kindness. He comes at half-past three—let me have your thoughts with me then—and the letter, farther on. Two letters, I am to have to-morrow. If Sunday is the worst day, Monday is the best,—of those I mean of course, on which I do not see you. May God bless you, my own beloved. I love you in the deepest of my heart; which seems ever to grow deeper. I live only for you; and feel that it is worth while.

Your Ba.

R. B. to E. B. B.

Monday Morning.
[Post-mark, August 10, 1846.]

You dearest Ba, do you write thus to put all thoughts of fear out of my head, and make me confident nothing can go ill with us if you feel so for me? I seem to have a presentiment that this afternoon, before this letter reaches you, Mr. Kenyon will have spoken—and if the whole world spoke its loudest, your words would be all I should hear. Or are they trials, every such word, of my vanity and weakness,—do you think, 'if anything can call them up, this will?' No, I very well know your entire truth in this and the other assurances I make my life bright with,—through any darkness that can come. What you choose to assert of yourself, *I* feel of myself every hour. But there must be this disproportionateness in a beloved object—before I knew you, women seemed not so much better than myself,—therefore, no love for them! There is no love but from beneath, far beneath,—that is the law of its nature—and now, no more of words—will there indeed be need of no more,—as I dare hope and believe, will the deeds suffice?—not in their own value, no!—but in their plain, certain intention,—as a clear advance beyond mere words? We shall soon know—if you live, you will be mine, I must think—you have put these dear arms too surely round my neck to be disengaged now. I cannot presume to suggest thoughts to you, resolutions for the future—you must impart to me always,—but I do lift up my heart in an aspiration to lead the life that seems accorded by your side, under your eyes.—I cannot write on this, dear Ba,—to say, I will live and work as I ought, seems too presumptuous. Understand all, and help me with your dearest hand, my own love!

As I say, I fancy Mr. Kenyon will speak—I only hope, the caution will act both ways, and that he will see as much inexpediency in altogether opposing as in encouraging such a step. That you should pass another winter and the risk of it—and perhaps many—*that* seems the *worst* fate. Can he apprehend any worse evil than that?

I observe in the *Times* to-day that the Peninsular & Oriental Steam Company have advertised a ship from Southampton to Genoa, Leghorn, Civita Vecchia and Naples on the 30th September, and that 'thenceforth the company will despatch a first-class steamer to those ports on the 15th of every month.' One more facility, should circumstances require it. Are you sure that the France journey with the delays and fatigue is preferable to this—where if the expenses are greater, yet the *uncertain* expenses are impossible? You are to think, beloved.

Now, will you write to-night? I may come to-morrow? Say one word—you have heard why I wanted to come, even if Mr. Kenyon's questions had not been put—otherwise, Friday will be impossible—I can say, 'I called on Saturday, and think of doing so next Friday—' I must see you to-morrow indeed, love!

Let me leave off here—I love you wholly, and bless you ever as now—Your own R.

E. B. B. to R. B.

Monday Morning.
[Post-mark, August 11, 1846.]

Then let it be Tuesday. It will correct, too, my stupidity to Mr. Kenyon, for easily you may reply to his certain question, that you had not been here on Wednesday but meant to go on Friday instead. Ah well! By the time all this is over we shall be fit to take a degree in some Jesuits' college—we shall have mastered all the points of casuistry. To wash one's hands of it, and then throw away the water, will be something gained at least.

Dearest, no, indeed!—there is nothing for your goodness to do in that badness I told you of, and which you describe so precisely in your word, 'drunkenness' of mind. It is precisely *that*, and no more nor less—a throwing off of moral restraint . . a miserable degradation. One may get angry, frightened, disgusted—but, after all, compassion comes in:—and who would think of fighting a delirious man with a sword? It would be a cruelty, like murder. There is a fine nature too, under these ruins of the will; and a sensibility which strikes inwards and outwards—(no one else should have any sensibility, within a thousand miles.) Think of a sort of dumb Rousseau,—with the 'Confessions' *in* him, pining evermore to get out! A miserable man, first by constitution and next by fortune—seeing only the shadow, for the sun,—the nettles in the field,—and breathing hard when he stands among garden-roses, to attain to smelling the onions over the wall. I have told him sometimes that he had a talent for anger!—'indignatio facit orationes:' and *that* is his pleasure, 'par excellence,'—to be let talk against this abuse or that abuse, this class of men or that class of men, this or that world's misery or offence:—he will rise up in it and be eloquent and happy. Otherwise . . mécréants we must be, he thinks, who dare to be happy in this vale of tears. Life is a long moan to him. And is not such a man enough punished? For me, I have not had the heart to take quite the position I ought to have done, looking only to his most outrageous bearing towards myself—although he talks of my scorn and sarcasms, as if I had shown myself quite equal to self-defence. An old, old friend, too!—known as a friend these twelve or thirteen years! And then, men are nearly all the same in the point of *wanting generosity to women*. It is a sin of sex, be sure—and we have our counter-sins and should be merciful. So I have been furiously angry, and then relented—by turns; as I could. Oh yes—it was he who followed you upstairs. There was an explosion that day among the many—and I had to tell him as a consequence, that if he chose to make himself the fable and jest of the whole house, he was the master, but that I should insist upon his not involving my name in the discussion of his violences. Wilson said he was white with passion as he followed you, and that she in fear trembled so she could scarcely open the door. He was a little ashamed afterwards, and apologized in a manner for what sufficiently required an apology. Before a servant too!—But that is long ago—and at that time he knew nothing for a certainty. Is it possible to be continuously angry with any one who proves himself so *much the weaker?* The slave of himself . . of his own passions—is too unhappy for the rod of another—man or woman.

Mr. Chorley—Mr. Chorley!—how could he utter such words! Men seem imbecile sometimes—understandings have they, and understand not.

Monday Night.

Dearest, I have your last letter. Thank you out of my heart—though you are not a prophet, dear dearest—not about Mr. Kenyon at least. See how far you are from the truth-well, with that divining hazel which you wave to and fro before my eyes. Mr. Kenyon, instead of too much remembering us, has forgotten me to-day. I waited an hour with my bonnet on, and he did not come. And then came a note! He had had business—he had forgotten me—he would come to-morrow. Which I, thinking of you, wrote back a word against, and begged him to come rather on Thursday or Saturday, or Monday. Is *that* right, dearest? Your coming to-morrow will be very right.

But when you say that there can be no love except '*from beneath*' . . is it right? is it comforting to hear of? No, no—indeed! How unhappy I should be if I accepted your theory! So I accept rather your love, beloved . .

Trusting to be yours.

R. B. to E. B. B.

Wednesday Morning.
[Post-mark, August 12, 1846.]

I have been putting all the letters into rings—twenty together—and they look now as they should—'infinite treasure in a little room'—note, that they were so united and so ranged from the beginning, at least since I began to count by twenties—but the white tape I used (no red tape, thank you!) was vile in its operation,—the untying and retying (so as to preserve a proper *cross* ) hard for clumsy fingers like mine:—these rings are perfect. How strange it will be to have no more letters! Of all the foolishnesses that ever were uttered that speech of mine,—about your letters strewing the house,—was the most thoroughly perfect! yet you have nothing to forgive in me, you say!

Just now I took up a periodical and read a few lines of a paper on the charm that there is in a contrariety of tempers and tastes, for friends and lovers—and there followed platitudes in a string—the clever like the stupid, the grave choose the likely, and so forth. Now, unless, the state of the liker and chooser is really considered by him as a misfortune,—what he would get rid of if he could in himself, so shall hardly desire to find in another—except in this not very probable case, is there not implied by every such choice, an absolute despair of any higher one? The grave man says (or would if he knew himself)—'except on my particular grounds such a serious humour would be impossible and absurd . . and where can I find another to appreciate them? Better accept the lower state of ignorance that they exist even, and consequent gaiety,—than a preposterous melancholy arising from no adequate cause.' And what man of genius would not associate with people of no talent at all, rather than the possessors of *mere* talent, who keep sufficiently near him, as they walk together, to give him annoyance at every step? Better go with Flush on his four legs, avowedly doglike, than with a monkey who will shuffle along on two for I don't know how many yards. Now for instance, is the writer of that wise notice of Landor in last week's *Athenæum*, one whit nearer your sympathy *in that precise matter*, than somebody who never heard of Landor or supposed him to have usually written under the signature of L. E. L.? With the exception of a word or two about the silly abuse of Plato, and on the occasional unfairness of statement, is there one word right and seasonable?

Here am I letting the words scratch themselves one after another while my thought as usual goes quite another way. Perhaps my wits are resting because of the great alacrity they are to display at Mr. Kenyon's this evening . . I shall take care not to be first comer, nor last goer.

Dearest, you are wrong in your fancy about my little caring whether he knows or does not. I see altogether with your eyes . . indeed, now that you engage to remove any suspicion of unkindness or mistrust which might attach to me in his thoughts (all I ever apprehended for *myself*), there is no need to consider him—at all. He can do no good nor harm. Did you ever receive such a letter? The dull morning shall excuse it—anything but the dull heart —for you fill it, however the *heat* may keep within, sometimes.

Bless you, Ba, my dearest, perfect love—now I will begin thinking of you again—let me kiss you, my own!

E. B. B. to R. B.

Wednesday Morning.
[Post-mark, August 12, 1846.]

Shall you pass through this street to Mr. Kenyon's, this evening? I have been sitting here these five minutes, wondering. But no answer is possible now, and if I go to the window of the other room and look up and look down about half-past five or a little later, it will be in vain perhaps. Just now I have heard from Mr. Kenyon, who cannot come to-day to drive with me though he may come to talk. He does not leave London, he says, so soon as he thought!—more's the pity. Ah! What unkind things one learns to write and meditate in this world, even of the dear Mr. Kenyons in it!— I am ashamed. Instruct your guardian angel to cover me with the shadow of his wings, —dearest.

Now I will tell you a curious thing which *Treppy* said to Arabel yesterday while you and I were together. Arabel was walking with her, and she was in one of her ill humours, poor Treppy, sighing and moaning over the wickedness of the people in Wimpole Street—she 'should go and live at Ramsgate, she thought, as nobody paid her the right attention!' *That's* the intermittent groan, when she is out of humour, poor Treppy. 'And besides' said she, 'it is much better that I should not go to Wimpole Street at this time when there are so many secrets. Secrets indeed! You think that nobody can see and hear except yourselves, I suppose; and there are two circumstances going on in the house, plain for any eyes to see! and those are considered *secrets*, I suppose.' 'Oh, Treppy'—interpolated Arabel . . 'you are always fancying secrets where there are none.' 'Well, I don't fancy anything now! I *know*—just as *you* do.'—Something was said too about 'Ba's going to Italy.' 'And, Treppy, do you think that she *will* go to Italy?' 'Why there is only one way for her to go—but she may go that way. If she marries, she may go.' 'And you would not be surprised?' '*I!* not in the least—*I* am never surprised, because I always see things from the beginning. Nobody can hide anything from *me*.' After which fashion she smoothed the darkness till it smiled, and boasted herself back into a calmer mood. But just observe how people are talking and inferring! It frightens me to think of it. Not that there is any danger from Treppy. She would as soon cut off her hand, as bring one of us into a difficulty, and *me*, the last. Only it would not do to *tell her*,—she must have it in her power to say 'I did not know this' . . for reasons of the strongest. To occasion a schism between her and this house, would be to embitter the remainder of her days.

Here is a letter from a lady in a remote district called Swineshead, who sends me lyrical specimens, and desires to know if *this be Genius*. She does not desire to publish; at any rate not for an indefinite number of years; but for her private and personal satisfaction, she would be glad to be informed whether she is a Sappho or George Sand or anything of that kind. What in the world is to be answered, now, to an application of *that* kind! To meddle with a person's opinion of himself or herself (quite a private opinion) seems like meddling with his way of dressing, with her fashion of putting in pins—like saying you *shall* put your feet on a stool, or you *shan't* eat pork. It is an interference with private rights, from which I really do shrink. Unfortunately too it is impossible to say what she wants to hear—I am in despair about it. When we are at Pisa we shall not hear these black stones crying after us any more perhaps. I shall listen, instead, to my talking bird and singing tree, and repose from the rest. How did you get home? And tell me of Mr. Kenyon's dinner! So nervous I am about Mr. Kenyon, when you or I happen to be *en rapport* with him.

Not only I loved you yesterday, but even to-day I love you; which is remarkable. To-morrow and to-morrow and to-morrow, what will *you* do? Is *that* an 'offence?' Nay, but it is rather reasonable that when the hour strikes, the fairy-gold should turn back into leaves, and poor Cinderella find herself sitting in her old place among the ashes, just as she had touched the hand of the king's son.

Don't think I mean anything by *that*, ever dearest—not so much as to teaze you—Robert!

I only love you to-day—that is, I love you and do nothing more. And the Fairy Tales are on the whole, I feel, the most available literature for illustration, whenever I think of loving you.

Your own Ba.

E. B. B. to R. B.

Wednesday Evening.
[Post-mark, August 13, 1846.]

Did I ever receive such a letter?' Never—except from *you*. It is a question easily answered.

As to [the] other question, about the communion of contrarieties, I agree with you, thought for thought, in all your thinking about it—only adding one more reason to the reasons you point out. There is another reason at the bottom of all, *I* think—I cannot but think—and it is just that, when women are chosen for wives, they are not chosen for companions—that when they are selected to be loved, it is quite apart from life—'man's love is of man's life a thing apart.' A German professor selects a woman who can merely stew prunes—not because stewing prunes and reading Proclus make a delightful harmony, but because he wants his prunes stewed for him and chooses to read Proclus by himself. A fulness of sympathy, a sharing of life, one with another, . . is scarcely ever looked for except in a narrow conventional sense. Men like to come home and find a blazing fire and a smiling face and an hour of relaxation. Their serious thoughts, and earnest aims in life, they like to keep on one side. And this is the carrying out of love and marriage almost everywhere in the world—and this, the degrading of women by both.

For friendship . . why Like seeks Like in friendship very openly. To 'have sympathy' with a person, is a good banal current motive for friendship. Yet (for the minor points) a man with a deficiency of animal spirits may like the society of a man who can amuse him, and the amusing man may have pleasure again in the sense of using a faculty and conferring a benefit. It is happily possible to *love down*, and even across a chasm—or the world would be more loveless than it is. I have loved and still love people a thousand souls off—as you have and do, of course;—but to love them *better* on that account, would be strange and difficult.

Always I know, my beloved, that I am unworthy of your love in a hundred ways—yet I do hold fast my sense of advantage in one,—that, as far as I can see, I see after you . . understand you, divine you . . call you by your right name. Then it is something to be able to look at life itself as you look at it—(I quite *sigh* sometimes with satisfaction at that thought!): there will be neither hope nor regret away from your footsteps. Dearest—I feel to myself sometimes, 'Do not move, do not speak—or the dream will vanish.' So fearfully like a dream, it is! Like a reflection in the water of an actual old, old dream of my own, too . . touching which, . . now silent voices used to say "That romantic child."

What did *you* mean to say about my not believing in your nature . . in your feelings . . what did you and could you mean yesterday? Was it because of my speech about the 'calm eyes'? Ah—*you!*—I did not think to make so impressive a speech when I made it . . for this is not the first time, Robert, you have quoted Hansard for it. Well! I shall not rise to explain after all. Only I do justice to the whole subject . . *eyes* inclusively . . 'whatever you may think' as you said yesterday with ever such significance.

No—yes—now I will ask you one thing. Common eyes will carry an emotion of a soul—and, so, not be calm, of course. Calm ones, I know, will carry the whole soul and float it up against yours, till it loses footing, and . . . . . *That* is a little of what I meant by the calm in the eyes, and so I will ask you whether I could wrong, by such meaning, any depth in the nature.

At this moment you are at Mr. Kenyon's—and you did not, I think, go up this street. Perhaps you will go home through it—but I shall not see—I cannot watch, being afraid of the over-watchers. May God bless you, my own dearest! You have my heart with you as if it lay in your hand! I told you once that I never could love (in *this* way of love) except *upward* very far and high—but you are not like me in it, I thank God—since you can love *me*. Love me, dearest of all—do not tire. I am your very own

Ba.

Another Bennett! !—yet the same.! *To Friday.*

R. B. to E. B. B.

Thursday.
[Post-mark, August 13, 1846.]

Dearest Ba, I love you wholly and for ever! How shall the charm ever break?

My two letters! I think we must institute solemn days whereon such letters are to be read years hence . . when I shall ask you,—(all being known, many weaknesses you do not choose to see now, and perhaps some strength and constancy you cannot be sure of—for the charm may break, you think) . . 'If you stood *there*' . . at Wimpole Street in the room . . would you whisper 'Love, I love you, as before?' Oh, how fortunately, fortunately the next verse comes with its sweetest reassurance!

When I have chosen to consider the circumstances of the altered life I am about to lead with you . . ('chosen,' because you have often suggested drawbacks, harms to my interest &c. which I have really been forced to take up and try to think over seriously, lest I should be unawares found treating what had undoubtedly come from you with disrespect), I never, after all the considering in my power, was yet able to *fancy* even the possibility of their existence. I will not revert to them now—nor to the few *real* inconveniences which I *did* apprehend at the beginning, but which never occurred to *you:* at present I take you, and with you as much happiness as I seem fit to bear in this world,—the one shadow being the fear of its continuance. Or if there is one thing I shall regret . . it is just that which I should as truly lose if I married any Miss Campbell of them all—rather, *then* should *really* lose, what now is only modified,—transferred partly and the rest retainable. There was always a great delight to me in this prolonged relation of childhood almost . . nay altogether—with all here. My father and I have not one taste in common, one artistic taste . . in pictures, he goes, 'souls away,' to Brauwer,

Ostade, Teniers . . he would turn from the Sistine Altar piece to these—in music he desiderates a tune 'that has a story connected with it,' whether Charles II.'s favourite dance of 'Brose and butter' or—no matter,—what I mean is, that the sympathy has not been an intellectual one. I hope if you want to please me especially, Ba, you will always remember I have been accustomed, by pure choice, to have another will lead mine in the little daily matters of life. If there are two walks to take (to put the thing at simplest) you must say, '*This* one' and not 'either' . . because though they were before indifferently to be chosen —after *that* speech, one is altogether better than the other, to *me* if not to you. When you have a real preference which I can discern, you will be good enough to say nothing about it, my own Ba! Now, do you not see how, with this feeling, which God knows I profess to be mine without the least affectation,—how much my happiness would be disturbed by allying myself with a woman to whose intellect, as well as goodness, I could *not* look up?—in an obedience to whose desires, therefore, I should not be justified in indulging? It is pleasanter to lie back on the cushions inside the carriage and let another drive—but if you suspect he cannot drive?

Nothing new at Mr. Kenyon's yesterday—I arrived late to a small party—Thackeray and Procter—pleasant as usual. I took an opportunity of mentioning that I had come straight from home. Did you really look from the window, dearest? I was carried the other way, by the new road, but I thought of you till you may have felt it!

And indeed you are 'out' again as to my notions of your notions, you dearest Ba! I know well enough that by 'calmness' you did not mean absence of passion—I spoke only of the foolish popular notion.

To-morrow there would seem to be no impediment whatever—and I trust to be with you, beloved—but before, I can kiss you as now,—loving you as ever—ever—

Your own.

E. B. B. to R. B.

Saturday Morning.
[August 15, 1846.]

A bright beautiful day this is, on which you do not come—it seems as if you ought to have come on it by rights. Dearest, you did not meet Mr. Kenyon yesterday after you left me? I fancied that you might, and so be detected in the three hours, to the fullest length of them—it seemed possible. Now I look forward to the driving instead of to you—and he has just sent to desire me to be ready at a quarter to three, and not later, as was fixed in your hearing. And why, pray, should you be glad that I am going on this excursion? I *should* have liked it, if we had been living in the daylight; but with all these 'shadows, clouds and darkness,' it is pleasanter to me to sit still and see nobody—and least, Mr. Kenyon. Oh, that somebody would spirit him away gently, very gently, so as to do him no manner of harm in achieving the good for me!—for both you and me. Did you say 'Do you pity me' to *me?* I did not tell you yesterday that I have another new fear . . an American lady who in her time has reviewed both you and me, it seems, comes to see me . . is about to come to see me . . armed with a letter of introduction from Mr. Mathews—and in a week, I may expect her perhaps. She is directed, too, towards Mr. Horne. Observe the double chain thrown across the road at my feet—I am entreated to show her attention and introduce her to my friends . . things out of the question as I am situated. Yet I have not boldness to say 'I will not see you.' I almost *must* see her, I do fear. Mr. Mathews ought to have felt his way a little, before throwing such a weight on me. He is delighted with your 'Bells and Pomegranates' (to pass from his frailties to his merits) and the review of them is sent to me, he says—only that I do not receive it.

Dearest, when I told you yesterday, after speaking of the many coloured theologies of the house, that it was hard to answer for what *I* was, . . I meant that I felt unwilling, for my own part, to put on any of the liveries of the sects. The truth, as God sees it, must be something so different from these opinions about truth—these systems which fit different classes of men like their coats, and wear brown at the elbows always! I believe in what is divine and floats at highest, in all these different theologies—and because the really Divine draws together souls, and tends so to a unity, I could pray anywhere and with all sorts of worshippers, from the Sistine Chapel to Mr. Fox's, those kneeling and those standing. Wherever you go, in all religious societies, there is a little to revolt, and a good deal to bear with—but it is not otherwise in the world without; and, *within*, you are especially reminded that God has to be more patient than yourself after all. Still you go quickest there, where your sympathies are least ruffled and disturbed—and I like, beyond comparison best, the simplicity of the dissenters . . the unwritten prayer, . . the sacraments administered quietly and without charlatanism! and the principle of a church, as they hold it, *I* hold it too, . . quite apart from state-necessities . . pure from the law. Well—there is enough to dissent from among the dissenters—the Formula is rampant among them as among others—you hear things like the buzzing of flies in proof of a corruption—and see every now and then something divine set up like a post for men of irritable minds and passions to rub themselves against, calling it a holy deed—you feel moreover bigotry and ignorance pressing on you on all sides, till you gasp for breath like one strangled. But better this, even, than what is elsewhere—*this* being elsewhere too in different degrees, besides the evil of the place. Public and social prayer is right and desirable—and I would prefer, as a matter of custom, to pray in one of those chapels, where the minister is simple-minded and not controversial—certainly would prefer it. Not exactly in the Socinian chapels, nor yet in Mr. Fox's—not by preference. The Unitarians seem to me to throw over what is most beautiful in the Christian Doctrine; but the Formulists, on the other side, stir up a dust, in which it appears excusable not to see. When the veil of the body falls, how we shall look into each other's faces, astonished, . . after one glance at God's!

Have I written to you more than too much about my doxy? I was a little, little, uncomfortable in the retrospect of yesterday, lest my quick answer should have struck you as either a levity or an evasion—and have you not a right to all my thoughts of all things? For the rest, we will be married just as you like . . *volo quod vis:* and you will see by this profession of faith that I am not likely much to care either way. There are some solemn and beautiful things in the Church of England Marriage-service, as I once heard it read, the only time I was present at such a ceremony—but I heard it then in the abbreviated customary form . . and not as the Puseyites (who always bring up the old lamps against a new) choose to read it, they say, in spite of custom. Archdeacon Hale with an inodorous old lamp, displeased some of the congregation from Fenton's Hotel, I hear. But we need not go to the Puseyites at least. And after all, perhaps the best will be what is easiest. Something is sure to happen—something must surely happen to put an end to it all . . . before I go to Greece!

May God bless you, ever dearest: Tell me if you get this letter to-day, Saturday.

Your very own Ba.

R. B. to E. B. B.

Saturday.
[Post-mark, August 15, 1846.]

My very, very dearest—many, if not all, of those things for which I want the words when too close to you, become quite clear at a little distance. How simple, for instance, it is to admit, that in our case,—my own, only Ba once discovered, the circumstances of the weakness and retirement were, on the whole, favourable rather than otherwise! Had they been unfavourable . . I do not think a few obstacles would have discouraged me . . but this way has been easier—better—and now all is admitted! *By themselves,* the circumstances could never obtain more than the feeling properly due to them—do you think one particle of love goes with the pity and service to a whole Hospital of Incurables? So let all the attraction of that kind pass for what it is worth, and for no more. If all had been different, and I had still perceived you and loved you, then there *might,* perhaps,—or probably—be as different an aim for me,—for my own peculiar delight in you . . I should want to feel and be sure of your love, in your happiness . . certainly in your entire happiness then as now —but I should aspire to find it able to support itself in a life altogether different from the life in which I had first seen you—if you loved me you would need to be happy in quiet and solitude and simplicity and privation . . then I should *know* you loved me, knowing *how* you had been happy before! But now, do you not see that my utmost pride and delight will be to think you are happy, as *you were not,*—in the way you were not: if you chose to come out of a whirl of balls and parties and excursions and visitings—to my side, I should love you as you sate still by me,—but now, when you stand up simply, much more walk . . I will consider, if you let me, every step you take that brings you pleasure,—every smile on your mouth, and light on your eyes—as a directest *obedience* to me . . all the obedience you *can* ever pay me . . you shall say in every such act 'this I do on purpose to content you!' I hope to know you have been happy . . that shall prove you loved me, at the end.

Probably you *will* not hear anything to-day from Mr. Kenyon, as your sister is to be present: do you really imagine that those eyes and spectacles are less effective than the perceptions of your 'Treppy?'

By the way, hear an odd coincidence—you heard that foolish story of Thackeray and Mr. 'Widdicombe' . . which I told just to avoid a dead silence and guilty blankness of face. As I was returning I met Thackeray (with Doyle—H.B.) and was energetically reminded of our dinner . . he is in very earnest, Mr. Kenyon may assure himself. Presently I reached Charing Cross—and stood waiting for my omnibus. There is always a crowd of waiters—in a moment there passes an extraordinary looking personage—a policeman on duty at this police-requiring spot saunters up to *me*, of all others, and says (on some miraculous impulse, no doubt)—with an overflowing impressible grin, 'D'ye know *him*, Sir?' 'No—who may he be?' 'He's Widdicombe!—He goes now to Astley's, and afterwards to Vauxhall—there's a good likeness of him in the painting of the Judge and Jury Club.' Here my omnibus arrives . . 'Thank you' I said—and there was an end of the communication. How for many thousand years may I walk the street before another inspired policeman addresses me without preface and tells me, *that* is the man I have just been talking of to somebody else? Let me chronicle Mr. W.'s glories . . his face is just Tom Moore's, *plus* two painted cheeks, a sham moustache, and hair curled in wiry long ringlets; Thackeray's friend was a friend indeed, 'warning every man and teaching every man'—the *tête-à-tête* would have been portentous.

Now, dearest, you cannot return me such delectabilities, so must even be content to tell me what happens to-day and what is said and done and surmised—and how you are . . three times over, how you are, dearest dearest! And I will write to-morrow, and kiss you meanwhile, as now as ever. Bless you, love—

your R.

E. B. B. to R. B.

Saturday Evening.
[Post-mark, August 17, 1846.]

How I thank for your letter, ever beloved. You were made perfectly to be loved—and surely I have loved you, in the idea of you, my whole life long. Did I tell you *that* before, so often as I have thought it? It is *that* which makes me take it all as visionary good—for when one's Ideal comes down to one, and walks beside one suddenly, what is it possible to do but to cry out . . 'a dream?' You are the best . . best. And if you loved me only and altogether for pity, (and I think that, more than *you* think, the sentiment operated upon your generous chivalrous nature), and if you confessed it to me and proved it, and I knew it absolutely—what then? As long as it was *love*, should I accept it less gladly, do you imagine, because of the root? Should I think it less a gift? should I be less grateful, . . or *more?* Ah—I have my 'theory of causation' about it all—but we need not dispute, and will not, on any such metaphysics. Your *loving* me is enough to satisfy me—and if you did it because I sate rather on a green chair than a yellow one, it would be enough still for me:—only it would not, for *you*—because your motives are as worthy always as your acts.—Dearest!

So let us talk of the great conference in Mr. Kenyon's carriage, in which joined himself, Arabel, Flush and I. First he said . . 'Did Browning stay much longer with you?' 'Yes—some time.' This was as we were going on our way toward some bridge, whence to look at the Birmingham train. As we came back, he said, with an epical leap *in medias res* . . 'What an extraordinary memory our friend Browning has.' 'Very extraordinary'—said I—'and how it is raining.' I give you Arabel's report of my reply, for I did not myself exactly remember the full happiness of it—and she assured me besides that he looked . . looked at me . . as a man may look . . And this was everything spoken of you throughout the excursion.

But he spoke of *me* and observed how well I was—on which Arabel said 'Yes—she considered me quite well; and that nothing was the matter now but *sham*.' Then the railroads were discussed in relation to me . . and she asked him—'Shouldn't she try them a little, before she undertakes this great journey to Italy?' 'Oh' . . he replied—'*she* is going on no great journey.' 'Yes, she will, perhaps—Ba is inclined to be a great deal too wild, and now that she is getting well, I do assure you, Mr. Kenyon.'

To sit upon thorns, would express rather a 'velvet cushion' than where I was sitting, while she talked this foolishness. I have been upbraiding her since, very seriously; and I can only hope that the words were taken for mere jest—*du bout des lèvres*.

Moreover Mr. Kenyon is *not* going away on Thursday—he has changed his plans: he has put off Cambridge till the 'spring'—he meets Miss Bayley nowhere—he holds his police-station in London. 'When *are* you going' I asked in my despair, trying to look satisfied. He did not know—'not directly, at any rate'—'I need not hope to get rid of him,' he said aside perhaps.

But we saw the great roaring, grinding Thing . . a great blind mole, it looked for blackness. We got out of the carriage to see closer—and Flush was so frightened at the roar of it, that he leapt upon the coach-box. Also it rained,—and I had ever so many raindrops on my gown and in my face even, . . which pleased me nearly as much as the railroad sight. It is something new for me to be rained upon, you know.

As for happiness—the words which you use so tenderly are in my heart already, making me happy, . . I am happy by you. Also I may say solemnly, that the greatest proof of love I could give you, is to be happy because of you—and even *you* cannot judge and see how great a proof *that* is. You have lifted my very soul up into the light of your soul, and I am not ever likely to mistake it for the common daylight. May God bless you, ever ever dearest!

I am your own—

R. B. to E. B. B.

Sunday.
[Post-mark, August 17, 1846.]

No, my own dearest, your letter does not arrive on Saturday, but this morning—what then? You will not be prevented from your usual ways of entire goodness to me by *that?* You will continue to write through the remainder of the writing-time? This one letter reaches me,—if another was sent, it stays back till to-morrow—so I *do* get a blessing by your endeavour, and am grateful as ever, my own Ba! After all, neither of us loses,—effectually loses —anything—for my letter always comes in its good time, —it is not cast hopelessly away—and do you suppose that *you* lose any of the gladness and thanks? Rather, you get them doubly—for all along, all through the suspense, I have been (invariably) sure of the deed, when promised, and of the unchanging love, when only expected . . so that when the letter finds me at last, the joy being unaccountably unabated do you not see that there is a *gain* somehow? I told you on Friday I loved you more at that instant than at any previous time—I will show you why, because I *can* show you, I think—though it seems at first an irrational word . . for always having loved you wholly, how can I, still *only* loving you wholly, speak of 'more' or 'less'?—This is why—I used to see you once a week, to sit with you for an hour and a half—to receive a letter, or two, or three, during the week—and I loved you, Ba, wholly, as I say, and reckoned time for no time in the intervals of seeing you and hearing from you. Now I see you twice in the week, and stay with you the three hours, and have letter on dear letter,—and the distance is, at least, the *same*, between the days, and between the letters—I will only affirm it is the *same*—so I must love you more—because if you were to bring me back to the old allowance of you,—the one short visit, the two or three letters,—I should be starved with what once feasted me! (If you do not understand Flush does!) Seriously, does not that go to prove, I love you more! Increased strength comes insensibly thus,—is only ascertained by such process of induction . . once you crossed the room to look out Shelley's age in a book, and were not tired—now you cross London to see the trains arrive, and (I trust) are not tired . . *So*—you are stronger.

Dearest, I know your very meaning, in what you said of religion, and responded to it with my whole soul—what you express now, is for us both . . those are my own feelings, my convictions beside—instinct confirmed by reason. Look at that injunction to 'love God with all the heart, and soul, and strength'—and then imagine yourself bidding any faculty, that arises towards the love of him, be still! If in a meeting house, with the blank white walls, and a simple doctrinal exposition,—all the senses should turn (from where they lie neglected) to all that sunshine in the Sistine with its music and painting, which would lift them at once to Heaven,—why should you not go forth?—to return just as quickly, when they are nourished into a luxuriance that extinguishes, what is called, Reason's pale wavering light, lamp or whatever it is—for I have got into a confusion with thinking of our convolvuluses that climb and tangle round the rose-trees—which might be lamps or tapers! See the levity! No—this sort of levity only exists because of the strong conviction, I do believe! There seems no longer need of earnestness in assertion, or proof . . so it runs lightly over, like foam on the top of a wave.

Chorley came and was very agreeable and communicative. You shall tell me more about Mr. Mathews and his review. And with respect to his lady-friend, you will see her, I think. But first tell me of Mr. Kenyon, and yourself—how you are, and what I am to do, when to see you.

Now goodbye, my own Ba—'goodbye.' Be prepared for all fantasticalness that may happen! Perhaps some day I shall shake hands with you, simply, and go . . just to remember the more exquisitely where I once was, and where you let me stay now, you dearest, dearest heart of my heart, soul of my soul! But the shaking-hands, at a very distant time! *Now*—let me kiss you, beloved—and so I do kiss you—

Ever your own.

E. B. B. to R. B.

Sunday Morning.
[Post-mark, August 17, 1846.]

Your sight of Widdicombe was highly dramatic—and the policeman 'intersit nodo' as well as any god of them all. What a personage Widdicombe must be! Think of the mental state of a man, who could gravely apply to his own face false moustachios and rouge before a looking-glass. There is something in it to wonder over, as over the megalosaurie and prodigions of ridicules. Mind—when I talked of rouge improving a complexion for the nonce, I was thinking of women; not of men, in whom that sort of colouring (even if it were natural) is detestable, or, to measure one's language, very ugly indeed. I have seen a man, of whom it was related that he *painted his lips*—so that at dinner, with every course, was removed a degree of bloom; the lips paled at the soup, grew paler at the mutton, became white at the fricandeau and ghastly at the pudding—till with the orange at dessert, his nearest neighbours drew back their chairs a little, expecting him to fall flat in a fainting-fit. But he was very rich, and could only talk charmingly out of those painted lips. There were women who 'couldn't conceive why people should call him a fool.' To every Bottom's head (not to wrong Bottom by such a comparison), there will be a special Titania—see if there will not!

So you go on Wednesday to this club-dinner, really. And you come to me also on Wednesday. Does *that* remain decided? I have had a letter from that poor Chiappino, to desire a 'last interview' . . which is promised to be 'pacific.' Oh—such stuff! Am I to hold a handkerchief to my eyes and sob a little? Your policeman is necessary to the full development of the drama, I think. And I forgot to tell you that there were *two* things in which I had shown great want of feeling—one, the venturing to enclose your verses—the other . . (now listen!) the other . . the having said that 'I was sincerely sorry for all his real troubles.' Which I do remember having said once, when I was out of patience—as how can any one be patient continually? and how was I especially to condole with him in lawn and weepers, on the dreadful fact of your existence in the world? Well—he has real troubles unfortunately, and he is going away to live in a village somewhere. Poor Chiappino! A little occupation would be the best thing that could happen for him; it would be better than prosperity without it. When a man spins evermore on his own axis, like a child's toy I saw the other day, . . what is the use of him but to make a noise? No greater tormentor is there, than self-love, . . even to self. And no greater instance of this, than *this!*

Dearest beloved, to turn away from the whole world to you . . *when* I do, do I lose anything . . or not rather gain all? Sometimes I feel to wish that I had more to sacrifice to you, so as to prove something of what is in me—but you do not require sacrifice . . it is enough, you say, that I should *be happy through you.* How like those words are to you!—how they are said in your own idiom! And for myself, I am contented to think that, . . if such things can really satisfy you, . . you would find with difficulty elsewhere in the world than here, a woman as perfectly empty of life and gladness, except what comes to her from your hands. Many would be happy through you:—but to be happy through only you, is my advantage . . my boast. In this, I shall be better than the others.

Why, if you were to drive me from you after a little, in what words could I reproach you, but just in these . . 'You might have left me to die *before*.' Still I should be your debtor, my beloved, as now I am

Your very own

Ba.

I told you that I was going to the chapel one Sunday —but I have not been yet. I had not courage. May God bless you!—

R. B. to E. B. B.

Monday Morning.
[Post-mark, August 17, 1846.]

I come home from Town for my letters . . the *two* I ventured to expect, and here they meet me. As I said, you *had* written, and I thanked you *then*, and *now*, too, just as if I had been despairing all along—and over and above, there are some especial thanks to pay,—for when I could not otherwise disengage myself from a dinner a little way out of town,—having unawares confessed to the day's being at my disposal, . . I said—'I expect letters at home which *must* be answered'—and here I am.

Or rather, here you are, dearest,—in, I do think, your dearest mood. I must shift my ground already, alter my moment of time, and avow that it is *now* I love you the best, the completest. Do you want to know how much kindness I can bear? If I ever am so happy as to speak so as to please you, it may be only your own kindness overflowing and running back to you—I feel every day, often in every day, the regret follow some thought of you, —that *this* thought, for instance, if I could secure and properly tell you *this* only, you would know my love for what it is,—and yet that *this* thought will pass unexpressed like the others! Well, I do not care—rightly considered, there is not so much to regret—the words *should* lead to acts, and be felt insufficient.

Now we collect then, from Mr. Kenyon's caution, or discretion, or pity, or ignorance, that he will not interpose, and that there will be one great effort, and acknowledgment *for all?* I should certainly like it *so* best. You seem stronger than to need the process of preparatory disclosures, now to one, now to another friend. It is clearly best as it is like to be . . for perhaps the chances are in our favour that the few weeks more will be uninterrupted.

My time is gone—and nothing said! For to-morrow, all rests with you . . if the note bids me go, I shall be in *absolute* readiness—otherwise on Wednesday . . just as you seem to discern the times and the seasons.

Bless you my own best, dearest Ba—your own R.

E. B. B. to R. B.

Monday.
[Post-mark, August 18, 1846.]

For these two dear letters, I thank you, dearest! You are best, as ever! And *that* is all I have to tell you, almost —for I have seen nobody, heard nothing . . except that *Eugene Sue can paint*, . . which Miss Mitford told me this morning in a note of hers, . . in which, besides, she complains of the fatigue she suffers from the visitors who go to see after her the Reading prison, as the next 'sight' of the neighbourhood. Better to live in Cheapside, than among the oaks, on such conditions! As to Mr. Kenyon, he does not approach me. So he may come to-morrow, perhaps, or even on Wednesday. Would it not appear the top of wisdom if you deferred our day to Thursday's sun! —now consider! It would be a decided gain, surely, to be able to say to him on Wednesday that you had not seen me since you and he saw me together. So I propose *Thursday* if you permit it. Next week we may take up our two days again, as one takes up so many dropt silken stitches, . . and we will be careful that the beads do not run off in the meantime. To-day George came from circuit. He asked, for nearly a first question, whether I had thought of Italy—'Yes, I had thought of it—but there was time to think more.' I am uneasy a little under George's eyes.

You did not tell me of Mr. Chorley . . whether he put questions about the Continent, or observed on the mysteries in you. Does he go himself, and when? A curious 'fact' is, that Mrs. Jameson was in the next house to us this morning, and also a few days ago; yet never came here—the reason certainly being a reluctance to seem to tread in upon the recalling confidence. I felt sorry, and obliged to her—both at once. Talking of confidences, I neglected to tell you when you were here last, that one more had escaped us. It was not by my choice, if by my fault. I wrote something in a note to Mr. Boyd some weeks ago, which nobody except himself would have paused to think over; but he, like a prisoner in a dungeon, sounds every stone of the walls round him, and discerns a hollowness, detects a wooden beam, . . patiently pricks out the mortar with a pin—all this, in his rayless, companionless Dark,—poor Mr. Boyd! The time before I last went to see him, he asked me if I were going to be a nun—there, was the first guess! On the next visit he puts his question precisely right—*I* tried to evade—then, promised to be frank in a little time—but being pressed on all sides, and drawn on by a solemn vow of secrecy, I allowed him to see the truth—and he lives such an isolated life, that it is perfectly safe with him, setting the oath aside. Also, he was very good and kind, and approved highly of the whole, and exhorted me, with ever such exhortation, to keep to my purpose, and to allow no consideration in the world or out of the world, to make any difference—quoting the moral philosophers as to the rights of such questions. Is there harm in his knowing? He knows nobody, talks to nobody, and is very faithful to his word. Just as *I*, you will retort, was foolish in mine! Yet I do assure you, mine was a sort of word, which to nine hundred and ninety nine persons, would have suggested nothing—only *he* mused over it, turned it into all lights, and had nothing to do but *that*. Afterwards he was proud, and asked . . 'Was I not acute?' It was a pleasure to him, one could not grudge.

Are you well, ever dearest? *I* am well. And yesterday, while they were at dinner, I walked out alone, or with Flush—twice to the corner of the street, turning it, to post your letter. May God bless you. Surely we feel alike in many, many things—the convolvuluses grow together; twisted together—and you lift me up from the ground; you! I am your very own—

Mr. Mathews said nothing more than I told you—very briefly—but he *sent* the review, he said—and it has not come.

R. B. to E. B. B.

Tuesday Morning.
[Post-mark, August 18, 1846.]

Let it be on Thursday then, dearest, for the reasons you mention. I will say nothing of my own desires to meet you sooner . . they are corrected by the other desires to spend my whole life with you. After all, these are the critical weeks now approaching or indeed present—there shall be no fault I can avoid. So, till Thursday—

Chorley said very little . . he is all discreetness and forbearance, here as on other points. He goes to Birmingham at the end of this week, and returning after some three or four days, leaves London for Paris—probably next Saturday week. From Paris he thinks of going to Holland . . a good step,—and of staying at Scheven . . ing . . what is the Bath's name?—not a good step, I told him, because of the mortal ugliness of the place—which I well remember . . it may have improved in ten years, to be sure. There, 'walking on the sands,' (sands in a heapy slope, not a traversable flat) he means to 'grow to an end' with his Tragedy . . there is a noble ardour in his working which one cannot help admiring—he has a few weeks' holiday, is jaded to death with writing, and yet will write away his brief time of respite and restoratives—for what? He wondered whether there was any chance of our meeting in Paris—'our' meaning him and myself.

As for your communication to Mr. Boyd—how could you do otherwise, my own Ba? I am altogether regardless of whatever danger there may be, in the great delight at his sympathy and approval of your intention: he probably never heard my name before . . but his own will ever be associated divinely in my memory with those verses which always have affected me profoundly . . perhaps on the whole, *more* profoundly than any others you ever wrote: *that* is hard to prove to myself,—but I really think so—the personal allusions in it went straight to my heart at the beginning. I remember, too, how he loved and loves you . . you told me, Ba: so I am most grateful to him,—as I ever shall feel to those who, knowing you, judge me worthy of being capable of knowing you and taking your impress, and becoming yours sufficiently for your happiness.

Are you so well, dearest, in your walks,—after your rides? Does that rejoice me or no, when I would rather hear you had been happy, than simply see you without such an assurance? I am very well, since you ask—but my mother is not—her head being again affected. Yet the late improvement gives ground for hope . . nor is this a very violent attack in itself.

I suppose it *was* in Mrs. Jameson's mind, as you apprehend—you must always be fond of her—(and such will be always my way of rewarding people *I* am fond of!)

God bless you, dearest—I love you all I can, Ba. I

see another ship is advertised to sail—(a steamer) for Naples, and other southern ports—but no higher. When you are well and disposed to go to Greece, take me, my love. I should feel too happy for this world, I think, among the islands with you.

My very own, I am yours—

E. B. B. to R. B.

Tuesday Evening.
[Post-mark, August 19, 1846.]

Your mother is not well, dearest? *that* is bad news indeed. And then, I think of your superstition of your being ill and well with her—take care and keep well, Robert, . . or of what use will it be that *I* should be well? Today we drove out, and were as far as Finchley, and I am none the worse at all for it. Do you know Finchley? It is pretty and rural; the ground rising and falling as if with the weight of verdure and dew! fields, and hedgerows, and long slopes of grass thick and long enough, in its fresh greenness, quite to hide the nostrils of the grazing cows. The fields are little, too, as if the hedges wanted to get together. Then the village of Finchley straggles along the road with a line of cottages, or small houses, seeming to *play* at a village. No butchers, no bakers—only one shop in the place—but gardens, and creepers round the windows. Such a way from London, it looked! Arabel wanted to call on a friend of hers, a daughter of Sir William Russell's, who married an adopted son of *Lamartine*, and was in the navy, and is now an Independent minister officiating in this selfsame metropolis of Finchley. A concatenation, *that* is, altogether. Very poor they are—living on something less than two hundred a year, with five children, and the eldest five years old. And the children came out to us, everybody else being away—so I, who would have stayed in the carriage under other circumstances, was tempted out by the children and the cottage, and they dragged us along to see the drawing room, and dining room, and 'Papa's flowers,' and their own particular book 'about the twenty-seven tailors'; and those of the children who could speak, thought Flush 'very cool' for walking upstairs without being asked. (The baby opened its immense eyes wider than ever, thinking unutterable things.) So as they had been so kind and hospitable to us, we could not do less (after a quantity of admiration upon the pretty house covered with roses, and the garden and lawn, and especially the literature of those twenty-seven tailors) we could not do less than offer to give them a drive . . which was accepted with acclamation. Think of our taking into the carriage, all five children, with their prodigious eyes and cheeks—the nurse on the coachbox, to take them home at the end of some quarter of a mile! At the moment of parting, Alphonse Lamartine thought seriously of making a great scream—but upon Arabel's perjuring herself by a promise to 'come again soon,' we got away without that catastrophe. A worse one is, that you may think yourself obliged to read this amusing history. To make amends, I send you what I gathered for you in the garden. 'Pansy!—that's for thoughts.'[1]

How wise we are about Thursday! or rather about Tuesday and Wednesday, perhaps.

As for Mr. Boyd, he had just heard your name, but he is blind and deaf to modern literature, and I am not anxious that he should know you much by your poetry. He asked some questions about you, and he enquired of Arabel particularly whether she thought we cared for each other enough. But to tell you the truth, his unqualified adhesion strikes me as less the result of his love for *you*, than of his anger towards another. I am sure he triumphs inwardly in the idea of a chain being broken which he has so often denounced in words that pained and vexed me—and then last year's affair about Italy made him furious. Oh—I could see plainly by the sort of smile he smiled—

[1] [The flower is enclosed with the letter.]

but we need not talk of it—I am at the end too of my time. How good you are to me not to upbraid me for imprudence and womanly talkativeness! You are too, too good. And you liked my verses to Mr. Boyd! Which *I* like to hear, of course. Dearest—

Shall we go to Greece then, Robert? *Let* us, if you like it! When we have used a little the charm of your Italy, and have been in England just to see that everybody is well, of yours and mine, . . (if you like *that!*) . . why straightway we can go 'among the islands'—(and *nearly* as pleasant, it will be for me, as if I went there alone, having left you!). I should like to see Athens with my living eyes . . Athens was in all the dreams I dreamed, before I knew you. Why should we not see Athens, and Egypt too, and float down the mystical Nile, and stand in the shadow of the Pyramids? *All* of it is more possible now, than walking up this street seemed to me last year.

Indeed, there is only one miracle for *me*, my beloved, —and *that* is your loving me. Everything else under the sun, and much over it, seems the merest commonplace and workday matter-of-fact. If I found myself, suddenly, riding in Paradise, on a white elephant of golden feet, . . I should shake the bridle, I fancy, with ever so much nonchalance, and absently wonder over 'that miracle' of the previous world. Because 'THAT'S *for thoughts*,' as my flower says! look at it and listen.

As for me, I am your very own—

R. B. to E. B. B.

Wednesday.
[Post-mark, August 19, 1846.]

See my one piece of available paper for the minute! Ought I to write on or wait? No, I will tell Ba at once how I love her for giving me this one more letter with its delights. 'Finchley'—I know very well—not that I ever saw the streets, and palaces, and cathedral, with these eyes . . but in 'Quarles' Emblems,' my childhood's pet book, I well remember that an aspiring Soul,—(a squat little woman-figure with a loose gown, hair in a coil, and bare feet—) is seated on the world, a 'terrestrial ball,'—which, that you may clearly perceive it to be our world, is somewhat parsimoniously scattered over with cities and towns—and one, the evident capital of the universe and Babylon's despair for size,—occupying as it does a tract quite equal to all Europe's due share on the hemisphere, is marked 'Finchley'—Do  you recognize? Yet, if you will have it only the pretty village with the fields you describe so perfectly, I accept the sweetness and give up the glory, and your Finchley is mine for ever, you dearest—whom I see in the house, and in the carriage . . but how is it you escaped the rain, Ba? Oh, it did not rain till later, now I think a little. Those are indeed strange circumstances . . and the 'independent ministry' at the end, seems hard to account for . . or, why hard? Well, *this* is *not* hard to feel and know, that it is perfect joy to hear you propose such travels and adventures—Greece *with you*, Egypt *with you!* Will you please and tell me . . (not *now*, but whenever your conscience prompts you on the recurrence of that notable objection, if Miss Campbell's desirableness *is* to recur) . . what other woman in the whole world and Finchley, would propose to go to Egypt instead of Belgravia? Do our tastes coincide or no? This is putting all on the lowest possible ground . . setting love aside even, to Miss Mitford's heart's fullest content; if I were to choose among women, without love to give or take, and only for *other* advantages, do you think *any* advantage would compete with this single one,—'she will feel happy in traveling with you to a distance.' Love alters the scale, overbalances everything—at the beginning I fancied you could not leave England, you know. But it singularly affects my imagination, such a life with you,—led *for* the world, I hope, all the more effectually for being not led *in* the world. If their ways are not to be ours, all is better at a distance, and *so* I have put this down as, surely, *one* palpable, unmistakable *advantage* even *you* must confess I shall gain in marrying you—(I may only love Ba's eyes and mouth in a sort of fearful secrecy so far as words go . . she stops all speech on that subject!)

Yes indeed, Ba, I always felt that 'Cyprus wine' poem fill my heart with unutterable desires to you. There is so much of you in it. Observe, I do no foolish injustice in criticisms . . I quite understand a charm *beside* the charm the world can see. Some of your pansies are entirely beautiful in themselves . . I can set them before the visitors of a flower-show and bid all pronounce on them—others, beside their beauty, come to me as *this* dear one, in a letter, with a story of the plucking, with a *sense* of the fingers that held it. Bless you, ever dearest, dear beyond words,—you have given me already in this year and a half the entirest faith and purest kindness my heart can comprehend. Do lovers 'abuse the beloved object'—'try to shake off their chains' &c. &c.? Mine is not love then! Not one minute or moment of your life with me could have been other than it was without seeming less dear, less perfect in my memory—and for all, God reward you.

To-morrow, Thursday! And to-night I will warily speak of not having seen you.

Your own.

E. B. B. to R. B.

Friday.
[Post-mark, August 21, 1846.]

Dearest, this is to be a brief letter, though my heart shall find room in whatever goes to you. Yesterday cost us nothing—no observation was made: we were in all security notwithstanding the forebodings on either side. May they find such an end in circumstances of still more consequence. Dearest, your flowers are beautiful beyond their beauty of yesterday which I praised—they think themselves still in the garden; we have done them no sort of wrong. What a luring thought you leave with me in the flowers! How I look at them as a sign of you, left behind—your footstep in the ground! It has been so from the beginning. And yet sometimes you try to prove that you are not always good. You!

If you are not good, it is because you are *best*. I will admit so much.

Oh, to look back! It is so wonderful to me to look back on my life and my old philosophy of life, made of the necessities of sorrow and the resolution to attain to something better than a perpetual moaning and complaint,—to that state of neutralized emotion to which I did attain—that serenity which meant the failure of hope! *Can* I look back to such things, and not thank you next to God? For you, who had the *power*, to stoop to having the will,—is it not worthy of thanks? So I thank you and love you and shall always, however it may be hereafter. I could not feel otherwise to you, I think, than by my feeling at this moment.

How Papa has startled me. He came in while I was writing . . (I shut the writing-case as he walked over the floor—) and then, after the usual talk of the weather, and how the nights 'were growing cold,' . . . he said suddenly . . looking to the table . . 'What a beautiful colour those little blue flowers have—' Calling them just *so*, . . 'little blue flowers.' I could scarcely answer I was so frightened—but he observed nothing and turned and left the room with his favourite enquiry *pour rire*, as to whether he 'could do anything for me in the City.'

Do anything for *me* in the City! Well—do *you* do something for me, by thinking of me and loving me, Robert. Dear you are, never to be tired of me, with so much reason for it as I know. May God bless you, very dear!—and ever dearest! I am your own too entirely to need to say so.

Ba.

R. B. to E. B. B.

Friday.
[Post-mark, August 21, 1846.]

I think—now that the week is over with its opportunities,—and now that no selfish complaining can take advantage of your goodness,—that I will ask you how *I* feel, do you suppose, without my proper quantity of 'morphine'? May I call you my morphine?

And speaking of 'proper quantities'—there were some remarks of yours which I altogether acquiesced in, yesterday, about a humiliating dependence in money-matters; though I should be the first to except myself from feeling *quite* with the world there—I have told you, indeed,—but my case is not everybody's. I hate being *master*, and alone, and absolute disposer in points where real love will save me the trouble . . because there are infinitely more and greater points where the solitary action and will, with their responsibility, cannot be avoided. I suppose *that* is Goethe's meaning when he says every man has liberty enough—political liberty and social: so that when they let him write 'Faust' after his own fashion, he does not mind how they dispose of his money, or even limit his own footsteps. Ah,—but there are the good thousands all round who don't want to write 'Fausts,' and only have money to spend and walks to take, and how do *they* like such an arrangement? Moreover, I should be perhaps more refractory than anybody, if what I cheerfully agree to, as happening to take my fancy, were forced on me, as the only reasonable course. All men ought to be independent, whatever Carlyle may say. And so, too, I like being alone, myself—but I should be sorry to see the ordinary friends I have, live alone. Do you understand all this, Ba? Will you make me say it, in your mind, intelligibly? And then will you say still more of your own till the true thing is completely said? And, after all, will you kiss me?

As I asked you yesterday . . because of a most foolish, thoughtless allusion,—which I only trust you never noticed . . do not you allude to it, not even to forgive me, dearest, dearest. I would rather be unforgiven than pain you afresh to do it . . but perhaps you did not notice my silly expression after all . . I wished your dear hands before my eyes, I know! Still you would know it was only thoughtlessness.

All this sad morning the blackness has been quite enough to justify our fire . . we have had one there two or three days. But now the sun comes out—and I will hope you follow him,—after Mr. Kenyon's visit? *That* is to be, I think!

I never write anything bearable, even for *me*, on these days when no letter from you leads me on phrase by phrase . . I am thrown too completely on the general feelings—'Do you love Ba?—then tell her *that!*' Yes, indeed! It is easier to leave all the love untold, having to speak for the moment of Finchley only! Finchley,—the cottage,—Ba entering it—Flush following her . . now I come to something I wanted to say! In the paper, this morning, is a paragraph about the bold villainy of *dog-stealers*. There is an 'organised society' of these fellows, and they seize and convey away everybody's Flushes, 'if such a one ever *were*,' as Iago rhymes of his perfect wife. So friend Flush must go his *high* ways only, and keep out of alleys and dark corners: beside in Pisa, he must guard the house. In earnest, I warn you, Ba!

Now tell me—will there be any impediment to Tuesday?

I think I will go out into this sunshine while it lasts. I am very well considering there are three days to wait, but a walk will do no harm,—nor will I.

All speech to you shall be ever simple, simplest. I can only love you and say so,—and I do love you, best beloved!

Your own, very own.

E. B. B. to R. B.

Friday Evening.
[Post-mark, August 22, 1846.]

Can I be as good for you as morphine is for me, I wonder . . even at the cost of being as bad also? Can't you leave me off without risking your life,—nor go on with me without running the hazards of all poison. Ah!—it will not do, so. The figure exceeds me, let *it* be ever so fatal. I may not be your morphine, even if I shall be your Ba!—you *see!*

You are my prophet though, in a few things. For instance, Mr. Kenyon came to-day, and sate here I really believe two hours, talking of poor Papa . . (oh! not of *us*, my prophet!) and at length, of the Pyrenees and of Switzerland, and of the characteristics of mountain scenery—full of interest it all was, and I thought (while he talked) that when you and I had done with the crocodiles, we might look for a chamois or two. If I 'drive,' I shall drive that way, I think still . . that is, ever since four o'clock, I *have* thought. Mr. Kenyon said . . 'You had a visitor yesterday!' 'Yes' said I—'Mr. Browning came.' 'You mean that he actually *did* come, through that pouring rain! Well—he told me he was coming: but when I saw the rain, I imagined it to be out of the question.' Just observe his subtlety. Imagining that you did not come yesterday he concluded of course that you would come to-day,—and straightway hurried here himself! Moreover he seems to me to have resolved on never again leaving London! Because Mr. Eagles goes to the seaside instead of to the Quantock hills, Mr. Kenyon has written to Landor a proposition toward a general renouncement of the adventure. Quite cross I felt, to hear of it! And it doesn't unruffle me to be told, even that he goes to Richmond on Tuesday and sleeps there and spends the Wednesday. Nothing *can* unruffle me. So tiresome it is! Then I am provoked a little by the news he brought me of 'Miss

Martineau's leaving the Lakes for a month or two'—seeing that *if* she leaves the Lakes, it is for London—there are nets on all sides of us. I am under a promise to see her, and I shrink both from herself and her consequences. Now, *is* it not tiresome? Those are coming, and these are *not* going away. The hunters are upon us . . and where we run, we run into the nets.

Dearest, I have been considering one thing, and do *you* consider whether, if we *do* achieve this peculiar madness of going to Italy, we should take any books, and what they should be. A few books of the small editions would be desirable perhaps—and then it were well for us to arrange it so that we should not take duplicates, and that the possession of the duodecimo should 'have the preference' . . do you understand? Also, this arrangement being made, and the time approaching, I had better perhaps send you *my* part of the books, so as to save the difficulty of taking more packets than absolutely were necessary, from this house. It will be very difficult to remove things without exciting observation—and *my sisters must not observe.* The consequences would be frightful if they were suspected of knowing; and, poor things, I could not drive them into acting a part.

My own beloved, when my courage seems to bend and break, I turn to you and look at you . . as men see visions! *It is enough, always.* Did you ever give me pain by a purpose of yours?—do you not rather keep me from all pain?—do we blame the wind that breathes gently, because a reed or a weed trembles in it? I could not feel much pain while sitting near you, I think—unless you suffered a little, . . or looked as if you did not love me. And *that* was not at least yesterday.

May God bless you dearest, ever dearest.

I am your own.

Say how your mother is—and how you are. *Don't* neglect this.

R. B. to E. B. B.

Saturday.
[Post-mark, August 22, 1846.]

Your first note reached me at six o'clock yesterday . . did the dear living spirit inside help it along in spite of all the post's hindrances? And this second comes duly. When you know I am most at a loss how to thank you, invariably you begin thanking *me!* Is that because of my own practice of saying a foolish thing and then, to cover it, asking you to kiss me? I think I will tell you now what that foolish thing was,—lest you, missing it, should go hunting and find worse, and far worse. I will just remind you, that on your enumerating your brothers and sisters, I said without a moment's thought 'so, *you are seven'!* . . And you know how Wordsworth applied that phrase . . and in the sudden fear of wounding dearest Ba, I took such refuge for myself, rather than her! Will you kiss me now, my own love? And say nothing, but let it die away here, this stupidity of mine.

I hardly conceive what Mr. Kenyon means . . except perhaps a sort of general exhortation to take care, and—I mean, if he came for the purpose of catching me *only*,—he ought either to know or not know, keep silence or speak, approve or condemn . . and to do *neither* being so easy, his own cautiousness would keep him away, I should have thought.

About your books, you speak altogether wisely: in this first visit to Italy we had better take only enough to live upon,—travelling books,—and return for the rest. And so with everything else. I shall put papers &c. into a room and turn the key on them and my death's heads—because when we come back (think of you and me . . why, we shall walk arm in arm,—would Flush object to carry an umbrella in his mouth? And so let Lough cut us in marble, all three!)—well, when we come back, all can be done leisurely and considerately. And *then*, Greece, Egypt, Syria, the Chamois-country, as Ba pleases!

Ba, Lord Byron is altogether in my affection again . . I have read on to the end, and am quite sure of the great qualities which the last ten or fifteen years had partially obscured. Only a little longer life and all would have been gloriously right again. I read this book of Moore's too long ago: but I always retained my first feeling for Byron in many respects . . the interest in the places he had visited, in relics of him. I would at any time have gone to Finchley to see a curl of his hair or one of his gloves, I am sure—while Heaven knows that I could not get up enthusiasm enough to cross the room if at the other end of it all Wordsworth, Coleridge and Southey were condensed into the little China bottle yonder, after the Rosicrucian fashion . . they seem to 'have their reward' and want nobody's love or faith. Just one of those trenchant opinions which I found fault with Byron for uttering,—as 'proving nothing'! But telling a weakness to Ba is not telling it to 'the world,' as poor authors phrase it!

By the way, Chorley has written another very kind paper, in that little journal of to-day, 'Colombe's Birthday'—I have only glanced at it however. See his goodwill: I will bring it on Tuesday, if you please in goodness. I was not *quite* so well . . (there is the bare truth . .) this morning early—but the little there was to *go*, *has* gone, and I am about to go out. My mother continues indisposed. The connection between our ailings is no fanciful one. A few weeks ago when my medical adviser was speaking about the pain and its cause . . my mother sitting by me . . he exclaimed 'Why, has anybody to search far for a cause of whatever nervous disorder you may suffer from, when *there* sits your mother . . whom you so absolutely resemble . . I can trace every feature &c. &c.' To which I did *not* answer, 'And will anybody wonder that the said disorder flies away, when there sits my Ba, whom I so thoroughly adore.'

Yes, there you sit, Ba!

And here I kiss you, best beloved,—my very own as I am your own—

E. B. B. to R. B.

Saturday.
[Post-mark, August 22, 1846.]

I begin to write before one this morning, with the high resolve that you shall have a letter on Sunday, to-morrow, at least,—it shall be put into the post so precisely at the right hour. At two I am going out in the carriage to Mr. Boyd's and other places,—and dining duties are to be performed before then, and before now I have had a visitor. Guess whom—Mrs. Jameson. So I am on a 'narrow neck of land' . . such as Wesley wrote hymns about; . and *stans in pede uno* on it—can make for you but a hurried letter.

She came in with a questioning face, and after wondering to find me visible so soon, plunged into the centre of the question and asked 'what was settled . . what I was doing about Italy.—' 'Just nothing,' I told her. 'She found me as she left me, able to say no word.'

'But what *are* you going to do—' throwing herself back in the chair with a sudden—'but oh, I must not enquire.'

I went on to say that 'in the first place my going would not take place till quite the end of September if so soon,—that I had determined to make no premature fuss,—and that, for the actual present, nothing was either to be done or said.

'Very sudden then, it is to be. In fact, there is only an *elopement* for you—' she observed laughing.

So I was obliged to laugh.

(But, dearest, nobody will use such a word surely to the *event*. We shall be in such an obvious exercise of Right by Daylight—surely nobody will use such a word.)

I talked of Mr. Kenyon,—how he had been with me

yesterday and brought the mountains of the Earth into my room—'which was almost too much,' I said, 'for a prisoner.' 'Yes—but if you go to Italy. .'

'But Mr. Kenyon thinks I shall not. In his opinion, my case is desperate.'

'But I tell you that it is not. Nobody's case is desperate when the will is not at fault. And a woman's will when she wills thoroughly as I hope you do, is strong enough to overcome. When I hear people say that *circumstances are against them,* I always retort, . . you mean *that your will is not with you!* I believe in the will—I have faith in it.'

There is an oracle for us, to remember for good! She goes to Paris, she says, with her niece, between the seventh and tenth of September,—and after a few days at Paris she goes to Orleans for the cathedral's sake—but what follows is doubtful . . Italy is doubtful. Only that my opinion is, as I told her, that if Italy is doubtful here in London, at Orleans, when she gets there, it will be certain. She will not resist the attraction towards the South. She looked at me all the while she told me this . . looked into my eyes, like a Diviner.

On Monday morning she comes to see me again. It is all painful, or rather unpleasant. One should not use strong words out of place, and there will remain too much use for this. How I teaze you now!

Believe me, through it all, that when I think of the very worst of the future, I love you the best, and feel most certain of never hesitating. As long as you choose to have me, my beloved, I have chosen—I am yours already—

and your own always—

Ba

E. B. B. to R. B.

Sunday Morning.
[Post-mark, August 24, 1846.]

But dearest—Did you not understand that I understood? I know your words better than you think, you see. Were you afraid to trust me to give a chase to them in my recollection, lest I should fall blindly upon some 'Secret Sin' of yours? a wild boar, instead of a poor little coney belonging to the rocks of my desolation?—such as it was before you made the yellow furze grow everywhere on it? Now, it is like me for wickedness, to begin talking of your 'Secret Sins,' just by this opportunity. You overcome me with goodness—there's the real truth, and the whole of it.

While I am writing, comes in Arabel with such a face. My brother had been talking, talking of me. Stormie suddenly touched her and said—'Is it true that there is an engagement between Mr. Browning and Ba—'? She was taken unaware, but had just power to say 'You had better ask them, if you want to know. What nonsense, Storm.' 'Well,' he resumed, 'I'll ask Ba when I go upstairs.' George was by, looking as grave as if antedating his judgeship. Think how frightened I was, Robert . . expecting them upstairs every minute,—for all my brothers come here on Sunday, all together. But they came, and not a single word was said—not on that subject, and I talked on every other in a sort of hurried way—I was so frightened.

Saturday Mr. Boyd and I talked on *it* for two hours nearly, he would not let me go with his kindness. Nothing, he said, would make him gladder than our having gone, and escaped the storms. In fact, what with affection for me, and disaffection in other directions, he thinks of nothing besides, I do believe. He only wishes that he had known last year, in order to exhort me properly. The very triumph of reason and righteousness, he considers the whole affair. But I told you what Mr. Boyd is—dear, poor Mr. Boyd! Talking such pure childishness sometimes, in such pure Attic—yet one of the very most upright men, after all, that I ever dreamt of—one of the men born shepherds—with a crook in the hand, instead of the metaphorical 'silver spoon in the mouth.' Good, dear Mr. Boyd,—I am very grateful to him for his goodness to me just now. I assure you that he takes us up exactly as if we were Ossian and Macpherson, or a criticism of Porson's, or a new chapter of Bentley on Phalaris. By the way, *do you believe in Ossian?* Let me be properly prepared for that question.

But I have a question for you of my own. Listen to me, my Famous in Council, and give me back words of wisdom. A long, long while ago, nearly a year since perhaps, I wrote to the Blackwoods of Edinburgh to mention my new 'Prometheus,' and to ask if they would care to use it in their magazine, *that,* and verses more my own; whether they would care to have them at the usual magazine terms—I had some lyrics by me, and people have constantly advised me to print in Blackwood, with the prospect of republishing in the independent form. You get at the public so, and are paid for your poems instead of paying for them. Did I tell you all this before—and about my having written the enquiry? At any rate, no reply came—I concluded that Mr. Blackwood did not think it worth while to write, and eschewed the poems—and the subject passed from my thoughts till last night. Then came a very civil note. The authorities receiving nothing from me, were afraid that their answer to my letter had not reached me, and therefore wrote again. They would 'like to see' my 'Prometheus' though apprehensive of its being unfit for the Magazine—but particularly desire to have all manner of lyrics, whatever I have by me. Now, what do you think? What shall I do? Would it not be well to let this door between us and Blackwood stand open. One is not in the worst company there—they pay well,—and you have the opportunity of standing face to face with the public at any moment—without hindering the solemner interviews. When we are in Italy, particularly . . ! Do you see? Tell me your thoughts.

Since I began this letter, I have been to the Scotch Church in our neighbourhood—and it has all been in vain —I could not stay. We heard that a French minister, a M. Alphonse Monod of Montauban, was to preach at three o'clock, in French—and counting on a small congregation, and Arabel (through a knowledge of the localities) encouraging me with the prospect of sitting close to the door, and retiring back into the entrance-hall when the singing began, so as to escape that excitement—I agreed to make the trial, and she and I set out in a cab from the cab-stand hard by . . to which we walked. But the church was filling, obviously filling, as we arrived . . and grew fuller and fuller. We went in and came out again, and I sate down on the stairs—and the people came faster and faster, and I could not keep the tears out of my eyes to begin with. One gets nervous among all these people if a straw stirs. So Arabel after due observations on every side, decided that it would be too much of a congregation for me, and that I had better go home to Flush—(poor Flush having been left at home in a state of absolute despair). She therefore put me into a cab and sent me to Wimpole Street, and stayed behind herself to hear M. Monod—there's my adventure to-day. When I opened my door on my return, Flush threw himself upon me with a most ecstatical agony, and for full ten minutes did not cease jumping and kissing my hands—he thought he had lost me for certain, this time. Oh! and you warn me against the danger of losing *him*. Indeed I take care and take thought too—those 'organised banditti' are not merely banditti *de comedie*—they are a dreadful reality. Did I not tell you once that they had announced to me that I should not have Flush back the *next time*, for less than ten guineas? But you will let him come with us to Italy, instead—will you not, dear, dearest? in good earnest, will you not? Because, if I leave him behind, he will be teazed for my sins in this house—or I could not be sure of the reverse of it. And even if he escaped that fate, consider how he would break his heart about me. Dogs pine to death sometimes—and if ever a dog loved a man, or a woman, Flush loves me. But you say that he shall keep the house at Pisa—and you mean it, I hope and I think?—you are in earnest. May God bless you,—*so*, I say my prayers though I missed the Church. To-morrow, comes my letter . . come my two letters! the happy Monday! The happier Tuesday, if on Tuesday comes the writer of the letters!

His very own Ba.

R. B. to E. B. B.

Sunday Afternoon.
[Post-mark, August 24, 1846.]

This time, they brought me your letter at six o'clock yesterday evening: was I startled, or no, do you think, as I received it? But all proved right, and kind as ever, or kinder. By the post-mark, I see you *did* go out. Can you care in this way for my disappointments and remedy them? If I did not love you, how I would begin *now!* Every day shows me more to love in you, dearest, and I open my arms as wide as I can . . 'incomprehensible' Ba, as Donne would say! Also he would say much better things, however.

What a visitation! Miss Martineau is the more formidable friend, however—Mrs. Jameson will be contented with a little confidence, you see, and ask no questions—but I doubt if you arrange matters so easily with the new-comer. Because no great delicacy can be kept alive with all that conceit—and such conceit! A lady told me a few weeks ago that she had seen a letter in which Miss M. gave as her reason for not undertaking *then*, during the

London season, this very journey which empty London is to benefit from now, 'that at such a time she should be *mobbed to death*': whereupon the lady went on to comment, 'Miss M. little knows what London is, and how many nearly as notable objects may be found to divert its truculence from herself'—Tom Thumb, and Ibrahim Pacha, to wit.

Why do you suspect that you 'teaze' me when you say 'there will remain too much use for the word "painful"'? Do you not know more of me by this time, my own Ba? When I have spoken of the probable happiness of our future life—of the chances in our favour from a community of tastes and feelings,—I have really done it on your account, not mine. I very well know that there would be an exquisite, secret happiness *through* pain with you, or for you—but it is not for me to insist on *that*, with that divine diffidence in your own worth which meets me wherever I turn to approach you, and puts me so gently aside . . so I rather retire and content myself with occupying the ground you *do* concede . . and since you will only hear of my being happy in the obvious, ordinary way, I tell you, with perfect truth, that you, and only you, can make me thus—that only you, of all women, look in the direction that I look, and feel as I feel, and live for the ends of my life; and beside that, see with my eyes the most natural and immediate way of reaching them, through a simple life, retirements from the world here (not from the real world), travel, and the rest. But all the while I know . . do not *you* know, Ba? . . that the joy's essence is in the life with you, for the sake of you, not of the mere vulgar happiness; and that if any of our calculations should fail, it will be a surprise, a delight, a pride to me to take the new taste you shall prescribe, or leave the old one you forbid. My life being yours, what matters the change which you effect in it?

Here, you mean not even so much as this by your 'painful'—'Elopement'! Let them call it 'felony' or 'burglary'—so long as they don't go to church with us, and propose my health after breakfast! Now you fancy this a gratuitous piece of impertinence, do you not, Ba? You are wrong, sweet: I speak from directest experience—having dreamed, the night before last, that we were married, and that on adjourning to the house of a friend of mine, his brother, a young fop I know slightly, made a speech, about a certain desk or dressing-case, which he ended by presenting to me in the name of the house! Whereto I replied in a strain of the most alarming fluency (. . all in the dream, I need not tell you)—'and then I woke.' Oh *can* I have smiled, higher up in the letter, at Miss Martineau's over-excitability on the subject of 'mobbing' here? The greatest coward is the wisest man . . even the suspicion of such mobs ought to keep people at their lakes, or send them to their Pisas.

By the way, Byron speaks of plucking oranges in his garden at Pisa . . I saw just a courtyard with a high wall—which may have been a garden . . but a gloomier one than the palace, even, warrants. They have painted the front fresh staring yellow and changed its name . . there being another Casa Lanfranchi on the other side of the Arno.

Now I will kiss you, dearest: used you to divine that at the *very* beginning, I have sometimes shortened the visit in order to arrive at the time of taking your hand?

You will write to me to-night, I think—Tuesday is our day, remember. May God bless you, my very very dearest—

Your R

That sonnet will not turn up—it is neither in Vasari, nor Dolce, nor Castiglione . . probably in Richardson's 'Painting' which somebody has borrowed—but I will find it yet, knowing that it must be near at hand.

R. B. to E. B. B.

Monday Morning.
[Post-mark, August 24, 1846.]

My own dearest, let me say the most urgent thing first. You hear these suspicions of your brothers. Will you consider if, during this next month, we do not risk too much in seeing each other as usual? We risk everything . . and what do we gain, in the face of that? I can learn no more about you, be taught no new belief in your absolute peerlessness—I have taken my place at your feet for ever: all my use of the visits is, therefore, the perfect delight of them . . and to hazard a whole life of such delight for the want of self-denial during a little month,—that would be horrible. I altogether sympathise with your brothers' impatience, or curiosity, or anxiety, or 'graveness'—and am prepared for their increasing and growing to heights difficult or impossible to be borne. But do you not think we may avoid compelling any premature crisis of this kind? I am guided by your feelings, as I seem to perceive them, in this matter; the harm to be apprehended is *through* the harm to *them*—to your brothers. If they determine on avowedly *knowing* what we intend, I do not see which to fear most; the tacit acquiescence in our scheme which may draw down a vengeance on them without doing us the least good,—or the open opposition which would bring about just so much additional misfortune. I *know*, now, your perfect adequacy to any pain and danger you will incur for our love's sake—I believe in you as you would have me believe: but give yourself to me, dearest dearest Ba, the entire creature you are, and not a lacerated thing only reaching my arms to sink there. Perhaps this is all a sudden fancy, not justified by circumstances, arising from my ignorance of the characters of those I talk about; that is for you to decide—your least word reassures me, as always. But I fear much for *you*, to make up, perhaps, for there being nothing else in the world fit to fear: I exclude direct visitations of God, which cannot be feared, after all—dreadful dooms to which we should bow. But the 'fear' *proper*, means with me an apprehension that, with all my best effort, it may be unable to avert some misfortune . . the effort going on all the time: and *this* is a real effort, dearest Ba, this letter: consider it thus. I will (if possible) send it to town, so as to reach you earlier and allow you to write *one line* in reply. You have heard all I can say . . say you, *shall I come to-morrow?* If you think it advisable, I will come and be most happy.

Another thing: you see your excitement about the church and the crowd . . My own love, are you able,—with all that great, wonderful heart of yours,—to bear the railway fatigues, and the entering and departure from Paris and Orleans and the other cities and towns? Would not the long sea-voyage be infinitely better, if a little dearer? Or what can be *dear* if it prevents all that risk, or rather certainty, of excitement and fatigue? You see, the packet sails on the 30th September and the 15*th October*. As three of us go, they would probably make some reduction in price. Ah, even here, I must smile . . will you affirm that ever *an approximation to a doubt* crossed your mind about Flush? I think your plans with respect to 'Blackwood' most excellent—I see *many* advantages.

. . . . .

Here is the carriage for my sister, who is going to stay in town at the Arnoulds' for a week,—with Mrs. A. in it to fetch her. I shall give this letter to be put in the post—I have *all* to say, but the *very* essential is said—understand me, my best, only love, and forgive my undue alarm, for the sake of the love that prompts it. Write the one line . . do not let me do myself wrong by my anxiety—if I *may* come, *let me!* Bless you, Ba.

E. B. B. to R. B.

Monday Evening.
[Post-mark, August 25, 1846.]

Dearest, how you frightened me with the sight of your early letter! But it is only your wisdom,—which by this time should scarcely startle me,—there's a compliment, to begin with, you see, in change for all the praises; . . my 'peerlessness' (! ! !) being settled like the Corn Law repeal!—oh, you want no more evidence of it, not you! (poor blind you!) and the other witnesses are bidden to 'stand down'—'I may smile even *now*' . . . as you say *quoad* Flush, . . smile at your certainty as you smile at my doubt. Will you let me smile, and not call it a peerless insolence, or ingratitude,—dearest you?

For dearest you are, and best in the world, . . it all comes to *that*, . . and considerate for me always: and at once I agree with you that for this interval it will be wise for us to set the visits, . . 'our days . . far apart, . . nearly a week apart, perhaps, so as to escape the dismal evils we apprehend. I agree in all you say—in all. At the same time, the cloud has passed for the present—nothing has been said more, and not a word to me; and nobody appears out of humour with me. They will be displeased of course, in the first movement . . we must expect *that* . . they will be vexed at the occasion given to conversation and so on. But it will be a passing feeling, and their hearts and their knowledge of circumstances may be trusted to justify me thoroughly. I do not fear offending them—there is no room for fear. At this point of the business too, you place the alternative rightly—their approbation or their disapprobation is equally to be escaped from. Also, we may be certain that they would press the applying for permission—and I might perhaps, in the storm excited, among so many opinions and feelings, fail to myself and you, through weakness of the body. . Not of the *Will!*

And for my affections and my conscience, they turn to you—and untremblingly turn.

Will you come on *Wednesday* rather than Tuesday then? It is only one day later than we meant at first, but it nearly completes a week of separation; and we can then go to next week for the next day. Also, on Wednesday we secure Mr. Kenyon's absence. He will be still at Richmond.

Your letter which startled me by coming early, yet came too late for you to receive the answer to it to-night. But I will send it to the post to-night; and I write hurriedly to be in time for that end.

My own beloved, you shall not be uneasy on my account.—I send you foolishnesses and you are daunted by them—but see! What affects me in those churches and chapels is something different, quite different, from railroad noises and the like. You do not understand, and I never explained, . . you could not understand—but the music, the sight of the people, the old tunes of hymns . . all these things seem to suffocate my very soul with the sense of the past, past days, when there was one beside me who is not here now—I am upset, overwhelmed with it all. I think I should have been quite foolishly, hysterically ill yesterday if I had persisted in staying. Next Sunday I shall go to the vestry, and see nobody, and get over it by degrees.

Well—but for the sea-voyage, it seems to me that the great thing for us to ascertain is the precise *expense*. I should not at all mind going by sea, only that I fear the expense, and also that it is necessary to take our passages some time before, . . and then, if anything happened . . I mean any little thing . . an obstacle for a day or two! Consider our circumstances.

I shall write again perhaps. Do not rely, though, on my writing. *Perhaps* I shall write. I shall think of your goodness certainly! May God bless you, dearest beloved, I love, love you! I cannot be more

Your own.

Don't forget to bring the paper on 'Colombe's Birthday,'—and say particularly how you are—and how your mother.

In such haste I write!—

R. B, to E. B. B.

Tuesday.
[Post-mark, August 25, 1846.]

When your letter came, my love, I could have easily borne the over-ruling its objections to a visit to-day, for all my cautious philosophy! But it seems best arranged as at present . . indeed it must be best, if you agree. To-morrow repays me: nor is very long to wait!

I will only write briefly because I want to go to Town, (since there is nothing better practicable), and enquire precisely about that steamboat and the prices. I see that one may go to Trieste, a much greater journey, for '£12 and £15,' according to Mr. Waghorn's bill. Besides, the advertisement speaks of the 'economy' of this way—and certainly under ordinary circumstances anybody would prefer the river-voyage with its picturesqueness. There is a long account, in the paper to-day, of the earthquakes in Tuscany—which have really been formidable enough to keep away the travelling English for the next month or two—whole villages were overthrown, Leghorn has suffered considerably, the inhabitants bivouac outside the walls—and at Pisa the roof of a church fell in . . also the villas in the vicinity have been damaged. Do you fear, dearest? If you do not,—*I fear* that the eligibility of Pisa as our place of abode is only doubled and tripled by all this. Think; there is a new lake risen, just by! and great puffs of sulphureous smoke came up through chinks in the plains. How do these wonders affect you?

You asked me about Ossian—now here is truth—the first book I ever bought in my life was Ossian . . it is now in the next room. And years before that, the first *composition* I ever was guilty of was something in *imitation* of Ossian, whom I had not read, but *conceived*, through two or three scraps in other books—I never can recollect *not* writing rhymes . . but I knew they were nonsense even then; *this*, however, I thought exceedingly well of, and laid up for posterity under the cushion of a great arm-chair. 'And now my soul is satisfied'—so said one man after killing another, the death being suggested, in its height of honour, by stars and stars (* * * *). I could not have been five years old, that's one consolation. Years after, when I bought this book, I found a vile dissertation of Laing . . all to prove Ossian was not Ossian . . I would not read it, but could not help knowing the purpose of it, and the pith of the hatefully-irresistible arguments. The worst came in another shape, though . . an after-gleaning of real Ossianic poems, by a firm believer whose name I forget—'if this is the *real*'—I thought! Well, to this day I believe in a nucleus for all that haze, a foundation of truth to Macpherson's fanciful superstructure—and I have been long intending to read once again those Fingals and Malvinas.

I remember that somewhere a chief cries 'Come round me, my thousands!'—There is an Achilles! And another, complaining of old age remarks '*Now*—I feel the weight of my shield!' Nestor; and both beautifully perfect, are they not, *you* perfect Ba?

I will go now. To-morrow I trust to see you face to face; dearest that you are!

Ever your own.

My poor mother suffers greatly. I am much better.

E. B. B. to R. B.

Tuesday, 6 P.M.
[Post-mark, August 26, 1846.]

I have just had a note from Mr. Kenyon, who, after his absence at Richmond, promises to come and see me on *Thursday afternoon*. Now . . would it be quite 'unco guid' of us . . and wise 'above what is written' (in your letter) if we put off our day to Friday, and gave me the power to answer to Mr. Kenyon's certain question, . . 'no, I have not seen him since I saw *you.*'? If you think it would be wise, my own dearest, why do not come to-morrow; do not come till Friday. See—to-day is Tuesday, and only two days more will intervene,—and we are agreed on the necessity of prudence for the coming weeks—particularly when my brothers have nothing particular to do, at this time of vacation, but to watch us on all sides. I am so nervous that my own footsteps startle me. But *quite well* I am, and you shall not have fancies about me—as to strength, I mean—as to what I cannot do, bear, and the like.

To-night I shall write a letter as usual. This is a bare *line*, which Henrietta will throw into the post, to speak to you of to-morrow. The letter follows.

How I miss you, and long for Friday. If you have an engagement for Friday, there is Saturday. '*Understand*' . . as you say, and I repeat.

To-night I will tell you where I went to-day.

Your own I am always

E. B. B. to R. B.

Tuesday Evening.
[Post-mark, August 26, 1846.]

'*Nor is it very long to wait*'—Alas!—My note went two hours ago to cross out the application of that phrase, and now it *is* very long to wait, . . all the days to Friday. Tell me, dearest, if you think it wise, at least, to make such an unhappy arrangement, . . considering, you know, Mr. Kenyon and my brothers. It ought to be wise, *I* think . . it is so unhappy and disappointing. Consider what I am without you all this long dreary while; and how little ever so much sense of wisdom can console anybody.

Friday will come however,—and I may as well go on to tell you that Mrs. Jameson came yesterday. 'Anything settled?' she asked; as she walked into the room. She looked at me with resolute, enquiring eyes. I wonder if she ever approaches to the divination of something like the truth—*not* the truth, but like it. Either she must see indistinctly 'something new and strange,' or attribute to me a strange delight in the mysterious. She half promised to see me again before she leaves England, and begged me to write and tell her all whenever I shall have it in my power to make the communication. Affectionate she was, as always.

To-day I have seen nobody, except Mr. Boyd for a little, after driving through street upon street, where I might have met you if I had been happy enough. Albemarle Street . . were you *there?* I sate there, in the carriage, opposite to the York Hotel, while Henrietta paid her visit to old Lady Bolingbroke, a full half hour . . Flush and I —Flush staring out of the window, and I . . doing what I generally do in this room, do you ask what it was? At the end of some twenty minutes, a boy passed, who had the impertinence to look full at Flush and whistle, whereupon Flush growled, and appealed to me with two immense eyes . . both seeming to say 'I hope you observe how I am insulted.' So my reverie was broken in the middle—but being better tempered, rather, than Flush, or having larger resources, I did not growl, but took your latest letter out instead, which lasted for the whole remainder of the time. Then at Mr. Boyd's . . oh, I must tell you . . he began to tell me some romantic compliment of several young ladies who desired to be disguised in servant's accoutrements, just to open the door to me (to have a good stare, I suppose) or, in good earnest, to be my maid! (to go with us to Pisa, dearest . . how would you like *that?*—Seriously now *do* just calculate the wonderful good fortune of such a person, in falling upon two lions instead of one—nay, on a great wild forest-lion, this time, in addition to the little puny lioness of the original bargain!) Well!—but when Mr. Boyd had done his report, I asked naturally, 'And what am I to say to all this?' 'Why you are to say that you will be good-natured, and give somebody pleasure at the cost of no pain to yourself, and go to the room downstairs and speak three words to Miss Smith who is there, waiting.' Imagine anybody having a Miss Smith ready in the drawing-room to let out upon one! Imagine *me* too (to be less abstract) walking in to that same Miss Smith, . . to the effect of—! 'Here I am! just come to be looked at. Is it at all what you expected, Miss Smith'?

The worst was, that dear Mr. Boyd would have set it down to a species of malignancy, if I had refused—so I took my courage up with both hands, and remembering that I had seen two or three times, years ago, the stepmother of the said Miss Smith, I thought I might enquire after her with a sort of propriety. And I got through it somehow. 'Will you let me shake hands with you and ask how Mrs. Smith is? Does she remember me, I wonder? I am Elizabeth Barrett.'—'Is it possible? Ah! I thought you were one of your sisters at first! Dear me! Why how much better, you must be, to be sure!—Oh dear me, what an illness you have had! Ah, quite shut up so long! How very, very interesting, to be sure.'—If Flush had swallowed her up in the middle, I might have forgiven him, to be sure. So interesting too, that catastrophe would have been! But you shall not set me down as a savage—it was all kindness on her side, of course—but one may be savage to a *situation* . . (which is just the way with me, . .) without being a born barbarian woman.

As to Miss Martineau, the expression which sounds so rampant with conceit, may yet be the plainest proof of a mere instinct of self-preservation. If three Smiths would be mob enough to mob *me* to death (and they may make a mob, as three fine days, a summer!), let us have some feeling for *her*, exposed, from various causes, to the thirties . . at the lowest comparative computation.

For Ossian, you admit the *nucleus*. Which is only like your Ba, dearest . . you will not stand higher as an Ossianic critic unless you believe the verbal authenticity, 'nothing extenuating.' The cushion of the armchair! *My* place of deposit used to be between the mattresses of my crib—a little mahogany crib with cane sides to it. You were like Lord Byron (another point of likeness!) in imitating Ossian, but you were still earlier at the work than he was.

It is very well to ascertain the prices by the steamers; though my expectation is that you will find them higher than you fancy them. *Nineteen guineas* was the charge last year, as far as Gibraltar only. Then, if you charmed ever so eloquently with the voice of the charmer, you never, as a passenger, would induce those people to diminish the rate, because of our being *three;* and a female servant is charged for at the higher rate . . if not the highest. Altogether the expenses will be, out of all comparison, beyond that of the passage through France . . . see if it will not. Ten pounds, as far as the travelling goes, seem to cover everything, in going from hence to Leghorn . . to Pisa . . taking Rouen and Orleans—and meaning of course, for one person. And if the advantages are, as you describe, besides . . why should we forego them? *Is* the fatigue so much greater? If there are more changes and shiftings, there is also more absolute rest—and the rivers are smoother than the seas. Still, it is well to consider—and there are good reasons on each side, worthy of consideration.

So much more I had to say—I break off suddenly, being benighted. How you write to me! how you wrote to me on Sunday and yesterday! How I wish for two hearts to love you with, and two lives to give to you, and two souls to bear the weight worthily of all you have given to *me.* But if one heart and one life will do, . . they are yours . . I cannot give them again.

Beloved, if your mother should be ill, we must not think of your leaving her, surely?

May God bless you, dearest beloved.

I am your Ba.

R. B. to E. B. B.

Wednesday Morning.
[Post-mark, August 26, 1846.]

Dearest, I *do* think it will be only prudent to stay away till Friday for those reasons. Oh, how I feel *what* a Ba, mine is . . how truly peerless a lady . . when I find instinctively at this minute while I write, that the proper course will be to seem as little affected by this enforced absence as possible . . that knowing my love she would understand any comfort I take from the eventful good of the arrangement—I have not to dwell on the present sorrow of it, lest she disbelieve me! I am your very own, dearest dearest, with you or away from you. Both your notes came together just now . . how can I thank and love you enough? I might have guessed that at the end you would thank *me* for my own letters . . that is your 'trick of fence,' discovered, remember! But when you read the 'red-leaved tablets of the heart' . . then be satisfied . . 'praise,' nothing in me to you can deserve.

I have learned all particulars about the steamer. There are only two classes of passengers . . *Servants* being the second. The first pay, for the voyage to Leghorn 21*l.* —the second, 14*l.* 5*s.* all expenses included except during the stay at Genoa. No reduction 'it is feared' could be made in the case of so small a party—but by booking early, a separate cabin might be secured, at no additional expense. In the event of any obstacle, the passage paid for may be postponed till the departure of the next, or any future vessel of the company. Now, you see, these rates, though moderate, I think—(the ordinary term of the passage to *Genoa* is eleven days)—are yet considerably above those of the other method by at least 20*l.*, I should say. The voyage is long, supremely tiresome, and in all respects so much less interesting than the French route, that the whole scheme *can* only be constructed for those to whom any other mode of travel is impossible. The one question to be asked therefore is . . are you really convinced that you need not be treated as one of these? And on further consideration, there arise not a few doubts as to whether the sea-voyage be not the more *difficult* of the two—the roughness is all between here and Gibraltar—and in the case of *that* affecting you more seriously than we hope, there would be no possibility of escaping from the ship—whereas, should you be indisposed on the other route, we can stop at once and stay for any period. Then, the 'shiftings' are only three or four, and probably accompanied by no very great fatigue beyond the *notion* that a shifting there *is*. Above all, you would get the first of the sea in a little experiment, soon made and over,—so that if it proved unfavourable to you there might be an end of the matter at once. So that after all, the cheaper journey may be the safer. But all does *not* rest with you *quite*, as I was going to say . . all my life is bound up with the success of this measure . . therefore, think and decide, my Ba!

Would there be an advantage in Mrs. Jameson accompanying us—to Orleans, at least? Would the circumstances of our marriage alter her desire, do you think? She has wished to travel with *me*, also—she must suspect the truth—I doubt whether it is not in such cases as hers, where no responsibility is involved, whether it is not better policy, as well as the more graceful, to communicate what is sure to be discovered—so getting thanks and sympathy instead of neither. All is for you to consider.

And now, dearest, I will revert, in as few words as I can, to the account you gave me, a short time since, of your income. At the beginning, if there had been the necessity I supposed, I should have proposed to myself the attainment of something like such an amount, by my utmost efforts, before we could marry. We could not under the circumstances begin with less—so as to be free from horrible contingencies,—not the least of which would be the application for assistance afterward. After we marry, nobody must hear of us. In spite of a few misgivings at first I am not proud, or rather, am proud in the right place. I am utterly, exclusively proud of you—and though I should have gloried in working myself to death to prove it, and shall be as ready to do so at any time a necessity shall exist, yet at present I shall best serve you, I think, by the life by your side, which we contemplate. I hope and believe, that by your side I shall accomplish something to justify God's goodness and yours—and, looking at the matter in a worldly light, I see not a few reasons for thinking that unproductive as the kind of literature may be, which I should aim at producing, yet, by judicious management, and profiting by certain favourable circumstances,—I shall be able to realise an annual sum quite sufficient for every purpose—at least in Italy.

As I never calculated on such a change in my life, I had the less repugnance to my father's generosity, that I knew that an effort at some time or other might furnish me with a few hundred pounds which would soon cover my very simple expenses. If we are poor, it is to my father's infinite glory, who, as my mother told me last night, as we sate alone, 'conceived such a hatred to the slave-system in the West Indies,' (where his mother was born, who died in his infancy), that he relinquished every prospect,—supported himself, while there, in some other capacity, and came back, while yet a boy, to his father's profound astonishment and rage—one proof of which was, that when he heard that his son was a suitor to *her*, my mother—he benevolently waited on her uncle to assure him that his niece would be thrown away on a man so evidently born to be hanged!—those were his words. My father on his return had the intention of devoting himself to art, for which he had many qualifications and abundant love—but the quarrel with his father,—who married again and continued to hate him till a few years before his death,—induced him to go at once and consume his life after a fashion he always detested. You may fancy, I am not ashamed of him.

I told my mother, who told *him*. They have never been used to interfere with, or act for me—and they trust me. If you care for any love, purely love,—you will have theirs—they give it you, whether you take it or no. You will understand, therefore, that I would not *accept* even the 100*l*. we shall want: I said 'you shall lend it me—I will pay it back out of my first literary earnings—I take it, because I do not want to sell my copyrights, or engage myself to write a play, or any other nuisance. Surely I can get fifty pounds next year, and the other fifty in due course!'

So, dearest, we shall have plenty for the journey—and you have only to determine the when and the how. Oh, the time! Bless you, ever dearest! I love you with all my heart and soul—

R.

E. B. B. to R. B.

Wednesday.
[Post-mark, August 27, 1846.]

'*If I care for any love*'—'*whether I take it or no.*' Now ought I not to reproach you a little, for bearing to write such words of me, when you could not but think all the while, that I should feel a good deal in reading what you wrote beside? Will you tell me that you did not know I should be glad and grateful for *tolerance* even?—the least significance of the kinder feeling affecting me *beyond*, perhaps, what you could know of me. I am bound to them utterly.

And if it is true, as it is true, that they have much to pardon and overlook in me, . . and among the rest, the painful position imposed on you by my miserable necessities, . . they yet never shall find me, I trust, unworthy of them and you by *voluntary* failures, and, least of all, by failures of dutiful affection towards themselves—'IF THEY CARE FOR ANY LOVE.'

For the rest of what you tell me, it is all the purest

kindness—and you were perfectly, perfectly right in taking so, and as a loan, which we ought, I think, to return when our hands are free, without waiting for the completion of other projects. By living quietly and simply, we shall surely have enough—and more than enough. Then among other resources is Blackwood. I calculated once that without unpleasant labour, with scarcely an effort, I could make a hundred a year by magazine-contributions—and this, without dishonour either. It does 'fugitive poems,' observe, no harm whatever, to let them fly through a periodical before they alight on their tree to sing. Then *you* will send perhaps the sweepings of your desk to Blackwood, to alternate with my sendings! Shall we do *that*, when we sit together on the ragged edge of earthquake chasms, in the midst of the 'sulphurous vapour.' I, afraid? No indeed—I think I should never be afraid, if you were near enough. Only that you never must go away in *boats*. But there is time enough for such compacts.

As to the sea voyage, *that* was *your* scheme, and not mine, from the beginning: and your account of the expenses, if below my fear . . (although I believe that 'servants' do not mean 'female servants' and that the latter are subject to additional charges), yet seems to me to leave the Rhone and Saone route as preferable as ever. And do you mark, dear dearest, that supposing me to be unfit for the short railroad passage from Rouen to Paris and from Paris to Orleans, I must be just as unfit for the journey to Southampton, which is necessary to the sea-voyage. Then . . supposing me to be unfit for the river-passage, I must be still more unfit for the sea. So don't suppose *either*. I am stronger than you fancy. I shall shut my eyes and think of you when there is too much noise and confusion, —the things which try me most,—and it will be easy to find a quiet room and to draw down the blinds and take rest, I suppose, . . which one might in vain long for in that crowded steamer at sea. Therefore, dearest, if I am to think and decide, I have decided . . let us go through

France. And let us go quick, quick, and not stop anywhere within hearing of England . . not stop at Havre, nor at Rouen, nor at Paris—*that* is how *I* decide. May God help us, and smooth the way before and behind. May your father indeed be able to love me a little, for *my* father will never love me again.

For *you* . . you will 'serve me best' and serve me only, by being happy not away from me. When I shall have none but you, if I can feel myself not too much for you,—not something you would rather leave—then you will have 'served' mo all you can. But this is more perhaps than you can—these things do not depend on the will of a man—that he should promise to do them. I speak simply for myself, and of what would give me a full contentment. Do not fancy that there is a *doubt* in the words of it. I cannot doubt now of your affection for me. Dearest, I *cannot*. Yet you make me uneasy often through this extravagance of over-estimation; forcing me to contract 'obligations to pay' which I look at in speechless despair —And here is a penny.

Of Mrs. Jameson, let me write to-morrow—I am benighted and must close. On Friday we shall meet at last, surely; and then it will be all the happier in proportion to the vexation. Dearest, love me—

I am your own—

E. B. B. to R. B.

Thursday Morning.
[Post-mark, August 27, 1846.]

Dearest, I am to write to you of Mrs. Jameson. First, as to telling her . . will it not be an embarrassment both to her and ourselves? If she cannot say 'I knew nothing of this,' she bears the *odium* of confidante and *adviser* perhaps—who shall explain the distinction to others? And to Mr. Kenyon, will it not seem as if we had trusted her more than him—and though there is a broad distinction too between their cases, who shall explain *that* to him so quickly and nicely that he shall not receive the shock of a painful impression? Consider a little—She is so *in medias res*—so in the way of all the conversation and the questionings. But it shall be as you like and think best. I am too nervous perhaps.

As for the travelling, she sets out between the seventh and tenth of September, a century before our æra, you know—but if she goes to Italy and is not too angry with me, we might certainly meet her in Paris or at Orleans . . take her up at Orleans, and go on together. That is, if you like it too. She would be pleased, I daresay, if it were proposed—and we might be kind in proposing it—and something I might say to her, if you liked it, on the condition of her not changing her mind. Certainly I do agree with you that she must have *some ideas*—she is not without imagination, and the suggestions are abundant,—though nothing points to you, mind!—if she could possibly think me capable of loving anyone else in the world, with you in it.

I had a letter to-day . . with a proposition to write ballads and other lyrics in order to the civilisation of the colonies . . especially Australia. It appears that a Mr. Angus Fife has a scheme on foot nearly, about sending missionary ballad-singers among the natives, and that I am invited to write some of them, or to *be* invited—for nothing is specified yet. Now what do you think of *that?* One should take one's mythology from the Kangaroos, I suppose.

Then a book of 'serious poems' is to be brought out in Edinburgh and contributions are desired so very politely that nobody can quite refuse.

I write to you of anything but what is in my thoughts. Your letter of yesterday took hold of me and will not let me go—it all seems too earnest for the mere dream I have been dreaming all this while—is it not a dream . . or what? And something I said in *my* letter, which was wrong to say and I am sorry to think of—forgive me *that*, ever beloved—but you have forgiven, I know. May God bless you, and not take from *me* my blessing in you.

I am your very own Ba.

We are going out in the carriage and shall post this note. You will come to-morrow unless you hear more? Is it a compact?

R. B. to E. B. B.

Thursday.
[Post-mark, August 27, 1846.]

The post's old fault, is it not, this letter that does not come? I have waited till nearly the time of the next arrival, 3 o'clock, and perhaps I begin writing now because I have observed that sometimes the letter comes just as I am trying hardest to resign myself. So may it be now, or presently!

Dearest, I did not thank you yesterday for the accounts of your visit and drive . . I always love you for such accounts; you know, I might *like*, we will say, a Miss Campbell, while she was in the very act of speaking Greek to Mr. Kenyon's satisfaction, or making verses, or putting them into action—but there would be no following her about the streets, and through bazaars, and into houses, and loving the walking and standing and sitting and companionship with Flush! I shall be satisfied to the full if you only live in my sight,—cross the room in which I sit, —not to say, sit down by me there,—always supposing that you also, for your part, seem happy and contented,—or at least could not become more so by leaving me. But I do believe you will be happy.

And here the letter comes! See, what I tell you does now fill my life with gladness,—*that*, the counterpart of that, you promise me shall make *you* glad too! My very own, entirely beloved Ba, there is no exaggeration, no overestimation—the case does not admit of any, indeed! If a man tells you he owns a peerless horse, the horse may go lame and the estimation sink upon that experience—but if I think, as I do, that the Elgin Horse is peerless (despite his ewe-neck) nothing further can touch it, nor change me. One of my comparisons! All I want to express is, that I love *you*, dearest, with a love that seems to separate you from your very qualities—the essential from its accidents. But you must wait to know—wait a life, perhaps.

I used those words you object to—(in your true way), because you shall love nothing connected with me for conventional reasons—and if I understated the amount of kind feeling which you might be led to return for theirs, be assured that I also expressed in the simplest and coldest terms possible my father and mother's affection for you. I told you, they *believe* me . . therefore, know in some measure what you are to me. They are both entirely affectionate and generous. My father is tender-hearted to a fault. I have never known much more of those circumstances in his youth than I told you, in consequence of his invincible repugnance to allude to the matter—and I have a fancy, to account for some peculiarities in him, which connects them with some abominable early experience. Thus,—if you question him about it, he shuts his eyes involuntarily and shows exactly the same marks of loathing that may be noticed while a piece of cruelty is mentioned . . and the *word* 'blood,' even, makes him change colour. To all women and children *he* is 'chivalrous' . . as you called his unworthy son! There is no service which the ugliest, oldest, crossest woman in the world might not exact of him. But I must leave off; to-morrow I do really see you at last, dearest! God bless you ever for your very own R.

The France-route seems in nearly every way the best—perhaps in every way—let it be as you have decided. Nothing is said in this letter, nothing answered, mind . . time presses so!

E. B. B. to R. B.

Thursday Night.
[August 27, 1846.]

Here is the bad news going to you as fast as bad news *will* go! for you 'do really (NOT) see me to-morrow,' Robert, —there is no chance of it for such 'too, two' wise people as we are! In the first place Mr. Kenyon never paid his visit to-day and will do it to-morrow instead; and secondly, and while I was gloomily musing over this 'great fact,' arrives the tidings of my uncle and aunt Hedley's being at Fenton's Hotel for two days from this evening . . so that not only Friday perishes, but even Saturday, unless there should be a change in their plans. We shall have them here continually; and there would neither be safety nor peace if we attempted a meeting. So let us take patience, dearest beloved, and let me feel you loving me through the distance. It is only for a short time, to bear these weeks without our days in them; and presently you will have too much of me perhaps,—ah, the ungrateful creature, who stops in the middle of the sentence, thunderstruck in the tenderest part of her conscience! So instead, I go on to say that certainly I shall be happy with you, as long as my 'sitting in the room' does not make you less happy—certainly I shall be happy with you. I thought once that the capacity of happiness was destroyed in me, but you have *made* it over again,—God has permitted you! And while you love me *so* . . *essentially*, as you describe, and apart from supposed and supposititious qualities, . . I will take courage and hope, and believe that such a love may be enough for the happiness of us both—enough for yours even.

Your father is worthy to be your father, let you call yourself his 'unworthy son' ever so. The noblest inheritance of sons is to have such thoughts of their fathers, as you have of yours—the privilege of such thoughts, the faith in such virtues and the gratitude for such affection.

You have better than the silver or the gold, and you can afford to leave those to less happy sons. And your mother —Scarcely I was a woman when I lost *my* mother—dearest as she was, and very tender, (as yours even could be), but of a nature harrowed up into some furrows by the pressure of circumstances: for we lost more in her than she lost in life, my dear dearest mother. A sweet, gentle nature, which the thunder a little turned from its sweetness—as when it turns milk. One of those women who never can resist; but, in submitting and bowing on themselves, make a mark, a plait, within,—a sign of suffering. Too womanly she was—it was her only fault. Good, good, and dear—and refined too!—she would have admired and loved you,—but I can only tell you so, for she is gone past us all into the place of the purer spirits. God had to take her, before He could bless her enough.

Now I shall not write any more to-night. You had my note to-day—the note written this morning? I went out in the carriage, and we drove to one or two shops and up the Uxbridge Road, and I was utterly dull. Shall I not really see you before Monday? It seems impossible to bear. Let us hope at any rate, for Saturday.

How could such an idea enter your head, pray, as that about selling your copyrights? That would have been travelling at the price of blood, and I never should have agreed to it. I shall be able to bring you a few pennies, I hope; only it would not be enough for the journey, what *I* could bring, under the circumstances of imprisonment. When we are free, we ought to place our money somewhere on the railroads, where the percentage will be better—which will not disturb the simplicity of our way of life, you know, though it will give us more liberty in living.

Now I expect to hear your decision about Mrs. Jameson —I expect to hear from you of yourself, though, most and chiefest—tell me how you are, and how your mother is. Dearest, *promise* me not to say to your family any foolishness about me—remember what the recoil will be, and understand that I must suffer in proportion to all the over-praises. It quite frightens me to think of it! And then, again, I laugh to myself at your excellent logic of comparison, between Miss Campbell and me; and how you did not care for walking the bazaars and looking at the dolls with her; to the discredit of the whole class of Miss Campbells . . whereas, with ME!! &c. No wonder that your father should give you books of logic to study, books on the 'right use of reason,' if you do not understand that I am not better than she, except by your loving me better; that the cause is not in her or me, but in you only. Can it indeed be so true that people, when they love other people, never see them at all? Yet it seems to me that I see *you* clearly, discern you entirely and thoroughly—which makes me love you profoundly. But you . . without seeing me at all, you love *me* . . which does as well, I think —so I am your very own.

R. B. to E. B. B.

Friday.
[Post-mark, August 28, 1846.]

I was beginning to dress, hours before the proper time, through the confidence of seeing you *now*,—after the letter which came early in the morning,—when this new letter changes everything. It just strikes me, what a comfort it is that whenever such a disappointment is inevitable, your hand or voice announces it, and not another's—no second person bids me stay away for good reasons I must take in trust, leaving me to deal with the innumerable fancies that arise—on the contrary, you contrive that, with the one misfortune, twenty kindnesses shall reach me—can I be very sorry *now*, for instance, that you tell me *why* it is, and how it affects you and how it will affect me in the end? Dear Ba, if you will not believe in the immortality of love, do think the poor thought that when love shall end, gratitude will begin!

I altogether agree with you—it is best to keep away—we cannot be too cautious now at the 'end of things.' I am prepared for difficulties enough, without needing to cause them by any rashness or wilfulness of my own. I really expect, for example, that out of the various plans of these sympathising friends and relations some one will mature itself sufficiently to be directly proposed to you, for your acceptance or refusal contingent on your father's approbation; the shortness of the remaining travelling season serving to compel a speedy development. Or what if your father, who was the first to propose, or at least talk about, a voyage to Malta or elsewhere, when you took no interest in the matter comparatively, and who perhaps chiefly found fault with last year's scheme for its not originating with himself . . what if he should again determine on some such voyage now that you are apparently as obedient to his wishes as can be desired? Would it be strange, not to say improbable, if he tells you some fine morning that your passage is taken to Madeira, or Palermo? Because, all the attempts in the world cannot hide the truth from the mind, any more than all five fingers before the eyes keep out the sun at noon-day: you see a red through them all—and your father must see your improved health and strength, and divine the opinion of everybody round him as to the simple proper course for the complete restoration of them. Therefore be prepared, my own Ba!

In any case—I trust in you wholly.

There is nothing to decide upon, with respect to Mrs. Jameson—the reasons for not sharing that confidence with her are irrefragable. I only thought of you, dearest, who have to bear her all but direct enquiries. You know, *I* undergo nothing of the kind. Any such arrangement as that of taking her up at Orleans would be very practicable. I rejoice in your desire (by the way) of going rapidly on, stopping nowhere, till we reach our appointed place—because that spirit *helps* the body wonderfully—and, in this case, exactly corresponds with mine. Above all, I should hate to be seen at Paris by anybody a few days only after our adventure—Chorley will be there, and the Arnoulds,—for *one* party!

What could it be, you thought should make you 'sorry,' in that letter of yesterday, love? What was I to 'forgive'? Certainly you are unforgiven hitherto, for the best of reasons.

And assure yourself, dearest, that I have told my family nothing that can possibly mislead them. Remember that I have the advantage of knowing those I speak to,—their tastes and understandings, and notions of what is advantageous and what otherwise. I spoke the simple truth about your heart—of your mind they knew something already—I explained your position with respect to your father . . unfortunately, a very few plain words do that . . I mean, a few facts, such as the parish register could supply . . sufficiently to exonerate you and me.

As to my copyrights, I never meant to sell them—it would be foolish—because, since some little time, and in consequence of the establishment of the fact that my poems, even in their present disadvantageous form, without advertisement, and unnoticed by the influential journals—do somehow manage to pay their expenses, I have had one direct offer to print a new edition,—and there are reasons for thinking, two or three booksellers, that I know, would come to terms. Smith & Elder, for instance, wrote to offer to print any poem about Italy, in any form, with any amount of advertisements, on condition of sharing profits . . taking all risk off my hands . . concluding with more than a hint that if that proposition was not favourable enough, they would try and agree to any reasonable demand.

Because Moxon is the 'slowest' of publishers, and if one of his books can only contrive to pay its expenses, you may be sure that a more enterprising brother of the craft would have sent it into a second or third edition—yet

Moxon's slow self even, anticipates success for the next venture. Now the fact is, not having really cared about anything except not losing too much money, I have taken very little care of my concerns in that way—not calling on Moxon for months together. But all will be different now—and I shall look into matters, and turn my experience to account, such as it is.

Well,—I am yours, *you* are mine, dearest Ba! I love you, I think, *perceptibly* more in these latter days! Is this absence contrived on purpose to prove how foolishly I said that I loved you the more from seeing you the oftener? Ah, you reconcile all extremes, destroy the force of all logic-books, my father's or mine—*that* was true, but this is also true (logical or no) that I now love you through not seeing you,—loving more, as I desire more to be with you, my best, dearest wife that will be! (*I* could not help writing it—why should it sound sweeter than 'Ba'?)

Your very own R.

E. B. B. to R. B.

Friday Evening.
[Post-mark, August 29, 1846.]

Will you come, dearest, after all? Judge for both of us. The Hedleys go to-morrow morning and we shall not see them after to-night when they are dining here—but Mr. Kenyon has not paid his visit, and *may* come to-morrow, or *may* take Sunday, which he is fond of doing—is it worth while to be afraid of Mr. Kenyon? What do you think? I leave it to your wisdom which is the greatest. Perhaps he may not come till *Monday*—yet *he may*.

Dearest, I have had all your thoughts by turns, or most of them . . and each one has withered away without coming to bear fruit. Papa seems to have no more idea of my living beyond these four walls, than of a journey to Lapland. I confess that I thought it possible he might propose the country for the summer, or even Italy for the winter, in a 'late remark'—but no, 'nothing' and there is not a possibility of either word, as I see things. My brothers 'wish that something could be arranged'—a wish which I put away quietly as often as they bring it to me. And for my uncle and aunt, they have been talking to me to-day—and she with her usual acuteness in such matters, observing my evasion, said, 'Ah Ba, you have arranged your plans more than you would have us believe. But you are right not to tell us—indeed I would rather not hear. Only *don't be rash—that* is my only advice to you.'

I thought she had touched the truth, and wondered—but since then, from another of her words, I came to conclude that she imagined me about to accept the convoy of Henrietta and Captain Cook! She said in respect to them—'I only say that your father's consent ought to be *asked*, as a form of respect to him.' Which, in their case should be, I think—and should also in ours, but for the peculiar position of one of us. My uncle urged me to keep firm and go to Italy, and my aunt, though she would not advise, she said, yet thought that I 'ought to go,' and that to live on in this fashion in this room was lamentable to contemplate. Both of them approved of the French route, and urged me to go to them in Paris—'And,' said my uncle kindly, 'when once we *have* you, we shall not bear to part with you, I think.'

Do you really imagine, by the way, that to appear in Paris for one half-minute, to a single soul, could be less detestable to me than to you? I shall take care that nobody belonging to me there shall hear of my being within a hundred miles—and why need we stay in Paris the half minute? Not unless you pause to demand an audience of Mr. Chorley at the Barrière des Étoiles.

While we were talking, Papa came into the room. My aunt said, 'How well she is looking'—'Do you think so?' he said. 'Why, do not *you* think so? Do you pretend to say that you see no surprising difference in her?'—'Oh, I don't know,' he went on to say.' 'She is mumpish, I think.' Mumpish!

'She does not talk,' resumed he—

'Perhaps she is nervous'—my aunt apologised—I said not one word . . When birds have their eyes out, they are apt to be mumpish.

Mumpish! The expression proved a displeasure. Yet I am sure that I have shown as little sullenness as was possible. To be very talkative and vivacious under such circumstances as those of mine, would argue insensibility, and was certainly beyond my power.

I told her gently afterwards that she had been wrong in speaking of me at all—a wrong with a right intention,—as all her wrongness must be. She was very sorry to have done it, she said, and looked sorry.

Poor Papa!—Presently I shall be worse to him than 'mumpish' even. But *then*, I hope, he will try to forgive me, as I have forgiven him, long ago.

My own beloved—do you know that your letter caught me in the act of wondering whether the absence would do me harm with you, according to that memorable theory.. And so in the midst came the solution of the doubt—you do *not* love me less. Nay, you love me more—ah, but if you say so, I am capable of wishing not to see you for a month added to the week! For did I not once confess to you that I loved your love as much as I loved you . . or very, very, very nearly as much? Not precisely so much. *Confiteor tibi*—but I will sing a penitential psalm low to myself and do the act of penance by seeing you to-morrow if you choose to come,—and then you shall absolve me and give me the *Benedicite*, which, *if* you come, you cannot keep back, because it comes with you of necessity.

Not a word of your head, nor of your mother! You should come I think, to-morrow, if only to say it. Yet let us be wise to the end. Be *you* wise to the end, and decide between Saturday and Monday. And I, for my part, promise to go to Italy, only with *you*—do not be afraid.

And for your poetry, I believe in it as '*golden water*'—and the 'singing tree' does not hide it from me with all the overdropping branches and leaves. In fact, the chief inconvenience we are likely to suffer from, in the way of income, is the having *too much.* Don't you think so? But in that case, we will buy an island of our own in one of those purple seas, and inherit the sun—or perhaps the shadow . . of Calypso's cave.

So do not be uneasy, dearest!—not even lest I should wish to spend three weeks in Paris, to show myself at the Champs Élysées and the opera, and gather a little glory after what you happily call 'our adventure.'

Our adventure, indeed! But it is *you* who are adventuring in the matter,—and as any Red Cross Knight of them all, whom you exceed in their chivalry proper.

Chiappino little knew how right he was, when he used to taunt me with my 'New Cross Knight.' He did—Ah! Even if he had talked of 'Rosie Cross,' he would not have been so far wide—the magic 'saute aux yeaux.'

And now, will you come to-morrow, I wonder, or not? The answer is in you.

And I am your own, ever and as ever!

And you thought I was dying with a desire to tell Mrs. Jameson!!—*I!*

E. B. B. to R. B.

Sunday.
[Post-mark, August 31, 1846.]

I have just come from the vestry of Paddington chapel, and bore it very well, and saw nobody except one woman. Arabel went with me, and during the singing we escaped and stood outside the door. Now, *that* is over; and the next time I shall care less. It was a rambling sermon, which I could hear distinctly through the open door, quite wanting in coherence, but with good and touching things in it, the more touching that they came from a preacher whose life is known to us—from Mr. Stratton, for whom I have the greatest respect, though he never looked into Shakespeare till he was fifty, and shut the book quickly, perhaps, afterward. He is the very ideal of his class; and, with some of the narrow views peculiar to it, has a heart of miraculous breadth and depth; loving further than he can see, pitying beyond what he can approve, having in him a divine Christian spirit, the 'love of love' in the most expansive form. How that man is beloved by his congregation, the members of his church, by his children, his friends, is wonderful to see—for everybody seems to love him *from afar*, as a man is loved who is of a purer nature than others. There is that reverence in the love—and yet no fear. His children have been encouraged and instructed to speak aloud before him on religion and other subjects in all freedom of conscience—he turns to his little daughter seriously 'to hear what she thinks.' The other day his eldest son, whom he had hoped to see succeed him at Paddington, determined to enter the Church of England: his wife became quite ill with grief about it, and to himself perhaps it was a trial, a disappointment. With the utmost gentleness and tenderness however, he desired him to take time for thought and act according to his conscience.—I believe for my part that there never was a holier man . . 'except those bonds' . . never a man who more resolutely trod under his feet every form of evil and selfish passion when it was once recognized—and looked to God and the Truth with a direct aspiration. Once I could not help writing to put our affairs into his hands to settle them for us—but *that* would be wrong—because Papa would forbid Arabel's going to the chapel or communicating with his family, and it would be depriving her of a comfort she holds dear—oh no. And besides, you are wise in taking the other view.

Think of our waiting day after day to fall into the net so, yesterday! How I was provoked and vexed—but more for you, dearest dearest, than for me—much more for you. As for me I *saw you*, which was joy enough, let the hours be ever so clipped of their natural proportions—and then, you know, you were obliged to go soon, whether Mr. Kenyou had come or not come. After you were gone, nothing was said, and nothing asked, and it is delightful to have heard of those intended absences one after another till far into October: which will secure us from future embarrassments. See if he means to put us to the question!—not such a thing is in his thoughts.

And I said what you 'would not have believed of me'! Have you forgiven me, beloved—for saying what you would not have believed of me,—understanding that I did not mean it very seriously, though I proved to be capable of saying it? Seriously, I don't want to make unnecessary delays. It is a horrible position, however I may cover it with your roses and the thoughts of you—and far worse to myself than to you, inasmuch that what is painful to you once a week, is to me so continually. To hear the voice of my father and meet his eye makes me shrink back—to talk to my brothers leaves my nerves all trembling . . and even to receive the sympathy of my sisters turns into sorrow and fear, lest they should suffer through their affection for me. How I can look and sleep as well as I do, is a miracle exactly like the rest—or would be, if the love were not the deepest and strongest thing of all, and did not hold and possess me overcomingly. I feel myself to be yours notwithstanding every other influence, and being yours, cannot but be happy by you. Ah—let people talk as they please of the happiness of early youth! Mrs. Jameson did, the other day, when she wished kindly to take her young niece with her to the Continent, that she might enjoy what in a few years she could not so much enjoy. There is a sort of blind joy common perhaps to such times—a blind joy which blunts itself with its own leaps and bounds; peculiar to a time of comparative ignorance and inexperience of evil:—but I for my part, with all the capacity for happiness which I had from the beginning, I look back and listen to my whole life, and feel sure of what I have already told you, . . that I am *happier now than I ever was before* . . infinitely happier now, through you . . infinitely happier; even now in this position I have just called 'horrible.' When I hear you say for instance, that you 'love me *perceptibly* more' . . why I cannot, cannot be more happy than when I hear you say *that*—going to Italy seems nothing! a vulgar walk to Primrose Hill after being caught up to the third Heaven! I think nothing of Italy now, though I shall enjoy it of course when the time comes. I think only that you love me, that you are the angel of my life,—and for the despair and desolation behind me, they serve to mark the hour of your coming,—and they *are* behind, as Italy is *before*. Never can you feel for me, Robert, as I feel for you . . it is not possible of course. I am yours in a way and degree which the tenderest of other women could not be at her will. Which you know. Why should I repeat it to you? Why, except that is a reason to prove that we cannot, as you say, 'ever be a common wife and husband.' But I don't think I was intending to give proofs of *that*—no, indeed.

To-morrow I shall hear from you. Say how your mother is, in the second letter if you do not in the first. May God bless you and keep you, dearest beloved—

Your very own Ba.

There is not much in the article by Mr. Chorley, but it is right and kind as far as it goes.

R. B. to E. B. B.

Sunday Morning.
[Post-mark, August 31, 1846.]

I wonder what I shall write to you, Ba—I could suppress my feelings here, as I do on other points, and say nothing of the hatefulness of this state of things which is prolonged so uselessly. There is the point—show me one good reason, or show of reason, why we gain anything by deferring our departure till next week instead of to-morrow, and I will bear to perform yesterday's part for the amusement of Mr. Kenyon a dozen times over without complaint. But if the cold plunge *must* be taken, all this shivering delay on the bank is hurtful as well as fruitless. I *do* understand your anxieties, dearest—I take your fears and make them mine, while I put my own natural feeling of quite another kind away from us both, succeeding in *that* beyond all expectation. There is no amount of patience or suffering I would not undergo to relieve you from these apprehensions. But if, on the whole, you really determine to act as we propose in spite of them,—why, a new leaf is turned over in our journal, an old part of our adventure done with, and a new one entered upon, altogether distinct from the other. Having once decided to go to Italy with me, the next thing to decide is on the best means of going—or rather, there is just this connection between the two measures, that by the success or failure of the last, the first will have to be justified or condemned. You tell me you have decided to go—then, dearest, you will be prepared to go earlier than you promised yesterday—by the end of September at very latest. In proportion to the too probable excitement and painful circumstances of the departure, the greater amount of advantages should be secured for the departure itself. How can I take you away in even the beginning of October? We shall be a fortnight on the journey—with the year, as everybody sees and says, a full month in advance . . cold mornings and dark evenings already. Everybody would cry out on such folly when it was found that we let the favorable weather escape, in full assurance that the Autumn would come to us unattended by any one beneficial circumstance.

My own dearest, I am wholly your own, for ever, and under every determination of yours. If you find yourself unable, or unwilling to make this effort, tell me so and plainly and at once—I will not offer a word in objection,—I will continue our present life, if you please, so far as may be desirable, and wait till next autumn, and the next and the next, till providence end our waiting. It is clearly not for me to pretend to instruct you in your duties to God and yourself; . . enough, that I have long ago chosen to accept your decision. If, on the other hand, you make up your mind to leave England now, you will be prepared by the end of September.

I should think myself the most unworthy of human beings if I could employ any arguments with the remotest show of a tendency to *frighten* you into a compliance with any scheme of mine. Those methods are for people in another relation to you. But you love me, and, at lowest, shall I say, wish me well—and the fact is too obvious for me to commit any indelicacy in reminding you, that in any dreadful event to our journey of which I could accuse myself as the cause,—as of this undertaking to travel with you in the worst time of year when I could have taken the best,—in the case of your health being irretrievably shaken, for instance . . the happiest fate I should pray for would be to live and die in some corner where I might never hear a word of the English language, much less a comment in it on my own wretched imbecility,—to disappear and be forgotten.

So that must not be, for all our sakes. My family will give me to you that we may be both of us happy . . but for such an end—no!

Dearest, do you think all this earnestness foolish and uncalled for?—that I might know you spoke yesterday in mere jest,—as yourself said, 'only to hear what I would say'? Ah but consider, my own Ba, the way of our life, as it is, and is to be—a word, a simple word from you, is not as a word is counted in the world—the word between us is different—I am guided by your will, which a word shall signify to me. Consider that just such a word, so spoken, even with that lightness, would make me lay my life at your feet at any minute. Should we gain anything by my trying, if I could, to deaden the sense of hearing, dull the medium of communication between us; and procuring that, instead of this prompt rising of my will at the first intimation from yours, the same effect should only follow after fifty speeches, and as many protestations of complete serious desire for their success on your part, accompanied by all kinds of acts and deeds and other evidences of the same?

At all events, God knows I have said this in the deepest, truest love of you. I will say no more, praying you to forgive whatever you shall judge to need forgiveness here,—dearest Ba! I will also say, if that may help me,—and what otherwise I might not have said,—that I am not too well this morning, and write with an aching head. My mother's suffering continues too.

My friend Pritchard tells me that Brighton is not to be thought of under ordinary circumstances as a point of departure for Havre. Its one packet a week from Shoreham cannot get in if the wind and tide are unfavourable. There is the greatest uncertainty in consequence . . as I have heard before—while, of course, from Southampton, the departures are calculated punctually. He considers that the least troublesome plan, and the cheapest, is to go from London to Havre . . the voyage being so arranged that the river passage takes up the day and the sea-crossing the night—you reach Havre early in the morning and get to Paris by four o'clock, perhaps, in the afternoon . . in time to leave for Orleans and spend the night there, I suppose.

Do I make myself particularly remarkable for silliness when confronted by our friend as yesterday? And the shortest visit,—and comments of everybody. Oh, Mr. Hunter, methinks you should be of some use to me with those amiable peculiarities of yours, if you would just dye your hair black, take a stick in your hand, sink the clerical character you do such credit to, and have the goodness just to deliver yourself of one such epithet as *that* pleasant one, the next time you find me on the steps of No. 50, with Mr. Kenyon somewhere higher up in the building. It is delectable work, this having to do with relatives and 'freemen who have a right to beat their own negroes,' and father Zeus with his paternal epistles, and peggings to the rock, and immense indignation at 'this marriage you talk of' which is to release his victim. Is Mr. Kenyon Hermes?

> *Εἰσελθέτω σε μήποθ' ὡς ἐγὼ Διὸς*
> *γνώμην φοβηθεὶς θηλύνους γενήσομαι,*
> *καὶ λιπαρήσω τὸν μέγα στυγούμενον*
> *γυναικομίμοις ὑπτιάσμασιν χερῶν,*
> *λῦσαί με δεσμῶν τῶνδε· τοῦ παντὸς δέω.*
> *Chorus of Aunts:* *ἡμῖν μὲν Ἑρμῆς οὐκ ἄκαιρα φαίνεται*
> *λέγειν, κ. τ. λ.*[1]

Well, bless you in any case—
Your own R.

R. B. to E. B. B.

Monday Morning.
[Post-mark, August 31, 1846.]

Here is dearest Ba's dearest letter, because the latest, and it is one of her very kisses incorporated and made manifest—so perfectly kind! And should this make me ashamed of perhaps an over-earnestness in what I wrote yesterday? or not rather justify me to myself and to her—since it was on a passing fear of losing what I hold so infinitely precious, that the earnestness happened! My own Ba, you lap me over with love upon love . . there is my first and proper love, independent of any return, and there is *this* return for what would reward itself. Do think how I must feel at the most transient suggestion of failure, and parting, and an end to all! You cannot expect I can lie

[1] ['Oh, think no more
That I, fear-struck by Zeus to a woman's mind
Will supplicate him, loathèd as he is,
With feminine upliftings of my hands,
To break these chains. Far from me be the thought!
Chorus. Our Hermes suits his reasons to the times;
At least I think so.'
Æschylus, *Prometheus*, 1002–6, 1036–7.]

quietly and let my life of life be touched. And ever, dearest, through the life which I trust is about to be permitted us,—ever I shall remember where my treasure is, and turn as vigilantly when it is approached. Beside, I was not very well, as I told you in excuse—I am much better now. Not that, upon reconsideration, I can alter my opinion on the proper course to take. We know all the miracles wrought in our favour hitherto . . are not the chances (speaking in that foolish way) against our expecting more? To-day is fine, sunny and warm, for instance, and looks as if cold weather were a long way off—but what are these fancies and appearances when weighed against the other possibility of a sudden *fall* of the year? By six months more of days like this we should gain nothing, nothing in the world, you confess—by the other misfortune we lose everything perhaps.

Will you have a homely illustration? There is a tree against our wall here which produced weeks ago a gigantic apple—which my mother had set her heart on showing a cousin of mine who is learned in fruits and trees. I told her, 'You had better pluck it at once—it will fall and be spoiled.' She thought the next day or two would do its cheeks good,—just the next—so there it continued to hang till this morning, when she was about to go out with my sister—I said 'now is the time—you are going to my aunt's—let me pluck you the apple'—'Oh,' she said 'I have been looking at it, trying it,—it hangs so firmly, . . not *this* time, thank you!' So she went without it, two hours ago—and just now, I turned to the tree with a boding presentiment—there lay our glory, bruised in the dirt, a sad wreck! 'Comfort me with apples, for I am sick of love!' Rather, counsel me *through* apples! Do you see the counsel?

Come, let me not be so ungrateful to the letter, to what you have done for me, as only to speak of what you are disinclined to do. I am very glad you succeeded in going to the chapel, and that the result was so favourable—see how the dangers disappear when one faces them! And the account of Mr. Stratten is very interesting, too—besides characteristic—do you see *how?* Find as great a saint as the world holds, who shall be acknowledged to be utterly disinterested, unbiassed by anything except truth and common justice,—a man of sense as well as piety—and succeed in convincing such an one of our right to do as we purpose,—and then—let *him* lay the matter before your father! To no other use than to exasperate him against Mr. Stratten, deprive your sister of the privilege of seeing his family, and bring about a little more pain and trouble!

Let me think of something else . . of the happiness you profess to feel—which it makes me entirely happy to know. I will not try and put away the crown you give me. I just say the obvious truth, . . even what I *can* do to make you happy, according to my ability, has yet to be experienced by you . . if my thoughts and wishes reach you with any effect at present, they will operate freelier when the obstruction is removed . . that is only natural. I shall live for you, for every minute in your life. May God bless me with such a life, as that it may be of use to you . . yours it must be whether of use or not, for I am wholly your R.

Here comes my mother back . . she is a little better to-day. I am much better as I said. And you? Let me get the kiss I lost on Saturday! (I dined at Arnould's yesterday with Chorley and his brother, and the Cushmans.) Chorley goes to-night to Ostend.

E. B. B. to R. B.

Monday Night.
[Post-mark, September 1, 1846.]

You are better, dearest,—and so I will confess to having felt a little inclined to reproach you gently for the earlier letter, except that you were not well when you wrote it. That you should endure painfully and impatiently a position unworthy of you, is the natural consequence of the unworthiness—and I do hold that you would be justified at this moment, on the barest motives of self-respect, in abandoning the whole ground and leaving me to Mr. Kenyon and others. What I might complain of, is another thing—what I might complain of is, that I have not given you reason to *doubt me* or my inclination to accede to any serious wish of yours relating to the step before us. On the contrary I told you in so many words in July, that, if you really wished to go in August rather than in September, I would make no difficulty—to which you answered, remember, that *October or November would do as well.* Now *is* it fair, ever dearest, that you should turn round on me so quickly, and call in question my willingness to keep my engagement for years, if ever? Can I help it, if the circumstances around us are painful to both of us? Did I not keep repeating, from the beginning, that they *must* be painful? Only you could not believe, you see, until you felt the pricks. And when all is done, and the doing shall be the occasion of new affronts, sarcasms, every form of injustice, will you be any happier then, than you are now that you only imagine the possibility of them? I tremble to answer that question—even to myself—! As for myself, though I cannot help feeling pain and fear, in encountering what is to be encountered, and though I sometimes fear, in addition, for *you*, lest you should overtask your serenity in bearing your own part in it, . . yet certainly I have never wavered for a moment from the decision on which all depends. I might fill up your quotations from 'Prometheus,' and say how no evil takes me unaware, having foreseen all from the beginning—but I have not the heart for filling up quotations. I mean to say only, that I never wavered from the promise I gave freely; and that I will keep it freely at any time you choose—that is, within a week of any time you choose. As to a light word . . . why now, dear, judge me in justice! If I had written it, there might have been more wrong in it—but I spoke it lightly to show it was light, and in the next breath I told you that it was a jest. Will you not forgive me a word so spoken, Robert? will you rather set it against me as if habitually I threw to you levities in change for earnest devotion?—you imply *that* of me. Or you *seem* to imply it—you did not mean, you could not, a thought approaching to unkindness,—but it looks like *that* in the letter, or *did*, this morning. And all the time, you pretended not to know very well, . . (dearest!) . . that what you made up your mind to wish and ask of me, I had not in my power to say 'no' to. Ah, you *knew* that you had only to make up your mind, and to see that the thing was possible. So if September shall be possible, let it be September. I do not object nor hold back. To sail from the Thames has not the feasibility—and listen why! All the sailing or rather steaming from London begins *early;* and I told you how out of the question it was, for me to leave this house early. I could not, without involving my sisters. Arabel sleeps in my room, on the sofa, and is seldom out of the room before nine in the morning—and for me to draw her into a ruinous confidence, or to escape without a confidence at that hour, would be equally impossible. Now see if it is my fancy, my whim! And as for the expenses, *they* are as nearly equal as a shilling and two sixpences can be—the expense of the sea-voyage from London to Havre, and of the land and sea voyage, through Southampton . . *or* Brighton. But of course what you say of Brighton, keeps us to Southampton, of those two routes. We can go to Southampton and meet the packet . . take the river-steamer to Rouen, and proceed as rapidly as your programme shows. You are not angry with me, dearest, dearest? I did not mean any harm.

May God bless you always. *I* am not angry either, understand, though I did think this morning that you were a little hard on me, just when I felt myself ready to give up the whole world for you at the holding up of a finger. And now say nothing of this. I kiss the end of the dear finger; and when *it* is ready, *I* am ready; I will not be reproached again. Being too much your own, very own

Ba.

Tell me that you keep better. And your mother?

R. B. to E. B. B.

Tuesday—3 p.m.
[Post-mark, September 1, 1846.]

Dearest, when your letter kept away, all this morning, I never once fancied you might be angry . . I knew you must feel the love which produced the fear. And I will lay to my heart the little, gentlest blame that there is, in the spirit which dictated it. I know, my own Ba, your words have given me the right to doubt nothing from your generosity—but it is not the mere bidding . . no, at the thousandth repetition—which can make me help myself to all that treasure which you please to call mine: I shall perhaps get used to the generosity and readier to profit by it.

I have not time to write much; all is divinely kind of you, and I love you for forgiving me.

You could not leave at an early hour under those circumstances . . the moment I become aware of them, I fully see that.

Ah, but, Ba, am I so to blame for not taking your diamonds, while you disclaim a right over my pebbles even? May I 'withdraw from the business'? &c., &c.

Kiss me, and do not say that again—and I will say you are 'my own,' as I always say,—my very own!

As for 'sarcasms' and the rest—I shall hardly do other than despise what will never be said *to* me, for the best of reasons—except where is to be exception. I never objected to such miserable work as that—and the other day, my annoyance was not at anything which *might* be fancied, by Mr. Kenyon or anybody else, but at what could not but be plainly seen—it was a fact, and not a fancy, that our visit was shortened &c., &c.

All which is foolish to think of—I will think of you and a better time.

You do not tell me how you are, Ba—and I left you with a headache. Will you tell me? And the post may come in earlier to-morrow,—at all events I will write at length . . not in this haste. And our day? When before have I been without a day, a fixed day, to look forward to?

Bless you, my dearest beloved—

Your own R.

I am pretty well to-day—not too well. My mother is no better than usual; we blame the wind, with or without reason. See this scrawl! Could anything make me write legibly, I wonder?

Ba.

BA.

βα.

Ba, Ba, Ba.

E. B. B. to R. B.

Tuesday.
[Post-mark, September 2, 1846.]

Here is a distress for me, dearest! I have lost my poor Flush—*lost* him! You were a prophet when you said 'Take care.'

This morning Arabel and I, and he with us, went in a cab to Vere Street where we had a little business, and he followed us as usual into a shop and out of it again, and was at my heels when I stepped up into the carriage. Having turned, I said 'Flush,' and Arabel looked round for Flush—there was no Flush! He had been caught up in that moment, from *under* the wheels, do you understand? and the thief must have run with him and thrown him into a bag perhaps. It was such a shock to me—think of it! losing him in a moment, *so!* No wonder if I looked white, as Aràbel said! So she began to comfort me by showing how certain it was that I should recover him for ten pounds at most, and we came home ever so drearily. Because *Flush* doesn't know that we can recover him, and he is in the extremest despair all this while, poor darling Flush, with his fretful fears, and pretty whims, and his fancy of being near me. All this night he will howl and lament, I know perfectly,—for I fear we shall not ransom him to-night. Henry went down for me directly to the captain of the banditti, who evidently knew all about it, said Henry, —and after a little form of consideration and enquiry, promised to let us hear something this evening, but has not come yet. In the morning perhaps he will come. Henry told him that I was resolved not to give much—but of course they will make me give what they choose—I am not going to leave Flush at their mercy, and they know that as well as I do. My poor Flush!

When we shall be at Pisa, dearest, we shall be away from the London dog-stealers—it will be one of the advantages. Another may be that I may have an opportunity of 'forgiving' you, which I have not had yet. I might reproach you a little in my letter, and I *did*, I believe; but the offending was not enough for any *forgiving* to follow—it is too grand a word. Also your worst is better than my best, taking it on the whole. How then should I be able to *forgive* you, my beloved, even *at Pisa?*

If we go to Southampton, we go straight from the rail-road to the packet, without entering any hotel—and if we do *so*, *no* greater expense is incurred than by the long water-passage from London. Also, we reach Havre alike in the morning, and have the day before us for Rouen, Paris and Orleans. Thereupon nothing is lost by losing the early hour for the departure. Then, if I accede to your *idée fixe* about the marriage! Only do not let us put a long time between that and the setting out, and do not you come here afterwards—let us go away as soon as possible afterwards at least. You are afraid for me of my suffering from the autumnal cold when it is yet far off—while *I* (observe this!) while *I* am afraid for myself, of breaking down under quite a different set of causes, in nervous excitement and exhaustion. I belong to that pitiful order of weak women who cannot command their bodies with their souls at every moment, and who sink down in hysterical disorder when they ought to act and resist. Now I think and believe that I shall take strength from my attachment to you, and so go through to the end what is before us; but at the same time, knowing myself and fearing myself, I do desire to provoke the 'demon' as little as possible, and to be as quiet as the situation will permit. Still, where things *ought* to be done, they of course *must* be done. Only we should consider whether they really *ought* to be done—not for the sake of the inconvenience to me, but of the consequence to both of us.

Do I frighten you, ever dearest? Oh no—I shall go through it, if I keep a breath of soul in me to live with. I shall go through it, as certainly as that I love you. I speak only of the accessory circumstances, that they may be kept as smooth as is practicable.

You are not well, my beloved—and I cannot even dream of making you better this time,—because you will think it wise for us not to meet for the next few days perhaps. Mr. Kenyon will come to see me, he said, before he leaves town, and he leaves it on the fourth, fifth or sixth of September. This is the first. So I will not let you come to be vexed as last time—no, indeed. But write to me instead—and pity me for Flush. Oh, I trust to have him back to-morrow. I had no headache, and was quite perfectly well this morning . . before I lost him.

Is your mother able to walk? is she worse on the whole than last week for instance? We may talk of September, but you cannot leave her, you know, dearest, if she should be *so* ill! it would be unkind and wrong.

More, to-morrow! But I cannot be more to-morrow, your very own—

R. B. to E. B. B.

Wednesday Morning.
[Post-mark, September 2, 1846.]

Poor Flush—how sorry I am for you, my Ba! But you will recover him, I dare say . . not, perhaps directly; the delay seems to justify their charge at the end: poor fellow—was he no better than the rest of us, and did all that barking and fanciful valour spend itself on such enemies as Mr. Kenyon and myself, leaving only blandness and waggings of the tail for the man with the bag? I am sure you are grieved and frightened for our friend and follower, that was to be, at Pisa—will you not write a special note to tell me when you get him again?

For the rest—I will urge you no more by a single word—you shall arrange everything henceforward without a desire on my part,—an expressed one at least. Do not let our happiness be caught up from us, after poor Flush's fashion—there may be no redemption from *that* peril.

There can hardly be another way of carrying our purpose into effect than by that arrangement you consent to—except you choose to sacrifice a day and incur all costs of risk. Of course, the whole in the way and with the conditions that you shall determine.

Do you think, Ba, I apprehend nothing from the excitement and exhaustion attendant on it? I altogether apprehend it,—and am therefore the more anxious that no greater difficulty should be superinduced than is absolutely necessary. Because the first part of our adventure will be dangerous in *that* way, I want the second part to be as safe as possible in another. I should care comparatively little about winter-travelling, even (knowing that one can take precautions)—if it were to be undertaken under really propitious circumstances, and you set forth with so much kindness to carry away as would keep you warm for a week or two—but the 'winter wind that is not *so* unkind as &c,' may prove,—by adding its share of unkindness to the greater,—intolerable. Now, my last word is said, however—and a kiss follows!

I thank you, dearest, for your enquiries about my mother; and for the sympathy, and proposal of delay. She is better this morning, I hope. From the time that my sister went to Town, she discontinued the exercise which does her such evident good—and on Monday the walks began again—with no great effect yesterday because of the dull weather and sharp wind . . she kept at home—but this morning she is abroad, and will profit by this sunshine, I hope. My head will not get quite well, neither. I take both effects to be caused by the turn of the year.

Bless you, dearest—I cannot but acquiesce in your postponing our day for such reasons. Only, do not misconceive those few foolish words of impatience . . a great matter to bear truly! I shall be punished indeed if they prevent you from according to me one hour I should have otherwise possessed.

Bless you once again, my Ba.

My mother is returned—very much better indeed. Remember Flush—to write.

E. B. B. to R. B.

Wednesday Evening.
[Post-mark, September 3, 1846.]

'Our friend and follower, that *was* to be'—is *that*, then, your opinion of my poor darling Flush's destiny—? Ah,—I should not have been so quiet if I had not known differently and better. I 'shall not recover him directly,' you think! But, dearest, I am *sure* that I *shall*. I am learned in the ways of the Philistines—I knew from the beginning where to apply and how to persuade. The worst is poor Flush's fright and suffering. And then, it is inconvenient just now to pay the ransom for him. But we shall have time to-morrow if not to-night. Two hours ago the chief of the Confederacy came to call on Henry and to tell him that the 'Society had the dog,' having done us the honour of tracking us into Bond Street and out of Bond Street into Vere Street where he was kidnapped. Now he is in Whitechapel (poor Flush). And the great man was going down there at half past seven to meet other great men in council and hear the decision as to the ransom exacted, and would return with their *ultimatum*. Oh, the villainy of it is excellent, and then the humiliation of having to pay for your own vexations and anxieties! *Will* they have the insolence, now, to make me pay ten pounds, as they said they would? But I must have Flush, you know—I can't run any risk, and bargain and haggle. There is a dreadful tradition in this neighbourhood, of a lady who did *so* having her dog's head sent to her in a parcel. So I say to Henry—'Get Flush back, whatever you do'—for Henry is angry as he may well be, and as *I* should be if I was not too afraid . . and talks police-officers against thieves, and finds it very hard to attend to my instructions and be civil and respectful to their captain. There he found him, smoking a cigar in a room with pictures! They make some three or four thousand a year by their honourable employment. As to Flush's following anyone 'blandly,' never think it. He was caught up and gagged . . depend upon that. If he could have bitten, he would have bitten—if he could have yelled, he would have yelled. Indeed on a former occasion the ingenuous thief observed, that he 'was a difficult dog to get, he was so distrustful.' They had to drag him with a string, put him into a cab, they said, before. Poor Flush!

Dearest, I am glad that your mother is a little better—but why should the turn of the year make you suffer, ever dearest? I am not easy about you indeed. Remember not to use the shower-bath injudiciously—and remember to walk. *Do* you walk enough?—it being as necessary for you as for your mother.

And as for *me* you will not say a word more to *me*, you will leave me to my own devices now.

Which is just exactly what you must *not* do. Ah, why do you say so, even, when you must not do it? Have I refused one proposition of yours when there were not strong obstacles, that you should have finished with me so, my beloved? For instance, I agreed to your plan about the marrying, and I agreed to go with you to Italy in the latter part of September—did I not? And what am I disagreeing in now? Don't let me pass for disagreeable! And don't, above all, refuse to think for me, and decide for me, or what will become of me, I cannot guess. I shall be worse off than Flush is now . . in his despair, at Whitechapel. Think of my being let loose upon a common, just when the thunder-clouds are gathering!! You would not be so cruel, *you*. All I meant to say was that it would be wise to make the occasions of excitement as few as possible, for the reasons I gave you. But I shall not fail, I believe—I should despise myself too much for failing—I should lose too much by the failure. Then there is an amulet which strengthens the heart of one,—let it incline to fail ever so. Believe of me that I shall not fail, dearest beloved—I shall not, if you love me enough to stand by—believe *that* always.

The heart will sink indeed sometimes—as mine does to-night, I scarcely know why—but even while it sinks, I do not feel that I shall fail *so*—I do not. Dearest, I do not, either, 'misconceive,' as you desire me not: I only infer that you will think it best to avoid the chance of meeting Mr. Kenyon, who speaks to me, in a note received this morning, of intending to leave town next Monday—of coming here he does not speak,—and he may come and he may not come, on any intermediate day. He wrote for a book he lent me. If I do not see you until Monday, it will be hard—but judge! there was more of bitterness than of sweetness in the last visit.

Mr. Kenyon said in his note that he had seen Moxon,

and that Tennyson was 'disappointed' with the mountains. Is not that strange? Is it a good or a bad sign when people are disappointed with the miracles of nature? I am accustomed to fancy it a bad sign. Because a man's imagination ought to aggrandise, glorify, consecrate. A man sees with his mind, and mind is at fault when he does not see greatly, I think.

Moxon sent a civil message to me about my books 'going off regularly.'

And now *I* must go off—it is my turn. Do you love me to-night, dearest? I ask you . . through the air. I am your very own Ba.

Say how you are, I beseech you, and tell me always and particularly of your mother.

They are all here, gone to a picnic at Richmond.

R. B. to E. B. B.

Thursday.
[Post-mark, September 3, 1846.]

I am rejoiced that poor Flush is found again, dearest—altogether rejoiced.

And now that you probably have him by your side, I will tell you what I should have done in such a case, because it explains our two ways of seeing and meeting oppression lesser or greater. I would not have given five shillings on that fellow's application. I would have said, —and in entire earnestness '*You* are responsible for the proceedings of your gang, and *you* I mark—don't talk nonsense to me about cutting off heads or paws. Be as sure as that I stand here and tell you, I will spend my whole life in putting you down, the nuisance you declare yourself —and by every imaginable means I will be the death of you and as many of your accomplices as I can discover—but *you* I have discovered and will never lose sight of—now try my sincerity, by delaying to produce the dog by to-morrow. And for the ten pounds—see!' Whereupon I would give them to the first beggar in the street. You think I should receive Flush's head? Perhaps—*so* God allows matters to happen! on purpose, it may be, that I should vindicate him by the punishment I would exact.

Observe, Ba, this course ought not to be yours, because it *could* not be—it would not suit your other qualities. But all religion, right and justice, with me, seem implied in such a resistance to wickedness and refusal to multiply it a hundredfold—for from this prompt payment of ten pounds for a few minutes' act of the easiest villainy, there will be encouragement to—how many similar acts in the course of next month? And how will the poor owners fare who have not money enough for their dogs' redemption? I suppose the gentleman, properly disgusted with such obstinacy, will threaten roasting at a slow fire to test the sincerity of attachment! No—the world would grow too detestable a den of thieves and oppressors that way! And this is too great a piece of indignation to be expressed when one has the sick vile headache that oppresses me this morning. Dearest, I am not inclined to be even as tolerant as usual. Will you be tolerant, my Ba, and forgive me—till to-morrow at least—when, what with physic, what with impatience, I shall be better one way or another?

Ever your own R.

R. B. to E. B. B.

Thursday Afternoon.
[Post-mark, September 4, 1846.]

When I had finished that letter this morning, dearest dearest, before I could seal it, even, (my sister did it for me . . and despatched it to the post at once) I became quite ill and so sick as to be forced to go up-stairs and throw myself on the bed. It is now six o'clock, and I feel better, and have some thoughts of breaking my fast to-day —but, first of all . . did whatever it may have been I wrote seem *cross*—unnecessarily angry, to you, dearest

Ba? Because, I confess to having felt indignant at this sample of the evils done under the sun every day . . . and as if it would be to no purpose though the whole world were peopled with Ba's, instead of just Wimpole Street; as they would be just so many more soft cushions for the villainously-disposed to run pins into at their pleasure. Donne says that 'Weakness invites, but silence *feasts* oppression.' And it is horrible to fancy how all the oppressors in their several ranks may, if they choose, twitch back to them by the heartstrings after various modes the weak and silent whose secret they have found out. No one should profit by those qualities in me, at least. Having formed a resolution, I would keep it, I hope, through fire and water, and the threatener of any piece of rascality, who (as commonly happens) should be without the full heart to carry it into effect, should pay me exactly the same for the threat . . which had determined my conduct once and for ever. But in this particular case, I ought to have told you (unless you divined it, as you might) that I would give all I am ever to be worth in the world to get back your Flush for you—for your interest is not *mine*, any more than the lake is the river that goes to feed it,—mine is only made to feed yours—I am yours, as we say—as I feel more and more every minute.

Are you not mine, too? And do you not forgive your own R

E. B. B. to R. B.

Thursday Evening.
[Post-mark, September 4, 1846.]

Ever dearest, you are not well—that is the first thing!—And that is the thing I saw first, when, opening your letter, my eyes fell on the ending sentence of it,—which disenchanted me in a moment from the hope of the day. Dearest—you have not been well for two or three days, it is plain,—and now you are very, very unwell—tell me if it is not so? I beseech you to let me hear the exact truth about you, for I am very uneasy, and it is dreadful to doubt about knowing the exact truth in all such cases. How everything goes against me this week! I cannot see you. I cannot comfort myself by knowing that you are well. And then poor Flush! You must let him pass as one of the evils, and you *will,* I know; for I have not got him back yet—no, indeed.

I should have done it. The archfiend, Taylor, the man whom you are going to spend your life in persecuting (the life that belongs to me, too!), came last night to say that they would accept six pounds, six guineas, with half a guinea for himself, considering the trouble of the mediation; and Papa desired Henry to refuse to pay, and not to tell me a word about it—all which I did not find out till this morning. Now it is less, as the money goes, than I had expected, and I was very vexed and angry, and wanted Henry to go at once and conclude the business—only he wouldn't, talked of Papa, and persuaded me that Taylor would come to-day with a lower charge. He has not come —I knew he would not come,—and if people won't do as I choose, I shall go down to-morrow morning myself and bring Flush back with me. All this time he is suffering and I am suffering. It may be very foolish—I do not say it is not—or it may even be 'awful sin,' as Mr. Boyd sends to assure me—but I cannot endure to run cruel hazards about my poor Flush for the sake of a few guineas, or even for the sake of abstract principles of justice—I cannot. *You* say that *I* cannot, . . but that *you would.* You would! —Ah dearest—most pattern of citizens, but you *would not* —I know you better. Your theory is far too good not to fall to pieces in practice. A man may love justice intensely; but the love of an abstract principle is not the strongest love—now is it? Let us consider a little, putting poor Flush out of the question. (You would bear, you say, to receive his head in a parcel—it would satisfy you to cut off Taylor's in return.) Do you mean to say that if the banditti came down on us in Italy and carried me off to the mountains, and, sending to you one of my ears, to show you my probable fate if you did not let them have . . how much may I venture to say I am worth? . . five or six scudi,—(is *that* reasonable at all?) . . would your answer be 'Not so many crazie'; and would you wait, poised upon abstract principles, for the other ear, and the catastrophe, —as was done in Spain not long ago? Would you, dearest? Because it is as well to know beforehand, perhaps.

Ah—how I am teazing you, my beloved, when you are not well. But indeed that life of yours is worthy of better uses than to scourge Taylor with, even if *I* should not be worth the crazie.

I have seen nobody and heard nothing. I bought a pair of shoes to-day lined with flannel, to walk with on the bare floors of Italy in the winter. Is not *that* being practical and coming to the point? I did it indeed!

May God bless you. I love you always and am your own.

Write of yourself, I *do pray you*—and also, how is your mother?

R. B. to E. B. B.

Friday Morning.
[Post-mark, September 4, 1846.]

You dearest, best Ba, I will say at the beginning of the letter, and not at the end, this time, that I am very much better—my head clear from pain, if a little *uncertain*—I was in the garden when your letter came. The worst is, that I am really forced to go and dine out to-day—but I shall take all imaginable care and get away early . . and be ready to go and see you at a minute's notice, should a note signify your permission to-morrow . . if Mr. Kenyon's visit is over, for instance. I have to attribute this effect to that abstinent system of yours. Depend on it, I shall be well and continue well now.

Dear Ba, I wrote under the notion (as I said) that poor Flush was safe by your side; and only took that occasion to point at what I must still consider the wrongness of the whole system of giving way to, instead of opposing, such proceedings. I think it lamentable weakness . . though I can quite understand and allow for it in you,—but weakness it essentially *is*, as *you* know perfectly. For see, you first put the matter in the gentlest possible light . . 'who would give much time and trouble to the castigation of such a fellow as *that!*' You ask—and immediately after, for another purpose, you very rightly rank this crime with that other enormous one, of the Spanish banditti—nay, you confess that, in this very case, any such injury to Flush as you dread would give you inexpressible grief. Is the threatening this outrage then so little a matter? Am I to think it a less matter if the same miscreant should *strike* you in the street because you would probably suffer less than by this that he *has* done? There is the inevitable inconsistency of wrong reasoning in all this. Say, as I told you on another subject,—'I determine to resist no injury whatever, to be at the disposal of any villain in the world, trusting to God for protection here or recompense hereafter'—or take my course; *which* is the easier, and in the long run, however strangely it may seem, the more profitable, no one can doubt—but I take the harder—in all but the responsibility—which, without any cant, would be intolerable to me. Look at this 'society' with its 'four thousand a year'—which unless its members are perfect fools they will go on to double and treble—would this have existed if a proper stand had been made at the beginning? The first silly man, woman or child who consented to pay five shillings, beyond the mere expense of keeping the dog (on the supposition of its having been found, *not* stolen), is responsible for all the harm—what could the thief do but go and steal another, and ask double for its ransom?

And see—dog-stealers so encouraged are the lowest of the vile—can neither write nor read, perhaps. One of the fraternity possesses this knowledge, however, and aims higher. Accordingly, instead of stealing your dog, he determines to steal your character; if a guinea (at the beginning) ransoms the one, ten pounds shall ransom the other; accordingly Mr. Barnard Gregory takes pen in hand and writes to some timid man, in the first instance, that unless he receives that sum, his character will be blasted. The timid man takes your advice . . says that the 'love of an abstract principle' must not run him into 'cruel hazards' 'for the sake of a few guineas'—so he pays them—who would bother himself with such vermin as Gregory? So Gregory receives his pay for his five minutes' penmanship —takes down a directory, and writes five hundred such letters. Serjeant Talfourd told me, counting them on his fingers, 'such and such' (naming them) cut their throats after robbing their families, employers &c., such fled the country—such went mad . . *that* was the commonest event.' At last, even so poor a creature as the Duke of Brunswick, with his detestable character and painted face,—even *he* plucks up courage and turns on Gregory, grown by this time into a really formidable monster by these amiable victims to the other principle of easy virtue,—and the event is that this execrable 'Abhorson's' trade is utterly destroyed—that form of atrocious persecution exists no longer. I am in no danger of being told, at next post delivery, that having been 'tracked up Vere Street, down Bond Street, &c.' into Wimpole Street my character and yours will be the subject of an article in the next *Satirist* unless' . .

To all of which you have a great answer—'What should I do if *you* were to be the victim?' That my note yesterday, the second one, told you. I sacrifice *myself* . . all that belongs *to me*—but there are some interests which I belong to—I have no right, no more than inclination, in such a case, to think of myself if your safety is concerned, and as I could cut off a limb to save my head, so my head should fall most willingly to redeem yours . . I would pay every farthing I had in the world, and shoot with my own hand the receiver of it after a chase of fifty years—

esteeming *that* to be a very worthy recompense for the trouble.

But why write all this string of truisms about the plainest thing in the world? All reformers are met at the outset by such dissuasion from their efforts. 'Better suffer the grievance and get off as cheaply as you [can]—You, Mahomet,—what if the Caaba *be* only a black stone? You need only bow your head as the others, and make any inward remark you like on the blindness of the people. You, Hampden, have you really so little wit as to contest payment of a paltry 20*s.* at such risk?'

Ah, but here all the fuss is just about stealing a dog—two or three words, and the matter becomes simply ludicrous—very easily got rid of! One cannot take vengeance on the 'great man' with his cigar and room of pictures and burlesque dignities of mediation! Just so, when Robert was inclined to be sorry for the fate of Bertha's sister, one can fancy what a relief and change would be operated in his feelings, if a good-natured friend send him a version of his mighty crime in Lord Rochester's funny account of 'forsaken damsels' . . with the motto 'Women have died ere now and worms have eaten them—but not for love—' or 'At lovers' perjuries Jove laughs' why, Robert is a 'lady-killer' like D'Orsay! Well, enough of sermonizing for the present; it is impossible for me to differ with you and treat *that* as a light matter . . or, what on earth would have been so little to wonder at, as that, loving Flush, you should determine to save him at any price? If 'Chiappino' were to assure you, in terms that you could not disbelieve, that in the event of your marrying me he would destroy himself,—would you answer, as I should, 'Do so, and take the consequences,'—and think no more about the matter? I should absolutely leave it, as not my concern but God's—nor should blame myself any more than if the poor man, being uncertain what to do, had said 'If a man first passes the window—yes—if a woman—no'—and I, a total stranger, had passed.

One word more—in all this, I labour against the execrable policy of the world's husbands, fathers, brothers, and domineerers in general. I am about to marry you . . how wise, then, to encourage such a temper in you! such was that divine Griselda's—a word rules the gentle nature —'Do this, or . . . .'

My own Ba, if I thought you could fear me, I think *I* should have the courage to give you up to-morrow!

Because *to-day* I am altogether yours, and you are my very own—and to-morrow never comes, they say. Bless you, my best dearest Ba—and if you think I deserve it, you shall test the excellence of those slippers on my cheek, (and not the flannelled side, neither), the next happy time I see you . . which will be soon, soon, I trust! who am more than

ever your own R.

E. B. B. to R. B.

Friday.
[Post-mark, September 5, 1846.]

You best! Was ever any in the world, in any possible world, so perfectly good and dear to another as you are to me! Ah! if you could know how I feel to you, when you write such words as came to me this morning—Dearest! It ends in that, all I can say. And yet I must say besides that the idea of 'crossness,' of hardness, never came to me, for one moment, from the previous letter. I just shook my head and thought how you would not act it out, if *you* had a Flush. Upon which I could not follow out my argument to myself, through thinking that you were ill.

You are better now, Robert, and you promise to take care of the dinner, where you should *not* go if I were near you. I should be 'afraid of you' far too much to let you, indeed! Such a wrong thing *that* dinner is . . as wrong as any dogstealer in his way . . drawing you out just when you ought to be at home and quiet, if not 'abstinent.' When did I ever tell you to be abstinent, pray?

You are too much so, it seems to me, in general: and to pass the whole of that day without eating! How unwell you must have been, dearest! How I long to see you and ascertain that you look tolerably well! How very, very happy I should be, to be able to look at you to-morrow. But no, no! Mr. Kenyon does not come, and we must be wise, I suppose, and wait till the ground is clear of him, which will not be till Monday. Probably he will visit me on Sunday—but the chance of Saturday is like the hat on a pole in gardens, set there to frighten away the birds. Still they may sing on the other side of the wall, not to be too far from the cherries and the hope of them. Monday surely will be a clear day. Unless Mr. Kenyon shall put off his journey just to despite us—who shall say?

I have not Flush yet. I am to have him to-morrow morning.

And for the Flush-argument, dear dearest, I hold that your theory is entirely good and undeniable. I agree with you throughout it, praising Mahomet, praising Hampden, and classing the Taylors, Gregorys, and Spanish banditti all together. Also I hope I should try, at least, to resist with you their various iniquities—and, for instance, I do not think that any Gregory in the world would draw a shilling from *me*, by a threat against my own character. I should dare *that*, oh, I am confident I should—the indignation would be far the stronger, where I myself only was involved. And even in the imaginary Chiappino-case, the selfish and dastardly threat would fall from me like a child's arrow from steel. I believe so.

But Flush, poor Flush, Flush who has loved me so faithfully; have I a right to sacrifice *him* in his innocence, for the sake of any Mr. Taylor's guilt in the world? Does not Flush's condition assimilate to my own among the banditti? for you agree that you would not, after all, leave me to the banditti—and I, *exactly on the same ground,* will not leave Flush. It seems to me that you and I are *at one* upon the whole question,—only that *I* am *your* Flush, and *he* is mine. You, if you were 'consistent' . . dearest! . . would not redeem me on any account. You do ever so much harm by it, observe—you produce catastrophe on catastrophe, just for the sake of my two ears without ear-rings! Oh, I entirely agree with your principle. Evil should be resisted that it may fly from you.

But Flush is not to be sacrificed—nor even is Ba, it appears. So our two weaknesses may pardon one another, yours and mine!

Some dog, shut up in a mews somewhere behind this house, has been yelling and moaning to-day and yesterday. How he has made me think of my poor poor Flush, I cannot tell you—'Think of Flush' he seemed to say.

Yes!— A blow in the street! I wish somebody *would* propose such a thing to me, in exchange! I would have thanked Mr. Taylor himself for striking me down in the street, if the stroke had been offered as an alternative for the loss of Flush. You may think it absurd—but when my dinner is brought to me, I feel as if I could not (scarcely) touch it—the thought of poor Flush's golden eyes is too strong in me.

Not a word of your mother. She is better, I trust! And you . . may God keep you better, beloved! To be parted from you so long, teaches me the necessity of your presence—I am your very, very own.

I was out to-day—driving along the Hampstead Road. What weather!

R. B. to E. B. B.

Saturday.
[Post-mark, September 5, 1846.]

Dearest Ba, I feel your perfect goodness at my heart—I can say nothing.

Nor write very much more: my head still teazes, rather than pains me. Don't lay more of it to the dinner than necessary: I got my sister to write a letter deprecatory of all pressing to eat and drink and such mistaken hospitality

—to the end that I might sit unpitied, uncondoled with, and be an eyesore to nobody—which succeeded so well that I eat some mutton and drank wine and water without let or molestation. Our party was reduced to three, by a couple of defections—but there was an immense talking and I dare say this continuance of my ailment is partly attributable to it. I shall be quiet now. I tell you the simple truth, that you may believe—and this also believe, that it would have done me great good to go to you this morning,—if I could lean my head on your neck, what could pain it, dear dear Ba?

I am sorry poor Flush is not back again—very sorry. But no one would hurt him, be quite sure . . his mere value prevents that.

Shall I see you on Monday then? This is the *first time* since we met at the beginning, that a whole week, from a Sunday to a Saturday, has gone by without a day for us. Well—I trust you are constant . . nay you *are* constant to your purpose of leaving at the end of this month. When we meet next, let us talk of our business, like the grave man and woman we are going to become. Mr. K. will be away—how fortunate this is! We need implicate nobody. And in the end the reasonableness of what we do will be apparent to everybody—if I can show you well and happy, —which God send!

Kiss me as I kiss you, my own Ba. I am all one wide wonder at your loving nature: I can only give it the like love in return, and as much limited as I am limited. But I seem really to *grow* under you,—my faculties extend toward yours.

May God bless you, and enable me to make you as happy as your dear generous heart will be contented to be made. I am your own R.

E. B. B. to R. B.

Saturday Morning.
[Post-mark, September 5, 1846.]

Dearest, I write just a few lines that you may know me for thinking of you to-morrow. Flush has not come and I am going on a voyage of discovery myself,—Henry being far too lukewarm. He says I may be robbed and murdered before the time for coming back, in which case remember that it is not my fault that I do not go with you to Pisa.

Just now came a kind little note from dear Mr. Kenyon, who will not come, he says, Flush being away, and has set out on his travels, meaning not to come back for a week. So I might have seen you after all, to-day! My comfort is, that it is good for you, beloved, to be quiet, and that coming through the sun might have made your head suffer. How my thoughts are with you—how all day they never fall from you! I shall have my letter to-night through your dear goodness, which is a lamp hung up for me to look towards. Aladdin's, did you say? Yes, Aladdin's.

As to being afraid of you ever—once, do you know, I was quite afraid . . in a peculiar sense—as when it thunders, I am afraid . . or a little different from *that* even—or, oh yes, *very* different from *that*. Now it is changed . . the feeling is—and I am not afraid even so—except sometimes of losing your affection by some fault of my own—I am *not* afraid that it would be a fault of yours, remember. I trust you for goodness to the uttermost—and I know perfectly that if you did not love me (*supposing* it) you are one who would be *ashamed* for a woman to fear you, as some women fear some men. For *me*, I could not, you know—I knew you too well and love you too perfectly, and everybody can tell what perfect love casts out.

So you need not have done with me for *that* reason! Understand it.

And if I shall not be slain by the 'society,' you shall be written to again to-night. Ah—say in the letter *I* am to have, that you are better! And you are to come on Monday—dear, dearest! mind *that!*

Your Ba.

Come back safe, but without Flush—I am to have him to-night though.

E. B. B. to R. B.

Sunday.
[Post-mark, September 7, 1846.]

Not well—not well! But I shall see you with my own eyes soon after you read what I write to-day; so I shall not write much. Only a few words to tell you that Flush is found, and lying on the sofa, with one paw and both ears hanging over the edge of it. Still my visit to Taylor was not the successful one. My hero was not at home.

I went, you know, . . did I tell you? . . with Wilson in the cab. We got into obscure streets; and our cabman stopped at a public house to ask his way. Out came two or three men, . . 'Oh, you want to find Mr. Taylor, I dare say!' (mark that no name had been mentioned!) and instantly an unsolicited philanthropist ran before us to the house, and out again to tell me that the great man 'wasn't at home! but wouldn't I get out?' Wilson, in an aside of terror, entreated me not to think of such a thing—she believed devoutly in the robbing and murdering, and was not reassured by the gang of benevolent men and boys who 'lived but to oblige us' all round the cab. 'Then wouldn't I see Mrs. Taylor,' suggested the philanthropist,—and, notwithstanding my negatives, he had run back again and brought an immense feminine bandit, . . fat enough to have had an easy conscience all her life, . . who informed me that 'her husband might be in in a few minutes, or in so many hours—wouldn't I like to get out and wait' (Wilson pulling at my gown, the philanthropist echoing the invitation of the feminine Taylor.)—'No, I thanked them all—it was not necessary that I should get out, but it *was*, that Mr. Taylor should keep his promise about the restoration of a dog which he had agreed to restore—and I begged her to induce him to go to Wimpole Street in the course of the day, and not defer it any longer.' To which, replied the lady, with the most gracious of smiles—'Oh yes certainly'—and indeed she *did* believe that Taylor had left home precisely on that business—poising her head to the right and left with the most easy grace—'She was sure that Taylor would give his very best attention.' . . .

So, in the midst of the politeness, we drove away, and Wilson seemed to be of opinion that we had escaped with our lives barely. Plain enough it was, that the gang was strong there. The society . . the 'Fancy' . . had their roots in the ground. The faces of those men!—

I had not been at home long, when Mr. Taylor did actually come—desiring to have six guineas confided to his honour!! . . and promising to bring back the dog. I sent down the money, and told them to trust the gentleman's honour, as there seemed no other way for it—and while the business was being concluded, in came Alfred, and straightway called our 'honourable friend' (meeting him in the passage) a swindler and a liar and a thief. Which no gentleman could bear, of course. Therefore with reiterated oaths he swore, 'as he hoped to be saved, we should never see our dog again'—and rushed out of the house. Followed a great storm. I was very angry with Alfred, who had no business to risk Flush's life for the sake of the satisfaction of trying on names which fitted. Angry I was with Alfred, and terrified for Flush,—seeing at a glance the probability of his head being cut off as the proper vengeance! and downstairs I went with the resolution of going again myself to Mr. Taylor's in Manning Street, or Shoreditch [or] wherever it was, and saving the victim at any price. It was the evening, getting dusk—and everybody was crying out against me for being 'quite mad' and obstinate, and wilful—I was called as many names as Mr. Taylor. At last, Sette said that *he* would do it, promised to be as civil as I could wish, and got me to be 'in a good humour and go up to my room again.' And he went instead of me, and took the money and fair words, and induced the 'man of honour' to forfeit his vengeance and go and fetch the dog. Flush arrived here at eight o'clock (at the very moment with your letter, dearest!), and the first thing he did was to dash up to this door, and then to drink his purple cup full of water, filled three times over. He was not so enthusiastic about seeing me, as I expected—he seemed bewildered and frightened—and whenever anyone said to him 'Poor Flush, did the naughty men take you away?' he put up his head and moaned and yelled. He has been very unhappy certainly. Dirty he is, and much thinner, and continually he is drinking. Six guineas, was his ransom—and now I have paid twenty for him to the dog-stealers.

Arabel says that I wanted *you* yesterday, she thought, to manage me a little. She thought I was suddenly seized with madness, to prepare to walk out of the house in that state of excitement and that hour of the evening. But now —*was* I to let them cut off Flush's head?—

There! I have told you the whole history of yesterday's adventures—and to-morrow I shall see you, my own dear, dear!—Only remember for my sake, *not* to come if you are not fit to come. Dearest, remember not to run any hazards!—That dinner! which I *will* blame, because it deserves it! Mind not to make me be as bad as that dinner, in being the means of working you harm! So I expect you to-morrow *conditionally* . . if you are well enough!—and I thank you for the kind dear letter, welcome next to you, . . being ever and ever your own

Ba.

I have been to the *vestry* again to-day.

R. B. to E. B. B.

Sunday Afternoon.
[Post-mark, September 7, 1846.]

No, dearest, I am not to see you to-morrow for all the happiness of the permission! It seems absurd, but perhaps the greater absurdity would be a refusal to submit, under circumstances. You shall hear—I got up with the old *vertiginousness*, or a little worse—and so, as I had in that case determined, went to consult my doctor. He thinks he finds the root of the evil and can remove it, 'if I have patience enough'—so I promised . . expecting something worthy that preamble—whereas I am bidden go to bed and keep there for a day or two—from this Sunday till Wednesday morning—taking nothing but a sip of medicine I can't distinguish from water, thrice a day—and *milk* at discretion—no other food! The mild queerness of it is amusing, is it not? 'And for this fine piece of self-denial,' says he, 'you shall be quite well by the week's end.'—'But may I go to town on Wednesday?'—'Yes.'—

Now, Ba, my own Ba, you know how often I have to sorrowfully disclaim all the praises your dearest kindness would attach to me; this time, if you will praise me a little for obeying you, I will take the praise—for the truth of truths is, that I said at once to myself—'have I a right to avoid anything which promises to relieve Her from this eternal account of aches and pains?' So here am I writing, leaning on my elbow, in bed,—as I never wrote before I think—and perhaps my head is a little better, or I fancy so. Mind, I may read, or write,—only in bed I must lie, because there is some temperature to be kept up in the skin, or some other cause as good—'for reasons, for reasons.'

'The milk,' answers Ba, is exactly to correct the superabundant gall of bitterness which overflowed lately about Flush. So it is, my own Ba—and for Flush, the victim of a principle, he is just saved from a sickness by cakes I meditated as a joy-offering on his safe return. Will you, among the other kisses, give him one for me? And save yet another for your own R.

How I shall need your letters, dearest!

E. B. B. to R. B.

Monday Morning.
[Post-mark, September 7, 1846.]

Ever, ever dearest, how was it that without presentiment of evil I got up this morning in the good spirits of '*our* days,' hoping to see you, believing to see you, and feeling that it would be greater happiness than usual? The sight of your letter, even, did not provoke the cloud—*that* was only the lesser joy, I thought, preceding the greater! And smiling to myself I was, both last night and this morning, at your phrase about the 'business' to be talked by the 'grave man and woman'; understanding your precaution against all unlawful jesting!—jesters forbidden in the protocol! And then, at last, to be made so suddenly grave and sad even! How am I to be comforted, my own dearest? No way, except by your being really better, really well—in order to which I shall not let you come as soon as Wednesday: it will not be wise for you to leave your bed for a journey into London! Rather you should be very quiet, and keep in the garden at farthest. Take care of yourself, dearest dearest, and if you think of me and love me, show it in that best way. And I praise you, praise you,—nay, I thank you and am grateful to you for every such proof of love, more than for *other* kinds of proof, —I will love you for it, my beloved! Now judge—shall I be able to help thinking of you every moment of the day? Could I help it, if I tried? In return, therefore, you will attend to the orders, submit to the discipline—ah, but will not the leaving off all food but milk weaken you out of measure? I am uneasy about that milk-diet for *you*, who always seem to me to want support, and something to stimulate. You will promise to tell me *everything*—will you, dearest?—whether better or worse, stronger or weaker, you will tell me? And if you should be too unwell to write, as may God forbid, your sister will write—she will have that great goodness? Let it be so, I beseech you.

But you will be better—oh, I mean to hope stedfastly toward your being better, and toward the possibility of our meeting before the week ends. And as for this day lost, it is not of importance except in our present thoughts: soon you will have more than enough of me, you know. For I am in earnest and not a jester *au fond*, and am ready to do just as you bid me and think best—which I tell you now, that you may not be vexed at a shadow, after my own fashion. May God bless you—'*and me in you.*' Have I not leave to say *that*, too, since I feel it more than *you* could . . (more intensely . . I do not say more sincerely . .) when you used it first? My happiness and life are in you,—I am your very own

Ba.

Your mother—how is she? Mind you get an amusing book . . something to amuse only, and not use you. Do you know the 'Mathilde' of Sue? I shall write again to-night.

R. B. to E. B. B.

Monday Morning.
[Post-mark, September 7, 1846.]

I had the greatest mind, when your letter came—(the most welcome of all letters—so much more than I could expect!)—to get up at once and be well in your dearest eyes or through them—but I checked myself and thought that I ought to be contented with one such a letter through whole long weeks of annoyance, instead of one day more.

I am delighted to know Flush is with you, if I am not. Did you remember my petition about him? But, dearest, it *was* very imprudent to go to those disgusting wretches yourself—they have had a pretty honour without knowing it!

Here I lie with a dizzy head—unable to read more than a page or two . . there is something in the unwonted position that tires me—but whenever the book is left off, I turn to the dark side of the room and see you, my very own Ba, —and so I am soon better and able to try again.

How hot, and thunder-like, this oppressive air! And you who are affected by such weather? Tell me, my dearest dearest, all you can tell me—since the real lips and eyes are away.

Bless you, my beloved. Remember, I count upon seeing you on Wednesday at farthest.

Your own R.

E. B. B. to R. B.

Monday Night.
[Post-mark, September 8, 1846.]

How unwell you are, dearest beloved! Ah no! It is not 'the position that tires you,' it is the illness that incapacitates you. And *you* to think of getting up and coming here . . you! Now, for my sake, for both our sakes, you *must* and *shall* be patient and quiet, and remember how my thoughts are with you conjuring you continually to quiet. As to the reading, . . you see it makes you dizzy,—and to provoke that sensation cannot plainly be right: and you will be right always, will you not, for my sake, dearest of all? And for the coming here on Wednesday, . . no, no, I say again,—you ought not to do it, and you shall not: we will see how you are, later in the week; but for Wednesday, certainly no. That violent transition from the bed to the omnibus would be manifestly wrong. Also I can be quite satisfied without seeing you, if I may but hear of your being well again. I wonder to-day how yesterday I was impatient about not having seen you so long. Oh, be well, be well, dearest! There is no need of your being ill to prove to me how I love you entirely, how I love you only!

For Flush, I did your commission, kissing the top of his head: then I took the kiss back again because it seemed too good for him *just now.* And you shall not say that you 'are glad *he* is with me' if *you* are not? It is more to Flush's disadvantage, that phrase is, than all your theories which pretended to leave him with the dogstealers. How can I be glad of anyone's being with me, if you are not? And how should *you* be glad for anything, if *I* am not? Flush and I know our logic better than to accept that congratulation of yours, with the spike pricking us out of it.

So hot, indeed, to-day! If you thought of me, I thought of you, through it all. This close air cannot be good for you while you are shut up. But *I* have not been shut up. I went out in the carriage and bought a pair of boots for Italy, besides the shoes—because, you see, we shall have such long walks in the forest after the camels, and it won't do to go in one's slippers. Does not *that* sound like 'a grave woman?' You need not make laws against the jesters, after all! You need only be well! And, gravely, quite gravely, is it not likely that going to Italy, that travelling, and putting an end to all the annoyances which lately have grown up out of our affairs, will do you good, substantial good, in this chief matter of your health? It seems so to me sometimes. You are always well, you say, in Italy, and when you get there once again. But in the meanwhile, try to be a little better, my own dearest! I cannot write to you except about you to-night. The subject is too near me—I am under the shadow of the wall, and cannot see over it. To-morrow I shall hear more, and *trust to you* to tell me the whole, unmutilated truth. May God bless you, as *I* would, *I* in my weakness! For the best blessing on your part, love your own Ba.

And do not tire yourself with writing. The least line—three words—I beseech you not to let me do you harm.

R. B. to E. B. B.

Tuesday Morning.
[Post-mark, September 8, 1846.]

Do you think your wishes, much less your blessings, fall to the ground, my own Ba? Here is your letter, and here am I writing to you, 'clothed and in my proper' room. My doctor bade me 'get up and do as I pleased'—and the perfect pleasure is to say, I may indeed see you to-morrow, dearest, dearest! Can you look as you look in this letter? So entirely my own, and yet,—what should never be my own, by right . . such a treasure to one so little worthy!

I have only a few minutes to say this,—the dressing and talking having taken up the time. To-morrow shall repay me!

The lightness, slight uneasiness of the head, continues, though the general health is much better, it seems.

Do you doubt I shall be well in Italy? But I must leave off. Bless you as you have blessed me, my best, dearest Ba, me who am your very own R.

E. B. B. to R. B.

Tuesday Evening.
[Post-mark, September 9, 1846.]

I write a word to say, . . dearest, do not run any risk about coming to-morrow. I mean, . . unless you are sure that the noise and exertion will not be too much for you,—unless, when the moment comes for setting off, you feel equal to it . . now, I do beseech you, very dear, not to persist in coming because you have said that you will come—I beseech you. Listen. At three o'clock I shall expect you doubtfully; at half-past three, the doubt will be the strongest; and at a quarter to four, I shall have said to myself cheerfully, that you were wise and good and had determined to stay at home. In that case, I shall have a line from you by five or six! Understand all this, and let it have the right influence and no more. Of course if I could see you without harm to yourself, and so to me, it would be a *great happiness:* it even makes me happy to think of, as a bare possibility, at this distance off! I am happy by your letter, twice over, indeed—once, for *that* reason, . . and again, for the thought of your being in some respects better. At the same time I do not see why your wise man did not follow his plan to the end. It looks as if he did not think you better essentially because of it. Ah well, I shall see with my eyes to-morrow—*perhaps* I shall: and I shall see in a dream to-night more certainly.

This shall go at once, though, that it may reach you in time in the morning. How I thank you for the precious note! You are so much too good to me, that your being also too *dear* is an excusable consequence—or would be, if it were possible. I write nonsense, I believe,—but it is half for gladness . . and half . . for what makes me your own

Ba.

E. B. B. to R. B.

Wednesday Night.
[Post-mark, September 10, 1846.]

Dearest, you are a prophet, I suppose—there can be no denying it. This night, an edict has gone out, and George is to-morrow to be on his way to take a house for a month either at Dover, Reigate, Tunbridge, . . Papa did 'not mind which,' he said, and 'you may settle it among you!!' but he 'must have this house empty for a month in order to its cleaning'—we are to go therefore and not delay.

Now!—what *can* be done? It is possible that the absence may be longer than for a month, indeed it is probable—for there is much to do in painting and repairing, here in Wimpole Street, more than a month's work they say. Decide, after thinking. I am embarrassed to the utmost degree, as to the best path to take. If we are taken away on Monday . . what then?

Of course I decline to give any opinion and express any preference,—as to places, I mean. It is not for my sake that we go:—if *I* had been considered at all, indeed, we should have been taken away earlier, . . and not certainly now, when the cold season is at hand. And so much the better it is for me, that I have not, obviously, been thought of.

Therefore decide! It seems quite too soon and too sudden for us to set out on our Italian adventure now—and perhaps even we could not compass—

Well—but you must think for both of us. It is past twelve and I have just a moment to seal this and entrust it to Henrietta for the morning's post.

More than ever beloved, I am
Your own Ba.

I will do as you wish—understand.

R. B. to E. B. B.

Thursday Morning.
[Post-mark, September 10, 1846.]

What do you expect this letter will be about, my own dearest? Those which I write on the mornings after our days seem naturally to *answer* any strong point brought out in the previous discourse, and not then completely disposed of . . so they generally run in the vile fashion of a disputatious 'last word'; 'one word yet'—do not they? Ah, but you should remember that never does it feel so intolerable,—the barest fancy of a possibility of losing you—as when I have just seen you and heard you and, alas—left you for a time; on these occasions, it seems so horrible—that if the least recollection of a fear of yours, or a doubt . . . anything which might be nursed, or let grow quietly into a serious obstacle to what we desire—if *that* rises up threateningly,—do you wonder that I begin by attacking *it?* There are always a hundred deepest reasons for gratitude and love which I could write about, but which my after life shall prove I never have forgotten . . still, that very after-life depends perhaps on the letter of the morning reasoning with you, teazing, contradicting. Dearest Ba, I do not tell you that I am justified in plaguing you thus, at any time . . only to get your pardon, if I can, on the grounds—the true grounds.

And this pardon, if you grant it, shall be for the past offences, not for any fresh one I mean to commit now. I will not add one word to those spoken yesterday about the extreme perilousness of delay. You *give* me yourself. Hitherto, from the very first till this moment, the giving hand has been advancing steadily—it is not for me to grasp it lest it stop within an inch or two of my forehead with its crown.

I am going to town this morning, and will leave off now.

What a glorious dream; through nearly two years—without a single interval of blankness,—much less, bitter waking!

I may say *that*, I suppose, safely through whatever befalls!

Also I will ever say, God bless you, my dearest dearest,—my perfect angel you have been! While I am only your R.

My mother is deeply gratified at your present.

12 o'clock. On returning I find your note,

'I will do as you wish—understand'—then I understand you are in earnest. If you *do* go on Monday, our marriage will be impossible for another year—the misery! You see what we have gained by waiting. We must be *married directly* and go to Italy. I will go for a licence to-day and we can be married on Saturday. I will call to-morrow at 3 and arrange everything with you. We can leave from Dover &c., *after* that,—but otherwise, impossible! Inclose the ring, or a substitute—I have not a minute to spare for the post.

Ever your own R.

R. B. to E. B. B.

4 p.m. Thursday.
[Post-mark, September 10, 1846.]

I broke open your sealed letter and added the postscript just now. The post being thus saved, I can say a few words more leisurely.

I will go to-morrow, I think, and not to-day for the licence—there are fixed hours I fancy at the office—and I might be too late. I will also make the arrangement with my friend for Saturday, if we should want him,—as we shall, in all probability—it would look suspiciously to be unaccompanied. We can arrange to-morrow.

Your words, first and last, have been that you 'would not fail me'—you will not.

And the marriage over, you can take advantage of circumstances and go early or late in the week, as may be practicable. There will be facilities in the general packing &c.,—your own measures may be taken unobserved. Write short notes to the proper persons,—promising longer ones, if necessary.

See the *tone* I take, the way I write to *you* . . but it is all through you, in the little brief authority you give me, —and in the perfect belief of your truth and firmness—indeed, I do not consider this an extraordinary occasion for proving those qualities—this conduct of your father's is quite characteristic.

Otherwise, too, the departure with its bustle is not unfavourable. If you hesitated, it would be before a little hurried shopping and letter-writing! I expected it, and therefore spoke as you heard yesterday. *Now your* part must begin. It may as well begin and end, both, *now* as at any other time. I will bring you every information possible to-morrow.

It seems as if I should insult you if I spoke a word to confirm you, to beseech you, to relieve you from your promise, if you claim it.

God bless you, prays your own R.

E. B. B. to R. B.

Thursday.
[Post-mark, September 11, 1846.][1]

Dearest, I write one word, and have one will which is yours. At the same time, do not be precipitate—we shall not be taken away on Monday, no, nor for several days afterward. George has simply gone to look for houses—going to Reigate first.

Oh yes—come to-morrow. And then, you shall have the ring . . soon enough and safer.

Not a word of how you are!—*you* so good as to write me that letter beyond compact, yet not good enough, to say how you are! Dear, dearest . . take care, and keep yourself unhurt and calm. I shall not fail to you—I do not, I will not. I will act by your decision, and I wish you to decide. I was yours long ago, and though you give me back my promise at this eleventh hour, . . you generous, dear unkind! . . . you know very well that you can do as well without it. So take it again for my sake and not your own.

I cannot write, I am so tired, having been long out. Will not this dream break on a sudden? Now is the moment for the breaking of it, surely.

But come to-morrow, come. Almost everybody is to be away at Richmond, at a picnic, and we shall be free on all sides.

Ever and ever your Ba.

[1] [The envelope of this letter is endorsed by R. B. 'Saturday, Septr. 12, 1846, ¾11–11¼ A. M. (91).' This is the record of his marriage with E. B. B. in Marylebone Church. The number 91 indicates that it was the ninety-first of their meetings, a record of which was always endorsed by Robert Browning on the letters received by him from Miss Barrett.]

R. B. to E. B. B.

1 p.m. Saturday.
[Post-mark, September 12, 1846.]

You will only expect a few words—what will those be? When the heart is full it may run over, but the real fulness stays within.

You asked me yesterday 'if I should repent?' Yes—my own Ba,—I could wish all the past were to do over again, that in it I might somewhat more,—never so little more, conform in the outward homage to the inward feeling. What I have professed . . (for I have performed nothing) seems to fall short of what my first love required even—and when I think of *this* moment's love . . I could repent, as I say.

Words can never tell you, however,—form them, transform them anyway,—how perfectly dear you are to me—perfectly dear to my heart and soul.

I look back, and in every one point, every word and gesture, every letter, every *silence*—you have been entirely perfect to me—I would not change one word, one look.

My hope and aim are to preserve this love, not to fall from it—for which I trust to God who procured it for me, and doubtlessly can preserve it.

Enough now, my dearest, dearest, own Ba! You have given me the highest, completest proof of love that ever one human being gave another. I am all gratitude—and all pride (under the proper feeling which ascribes pride to the right source) all pride that my life has been so crowned by you.

God bless you prays your very own R.

I will write to-morrow of course. Take every care of *my life* which is in that dearest little hand; try and be composed, my beloved.

Remember to thank Wilson for me.

E. B. B. to R. B.

Saturday. Sept. 12.—4½ p.m.
[Post-mark, September 12, 1846.]

Ever dearest, I write a word that you may read it and know how all is safe so far, and that I am not slain downright with the day—oh, *such a day!* I went to Mr. Boyd's directly, so as to send Wilson home the faster—and was able to lie quietly on the sofa in his sitting-room downstairs, before he was ready to see me, being happily engaged with a medical councillor. Then I was made to talk and take Cyprus wine,—and, my sisters delaying to come, I had some bread and butter for dinner, to keep me from looking too pale in their eyes. At last they came, and with such grave faces! Missing me and Wilson, they had taken fright,—and Arabel had forgotten at first what I told her last night about the fly. I kept saying, 'What nonsense, . . what fancies you do have to be sure,' . . trembling in my heart with every look they cast at me. And so, to complete the bravery, I went on with them in the carriage to Hampstead . . as far as the heath,—and talked and looked—now you shall praise me for courage—or rather you shall love me for the love which was the root of it all. How necessity makes heroes—or heroines at least! For I did not sleep all last night, and when I first went out with Wilson to get to the fly-stand in Marylebone Street I staggered so, that we both were afraid for the fear's sake,—but we called at a chemist's for sal volatile and were thus enabled to go on. I spoke to her last night, and she was very kind, very affectionate, and never shrank for a moment. I told her that always I should be grateful to her.

You—how are you? how is your head, ever dearest?

It seems all like a dream! When we drove past that church again, I and my sisters, there was a cloud before my eyes. Ask your mother to forgive me, Robert. If *I* had not been there, *she* would have been there, perhaps.

And for the rest, if either of us two is to suffer injury and sorrow for what happened there to-day—I pray that it may all fall upon *me!* Nor should I suffer the most pain *that* way, as I know, and God knows.

Your own

Ba.

Was I very uncourteous to your cousin? So kind, too, it was in him! Can there be the least danger of the newspapers? Are those books ever examined by penny-a-liners, do you suppose?

E. B. B. to R. B.

Sunday.
[Post-mark, September 14, 1846.]

My own beloved, if ever you should have reason to complain of me in things voluntary and possible, all other women would have a right to tread me underfoot, I should be so vile and utterly unworthy. There is my answer to what you wrote yesterday of wishing to be better to me . . you! What could be better than lifting me from the ground and carrying me into life and the sunshine? I was yours rather by right than by gift (yet by gift also, my beloved!); for what you have saved and renewed is surely yours. All that I am, I owe you—if I enjoy anything now and henceforth, it is through you. You know this well. Even as *I*, from the beginning, knew that I had no power against you, . . or that, if I *had*, it was for your sake.

Dearest, in the emotion and confusion of yesterday morning, there was yet room in me for one thought which was not a feeling—for I thought that, of the many, many women who have stood where I stood, and to the same end, not one of them all perhaps, not one perhaps, since that building was a church, has had reasons strong as mine, for an absolute trust and devotion towards the man she married,——not one! And then I both thought and felt, that it was only just, for them, . . those women who were less happy, . . to have that affectionate sympathy and support and presence of their nearest relations, parent or sister . . which failed to *me*, . . needing it less through being happier!

All my brothers have been here this morning, laughing and talking, and discussing this matter of the leaving town, —and in the room, at the same time, were two or three female friends of ours, from Herefordshire—and I did not *dare* to cry out against the noise, though my head seemed splitting in two (one half for each shoulder), I had such a morbid fear of exciting a suspicion. Trippy too being one of them, I promised to go to see her to-morrow and dine in her drawing-room if she would give me, for dinner, some bread and butter. It was like having a sort of fever. And all in the midst, the bells began to ring. 'What bells are those?' asked one of the provincials. 'Marylebone Church bells' said Henrietta, standing behind my chair.

And now . . while I write, having escaped from the great din, and sit here quietly,—comes . . who do you think?—Mr. Kenyon.

He came with his spectacles, looking as if his eyes reached to their rim all the way round; and one of the first words was, '*When did you see Browning?*' And I think I shall make a pretension to presence of mind henceforward; for, though *certainly* I changed colour and he saw it, I yet answered with a tolerably quick evasion, . . 'He was here on Friday'—and leapt straight into another subject, and left him gazing fixedly on my face. Dearest, he saw something, but not all. So we talked, talked. He told me that the 'Fawn of Sertorius,' (which I refused to cut open the other day,) was ascribed to Landor—and he told me that he meant to leave town again on Wednesday, and would see me once before then. On rising to go away, he mentioned your name a second time . . 'When do you see Browning again?' To which I answered that I did not know.

Is not *that* pleasant? The worst is that all these combinations of things make me feel so bewildered that I cannot make the necessary arrangements, as far as the letters go. But I must break from the dream-stupor which falls on me when left to myself a little, and set about what remains to be done.

A house near Watford is thought of now—but, as none is concluded on, the removal is not likely to take place in the middle of the week even, perhaps.

I sit in a dream, when left to myself. I cannot believe, or understand. Oh! but in all this difficult, embarrassing and painful situation, I look over the palms to Troy—I feel happy and exulting to belong to you, past every opposition, out of sight of every will of man—none can put us asunder, now, at least. I have a right now openly to love you, and to hear other people call it *a duty*, when I do, . . knowing that if it were a sin, it would be done equally. Ah—*I* shall not be first to leave off *that*—see if I shall! May God bless you, ever and ever dearest! Beseech for me the indulgence of your father and mother, and ask your sister to love me. I feel so as if I had slipped down over the wall into somebody's garden—I feel ashamed. To be grateful and affectionate to them all, while I live, is all that I can do, and it is too much a matter of course to need to be promised. Promise it however for your very own Ba whom you made so happy with the dear letter last night. But say in the next how you are—and how your mother is.

I did hate so, to have to take off the ring! You will have to take the trouble of putting it on again, some day.

R. B. to E. B. B.

Sunday Afternoon.
[Post-mark, September 14, 1846.]

Thank you a thousand times for the note, my own Ba. I welcomed it as I never yet welcomed even *your* notes; entirely kind to write, and write *so!* Oh, I know the effort you made, the pain you bore for my sake! I tell you, once and for ever, your proof of love to me is *made* . . I *know* love, my dearest dearest: my whole life shall be spent in trying to furnish such a proof of *my* affection; such a perfect proof,—and perhaps vainly spent—but I will endeavour with God's help. Do you feel what I mean, dearest? How you have dared and done all this, under my very eyes, for my only sake? I believed you would be capable of it—what then? What is a belief? My own eyes have seen—my heart will remember!

Dearest, nothing needs *much* trouble you farther: take your own time and opportunity. I confide in your judgment—(for I am not going to profess confidence in *you!*)—I am sure you will see and act for the best. My preparations are made; I have only to await your desires. I will not ask to see you, for instance—though of course a word brings me as usual to you—your will is altogether my will.

The first obvious advantage of our present relation, I will take. You are mine—your generosity has given to me my utmost claim upon your family—so far as I am concerned, putting aside my sympathy with you, there is nothing more they *can* give me: so, I will say, perhaps a little less reservedly than I could have brought myself to say before, that there is no conceivable submission I will refuse, nor possible satisfaction I will hesitate to make to those feelings I have been forced to offend, if by any means I may preserve, for *you*, so much of their affection as you have been accustomed to receive; I do not require anything beyond *toleration* for myself . . I will cheerfully accept as the truest kindness to me, a continuance of kindness *to you*. You know what I would have done to possess you:—now that I *do* possess you, I renew the offer to *you* . . judge with what earnest purpose of keeping my word! I do not think . . nor do you think . . that any personal application, directly or by letter, would do any good—it might rather add to the irritation we apprehend: but my consent is given beforehand to any measure you shall ever consider proper. And your father may be sure that while I adore his daughter it will be impossible for me, under any circumstances, to be wanting in the utmost respect for, and observance of, himself. Understand, with the rest, why I write this, Ba. To your brothers and sisters I am bound for ever,—by every tie of gratitude: *they* may acquiesce more easily . . comprehending more, perhaps, of the dear treasure you are, they will forgive my ambition of gaining it. I will write to Mr. Kenyon. You will probably have time to write all the letters requisite.

Do not trouble yourself with more than is strictly necessary—you can supply all wants at Leghorn or Pisa. Let us be as unencumbered with luggage as possible.

What is your opinion about the advertisements? If our journey is delayed for a few days, we had better omit the *date*, I think. And the *cards?* I will get them engraved if you will direct me. The simplest form of course:—and the last (or among the last) happens to be also the simplest, consisting merely of the words 'Mr. and Mrs. R. B.' on *one* card—with the usual 'at home' in a corner. How shall we manage *that*, by the way? Could we put 'In Italy for a year?' There is precedent for it—Sir—Fellow's (what is the traveller's name?)—*his* were thus subscribed. By which means we should avoid telling people absolutely, that they need never come and see us. Choose your own fashion, my Ba, and tell me how many you require.

I only saw my cousin for a few minutes afterward—he came up in a cab immediately—he understood all there was need he should. *You* to be 'uncourteous' to anybody! no, no—sweetest! But I will thank him as you bid, knowing the value of Ba's thanks! For the prying penny-a-liners . . why, trust to Providence—we must! I do not apprehend much danger . .

Dearest, I woke this morning *quite well*—quite free from the sensation in the head. I have not woke *so*, for two years perhaps—what have you been doing to me?

My father and mother and sister love you thoroughly—my mother said this morning, in my room, 'If I were as I have been, I would try and write to her'—I said, 'I will tell her what I know you feel.' She is much better—(I hear her voice while I write . . below the open window). Poor Pritchard came home from the country on Friday *night*—late—and posted here immediately—he was vexed to be made understand that there was some way in which he might have served me and did not. It was kind, very kind of Wilson.

I will leave off—to resume to-morrow. Bless you, my very own, only Ba—my pride, and joy, and utter comfort. I kiss you and am ever your own.

R. B. to E. B. B.

Monday Morning.
[Post-mark, September 14, 1846.]

You go on to comfort me, love—bless you for it. I collect from the letter that you are recovering from the pain and excitement; that is happy! I waited to hear from you, my own Ba, and will only write a word—then go out —I *think*.

Do you feel *so*, through the anxieties and trouble of this situation? You take my words from me—*I* 'exult' in the irrevocability of this precious bestowal of yourself on me—come what will my life has borne flower and fruit —it is a glorious, successful, felicitous life, I thank God and you.

All has been for the best, you will see, even in these apparently untoward circumstances—this particular act was *precipitated* by them, certainly—but it is done, and well done. Does it not simplify our arrangements that this is *done?* And surely there was every justification for the precipitancy in that proposed journey, and uncertain return,—(in Winter to a freshly-painted house!) But every moment of my life brings fresh proof to me of the intervention of Providence. How the *natural* course would have embarrassed us!—any consultation with you respecting your own feelings on a removal at present—any desire to gratify them . .

Will not Mr. Kenyon understand at least? Would it not be well to ascertain his precise address in the country,—so as to send your letter there, before the newspaper reaches him,—or any other person's version? I will send you my letter to accompany yours—just a few words to explain why he was not consulted—(by *me*) . . what is strictly *my own* part to be excused. What do you intend to do about Mrs. Jameson? I only want to know in the case of our mutual friends, of course, so as to avoid the necessity of going over the same ground in our letters.

I confided my approaching marriage to that kind old Pritchard, lest he should be too much wounded—if his surprise was considerable, his delight kept due proportion. You may depend on his secrecy—I need not say, I mentioned the fact *simply* . . without a word about any circumstances. If your father could be brought to allow the matter to pass as *indifferent* to him . . what he did not choose to interfere with, however little he approved it,—we should be fortunate? Perhaps pride, if no kinder feeling, may induce him to that.

My family all love you, dearest—you cannot conceive my father and mother's childlike faith in goodness—and my sister is very high-spirited, and quick of apprehension—so as to seize the true point of the case at once. I am in great hopes you will love them all, and understand them. Last night, I asked my father, who was absorbed over some old book, 'if he should not be glad to see his new daughter?'—to which he, starting, replied 'Indeed I *shall!*' with such a fervour as to make my mother laugh—not abated by his adding, 'And how I should be glad of her seeing Sis!' his other daughter, Sarianna, to wit—who was at church.

Trifles, trifles, only commended to your dear, affectionate heart. Do you confide in me, Ba? Well, you *shall!*—in my love, in my pride, in my heart's purposes; but not in anything else. Give me your counsel at all times, beloved: I am wholly open to your desires, and teaching, and direction. Try what you can make of me,—if you can in any way justify your choice to the world. So *I* would gladly counsel you on any point! See how I read lectures about Flush! Only give a kiss before beginning, and promise me another upon my profiting,—and I shall be twice blessed beside the profit. So, *my* counsel being done, here begin the kisses, you dear dear Ba of mine. Bless you ever, Ba! I continue *quite well*—is it not strange . . or *is* it? And my mother is better decidedly. When she comes back from town (where she and my sister are caring for me) I will tell her what you bade me promise to give her—in return for what she has long given you. Good-bye, my own—very own Ba, from your R.

E. B. B. to R. B.

Monday Morning.
[Post-mark, September 14, 1846.]

Ever dearest, this one word goes to you to say about Mr. Kenyon's letter—oh, do not send any letter, dearest, till we are out of hearing of the answer. It terrifies me to think of your sending a letter, perhaps, without delay. Do let no letter nor intimation be given till the very last. Remember that I shall be *killed*—it will be so infinitely worse than you can have an idea.

Afterwards—yes!—you will, for my sake, forget some natural pride, as I, for yours, have forgotten some as natural apprehensiveness. That kindness, I expected from you, . . and now accept . . thanking you, dearest. In the meanwhile, there seems to remain the dreadful danger of the newspapers—we must trust, as you say.

Your mother's goodness touches me very deeply. I am grateful to her and to all your family, beyond any power of mine to express my feelings. Let me be silent therefore, instead of trying.

As to the important business of the cards, you know I have heard the whole theory of etiquette lately on that subject, and you must not think of putting any '*At home*' anywhere, or any other thing in the place of it. A Fellows is an authority in Asia Minor, but for the *minora* of the cards, not at all. Put simply the names, as you say, on one card, only without abbreviation or initial, and no intimation of address, which is not necessary, and would be under our circumstances quite wrong. Then I had better perhaps send you a list of names and addresses. But for this, enough time.

They hasten me—I must go. Not from the thought however of you . . being your very own Ba.

I shall write of course in the evening again.

E. B. B. to R. B.

Monday Evening.
[Post-mark, September 15, 1846.]

First, God is to be thanked for this great joy of hearing that you are better, my ever dearest—it is a joy that floats over all the other emotions. Dearest, I am so glad! I had feared that excitement's telling on you quite in another way. When the whole is done, and we have left England and the talkers thereof behind our backs, you will be well, steadfastly and satisfactorily, I do trust. In the meantime, there seems so much to do, that I am frightened to look towards the heaps of it. As to accoutrements, everything has been arranged as simply as possible that way—but still there are necessities—and the letters, the letters! I am paralysed when I think of having to write such words as . . 'Papa, I am married; I hope you will not be too displeased.' Ah, poor Papa! You are too sanguine if you expect any such calm from him as an assumption of indifference would imply. To the utmost, he will be angry,—he will cast me off as far from him. Well—there is no comfort in such thoughts. How I felt to-night when I saw him at seven o'clock, for the first time since Friday, and the event of Saturday! He spoke kindly too, and asked me how I was. Once I heard of his saying of me that I was 'the purest woman he ever knew,'—which made me smile at the moment, or laugh I believe, outright, because I understood perfectly what he meant by *that*—viz—that I had not troubled him with the iniquity of love affairs, or any impropriety of seeming to think about being married. But now the whole sex will go down with me to the perdition of faith in any of us. See the effect of my wickedness!—'Those women!'

But we will submit, dearest. I will put myself under his feet, to be forgiven a little, . . enough to be taken up again into his arms. I love him—he is my father—he has good and high qualities after all: he is my father *above* all. And *you*, because you are so generous and tender to me, will let me, you say, and help me to try to win back the alienated affection—for which, I thank you and bless you,—I did not thank you enough this morning. Surely I may say to him, too, . . 'With the exception of this act, I have submitted to the least of your wishes all my life long. Set the life against the act, and forgive me, for the sake of the daughter you once loved.' Surely I may say *that*,—and then remind him of the long suffering I have suffered,—and entreat him to pardon the happiness which has come at last.

And *he* will wish in return, that I had died years ago! For the storm will come and endure. And at last, perhaps, he will forgive us—it is my hope.

I accede to all you say of Mr. Kenyon. I will ask him for his address in the country, and we will send, when the moment comes, our letters together.

From Mrs. Jameson I had the letter I enclose, this morning, (full of kindness—is it not?) and another really as kind from Miss Bayley, who begs me, if I cannot go to Italy, to go to Hastings and visit her. To both I must write at some length. Will *you* write to Mrs. Jameson, besides what I shall write? And what are we to say as to travelling? As she is in Paris, perhaps we may let her have the solution of our problem sooner than the near people. May we? shall we? Yet we dare not, I suppose, talk too historically of what happened last Saturday. It is like the dates in the newspaper—advertisements, which we must eschew, as you observe.

Other things, too, you observe, my beloved, which are altogether out of date. In your ways towards me, you have acted throughout too much 'the woman's part,' as that is considered. You loved me because I was lower than others, that you might be generous and raise me up: —very characteristic for a woman (in her ideal standard) but quite wrong for a man, as again and again I use to signify to you, Robert—but you went on and did it all the same. And now, you still go on—you persist—you will be the woman of the play, to the last; let the prompter prompt ever so against you. You are to do everything I like, instead of my doing what *you* like, . . and to 'honour and obey' *me*, in spite of what was in the vows last Saturday,—is *that* the way of it and of you? and are vows to be kept *so*, pray? after that fashion? Then, *don't* put 'at home' at the corner of the cards, dearest! It is my command!

And forgive the inveterate jesting, which jests with eyes full of tears. I love you—I bless God for you. You are too good for me, as always I knew. I look up to you continually.

It is best, I continue to think, that you should not come here—best for *you*, because the position, if you were to try it, would be less tolerable than ever—and best for both of us, that in case the whole truth were ever discovered (I mean, of the previous marriage) we might be able to call it simply an act in order to security. I don't know how to put my feeling into words, but I do seem to feel that it would be better, and less offensive to those whom we offend at any rate, to avoid all possible remark on this point. It seems better to a sort of instinct I have.

Then, if I see you—farewell, the letter-writing. Oh no—there will be time enough when we are on the railway!—We shall talk then.

Ah—you say such things to me! Dearest, dearest*est!* —And you do not start at that word, 'Irrevocable,' as I have had fancies that you might, when the time came! But you may recover, by putting out your hand, all you have given me, . . nearly all. I never, never, being myself, could willingly vex you, torment you. If I approach to it, you will tell me. I will confide in you, to that end also. Dearest.

And your father's goodness, and the affectionateness of them all. When they shall have learnt most that I am not worthy of you, they will have learnt besides that I can be grateful to *them* and you. Certainly I am capable, I hope, of loving them all, well and with appreciation. And then . . imagine the comfort I take to the deepest of my heart from these hands held out to me! For your sake! Yes, for your sake entirely!—and, so, the more dearly comforting to

Your very own Ba.

There is still difficulty about the house. They think of Tunbridge Wells.

R. B. to E. B. B.

Tuesday Morning.
[Post-mark, September 15, 1846.]

My own Ba, could you think me capable of such a step? I forget what I exactly said in the first letter, but in the second, which you have received by this, I know there is mention made of *your* account which is to accompany mine. You never quite understood, I think, my feeling about Mr. Kenyon and desire to tell him earlier. In the first place, at the very *beginning*, he seemed to stand (as he did) in closer connection with you than any other person I could communicate with,—therefore to represent, in some degree, your dear self in the worldly sense, and be able to impose on me any conditions &c. which your generous nature might be silent on, and my ignorance and excitement overlook: then there was another reason, the natural one, of our own . . *his* friendship, rather, for me, and the circumstance of his having in a manner introduced me to your acquaintance,—at all events, facilitated my introduction,—and so being after a fashion responsible in some degree for my conduct. These two reasons, added to a general real respect for his circumspection and sagacity, and a desire to make both of them instruct me in the way of doing you good. But you effectually convinced me that in neither case would the benefit derivable balance the certain injury, or at least, annoyance, to himself—while you showed me that I should not be so truly serving you, as I had intended, by the plans I used to turn over in my mind.

In brief, it was written that your proof of love and trust to me was to be complete, the *completest*—and I could not but be proud and submit—and a few words will explain the mere sin against friendship. I quite, quite feel as you feel, nor ever had the least intention of writing . . that is, of sending any letter,—till the very last. Be sure of it.

For the cards, I have just given orders, as you desire and as I entirely agree. The notion of a word about our *not being in England* was only a fancy for your family's sake —just to save people's application to *them*, to know what had become of us—and I had heard Mr. Kenyon commend the considerateness of those 'Lydian measures' . . albeit there was . . or narrowly escaped being—an awful oversight of the traveller's which would have made him the sad hero of a merry story for ever . . as I will tell you some day. If you will send the addresses, at any time, that trouble will be over. In all these mighty matters, be sure I shall never take the least step without consulting you—will you draw up the advertisement, please? I will supply the clergyman's name &c. &c.

I shall not see one friend more before I leave with you. So that nobody needs divine that since the 12th, we have not been at Margate—seeking 'food for the mind.'—

11¾ A.M.

Dearest, I agree to all—I will not see you, for those reasons. I think, as you may, that it will be a point in excuse of the precipitancy that a removal was threatened for 'next Monday perhaps' . . which, finding us unprepared, would have been ruinous. Say all you would have me say to your father,—no concession shall be felt by the side of your love. I will write a few words to Mrs. J.—her kindness is admirable and deserves the attention. For the *date*,—you will have seen the precautions I take,—I hope to see nobody know; but I don't know that it will be necessary to suppress it in the advertisement, if we can leave England by the end of the week, as I hope . . do you not hope, too? For I see announcements, in to-day's *Times*, of marriages on the 8th and 9th and our silence on that particular might be only the beginning of some mystery . . as if it had happened half a year ago, for instance. Beside, your relations will examine the register. All rests with you, however—and *will* rest, Ba! I shall ask you to do no more of my business that I can manage myself; but where I can *not* manage . . why, then you shall think for me,—that is my command!

I suppose when a man buys a spinning-machine he loses dignity because he lets *it* weave stockings,—does not keep on with his clumsy fingers! No, I will retain my honours, be certain,—you shall say, *Ego et rex meus* like Wolsey—or rather, like dear, dear Ba—like yourself I will ever *worship!* See the good of taking up arms against me out of that service! If you 'honour and obey' me, 'with my body I thee worship'—my best, dearest, sweetest Ba, and that I have avowed thus 'irrevocably'—is the heart's delight of your own R.

E. B. B. to R. B.

Tuesday.
[Post-mark, September 16, 1846.]

Dearest, you were in the right as usual, and I in a fright as sometimes. I took a mere fancy into my head about your writing to Mr. Kenyon. To-day he came, and I did not see him—on the ground of a headache, which, though real, was not really sufficient of itself to keep me from seeing him, if I had not distrusted my self-control—so I did not see him. To-morrow he goes away. His letters will of course be made to follow him, and we may easily precede the newspapers by a day or two.

As for the advertisements, you quite amuse me by telling me to compose an advertisement. How should I know better than you, dearest, or as well even? All I intermeddle with willingly is the matter of the date—although there is something in what you say about the mystery, and the idea of our being six months married—still it is our disquieted conscience that gives us such thoughts—and when the advertisement appears and the cards come out so very properly, people will not have enough imagination to apprehend a single mystery in the case: and the omission of the date will not be so singular . . will it? On the other hand I apprehend evil from the date of the marriage being known. One of my brothers may be sent to examine the register, but would not betray the fact in question, *I think*, to my father; would not, I am certain, willingly give cause for additional irritation against me. But if the date be publicly announced, Papa must know it and most of my personal friends will be sure to know it. I have written letters and seen people since the twelfth . . Mr. Kenyon on Sunday, Miss Bordman on Monday. Moreover Papa would be exposed to unpleasant observations—he going every day among his City friends, and on Saturday among the rest. What quantities of good reasons, . . till you are tired of them and me!

Would you put it this way . . At such a church, by such a minister, Robert Browning Esquire, of New Cross, author of 'Paracelsus,' to Elizabeth Barrett, eldest daughter of Edward Moulton Barrett Esquire of Wimpole Street. Would you put it so? I do not understand really, . . and whether you should be specified as the author of 'Paracelsus' . . but, for *me*, it ought to be, I think, simply as I have written it. Oh, and I forgot to tell you that what we did on Saturday is quite *invalid*, so that you may give me up now if you like—it isn't too late. You gave me a wrong name—*Moulton* is no Christian name of mine. Moulton Barrett is our family name; Elizabeth Barrett, my Christian name—Behold and see!

I will send the list if I can have time to-night to write it—but the haste, the hurry—do you think, when in your right mind, of getting away this week? Think of the work before us! Next Monday is the day fixed for the general departure to a house taken at Little Bookham or Hookham . . what is it? Well—we must think. Tell me when you want me to go. I might go from the new house, perhaps. But you will think, dearest, and tell me. Tell me first, though, how your head continues or begins again . . for I fear that the good news is too sudden to last long —I fear.

Thankful, thankful I shall be when we are gone out of reach of evil, when I shall have heard that my poor dearest Papa is only angry with me, and not sorry because of me, and that Henrietta and Arabel are not too miserable. They come between me and the thought of you often—but I do not, for *that*, love you less—oh no. You are best and dearest in saying what you say—only, observe, there is not any practicable 'concession' now for you. All you can do now, is what you will do . . in being tolerant, and gentle, for my sake. My own dearest, I am your

Ba.

The list to-morrow.

R. B. to E. B. B.

Wednesday.
[Post-mark, September 16, 1846.]

Ever dearest, you are right about the date . . so it shall be—and so the advertisement shall run, save and except the avowal of 'Paracelsus' . . I avow *you*, and to add another title of honour would succeed no better than in Dalhousie's case, who was 'God of War and Lieutenant-general to the Earl of Mar.' I wanted the description &c. of your father. What a strange mistake I made—(but as for invalidation, oh no!)—I save your every word and then apply them thus! (In to-day's *Times* is a notice without a date . . not looking at all singular. It is far better).

It is absolutely for yourself to decide on the day and the mode—if for no other reason, because I am quite ready, and shall have no kind of difficulty; while you have every kind. Make the arrangements that promise most comfort to yourself. Observe the packets and alter the route if necessary. There is one from Brighton to Dieppe every day, for instance . . but then the getting to Rouen! The Havre-boat leaves Southampton, *Wednesdays* and *Saturdays*—and Portsmouth, *Mondays* and *Thursdays*. The boat from London, Thursdays and Saturdays at 9 A.M.

I do not know where 'Bookham' is—you must decide . . I am sure you will be anxious to get away.

The business of the letters will grow less difficult when once begun—see if it will not! and in these four or five days whole epics might be written, much more letters. Have you arranged all with Wilson? Take, of course, the simplest possible wardrobe &c.—so as to reduce our luggage to the very narrowest compass. The expense—(beside the common sense of a little luggage)—is considerable—every ounce being paid for. Let us treat our journey as a mere journey—we can return for what else we want, or get it sent, or procure it abroad. I shall take just a portmanteau and carpet bag. I think the fewer books we take the better; they take up room—and the wise way always seemed to me to read in rooms at home, and open one's eyes and *see* abroad. A critic somewhere mentioned *that* as my characteristic—were two other poets he named placed in novel circumstances . . in a great wood, for instance, Mr. Trench would begin opening books to see how woods were treated of . . the other man would set to writing poetry forthwith, from his old stock of associations, on the new impulse—and R. B. would sit still and learn how to write after! A pretty compliment, I thought that!—But seriously there must be a great library at Pisa . . (with that university!) and abroad they are delighted to facilitate such matters . . I have read in a chamber of the Doges' palace at Venice painted all over by Tintoretto, walls and ceiling—and at Rome there is a library with a learned priest always kept ready 'to solve any doubt that may arise!' Murray's book you have, I think? Any guide-books &c.

Be sure, dearest, I will do my utmost to conciliate your father: sometimes I could not but speak impatiently to you of him . . that was while you were in his direct power—now there is no *need* of a word in any case . . I shall be silent if the *worst imaginable* happens; and if anything better, most grateful. You do not need to remind me he is your father . . I shall be proud to say *mine* too. Then, he said *that* of you—for which I love him—love the full prompt justice of that ascription of 'perfect purity'—it is another voice responding to mine, confirming mine.

Good-bye, dearest dearest; I continue *quite* well . . I thank God, as you do, and see his hand in it. My poor mother suffers greatly, but is no worse . . rather, better I hope. They (all here) will leave town for some quiet place at the beginning of October for some three weeks at least. Dear, kind souls they are.

Kiss me as I kiss you, dearest Ba. I can bring you no

flowers but I pluck this bud and send it with all affectionate devotion.

Your own
R. B.

E. B. B. to R. B.

[Post-mark, September 17, 1846.]

Dearest, the general departure from this house takes place on Monday—and the house at Little Bookham is six miles from the nearest railroad, and a mile and a half from Leatherhead where a coach runs. Now you are to judge. Certainly if I go with you on Saturday I shall not have half the letters written—you, who talk so largely of epic poems, have not the least imagination of my state of mind and spirits. I began to write a letter to Papa this morning, and could do nothing but cry, and looked so pale thereupon, that everybody wondered what could be the matter. Oh—quite well I am now, and I only speak of myself in that way to show you how the inspiration is by no means sufficient for epic poems. Still, I may certainly write the necessary letters, . . and do the others on the road . . could I, do you think? I would rather have waited—indeed rather—only it may be difficult to leave Bookham . . yet *possible*—so tell me what you would have me do.

Wilson and I have a light box and a carpet bag between us—and I will be docile about the books, dearest. Do you take a desk? Had I better not, I wonder?

Then for box and carpet bag . . Remember that we cannot take them out of the house with us. We must send them the evening before—Friday evening, if we went on Saturday . . and where? Have you a friend anywhere, to whose house they might be sent, or could they go direct to the railroad office—and what office? In that case they should have your name on them, should they not?

Now think for me, ever dearest—and tell me what you do not tell me . . that you continue better. Ah no—you are ill again—or you would not wait to be told to tell me. And the dear, dear little *bud!*—I shall keep it to the end of my life, if you love me so long, . . or *not*, sir! I thank you, dearest.

Your mother!—I am very, very sorry. Would it be better and kinder to wait on *her* account?—tell me that too.

Yes, they are perfectly kind. We must love them well: —and *I* shall, I am sure.

Mr. Kenyon sends the 'Fawn,' *which is Landor's Fawn*, and desires me to send it to you when I have done with it. As if I could read a word! He directs me to write to him to Taunton, Somersetshire. May God bless you, beloved.

No more to-night from your very own

Ba.

Are not passengers allowed to carry a specific proportion of luggage? What do you mean then, by paying for every ounce? As to Dieppe, the diligence would be more fatiguing than the river, and, without strong reasons, one would prefer of course the Havre plan. Still I am not afraid of either. Think.

You might put in the newspaper . . of Wimpole Street and Jamaica, or . . and Cinnamon Hill, Jamaica. That is right and I thought of it at first—only stopped . . seeming to wish to have as little about poor Papa as possible. Do as you think best now.

R. B. to E. B. B.

[Post-mark, September 17, 1846.]

My only sweetest, I will write just a word to catch the earlier post,—time pressing. Bless you for all you suffer . . I *know* it though it would be very needless to call your attention to the difficulties. I know much, if not all, and can only love and admire you,—not help, alas!

Surely these difficulties will multiply, if you go to Bookham—the way will be to leave at once. The letters may easily be written during the journey . . at Orléans, for example. But now,—you propose *Saturday* . . nothing leaves Southampton according to *to-day's* advertisement till *Tuesday* . . the days seemed changed to *Tuesdays* and *Fridays*. To-morrow at 8¼ P.M. and Friday the 22, 10¼. Provoking! I will go to town directly to the railway office and enquire particularly—getting the time-table also. Under these circumstances, we have only the choice of Dieppe (as needing the shortest diligence-journey)—or the Sunday morning Havre-packet, at 9 A.M.—which you do nŏt consider practicable: though it would, I think, take us the quickliest out of all the trouble. I will let you know all particulars in a note to-night . . it shall reach you to-night.

If we went from London only, the luggage could be sent here or in any case, perhaps . . as one fly will carry them with me and mine, and save possibility of delay.

I am *very* well, dearest dearest—my mother no worse, better, perhaps—she is out now. Our staying and getting into trouble would increase her malady.

As you leave it to me,—the name, and 'Wimpole St.' will do. Jamaica sounds in the wrong direction, does it not? and the other place is distinctive enough.

Take no desk . . I will take a large one—take nothing you can leave—but secure letters &c. I will take out a passport. Did you not tell me roughly at how much you estimated our expenses for the journey? Because I will take about *that* much, and get Rothschild's letter of credit for Leghorn. One should avoid carrying money about with one.

All this in such haste! Bless you, my dearest dearest Ba

Your R.

All was right in the licence, and Certificate and Register—the whole name is there, E.B.M.B. The clergyman made the mistake in not having the *two* names, but all runs right to *read* . . the essential thing.

R. B. to E. B. B.

5 o'clock.
[Post-mark, September 17, 1846.]

My own Ba, I believe, or am sure the mistake has been mine—in the flurry I noted down the departures from *Havre*—instead of *Southampton*. You must either be at the Vauxhall Station by *four* o'clock—so as to arrive in 3 hours and a half at Southampton and leave by 8¼ P.M.—or must go by the Sunday Boat,—or *wait* till Tuesday. Dieppe is impossible, being too early. You must decide —and let me know directly. To-morrow *is* too early—yet one . . that is, *I*—could manage.

Ever your own, in all haste
R. B.

R. B. to E. B. B.

7½—Thursday.
[Post-mark, September 18, 1846.]

My own Ba—forgive my mistaking! I had not enough confidence in my own correctness. The advertisement of the Tuesday and Friday Boats is of the South of England Steam Company. The Wednesday and Saturday is that of the *South Western*. There must be then *two* companies, because on the Southampton Railway Bill it is expressly stated that there are departures for Havre on all four days. Perhaps you have seen my blunder. In that case, you can leave by 1-12½ as you may appoint—

Your R.

E. B. B. to R. B.

[Post-mark, September 18, 1846.]

Dearest take this word, as if it were many. I am so tired—and then it shall be the right word.

Sunday and Friday are impossible. On Saturday I will go to you, if you like—with half done, . . nothing done . . . scarcely. Will you come for me to Hodgson's? or shall I meet you at the station? At what o'clock should I set out, to be there at the hour you mention?

Also, for the boxes . . we cannot carry them out of the house, you know, Wilson and I. They must be sent on Friday evening to the Vauxhall Station, 'to be taken care of.' Will the people keep them carefully? Ought some-one to be spoken to beforehand? If we sent them to New Cross, they would not reach you in time.

Hold me my beloved—with your love. It is very hard—But Saturday seems the only day for us. Tell me if you think so indeed.

Your very own Ba.

The boxes must have your name on them of course. Let there be no great haste about sending out the cards. *Saturday* might be mentioned in the advertisement, *without* the date—might it not?

E. B. B. to R. B.

[Post-mark, September 18, 1846.]

Dearest, here is the paper of addresses. I cannot remember, I am so confused, half of them.

Surely you say wrong in the hour for to-morrow. Also there is the express train. Would it not be better?

Your Ba.

R. B. to E. B. B.

11¼ Friday.
[Post-mark, September 18, 1846.]

My own best Ba. How thankful I am you have seen my blunder—I took the other company's days for the South Western's changed. What I shall write now is with the tables before me (of the Railway) and a transcript from *to-day's* advertisement in the *Times*.

The packet will leave to-morrow evening, from the

Friday morning ..

Let it be this way, ever dearest. If in the time of fine weather, I am not ill, .. then .. *not now* .. you shall decide, & your decision shall be duty & desire to me, both — I will make no difficulties. Remember, in the meanwhile, that I *have* decided to let it be as you shall choose .. *shall* choose .. That I love you enough to give you up "for your good," is proof (to myself at least) that I love you enough for any other end: — but you thought too much of me in the last letter. Do not mistake me. I believe & trust in all your words — only you are generous unawares, as other men are selfish ..

More, I meant to say of this, but you moved me as usual yesterday into the sunshine, & then I am dazzled & cannot see clearly. Still I see that you love me & that I am bound to you! — & "what more need I see" you may ask, — while I cannot help looking out to the future, to the blue ridges of the hills, to the chances of your being happy with me. Well! — I am yours as you see .. & not yours to teaze you — you shall decide everything when the time comes for doing anything — and from

And you? how are you? Mind to tell me.. May I hold Thursday [illegible] to monday or tuesday to be my day?— If it were not for the Kenyons I should take courage & say monday— but tuesday or saturday would do as well— would they not? Ever your own Ba—

Shall I have a letter?

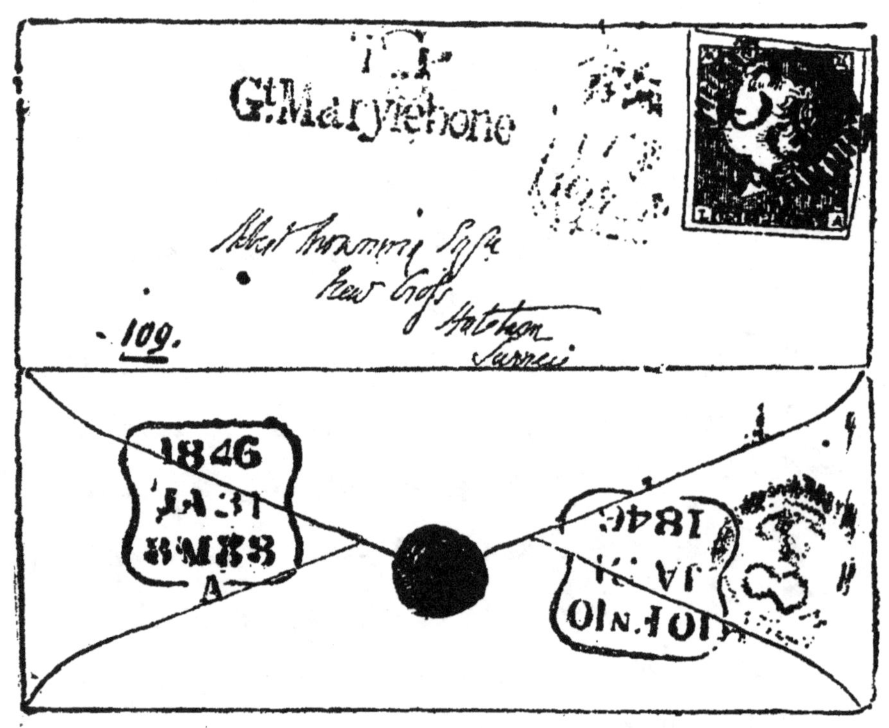

Royal Pier, Southampton at *nine*. We leave Nine Elms, Vauxhall, at *five*—to arrive at *eight*. Doors close *five* minutes before. I will be at Hodgson's *from* half-past three to *four precisely* when I shall hope you can be ready. I shall go to Vauxhall, apprise them that luggage is coming (yours) and send *mine* there—so that we both shall be unencumbered and we can take a cab or coach from H's.

Never mind your scanty preparations . . we can get everything at Leghorn,—and the new boats carry parcels to Leghorn on the 15th of every month, remember—so can bring what you may wish to send for.

I enclose a letter to go with yours. The cards as you choose—they are here—we can write about them from Paris or elsewhere. The advertisement, as you advise. All shall be cared for.

God bless and strengthen you, my ever dearest dearest—I will not trust myself to speak of my feelings for you—worship well belongs to such fortitude. One struggle more—if all the kindness on your part brought a strangely insufficient return, is it not possible that this step may produce all you can hope? Write to me one word more. Depend on me. I go to Town about business.

Your own, own R.

E. B. B. to R. B.

Friday Night.
[Post-mark, September 19, 1846.]

At from half-past three to four, then—four will not, I suppose, be too late. I will not write more— *I cannot*. By to-morrow at this time, I shall have *you* only, to love me—my beloved!

You *only!* As if one said *God only*. And we shall have *Him* beside, I pray of Him.

I shall send to your address at New Cross your Hanmer's poems—and the two dear books you gave me, which I do not like to leave here and am afraid of hurting by taking them with me. Will you ask *our* Sister to put the parcel into a drawer, so as to keep it for us?

Your letters to me I take with me, let the 'ounces' cry out aloud, ever so. I *tried* to leave them, and I could not. That is, they would not be left: it was not my fault—I will not be scolded.

Is this my last letter to you, ever dearest? Oh—if I loved you less . . a little, little less.

Why I should tell you that our marriage was invalid, or ought to be; and that you should by no means come for me to-morrow. It is dreadful . . dreadful . . to have to give pain here by a voluntary act—for the first time in my life.

Remind your mother and father of me affectionately and gratefully—and your Sister too! Would she think it too bold of me to say *our* Sister, if she had heard it on the last page?

Do you pray for me to-night, Robert? Pray for me, and love me, that I may have courage, feeling both—

Your own
Ba.

The boxes are *safely sent.* Wilson has been perfect to me. And *I* . . calling her 'timid,' and afraid of her timidity! I begin to think that none are so bold as the timid, when they are fairly roused.

INDEX

ACTON, Cardinal, i. 148.
Adams, Mrs., i. 550.
Ælian, i. 369, 375, 535; ii. 195, 201.
Æschylus, i. 15, 31ff., 34, 35ff., 38ff., 45, 61, 87, 171, 312.
Alfieri, Vittorio, i. 52.
Andersen, Hans Christian ('The Dane'), i. 52, 160.
his 'Improvisatore,' i. 45, 50, 51, 54; his 'Only a Fiddler,' 1, 154, 160.
Angelico, Fra, i. 196.
Apuleius, E. B. B.'s translations from, i. 167.
'Athenæum,' the, i. 154, 161, 166, 288, 322, 325, 387, 393, 410, 413, 537, 553, 566; ii. 33, 35, 102, 157, 175, 306, 342, 418.
Arnould, Joseph (afterwards Sir), ii. 102, 115, 410, 463, 485.
Asolo, i. 113.
Australia (proposals for E. B. B. to write ballads, &c., for), ii. 478.
'Autography,' i. 318, 319, 322; ii. 187.

BABBAGE, C., i. 24.
Bacon, Lord, i. 478, 481.
Bailey, P. J., his 'Festus,' i. 373, 382.
Balzac, H. de, ii. 35, 91, 93, 107, 113.
Barrett, Alfred, brother of E. B. B., i. 192, 195; ii. 176.
Barrett, Arabel, sister of E. B. B., i. 101, 193, 215, 219, 329, 537; ii. 327, 332 and passim.
Barrett, Charles John ('Stormie'), brother of E. B. B., i. 219, 415, 570; ii. 108, 111, 406, 456.
Barrett, Edward ('Bro'), brother of E. B. B., his death, i. 175ff.
Barrett, Edward Moulton, father of E. B. B., i. 122, 131, 141, 167, 174, 190, 192, 212, 218, 235, 240ff., 407, 502, 526; ii. 26, 109, 151, 269, 292, 330, 333, 338, 340, 382, 447, 484, 489, 551.
Barrett, Elizabeth Barrett:
on poetic composition, i. 21.
on her translation of 'Prometheus Bound,' i. 31.
proposes to write a 'novel' or 'romance' poem, i. 32, 150, 153, 271.
project of writing a drama ('Psyché Apocalypté') with R. H. Horne, i. 61.
American appreciation, i. 115, 306; ii. 152, 165, 183, 426.
proposals for wintering abroad, i. 131ff., 135, 167, 190, 208, 218, 225, 229, 234ff., 240.
religious views, i. 145; ii. 427.
on George Sand, i. 164.
on the death of her brother Edward, i. 175ff.
references to her dangerous illness, i. 43, 175; ii. 26.
American publishers, i. 187, 189, 258, 260.
on her pet name 'Ba,' i. 192, 195, 340, 345.
her portrait, i. 195; ii. 12, 19.
requests R. B's autograph for a friend, i. 227.
on R. B's. poetry, i. 268ff.; ii. 488.
sends a ring and lock of hair to R. B., i. 307, 308.
opinions on French fiction, i. 340; ii. 102.

Barrett, Elizabeth Barrett, (*cont.*):
on women's position and married life, i. 350ff.; ii. 422.
early reading, i. 404.
French verses, i. 403.
on R. B.'s letters, i. 415, 420, 482, 489; ii. 18.
on the publication of letters, i. 480.
on autograph collectors, i. 531.
on the difficulties of her engagement with R. B., ii. 32, 78, 81, 121, 140, 219, 221, 227, 228, 231, 334, 339, 372, 376, 381, 383, 394, 414, 456, 462, 491, 494.
on artistic Bohemianism, ii. 30.
on the curiosity of strangers, their visits, letters, &c., ii. 31, 73, 168, 420, 470.
on duelling, ii. 41ff., 45, 53ff.
on Raffael's portrait, ii. 149.
plans for going to Italy with R. B., ii. 207, 209, 274, 277ff., 287, 319, 377, 389, 414, 471, 476, 478, 487, 499ff., 503, 508.
proposal for her to visit New Cross, ii. 225, 229.
her money affairs, ii. 227, 233, 363, 366, 398ff., 406, 473ff.
visit to the Great Western Railway, ii. 233, 432.
visit to Mr. Rogers' picture gallery, ii. 249, 261.
visits to H. S. Boyd described, ii. 258, 281.
on the death of B. R. Haydon, ii. 264, 270; on Horne's verses on Haydon, ii. 298; bequest of his MSS. to E.B.B., ii. 303ff., 306, 308ff., 314ff., 321ff., 325.
on women and politics, ii. 282.
her visit to Finchley, ii. 442, 444, 449.
'Blackwood's Magazine's' offer to print her lyrics, ii. 457, 463, 476.
visit to church, and the effect of music on her, ii. 458, 465, 489.
proposal to write ballads, &c., for Australia, ii. 478.
her marriage, ii. 535 *n*, 537.
Barrett, Elizabeth Barrett, works:
'Bertha in the Lane,' i. 10, 148, 270.
'Catarina to Camoens,' i. 148, 422.

Barrett, Elizabeth Barrett, works (*cont.*):
'The Cry of the Children,' proposals for musical setting, i. 519, 532.
'A Drama of Exile,' i. 10, 19.
'An Essay of Mind,' i. 129, 132, 134, 135, 381.
'Lady Geraldine's Courtship,' i. 32, 148, 162, 270.
'Past and Future,' i. 281.
'Poems,' 2 vols. 1844, i. 9, 189, 280; ii. 284; American edition, i. 185, 186.
'Rhyme of the Duchess May,' i. 10.
'The Romaunt of Margret,' i. 381.
'The Romaunt of the Page,' i. 10.
'The Seraphim,' i. 129, 189, 381.
'Two Sketches,' i. 192.
'The Vision of Fame,' i. 132.
'A Vision of Poets,' i. 147, 381.
'Wine of Cyprus,' ii. 441, 444, 446.
Translations from Bion, Theocritus, Apuleius, Nonnus, i. 167, 170ff., 493; ii. 8; from Homer, i. 574; ii. 8, 22, 25, 31, 69, 138, 160; from Æschylus, i. 34, 75, 140, 142, 148, 150; ii, 456; from Pietro d'Abano, i. 458, 459.
Barrett, George, brother of E. B. B., i. 192, 195, 215, 218, 219, 229, 234, 240, 288, 318, 321, 402, 436, 441, 488, 492, 496; ii. 115, 439.
Barrett, Henrietta, sister of E. B. B., i. 128, 193, 329, 405, 430, 434, 512; ii. 141, 332, 385, 487 and passim.
Barrett, Henry, brother of E. B. B., i. 157.
Barrett, Lizzie, cousin of E. B. B., i. 518; ii. 244.
Barrett, Mary (E. B. B.'s mother), ii. 482.
Barrett, Octavius ('Occy'), brother of E. B. B., his illness, i. 236ff., 240ff., 246ff., 265.
Barrett, Sam, cousin of E. B. B., i. 517.
Bartoli, his 'Simboli,' i. 535, 536, 540.
Bayley, Miss, i. 299, 302, 303; ii. 22, 109, 111, 114, 120, 136, 195, 547; her plans for taking E. B. B. to Italy, ii. 189, 197, 207, 243.
Beethoven, i. 528; ii. 153; his 'Fidelio,' i. 161.
Benjamin of Tudela, R., i. 153 *n*.

Bennet, Miss Georgiana, ii. 73, 80, 110, 224, 327, 367.
Bennett, W. C., ii. 106, 124, 329, 364, 387.
Bevan, Mr., ii. 333.
Bezzi, Mr., ii. 139, 190.
'Blackwood's Magazine,' i. 23; ii. 457, 463, 476.
Blake, William, ii. 317.
Blessington, Lady, i. 157.
Boccaccio, Giovanni, i. 45, 390.
Boyd, Hugh Stuart, i. 100, 235, 340; ii. 258, 259, 281, 405, 439, 441, 443, 456, 469, 537.
Bremer, Miss, ii. 118.
'British Quarterly,' the, i. 268.
Browne, Sir Thomas, ii. 52.
Browning, Miss, i. 146, 152, 189, 514; ii. 164, 167, 203, 410, 562.
Browning, Mrs., senior, i. 146; ii. 453, 480, 497.
Browning, R., senior, i. 28, 146, 493; ii. 424, 544; his drawings for R. B.'s poems, i. 413, 431; his early life, ii. 474, 480, 481.
Browning, Robert:
- Mr. Kenyon's offer of introduction to Miss Barrett, i. 2, 280.
- on E. B. B.'s poems, i. 9, 147.
- helps Carlyle with his 'Cromwell,' i. 16.
- on the attitude of the public towards his work, i. 17ff.
- first visit to E. B. B., i. 72 *n.*
- account of the 'bora' at Trieste, i. 126.
- on 'The Flight of the Duchess,' i. 138.
- on George Sand, i. 163.
- baptised at an Independent Chapel, i. 147.
- reference to his visit to St. Petersburg, i. 154.
- on dramatic poetry and novels, i. 155, 160.
- on reading law with Basil Montagu, i. 199.
- his early life, i. 200, 347.
- on the performance of 'Every Man in his Humour,' i. 212, 217.
- his portrait in the 'New Spirit of the Age,' i. 315; ii. 218.
- sends a lock of hair to E. B. B., i. 303, 331.
- his visit to R. H. Horne, i. 364ff.
- on R. H. Horne's 'Ballad Romances,' i. 368.

Browning, Robert (*cont.*):
- French verses, i. 417.
- on a proposal of a journey to St. Petersburg, i. 485, 503.
- on music, i. 539.
- plants rose-trees, ii. 10.
- thoughts for future work, i. 454; ii. 25, 388.
- on duelling, ii. 33, 46ff., 58.
- on the rearrangement of his poems, ii. 71.
- on French romance, ii. 107.
- his birthday, ii. 135.
- at the Royal Literary Fund Dinner, ii. 143, 144, 147, 150, 157.
- proposal to write a long poem, ii. 175, 179.
- 'Mr. Forster's "Strafford,"' ii. 214.
- meets a phrenologist, ii. 215, 217.
- on his engagement with E. B. B., ii. 225.
- proposes to seek Government employment, ii. 227, 230, 234, 246.
- on the death of B. R. Haydon, ii. 263, 267, 316ff.
- plans for his marriage, ii. 268, 374.
- on Parliament, ii. 280.
- on his name, ii. 284, 285.
- on Italian post offices, ii. 110, 288.
- on Horne's verses on Haydon's death, ii. 302.
- on Haydon's bequest of MSS. to E. B. B., ii. 305, 314ff., 325.
- on strangers' letters, ii. 329.
- his dream on Haydon, ii. 329.
- on E. B. B.'s letters, i. 295, 417; ii. 8, 248, 417, 434.
- on E. B. B.'s religious opinions, ii. 434.
- on Lord Byron, ii. 453.
- final preparations for their journey to Italy, ii. 463ff., 472, 492ff., 533, 551, 554 and ff.
- early compositions in imitation of Ossian, ii. 466.
- his marriage, ii. 535 *n.*
- his family's attitude towards E. B. B., ii. 542, 544.

Browning, Robert, works:
- 'Bells and Pomegranates, i. 9, 13, 98, 131, 135, 144, 148, 319, 359; ii. 426; see also 'Dramatic Romances and Lyrics,' 'Luria,' and 'A Soul's Tragedy.'

Browning, Robert, works (*cont.*):
meaning of the phrase, i. 248, 249, 250, 569; ii. 2, 67.
'The Bishop orders his Tomb at St. Praxed Church,' i. 134, 252, 277.
'The Blot in the Scutcheon,' i. 323.
'The Boy and the Angel' ('Theocrite,' 'Angel and Child'), i. 134, 261.
'Claret and Tokay' ('Nationality in Drinks'), i. 131, 135.
'Colombe's Birthday,' ii. 453, 466.
'Count Gismond,' i. 176.
Dante, Translation from, i. 347, 353.
'Dramatic Romances and Lyrics' ('Bells and Pomegranates' No. VII.), i. 58, 66.
proof of, i. 258, 260, 261, 262.
its publication, i. 265, 266, 267.
E. B. B. on, i. 268ff. to C. Mathews, i. 319.
Mr. Kenyon on, i. 273.
Mr. Fox on, i. 276, 277.
noticed in the 'Examiner,' i. 285.
noticed in the 'New Monthly,' i. 359.
noticed in the 'Athenæum,' i. 410, 413.
'Earth's Immortalities,' i. 261.
'The Englishman in Italy ('England in Italy,' 'Fortú,' 'Sorrento Lines'), i. 253, 267, 269, 277.
'The Flight of the Duchess,' i. 54, 58ff., 62, 76, 97, 104ff, 114, 115, 120, 121, 123, 128, 131, 135, 138, 147, 149ff., 244, 253, 261, 273, 277; ii. 90.
French Book, An Elementary, i. 208.
'Garden Fancies,' i. 134.
'The Glove,' i. 261, 277.
'Home Thoughts from Abroad' ('Spring Song'), i. 229ff.
'Home Thoughts from the Sea,' i. 253.
'How we brought the Good News from Ghent to Aix' ('The Ride'), i. 273, 277ff.
'The Italian in England' ('Italy in England'), i. 159, 277.
'The Laboratory,' i. 134.
'The Lost Leader,' i. 252.

Browning, Robert, works (*cont.*):
'The Lost Mistress,' i. 252, 269.
'Luria: a Tragedy' ('Bells and Pomegranates' No. VIII.), i. 17, 22, 26, 30, 58, 59, 80, 83, 85, 260, 271, 423, 466, 471; ii. 2, 13, 21, 367.
E. B. B. on, i. 276ff., 285, 312, 353, 358ff., 418ff., 459, 468, 540, 574; ii. 76ff.
proof of, ii. 12, 17.
dedication of, ii. 12, 18, 44, 66ff.
publication of, ii. 66.
Mr. Kenyon on, ii. 82.
Carlyle on, ii. 90.
Mr. Chorley on, ii. 92.
noticed in the 'Examiner,' ii. 108, 410.
'Night and Morning,' i. 261.
'Only a Player Girl,' i. 155, 160.
'Paracelsus,' i. 62, 208, 246, 322 326, 380, 392.
'Pauline,' i. 386, 390, 397, 400, 403, 417, 420.
reviewed by J. S. Mill, i. 28, 33.
'Pictor Ignotus,' i. 252, 277.
Pietro d'Abano, Translation from, i. 458, 463.
'Pippa Passes,' i. 12, 22, 24, 28, 100; ii. 348.
'Saul,' i. 60, 76, 179, 182, 191, 261, 277, 325.
Blue lilies in, i. 523, 553, 566.
'Soliloquy of the Spanish Cloister,' i. 22.
'Song,' i. 261.
'Sordello,' i. 134, 193, 247, 346, 454, 468.
'A Soul's Tragedy ('Bells and Pomegranates' No. VIII.), i. 26, 30, 97, 467, 470; ii. 16, 34, 67, 92.
E. B. B. on, i. 540; ii. 13ff., 17, 34, 77.
publication of, ii. 66.
Mr. Kenyon on, ii. 82.
Mr. Chorley on, ii. 92.
noticed in the 'Examiner,' ii. 108.
Buckingham, Mr., i. 558, 560, 565, 571.
Bulwer, Sir Edward Lytton, afterwards first Lord Lytton, i. 245.
his 'Alice,' i. 160.
his 'Ernest Maltravers,' i. 160, 165.
his 'Last Days of Pompeii,' i. 155.

Bunn, Alfred, i. 567; ii. 135.
Bunyan, J., ii. 37.
Burdett-Coutts, Miss, i. 559.
Burges, George, i. 167, 169, 171, 493, 544, 548.
Burns, R., i. 477.
Bury, Lady Charles, her 'Reminiscences,' i. 228.
Butler, Mrs. (Fanny Kemble), her poems, ii. 27, 37, 386, 389.
Butler, Samuel, his 'Hudibras' quoted, i. 562.
Byron, Lady, i. 130.
Byron, Lord, i. 125; ii. 453, 461, 471.

CALDERON, i. 65.
'Cambridge Advertiser,' the, ii. 28.
Campbell, Miss, ii. 169, 171, 173, 177, 182.
Campbell, Thomas, ii. 285.
Carlyle, Mrs., i. 194, 238; ii. 251, 253.
Carlyle, Thomas, i. 25, 27, 29, 30, 151, 157, 194, 260, 315, 454, 456; ii. 8, 80, 81, 84, 90, 92, 98, 159, 184, 236, 276.
'Oliver Cromwell,' i. 16, 25, 447; ii. 2, 285.
Cerutti's Italian Grammar, i. 464.
Cervantes 'Don Quixote,' i. 46.
Chambers, Dr., i. 122, 125, 157, 175, 186, 188; ii. 253.
Chapman, George, i. 97, 335.
Chaucer, Geoffrey, i. 159, 266, 335, 391, 426.
Chesterfield, Lord, i. 525; ii. 105.
Chorley, H. F., i. 45, 107, 108, 144, 148, 154, 287, 295, 297, 315, 386, 392ff., 397, 479, 483, 489, 492, 544, 550ff., 568; ii. 92, 102, 106, 131, 135, 344, 348, 349, 351, 409, 435, 439, 440, 453, 485.
his 'Pomfret,' i. 272, 279, 282, 290, 291.
'Christus Patiens,' i. 171.
Cimarosa, D., i. 539.
Claude le Jeune, i. 539, 540.
Clayton, John, i. 525.
Cockers, the Misses, ii. 176, 182.
Cocks, Lady Margaret, ii. 126, 130, 240.
Colburn, Henry, i. 200.
Coleridge, S. T., i. 279, 335, 364; ii. 83, 453.
Colonna, Vittoria, i. 116.
Compton, Lord, ii. 28, 29.
Cook, Surtees, Captain, i. 421, 436, 512, 526; ii. 353, 385, 487.
Corelli, A., i. 539.
Crashaw, Richard, i. 335.
Cushman, Miss, i. 154, 160, 393, 443.

'DAILY NEWS,' i. 400, 407, 421; ii. 28.
Dante, i. 52, 54, 56, 116, 309, 347, 353, 570; ii. 276.
Darwin, Erasmus, i. 381.
134, 175, 298, 337.
De Lamennais, L'Abbe, ii. 107.
De Musset, Alfred, ii. 107.
Dickens, Charles, i. 69, 217, 260, 392, 441; ii. 115, 122, 135.
his 'Cricket on the Hearth,' i. 344, 354.
his 'Pictures from Italy,' ii. 167, 168.
Diderot, Denis, i. 113, 118.
Dilke, C. W., i. 393; ii. 134, 175.
D'Israeli, Benjamin, his 'Sybil,' i. 124.
his 'Vivian Grey,' i. 52, 53ff., 56.
Domett, Alfred, i. 16, 295, 526; ii. 349.
Donne, Dr. John, i. 27, 145, 196, 417, 437; ii. 115.
D'Orsay, Count, ii. 135, 137.
Dowland, John, i. 540.
Doyle, John ('H. B.'), ii. 430.
Drayton, M., his 'Nymphidia,' i. 371.
Dryden, John, i. 23.
Dulwich Galleries, the two, i. 514, 518, 520, 524.
Dumas, Alexander, ii. 103, 344.
his 'Monte Cristo,' ii. 213, 338.

EAGLES, Mr., ii. 372, 450.
Elliotson, Dr., i. 117.
Etty, William, ii. 188, 190.
Euripides, i. 21.
'Examiner,' the, i. 288, 322, 373, 463; ii. 106, 107, 108, 410.

FERRERS case, the, i. 488.
Fife, Angus, ii. 478.
Fisher, Miss Emma, i. 381.
Fletcher, J., i. 371.
Florence, ii. 195, 253.
Flush, Miss Barrett's dog, i. 54, 150, 167, 236, 263ff., 544; ii. 320, 324, 356; the loss of, 502–524, passim.
Ford, J., i. 335.
Forster, John, i. 217, 245, 268, 292, 293, 294, 297, 299, 322, 373, 393, 400, 403; ii. 67, 81, 106, 107, 108,

111, 214, 239, 304, 307, 311, 314, 315, 363, 372.
Forsyth Joseph, quoted, ii. 278.
Fox, Mrs., ii. 345.
Fox, W. J., i. 276, 500, 551.
French and English criticisms on foreign books, i. 553, 561.
Fuller, Miss Margaret Sarah (afterwards Mme. Ossoli), i. 373.
Fuseli, H., i. 65.

Garrow, Miss, i. 156, 288.
Gill, Rev. Thomas Hornblower, i. 570; ii. 3.
Godwin, William, i. 196.
Goethe, J. W., i. 272; ii. 52, 312, 314, 448.
Grey, Lord, ii. 411.
Gurney, A., i. 73, 563.

Hahn-Hahn, the Countess, ii. 211, 249, 251, 254, 262, 267.
Hall, Robert, i. 510.
Hall, Spencer, i. 246.
Handel, G. F., i. 539.
Hanmer, Sir John, i. 287, 293, 396, 528.
Harness, Rev. William, i. 373.
Haworth, Miss, ii. 171.
Haydon, B. R., i. 85; ii. 364; his death, ii. 263, 264ff., 267, 270ff., 316ff.; bequest of his MSS. to E. B. B., ii. 303, 306, 314ff., 321ff., 325.
Horne's verses on his death, ii. 298, 299, 302, 337.
Hazlitt, William, i. 336; ii. 251.
Heaton, Miss, ii. 127, 133, 154, 156, 169, 171.
Hedley, Arabella, her marriage, ii. 193, 303, 360, 390, 393, 428.
Hedley, Mrs., i. 84, 108ff., 192; ii. 330, 332, 385.
Hedley, Robert, ii. 237, 286, 319, 343.
Hemans, Charles (son of Mrs. Hemans), i. 115.
Heraud, John Abraham, i. 386, 390, 568.
Hood, Thomas, i. 58, 63, 456.
'Hood's Magazine,' i. 58, 131, 133, 134ff.
Horne, R. H., i. 7, 11, 28, 32, 61, 62, 64, 81, 94, 96, 120, 121, 265, 267, 269, 314, 363ff., 391; ii. 392, 401, 405, 410.
and Miss Mitford, i. 462ff., 465ff., 470.
Horne, R. H., verses on the death of B. R. Haydon, ii. 298, 299, 302, 337.
'Ballad Romances,' i. 368ff., 370ff., 378ff., 384.
his 'Cosmo de Medici,' i. 65, 371.
'Death of Marlowe,' i. 371.
'Gregory VII.,' i. 65.
'New Spirit of the Age,' i. 69.
'Orion,' i. 371.
Howitt, Mary, i. 45, 55, 160; ii. 119, 124.
Howitt, Richard, i. 246.
Howitt, William, ii. 118, 120, 124.
Hugo, Victor, his portrait, ii. 344, 357.
Hume, David, quoted, ii. 327.
Hunt, Leigh, i. 125, 170, 227, 228, 336, 364, 366, 391; ii. 313.
his translation of lines on Pulci, i. 458, 463.
Hunter, Mary, i. 229.
Hunter, Mr., i. 227; ii. 495.

Jameson, Mrs., i. 116, 130, 150, 17[illegible], 311, 497, 512, 514; ii. 4, 11, 27, 69, 72, 130, 137, 143, 148, 154, 157, 160, 194, 218, 243, 249, 261, 287, 288, 289, 300, 343, 372, 454, 459, 468, 473, 477, 482, 547.
her etchings, ii. 8ff., 56, 138.
plan for taking E. B. B. to Italy, ii. 190, 269, 286, 368, 403ff.
Janin, Jules, i. 553; ii. 345.
Jerrold, Douglas, i. 217, 441.
Jones, Commodore, ii. 143, 168, 184.
Jonson, Ben, performance of 'Every Man in his Humour,' i. 212, 216, 217ff.
Junius, ii. 170, 173.

Kean, Charles, i. 200.
Kean, Edmund, i. 77.
Keats, John, i. 13, 18, 194, 238, 244, 364, 388; ii. 150, 313.
Keats, John, his 'Eve of St. Agnes,' i. 194.
Kelly, Mr. Fitzroy, i. 200, 211, 488.
Kemble, Fanny. *See* Mrs. Butler.
Kenyon, John, i. 2, 4, 6, 9, 21, 47, 134, 143, 188, 306, 359ff., 446, 480, 482, 537; ii. 62ff., 82, 165, 211, 233, 269, 281, 307, 363, 368, 371, 378, 384, 412, 432, 450, 549 and passim.
Kinglake, A. W., ii. 134.

LA CAVA, ii. 288, 291, 319, 321, 323.
Lamb, Charles, i. 336, 393, 449.
'Lancet,' the, i. 245.
Landelle, ii. 115.
Landor, Walter Savage, i. 20, 131, 282, 289, 294, 297, 299, 361; ii. 44, 81, 83, 85, 185, 199, 211, 239, 307, 311, 313, 370, 372, 418, 450.
his 'Count Julian,' i. 560, 561.
his 'Dialogue between Tasso and his Sister,' ii. 260, 262.
his 'Pentameron,' i. 131.
verses to Robert Browning, i. 286ff., 319, 493; ii. 242.
Lawes, Henry, i. 540.
'League,' the, ii. 105, 111, 112.
Lee, Nathaniel, i. 514.
Leech, John, i. 217.
Lewis, 'Monk,' i. 228.
Londonderry, Lady, i. 196.
Longfellow, H. W., ii. 137.
Longman, Mr., ii. 364.
Lough, John Graham, ii. 193, 195, 212, 217, 219, 220, 223, 450.
Lowell, J. R., his 'Conversations on some of the Old Poets,' i. 335ff., 342ff.
Lytton, Sir Edward. *See* Bulwer.

MACHIAVELLI, N., i. 302, 309; ii. 213.
Mackay, Charles, i. 386, 393, 398.
Maclise, David, i. 217; ii. 306.
Malherbe, i. 257.
Manners, Lord John, i. 387.
Marc-Antonio's etchings, ii. 143, 149.
Markham, Mrs., i. 343.
Marlowe, Christopher, i. 96.
Martineau, Harriet, i. 112, 114, 116, 246, 263, 315, 357, 361, 373, 428, 438, 466, 477; ii. 69, 282, 451, 459.
her letter on Wordsworth, i. 461, 476ff., 486.
Mathews, Cornelius, i. 307, 319, 323, 343, 493; ii. 426, 435, 440.
Matthew, Father, i. 77.
Medwin, Capt. Thomas, his 'Conversations of Lord Byron,' i. 228.
'Methodist Quarterly,' the, ii. 152, 176.
Mill, John Stuart, i. 28, 33, 78.
Milner, Mrs., ii. 74.
Milnes, R. Monckton (afterwards Lord Houghton), i. 528, 530; ii. 134, 246, 407.
Milton, John, i. 45, 194; ii. 261.
Mitford, Miss M. R., i. 11, 22, 61, 68, 85, 95, 106, 108, 109, 110, 147, 160, 263, 452, 453, 456, 482, 489, 496; ii. 22, 27, 241, 287, 290, 314, 357, 413, 438.
on R. H. Horne, i. 462ff., 465ff., 470.
Molière, i. 188.
Monod, Rev. A., ii. 458ff.
Montagu, Basil, i. 199.
Montagu, Lady Mary, her 'Septennial Act,' ii. 237.
Montagu, Mrs., i. 528.
Montaigne, Michel de, i. 131.
Montefiore, Sir Moses, i. 485, 500, 506, 511, 522.
Moore, Thomas, ii. 376; his 'Life and Letters of Byron,' ii. 453.
'Morning Chronicle,' the, i. 297, 387.
Moxon, Edward, i. 18, 115, 187, 235, 238, 265, 292, 297, 323, 471, 528; ii. 118, 122, 150, 284, 335, 372, 485, 509.
on reviewers, ii. 342.

NAPOLEON I., i. 24, 200, 238.
'New Monthly Magazine' (Colburn's), i. 52, 53, 69, 120, 359.
'New Quarterly Review,' i. 375, 379.
Northampton, Lord, i. 492.
Norton, Hon. Mrs., i. 48, 51, 357 *n.*; ii. 308, 399.

O'CONNELL, D., ii. 42.
Osgood, Mrs., ii. 133.
Ossian, ii. 89, 258, 282, 457, 467, 470.
Ovid, i. 271.

PADUA, i. 196.
Paine, Mrs., ii. 31, 74, 83, 85, 367.
Palmella, the Duke of, i. 229, 230, 240.
Patmore, Coventry, ii. 134.
Peel, Sir Robert, ii. 265, 270, 280.
'Peoples' Journal,' the, i. 542, 550; ii. 123.
Pietro d'Abano, i. 458, 463.
Pisa, i. 189, 192, 196, 200, 209, 231, 236, 254, 257; ii. 461.
Plato, i. 468, 536.
Poe, Edgar A., i. 307, 384, 400, 443, 565; ii. 133, 218.
dedication of his poems to E. B. B., i. 428.
his 'Raven,' i. 537.
Polidoro, i. 28; ii. 153.
Polk, President, ii. 98.

Porta, J. Baptista, i. 497.
Possagno, i. 125.
Powell, T., i. 391, 395, 568; ii. 156.
Priessnitz, i. 246.
Pritchard, Captain, ii. 39, 83, 345, 495, 543.
Procter, B. W., i. 311, 493, 496; ii. 133, 254, 425.
Procter, Mrs. B. W., ii. 62, 70, 72, 75, 134, 211, 326.
Purchas, J., i. 357 *n.*
Pusey, Dr., ii. 345.

Quarles, Francis, i. 416; ii. 187, 444.
'Quarterly Review,' the, i. 19, 293, 310, 313.
Quintilian, i. 35.

Rabelais, François de, i. 46.
Rachel, Mlle., ii. 326, 339, 345, 410.
Ravenna, ii. 232, 251, 254.
Reade, J. Edmund, ii. 285, 370, 372, 376.
'Retrospective Review,' i. 342, 344, 380.
Reybaud, Mme. Charles, i. 553.
Robinson, Crabb, i. 480.
Rogers, Samuel, i. 85ff., 196; ii. 249ff., 261, 262.
Ronsard, Peter, i. 261, 271.
Rossini, G. A., i. 540.
Royal Society's soirée, i. 492.
Russell, Henry, i. 519, 532.

Sand, George, i. 115, 118, 160, 164; ii. 102, 107, 347, 350.
her 'Comtesse de Rudolstadt,' i. 165.
her 'Consuelo,' i. 117, 155, 162ff., 165.
her 'Leila,' i. 117.
her 'Spiridion,' i. 99.
Schiller, Friedrich, i. 395.
Schmitz, Dr. Leonhard, i. 171.
Severn, Joseph, ii. 151.
Sévigné, Mme. de, i. 258.
Shakespeare, William, i. 23, 43, 65, 99, 371; ii. 87.
'Romeo and Juliet,' i. 15.
Shaw, Sir James, ii. 153.
Shelley, Mrs., i. 185, 196, 226, 286.
Shelley, P. B., i. 38, 57, 65, 96, 116, 196, 214, 322, 326, 364, 476, 562; ii. 79, 151, 153, 254, 313.
his 'Cenci,' i. 228.
his 'Marianne's Dream,' i. 215.
Shelley, P. B., his 'Prometheus Unbound,' i. 228.
his 'St. Irvyne, or the Rosicrucian,' i. 226, 228.
Shirley, James, quoted, ii. 174.
Sidney, Sir Philip, i. 23.
Sigourney, Mrs., i. 343.
Simpson, Mr., i. 70ff.; ii. 31.
Smith, Elder & Co., ii. 485.
Smith, Rev. Sydney, i. 59; ii. 364.
Socrates, i. 535, 536.
Sorrento, i. 196.
Soulié, Frédéric, i. 340; ii. 107.
his 'Sept Jours au Château,' ii. 108.
Southey, Robert, ii. 453.
Stael, Mme. de, i. 337.
Stanfield, Clarkson, i. 217.
Starke, Mrs., quoted, ii. 279.
'Statesman,' the, ii. 170, 173, 174, 183, 190, 198.
Stewart, Dugdale, i. 168; ii. 27.
Stilling, Heinrich (autobiography of), i. 112.
Stratten, Rev. James, ii. 491, 498.
Sue, Eugène, ii. 438, 527.

Talfourd, Mr. Serjeant, i. 320, 391, 438, 568; ii. 81, 304, 306, 308, 311, 315, 319, 363.
his 'Ion,' i. 316ff., 319, 322.
Tasso, T., i. 5; ii. 260.
Tennyson, Alfred, i. 19, 24, 27, 69, 100, 238, 244, 260, 315, 320, 381, 402, 441, 443; ii. 81, 115ff., 122, 135, 151, 176, 227, 335, 509.
his 'Œnone,' i. 96; 'Morte d'Arthur,' i. 96.
Thackeray, W. M., i. 260; ii. 407, 425, 430.
Thiers, M., i. 343.
Thomson, Miss, i. 167, 171ff., 497, 500; ii. 8, 22.
Thucydides, i. 171.
Tieck, i. 458.
'Times,' the, i. 245, 247; ii. 342.
Titian, i. 5.
Trepsack, Miss ('Treppy'), ii. 200, 208, 209, 404, 419, 430.
Trieste, i. 126.
Trollope, Mrs., i. 111.
Tuckerman, H., his 'Thoughts on the Poets,' ii. 183.

Vasari, G., i. 570.

Venables, George Stovin, i. 402; ii. 115.
Vidocq, i. 113, 117.
Voltaire, i. 408, 481, 490.

WALES, Prince of (afterwards George IV.), i. 48.
Warburton, Eliot, i. 287, 293, 396; ii. 372.
Ward, R. P., his 'Tremaine,' i. 501.
Watts, Dr. Isaac, i. 200.
Whately, Archbishop, i. 112; ii. 392.
White, Dr., i. 492.
White, Henry Kirke, i. 29.
Widdicombe, Harry, ii. 430, 435.
Wilkie, David, i. 86.
Wilson, Miss Barrett's maid, i. 177, 473; ii. 354, 357, 537, 562.
Wilson, Professor ('Christopher North'), i. 23.
Wordsworth, William, i. 73, 85, 87, 315, 361, 461ff., 480, 482; ii. 47, 63, 75, 76, 83, 118, 312, 453.
Miss Martineau's letter on, i. 461, 475ff.
Wordsworth, William, *junr.*, i. 544, 549; ii. 118.
Wylie, Sir James, i. 154, 161.

THE END

By THOMAS HARDY

Desperate Remedies.
Two on a Tower.
The Woodlanders.
Far from the Madding Crowd.
Wessex Tales.
A Laodicean.
Tess of the D'Urbervilles.
Jude the Obscure.
The Hand of Ethelberta.
A Pair of Blue Eyes.
The Mayor of Casterbridge.
The Trumpet-Major.
Under the Greenwood Tree.
Return of the Native.
The Well-Beloved.

Uniform Edition. Illustrated. Crown 8vo, Cloth, $1 50 per Volume.

Wessex Poems, and Other Verses. Illustrated by the Author. Crown 8vo, Cloth, $1 75.

Life's Little Ironies. Tales. Post 8vo, Cloth, Ornamental, $1 25.

A Group of Noble Dames. Illustrated. 12mo, Cloth, Ornamental, $1 25.

Fellow-Townsmen. 32mo, Cloth, 35 cents.

Hardy has an exquisite vein of humor. . . . He has a reserve force, so to speak, of imagination, of invention, which keeps the interest undiminished always, though the personages in the drama may be few and their adventures unremarkable. But most of all he has shown the pity and the beauty of human life, most of all he has enlarged the boundaries of sympathy and charity.—*New York Tribune.*

HARPER & BROTHERS, Publishers
NEW YORK AND LONDON

☞ *Any of the above works will be sent by mail, postage prepaid, to any part of the United States, Canada, or Mexico, on receipt of the price.*

www.ingramcontent.com/pod-product-compliance
Lightning Source LLC
Chambersburg PA
CBHW081322090726
47907CB00010B/2342

* 9 7 8 1 5 9 4 6 2 1 0 2 4 *